Tutorial:
SOFTWARE REUSE: EMERGING TECHNOLOGY

Will Tracz

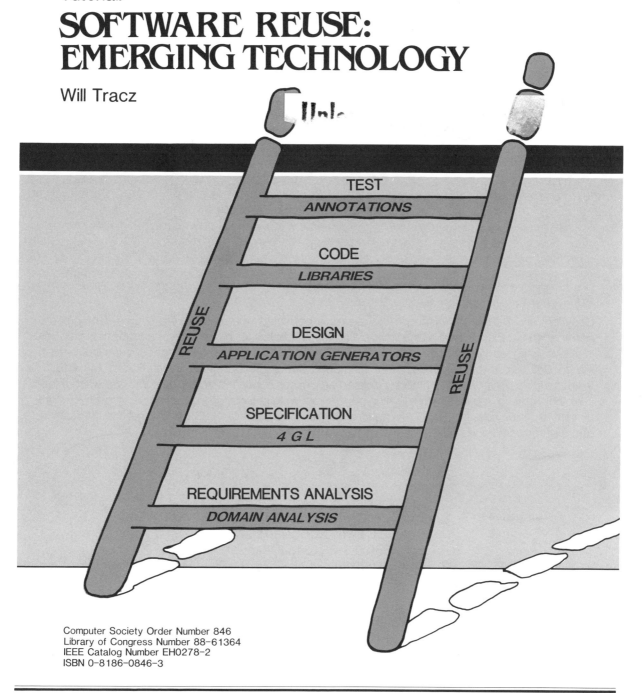

Computer Society Order Number 846
Library of Congress Number 88-61364
IEEE Catalog Number EH0278-2
ISBN 0-8186-0846-3

 THE COMPUTER SOCIETY
OF THE IEEE

 IEEE   THE INSTITUTE OF ELECTRICAL AND ELECTRONICS ENGINEERS, INC.

 COMPUTER
SOCIETY
PRESS

Published by Computer Society Press
1730 Massachusetts Avenue, N.W.
Washington, D.C. 20036-1903

Cover designed by Jack I. Ballestero

The Computer Society Order Number 846
Library of Congress Number 88-61364
IEEE Catalog Number EH0278-2
ISBN 0-8186-0846-3 (Paper)
ISBN 0-8186-4846-5 (Microfiche)
SAN 264-620X

10-10-90

Order from: Computer Society
Terminal Annex
Post Office Box 4699
Los Angeles, CA 90080

IEEE Service Center
445 Hoes Lane
P.O. Box 1331
Piscataway, NJ 08855-1331

Computer Society
13, Avenue de l'Aquilon
B-1200 Brussels
BELGIUM

 THE INSTITUTE OF ELECTRICAL AND ELECTRONICS ENGINEERS, INC.
IEEE

Dedication

To my loving wife Sharon, for 15 years of patience in being married to a student; and to my children, Matt, Nick, and Meg, for helping me in more ways than they know.

Preface

This tutorial presents a state-of-the-art/state-of-the practice look at software reuse. I have selected the material to compliment the basic foundational work found in Peter Freeman's tutorial *Software Reusability,* which was published by Computer Society Press in 1987.

Part of the motivation for organizing this volume can be summarized in the following quotation: "It is amazing that three months in the lab can save you one hour in the library." Having invested much time and effort to research the underlying principles and concepts of software reuse, I realized there was a pressing need to "practice what I preached," to save others from rediscovering what I had uncovered. Therefore, found within this tutorial is a discussion of the technical and nontechnical barriers facing wide-spread reuse of software along with the emerging technology, methodology, and mind set to facilitate its transition into the software development life cycle.

The programming community has recently witnessed a flurry of activity in the field of software reuse. Numerous conferences, workshops, seminars, and colloquia have either featured sessions on or have been devoted entirely to software reusability. The goal of this tutorial is to present the material that best reflects the contributions of software researchers and developers in the field of software reuse.

The following is a list of the conferences, workshops, seminars, tutorials, and colloquia from which the material in this tutorial is drawn:

- *Tutorial on Software Reuse: The State of the Practice* by Will Tracz at COMPCON 87, February 23-27, 1987, San Francisco, California.

- *Tutorial on Reusable Software Engineering* by Peter Freeman at COMPCON 87, February 23-27, 1987, San Francisco, California.

- *Software Reuseability and Maintainability Conference,* March 4-5, 1987, Tysons Corner, Virginia. Presented by the National Institute for Software Quality and Productivity, Inc.

- *Tutorial on Software Reusability* by John Goodenough, at the Ninth International Conference on Software Engineering, March 30-April 2, 1987, Monterey, California.

- *Colloquium on Reusable Software Components,* May 22-23, 1987, London, England. Sponsored by IEE.

- *Tenth Minnowbrook Workshop on Software Reuse,* July 28-31, 1987, Blue Mountain Lake, New York. Sponsored by Syracuse University and the University of Maryland in cooperation with RADC and the IEEE/CS Software Engineering Technical Committee.

- *Software Reusability and Portability Conference,* September 16-17, 1987, Bethesda, Maryland. Presented by the National Institute for Software Quality and Productivity, Inc.

- *Workshop on Software Reuse,* October 14-16, 1987, Boulder, Colorado. Sponsored by SEI, SPC, and MCC in cooperation with the RMISE.

- *Software Reuse Satellite Seminar,* October 20-21, 1987. Sponsored by the Association for Media-Based Continuing Education for Engineers, Inc.

In addition, the following conferences featured sessions devoted to software reusability:

- *HICSS-20,* January 6-9, 1987, Kailua-Kona, Hawaii.

- *COMPCON 87,* February 23-27, 1987, San Francisco, California.

- *Joint Ada Conference,* March 16-19, 1987, Arlington, Virginia.

- *Ninth International Conference on Software Engineering,* March 30-April 2, 1987, Monterey, California.

- *Fourth International Workshop on Software Specification and Design,* April 3-4, 1987, Monterey, California.

- *1987 Ada-Europe Conference on Ada Components: Libraries and Tools,* May 26-28, 1987, Stockholm, Sweden.
- *NCC-87,* June 15-18, 1987, Chicago, Illinois.
- *COMPSAC 87,* October 5-9, 1987, Tokyo, Japan.
- *FJCC,* October 25-29, 1987, Dallas, Texas.

Finally, numerous articles on software reusability have appeared in *ACM SIGSOFT Software Engineering Notes* and *IEEE Software,* with the July 1987 issue of *IEEE Software* devoted to reusability tools. An extensive bibliography is included in the final section of this tutorial.

Will Tracz
Stanford, California

Acknowledgments

I wish to thank the authors for their efforts and interests in creating the material and permitting me to reuse it here. I also wish to thank my management especially Ray Brisson, Jack Florio, and Roger Fritz, at IBM Systems Integration Division in Owego, New York, for providing me with the opportunity to pursue research and studies in this area. I would like to express my sincere appreciation to my thesis advisors, David Luckham at Stanford University, and Joseph Goguen at SRI International, for their continued guidance and support. I would also like to thank Doug Bryan, Geoff Mendal, Randy Neff, Rosemary Brock, and all of the members of the Program Analysis and Verification Group at Stanford for their stimulating conversation, thought-provoking comments, and general harassment. Finally, I would like to acknowledge the efforts of the production staff at The Computer Society Press, especially Margaret Brown, for their unwavering support and encouragement and of the reviewers, whose comments have made this a better publication than originally planned.

Table of Contents

Part 1: Overview

This tutorial is organized into five parts. This first part gives an overview of the basic issues concerning software reuse. The second part contains motivational material that discusses the reasons why software is, isn't, and should be reused. The third part focuses on "mental and supplemental" tools (in the words of David Gries) that support software reuse. This part is divided into four subsections that focus on components, software libraries, methodologies, and Ada reuse experience. The fourth part is composed of papers that reflect emerging technologies that show promise for software reuse. The last part contains an extensive bibliography.

The papers that follow in this part provide the reader with an overview of the practice of software reuse. The first three papers discuss general issues and directions. The fourth paper focuses on the impact of the programming language Ada on software reuse. The last three papers summarize the activities at recent workshops on software reuse in the United States and abroad.

The first paper, "Reusability Framework, Assessment, and Directions" by Ted Biggerstaff and Charles Richter, is an outgrowth of Ted Biggerstaff and Alan Perlis's seminal work, which appeared as the foreword to the September 1984 special issue on software reusability in *IEEE Transactions on Software Engineering*. It starts out with a description of composition and generative technologies and the relative payoffs of each. Next, the paper contrasts the problems with code reuse versus design reuse. Finally, the paper focuses on reuse research directions including representational issues concerning the separation of concept from context for the reuse of designs. The reader should note Figure 1, "Characterization of reusability technologies," which succinctly lists and contrasts current software reuse approaches. An expanded version of this paper, along with updates and new contributions, based on the landmark ITT Workshop on Software Reusability in 1983, may be found in the book titled *Software Reusability* edited by Ted Biggerstaff (MCC) and Alan Perlis (Yale) to be published by Addison-Wesley and projected to be available late fall 1988.

In the second paper, "Software Components and Reuse—Getting More out of Your Code," Patrick Hall offers the British government's perspective on software reuse along with an approach used by his company, GenRad, to create reusable components for CAE tools. The paper describes how interface design can effect component connection and cites eight ways of solving this problem. The paper concludes by listing the technical, legal, economic, and social barriers that need to be resolved before "second-hand software" becomes a viable industry. One novel approach suggested in this paper is the addition of a "dongle," a hardware monitoring device that permits the execution of licensed software.

The next paper, "Software Reuse Myths" by Will Tracz, analyzes nine commonly believed software reuse myths. These myths focus on technical (e.g., tools, AI, programming languages, software development methodologies), cultural (Japanese software factories, management), and pedagogical issues of software reuse.

The impact of the programming language Ada on software reuse is presented in the paper, "Ada Reusability Efforts: A Survey of the State of the Practice," by Will Tracz. The language features that support reuse are first described and analyzed and then the current Ada reuse activity of 16 corporations and research consortia are summarized. The final section of this paper identifies and examines Ada reusability guidelines generated by five organizations/individuals.

The final three papers are summaries of recent workshops on software reuse. The first report by Bill Agresti and Frank McGarry summarizes the Minnowbrook workshop on software reuse. This workshop featured four working groups that addressed issues related to (1) defining the scope of reuse, (2) contrasting the state-of-the-art versus the state-of-the-practice of software reuse, (3) identifying tools and environments that support reuse, and (4) analyzing the technical and nontechnical foundations of reuse and identifying future directions.

The RMISE workshop on software reuse took place three months after the Minnowbrook workshop. It tried to build on the success of Minnowbrook.

Invited speakers addressed social and cultural issues, economic and legal issues, software methods that support reuse, design representations that enhance reuse, code representations, tools and environments, constructive and generative approaches, and domain analysis. The last six topics were also the focus of special working groups whose summaries are included in the report.

The final report, by M. Ratcliffe, describes the workshop on software reuse held in Hereford, England. It contains results from some of the reuse research projects sponsored by the Alvey Software Engineering Programme and the Esprit Software Technology Initiative. Of interest are the use of Ada and other languages, the standards that have been created, and the formal methods and tools proposed to support software reuse. One comment made in the report was the observation that the whole western (U.S.) economic system may be against reuse.

EH0278-2/88/0000/0001$01.00 ©1988

Reusability Framework, Assessment, and Directions

Ted Biggerstaff and Charles Richter
Microelectronics and Computer Technology Corp.

Reusability remains a puzzle despite its promise. Why? What can be done? The authors discuss some answers and possibilities.

Reusability is widely believed to be a key to improving software development productivity and quality. The reuse of software components amplifies the software developer's capabilities. It results in fewer total symbols in a system's development and in less time spent on organizing those symbols.

However, while reusability is a strategy of great promise, it is one whose promise has been largely unfulfilled.

Framework

You can address the question of reusability from a variety of different viewpoints. We consider it here from the technology viewpoint: What technologies, either mature or emerging, are available to address reusability? How do they work and how do they differ? If we can answer these questions, we can provide a basis for judging many other facets of reusability. (A more in-depth look at results in these technological areas can be found in Biggerstaff.[1,2])

The technologies applied to the reusability problem can be divided into two major groups that depend on the nature of the components being reused. These two major groups are composition technologies and generation technologies. Table 1 shows a framework for classifying the available technologies.

Composition technologies. The first major group is characterized by the fact that the components are largely atomic and, ideally, are unchanged in their reuse. Of course, the ideal is not always achieved, and these components may be modified or changed to fit the computational purposes of the reuser better. However, in the ideal they are passive elements operated on (composed) by an external agent. Examples of such items are code skeletons, subroutines,[3,4] functions, programs, and Smalltalk-style objects.

Deriving new programs from building blocks is a matter of composition: A few, well-defined composition principles are applied to the components. The Unix pipe mechanism is a good example: Constructing more complex programs from simpler ones requires connecting one program's output to another program's inputs.

Another example is Smalltalk, where the two principles of component composition are message-passing and inheritance. Message-passing is a generalization of function calls, a static binding of caller to callee. Inheritance permits a dynamic determination of the method (callee) to be invoked.

Generation technologies. The other major group of systems that incorporate reusability is not as easy to characterize because the reused components are not easily identifiable as concrete, self-contained entities. In the composition group, we could point at a building block both before and after its use. It was immutable in the sense that, for the most part, it kept its form and identity after use.

However, in the generation group, the reused components are often patterns woven into the fabric of a generator program. The resulting structures often bear only distant relations to the patterns of the programs that generated them. Further, each resulting instance of such a pattern may be highly individualistic, bearing only scant resemblance to other instances generated from the same seed code. In this case, reuse is less a composition matter (of components) than it is an execution matter (of component generators).

Reusable patterns take at least two different forms: patterns of code and patterns in transformation rules. An example of code patterns is application generation, where reusable patterns of code exist in the generator itself. Transformation systems (which use sets of transformation rules) are examples of rule patterns.

In both cases, the effects of the reusable components in the target program tend to be more global and diffuse than the effects of building blocks. Similarly, we cannot easily characterize the principle whereby patterns are reused, except to say that it is a kind of reactivation of the patterns. Neighbors' Draco system[5] provides an example of both an application generator and a transformation-based system.

Assessment

Dilemmas. Reusability presents several dilemmas. The general form of the dilemma is that a positive change in one parameter often leads to a negative change in another.

Generality of applicability versus payoff. The first dilemma is illustrated in Figure 1. Technologies that are very general (in that they can be applied to a broad range of application domains) have a much lower payoff than systems that are narrowly focused on one or two application domains.

For example, if an application generator has facilities for generating both screen and database interfaces for the user, it amplifies the user's capabilities much more than does a straight high-level language because there are fewer keystrokes and fewer compositions of architectural pieces for building the screen and data interfaces. In other parts of the application, there is no noticeable increase in productivity.

Figure 1's diagram is not based on rigorous data, but reflects our opinion about the relative characteristics of the various technologies. Nevertheless, it seems that there is a clearly discernible grouping that defines a curve from the upper left to the lower right. Even though the placement of individual points may be debatable, we believe the general characteristic of the curve is intuitively correct and that most readers would concur with its general shape.

It is unclear whether the curve is hyperbolic or linear. But its exact form is not as important as the general relationship between the axis variables. As you maximize the parameter on one axis, you minimize the parameter on the other axis. Breaking away from the restrictions implied by this figure is one of the key breakthroughs required to make reusability successful.

Component size (and payoff) versus reuse potential. The second dilemma is based on component mean size. As a component grows, the payoff involved in reusing that component increases more than linearly (because of the additional costs introduced as the complexity of the object grows).

However, as the component grows, it also becomes more and more specific, which narrows its application and increases the cost of reusing it when modifications are required. (This dilemma has been independently noticed by several others.)

This dilemma is amplified when we try to reuse code because code, by it very nature, requires great specificity.

Table 1.
A framework for reusability technologies.

Features	Reusability approaches				
Component reused	Building blocks		Patterns		
Component nature	Atomic and immutable Passive		Diffuse and malleable Active		
Reuse principle	Composition		Generation		
Emphasis	Application component	Organization and composition priciples	Language-based	Application generators	Transformation systems
Typical systems	Subroutine libraries	Object-oriented	Very high-level languages	Terminal-display formatters	Language transformers
		Pipe architectures	Problem-oriented languages	File management	

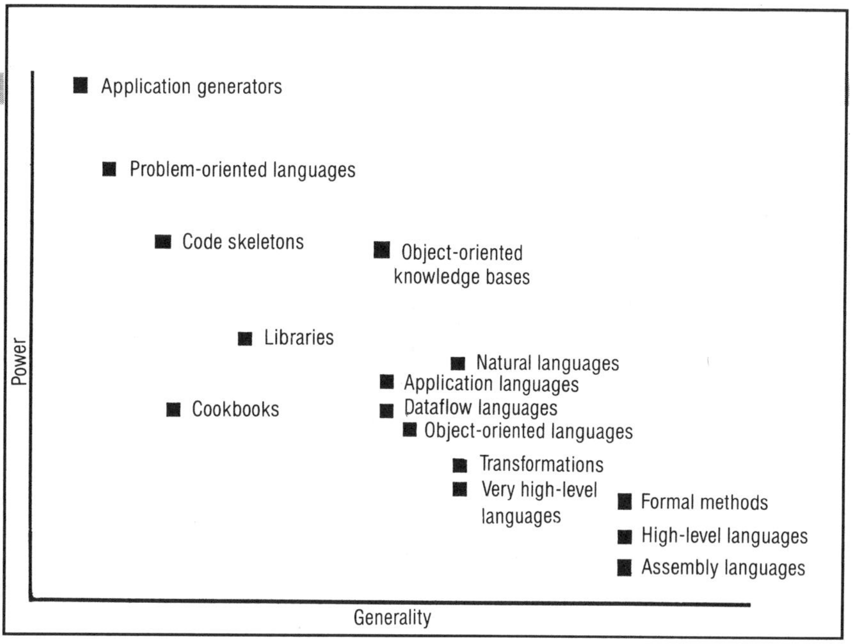
Application generators
Problem-oriented languages
Code skeletons
Object-oriented knowledge bases
Libraries
Natural languages
Application languages
Cookbooks
Dataflow languages
Object-oriented languages
Transformations
Very high-level languages
Formal methods
High-level languages
Assembly languages
Power
Generality

Figure 1. Characterization of reusability technologies.

The cost of library population. The third dilemma is that we must invest a great deal of intellectual capital, real capital, and time before reuse begins to pay off significantly. The organizational structure of most companies precludes such large initial capital investment — regardless of the potential long term payoff. Therein lies the dilemma.

Generally, such organizational structures consist of teams of people working on projects. Those projects are budgeted to meet a set of goals. Those goals generally do not include any extra work to generalize and capture the project results for reuse by other groups.

Developing a viable reusability system is an investment that does not have an early payoff. Therefore, populating the library blocks development of a working reusability system.

Operational problems. To operate successfully, a reusability system must address four fundamental problems:

- finding components,
- understanding components,
- modifying components, and
- composing components.

Finding components. The finding process is more than just locating an exact match. It includes locating highly similar components, because even if a target component must be partially redeveloped — rather than be reused in total — an example similar to the ideal component can reduce the effort and eliminate many defects.

Several approaches to this problem have been proposed. Rubén Prieto-Díaz has developed a classification scheme for a component library,[6] while William Jones has proposed using M. Ross Quillian's spreading activation search paradigm in his Memory Extender system to accomplish much the same purpose.

A different approach was taken in the Paris system for reusing partially interpreted schemes.[7] In Paris, the finding operation used preconditions and postconditions plus assertions about component properties to form clauses to be proved with the Boyer-Moore theorem prover. The resulting proof developed a list of candidate components.

The importance of the finding function is closely related to the dilemma of size versus reuse potential. Size is a metric that closely correlates with specificity, and specificity is the factor that really affects reusability. So we might better have defined the dilemma as specificity versus reuse potential.

Modules become less and less reusable the more specific they become because it is more and more difficult to find an exact (or even close) match of detailed specifics. Modules subtly encode very specific information about a variety of things: operating system, runtime library, hardware equipment availability, data packaging, interface packaging, and so forth.

Thus, if we have highly specialized modules, we can expect that we must have very many of them to make reuse work. In this circumstance, the finding component takes on added importance.

If, on the other hand, ways can be found to factor out such specificity while still providing reasonably large components, the importance of the finding component is diminished. In fact, if the components are sufficiently abstract so they capture only one aspect or principle of an algorithm, we may end up with a relatively small search space — and the finding problem may be only a minor operation in a reusability system. The search for such an abstraction scheme is one of the avenues being pursued at MCC.

Understanding components. The understanding process is required whether or not a component is to be modified, but especially if the component *is* to be modified. The component user needs a mental model of the component's computation to use it properly. Such a mental model takes some effort to acquire. This is probably the fundamental operational problem that must be solved in the development of any reuse system regardless of the underlying technology chosen for its implementation.

An approach to this problem is represented by hypertext systems such as Neptune[8] and PlaneText.[9] Hypertext systems provide a tool for building a web of information that smoothly integrates text, graphics diagrams, and other information such as existing code.

Each element is a node of information that can be examined by the user. The node can be annotated with pointers to other nodes that can contain descriptions, diagrams, explanations of decisions, invariant equations, and design information often lost when designing a system.

Happily, systems such as PlaneText let existing files be annotated without altering them. Thus, a code file can be annotated for hypertext purposes without affecting its use as a compilable file.

Figure 2 contains an example of a small hypertext web. In the example, we have a node containing the requirements for a product. Some requirements are linked (by defn links) to definitions of those requirements, while others contain links to the code that realizes them. One requirement

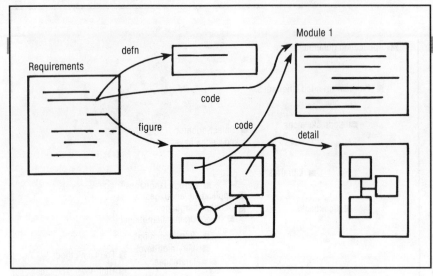

Figure 2. A PlaneText example.

is also annotated with a figure, a piece of which is further refined, and so on.

These systems support understanding by providing the component's user with instant access to supporting information. Decisions associated with some portion of the component can be called up to the screen with two or three keystrokes or with the touch of a mouse. While such systems are not a panacea, they represent a start at taming the understanding problem.

Modifying components. The modifying process is the lifeblood of reusability. It changes the perception of a reusability system from a static library of rock-like building blocks to a living system of components that spawn, change, and evolve new components with the changing requirements of their environment.

It is overly optimistic to expect that we can build a reusability system that allows significant reuse without the need to modify some portion of the components. However, modification is largely a human domain. There are few tools that provide any measure of help in modifying components.

Composing components. The composition process introduces the most challenging requirements on the representation used to specify components: The representation must have a dual character. It must provide the ability to represent composite structures as independent entities with well-defined computational characteristics. It must also provide the capability for these composite structures to be further composed into new computational structures with a different set of computational characteristics.

To some extent, these two goals are mutually antagonistic because the notions of functional composition drawn from mathematical theory are largely inadequate. Mathematical compositions produce their results through straightforward combination of the local effects of individual components: The whole is simply the sum of the parts.

Unfortunately, such composition systems are too limited. Human designers compose components that have both global and local effects, and this leads to more powerful, flexible, and practical modes of reuse.

An interesting approach to the problems of composition is Volpano's Software Templates.[10] This approach divides the component information into two parts: the essential algorithm and the data implementation decisions. By separately choosing an algorithm and its implementation decisions for the data types used, the system generates a customized implementation of the algorithm, often producing a significant code expansion. It remains to be seen how far this work can be pushed.

These four processes have typically been an informal part of design. A focus on reusability requires that they be formalized and defined so automated support structures can be engineered.

Code reuse versus design reuse. The obvious first approach to reusability is to use components expressed in some programming language and to form them into libraries. There are at least two problems with this strategy.

First, the payoff quickly reaches a ceiling that is difficult to surpass. Our experi-

ence has been that the amount of any system that can be formed from reused components is relatively small (well under half the system).

Second, if it is forced to be greater than this ceiling, the target system does not perform to specification. At the very least, they have problems of inappropriate functionality. Programs built completely from reused components typically have performance problems.

Limited code-reuse success. There are some limited success stories with reuse of code, however. The classic example is the reuse of numerical computation routines. Indeed, this is one of the few clear successes in the code reuse. But the numerical computation domain is unique in several ways:

• The domain is very narrow: It contains only a small number of data types.

• The domain is well-understood: Its mathematical framework that has evolved over hundreds of years.

• The underlying technology is quite static: It grows and evolves only very slowly and, importantly, it evolves so existing parts of the technology remain unchanged (upward compatibility of the technology).

These characteristics allow the establishment of standards in the domain, and these standards lead to the success of reusability in this domain. The narrowness of the domain simply makes the reuse of code manageable. The cost of developing the reusable parts is small, and because there are only a few data types, components in the library have a higher probability of reuse.

The fact that the domain is well-understood reduces the amount of investment needed to create a reusable library. It also positively affects the understanding problem. Many people understand the domain and, therefore, readily understand what function a component performs with only the barest description of that function.

The fact that the domain is largely static

and unchanging (except over long periods of time) means that the library of parts can be quite stable, so the using organization can amortize the investment over a much longer period of time.

The worst kind of domain for reusability is one where the underlying technology is rapidly changing. An example of such a domain is the personal computer and workstation domain. Systems software for this domain has a very short half-life and is therefore not very reusable.

Design representation problems. But while the code itself is not reusable, the general design ideas often are quite reusable. This observation has led to the notion of reusing design information. The idea is good in principle, but has problems in practice.

The problems center around the question of how to represent the design information. Code has well-defined representation schemes, as realized in today's high-level programming languages. However, there is no such representation system for designs. Each potential choice suffers some fatal flaw:

• Many machine-processible design languages are too close to programming languages and, therefore, too specific, leading to the same problems that arise with reusing code.

• Languages that are not overly specific are often only processible by machines in very limited ways. This leads to the requirement of much manual activity in the reuse of such designs — and this reduces the payoff.

Since the payoff potential is so high for design reuse, we believe research is required to realize that potential. Design reuse is the only way we can come even close to an order of magnitude increase in productivity or quality.

Why? Because reuse and design are really facets of the same activity. When we watch power designers, we are struck by the fact that the same patterns occur again and again in their designs. They will say something like "Oh, that structure is very similar to a widget and, typically, you handle widgets this way." They bring a lot of pre-

structured information (partially specified architectures) to bear on the problem.

Very few designers, except total novices, start from scratch. The difference in their productivity can be directly correlated with their experience, as modulated by their basic intelligence.

Unfortunately, to put that kind of experience on machines in useful forms, and to help apprentice designers to take advantage of it, we must overcome some factors that inhibit reuse.

> *Technologists are confounded because reusability is a multiorganization problem and requires a critical mass of components before it can really pay off. These issues prevent spontaneous use of reuse.*

Inhibiting factors. Several factors inhibit the advancement of reusability technology: representation technology, lack of a clear and obvious direction, the "not invented here" factor, and the high initial capitalization required to exploit reusability.

The first and most important inhibitor across a wide range of domains is that we do not have a representation for design that fosters reusability.

The second inhibitor is that it is not clear exactly what strategy represents the optimum approach to reusability. Management will generally not take positive steps until it has a strong notion of what seems like the obviously best path. In such cases, technologists often lead the way, but in this case, the nature of the problem prevents that from working.

The aspects of the problem that confound the technologists are (1) that reusability is a multiorganization problem and (2) that it requires a critical mass of com-

ponents before it really begins to pay off. Both aspects prevent the technology from arising spontaneously out of the ranks of the technologists.

The third factor, "not invented here," is a strong inhibitor among the program developers. Nevertheless, this is largely cultural, and when compared to the difficulty of solving some of the technical problems (such as the representation problem), this is a reasonably easy problem to cure.

The cure is largely a matter of management establishing the proper culture, one that makes a point of rewarding reuse. Once management establishes the proper culture, the developers rapidly learn that reuse does not inhibit their creativity after all — they are now free to attack more challenging problems. Once this fact is realized, resistance to reuse rapidly disappears. This has certainly been the case at Hartford Insurance[4] and in Japan.

The fourth inhibiting factor, initial capitalization, was discussed with the cost of library population (in the section on dilemmas). Effective reuse requires a very large initial commitment: Libraries of reusable parts must be stocked. And a lack of enough library components prevents reuse technology from arising spontaneously.

Activating factors. The factors that will foster the evolution of reusability technology are largely economic. While other technological improvements can provide marginal improvements, those improvements will (and indeed already are) reaching a point of diminishing returns.

For example, providing sufficient personal computing power in terms of workstations or shared computer time has provided some improvement, but there is a limit to the improvement you can get from such measures.

In the end, if the compiler requires a string of several million characters to produce the target system, there is a minimum amount of time required to produce and organize those several million characters — and you cannot get below that minimum without a fundamental change in technology.

7

Another primary activator will likely be the successful application of reuse by competitors. The Japanese have been emphasizing reuse for some time now and have been having some success with it.

Initially, US developers will deny that the Japanese are having any success, but when the competitive pressures make it obvious, they will grudgingly admit that maybe the Japanese have made some progress. Once this happens, US software developers will put more emphasis on reuse.

Speculations. We do not expect much immediate progress in generally applicable reuse systems because of the high initial capitalization required, management indifference, and lack of a mature technology base.

A few special cases of high-redundancy domains (such as Cobol development environments) will show good payoffs just by using simple tools (like short-form tools) that eliminate much of the redundancy and allow storage of common system specification information in one place (like data dictionaries and their progeny).

Several parallel approaches and their associated technologies will evolve:

• Ad hoc general reuse. This approach uses existing technology and just accumulates parts (including both design and code) ad hoc. It is not based on any theory nor dependent on any technology breakthroughs.

The Japanese are likely to work this avenue and achieve a very credible — but modest — payoff with it. The payoffs will probably be less than a 25 percent increase in productivity, where this 25 percent is a part of (not in addition to) other increases due to other improvements (like design tools). This approach will pay off in two to five years from the start time.

• Program generator reuse. Growth in program generators will occur in narrowly defined application domains. The main activity here will be seen in the personal computer market, with somewhat less activity in the workstation market. Today, and in the near future, we see very little reusability activity on mainframes and

minis, except for the porting of facilities developed in the small-machine market.

The time to payoff with this approach is very short — less than a year to two years. The narrower the domain, the faster the payoff. Further, the payoff with this approach will be very large — between 60 percent and 90 percent depending on how stereotyped the application architecture is.

If a fair amount of logic must be developed outside of the application generator, which often happens, the payoff will be closer to 60 percent. If not, it will be close to 90 percent. However, the domain of application of these generators is very narrow, and they are aimed largely at the end user, not the professional programmer.

• Theory-based general reuse. Representation breakthroughs are necessary for payoffs approaching or exceeding an order of magnitude. These representations must allow factored forms of design information. Designers must be able to store and deal separately with design aspects (or factors) such as function, implementation data structures, and interfaces.

These factors will be woven together to generate a design implementation. Such a breakthrough will allow reusability to be applied to a wide set of application domains with the expectation of order of magnitude (or greater) increase in productivity and quality.

Of course, a significant amount of preinvestment is necessary to populate the domains of interest before any payoff can be expected. The preinvestment will be an

inhibitor, at least until some corporation has demonstrated the commercial viability of the technology. The time to payoff is five to ten years.

(The figures for percentage improvement in productivity and for time to payoff are based largely on our intuition and experience. We do not have any scientifically derived data that pin these numbers down.)

We are most interested in the third area, a theory of general reuse of design information. Earlier, we cited several factors that inhibit reuse. One of those, representation, is an important key in such a theory.

Research issues. The fundamental problem preventing the successful reuse of design information is finding the right representation of that design information: a representation that allows designs to be captured in a form that is richly machine-processible. The need for rich machine processing eliminates English-language text and most of the block-and-connector styles of graphical representations (these forms allow only relatively superficial forms of machine processing). The representation we seek must exhibit the following properties:

• the ability to represent knowledge about implementation structures in factored form,

• the ability to create partial specifications of design information, specifications that can be incrementally extended,

• the ability to allow flexible couplings between instances of designs and the various interpretations those instances can have, and

• the ability to express controlled degrees of abstraction and precision (degrees of ambiguity).

Factored forms. Code components represent a variety of information in unfactored form. Once we have created a code component, information about many domains is woven (encoded) into that component in subtle and nonobvious ways.

For example, the control structure of a code component often takes a particular form because of the structure of the data it operates on. As an example, if we want to loop through a list of items, we would probably use a for loop if the list is an array. If it is a linked list, however, we'd more likely chose a while or repeat-until loop. Thus, by the time we have created code, a variety of requirements and design structures have been thoroughly mixed so that their individual structures may not be at all apparent.

Such a form is not optimal for reuse, since it is difficult to separate the individual design factors to understand the component, modify the component, etc. People deal well with the individual design factors, but not with the integrated whole. Therefore, a design representation must let the designer edit individual factors and combine several factors, obtaining a new component.

For example, suppose a designer must design a process table for a multitasking system — a table containing the description of each process running under the multitasking system. The designer will deal with this process table from at least two points of view: (1) an application-domain view, because it is a process table, and (2) a data-structure view, because it is an indexed table.

These points of view focus on two distinct design factors of a process table — and the representation must let the designer deal with these two factors separately. Future designers may want to reuse the concept of, say, a process table without the accompanying notion of an indexed table.

Partial specifications. People, and designers in particular, evolve their notions of design incrementally. First, they express the broad framework of the design, specifying only the major structures. Then, over a period of time, they fill in the details, probably reorganizing the broad framework while filling in the details.

The broad structures (partial architectures) are highly reusable; the details typically are not. In fact, inclusion of too much detail significantly reduces reusability of the overall component.

The broad structures must be precisely

described, while the details must be left incomplete and partly ambiguous: The details are constrained, but only minimally so. It is the requirement for *partial* constraints on the details that makes the problem difficult. Specification languages usually insist on specifying the details precisely or not at all.

If we insist on specifying the details too precisely, we overcommit to the details of the resulting component, reducing its reuse potential. If we leave too many details completely unconstrained, we have significantly fewer hooks for automation, and we reduce the payoff of reusing the component because so much manual labor is involved.

Without a representation that allows a mix of precision and fuzziness, we lose much of the advantage of reuse. The ideal representation must allow such partial architectures.

Without a representation that allows a mixture of precision and fuzziness, we lose much of the advantage of reuse. The ideal representation must allow the specification and storage of such partial architectures, and it must allow incremental completion of the details over time. No representations exist today that allow this kind of flexibility but still provide the other properties we desire.

Couplings between instances and their interpretations. Once we have individual factors, we want to combine them by creating component instances that incorporate several factors.

For example, suppose again that we are designing a process table. From the point of view of the process-table domain, we will want to choose a process identifier (a method for uniquely identifying or nam-

ing the process represented by a specific entry in the table). We will probably want the capability to search for any particular entry in the table with this identifier. Similarly, from the data structure point of view, we need to talk about the table index (the conceptual entity that identifies an entry in the table).

Thus, the process identifier and the table index will be the same entity, viewed from two separate points of view. Most design languages require us to choose a single name for the field that contains the process identifier (also called the table index). This means that we have to foresee all such possible intersections and choose the same name for the field or that we have to defer this naming decision until design time and let the designer indicate that these two different interpretations (or points of view) really apply to the same design structure.

The first option is not only undesirable, but impossible. It essentially requires that we use a global name space — a name space self-consistent over all possible intersections of factors. Some factor intersections chosen for one particular design may be inconsistent with factor intersections chosen for some other design. It is impossible to choose a global-naming convention that is totally consistent in the infinite number of possible factor combinations.

The second option provides more hope, but also presents a very difficult research problem. While difficult, however, our early research indicates that the problem is solvable.

Controlled degrees of abstraction. This property is more fundamental than the previous three — indeed, its existence implies the existence of the other three. Simply stated, it requires that design specifications in the early phases of software development have many of the same characteristics as natural language: abstraction to the point of ambiguity (although carefully controlled ambiguity).

The designer must be able to define conceptual structures that initially are largely free of details. These conceptual structures must be rigorous in the following sense: If information can be known based on completed design decisions, that information must be capturable by the representation scheme.

For example, suppose a designer has decided to use a binary search on a data structure. We do not yet know the exact control structure of that algorithm, but we do know that it will have three distinct parts:

- a section of code that searches the left portion of the search space,
- a section of code that searches the right portion of the search space,
- and a section of code that tests the search item against the left-right boundary item to eliminate either the left or the right portion of the search space from the

that is simultaneously a table index and a process identifier.

As a further example, suppose that we intend to create a reusable component to suspend a process, and this process will be referring to items in an as-yet-undefined process table. This component must have a form something like the following (we use pseudocode to avoid a lengthy definition and discussion of the actual representational form):

```
if (state of process is suspended)
    then return error;
    else {remove process from ready queue
        if there;
        set state of process to suspended;
        relinquish control to the
        scheduler;}
```

above component with more precise references, we are bound to introduce specializations that limit its use in many contexts, vastly increasing the number of specialized forms we would need to keep in our component library, or, alternately, onerously increasing the amount of modification required to fit the component to each slightly different context.

A representation mechanism with such a reference mechanism allows semantic binding of its objects and operations. This notion is an abstraction mechanism fundamental to effective and highly productive design reuse.

We are working on a computer-processible representation called Prep that incorporates the idea of semantic binding and allows the expression of reusable design components in factored form. While the details of Prep are beyond the scope of this article, we believe it possesses the properties discussed above.

What we are really advocating is a representation system that permits semantic binding.

---

search. This section concurrently redefines the left and right portions of the new, smaller search space.

The fact that these three distinct areas of the control structure exist must be captured by the design representation even before the details of the control structure are worked out. Indeed the ideal representation must let us refer to these three portions of the target algorithm, even though they are quite fuzzy.

Directions

Semantic binding. What we are really advocating is a representation system that permits semantic binding. We want to represent the essence of a design component (factor) rather than just its details, letting us apply concepts from one domain to structures in an entirely different context.

But to move a component from one domain to another, the component must have great referential flexibility. The component must refer to items it expects in its context, and, since it cannot know beforehand the items' names, it must be able to refer to them semantically. Drawing on our earlier example, a multitasking scheduler will expect to find a target system data item

This example references the state of the process, which must eventually be resolved into a reference to an instance variable that names the process-state field of a process entry (or alternatively, a local variable that previously acquired the value of this instance variable).

Similarly, this example references one value that the process state can have: suspended. This value will eventually be resolved into one of several implementation values (probably integers) decided on during the design.

Now, if we had a method by which such a reference could be easily associated with (bound to) any design entity in a given context that represented the state of the process, we would have a mechanism allowing the above specification to be used in many contexts where the details might differ but the essential intent is the same. Then, as the design process proceeds, the above component could be evolved to include the details specific to the emerging design.

A reference structure of this level of flexibility provides a component that can be used with and adapted to most process-table organizations and process-state value sets that the designer might dream up.

If on the other hand, we specify the

Code reuse is a reasonable first step toward reuse, but the implementer must be aware that the leverage gained is constrained by a rather low upper threshold. On the positive side, that leverage threshold is strongly and inversely coupled to the width of the domain. By narrowing the domain, the payoff can be significantly increased.

Design reuse has the greatest potential leverage, but it requires significant representational breakthroughs to realize its full potential. Some of this leverage may be realized with a mostly manual system, but the overhead of the manual processing will significantly reduce the overall leverage of design reuse.

We strongly believe that the representational breakthroughs with the greatest potential payoff will be those that solve the problems of factored forms, partial specification, the coupling of instances and their interpretations, and controlled degrees of abstraction. The mechanism central to solving these four problems is the notion of semantic binding, or, in a sense, binding by analogy. This form of binding — applying a design from one context to a new and different context — will provide the most general form of reuse. □

References

1. *Proc. Workshop on Reusability in Programming*, Ted Biggerstaff, ed., ITT, Shelton, Conn., 1983.

2. *IEEE Trans. Software Engineering*, software reusability special issue, Sept. 1984.

3. Robert G. Lanergan and Charles A. Grasso, "Software Engineering with Reusable Designs and Code," *IEEE Trans. Software Engineering,* Sept. 1984, pp. 498-501.

4. Michael J. Cavaliere and Philip J. Archambeault, "Reusable Code at the Hartford Insurance Company," *Proc. Workshop Reusability in Programming*, ITT, Shelton, Conn., 1983.

5. James M. Neighbors, "The Draco Approach to Constructing Software from Reusable Components," *IEEE Trans. Software Engineering,* Sept. 1984, pp. 564-574.

6. Rubén Prieto-Díaz and Peter Freeman, "Classifying Software for Reusability," *IEEE Software*, Jan. 1987, pp. 6-17.

7. Schmuel Katz and Khe-Sing The, "A Preliminary Report on the Paris System," Tech. Report STP-114-85, MCC, Austin, Texas, 1985.

8. Norman Delisle and Mayer Schwarz, "Neptune: A Hypertext System for CAD Applications," Tech. Report CR-85-50, Tektronix Laboratories, Beaverton, Ore., 1986.

9. Eric Gullichsen et al., "The PlaneText-Book," Tech. Report STP-333-86, MCC, Austin, Texas, 1986.

10. Dennis M. Volpano and Richard B. Kieburtz, "Software Templates," *Proc. Eighth Int'l Conf. Software Engineering*, Computer Society Press, Los Alamitos, Calif., 1985.

Ted Biggerstaff is director of design information at the Microelectronics and Computer Technology Corp. Before joining MCC in 1985, he worked for Boeing and ITT's Advanced Technology Center. His research interests include software engineering, program-synthesis techniques, and knowledge-based approaches to reusability.

Biggerstaff received a PhD in computer science from the University of Washington at Seattle. He wrote the book *Systems Software Tools.*

Charles Richter is on assignment from Control Data Corp. to the MCC Software Technology Program, where he works in the design information group. His research interests include specification of concurrent programs and application of knowledge-representation techniques to software design.

Richter received a BS in computer science from Purdue University and is pursuing a PhD in computer science at the University of Texas at Austin.

The authors can be contacted at MCC Software Technology Program, 3500 W. Balcones Center Dr., Austin, TX 78759-6509.

Software components and reuse — getting more out of your code

by PATRICK A V HALL

Abstract: Software reuse is becoming an important factor to meet user demand. A UK company specializing in CAE products conducted a requirements analysis for its products. This led to a need to have more control over the building of software. A procedure call paradigm for interfaces was used, with rigid standards for naming conventions. The paper also discusses the Advisory Council for Applied Research and Development (ACARD) proposals on software reuse.

Keywords: data processing, software techniques, programming languages, software reuse.

Software components and software reuse have become very fashionable in recent years. Yet, despite recent initiatives, it is argued that the software industry has not been concerned with the reuse of software.

This paper will survey the current practice in reuse, and two aspects of this will be discussed in further depth:

- reuse of programming languages,
- the approach taken to reuse in GenRad Fareham.

From this base, possible future developments will be considered.

Recent initiatives on reuse

Over the past few years, reuse has become topical. A special issue of the IEEE Transactions on Software Engineering on reuse was published in 1984[1]. During 1986 a number of meetings on reuse were held:

- April 1986, British Computer Society Software Engineering Specialist Group

GenRad Fareham Ltd, Waterside Gardens, Fareham, Hants. PO16 8RR, UK

- May 1986, Alvey sponsored workshop
- July 1986, Alvey reliability and metrics club meeting

Funding agencies have been seeking projects in the field:

- Alvey — a project to survey the field, particularly the practices in the US and Japan
- Esprit sought proposals at mid-1986
- Alvey II is rumoured to be making reuse a major theme

Recommendations

The Advisory Council for Applied Research and Development (ACARD) in the UK has offered a number of recommendations to industry concerning software reuse[2].

Bespoke software should be built with reusability, product spin-off and export potential in mind.

Stocks of reusable software components must be built and maintained: this will require investment. The development of products from these components will require significant investment, ...

The Council's recommendations to government include the:

Encouragement for the construction and use of re-usable components. Purchasing departments should encourage the construction of software which can be reused on later projects. This will require some additional cost on any specific project but over time will lead to spin-off creation of a national asset base of re-usable components. Industry can then exploit these re-usable components to reduce the cost of subsequent public contracts and win new non-public contracts. Re-use is an important software engineering technique which requires demand-side leadership to pull it through into commercial practice.

Also, the following activities are suggested:

The Software Re-usable Components Brokerage (SRCB) should be a database holding requirements, specification, code, test data, documentation, etc. Components should be collected from publicly funded projects and be made available to other projects, thereby exploiting the benefits of the public purchasing recommendations encouraging the funding of re-usable components (para 9.13). The SRCB's facilities should be made available via a communications network.

0950-5849/87/010038–06$03.00 © 1987 Butterworth & Co (Publishers) Ltd.

The implication of this is that the reuse of software is currently neglected. One objective of this paper will be to show that this is not correct and that reuse has been a major theme in the development of software technology.

Acard proposes a software components industry, and proposes government action to bring it about. The second objective of this paper will be to consider possible future directions in software reuse, and appraise the likelihood of a software components industry emerging.

Current practice

The reuse of software is now new. It has been practised since the beginning of computing through a number of ways:

The reuse of ideas. The normal process of technology development is to publish methods and techniques including algorithms, and to hold seminars. This disseminates the ideas, so that they are made available to other scientists and engineers. It should be remembered that Algol60 was conceived for the publication of algorithms and not for programming.

*Vertical reuse.** Programming languages form the major source of reusable code, providing an abstraction above the level of the hardware, and closer to the applications that need to be built. Libraries of standard functions further extend this abstraction. Newer languages, such as the object-oriented languages[3], and generics in ADA[4], provide powerful facilities for the user to continue this process of abstraction themselves.

*Horizontal reuse.** Within a level of abstraction, components of software might be reused. The most common example of this is the sort utility in batch data processing, with communication via files. Unix pipes and filters[6,7] are advances on this, and other examples can be found in MASCOT[8] and Conic[9,10].

Total reuse. Complete packages of software can be reused, usually after some customization. This can be done within a company, such as Logica's System Kernels, or on the open market. Customization can take the form of setting a few parameters, generating the actual system from a lot of parametric information, adding a 'shell' round a central core, or even through the modification of some or all of the sources possibly delivered as 'kits'[11].

Programming languages as reuse

It is worth working through some of the rationale underlying the development of programming languages.

---

*Terms 'vertical' and 'horizontal' reuse due to Goguen[5].

Originally programming was in Assembler, but as particular constructs, such as subroutine linkage and data structures were found to recur, it was found advantageous to reuse the assembly constructs used for these. In one direction macro-preprocessors were developed as aids for this, in the other direction programming languages arose where the constructs were built-in. In languages, subroutines provided a do-it-yourself facility for further extending reuse, with libraries providing frequently used routines.

Operating systems can be viewed as further developments in reuse, where a lot of the access to system facilities were packaged and made available to the programmer through run-time libraries.

Thus a programming language can be viewed as a collection of components together with the technology for adding your own components, and for combining the components together to make complete software systems. For example, the **if** ... **then** ... **else** ... construct is a component which allows three other components to be combined to form another larger component. The conventional view is that programming languages are tools: this is a legitimate way of looking at them, but not the only way.

Current trends continue to build on this, object-oriented programming providing a more sophisticated do-it-yourself capability, and functional programming and fourth-generation languages (4GLs) providing yet higher level languages closer to the application and heavily reusing code.

Reasons for reuse

The reasons for this rise in reuse are various. It is part of the scientific ethic to publish findings, to make them available to others. Many early computer practitioners were trained scientists, and to not share techniques would have been unthinkable.

Reuse also reduces the work of repeatedly spelling out in detail the same constructs to achieve the same end. This constructive laziness has been a very powerful force in moving software components forward. This also leads to economies in the development process, important in the face of competitive pressure when competition is on price.

Reuse has not arisen because of government initiatives, and therefore it has become a focus of research and development.

Case study: GenRad

To illustrate how commercial considerations can lead to reuse, with the need to solve quite basic technical problems, here is how one UK company approached software reuse.

GenRad was led into software reuse by marketing

requirements. In the early 1980s the company was concerned with electronic CAE products such as:

- Hilo a logic simulator
- Hitest a test program generator

In 1983–1984 it began to investigate relational databases as key to CAE tools integration. In December 1984 it reconsidered the nature of the OEM side of its business. The company was under pressure to allow the OEMs to replace its user interface by one of their own construction. OEMs and other customers complained about the delays in starting up the software, and the company conjectured that what was really needed was to replace its data storage mechanisms by the OEM data storage mchanisms. The conventional way in which third party software is connected into an existing set of CAE tools is shown in Figure 1. The environment communicates with the tool through intermediate files which is slow and awkward.

GenRad decided to conduct a requirements analysis in the first quarter of 1985, which in turn led to an architectural proposal containing some novel features.

Requirements analysis

GenRad found there were a number of distinct requirements that were needed to meet the product architecture: including being able to interchange or replace major components. For example, at one time the company had two simulators, which should have been interchangeable but were not.

The company needed to handle a variety of input and output formats, for hardware description languages and waveform languages. Although GenRad had its own proprietary languages it is necessary to be able to handle industry standard languages as they emerge.

Another requirement was to replace user interfaces, allowing OEM and end-user customers to make the user interfaces to GenRad's products correspond with their own.

GenRad wanted to replace data storage mechanisms, allowing its tools to work directly off the circuit and waveform descriptions stored by the customer in his/her own database. Also, it needed to add externally procured components to its tools to develop total CAE systems. The company needed to reconfigure existing components and bought-in components into new products. For example, arranging for two different simulators to run in tandem and compare their results.

Finally, GenRad needed to change the mapping of components onto processes and processors, so that it could exploit parallelism in hardware.

Interfaces and components

Some may think that modularization is the answer. However the problem is the reconfiguration of old components and new components to form new products. They require interfaces which are separated from components and given a life of their own.

The developer should not have to distinguish between interfaces that are *within* a process and interfaces that are *between* processes. This means that interfaces should follow a single paradigm to avoid confusion. At GenRad the decision was to choose function calls and use remote procedure calls for communication between processes and processors[12].

The developer should not develop his or her component with its connection to some other particular component in mind. Instead, he or she should always design for reuse, using standard interfaces. These should be independent of components as in Figure 2.

Component connection

The need to develop components independently of each other, with connections between them employing standard interfaces leads to changes in naming conventions. This is illustrated in Figure 3. Figure 3(a) shows the conventional position where the developer of A builds into this code the fact that it connects to B, by writing the name of B's function b func in his/her code. Developers have to break from that convention, and make all names local to a component, as in Figure 3(b). However, developers should also recognise the independent existence of the interface, and incorporate this into the names that are used, as in Figure 3(c). There is still the possibility that the same interface is used several times by a component and the naming convention needs to distinguish between these uses.

The next stage is to consider linking together components through their common interfaces. Normally the linker binds together names that are the same, but here

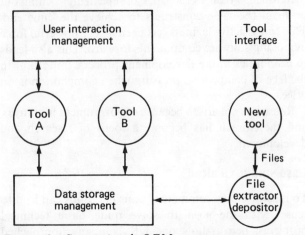

Figure 1. Conventional OEM arrangement — a tool embedded into an alien environment

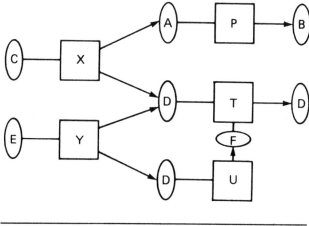

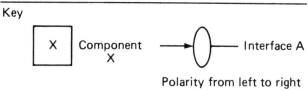

Key

Figure 2. Interfaces and components. Note the use of interface D in three places

the names have been made different, deliberately. Some possible solutions that have been considered are:

- using a tool to change the names within the component so that they do match, then recompile and link normally,
- using macros to rename, recompile and then link normally,
- supplying an interface procedure with the name used by caller, which in turn calls the target,

(a) Normal interconnection

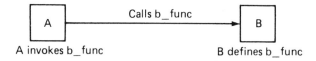

(b) Making names local to a component, binding the names handled later

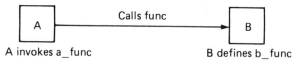

(c) Introducing the name of the interface

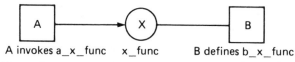

Figure 3. Naming conventions

- developing a special tool which can change the external names in the object files, then link normally,
- developing a special linker which can make equivalent external names,
- using an indirect function call, a function pointer, which is initialized to the target at build time,
- using an indirect function call, a function pointer which is initialized to the target at run time,
- using an object-oriented message passing system like that of Objective C.

At GenRad, the developers chose the seventh option.

Implementation

The implementation of this architectural mode, caused a number of problems. Firstly, the engineers at GenRad proved to be surprisingly conservative. They preferred to discuss problems with another engineer while working with a component and they were used to linking by name association. They legitimately feared performance costs, even for indirect function calls, though costs would be minimal. They also questioned the benefits gained from the proposed changes.

However, once the ideas had been adopted, and its potential grasped, some of the senior engineers saw the possibility of solving other problems with these mechanisms. One of GenRad's components acts as a switch, collecting the output from one component and forwarding selected parts of the output to several other components. The next problem was, should the switch be a fixed 2-way or 3-way, switch, or should it be a generic n-way switch? If it was generic, should n be fixed at compile time or run-time? The answer was to use linked lists of structures containing function pointers. However this complicated the whole component interface area, making it a difficult problem to apply the architectural model uniformly across the products.

Future developments

Measuring reuse

Can reuse be measured? Peter Wegner[13] says:

... any reusable resource may be thought of as a capital good whose development cost may be recovered over its set of uses.

Another way to measure reuse would be to monitor how often software components can be used. However, the developer needs to ascertain what sort of reuse is meant. Is it:

- the number of times the code is incorporated into other code?
- the number of times the code is executed?

- a combination, the number of times the incorporating code is executed?
- a figure of merit reflecting value or utility or saving rather than being a simple count of uses?

The simplest criteria is the number of times executed, which makes the reuse measure of basic software like operating systems very high.

However reuse is measured, the software industry has been conscientious in the reuse of software.

Trends

Future trends indicate that there will be an increase in development in:

- proven algorithms
- higher level languages
- generic packages
- customized packages, kits, sources
- in-house reuse of kernels and components

But should we expect a software components industry to emerge, as in other engineering industries?

Analogies with other engineering industries have very doubtful validity. It is difficult to expect software to behave like electronics and mechanical engineering.

In civil engineering reuse is simple, with the same basic components and materials being used repeatedly, using the same methods and designs.

In mechanical engineering, automobile, ships, and aircraft small or special components like motors and aero-engines are reused, but larger components are only very exceptionally used. Again, methods and designs are widely reused.

For electronics purposes, reuse is mostly of 'small' chips, with some reuse of large components, boards and boxes.

Technical barriers to a software components industry

To make software reusable, it must be possible to specify the software with sufficient precision and completeness for a potential user to be able to make his/her selection. The separation of interfaces from components is probably not important. The state of development of specification methods like Z^{14} and VDM[15] is sufficiently advanced for precision to be achievable for functional specification, though other attributes like performance may not be specifiable yet. It could be appropriate now to determine standards for specifying components.

If components are going to be used, we need some standard method of connecting them. Decisions must be taken about the form of interface, whether it consists of a set of procedures and, possibly, shared data, or whether it consists of messages in some communications style of protocol. Some simple interconnection technology needs to be set down, independently of particular programming languages or equipment suppliers. An international standard for subroutine linkage may be helpful. Manufacturers already define standards for their operating systems to enable the building of mixed language systems.

If any volume of reusable software components arise, there is going to be a problem concerned with cataloguing them, and searching indexes to find the appropriate one. This requires knowledge of how to describe components in a way that is helpful to would-be users. However, this may not be the same as specification. For example, if we consider how users find the appropriate subroutines in a library of numerical routines, a lot of high level understanding and descriptive terms are used. We do not have this kind of taxonomy for software in general. It should be noted that such a taxonomy would also be necessary for comparative studies of software, for example in work-content estimation.

In making a search, we may not be looking for exact matches, but approximate matches. To some degree we can adapt to the component, converting data, accepting attributes and functions which are not exactly what was desired. Again, this problem is not unique to software components, and arises in the proper consideration of conformance of a system to its requirements.

Software is notoriously easy to steal. A components industry relies on obtaining a return on investment, and a way of preventing piracy is critical. No other branch of engineering suffers in quite the same way, the nearest equivalent elsewhere is the theft of designs and blueprints. Legal and social measure will be addressed later. A limit could be placed on the uses of software, even having a meter which counts the number of times the software is executed and charging accordingly. There are already moves in this direction with dongles which in effect transform the software into hardware. The possession of the special piece of hardware, the dongle, enables the software to be executed. Much further research and development in this area is needed.

Social and legal barriers to a software components industry

If a software components industry is to happen, then the social, legal and economic environment must encourage this industry. In this area there is a significant difference between what can be achieved within a company or group of collaborating companies, and what can be achieved in the open market place.

Preparing software for reuse as a component does require extra effort. This extra effort needs to be rewarded. In the open market this reward would be some form of royalty or licence fee. However there may be problems in enforcing these payments. In the closed confines of a company, or group of companies, it is possible to reward individuals for the level of reuse of their software.

To maintain competitive advantage, some parts of a company's software may always be proprietary. The proprietary software may not even be particularly sophisticated, but comparable to the way application specific integrated circuits are used in hardware designs to make designs difficult to reproduce from inspection of an example. We must always expect some level of non-reuse.

A particular problem with software is that it is not a commodity. It does not become an asset of a company that purchases it. Software may be written off in its year of purchase, whereas hardware may be written off over three to five years, or more. Software may not be allowed to be sold on, as with recent public announcement that a computer manufacturer required the purchasers of second-hand hardware to relicense the software. There is no market in second-hand software. This could be changed and third-party maintenance could then find a market. Copyright protection of software is emerging, but clearly needs to be practised internationally.

The ability to build software oneself is an enormous barrier to reuse. The cost of designing and fabricating your own microprocessor is so enormous that it is only undertaken in very special circumstances, the margin between buying and building is several orders of magnitude. By contrast the margins between buying and building software are not so great, except in the large volume microcomputer marketplace.

Frequently software is acquired on the basis of futures, and if the software is bought, its future development may not turn out to be the way it was intended. If it is built in-house, the developer is in total control over its development. However, maintenance of in-house software is likely to be more expensive; the software is likely to be less robust and it may be subject to uncontrolled voluntary 'improvements' that are not required and add to cost.

It is clear to avoid some of these issues, a software components industry should be high-volume and low-cost, producing robust and stable products with low or zero maintenance costs.

Conclusions

There already exists a lot of reuse of software, through:

- algorithms and methods
- languages and systems
- packages and kits

these practices are likely to continue and evolve towards yet higher levels of reuse.

However, a software components industry as envisaged by ACARD is likely to meet severe technical, social, economic and legal barriers. The UK government could have some influence by encouraging research in:

- standardization of component interface mechanisms
- methods for protection against software piracy
- methods for cataloguing software components, and searching for best fits within the catalogue

and by considering what legal and fiscal measures could be taken to enable a market is second-hand software and third-party maintenance of software.

The software development industry could be encouraged into further reuse at the level of software components, focusing on internal reuse through the exploitation of methods used in some other companies.

References

1 *IEEE Trans. Software Engin.* Special Issue on Software Reusability Vol SE-10 No 5 (September 1985)
2 ACARD, Cabinet Office: Advisory Council for Applied Research and Development. *Software: A Vital Key to UK Competitiveness* HMSO (1986)
3 **Cox, B J** *Object-Oriented Programming* Addison-Wesley (1986)
4 **Ledgard, H** ADA: *An Introduction* Ada Reference Manual Springer-Verlag (1981)
5 **Goguen, A** 'Reusing and Interconnecting Software Components' *IEEE Computer* (February 1986) pp 16–28
6 **Bourne, S R** *The UNIX System*, Addison-Wesley (1983)
7 **Kernighan, B W** 'The UNIX System and Software Reusability' *IEEE 84* pp 513–519
8 **Simpson, H R and Jackson, K** 'Process Synchronisation in MASCOT' *The Comput J.* Vol 22 No 4 (November 1979) pp 332–345
9 **Kramer, J and Magee, J** 'Dynamic Configuration for Distributed Systems' *IEEE Trans. Software Engin* Vol SE-11 No 4 (April 1985) pp 424–436
10 **Sloman, M Kramer, J Magee, J** *The Conic Toolkit for Building Distributed Systems* 6th IFAC Distributed Computer Control Systems Workshop, Monterey, California, Pergamon Press (May 1985)
11 **Mill, J** 'Software solutions without re-inventing the wheel' *Computing* (November 6 1986) pp 35
12 **Bacarisse, B** 'Using Remote Procedure calls in C', *University College London Internal Working Paper 1616* (July 1984)
13 **Wegner, P** 'Capital-Intensive Software Technology' *IEEE Software* Vol 1 (July 1984)
14 **Sufrin, B** *Mathematics for System Specification* Oxford University Programming Research Group, Oxford, UK (18 January 1984)
15 **Jones, C B** *Systematic Software Development Using VDM* Prentice-Hall (1986) □

Software Reuse Myths

Will Tracz

Program Analysis and Verification Group[1]

Computer Systems Laboratory - ERL 402

Stanford, California 94305

TRACZ@SIERRA.STANFORD.EDU

Abstract

Reusing software is a simple, straightforward concept that has appealed to programmers since the first stored-program computer was created. Unfortunately, software reuse has not evolved beyond its most primitive forms of subroutine libraries and brute force program modification. This paper analyzes nine commonly believed software reuse myths. These myths reveal certain technical, organizational, and psychological software engineering research issues and trends.

1. Introduction

The concept of software reuse has been part of the programming heritage since the origins of the stored-program computer EDSAC at the University of Cambridge in 1949 where the first subroutine library was proposed. Until recently, little has been done to extend program reusability beyond this rather simple level. McIlroy [14] in 1968 envisioned software component factories, but apparently the only the Japanese listened. As this decade draws to a close, interest in applying this simple, but effective concept of not reinventing the wheel has been reborn. Again and again the role of reusable software has been recognized and discussed [9], [11], [2].

This paper identifies and examines nine myths that surround reusable software. These myths partially explain why software reuse has not had, to date, the broad sweeping effects envisioned by the programming prophets. The myths are as follows:

1. *Software reuse is a technical problem.*
2. *Special tools are needed for software reuse.*
3. *Reusing code results in huge increases in productivity.*
4. *Artificial intelligence will solve the reuse problem.*
5. *The Japanese have solved the reuse problem.*
6. *Ada[2] has solved the reuse problem.*
7. *Designing software from reusable parts is like designing hardware using integrated circuits.*
8. *Reused software is the same as Reusable software.*
9. *Software reuse will just happen.*

Each of these myths will be examined individually in the sections that follow.

---

[1]The author is an employee of the IBM Federal Systems Division, Owego, NY, participating in the IBM Resident Study Program at Stanford University.

[2]Ada is a registered trademark of the U.S. Government-Ada Joint Program Office.

2. Myths Revealed

2.1. Myth #1: Software Reuse Is a Technical Problem

Many good people have been lead astray by assuming that the software reuse problem needs a technical solution. While there are both technical and non-technical barriers inhibiting software reuse, if one looks at the most-often-stated reasons why software is not reused [20], the overwhelming majority of them may be classified as psychological, sociological, or economic. The only technical reasons cited are the lack of search methods to find the right pieces or the lack of quality components (to put in the library in the first place) to reuse. In the latter case, management plays a critical role in setting and enforcing standards, as well as motivating programmers to develop components, and to design software based upon them. The library issue will be addressed in the following myth. Finally, as stated by Ratcliffe [17], "... the whole western economic system may be against reuse." The development of software reuse has been stunted by intra-company and inter-company legal, contractual as well as political conflicts.

2.2. Myth#2: Special Tools Are Needed for Software Reuse

The term *special* is meant to imply tools tailored specifically to facilitate the reusable software engineering process. When reviewing the tools proposed to support software reuse, researchers generally include a library facility and perhaps a standards-checking program or syntax-directed editor. If one examines the most successful applications [12], [13] of software reuse to date, one finds that few, if any, tools at all are used. The Japanese software factories use a simple Key Word In Context (KWIC) index to locate the desired function. Furthermore, production software libraries seldom exceed 100-200 components in size, a number that is very easily managed manually by most programmers. (There are instances of very large repositories of subroutines as with the National Bureau of Standards Library, which contains over 2800 entries. In this case, a library system is a necessity.) In the instances where prototype reusable software libraries have been developed, they have either been created using a relational data base system [5], [15], or an information retrieval system [8], [1]. Finally, in most instances of software reuse, programmers modify existing programs, written by themselves or by a programmer on the same project [10]. In this case, because of the proximity and accessibility to the resource, the programmer does not need a sophisticated tool to locate the software to reuse.

2.3. Myth #3: Reusing Code Results in Huge Increases in Productivity

What is *huge*? Studies have shown [11] that even if 40% of a design and 75% of the code on a given project is reused, the resulting 50% reduction in testing, and comparable reductions in integration test, documentation, and system test, result in a net productivity gain of only 40%. In order to achieve an order-of-magnitude improvement in software productivity, one must resort to application generators, or highly parameterized components. (Still, cutting software development time roughly in half is not bad.) The real payoff is realized by the decreased maintenance costs! Maintenance cost reductions of up to 90% have been reported when reusable code, code templates, and application generators have been used to develop new systems.

On the other hand, one cannot ignore the initial start-up costs. Software designed for reuse costs between 20% and 25% more to develop and learn to use. The break-even point is not reached until after the second or third use.

2.4. Myth #4: Artificial Intelligence Will Solve the Reuse Problem

How can we automate something we have no expertise in? Actually such a statement is not entirely fair, because AI does have something to offer. There are strong similarities between the problem domain analysis performed by systems analysts trying to extract common components for reuse in similar applications and the domain analysis performed by heuristic search algorithms trying to match requirement specifications to program frames or schemas. However, automatic generation of code from requirements is still a research area. Expert systems have been designed to assist programmers in locating components [4] that match desired functions, and instantiate them [6], but the lack of a good notation to represent the semantics of software is still the major roadblock to unleashing the power of AI approaches.

2.5. Myth #5: The Japanese Have Solved the Reuse Problem

Many hold the somewhat mystical belief that the Japanese have solved the   problem (fill in the blank). The success of the Japanese software factories is not based on any technological breakthroughs, but on the formalization of the process and the product. A question that gets answered "no" only once in a Japanese software factory is "Does a part exist that performs this function?" Japanese programmer training and sense of commitment to standards also strongly facilitate reusable software engineering.

Another reason for the success of the Japanese software factory may be summarized in the following paraphrased motto: "Ask not what you can do for your software, but what your software can do for you." By making a business decision to address a particular problem domain and recognizing the leverage software reuse plays, the Japanese have justified amortizing the cost of developing the **critical mass** of reusable software and the associated software engineering environment ultimately necessary to succeed.

2.6. Myth #6: Ada Has Solved the Reuse Problem

Writing a generic package in Ada does not necessarily make it reusable any more than writing a Fortran subroutine or assembly language macro. The adaptability (and reuse potential) of a software component depends on the amount of domain analysis performed and the degree a module is parameterized to reflect this. Furthermore, the type of parameterization facilities provided by the programming language may not always support the degree or form of adaptability desired, as is the case with Ada generics. The same holds for a class in Smalltalk or other object-oriented languages. While certain language features do facilitate the development of reusable software, the language, in itself, is not enough to solve the problem.

2.7. Myth #7: Designing Software From Reusable Parts is Like Designing Hardware Using Integrated Circuits

Why don't there exist software building blocks which programmers can wire together to build systems similar to integrated circuits If they did exist, what type of CASE (Computer Aided Software Engineering) environment would be necessary to support them? Are electrical engineers that much smarter than software engineers? Superficially, comparing software design and hardware design [7] is a very appealing analogy. At one level of complexity, the analogy holds. Structured programming relies on a select handful of basic structures (e.g., An "if-statement" is similar to a 2-way multiplexor. A "for-loop" is like a counter). Unfortunately, the analogy breaks down [16] when one realizes that both the number and the complexity of software components far exceeds those currently used by logic designers. Because of the variety of applications, the wide spectrum of problem-domain-specific components, and, most of all, the amount of "glue" necessary to connect software components together, the similarities between software and hardware design have yet to be fully exploited. Other hard problems include identifying the building blocks and defining (and documenting) the interfaces and parameterization. Finally, economic factors that differentiate hardware design from software design. For practical reasons hardware designers must constrain their design to be based on available components, whereas software designers can create designs based on custom components. Furthermore, unused functionality in a hardware chip doesn't effect the chip's performance, whereas excess code can effect program size as well as performance.

2.8. Myth #8: Reused Software is the Same as Reusable Software.

A corollary to this myth is that "A good way to develop reusable software is to take an existing program and add parameters." Both these myths fail to emphasize the need to design for and document for reuse. Unplanned reuse of software (also called software salvaging) occurs frequently in the software community. Programmers often extract modules or code segments, and then modify them to meet their needs. This is an error-prone and time-consuming process, which could be avoided if the software were designed initially with reuse in mind.   As the corollary implies, reuse should be considered at design time, not after the implementation has been completed. The emphasis should be on *planned* reuse. Special attention needs to be placed on interface design and modularization (e.g., low coupling and high cohesion).

2.9. Myth #9:Software Reuse Will Just Happen

Judging from the limited success software reuse has enjoyed to date, most software reuse is not planned; therefore, the full potential has not been realized. Yet, times are changing. As hardware costs decrease and performance increases, customers are becoming less willing to buy a costly customized piece of software when a slightly more inefficient (due to some overhead in parameterization) but less costly software may do. In order to reach this goal, components need to be designed, documented and implemented for reuse [3] according to some guidelines [18], [3], [19]. Finally, management needs to provide the incentives to motivate and reward the application of this technology [21].

3. Conclusion

This paper has presented one perspective on why software reuse has not played a major role in improving programmer productivity. The realities of the myths discussed are as follows:

1. *Software reuse is a technical and non-technical problem.*
2. *No "special "tools are needed for software reuse. Available data base technology can be applied to help organize and retrieve software in large repositories.*
3. *Reusing code will not result in an order-of-magnitude increase in productivity and quality.*
4. *Artificial intelligence technology can play a role in solving the reuse problem.*
5. *The Japanese have taken the first steps toward solving the reuse problem.*
6. *No single language alone can solve the reuse problem.*
7. *Designing software from reusable parts is not like designing hardware using integrated circuits.*
8. *Reusing software that was not planned for reuse is harder than reusing software that was designed for reuse.*
9. *Software reuse will not just happen.*

While reusable software solve the software crisis by itself, it has the potential to make a significant impact. By exposing the preconceived myths about software reuse, this paper should help programmers and managers direct their efforts and resources more effectively and, thus, achieve more readily the goal of reusable software engineering.

References

1. Arnold, S.P., and Stepoway, S.L. The Reuse System: Cataloging and Retrieval of Reusable Software. Proceedings of COMPCON '87, February 23-27, 1987, pp. 376-379.

2. Biggerstaff, T. and Richter, C. Reusability Framework, Assessment and Directions. Proceedings of The Hawaii International Conference on System Sciences, January 7-10, 1987, pp. 502-512.

3. Braun, C.L., Goodenough, J.B., Eanes, R.S. Ada Reusability Guidelines. 3285-2-208/2, SofTech, Inc., April, 1985.

4. Braun, U. An Expert System for the Retrieval of Software Building Blocks. TR 05.373, IBM Laboratory Boeblingen, 1986. In German.

5. Burton, B.A., and Broido, M.D. A Phased Approach To Ada Package Reuse. Proceedings of Software Technology for Adaptable Reliable Systems (STARS) Workshop, April 9-12, 1985, pp. 83-98.

6. Defense Technical Information Center. CAMP: Common Ada Missile Packages. Pamphlet.

7. Cox, B.J. Object-oriented Programming, Software-ICs and System Building. Proceedings of National Conference on Software Reuseability and Maintainability, September 10-11, 1986.

8. Frakes, W.B., and Nejmeh, B.A. Software Reuse Through Information Retrieval. Proceedings of The Hawaii International Conference on System Sciences, January 7-10, 1987, pp. 530-535.

9. Freeman, P. Reusable Software Engineering: Concepts and Research Directions. Proceedings of ITT Workshop on Reusability in Programming, September 7-9, 1983.

10. Grabow, P.C., and Nobles, W,B. Reusable Software Concepts and Software Development Methodologies. Proceedings of National Conference on Software Reuseability and Maintainability, September 10-11, 1986.

11. Horowitz, E., and Munson, J.B. "An Expansive View of Reusable Software". *IEEE Transactions on Software Engineering SE-10*, 5 (September 1984), 477-487.

12. Lanergan,R.G. and Grasso, C.A. "Software Engineering with Reusable Design and Code". *IEEE Transactions on Software Engineering SE-10*, 5 (September 1984), 498-501.

13. Matsubara, T., Sasaki, O., Nakajim, K., Takezawa, K., Yamamoto, S. and Tanaka, T. SWB System: A Software Factory. In *Software Engineering Environments*, North-Holland Publishing Company, 1981, pp. 305-318.

14. McIlroy, M. D. Mass Produced Software Components. Proceedings of 1969 NATO Conference on Software Engineering, 1969, pp. 88-98.

15. Onuegbe, E.O. Software Classification as an Aid to Reuse: Initial Use as Part of a Rapid Prototyping System. Proceedings of The Hawaii International Conference on System Sciences, January 7-10, 1987, pp. 521-529.

16. Polak, W. Maintainability and Reusable Program Designs. Proceedings of National Conference on Software Reuseability and Maintainability, September 10-11, 1986.

17. Ratcliffe, M. "Report on a Workshop on Software Reuse held at Hereford, UK on 1,2 May 1986". *SIGSOFT Software Engineering Notes 12*, 1 (January 1987), 42-47.

18. STARS. STARS Reusability Guideline V4.0.

19. St. Dennis, R. J., Stachour, P., Frankowski, E., Onuegbe, E. "Measurable Characteristics of Reusable Ada Software". *Ada Letters 5*, 2 (March-April 1986), 41-49.

20. Tracz, W.J. Why Reusable Software Isn't. Proceedings of Workshop on Future Directions in Computer Architecture and Software, May, 1986.

21. Tracz, W.J. Software Reuse: Motivators and Inhibitors. Proceedings of COMPCON87, February, 1987.

Ada Reusability Efforts:

A Survey of the State of the Practice

Will Tracz

Program Analysis and Verification Group[*]
Stanford University, ERL 402
Stanford, California 94305

Abstract

Ada[**] is a programming language designed to help alleviate a portion of the "Software Crisis" currently being experienced by the US Department of Defense. **Software Reuse** is one aspect of program development that Ada's features were envisioned to support. This paper evaluates the progress being made on realizing software reuse with Ada. The efforts of 16 corporations and research consortiums are summarized and analyzed. Ada building blocks and reusability guidelines are discussed in detail.

1. Introduction

Software reusability is an appealing concept with obvious benefits in programmer productivity and program quality. Reuse manifests itself in many forms[1,2], yet software developers have not capitalize on it for a multitude of technical, social, and economic reasons[3]. Ada is a programming language designed to facilitate reusability. As stated in the Ada Language Reference Manual[4], section 1.3, paragraph 5, "the ability to assemble a program from independently produced software components has been a central idea in this design." Yet, a programming language alone is not enough to solve the "Software Crisis[5]."

Since the introduction of Ada in the early 80s, a growing base of experience has accumulated with its application. This experience has been documented and distributed only sporadically. Furthermore, the information that has been published has tended to be redundant, partially due to parallel proprietary efforts and first-time learning-curve considerations. This paper gathers together the scattered results of the Ada reusability efforts to date. It extracts the essence of the activities and summarizes the projects, products, ideas, and achievements. This paper condenses the research and development activities that constitute the state of the practice of Ada and software reusability.

---

[*]The author is an employee of the IBM Federal Systems Division, Owego, NY, participating in the IBM Resident Study Program at Stanford University.

[**]Ada is a trademark of the US Department of Defense (Ada Joint Program Office).

1.1. Organization

This paper is divided into three sections. The first section describes the characteristics of Ada, as a language, which lend themselves to developing reusable software components. The second section summarizes the efforts of various corporations and research consortiums to move toward a reusable Ada component-based software development paradigm. In particular, the work done by the following is described:

1. Ada Software Repository[6]
2. Boeing[7,8]
3. EVB Software Engineering[9]
4. Ford Aerospace[10]
5. General Dynamics[11]
6. GTE[12]
7. Honeywell[13]
8. IBM[14]
9. Intermetrics[15]
10. Lockheed[16]
11. Rockwell[17]
12. SofTech[18]
13. SEI[19]
14. STARS[20]
15. Toshiba[21]
16. TRW[22]

The final section identifies and examines the efforts by Ada practitioners to formalize the development of reusable components and to generate Ada reusability guidelines. The work of the following individuals/corporations represents the most significant, detailed and accessible contributions available.

- Booch[23]
- EVB Software Engineering[9]
- Honeywell[24]
- SofTech[18]
- STARS[25]

This paper concludes with a list of open issues that face the Ada programming community regarding software reusability.

2. Reusability and Ada

What features of Ada make it appropriate for developing reusable software?

Ada supports software reuse for several reasons[26, 27,18,17,28,29]. The existence of one stable[23], "standardized" language for developing "portable" programs, implies that programs should be able to "rerun" on different hosts over a long period of time. While this is clearly one aspect of software reuse, the key issue, and the one this paper focuses on, deals with reusing Ada software modules on different applications. To this end, Ada has several language constructs which facilitate the development of reusable software. They include

1. the **package** construct that supports modularization and separation between specification and implementation,
2. the **strong typing** that enforces consistency between formal and actual parameters,
3. the **generic** construct that supports parameterization, and
4. **overload resolution** that provides some syntactic as well as semantic reuse of function.

The package construct supports information hiding and the creation of abstract data types. Separating the program body and specification allows the programmer to create families of implementations using the same interface[9]. These program libraries can vary in performance characteristics and other attributes, including the actual language of implementation. Strong typing assists in the self documentation of a module and assures its proper composition. The generic construct provides additional flexibility and adaptability*** of a program unit to be reused under a variety of conditions and data types. Finally, overload resolution increases program readability and provides for an efficient, though somewhat restricted, compile-time implementation of the Smalltalk class concept.

In summary, Ada provides both syntactic and semantic facilities that *may***** be used to create reusable software. These, along with DoD directives (standardization, validation, and mandated use), enhance the chances of software reuse making a significant impact on the software crisis.

3. Industry Efforts

The programming community has committed relatively small amounts of research and development efforts (6-10 person years per company) related to Ada-based software reusability. In general, the approach taken by most projects consists of the following steps:

1. Identifying motivators and inhibitors of software reuse.

***Missing from the language is a means to handle conditional implementation (e.g., PL/I Pre-Processor). This could be remedied by a simple pre-processor, at the sacrifice of compromising the standardization of the language

****The degree reusability that software exhibits depends almost entirely on how it was designed.

2. Studying library mechanisms for storing and retrieving reusable components. In some instances, a classification schema is generated.
3. Developing a prototype project, Ada package library, or library system.
4. Studying how to fit software reusability into an existing software development methodology.

Finally, some researchers have entered a second phase of development. Full-scale production systems, reusability guidelines and environments are being specified, designed, and in some cases, implemented.

A major portion of the references cited in this section can be found in these three sources:

1. The proceedings of the *National Conference on Software Reuseability and Maintainability*, September 10-11, 1986, presented by the National Institute for Software Quality and Productivity.

2. The proceedings of the *First International Conference on Ada Programming Language Applications for the NASA Space Station*, June 2-5, 1986, hosted by the University of Houston-Clear Lake and NASA Lyndon B. Johnson Space Center.

3. The proceedings of the *Software Technology for Adaptable Reliable Systems (STARS) Workshop*, April 9-12, 1985.

The best reference covering general software reusability topics is the proceedings of the *ITT Workshop on Reusability in Programming*, September 7-9, 1983. (See also the September, 1984 issue of *IEEE Transactions on Software Engineering*, which reprints several of the articles.)

What follows is a summary of the research and development projects, tools and management philosophies of 16 companies or software consortiums. Their key accomplishments have been extracted and any significant results emphasized.

3.1. Ada Software Repository

The Ada Software Repository (ASR) is a collection over 25.5M bytes of source code and 10M bytes of documentation (as of 6/86) accessible over the ARPA net on SIMTEL20. Since its foundation in 1984, it has been growing with fairly unconstrained contributions of Ada tools and components. Each contribution is required to have a predefined header/disclaimer. One of the reasons for the success of the repository is the "trust-level" method of handling contributions. Each subscriber to the repository understands the limited conditions/warranty of the software within.

The following is a partial list of the contents and organization of the repository:

- **Ada-SQL** - standard Ada DBMS interface
- **AI** - expert systems, LISP, pattern recognition
- **CAIS Tools** - Mitre supplied Common APSE Interface Set tools

- **Compilation Order** - determines interrelationships
- **Components** - general purpose procedures, generics (data structures) sort/search, compare
- **Cross Reference** - cross-reference listing generator
- **Data Base Management** - DBM functions
- **DDN** - Defense Data Network communication facilities
- **Debuggers** - source level
- **Editors** - text editing
- **Education** - sample programs, tutorials, online courseware.
- **External Tools** - miscellaneous non-Ada tools (EMACS)
- **Forms Generator** - screen/form oriented menu system
- **Graphical Kernel System** - GKS routines
- **Management Tools** - Status tracking, manpower estimates
- **Math Library** - trig, matrix, bit/string manipulation etc.
- **Menu** - front end menus
- **Message Handling** - facilities
- **Metrics** - analysis (Halstead and McCabe) plus more
- **Pager** - paged file manipulation
- **PDL** - design support tools
- **Pretty Printers** - source reformatter
- **Program Stubber** - body creation from specification section
- **Simulation** - tools
- **Spelling Checkers** - written in Ada
- **Style Checkers** - checking tools
- **WIS ADA Tools** - NOSC tools paid for by WWMCCS Information Systems

3.2. Boeing

3.2.1. Boeing Aerospace Company
Researchers at the Boeing Aerospace Company have been involved in two projects related to Ada and software reuse. First, Boeing has completed an ongoing study[30] for the Rome Air Development Center (RADC) determining the factors, criteria, characteristics, and interrelationships of software *Interoperability and Reusability*. The study includes general guidelines for the development of reusable software and cites three application areas that would benefit from software reuse: 1) Command and Control, 2) Support Software, and 3) Business Applications.

The Boeing Automated Software Engineering Project[8] (BASE) is the second relevant effort. It addresses the full software life cycle with a consistent, user-friendly Ada programming environment. The BASE Project integrates commercial and internal tools and components

3.2.2. Boeing Commercial Airplane Company
Boeing Commercial Airplane Company (BCAC) subcontracts a large portion of its software projects to vendors. Each vendor is supplied with a set of development guidelines to follow and standards to comply with. BCAC has recently completed a study[7] updating the guidelines to reflect the implications of programming in Ada and using/contributing to a library of reusable software.

3.3. EVB Software Engineering Inc.
EVB Software Engineering Inc. provides a collection of reusable Ada components in the form of a product. GRACE™ (Generic Reusable Ada Components for Engineering) consists of over 200 well-documented***** and tested reusable Ada packages based on Booch's Reusable Structure Taxonomy(see section 4.1). For a flat fee, subscribers receive the components (mostly data structures) in several installments. A partial list of the components follows. Note that each item might have several implementations reflecting run-time tradeoffs (e.g., space or time) and different operating environments (e.g., sequential or concurrent).

- Stack (13 Variations)
- Queue (21 Variations)
- String (14 Variations)
- List (Singly-Linked, Doubly-Linked, Circular Doubly-Linked)
- Binary Tree (6 Variations)
- Graph (Directed, Un-Directed, Weighted Undirected, Weighted Directed)
- Set (12 Variations)
- Discrete Set (4 Variations)
- Binary Search Tree (9 Variations)
- Ring Structure (15 Variations)
- Matrix (10 Variations)
- B-Tree (3 Variations)
- Priority Queue (6 Variations)
- Tree (12 Variations)
- Bag (12 Variations)
- Deque (12 Variations)
- Map (12 Variations)
- Hash Table (6 Variations)

3.4. Ford Aerospace
Researchers at Ford Aerospace and Communication Corporation in Newport Beach, California, have taken a very pragmatic approach[10] to software reuse and Ada. Software engineers first redesigned an existing system to produce reusable Ada components. This included generating standard Ada packages such as a generic fixed point math library, a generic transformation package, and a table lookup math library. From this experience, researchers designed the **CAP System** (Computer Aided Programming) which consists of an icon-based, interactive graphics environment with a library of reusable components.

3.5. General Dynamics
General Dynamics has been successful applying AI/Object-oriented methodology to software reuse in the DARTS[31] system. At last word, researchers were investigating how to

---

*****The documentation is extensive and detailed. It not only describes the design and capability of the component, but shows how to reuse it also.

adapt this technology to Ada[11]. The DARTS system relies on software domain experts to develop *archetypes* or templates of applications. Then, with a specially developed language and translator, new systems are generated. Currently, the Ada reuse project is studying Ada generic units and specifications to determine what additional information needs to be recorded (e.g., performance and exceptions) and the limitations of Ada syntax in applying this paradigm.

3.6. GTE
GTE is under DoD contract to collect/develop a library[12] of reusable Ada software. This includes tools, programs, and compcnents.

3.7. Honeywell
Honeywell Computer Sciences Center's resuability effort has centered on the RaPIER[32] (Rapid Prototyping to Investigate End-user Requirements) Project, sponsored in part by the Office of Naval Research. The projects goals were to

- "define a methodology for prototype construction[32]" and
- "develop a prototype of a software engineering environment that supports end-user requirements prototyping[32]."

A secondary result of the project was the generation of the Ada reusability guidelines (see section 4.6).

The RaPIER system is based on an object-oriented prototype construction technique[13]. It uses a relational data-base[33] management system (referred to as the software base) to handle the classification and storage/retrieval of Ada components.

3.8. IBM
Ada does not play a major role as an implementation language within the main programming community of IBM. It has been explored by some sites for its tasking capability. The most significant impact that Ada has made on the programming process within IBM is its selection (and extension) as the common design language for all programming projects.

3.8.1. Federal Systems Division
The IBM Federal Systems Division supports all DoD-related business activities. Ada and software reuse have been deemed important technology thrusts. The Houston, Texas, Manassas, Virginia, and Owego, New York facilities have spent much effort to gain expertise. In particular, an advanced program development environment with a library of reusable Ada components[34] is being designed and implemented.

3.9. Intermetrics
Bruce Burton and his research team at Intermetrics have spent the last three years studying the Ada software reusability problem. Besides determining the factors inhibiting software reuse, they have laid out a detailed seven phase approach[35] to developing a production-quality

commercial reusable software library system - **ASCAT** (Ada Software Catalog). After completing the study, a prototype system[15] - **RSL** (Reusable Software Library) was built. The system relies on a Configuration Management System (CMS) and relational data base with a natural language front end (CLOUT) as the underlying technology. The prototype implements the first three phases of the proposed commercial library system described as follows:

1. *Analysis and Requirements Definition*: Examine existing software libraries (COSMIC, IMSL and SPSS). Identify types of information to be stored (e.g., specifications, or designs).
2. *Initial Software Catalog*: Design data-base record and tools to automate the data collection and entry process.
3. *Automated ASCAT/CMS Interface*: Tie the library system into the configuration management system to handle authorization control, distribution control, and identification.
4. *Integration of Standardization Support Tools*: Develop tools to enforce coding and documentation standards. Integrate **BRYON**[TM] into the library system
5. *Expand User Community*: Add an Email system and some security features.
6. *Automated Catalog and Library Interaction*: Automate the distribution and authorization of parts. Develop an ordering system data base.
7. *Multi-Site/Multi-Company Extensions* Add licensing, purchase agreement, and restrictions to the Order System along with enhanced security. Incorporate distributed libraries and a bulletin board for broadcasts and user forums.

3.10. Lockheed
The Ada Technology Support Lab (ATSL) at Lockheed Missiles and Space Company, Sunnyvale, CA, was originally organized to support the **MILSTAR** project. They have investigated the limits of generics[36] and the management of reusable software. One noteworthy study[16] focused on analyzing the impact of reusing Ada versus Jovial software for reducing maintenance costs.

3.11. Rockwell
The Rockwell reusability effort focuses on two projects:

- **ROSES** - Rockwell Operational Software Engineering System[17]
- **ATOP** - Ada Technology Objectives and Plans

ROSES consists of a cluster of VAX[TM], 150 workstations and an integrated support environment for developing and warehousing reusable Ada software. Researchers are studying the use of object-oriented design and the types of standards needed for analyzing, tracing and maintaining reusable software.

ATOP is a study Rockwell did for NASA to specify the design considerations for reusable Ada packages. Their findings include the following recommendations for developing reusable software:

- Find common aerospace applications.
- Determine general functional areas.
- Determine type of components to develop.
- Determine visible objects and operations.
- Determine private objects and operations.
- Determine generic aspects.
- Determine exception handling.
- Investigate software generator systems.
- Study effects of target machine dependency.

The study also investigated configuration and management control mechanisms as well as methods for pooling, documenting, indexing, cataloging, and distributing the reusable software.

3.12. SEI

The mission of the Software Engineering Institute (SEI) is to - "Bridge the gap between practice and potential[37]." The long-range goal is to support technology transition. One of the areas of technology identified and assessed is reusability and automation. In particular, researchers at the institute are looking at ways to reuse

- *Passive Knowledge* through software component libraries, and
- *Active Knowledge* through the use of expert systems, program generators, and transformation systems.

One of the short-term projects completed by SEI was the Software Factory Workshop held in February, 1986. This brought together leading practitioners to assess and evaluate programming-in-the-large, Japanese software factories, and integrated software development environments targeted toward Ada. Other short-term goals focus on licensing software (a key issue in developing reusable software for profit), evaluating Ada environments, and developing a showcase programming environment.

MELD[19] (Multiple Elucidations of Language Descriptions) is a project directed at language independent development of software systems based on object-oriented composition. The software developer specifies the behavior of the desired software using language constructs called *features* and *action equations*; then a translator synthesizes the Ada source code from the specifications.

3.13. STARS

STARS (Software Technology for Adaptable, Reliable Systems) was initiated in 1980 to follow the DoD's Ada effort to address complete software life cycle support, not just the programming language proliferation issue. Its goal was to improve productivity, reliability, and adaptability of software through sponsoring educational activities, creating incentives for new developments, and formating SEI.

As a result of biannual working group meetings over the past two years, a *Reusability Guidebook* (discussed in section 4.4) was created. STARS also sponsored the CAMP (Common Ada Missile Packages) Project at MacDonnell Douglas[38]. This pilot project advanced the concepts of horizontal and vertical domain analysis in creating a library of over 800 reusable software components, written in Ada, to support future contracts in this application area. A parts composition system based on the ART (Automated Reasoning Tool), an expert system by Inference Corp., was developed to help locate parts, suggest how to use parts efficiently, generate new parts, and manage parts in the data base. These parts were separated into two categories: Domain Independent parts (e.g., abstract data structures, math routines, and general utilities), and Domain Dependent parts (e.g., missile functions, navigation, guidance and telemetry).

The four STARS workshops were-well attended and productive gatherings. The partial list of participants that follows includes many of the companies covered in this paper.

- Honeywell
- Air Force Armament Lab
- E-Systems
- National Bureau of Standards
- General Dynamics
- Hughes Aircraft
- McDonnell Douglas
- IBM FSD
- Raytheon
- Rockwell International
- Allied Canada Inc.
- Boeing
- GTE
- Advanced Software Methods
- Westinghouse

3.14. Toshiba

Toshiba has adopted Ada as its program design language. All modules are designed with concurrency in mind; therefore, the tasking construct of Ada is heavily utilized. A sophisticated graphics system has been developed to support the documentation of Ada program units. The Ada package construct is extended for reusable components by requiring a Description For Reusers (DFR)[21] document that describes the constraints and dependencies of each module along with how to modify/reuse it. Tools to support the retrieval of components are part of a well-integrated and instrumented programming environment (i.e., Software Factory). Toshiba claims up to an order of magnitude better productivity through reuse and this software "production" environment.

Other tools that support software reuse at Toshiba are:

- **RCPS** - Reusable Code Promoting Section - Receives, reviews, catalogs, and publishes **DFRs**.

- **SPISE-II** - Software Production by Interactive Synthesis Engineering - an integrated editor for design and code specifications. It also assists in locating software components.

- **PARTNER** - PARTs desigNER - helps create parts by generalizing existing software modules. It also serves as a centralized control mechanism.

- **IMAP** - Integrated software Management And Production support system - used for parts storage, retrieval, and control. It contains a classification system and supports a program design methodology using parts synthesis.

3.15. TRW

TRW is embarking on the **Quantum Leap** project. It consists of a three-phased approach to generating an order-of-magnitude improvement in programmer productivity and program quality. The first phase calls for the development of an advanced, integrated programming environment based on a high resolution bit-mapped graphics workstation. The second phase focuses on software reuse issues with all reusable software components being written in Ada. The third phase addresses the instrumentation and measurement of productivity and quality.

4. Ada Reusability Guidelines

In reading and writing, you cannot lay down rules until you have learnt to obey them. - Marcus Aurelius

This section summarizes the software reuse guidelines that have been initially proposed. These guidelines are generally structured to include the following sections:

1. **Design Guidelines**: designing for reuse, parameterization, and domain analysis.

2. **Coding Guidelines**: using Ada constructs, portability issues, and compiler considerations.

3. **Documentation Guidelines**: enhancing readability, commenting, mnemonics, prologs, and style.

4. **Management Guidelines**: motivating, controlling, contracting, and maintaining reusable software.

(Note: Guidelines and standards, while well intentioned, often reduce the availability of software for reuse due to the additional development effort and cost of conformity. The solution to this problem lies outside the technical arena, although certain tools that automate the specification, design, fabrication, and documentation of software can help.)

4.1. Booch

Grady Booch has made numerous contributions to the successful migration of Ada into the programming community. His new book, *Software Components with Ada*[23], details how object-oriented design can be extended to object-oriented software development through the use of reusable software components. His taxonomy of primitive reusable software modules (as marketed by EVB Software Engineering, Inc.) is the cornerstone of this analysis. It provides insight into understanding the attributes that can be associated with families of components. The taxonomy consists of the following primitive reusable modules attributes:

- **Bounded vs. Unbounded**: A data structure may have fixed or virtually unbounded size.
- **Iterator vs. Non-Iterator**: An operator exists to step through all elements of the structure.

- **Managed vs. Unmanaged**: The component does its own garbage collection.
- **Sequential vs. Concurrent vs. Guarded vs. Controlled**: The type of concurrent operations that might access the component.
- **Priority vs. Non-Priority**: A scheme exists to order the elements within the data structure.
- **Balking vs. Non-Balking**: The data structure allows the removal of elements in a non-sequential manner.
- **Limited vs. Non-Limited**: The size of the component is conceptually limited, but the implementation relies on dynamic storage allocation.

Domain analysis reveals that a software component can exhibit any of a number of combinations of these attributes, depending on space/time tradeoffs and the degree of parallelism required in the system. Therefore, while each component is similar semantically, different implementations are necessary to meet these needs. Booch's taxonomy is a first step in recognizing the importance of classifying reusable components.

4.2. EVB Software Engineering Inc.

Ed Berard, in his tutorial on *Creating Reusable Ada Software*[39], states several reusability axioms and style guidelines for writing reusable Ada code. The reusability axioms can be summarized into five fundamental axioms:

1. Ada provides reusability constructs different from other programming languages.
2. **Code that is designed to be reused generally is.**
3. Sometimes reusability is not important.
4. Reusability should be: defined, measured, recorded, and increased.
5. The following *increase* reusability:

    - Following standards
    - Management encouragement
    - Code without language or implementation tricks
    - Portable code
    - Reliable code
    - Functionally cohesive and loosely coupled modules
    - Well-defined interfaces
    - Generality
    - Robustness
    - Conceptual Integrity

The Ada coding style guidelines for reusability may be summarized into two (somewhat long) guidelines:

1. Reusability is *increased* when using

    a. meaningful mnemonics
    b. attributes
    c. named parameters
    d. fully qualified names
    e. precise, concise comments
    f. subunits and separate compilation
    g. packages
    h. generics

i. isolated machine dependencies
j. isolated   application   specific
   dependencies

2. Reusability is *decreased* when using

   a. literal constants
   b. use clauses
   c. default values for discriminants, record
      field values, and formal parameters
   d. optional language features such as
      pragmas, unchecked-deallocation, and
      unchecked-conversion
   e. anonymous types
   f. pre-defined and implementation-defined
      types
   g. attention to underlying implementation
   h. restrictive modules
   i. assumptions about garbage collection

These guidelines are concise and directed. They may be applied, in general, to developing reusable components in any programming language.

4.3. SofTech

The *Ada Reusability Guidelines*[18], as described by Christine Braun and John Goodenough, provide insight into designing, implementing, documenting, and managing reusable Ada software. In addition, the report distinguishes and defines reusability and portability and, provides a small survey of previous reusability efforts and studies. Guidelines for many aspects of the software developed process are identified and illustrated. A summary of the topics and some key points follow.

- **Design**: A layered approach with a well-documented interface is recommended. The need to "design for reuse" is emphasized.
- **Interfaces**: Over 20 types of interfaces are defined (similar to those in the Booch Taxonomy). The robustness and semantic richness of the interface is crucial to its reuse.
- **Efficiency**: Several suggestions are made to overcome some of the inefficiencies attributable to the generalness of reusable code.
- **Libraries**: Facilities are recommended to allow retrieval of different versions.
- **Package and Subprograms**: The concept of abstraction is emphasized.
- **Generics**: Several suggestions are made on parameterization and the use of defaults.
- **Error Handling and Exceptions**: The distinction between exception handling and propagation is defined along with recommendations for increasing the reusability of a module by proper mapping of exceptions to assumptions.
- **Parameters and Types**: Examples of designing subprogram interfaces are presented.
- **Documentation**: "Good documentation is essential to software reusability. Without it, reusability will not happen[18]."
- **Management**: "Reusability will not occur automatically; designers and programmers must be explicitly directed and motivated[18]".

- **Testing and Tools**: Quality Assurance should verify the reusability of a component.

To summarize, this report contains the most comprehensive set of guidelines for designing and developing reusable software to date. Although there is some redundancy among the guidelines, and many of them can be considered to fall under the category of good software engineering practices, this report serves as a valuable reference.

4.4. Honeywell

A Guidebook for Writing Reusable Source Code in Ada[24] was developed at Honeywell Computer Sciences Center as a result of the work being done on the RaPIER project. It contains three reusability metacharacteristics, fifteen measurable reusability characteristics, and 63 programming and documentation guidelines. The guidelines are organized to follow the Ada Language Reference Manual organization (14 Chapters). Chapters 6 (Subprograms), 7 (Packages), 8 (Visibility Rules), 9 (Tasks), 10 (Program Structure and Compilation Issues), and 12(Generic Units) are covered in detail. The remaining seven chapters are not complete at this time.

The reusability metacharacteristics identified can be summarized as follows:

1. Reusable components must be locatable (in a library system).
2. Reusable components must understandable and useful (properly documented and designed).
3. It must be economically feasible to build systems from reusable components (faster/cheaper to reuse/rework than to rebuild from scratch).

While the metacharacteristics described above are qualitative in nature, the reusable software characteristics identified are "quantitative" and measurable. The characteristics of reusable software include (in a somewhat abbreviated form):

1. Syntactically and Semantically clear interfaces
2. Interfaces written at an appropriate (abstract) level
3. Components with no environmental side effects
4. Components of object oriented design
5. Components designed using levels of abstraction
6. Components with scaffolding for ease of debug
7. Components with specifications separate from bodies
8. Components that exhibit high cohesion and low coupling
9. "Components and interfaces readable by someone other than author[24]"
10. Components that exhibit a "balance between generality and specificity[24]"
11. Components with sufficient documentation
12. Black box and white box components
13. Components insulated from host/target dependencies
14. Components using standard invocation, error handling and communication
15. Components that exploit their "domain of applicability"

Further information on these metacharacteristics may be found in St.Dennis[40,41]. The Honeywell effort represents a systematic attempt to quantify and qualify reusability guidelines and the rational behind them.

4.5. STARS

The STARS *Reusability Guidebook* is a managerial as well as technical reference. It is broken down into seven sections. The first section covers definitions and identifies the roles played by key individuals involved with the development, distribution, and procurement process. Section 2, *Conceptual Framework for the Reuse of Software*, identifies what to reuse, why to reuse it, how to get things to reuse, and incentives for reuse. The next section, *Procurement Process and Related Issues*, lists three categories of reusable parts: government ownership, shared ownership, and private ownership. Contractual considerations and guidelines are cited along with recommendations for acquiring reusable parts. Section 4, *Software Part Engineering*, presents guidelines for analyzing, designing, coding, testing, documenting, and managing reusable parts. Domain analysis plays a crucial role in determining what functions should be packaged for reused, and how they should be parameterized. Once the part has been identified, a Reusable Parts Requirements Specification (RPRS) is generated explicitly stating under what circumstances the part can be reused.

Section 5, *Software Engineering with Parts*, describes how to build systems from reusable software parts. Reuse of requirements, designs, source code and other ancillary parts are covered, as well as a methodology for parts integration. The next section, *Specification and Evaluation of Software Part Characteristics*, summarizes the results of the RADC quality framework study (RADC-TR-37)[30]. This study enumerates the characteristics of reusable software and proposes metrics for measuring reusability (and generality, modularity, and augmentability). The last section, *Library of Reusable Software Parts*, describes the requirements for a reusable software components library. Besides part classification, cataloging, search/retrieval, configuration management, library access policies, and administration, this section introduces the concept of "trust vector" as an indicator of the value of a reusable part. A trust vector has five values:

1. Library part constituent completeness
2. Reliability and test history
3. Reusability metrics
4. Quality metrics
5. Usage metrics

By evaluating the trust vector on library entries with similar function, a user may better be able to identify the part best suited for an application.

The STARS *Reusability Guidebook* analyzes software reusability issues from many perspectives. This breadth of scope makes it an invaluable reference.

5. Conclusion

Few things are of themselves impossible, and we lack the application to make them a success rather than the means. -
La Rouchefoucauld

Software reuse is a simple concept that has yet to significantly influence programmer productivity and program quality. Some of the more often cited technical barriers inhibiting software reuse concern

1. the lack of appropriate reusable software components to use as building blocks,

2. the lack of mechanisms for both locating such components and assessing their worth, and

3. a methodology for developing software based on reusable components.

This paper has focused on the first technical problem, how Ada, the language, provides facilities for the generation of reusable software components and what efforts are being made to achieve this goal. The remaining two issues are language independent and are still open areas of research. Relational, information retrieval and knowledge-based library systems are being proposed to address the second issue. Object-oriented design displays the most promise as a methodology for generating reusable components and composing systems. Finally, non-technical issues such as motivating programmers and convincing management about the long-term benefits of reusable software may surmount the technical issues in their magnitude of difficulty.

Will Tracz is an advisory programmer for the IBM Federal Systems Division, Owego NY and is currently an IBM Resident Study Fellow at Stanford University. He was responsible for designing and developing microcode support software for military and aerospace processors. He is newsletter editor of ACM SIGMICRO/IEEE TC-MICRO. He has an M.S. in Computer Science from the Pennsylvania State University, an M.S. in Computer Engineering from Syracuse University, and is currently completing his Ph.D. at Stanford University. Tracz has taught at Syracuse University and the Rochester Institute of Technology.

References

1. Biggerstaff, T.J. and Perlis, A.J., "Forward: Special Issue on Software Reusability", *IEEE Transactions on Software Engineering*, Vol. SE-10, No. 5, September, 1984, pp. 474-476.

2. Jones, T.C., "Reusability in Programming: A Survey of the State of the Art", *IEEE Transactions on Software Engineering*, Vol. SE-10, No. 5, September, 1984, pp. 488-493.

3. Tracz, W.J., "Why Reusable Software Isn't", *Proceedings of Workshop on Future Directions in Computer Architecture and Software*, May 1986.

4. US Department of Defense, US Government Printing Office, "The Ada Programming Language Reference Manual". ANSI/MIL-STD-1815A-1983 Document

5. Boehm, B., *Software Engineering Economics*, Prentice Hall, Englewood Cliffs, NJ, 1981.

6. Conn, R., "Overview of DoD Ada Software Repository", *Dr. Dobbs Journal*, February, 1986, pp. 60-61,86-91.

7. Rainboth, C., "Boeing Reusability Effort". Personal conversation, June, 1986

8. Elston, J.R., "The Boeing Automated Software Engineering (BASE) Environment", *Proceedings of Software Factory Forum*, February 18-19 1986.

9. EVB, "GRACE Bounded Stack", Pamphlet.

10. Bieniak, R.M., Griffin, L.M., and Tripp, L.R., "Automated Parts Composition", Ford Aerospace and Communication.

11. Hansen, G.A., Spaulding, S.D., and Edgar, G., "Certification of Ada Parts for Reuse", *Proceedings of First International Conference on Ada Programming Language Applications for the NASA Space Station*, June 2-5 1986, pp. E.1.2.1-E.1.2.6.

12. Kroenert, K., "GTE Reusability Project". Personal conversation at Future APSE Workshop, September, 1986

13. Onuegbe, E.O., "Software Classification as an Aid to Reuse: Initial Use as Part of a Rapid Prototyping System", *Proceedings of The Hawaii International Conference on System Sciences*, January 7-10 1987, pp. 521-529.

14. McCain, R., "Software Development Methodology for Reusable Components", *Proceedings of the Eighteenth Hawaii International Conference on System Science*, January 2-4 1986, pp. 319-324.

15. Burton, B., and Broido, M., "Development of an Ada Package Library", *Proceedings of First International Conference on Ada Programming Language Applications for the NASA Space Station*, June 2-5 1986, pp. E.1.3.1-E.1.3.13.

16. Arkwright, T.D., "Macro Issues In Reuse From A Real Project", *Proceedings of Software Technology for Adaptable Reliable Systems (STARS) Workshop*, April 9-12 1985, pp. 55-74.

17. Dillehunt, D., Nise, N.S., and Giffin, C., "Reusable Software Development", Rockwell International.

18. Braun, C.L., Goodenough, J.B., Eanes, R.S., "Ada Reusability Guidelines", Tech. report 3285-2-208/2, SofTech, Inc., April 1985.

19. Kaiser, G.E., and Garlan, D., "Composing Software Systems from Reusable Building Blocks", *Proceedings of The Hawaii International Conference on System Sciences*, January 7-10 1987, pp. 536-545.

20. Druffel, L.E. Redwine, S.T. Riddle, W.E., "The STARS Program: Overview and Rationale", *Computer*, Vol. 16, No. 11, November, 1983, pp. 21-29.

21. Matsumoto, Y., "Management of Industrial Software Production", *IEEE Computer*, February, 1984, pp. 59-70.

22. Boehm, B., "Quantum Leap Project". Personal Conversation at Arcadia Consortium Meeting, September, 1986

23. Booch, G., *Software Components with Ada*, Benjamin/Cumming, 1987, In progress

24. St. Dennis, R., "A Guidebook for Writing Reusable Source Code in Ada", Tech. report, Honeywell Inc., March 1986.

25. Wald, E., et al, "Reusability Guidebook".

26. Burton, B.A., "A Practical Approach to Ada Reusability", *Proceedings of National Conference on Software Reuseability and Maintainability*, September 10-11 1986.

27. Litvintchouk, S.D., and Matsumoto, A.S., "Design of Ada Systems Yielding Reusable Components: An Approach Using Structured Algebraic Specification", *IEEE Transactions on Software Engineering*, Vol. SE-10, No. 5, September, 1984, pp. 544-551.

28. Polak, W., "Maintainability and Reusable Program Designs", *Proceedings of National Conference on Software Reuseability and Maintainability*, September 10-11 1986.

29. Wegner, P., "Varieties of Reusability", *Proceedings of ITT Workshop on Reusability in Programming*, September 7-9 1983.

30. Presson, P.E., Tsai, J., Bowen, T.P., Post, J.V., and Schmidt, R., "Software Interoperability and Reusability", Tech. report RADC-TR-83-174, Boeing Aerospace Company, July 1983, Two volumes.

31. Przybylinski, S.M., "Archetyping - A Knowledge-Based Reuse Paradigm", *Proceedings of Workshop on Future Directions in Computer Architecture and Software*, May 1986.

32. Frankowski, E.N., Abraham, C.L., Onuegbe, E., Spinrad, M., St.Dennis, R., Stachour, P., "PaPIER (Rapid Prototyping to Investigate End-user Requirements: A Report of 1985 Technical Activities", Tech. report CSC-86-4:82313, Honeywell Computer Sciences Center, March 1986.

33. Yeh, R.T., Roussopoulos, N., and Chu, B., "Management of Reusable Software", *Proceedings of COMPCON 84 Fall: The Small Computer (R)Evolution*, September 16-20 1984, pp. 311-320.

34. McCain, R.C., "Reusable Software Component Engineering", *Proceedings of National Conference on Software Reuseability and Maintainability*, September 10-11 1986.

35. Burton, B.A., and Broido, M.D., "A Phased Approach To Ada Package Reuse", *Proceedings of Software Technology for Adaptable Reliable Systems (STARS) Workshop*, April 9-12 1985, pp. 83-98.

36. Mendal, G.O., "Micro Issues In Reuse From A Real Project", *Proceedings of Software Technology for Adaptable Reliable Systems (STARS) Workshop*, April 9-12 1985, pp. 443-520.

37. Barbacci, M.R., Habermann, A.H., and Shaw, M., "The Software Engineering Institute: Bridging Practice and Potential", *IEEE Software*, November, 1985, pp. 4-21.

38. McNicholl, D.G., et. all, "Common Ada Missile Packages", Tech. report AFATL-TR-85-17, Eglin Air Force Base, FL, June 1985.

39. Berard, E.V., "Creating Reusable Ada Software", *Proceedings of National Conference on Software Reuseability and Maintainability*, September 10-11 1986.

40. St. Dennis, R. J., Stachour, P., Frankowski, E., Onuegbe, E., "Measurable Characteristics of Reusable Ada Software", *Ada Letters*, Vol. 5, No. 2, March-April, 1986, pp. 41-49.

41. St. Dennis, R.J., "Reusable Ada (R) Software Guidelines", *Proceedings of The Hawaii International Conference on System Sciences*, January 7-10 1987, pp. 513-520.

The Minnowbrook Workshop On Software Reuse: A Summary Report

William W. Agresti
Computer Sciences Corporation
8728 Colesville Rd.
Silver Spring, Maryland 20910

Frank E. McGarry
National Aeronautics and Space Administration
Goddard Space Flight Center, Code 552
Greenbelt, Maryland 20771

Abstract

This paper summarizes the working group sessions at the 1987 Minnowbrook Workshop on Software Reuse. The 62 participants representing industry, government, and universities were organized into 4 working groups, which addressed issues related to (1) the scope of reuse, (2) the state-of-the-art (SOA) and state-of-the-practice (SOP), (3) tools and environments supporting reuse, and (4) foundations for reuse and future directions.

The Tenth Minnowbrook Software Workshop held on July 28-31, 1987, focused on software reuse. It took place at the Minnowbrook Conference Center of Syracuse University, Blue Mountain Lake, New York. Syracuse University and the University of Maryland sponsored the workshop in cooperation with the Rome Air Development Center and the Software Engineering Technical Committee of the Computer Society of the Institute of Electrical and Electronics Engineers (IEEE). The workshop chairpersons were Frank McGarry of National Aeronautics and Space Administration's (NASA's) Goddard Space Flight Center (GSFC) and Amrit Goel of Syracuse University. Sixty-two participants represented industry (44), government (5), and universities (13).

The program included 12 presentations* on various aspects of software reuse, but the emphasis was on a series of four parallel working groups. Each workshop participant joined one of the four groups, which met extensively during the workshop, and shared their findings with the other working groups at the final session. The working groups addressed the following issues:

- Working Group 1: scope of reuse
- Working Group 2: state-of-the-art (SOA) and state-of-the-practice (SOP)

---

*Workshop presentations are identified with an asterisk in references.

- Working Group 3: tools and environments for reuse
- Working Group 4: foundations for reuse and future directions

This paper summarizes the results of the working group sessions as presented at the final session. A more comprehensive report of the workshop is in preparation.

1: Working Group 1: Scope of Reuse

The first group was chaired by Victor Basili of the University of Maryland and Mary Shaw of the Software Engineering Institute, Carnegie Mellon University. This working group addressed several issues related to the definition of reuse, the reasons for seeking to increase reuse, and the context of reuse in the software development process. Three of the key topics are summarized as follows:

- Definition and framework for reuse
- Benefits of reuse
- Classification of reused objects

1.1: Definition and Framework for Reuse

Reuse is employing knowledge that has been compiled through previous experience. Three different types of reuse (from [Basili et al. 87]) are the reuse of

- Knowledge that exists solely in people (informal knowledge)
- Plans or procedures; e.g., how to perform certain activities or how to structure and document certain products (schematized knowledge)
- Tools and products (productized knowledge)

One of the obstacles to reuse is that a large portion of potentially reusable knowledge is of the first type—residing solely in people's minds. Another obstacle is the lack of support for identifying information that would be most beneficial in a particular situation.

Table 1: Classification of Reusable Objects Using Products and Process Descriptors

Method or System [Reference]	Product Descriptors			Process Descriptors			
	Type	Medium	Maturity	Activity	Mechanism	Extent of Modification	Granularity
CAMP [McDonnell Douglas 86]	Machine proc	Formal	New (1 project)	Development	Parameterized or templates	Minor	Major subsegment
Ada Validation Suite	Machine proc	Formal	50-100 users	Development	Verbatim	None	Complete system
Cannibalization	Document	Personal knowledge	Varies	Development	Unconstrained	Major	Small fragments to complete system
COCOMO [Boehm 81]	Document	Formal	Corporate	Planning	Parameterized	None	Complete system
ACM Surveys "Sorting" [Martin 71]	Knowledge	Institutional	Frequently used	Development	Templates	Minor	Major subsegment
Math Subroutine Library	Machin proc	Formal	Frequently used	Development	Verbatim or parameterized	None	Major subsegment
MFPL [Pollack 87]	Knowledge	Formal	Few	Development	Templates	Minor	Major subsegment
PFM [White 87]	Document	Institutional	Few (research)	Development	Templates	Minor-major	Small fragments
Proto [Welch 87]	Machine proc	Formal	Few (in-house tool)	Development	Verbatim	None	Major subsegments
LARCH [Guttag 85]	Document	Formal	Few	Development	Templates, unconstrained	Major	Small fragments

An SOA technology is one that is implemented and used at one to five installations outside the developer's (of the technology) own installation. This definition may exclude some of the most advanced technical contributions, at the "cutting edge" of technology, which may be in use only by the developer of the technology. An SOP technology is one that is in use in 50 percent or more of the organizations that are actively engaged in the business for which the technology is appropriate. Certainly, the SOA/SOP definitions could be more precise, but they succeeded in providing a basis for the workshop participants to begin addressing the SOA/SOP technologies for reuse. The following four areas were discussed:

- Component libraries/life-cycle products
- Support software
- Development methods and standards
- An engineering workflow model for reuse

The working group identified characteristics and examples of SOA and SOP technologies. The group also assessed obstacles that inhibit progress in moving the SOP nearer to the SOA and recommended actions for accelerating the process of closing the gap.

2.1: Component Libraries/Life-Cycle Products

The SOA in component libraries is represented by examples from the emerging commercial components industry (e.g., GRACE™ [EVB]) and government-sponsored libraries (e.g., Common Ada[1] Missile Package (CAMP) [McDonnell Douglas 86]). For GRACE and CAMP, Ada helped with the standardization of interface descriptions critical to effective component reuse. A valuable extension to the concept of component libraries is an online repository of all life-cycle products (documents, test cases, etc.) associated with the software.

The SOP is the use of relatively low-level components contained in libraries developed within an organization, sold by an external supplier (e.g., IBM's SSP, SAS, and IMSL), or distributed by a user's group. Software practitioners have been more successful in the reuse of communication protocols and screen-windowing packages.

Impediments to the expanded use of component libraries include the following:

- Components are usually language specific
- Methods to classify and catalog components lack uniformity
- Accessibility of noncode project elements is limited
- Components reflect different design and construction methods

[1]Ada is a registered trademark of the U.S. Government, Ada Joint Program Office.

A measurement-based framework for classifying and organizing reusable knowledge will help address both obstacles. Measurement will help capture various kinds of knowledge with increasing degrees of objectivity (from people to plans to tools). Also, an appropriate measurement scheme will support a more objective assessment of the potential benefit of reusable objects (e.g., tools or procedures) to a particular project.

The framework for reuse includes a reuse-oriented model of software development. The potentially reusable knowledge of all three types is an integral and visible part of this model. Other important features include the measurement mechanism and the knowledge base for retaining the results of applying measurement to reuse.

1.2: Benefits of Reuse

The reasons for reusing software are as taken from the Minnowbrook presentation by Mary Shaw, "Purposes and Varieties of Software Reuse." The reasons correspond to various aspects of software development: productivity, reliability, consistency, manageability, and standardization. The contribution of software reuse in each case is as follows:

- Productivity—Use existing components. Increased reuse helps reduce the effort needed to develop software systems.

- Reliability—Use proven components. Developing reliable software is difficult, especially for large, complex systems. Software reuse helps by providing components whose reliability is already demonstrated.

- Consistency—Use the same components in many places. Through a set of generally useful components, software reuse helps reduce the need for fresh, and possibly idiosyncratic, design.

- Manageability—Use well-understood components. Increased reuse helps lessen the likelihood of cost and schedule overruns by providing already developed components whose behavior is understood.

- Standardization—Use standard components. With reuse, software components are in place early to help users and developers with specification and implementation.

1.3: Classification of Reused Objects

Classifying reused and reusable objects can be useful in the following ways [Shaw 87]:

- To simplify communication by providing a common frame of reference

- To encourage comparison of domains in which techniques apply or comparison of the power or generality of techniques

- To support analysis by providing a basis for evaluation criteria

Reused objects are classified by product and process descriptors. Product descriptors identify what is reused by type, medium, and maturity as follows:

- Type (What types of objects are reused?)
  - Knowledge (application, etc.)
  - Documents (requirements, code, test plans, etc.)
  - Machine processible items (tool, libraries, etc.)

- Medium (How formal are the reused objects?)
  - Formal (syntax and semantics, syntax only, etc.)
  - Institutional knowledge (guidebook, etc.)
  - Personal knowledge (borrowing from a friend, experience, etc.)

- Maturity (How broadly is the object used?)
  - Industry wide
  - Corporation wide
  - Department wide
  - One project

Process descriptors define how the object is reused:

- Activity (When do we reuse?)
  - Planning (cost modeling, risk analysis, etc.)
  - Development (requirements, specification, etc.)
  - Maintenance (functional change, error correction, etc.)

- Mechanism (How do we accomplish reuse?)
  - Verbatim
  - Parameterized
  - Templates
  - Unconstrained

- Extent of Modification (How much change is needed?)
  - None
  - Trivial (less than 5 percent)
  - Minor (less than 25 percent)
  - Major (more than 25 percent)

- Granularity (How much of the product is needed?)
  - Entire system
  - Subsegment
  - Small fragment

Table 1 gives examples of reusable objects and how they might be classified using the product and process descriptors.

2. Working Group 2: State-of-the-Art/State-of-the-Practice of Software Reuse

Working group 2 was chaired by Lorraine Duvall of Duvall Computer Technologies, Inc., and Michael Evans of Expertware, Inc. This group adopted the following working definitions of SOA and SOP.

- Reusing components is not as satisfying as designing new software

To help address these obstacles, software engineers need to be trained in the synthesis of systems from existing building blocks. Also, expert systems can help users access objects from libraries by exploring relationships and associations between the objects and the user's needs.

2.2: Support Software

This technology area includes tools, languages, and environments for software reuse, as well as systems for module interconnection and system composition.

Some environments that are oriented to reusability and system composition made the transition from "cutting edge" to SOA: the frame-based Netron/CAP Development Center [Bassett 87], TEDIUM [Blum 87], and CAMP [McDonnell Douglas 86]. Many examples of reuse support software are at the cutting edge and, to the knowledge of workshop participants, had not yet transitioned to one to five installations outside the developer's own installation. The cutting-edge reuse support software technologies most likely to move to SOA in the near future are KBEmacs [Waters 85], Meld [Kaiser, Garlan 87], LIL [Goquen 86], Objtalk [Fischer 87], Draco [Neighbors 84], and BB/LX [Lenz et al. 87].

Some widely used environments, especially UNIX and Smalltalk, are oriented to reuse and the building of systems from components. Also, many of the standard tools to support software development (e.g., configuration management and database management) contribute to the reuse of code.

Application generators are widely used, but in specific domains such as query and reporting applications.

The SOA/SOP gap is characterized by SOA support software possessing an overall system concept of reuse and system construction from components. While some SOP tools, such as source code management systems, certainly aid reuse, their effects are limited because they are associated with one phase in a "waterfall" life-cycle development process that is not oriented to reuse.

An obstacle to making progress in software support for reuse is the organizational inertia associated with current nonreuse-oriented development methods. It is not always clear how to evaluate or compare new tools or environments. The development support software should derive from the methodology used for development. New reuse-oriented tools may not fit with current development practices.

A promising area to pursue is the reuse support software that arises from domain analysis. Organizations would benefit from reuse tools and environments that are application specific, but are as unaffected as possible from the choice of particular development methods or practices.

2.3: Development Methods and Standards

An example of an SOA development practice is the use of Ada generics to significantly increase the levels of reuse on a project [Gargaro, Pappas 87] [St. Dennis 87]. Object-oriented development can facilitate reuse through the encapsulation of both operations and state data within objects.

The SOP is an overall lack of reuse orientation among the methods used in software development, procurement, and productivity measurement. Among development practices, top-down specification and design discourage reuse. Reuse-oriented design would aim to bridge the gap between a new need and existing building blocks. Procurement practices on large systems often impede reuse by interposing the prime contractor's standards between those of the software developer and the using agency. Productivity measures based on lines of code per staff-month reward new coding and discourage efforts to find and adapt old code.

To accelerate reuse, it must be identified explicitly as an objective for software development. Incentives should be defined to award productivity credit for time spent analyzing and adapting existing code.

Software engineers and managers must be educated on the benefits and techniques of reuse. Development standards and guidelines must be modified to recognize the role of software reuse.

2.4: Engineering Workflow Model for Reuse

An overall recommendation to accelerate the closing of the SOA/SOP gap was the definition of an engineering workflow model for reuse. The model must be based on the workflow used in more traditional engineering development. Method consistency, data standardization, and process compatibility will have much greater emphasis in an engineering approach.

The adoption of this workflow model must proceed and provide the unifying concept for efforts to define reuse-oriented methods or tools. The SOP is extremely limited when it can only support the reuse of code from one application to another. Organizations must shift their orientation to an engineering workflow model that provides for building and controlling reusable applications. These reused and reusable applications require more stringent process definition and control. Continuous configuration management is needed throughout development and sustaining engineering. Testing, certification, and acceptance/rejection must be applied at the level of applications, not systems or subsystems. Applying effort toward the development of such a reuse workflow model is the necessary first step to improve software reuse.

3. Working Group 3: Tools and Environments for Software Reuse

Working group 3 was chaired by Anthony Norcio of the Naval Research Laboratory and Sidney Bailin of Computer Technology Associates, Inc. The group approached the subject of reuse tools and environments by first recognizing the classes of reuse-related activities that need to be supported. Of the following six identified activities, the first three are concerned with creating reusable objects; the last three relate to using reusable objects:

- Domain analysis
- Development and refinement of reusable products
- Classification
- Searching
- Evaluation and assessment
- Incorporation of reusable items

3.1: Domain Analysis

"In domain analysis, common characteristics from similar systems are generalized, objects and operations common to all systems within the same domain are identified, and a model is defined to describe their relationships" [Prieto-Diaz 87]. Because the resulting domain model is used in requirements analysis, domain analysis can be viewed as a phase that precedes the conventional development process.

Key subactivities of domain analysis are

- Knowledge extraction
- Identification of objects and operations
- Abstraction and relationships
- Classification and taxonomy
- Domain languages and synthesis

Tools that support these subactivities of domain analysis, along with a characterization as being mature (M), developed but unproven (D), or undeveloped (U), are as follows:

- Knowledge extraction tools (e.g., expert system building tools) (D)
- Entity-relationship diagramming tools (D)
- Object-oriented development tools (U)
- Semantic clustering and automatic classification tools (U)
- Computer-added software engineering (CASE) tools (D)
- Parsing tools (M)

3.2: Development and Requirement of Reusable Products

Extra effort is required to develop products for reuse or to refine existing products to enhance reusability.

Several subactivities are critical to building and refining reusable products. These subactivities, listed with tools that provide support, are to

- Isolate replaceable features. Tools: object oriented languages (D); historical data collection (M)
- Make products self contained. Tools: dependency analyzers (e.g., cross-reference generators) (D); structure analyzers (D)
- Parameterize. Tools: software and language features such as table-driven software, macro expansion, preprocessors, and generics (D)
- Enrich (add features to a product to widen its range of application). Tools: object-oriented languages (D); configuration management tools to manage multiple versions of a product (M)
- Abstract and specialize. Tools: languages that support class hierarchies and inheritance (e.g., Smalltalk) (M)
- Test and validate (to mitigate risk in reuse—the not-invented-here syndrome). Tools: test coverage analyzers (M)
- Formally verify. Tools: verification environment (U)
- Assess quality. Tools: quality metrics (D); standands checkers (M)
- Restructure (for multilevel reusability). Tools: reusability metrics (U)

3.3: Classification

Three approaches to classifying reusable products are controlled vocabulary [Jones, Prietro-Diaz 87], uncontrolled vocabulary [Frakes, Nejmeh 87], and knowledge representation [Winston 84].

The tools to support these approaches appear to be chiefly in the developed but unproven category:

- Context clarification tool (D)
- Semantic closeness tool (D)
- Thesaurus construction tool [McCune et al. 85] (D)
- Boolean information-retrieval system [Salton et al. 83] (D)
- Vector space information-retrieval system (D)
- Word processing tools (M)
- Semantic net shell [Oddy 77] (D)
- Frame shell (D)
- Rule-based expert system shell (D)

3.4: Searching

Alternative searching approaches and support tools are

- Natural language: CATALOG tool [Frakes, Nejmeh 87] (D)
- Structured queries: CATALOG tool [Frakes, Nejmeh 87] (D)
- Browsing: Hypertext (D)
- Hierarchical: IMS, Smalltalk (D)

- Semantic search: Automated Library System (ALS) (D); SEMANTX (D)
- Citation search: Alicia (RADC) (D)

3.5: Evaluation and Assessment

Effective methods for evaluation and assessment of reusable products are essential for increasing the level of reuse. The following tools and environments support assessment:

- Standard test sets (U)
- Reuse-level measurement tools (U)
- Attitude measurement tools (U)
- Usage measurement tools (D)
- SMART environment [Rocchio 71] (D)

3.6: Incorporation of Reusable Items

Subactivities and tools related to the objective of incorporating reusable items include the following:

- Selection of variants. Tools: source code difference tools (M)
- Instantiation. Tools: compilers (M)
- Provision of data. Tools: data generation (D); forms management (M)
- Template completion. Tools: prompters (M); macro expanders (M)
- Modification safety. Tools: maintenance support (M)
- Integration of items: Tools: linkers (M); smart editors (D); environments with integration paradigm (e.g., UNIX shell, Common Lisp; Smalltalk) (M)

4. Working Group 4: Foundations for Reuse and Future Directions

Working group 4 was chaired by Marvin Zelkowitz of the University of Maryland. This group addressed the shortcomings in current reuse technology and proposed avenues for increasing reuse. Research approaches in computer science and software engineering were identified to address various reuse problem areas. The group also considered inhibitions to reuse arising from nontechnical issues such as social, legal, and business practices.

Four discussion areas are summarized:

- Language features
- Precise specifications
- Retrieval of existing code
- Nontechnical issues

4.1: Language Features

The focus in language features arises from the realization that the reusability of source code is affected by the language used. Various design approaches (e.g., information hiding and data abstraction) and language features (e.g., type polymorphism, dynamic binding, and inheritance) make reuse easier. No single programming language has all the desirable features for reuse, although Ada comes closest. To increase the level of reuse, those who design new languages or enhance existing ones need to introduce language features that facilitate reuse. Validation and evaluation of Ada compilers should emphasize reuse capabilities. Languages should also support design approaches that promote reuse.

Specification languages (e.g., Gist [Balzer et al. 83], PAISLey [Zave 82]) and module interconnect languages (e.g., MIL [Purtilo 86]) offer potential for increasing use, but are not yet widely used outside research environments.

4.2: Precise Specifications

Research on specification systems is relevant to reuse because of the prerequisites needed to understand what function the software computes. Current research is based on preconditions, algebraic specifications, and term rewriting systems. Several languages are in development or limited research use (e.g., Gist, Larch, and PAISLey).

Efforts in formal verification (e.g., AFFIRM [Musser 80], GYPSY [Good 77], and Boyer-Moore [Boyer, Moore 77]) are of interest because the goal is to automate the conversion of a formal process description into an executable source program. However, such systems are only narrowly applicable.

Several practical approaches that work with specifications as a starting point but have restricted domains are application generators, fourth-generation languages, and parser generators such as YACC on UNIX.

Increased research on specification languages and systems can benefit software reuse in the following areas:

- Understanding the function and performance of source code units
- Providing (automatically) concise and accurate documentation
- Understanding algorithmic dependencies and constraints

4.3: Retrieval of Existing Code

The major problems with taking advantage of the vast quantity of existing source code are determining what the code does and knowing how to retrieve it. Research is needed in both areas. Software archeologists are needed to sift through the large collections of existing code to identify potentially reusable components.

4.4 Nontechnical Issues

Progress in three nontechnical areas—corporate culture, education, and intellectual property rights—will improve software reuse. The reality of managing software projects in industry is that no incentives exist for a manager to spend extra funds to make products reusable. Software needs to be viewed the same as capital equipment items are—as a reusable component that has a life beyond the current project. Costs to develop a reusable component should be amortized over its expected lifetime.

Education must address the building of reusable components and their effective reuse on new systems. Universities and companies should be encouraged to move from an orientation of new development to one of software reuse.

The software engineering community should express its expert opinion on several issues related to intellectual property rights, such as

- Who, among designer, programmer, and company, owns software and gets paid if software is reused?

- What are the antitrust implications of companies sharing of source code?

- Who is liable for consequential damages owing to a reused component?

Determinations on such questions should not be left solely to the legal community without thoughtful opinion from software technologists.

5. Summary and Conclusions

The reports of the four working groups had two common themes for increasing software reuse:

1. An overall orientation to reuse must guide proposed methods, tools, and environments. It is not sufficient for improved reuse to be merely a welcome by-product or side-effect of technologies whose purposes lie elsewhere. Technologies must explicitly seek to improve reuse as their primary objective.

2. The conventional waterfall life-cycle model does not serve as an effective framework for structuring the development process based on reuse. The basic weakness of the waterfall model—its imbalance of analysis over synthesis [Agresti 86]—directly and detrimentally affects software reuse: developers are not trained in the synthesis of systems from reusable building blocks. That the waterfall model is so entrenched in organizational standards makes it especially difficult to restructure the process model to one that is oriented to reuse. However, such a restructuring is the key to providing an organizing context for the proposed reuse-improving technologies.

The Minnowbrook workshop succeeded in bringing interested software professionals together in a set of highly interactive working groups. The discussions raised questions, clarified issues, and sharpened the focus on software reuse.

Acknowledgments

Thanks go to all of the participants of the Minnowbrook workshop for contributing their ideas and observations in the working group sessions.

This report is a summary of their insights. The contribution of written draft material by the following working group chairs and other participants also provided assistance to the authors in preparing this summary report: Victor Basili, Mary Shaw, Ed Seidewitz, Tony Norcio, Sidney Bailin, Lorraine Duvall, Michael Evans, Herbert Hecht, Ruben Prieto-Diaz, Ed Presson, and Marvin Zelkowitz.

References

[Agresti 86] W. Agresti (ed.), *New Paradigms for Software Development*, Washington, D.C.: IEEE Computer Society Press, 1986

*[Agresti, McGarry 87] W. Agresti and F. McGarry, "Defining Leverage Points for Increasing Reuse," Minnowbrook Workshop on Software Reuse, 1987

*[Antoy et al. 87] S. Antoy, P. Forcheri, B. Kowalchack, M. Molfino, S. Pearlman, and M. Zelkowitz, "Executable Specifications as a Basis for Software Reuse," Minnowbrook Workshop on Software Reuse, 1987

[Balzer et al. 83] R. Balzer, T. Cheatham, and C. Green, "Software Technology in the 1990's: Using a New Paradigm," *IEEE Computer*, November 1983

*[Barnes et al. 87] B. Barnes, T. Durek, J. Gaffney, and A. Pyster, "Cost Models for Software Reuse," Minnowbrook Workshop on Software Reuse, 1987

*[Basili et al. 87] V. Basili, J. Barley, B. Joo, and H. Romback, "Software Reuse: A Framework," Minnowbrook Workshop on Software Reuse, 1987

[Bassett 87] P. Bassett, "Frame-Based Software Engineering," *IEEE Software*, July 1987

[Blum 87] B. Blum, "The TEDIUM Development Environment for Information Systems," *IEEE Software*, March 1987

[Boehm 81] B. Boehm, *Software Engineering Economics*, Englewood Cliffs, NJ: Prentice-Hall, 1981

[Booch 87] G. Booch, *Software Components With Ada*, Menlo Park, CA: Benjamin/Cummings, 1987

*[Bowen 87] T. Bowen, "E-3 Reusable Software Catalog," Minnowbrook Workshop on Software Reuse, 1987

[Boyer, Moore 77] R. Boyer and J. Moore, "A Lemma Driven Automatic Theorem Prover for Recursive Function Theory," *Proceedings of the International Joint Conference on Artifical Intelligence*, 1977

*[Carle, Fischer 87] R. Carle and L. Fischer, "Missile Software Reusability," Minnowbrook Workshop on Software Reuse, 1987

[Conn 86] R. Conn, *The Ada Software Repository Master Index*, Echelon, Inc., Los Altos, CA, 1986

*Presentation at the Minnowbrook workshop; may not be cited in the text.

[COSMIC] *Computer Software Management and Information Center (COSMIC) Software Catalog,* National Aeronautics and Space Administration, Operated by University of Georgia

[EVB] Generic Reusable Ada Components for Engineering (GRACE) (TM), EVB Software Engineering, Inc., Frederick, MD

[Fisher 87] G. Fischer, "Cognitive View of Reuse and Redesign," *IEEE Software*, July 1987

*[Frakes, Nejmeh 87] W. Frakes and B. Nejmeh, "An Information System for Reuse," Minnowbrook Workshop on Software Reuse, 1987

[Gargaro, Pappas 87] A. Gargaro and T. Pappas, "Reusability Issues and Ada," *IEEE Software*, July 1987

[Goguen 86] J. Goguen, "Reusing and Interconnecting Software Components," *IEEE Computer*, February 1986

[Good 77] D. Good, "Constructing Verified and Reliable Communications Systems," *ACM Software Engineering Notes*, May 1977

[Guttag et al. 85] J. Guttag, J. Horning, and J. Wing, "The Larch Family of Specification Languages," *IEEE Software*, September 1985

*[Jones, Prieto-Diaz 87] G. Jones and R. Prieto-Diaz, "Classification and Library Support for Reusability," Minnowbrook Workshop on Software Reuse, 1987

[Kaiser, Garlan 87] G. Kaiser and D. Garlan, "Melding Software Systems From Reusable Building Blocks," *IEEE Software*, July 1987

*[LeBlanc 87] R. LeBlanc, "Software Reuse Position Paper," Minnowbrook Workshop on Software Reuse, 1987

[Lenz et al. 87] M. Lenz, H. Schmid, and P. Wolf, "Software Reuse Through Building Blocks," *IEEE Software*, July 1987

[Martin 71] W. Martin, "Sorting," *ACM Computing Surveys*, December 1971

[McDonnell Douglas 86] McDonnell Douglas Astronautics Company, *Technical Report AFATL-TR-85-93*, Common Ada Missile Packages (CAMP), McDonnell Douglas Astronautics Company, St. Louis, MO, May 1986

[Musser 80] D. Musser, "Data Types in the AFFIRM System," *IEEE Transactions on Software Engineering*, January 1980

*[Musser, Stepanov 87] D. Musser and A. Stepanov, "Generic Algorithms + Generic Data Structures = Reusable Software," Minnowbrook Workshop on Software Reuse, 1987

[Neighbors 84] J. Neighbors, "The Draco Approach to Constructing Software From Reusable Components," *IEEE Transactions on Software Engineering*, September 1984

[Pollack et al. 87] R. Pollack, J. Solderitsch, and W. Loftus, "MFPL: A Case Study in Software Generation From Specification," *UNISYS Internal Report*, 1987

[Prieto-Diaz 87] R. Prieto-Diaz, "Domain Analysis for Reusability," *Proceedings: IEEE COMPSAC*, October 1987

[Purtilo 86] J. Purtilo, "Applications of a Software Interconnection System in Mathematical Problem Solving Environments," *Proceedings of the Symposium on Symbolic and Algebraic Computing*, July 1986

*[Shaw 87] M. Shaw, "Purposes and Varieties of Software Reuse," Minnowbrook Workshop on Software Reuse, 1987

[St. Dennis 87] R. St. Dennis, "Reusable Ada Software Guidelines," *Proceedings of the Hawaii International Conference on System Sciences*, 1987

*[Stotts 87] D. Stotts, "Achieving Software Reusability With Formal Semantic Model of Real-Time, Concurrent Computation," Minnowbrook Workshop on Software Reuse, 1987

[Waters 85] R. Waters, "The Programmer's Apprentice: A Session With KBEmacs," *IEEE Transactions on Software Engineering*, November 1985

[Welch 87) T. Welch, "Very High Level Language (VHLL) System Prototyping Tool," *International Software Systems, Inc.*, July 1987

[White 87] S. White, "A Pragmatic Formal Method for Computer System Definition," Ph.D, thesis, Polytechnic University, New York, NY, 1987

[Zave 82] P. Zave, "An Operational Approach to Requirements Specification for Embedded Systems," *IEEE Transactions on Software Engineering*, May 1982

RMISE Workshop on Software Reuse Meeting Summary

Will Tracz

Stanford University

Summary
A three day workshop focused on software reuse brought together a small group of leading researchers and practitioners. The goal of the meeting was to identify the current state-of-the-art and state-of-the-practice in software reuse and to suggest ways of closing the gap between the two. The meeting consisted of ten invited presentations addressing a broad range of technical, economic, legal and social issues The results of the workshop included six working group reports and a list of software reuse issues that the attendees reached consensus on. The most significant conclusion of the workshop was that tools and technology are emerging today that show great promise in capturing the design and implementation tradeoff knowledge that can be reused to gain an order of magnitude more productivity over simple forms of reuse (subroutine libraries and code templates).

1. Overview
The first jointly planned and sponsored workshop by SPC (Software Productivity Consortium), MCC (Microelectorics and Computer Technology Corporation), and SEI (Software Engineering Institute) in conjunction with the RMISE (Rocky Mountain Institute on Software Engineering) was held October 14-16 in Boulder, Colorado. The goal of the meeting was to identify the current state-of-the-art and state-of-the-practice in software reuse and suggest ways of closing the gap between the two. The meeting consisted of ten invited presentations:

1. **Issues and Overview** -- *J. Goodenough (SEI)*
2. **Methods** -- *G. Booch (Rational)*
3. **Representations** -- *C. Richter (MCC)*
4. **Report on Minnowbrook** -- *S. Bailin (Computer Technology Associates, Inc.)*
5. **Tools and Environments** -- *W. Riddle (SPC)*
6. **Constructive vs Generative Approaches** -- *T. Biggerstaff (MCC)*
7. **Domain Analysis** -- *J. Neighbors (Systems Analysis, Design and Assessment)*
8. **Social Issues** -- *W. Tracz (IBM)*
9. **Economics** -- *J. Gaffney (SPC)*
10. **Legal Issues** -- *J. Goodenough (SEI)*

The rest of the program was allocated to working groups and general discussion on the following topics:

- **Software methods which support reuse** -- *Jones (GTE)*,
- **Design representations which enhance reuse** -- *Baxter (MCC)*,
- **Code representations which support reuse** -- *Goodenough*,
- **Tools and environments which support reuse** -- *Williams (RMISE)*,
- **Constructive and generative approaches to reuse** -- *Bailin*, and
- **Domain analysis** -- *Neighbors*.

This report summarizes each presentation and the results of each working group along with the issues which achieved consensus. The final section includes a summary of the key statements made by the attendees.

1.1. Demographics/Background
Of the 30 attendees, four were from SEI, five from MCC, four from SPC and two from RMISE. The remaining invited attendees were split 9:4, industry to academia. (Of these attendees, only 2-3 were what I would call *"window shoppers"*, i.e., they came to observe rather than participate. This left 95% of the attendees who were researchers or software developers actively pursuing reuse technology and tools.) The mix of industry to academia resulted in a "down in the trenches" rather than ivory tower atmosphere.

MCC was addressing software reuse technology, looking 5-10 years out. SPC was looking for tools and methodology in the 3-5 year time frame. SEI, besides addressing the technology transfer issue, was evaluating current technology. The academians offered empirical evidence, and, in general, there was no one "political or religious" view that dominated. Because roughly a third of the attendees also were at the Minnowbrook workshop this past July 28-31, there was strong guidance to avoid some of the thrashing and biased views that had occurred during some of the sessions there. As Lloyd Williams, the director of the RMISE and chairman of the workshop committee, put it, "The workshop was the right people, at the right place at the right time."

2. Consensus Items
The following conclusions were agreed upon by those present at the workshop:

2.1. Domain analysis is at the heart of reuse.
This is the Catch-22 in any engineering discipline: "Before you can reuse something, you have to have something to reuse." The more effort spent in analyzing what is reusable, and how it can be reused, the more likely it is to be reused.

2.2. The largest payback is on "vertical" domains.
The message here reflects something that the Japanese software factories as well as small PC software houses have capitalized on well, that is, if you go after a small, well defined market, you can make a good business case to justify the increased expenses involved in developing a good set of parameterized components or templates that address that problem domain and the tools for generating applications from them.

2.3. There exists a small number of abstractions for each problem domain.
This conclusion was reluctantly accepted by some attendees. It was felt by some that a large number of abstractions (>1000) would be necessary for programmers to effectively construct new applications. From the data presented, and the experience of those in attendance, it was observed that somewhere under 100 abstractions are all that exist in most problem domains. Furthermore, if a larger number of abstractions did exists, then there was probably just cause for further analysis and parameterization to cut down the total number.

2.4. Object-oriented approaches are the best for reuse.
Object-oriented software design and development appeared to be the best "yet" known method of software development for reuse. It was agreed that the data encapsulation and information hiding, along with inheritance were the features that promoted reuse.

2.5. Non-technical reasons inhibit widespread reuse.
There was unanimous consensus on this issue. The general feeling was that management had a short sighted view on software development and wasn't about to commit the resources for tools and training in reuse technology. The "not-invented-here" problem was felt to be easily overcome with proper management incentive. The GTE experience appears to be a good case in point.

Gerry Jones and Ruben Prieto-Diaz from GTE Laboratories described how their research center helped set up a small library for reusable software (ORACLE on a PC) for one division in GTE. Management offered $25.00 for each component accepted into the library. It set up a certification group to screen the contributions, and contracted SofTech to adapt their Ada Reuse Guidelines [5] for COBOL and C. A separate Software Asset Group maintained the library and monitored its usage. Initially 300 components were accepted. Currently (one year later), the number is down to 150 due to redundancy and lack of use.

Furthermore the Software Asset Group is soliciting (build or buy) for strategic contributions to further populate the library. Management was directed to plan for reuse. Currently 25% of each delivered software product is reused code. The goal is 50%. Two other divisions in GTE are setting up similar reuse libraries and their corporate research center is developing domain analysis tools and techniques to support populating them.

2.6. Recording design/code decisions helps maintenance and reuse.

Software maintenance and software reuse are very similar in nature. Tools that support one, often support the other. It was widely recognized that in order to move software reuse out of programming-in-a-small-group to programming-at-large, there is a need for tools to capture the loose, unstructured process of evolving design from specifications and into code. This "traceability" (see *"Preventing the most-probable errors in design"* by Bob Poston in the November issue of **IEEE Software**, page 87) of what part of the requirements is satisfied by what part of the design and implemented by what part of the program (and what the design or implementation tradeoffs that were made to arrive at this design) have eluded most developers, partially because it is time consuming, but also because there are no tools to support the process -- *until now*. Ted Biggerstaff (MCC) described the gIBIS (Graphical Issue Based Information System) based on HyperText technology and a design theory based approach by Horst Rittel of Berkeley. Hypertex allows you to create a web of different types of information. This web can connect documentation with design, requirements specs and code, etc.. The power of gIBIS lies in the email system placed on top of the web. The mail system supports programming-in-the-large. Large systems are composed of several subsystems. Each subsystem may have certain hardware and software dependencies on other components. The web provides a mechanism for organizing decision/tradeoff points. At each point several possible positions (solutions) are stated along with the arguments for and against. Individuals concerned about certain issues can subscribe to these decision points. Whenever a new position is stated, a new issue raised, a new argument made for or against an existing issue, or decision made that may affect others, the subscribers are automatically notified. Underlying this scheme is a mechanism for capturing design decisions -- answering the question "Why was it done this way?", or "Why wasn't it done this other way?"

3. Invited Presentations

3.1. Issues and Overview

As lead presenter John Goodenough gave a "provocative rather than definitive" statement on software reuse. The issues that were raised served to contrast the differences between undisciplined program development and reuse-oriented programming. Also, no definition of software reuse, or classification of what can be reused was given. This was strategic in that some of the attendees felt that an unfortunately large amount of time was spent at the Minnowbrook conference arguing over these points. For purposes of the workshop, reuse consisted of reusing any knowledge that was codified.

The following is a summary of some key points in this presentation

- **Reuse Goals**: The goals of reuse are to improve productivity, reliability, schedule and reduce maintenance cost -- "to exploit what has been learned and used for similar programs in the past."

- **Capturing and Applying Programming Knowledge**: There are many ways to reuse code: parameterization, program generators, fourth generation languages, transformation systems. A new paradigm should be observed: concentrating on the difference between existing software and a new system.

- **Technology Readiness/Impediments**: Knowledge-base tools, program transformation system and formal specifications are research areas which show promise. Program generators and generic software designs/architectures are technologies that work in specific domains. Component libraries and retrieval systems raise legal issues. Training, tools and techniques need to be developed. Finally, an unanswered issue concerns whether these techniques scale.

- **Non-technical Impediments**: Government procurement regulations and other legal issues as well as the momentum of traditional programming development styles inhibit reuse. The costs of capturing, developing, maintaining and learning to design with reusable software also need to be addressed.

3.2. Methods

Grady Booch from Rational cited the importance of methodology in handling complexity and communication. He cited the trend to build reusable software components as risk reduction (error reduction) technique and a way to justify their costs. The following domains of reuse were observed in regards to targets of opportunity:

- inside the head,
- inside a program,
- between programs,
- between programmers,
- between projects,
- between divisions, and
- between companies.

As stated in his book **Software Components with Ada** [4], a package does not capture large enough abstractions, and so the concept of reusable subsystems needs to be addressed.

3.3. Representations

Charlie Richter (MCC) presentation gave an AI slant to reuse. His view of reuse was broken down into two sides: *Producers* and *Consumers*. The producers

- identify,
- capture,
- organize, and
- describe

software for reuse. The consumers

- find,
- browse,
- understand, and
- compose

reusable software. If one analyzes the operations cited from these two perspectives, one needs to ask the question, who are the producers and consumers, what are their backgrounds, and what tools can assist in each step? The more fundamental issues are how can the knowledge/information be represented to facilitate each of these operations and what limitations does a representation pose?

Domain analysis serves to identify software for reuse. Frame-based knowledge representation systems (CAPS-Netron) and object-oriented programming systems (Smalltalk) with inheritance and classes offer representational support for taxonomies. Abstract data types, Ada generics and software templates offer a lower level of representational support. HyperText systems help organize documentation and facilitate describing for reuse.

On the consumer side, pattern matching serves as underlying approach to locating software for reuse, but, pattern matching is driven by the representation, or vice versa. MCC has two tools to assist in finding software: PARIS is based on matching pre- and post-conditions on components, and ROSE, matches data flow diagrams. In each case the representation affects the domain. Composing new systems from reusable artifacts is still an open problem. Superimposition of code or designs was one technique proposed (automatically combining and optimizing two algorithms).

3.4. Report on Minnowbrook

Sid Bailin from Computer Technology Associates, Inc. gave a summary of results generated by four working groups at the Minnowbrook Workshop on Software Reuse, which was held July 28-31, 1987 and sponsored by Syracuse University and the University of Maryland in cooperation with RADC. There were 12 presentations, and 11 position papers. The four working groups were:

1. **Scope of Software Reuse** -- Basili(UM) and Shaw(SEI)
2. **State-of-the-Art/State-of-the-Practice** -- Duvall (Duvall Computer Technologies) and Evans (Expertware)
3. **Tools and Environments** -- Norcio(NRL) and Bailin (CTA)
4. **Future Directions/Foundations** -- Zelkowitz(UM) and Musser(GE)

The **Scope of Software Reuse** working group generated the following (broad) definition: **Reuse** *is a matter of employing knowledge that has been previously compiled. This information may take the form of information passed between people, knowledge recorded in plans or knowledge embodied in code, tools and products.* They also derived a classification system to document forms of reuse. Information gathered include: activity (e.g., specification, design, code), type of artifact (e.g., document, processable document), medium availability (e.g., institutional, department, personal), maturity of use (e.g., used by single person, a department, etc.), mechanism/representation (e.g., parameterize, template, black box), extent of modification, and granularity (e.g., small fragment). They further identified three forms of knowledge that is commonly reused: people, methods and tools. Defining the relationship between these three areas and capturing the knowledge about them formed the framework for future research.

The **State-of-the-Art/State-of-the-Practice** working group arrived at two related conclusions:

1. Reusable components are really programming language or ISA extensions.
2. "We are focussed on the easy problem - not dealing with the conceptual level."

These statements emphasize the differences between the SOA (State-Of-the-Art) (reusing abstractions) versus the SOP (State-Of-the-Practice) (reusing code).

Other comparisons made were:

- Libraries
    - **SOA** - commercial libraries of requirements, design, code and tests.
    - **SOP** - low level repositories of math, and IO routines.
    - **Obstacles** - not a standard language, no methodology, no standard interfaces, no useful abstractions.
- Tools
    - **SOA** - mostly domain specific
    - **SOP** - collections of small unintegrated tools
- Development methods and practices
    - **SOA** - Ada generics, reuse of architectures, recognized need for standards.
    - **SOP** - code not designed for reuse, unorganized reuse of specs and designs, no standards or guidelines.

The **Tools and Environments** working divided the basic activities of reuse into two categories: *Creation* and *Use.* The creation activity focused on

- **Domain Analysis**,
- **Development/Refinement**, and
- **Classification/Storage**.

The use activity focused on

- **Search/Retrieval**
- **Assessment**, and
- **Incorporation**.

The proposed approach to **Domain Analysis** was modeled after DRACO [6] as modified by

Prieto-Diaz [7]. No mature tools were assessed to be currently available to assist in this process. **Development/Refinement** tools include object-oriented languages, configuration management tools, structure analyzers and quality metric or standards checkers. Various controlled and uncontrolled vocabulary as well as knowledge based tools are available to support software **Classification/Storage**.

Search/Retrieval is supported by some natural language and structured query tools along with some semantic search capabilities. Browsing can be found in HyperText systems and programming environments such as Smalltalk. No tools are available to help the user evaluate/**assess** the components once they are retrieved, but several language processors and application generators help **incorporate** the components in applications (assuming reuse is at the code level).

3.5. Tools and Environments
Bill Riddle (SPC) made several points on the SOA versus SOP of tools and environments. There are currently no high level stand-alone, broad-scope, integrated environments. People are looking into tools that support the selection, adaptation, and assembly of systems at a high level of granularity. Reuse at a high level results in large improvements in productivity at the cost of flexibility, therefore tools are needed to assist in the adaptation (extensibility, customization, tuning and portability) of components. The mechanisms for adaptation identified were *substitution*, *transformation*, and *generation*. Tools play a key role in affecting the way programmers think about solving problems, and the methods that they use in arriving at implementations.

3.6. Constructive vs Generative
Ted Biggerstaff's presentation was split between a review of his seminal framework [2] for reusability technologies in which the composition and generation approaches to reuse were originally stated, and an overview of the reuse projects currently under development at MCC. Most of the points covered in the first part of the presentation can be found in his most recent article in the March issue of IEEE Software [3]. In particular he emphasized the representational (components and composition), operational (tools to find, understand, modify, and compose), and organizational (retrieval and inheritance) aspects of reuse (initially described by Charlie Richter in his presentation), then cited the tradeoff dilemmas of reusability -- generality versus payoff, component size versus reuse potential, implementation effort versus maximum payoff, and capital investment for library population versus payoff. While reuse of code has given some limited success (25% payoff threshold) in narrow, well defined and understood domains, the reuse of designs needs a representational breakthrough to capture and manipulate domain knowledge and achieve an order of magnitude improvement in productivity.

The second part of his presentation focused on moving reuse upstream in the software development life cycle. All the systems described (Prep, ROSE and gIBIS) focus on the reuse of requirements, specifications and designs by having a library of design schemas and abstract algorithms with domain types and constraints to help synthesis new applications (or to assist the user in the construction of new applications). Several applications of HyperText systems were describe. The most notable was gIBIS. Other projects include support for "vivisection" or reverse-engineering a design or code. The key point was the capture of knowledge to assist in the "understanding problem".

3.7. Domain Analysis
Jim Neighbors presented a summary of the DRACO approach to domain analysis. Draco is a generative approach to reuse. It can be viewed as an application generator generator. Basically, a domain is analyzed, and vocabulary defined consisting of objects and operations. A grammer is then defined from the vocabulary and various components associated with the vocabulary identified. A generator is created that takes "specifications" written in the grammer and generates code. The code generation may require more sophisticated domain analysis such as scripts, plans and goals, in order to refine and parameterize the code fragments and components that will be reused.

3.8. Social Issues

Will Tracz presented a summary of the most often cited reasons why software isn't reused: lack of tools, training, education, methodology, motivation -- both financial and psychological (see COMPCON Paper [8] for more details). The Japanese software factory approach was then analysed, and their training methods, management style and tools contrasted with current US software development practices. The conclusion was that, while the Japanese may not be using the most current state-of-the-art methods and facilities, they have developed expertise in using the tools they have and understanding the marketplace they address and are willing to standardize their process and invest the capital necessary to develop reusable software components and code templates, along with component development and certification groups necessary to support them.

3.9. Economics

John Gaffney presented a simple cost model for calculating the cost (C) of developing software given that R% of the code was reused, and that the cost of reusing a line of code is b% of the cost to develop new code. The simple cost model is as follows:

$$C = (1-R)^*1 + b^*R \text{ -- cost of new SW plus cost of reused software}$$

A second model was introduced that take into account the cost of developing the reusable software originally (E). Given this factor, it the minimum number of times that software needs to be reused in order to break even (N_0) can be determined.

$$C = (1-R)^*1 + R(b+E/n) \text{ -- where n is number of times reused}$$

$$N_0 = E/[1-b] \text{ -- Break even point = Cost to generate/cost savings per reuse}$$

The final model reflects the cost of developing software on a given project for reuse (Rc% of total) over "m" projects along with the R% reused and (1-Rc-R)% new.

$$C = (1-Rc-R) + (Rc^*(E/m)) + R^*((E/n)+b)$$

Possible values for b (the cost savings of reuse) are:

- For reusing code only: *0.85*

- For reusing design and code: *0.35*

- For reusing requirements, design and code: *0.08* (testing = 8% remaining cost)

3.10. Legal Issues

John Goodenough summarized some of work being done at SEI by Pamela Samuleson along with the results of the SEI sponsored workshop on legal issues in software. Two topics were covered: the role of government rights, and the current judicial view of protecting software. Ideally the law should protect the vendor by preventing competitors from selling identical, improved or corrupted versions of their software, and establish who is liabile for errors. Similarly, the reuser should have the ability to use, modify, extend and correct purchased software, and in turn provide software to others. There is currently disagreement about the best legal basis for protecting and rewarding each party and no clear cut incentives to the developer or the end user and maintainer of the end user system.

Part of the problem is the unlimited government rights to software and its documentation. The government can use, duplicate and disclose any software developed under contract. Restricted government rights have been proposed that limit revealing the software only for such purposes as maintenance, thus protecting the investment of the original contractor.

The US justice system is also sending mixed signals to software developers. Existing forms of software "protection" have proven inadequate. While it is legal to reverse engineer hardware and even analyze and reproduce a chip mask. The Whelan case demonstrated that even if a program is rewritten in a different language, using different algorithms, if the logic and structure are the same, then the original programs copyright was infringed. Yet a copyright is traditionally interpreted to only protect "expression" (i.e., source) not "ideas". Numerous other cases were cited and reference documents listed.

4. Working Groups Results
Six working groups were planned originally for the workshop but Domain Analysis became such a hot topic that a new working group was formed and the Construction and Generative working groups combined.

4.1. Software Methods Which Support Reuse
The goal of the software methods working group was to identify the characteristics of the methods that support software reuse. It was recognized that "methods" encompass the entire software life cycle, not just software design. Certain "brand name" (JSD, SADT, and OOD) methods were discussed and it was agreed that reuse could be mapped on to them, but that some supported reuse better than others. The reasons that some methods support reuse better than others is that systems developed from these methodologies tend to be based on concepts that are more stable than functional decomposition (i.e., JSD is takes an environmental view, SADT looks at data flow, and OOD focuses on objects).

In general, a method needs to help develop a conceptual model, represent it and canonicalize it. The method should support suitable levels of abstraction and facilitate synthesis of new applications through clean adaptable interfaces. It was pointed out that there are no physical rules (yet) that impose restrictions on specifying software abstractions and the multiplicity of representations inhibits reuse. (Note: part of the problem with the lack of significant results of this group was the fear of overlapping the design group.)

4.2. Design Representations Which Enhance Reuse
The design group recognized that the design process applies to not only code, but specifications, documents, tests and even designs. Even though design spans several concepts: domain analysis, constraints, architectures, plans and goals, process programs, and specifications/requirements, one tool/methodology/representation supports them all -- gIBIS (see section 2.6).

4.3. Code Representations Which Support Reuse
The code reuse working group addressed two separate issues:
1. What information is needed to reuse code?
2. What are the characteristics of language support for reuse?

A potential reuser of software is interested in a number of characteristics of the code. Its functionality, performance, dependence on other units, and overall correctness are of primary importance. This information can be represented as textual documentation, diagrams, benchmark reports, call graphs, usage history and validation certification.

A programming language affects the granularity and style of reuse. It affects the modularization and interface design as well as the ability to add or remove operations from an existing module.

4.4. Tools And Environments Which Support Reuse
The tools and environments group built upon the results of the Minnowbrook working group (see section 3.4). They concluded that future reuse systems would depend upon an information repository consisting of project (application specific), domain specific, and general knowledge/components. Current SOA provides some tool support for code reuse, but SOP tool support was projected for 1995. Tool support for reuse of design was projected to reach SOA by 1995, with no guesses made on SOP of design tool support. The group felt that transformational approaches would make the most significant impact in the future. For example, if a portion of a parts library became crowded with several versions of the same

component, then the copies might be replaced by a parts generator. The importance of traceability was emphasized to determine what tools/components are actually being used[1].

Integration was the basis of an software development environment. The environment consists of a notation that drives the tools that support the methodology that uses the notation. Two forms of integration are important: *internal integration*: tool-to-tool and tool-to-information-repository through an object management system, and *external integration*: a uniform user interface to the tools and a process management system.

4.5. Constructive And Generative Approaches To Reuse

It was fortuitous that the constructive and generative working groups were combined because, as a result of considering both, certain dualities surfaced. A generative approach is the evolution of a constructive approach. Black boxes may be thought of as the purest form in a constructive approach, but macros are both constructive and generative. An application generator uses templates and building blocks to create a new program. With black boxes there is more flexibility to glue them together in different combinations, while with application generators and 4GLs, the combinations are more restricted because the system supplies the glue and it only knows how to glue things together in certain patterns. (A constructive approach requires the domain knowledge be supplied by the user while a generative approach has the domain knowledge built in.) The output of an application generator is harder to extend or modify than a system constructed from building blocks. (Note the CAPS system from Netron [1] handles all these situations nicely.) Finally, a constructive approach is more imperative or procedural, while a generative approach is declarative.

Different forms of "glue" or component composition mechanisms include:
- inheritance,
- instantiation,
- sequence,
- pipes,
- functional composition,
- superimposition,
- binding, and
- module interconnect languages.

Many of the remarks in section 5.2 focus on the applicability of using a constructive versus a generative approach. In general one starts off with identifying the building blocks for a constructive approach, then, through recognizing patterns for putting them together, a parameterized framework is constructed in the form of an application generator.

4.6. Domain Analysis

Domain analysis can be used to match requirements to specifications and to create a model that can be used to educate new programmers. The domain analysis working group selected a sample domain to analyze (The library problem as posed for the ICSE-87). Domain analysis proceeded from several approaches (DRACO, SADT, OOD, Flow-oriented, semantic net, and GTE [7]) As a result, a richer analysis of the domain was achieved. While this result is not surprising, it highlighted the fact that certain approaches may bias the overall analysis of the system. In order to develop a truly robust abstraction, the problem domain should be analyzed from several perspectives.

Two domain analysis procedures were proposed:
    1. Analysis by Domain Experts Approach

---

[1]As a sidepoint in the discussion, the Ada Software Repository was cited as being the greatest counter collection of examples of how not to write good software.

- Establish domain subject area
- Collect experts in one room
- Free associate on what we might account for in the domain
- Distinguish significant things; constrain the domain
- Elaborate foundational things
- Define objects, relationships and constraints
- Clean up the diagrams
- Re-express for reusability

2. Analysis of Implementations Approach

- Select a set of examples - existing implementations.
- Identify similar functions across examples, collect names and terminology.
- For identified routines, map between them using parameters.
- Identify levels of abstraction used to implement the functions.
- Look for layering among functions.
- Graph distribution of instances of functions against possible reuse factors.
- Depending on the distribution, use a generative approach (even distribution) or a constructive approach (clusters).

5. Key Statements

The following quotes are excerpts of presentations and discussions that took place at the workshop. They reflect the personal philosophies of some of the attendees, as well as general statements about software reuse. They have been organized by topic.

5.1. Comments on Non-Technical Issues of Software Reuse

- "Code reuse in the small happens all the time with a small group." -- *Unattributed*

- "The problem is to make reuse fun!" -- *Bailin*

- "There is a fear reuse doesn't allow fresh ideas." -- *Jones*

- "US management reward for working hard, the Japanese reward for productivity" -- *Pyster*

- "Managers should note: there is no silver bullet, no free lunch. Reuse is like a savings account, you have to put a lot in before you get anything out." -- *Biggerstaff*

- "Management understands the tradeoff between less labor and more tools." -- *Booch*

- "Software is viewed as an expense not as a capital investment" -- *Pyster*

- "Software gives a false sense of economy because it is easy to change" -- *Woodfield*

- "If we only solve the technical problems (of reuse), we won't solve the problem." -- *Goodenough*

- "Current government contract clauses disincentivecise reuse." -- *Goodenough*

- "The Japanese do not have any non-technical inhibitors to reuse" -- *Tracz*

- "This graph shows you need a lot of reuse before you get fantastic cost savings" -- *Gaffney*

- "Reuse provides savings in cost, quality and schedule" -- *Gaffney*

- "People won't do it (reuse) to be altruistic" -- *Gaffney*

- "The greatest barriers to effective reuse (i.e., > 25%) are not technical; they are cultural, organizational, legal, and economic." -- *Pyster*

5.2. Comments on Software Reuse Tools and Methodology

- "Code reuse is here today, the question is how to do it better" -- *Williams*
- "Reuse of code is a good way to get started -- not a good way to end up." -- *Riddle*
- "Reuse follows abstraction -- abstraction follows practice" -- *Booch*
- "Before tools, you need to understand the process, you need to codify." -- *Booch*
- "There is nothing worse than a dumb tool that tries to be smart" -- *Simos*
- "Some methods put impediments in the way of reuse." -- *Jones*
- "Using a standard method is more important than using the best method" -- *Pyster*
- "A simple mechanism seems sufficient for construction new systems. " -- *Neighbors*
- "A generative approach .. only a matter of time until you run into the brick walls" -- *Goodenough*
- "The ability to produce garbage is a sign of power (in generative approaches)." -- *Goodenough*
- "A constructive approach is more easily completed or extended than a generative approach when the requirements are not immediately known" -- *Perry*
- "If you only have a problem, then use a constructive approach; if you have solutions, use a generative approach." -- *Perry*
- "The only problem with parameterization is you never have enough parameters." -- *Goodenough*
- "Think of a code generator as a pre-processor, then is your program code with pre-processor calls, or pre-processor calls with code." -- *Simos*
- "You establish standards within a technology window. As technology changes, standards change, and reuse falls off." *Biggerstaff*
- "The (reuse) tools which are best to create in the next 6 years are: a repository, a configuration management tool, and an integration tool." -- *Booch*

5.3. Comments on Domain Analysis

- "There are two kinds of knowledge: Domain Knowledge and Implementation Knowledge" -- *Embley*
- "Not all domains are the same, some are broad and expanding. Reuse is better in restricted domains." -- *Biggerstaff*
- "What needs to be done is the hard work (Domain Analysis") -- *Baxter*
- "We want a method to find canonical representations" -- *Durek*
- "Reverse engineering is one way of mining components, ... but modified systems become a blur." -- *Neighbors*
- "Reverse Engineering is a rats nest if you have to analyze code." -- *Iscoe*
- "99% of the effort is taking domains and extracting objects." -- *Biggerstaff*
- "I don't care how (domain analysis is performed), just get these results (objects and operations)." -- *Neighbors*
- "You benefit from different models of the same domain." -- *Neighbors*
- "Scenarios are the glue that hold objects together" -- *Potts*

- **"Methods for capturing and representing domain knowledge are the key."** -- *Baxter*

- **"Biggerstaff's 3-system rule: If you have not built three real systems in a particular domain, you are unlikely to be able to derive the necessary details of the domain required for successful reuse in that domain. In other words, the expertise needed for reuse arises out of 'doing' and the 'doing' must come first."** -- *Biggerstaff*

- **"The unifying concept is knowledge capture."** -- *Goodenough*

- **"It all comes back to Domain Analysis"** -- *Baxter*

5.4. Miscellaneous Remarks

- **"We successfully built on the results of Minnowbrook rather than replaying them."** -- *Simos*

- **"I measure how good a workshop is by the amount of other things I get done."** -- *Williams*

6. Summary/Personal Observations

The workshop reinforced the basic conclusions I had arrived at in my observations of the state-of-the-practice. It was disappointing, and at the same time encouraging, that the emerging technology is based on fairly simple (but not cheap) technology: high resolution graphics workstations, object-oriented programming languages and formal methods of specifying pre- and post-conditions. I believe momentum is gathering in industry and government to foster the proper environment for software reuse (i.e., create the proper financial incentives). Domain analysis is essential in populating reusable component libraries (constructive approach), or developing application generators (generative approach). Expert system technology is assisting in developing approaches analyzing application domains and representing and manipulating such knowledge to assist in the development or synthesis of new applications.

One personal revelation was stated by John Goodenough in one of the working group sessions. The topic of conversation was centered on what is the glue that holds things together in a constructive approach versus a generative approach. His observation was that as one moves more and more to a generative approach, the programming style becomes *declarative*. This reflects back on a statement he made in his opening remarks to the attendees that we should focus on what is different between one application and previous applications. Again, the importance of *scenarios* in domain analysis; if one can foresee how the components will be used, one can create the architecture and mechanism to instantiate it given certain parameters (e.g., an application generator).

The second significant outcome of the workshop was the overall excitement generated by gIBIS. This simple tool supports the capture of transformation knowledge and design decisions that, before this time, was unmanageable.

In closing, I have concluded that reuse is not an end in itself, but it is a means to an end. Furthermore, reuse is a side effect of the methodology as supported by the environment. Reuse is intuitive when the proper mechanisms are provided. It is part of a more nebulous concept called software engineering, which is another form of general problem solving. It is time the software community agree upon some basic abstractions and build upon them rather than reinvent them each time we build a new system.

References

1. Bassett, P.G. "Frame-Based Software Engineering". *IEEE Software 4*, 4 (July 1987), 9-16.

2. Biggerstaff, T.J. and Perlis, A.J. "Forward: Special Issue on Software Reusability". *IEEE Transactions on Software Engineering SE-10*, 5 (September 1984), 474-476.

3. Biggerstaff, T., and Richter, C. "Reusability Framework, Assessment and Directions". *IEEE Software 4*, 2 (March 1987), 41-49.

4. Booch, G.. *Software Components with Ada.* Benjamin/Cumming, 1987.

5. Braun, C.L., Goodenough, J.B., Eanes, R.S. Ada Reusability Guidelines. Tech. Rept. 3285-2-208/2, SofTech, Inc., April, 1985.

6. Neighbors, J.M. "The Draco Approach to Constructing Software from Reusable Components". *IEEE Transactions on Software Engineering SE-10*, 5 (September 1984), 564-573.

7. Prieto-Diaz, R. Domain Analysis for Reusability. Proceedings of COMPSAC 87, 1987.

8. Tracz, W.J. Software Reuse: Motivators and Inhibitors. Proceedings of COMPCON87, February, 1987.

Report on a Workshop on Software Reuse
held at Hereford, UK on 1,2 May 1986

M. Ratcliffe.
Computer Science Dept.,
UCW Aberystwyth.

Introduction.

It is generally acknowledged that one of the most effective means of improving the productivity of software development staff would be to increase the proportion of software which is reused. Not only should this increase productivity but it should also improve the reliability of software and reduce the elapsed time needed for its development. However, there appear to be major technical and organisational problems to be overcome before significant progress can be made in this direction.

Work addressing the problems of software reuse now has high priority within both the Alvey Software Engineering programme and the Esprit Software Technology initiative. This workshop was organised by the Computer Science Department of the University College of Wales, Aberystwyth, with the support of the Alvey Directorate, in order to bring together people in the United Kingdom who are working in this area or who have an active interest in it. The major objectives of the workshop were to encourage the exchange of ideas and information and to suggest ways in which work in the area might be encouraged.

The workshop was run very informally so that, although most of the programme was given over to presentations, a lot of discussion took place during the presentations. This report summarises the contents of both the presentations and the discussions. A list of participants is attached.

Introduction: A Survey of Reuse and its Problems.
Frank Bott (U.C.W. Aberystwyth)

This presentation was primarily concerned with outlining the issues which needed to be addressed. Frank identified the following list of technical issues:

- what is the appropriate granularity for software components ?
- what are the appropriate forms for reusable components (specifications, designs, code, etc) ?
- how should we describe components ?
- how can we identify and locate components to meet our needs ?
- what characteristics make a component reusable ?
- should we be seeking to reuse existing components or should we start from scratch ?
- what is the role of formal specifications ?
- how do we put reusable components together ?
- what effect does a component-rich environment have on design methods ?
- what new configuration control problems arise and how can we solve them ?
- how can components be certified ?

Most of these issues were to be addressed in other presentations or discussions during the two days.
On the non-technical side, Frank raised the following points:

- how can we motivate people to produce reusable software ?
- how do we motivate people to use reusable software ?
- how can we quantify the benefits of reuse ?

- what are the economics of producing components ?
- what are the legal, contractual and security problems of reuse ?
- does the future lie with the development of a software components industry or with the reuse of components developed in-house - or both ?

Frank emphasised the importance of these organisational issues. This was echoed by Mike Falla (Alvey) who said he was rather disappointed that the rest of the presentations were oriented towards 'technological fixes' rather than addressing the organisational problems.

The BSI Working Party on Reuse.
Phil Mair (National Computer Centre)

In 1984 The British Standards Institute committee on information technology set up a working group on software reusability.

This presentation was based on a paper produced by the Reuse working group which outlines their findings in the form of an informal taxonomy on the various types of reusability.

Phil first outlined the general case which involves direct reuse comprising the usual idea of code reuse, subdivided into immutable objects and derived components, and the reuse of design concepts.

Phil then went on to discuss the roles of libraries identifying the following categories of libraries, all of which aim to encourage reuse:

- public libraries containing general purpose components with a guarantee of quality;
- specialist libraries adapted for particular needs. These components are treated as immutable objects because of the skill involved in manufacture; pools in which developers put their software with minimal support and no guarantees;
- in-house libraries which are used to store software developed by a number of projects. This form of library was found to be least successful, though this is likely to change with the introduction of IPSEs.

On the subject of portability, Phil discussed virtual target machines comprising the machine architecture, programming language and operating system. He then covered the area of interfaces which range from the general purpose UNIX pipe to interfaces suitable for specific application areas, such as the Graphics Kernel System (GKS).

Operating Systems provide all sorts of obstacles to reusability but Phil outlined the following points which can be worked upon to reduce the problems:

- user friendliness/ user acceptability;
- interconnectivity;
- provision of user extendible operating system;
- design of system development languages enabling users to utilise available languages to the full;
- incentives to generate reusability;
- reliability and quality.

In conclusion, Phil emphasised the need to improve cataloguing specifications so as to provide reliable, unambiguous and accurate definitions of what a software component does and how it does it. It will be necessary to encourage standards in a manner not open to diverse interpretation.

"Report on a Workshop on Software Reuse Held at Hereford, UK on 1,2 May, 1986" by M. Ratcliffe from *ACM SIGSOFT Software Engineering Notes,* Volume 12, Number 1, January 1987, pages 42-47. Published 1987, Association for Computing Machinery, Inc., reprinted by permission.

The working paper produced by the BSI is available from John Souter at the following address:

        Quality Assurance Services,
        British Standards Institution,
        PO Box 375,
        Milton Keynes,
        MK14 6LO.

Ada and Software Reuse.
Peter Wallis (University of Bath)

Peter started his presentation by emphasising the cost reduction that reusability promises to give us and the effects that component granularity has on such savings. FB added that, despite the larger cost savings obtainable from large components, components which have coarse granularity, are less likely to be reusable. MT commented that the larger an item is, the smaller in proportion is the surface area. Interfacing problems may therefore well turn out to be smaller in relative scale.

Peter then moved on to discuss the Ada Europe Working Group. The Reuse Working Group itself is producing a book for the Ada Companion Series to contain a collection of papers entitled "Studies in Ada Reuse", this will be completed early in 1987. He stated also that two guidelines have so far been produced on Ada and Reusability:

–   Softech 'Ada Reusability Guidelines'
–   Eclipse 'Guideline for Writing Reusable Ada'

Both of these are available and can be obtained from the authors.

Peter then described specific examples of reuse, to see if there was anything to learn from their success. He explained that the success of NAG was attributed to the fact that though its components have complicated interfaces requiring a detailed user knowledge; it succeeds because it addresses a specialised problem domain with which a lot of people are familiar, the routines are well defined but are difficult to write giving obvious economic benefits to users of the library.

Peter explained that UNIX succeeds in the area of reusability because of the low perceived complexity of its interface (files and pipes). The actual interface is complicated but because most of the details are hidden away in the environment, the user is given a simpler 'user model'. The concept of the user model is also responsible for the suitability of fourth generation languages for building complicated programs from a number of simple components.

PM thought that reuse is more successful in the commercial world because the program designers are not pushing their software/machines to the limits; they are not as concerned about efficiency to the same extent as those working in the scientific world.

MF introduced the point that the language in which reusable components are written is not necessarily the language in which components are reused. There could well be a generation process which takes place from the meta component, which is the reusable thing and which is specialised in some way, into the generated system. It may be necessary to deliver the generated system in Ada but the meta components might be written in Meta Ada.

Some discussion followed on the implications such automatic generation had on program maintenance. Peter then moved on to identify the following reasons as to

why reuse isn't undertaken on a much larger scale:

–   not invented here syndrome – there is a general lack in confidence in other people's products;
–   wrong level of generality in a product or lack of availability;
–   management and organisation.

IS thought that the whole western economic system may be against reuse. MT added that there are now people in the States recommending the Department of Defence to change its whole procurement policy if it really wants to encourage reuse.

Summing up his presentation, Peter stated that reuse has the potential to provide huge cost benefits but that managerial and cultural problems are a major stumbling block. On the technical side, the important thing is the user model and standard design.

Building Systems out of Reusable Processes.
Peter Welch (University of Kent)

Peter began his presentation by discussing the point that to maximise a components reusability it is necessary to minimise complexity, suggesting that systems having complex properties should be built up from systems which have simple properties. If we can build our complete systems using these techniques, then we should produce a comprehensible system possessing arbitrary levels of complexity.

IS thought that a useful analogy is that of the human body. It is a very complex system that is built up from very simple cells. The thing that makes the human body so incomprehensible is the complexity of the connections between these simple cells.

Peter then moved on to parallelism, an area which he felt would aid in reducing system complexity. Peter identified the following software engineering principles which are supported by parallel processes.

–   components are discrete;
–   interfaces are well defined with low coupling between components;
–   there are no subtle side effects;
–   information hiding is used to a large extent.

These principles result in systems which are understandable, efficient, provable, maintainable and reusable. Concurrency gives a key to handling larger systems by viewing the constituent components as discrete modules running in parallel. The advantages of using such an approach as far as Ada applications are concerned has not been exploited.

Peter introduced the idea of 'processes' which are effectively generic tasks from which have been abstracted (into the specification) the calls that it makes to its network environment. These processes are reusable across network systems and hierarchies of nested networks may be built. He then proceeded to discuss the merits of Occam and whether it had anything to offer Ada programmers.

FB found Peter's system very elegant but was concerned that it was quite easy to provide formalisms for not very interesting subsets of the world. Previous experience with similar methodologies carried out at Aberystwyth showed that the elegance was soon lost on more complicated systems.

Peter said that he had tried the system on a larger variety of examples but testing with Ada had failed due to bugs in the compiler.

Guidelines for Writing Reusable Components in Ada.
Bob Gautier (U.C.W. Aberystwyth)

This presentation outlined some of the guidelines for writing reusable software components in Ada, that had been produced by Frank Bott, Tony Elliott and Bob Gautier for the Alvey ECLIPSE project.

Bob explained that the guide was produced not only because it was expected that ECLIPSE would produce a considerable amount of Ada code, but also because the coding level of a project seemed a good point at which to start solving reuse problems. The guidelines were produced with the assumptions that, components would be 'directly reused', with no source editing allowed and, all components would be capable of coexisting in a single Ada program library.

Bob said that the guidelines indicated the usefulness of deferring decisions to the reuser of a component. In this respect, object oriented design was considered important; it was felt that two designers attempting to model a given object would arrive at similar interfaces to the object, and therefore a similar software component requirement.

Bob added that when developing a package interface, a programmer had the choice between a package which would hold internal state and one which would export an abstract data type; he argued that reusable components should be packages which export an abstract data type.

Bob moved on to discuss more specific guidelines; in particular he described the guidelines for exception handling and tasks. The main problem with exceptions is that Ada does not allow them to be passed as parameters to generic packages. As generic formal exceptions would have improved reusability, Bob discussed some of the guidelines which help the programmer to work around this problem. The guidelines also provide suggestions for improving the documentation within a specification, e.g.

```
    procedure PUSH(S:STACK;IT:ITEM);
    -- raises STACK FULL
    -- when IS_FULL(S)
```

describing not only the exceptions which may be raised by a given operation, but also the method by which the exceptional condition may be tested (if possible).

Turning to the subject of tasks, Bob said that the guidelines recommended that tasks be hidden behind procedural interfaces. He pointed out that no restrictions on tasking operation resulted from this; timed and conditional entry calls were still possible, for example, as long as the procedural interface allowed them. Additional documentation was necessary, however, to indicate use of tasking within components.

Bob summed up with the following:

- Ada components should be generic packages which model objects as abstract data types;
- Object interfaces should be made as implementation independent as possible;
- The preferred method of component interconnection is generic instantiation;
- The guidelines produce verbose and in some cases tortuous Ada; some tools are needed to help.

IS asked if the conclusion to be drawn was that Ada was not suitable for reusable components; do we need another language that can be compiled into Ada? Bob agreed to some extent; he said that reusable components could be produced in Ada, but care was necessary to avoid certain features which conspire against reusability.

There were also areas in which Ada was lacking in its support for reusability. Bob listed a few features which would have been useful, such as generic formal exceptions.

MT pointed out that, like everyone else, the Aberystwyth group were acutely aware of the deficiencies in Ada, but were looking for ways to help people who will be using Ada in the real world. It didn't seem useful to say "don't use Ada; its not the best we can do", because people will have to use Ada.

IS expressed concern that there had been some trading off of safety in favour of generality; there was no way of checking that a set of actual parameters to a generic package actually implemented the function expected by the generic. Bob agreed that this was a problem, but not one that could be solved with Ada or simple tool support.

A copy of the guidelines can be obtained from any of the authors mentioned above.

Some Practical Aspects of Software Reuse.
Margaret Stanley (R.S.R.E)

This presentation was based on a paper by Margaret Stanley and Steve Goodenough at Malvern and presented at the Alvey IPSE conference held at Lancaster. It considers the factors present in programming support environments which may effect the reuse of software components and how such problems are tackled in the Flex Programming Support Environment.

Margaret's presentation identified three major features of the Flex PSE which specifically encourage reuse of software components:

- treatment of procedures as "first class" values.
  This means that a procedure is a storable context independent value that points not only to its code and constants but also to its non-local values; with procedure values, single purpose procedures can exist as executable entities no matter what non-local values or parameter structures are involved thus the artificial distinction between main programs and other procedures disappear, any procedure including system utilities then become reusable;
- separate compilation and software construction system which ensure that interfaces match their use.
  Every module holds a reference to the components that it uses, so if a component is accessible for reuse, the components it needs come with it;
- ability of the Flex command interpreter to handle complex data structures.
  It also contains a mode (type) system that is more general than that of most programming languages and includes procedure types, and facilities for handling objects of any type.

The Flex Programming Support Environment demonstrates that it is possible to achieve a high degree of software reuse, both product reuse and component reuse, with minimal risk. Future work is aimed at making the PSE more widely available, and at improving the facilities.

MF said that Flex appears to provide workable solutions to many of the points raised in earlier presentations but he was concerned that as Flex is both host and target, there would be a major problem in delivering a product to a customer. He wondered how much of Flex would need to be ported.

Margaret said that there was a current research project at Malvern to put the complete Flex system on a conventional machine.

A Component Description Language.
Bob Gautier (U.C.W Aberystwyth)

In Bob Gautier's second presentation, he described CDL (pronounced "cuddle"), a Component Description Language for Ada. CDL and its tools provide some support for application of the guidelines he had described in his first talk.

Bob explained that CDL was only about 3 months old, and that as a result the syntax of CDL showed rather too much evidence of the origins of the language, in OBJ and MASCOT3 particularly. The main objectives of CDL are to make generic components easy to instantiate and to remove the need to manually copy specifications of interfaces, for example, when writing generic packages that import abstractions via parameters.

CDL provides the necessary constructs for the separation of specification and implementation. A package is considered in CDL to be an implementation of one or more specifications. The specifications exist independently of the package bodies which implement them; they are themselves reusable components.

Bob gave a simple introductory example of how CDL can be used to convert a component which was not very reusable into a parameterised generic component which had improved reusability because it could be instantiated for many different item types and also because the operations required on the items were made explicit in the parameter list.

Bob moved on to identify the three types of entity in CDL:

1) Theories
In CDL, the (generic) parameter list of a component is not specified in terms of types and subprograms, but in terms of specification modules, called theories (due to the influence of OBJ and LIL). In addition, a package specification indicates which theories are satisfied by the types and subprograms provided by the package;

2) Components
A CDL component is effectively an Ada package. A component may have any number of ports and windows (these terms being borrowed from MASCOT3). A port indicates that a component requires a connection to some component implementing a given interface, and a window indicates that a component provides a given interface;

3) Views
A CDL view (again using OBJ terms) is a mapping from one interface to another. It is a device for allowing connection between ports and windows which require different (but compatible) interfaces. Bob pointed out that CDL views are relationships between interfaces, not between components and interfaces, as in OBJ. CDL views therefore have better status as reusable components, compared to their OBJ counterparts.

Two tools have been built to support CDL. The first is a librarian, which compiles CDL and stores it in a structure from which Ada package specifications can be generated. The second is a diagram editor, running on a SUN-2 workstation, which allows component interconnections to be drawn, or new components to be specified diagrammatically. The capability to convert diagrams into Ada is expected shortly.

In conclusion, Bob described some of the future work to be done on CDL. This included improvements in the checking performed by the compiler, and the addition of some sort of semantic annotation to help define the function of interfaces. Certain Ada-specific features have to be added, for example exception support.

Bob pointed out that the Ada guidelines had shown how this could be done, and that CDL would hide a lot of complex Ada.

IS asked if CDL wasn't really just Ada-flavoured MASCOT3. Bob replied that to some extent it was, but that many MASCOT features had been removed in order to support a component-oriented viewpoint. When pressed to justify the invention of a new language, in preference to simply using the MASCOT3 design language, Bob said that to some extent history and evolution had caused CDL to differ syntactically from the MASCOT3 language, but in any case there were certain features that would eventually be added to CDL (such as exceptions and tasking) that would never be in the MASCOT language.

A paper describing CDE and its tools is available from the author.

Knowledge Based Techniques for Cataloguing Components.
Murray Wood (University of Strathclyde)

This presentation was based on Strathclyde's experience in trying to develop methods for storage and retrieval of software components held within a component catalogue.

Murray identified the following requirements necessary for a usable software component catalogue:

- the retrieval mechanism must be able to match requests against components satisfying those requests;
- the retrieval mechanism must be capable of determining close matches when exact matches cannot be found;
- the catalogue interface must be simple to use;
- the catalogue should be extensible.

Though it is thought by many that formal methods provide the most satisfactory solution for component specification within a catalogue, these ideas were refuted by Murray on the following grounds:

- learning time required to use formal methods is prohibitive;
- many components are difficult to describe;
- formal methods cannot help in determining close matches. Two syntactically different yet semantically equivalent components cannot be equated automatically;
- retrieval doesn't need to be as precise as that required by formal methods.

Having explained why he thought that a keyword system, creating a network classification, is not a satisfactory solution for the majority of software components, Murray went on to explain the concept of 'software function frames'. These frames are based on 'conceptual dependency', a method used by natural language understanding systems to represent the text of natural language that they are trying to understand. The idea is to represent the meaning of natural language using the basic concepts of any domain and the relationships between those concepts. There are three fundamental types of concepts that can be recognised:

- actions which correspond to the functions that a software component performs;
- nominals representing the objects that perform the function;
- modifiers that describe actions and nominals.

At least one software function frame is constructed for each basic function that the software performs, based around the action, with slots for the objects manipulated by the component. Retrieval first tries to find an exact match with a component in the catalogue, if this fails the criteria used are gradually relaxed first by ignoring the action and then, if necessary, the nominals. It is only in the worst possible case that the system behaves as if it were keyword based.

Murray argued that a software component library based around these ideas has a better capability for matching requests than that provided by independent keywords. The system has a simple interface, is flexible and also extensible matching all the previous requirements.

Murray concluded his presentation by stating that an experimental system running on a limited domain had been developed at Strathclyde and was being evaluated.

Formal Notations for Representing Software Components - Some Problems.
Mel Jackson (Praxis)

The aim of this presentation was to look at some aspects of the use of formal specification techniques for software reuse and determine some of the problems. Mel's main concern was that despite much research being carried out into formal methods, formalisms for software reuse are still an unexplored area. Ideally one needs a linguistic framework in which it is possible to take a component specification, adapt it for some new use and at the same time manipulate the corresponding implementations that we already have.

Mel suggested that for the reuse of software to be beneficial, emphasis must be placed on using large components. It should be possible to reuse whole parts of existing systems, effectively getting more than 50% of a system from previous work. He added that in reusing such components, some form of modification would be required; components at this scale are not suitable for direct reuse. Mel stated that in order to successfully reuse these components it would be necessary to provide formal specifications, in particular:

- one must be able to understand the behaviour of existing components in order to understand whether they can meet the new requirements;
- it must be possible to relate the specification of existing components to the specification of the new requirements in order to identify required changes.

Formal specifications help in both of the above areas. To illustrate this point, Mel gave an example specification in VDM considering how one might want to massage the specification in order to meet the new requirements and then, how such changes might be reflected in the corresponding implementation. It is this latter operation that is the main problem. What is needed, in order to tackle the use of formal notation for representing reusable software, is a methodological linguistic framework which encompasses specification and code and which supports, in a uniform way, the operations such as inclusion, strengthening and instantiating a specification in the corresponding implementation.

FB stated that he had studied a case where large components were reused in a project for office automation. This had been achieved without the use of formal specifications.

Mel agreed that there are many systems developed in this way but, due to the lack of formal specifications, substantial amounts of time are wasted in determining what the components actually do. Toshiba, for example, build large systems with 70% of the components being reused from elsewhere. They do not use formal specifications.

Reuse of Specification Components.
Cydney Minkowitz (I.C.L)

This presentation was concerned in describing the experiences obtained from using the functional language 'me too' as a design and prototyping methodology for intelligent business systems.

The project undertaken at the University of Stirling and headed by Peter Henderson aimed at industrialising functional programming. The development of software using this method combines the principle of rapid prototyping of software using executable formal specifications; Cydney identified the following four steps:

- declare abstract data types and give natural language descriptions;
- formally define data types by modelling the objects on mathematical types such as sets and maps;
- validate and evaluate the system by executing the specification;
- iterate and refine.

Me too is a formal specification language similar to a subset of VDM. It is actually restricted to the constructive part of VDM for the sole purpose of supporting the execution of component specifications. Using me too, one is able to create rapid prototypes in the form of formal specifications which can then be executed for the developer to examine the results. Me too leads to clear and concise design.

The conclusions which Cydney came to are based on eighteen months work and development of twelve projects. The results showed that components required a lot of refining to make them general enough to be reusable. In some cases components were found to be too general. It was found to be much more difficult to try to design in isolation than when designing for a particular application.

MJ asked whether the presence of a library of reusable components made it easier to create new systems or was it easier to start from scratch. Cydney stated that once one becomes accustomed to system development using library components it becomes very easy; often concepts are reused rather than actual code.

Position Statements.

Keith Bennett (University of Keele)

Keith stated that he was about to start up a project entitled 'Software Archaeology' which is to look at reuse in practice. The idea is to examine a project which had, as one of its objectives, the intention of reusing components and to see how successful it was in achieving this aim.

It is intended that the project to be examined will be the Software Science development of SDS-2 and the Gamma system.

Patrick Hall (Cirrus Computers Ltd)

Cirrus Computers is subsidiary of a U.S. company and manufactures test equipment for VLSI. Patrick identified the problem that, as components are glued together creating larger components, there comes a point at which communication methods change.

Cirrus took the view that they did not want to differentiate between procedures and processes and would provide cross-process procedure call interfaces throughout by supporting remote procedure calls. Patrick went on to discuss a number of problems which arose such as naming conventions. These problems and further details are described in a paper available from the author.

John Mariani (University of Lancaster)

John is currently setting up a research project at Lancaster to implement the 'myop' language which, following the software chips paradigm, encourages the development of reusable components. The associated programming environment will provide graphic tools capable of supporting a universal test harness in which one can 'plug in' components for testing.

Discussion Group Reports.

Earlier in the workshop, the group had split into two discussion groups. One group, chaired by Mike Tedd discussed formal methods and their relevance to reuse. The other, chaired by Peter Wallis, were told that the Alvey directorate were considering commissioning a study of reusability practice and experience in the UK and abroad. This group was asked to propose terms of reference for such a study.

The following reports are the presentations, of the two groups, given to the whole workshop.

Formal Methods and Reuse.

Mike Tedd, on behalf of the first study group, identified the following roles that formal specifications may play in component reuse:

- help design components which are inherently more reusable. Formal specifications help with the coherence/clarity of components and when one is interested in reusing design, it helps capture that design;
- retrieval from a component catalogue. Formal specifications, though of little use for actual retrieval may help derive properties of a component which may be of use. Once a component has been retrieved, the formal specification may help in verifying the suitability of the selected component for a specific task;
- as a basis for modification. There is a definite role in this area providing the specification captures the process of movement from the specification to the code;
- as a basis of trust, overcoming the not-invented-here syndrome;
- design with reusable components. The presence of formal specifications helps the design process by giving the designer something to work with, perhaps allowing one to explore designs;
- protection against misuse;
- documentation. This is the most important role in that it helps the user in his understanding of what is going on. It is probably the basis for all the points discussed above.

Proposed Study.

Peter Wallis presented the following proposal on behalf of the second discussion group:

To prepare a report aimed at senior management in the UK Information Technology supply industry which will survey the state of the art of software reuse worldwide, present the benefits to be derived from it and suggest how the UK industry can best realise these benefits. The report will address both technical and organisational issues and will include a number of case studies.

The study team will be expected to visit appropriate organisations in the UK, North America, Japan and Europe. The team must include both managerial and technical expertise.

A budget of £ 45,000 is envisaged to cover all costs except physical production, distribution and marketing of copies of the report. The project is expected to take two hundred man days to complete.

MF asked whether the workshop felt that there was any other sensible action which could be taken at this time. He remarked that examples of outstanding problems include:

- how can we determine the extra costs involved in designing for reusability ?
- can we develop conceptual models to help as a means of discussing systems ?
- how do we design architecture required for a product line incorporating reusability ?
- what can be done to improve our knowledge of the effects of reusability on the software engineering process ?

MT expressed the view that until the results of the study were known, further initiatives would be premature. The workshop concurred.

At this point, the workshop closed.

Participants

(KB)	Keith Bennett	University of Keele
(FB)	Frank Bott	University College of Wales, Aberystwyth
(DD)	David Duxbury	British Aerospace, Warton, Nr. Preston
(MF)	Mike Falla	Alvey Directorate
(BG)	Bob Gautier	University College of Wales, Aberystwyth
(PH)	Patrick Hall	Cirrus Computers Ltd.
(MJ)	Mel Jackson	Praxis, Bath
(PM)	Phil Mair	N.C.C.
(JM)	John Mariani	University of Lancaster
(CM)	Cydney Minkowitz	University of Stirling
(BP)	Brian Passingham	Software Sciences, Macclesfield
(MR)	Mark Ratcliffe	University College of Wales, Aberystwyth
(NS)	Nick Sharman	Software Sciences, Macclesfield
(IS)	Ian Sommerville	University of Strathclyde
(MS)	Margaret Stanley	RSRE, Malvern
(MT)	Mike Tedd	University College of Wales, Aberystwyth
(PWa)	Peter Wallis	University of Bath
(PWe)	Peter Welch	University of Kent
(MW)	Murray Wood	University of Strathclyde

Part 2: Motivation

Much effort has been spent understanding the technical and nontechnical barriers of software reuse. The papers and short articles in this part summarize and place in perspective the problems and potential economic paybacks of reusing software.

The first paper, "Software Reuse: Motivation and Inhibitors" by Will Tracz, describes the reasons why software is, isn't, and should be reused.

It analyzes software reuse from the perspective of a programmer, software manager, computer scientist, and cognitive psychologist. Finally, it contains a section analyzing the success of Japanese software factories.

The second paper, "Reusability in the Large versus Code Reusability in the Small" by Mitch Lubars, first contrasts the technical and non-technical problems of software reuse in the small versus software reuse in the large and at large. Next, approaches to locating and modifying software to be reused are described followed by a discussion of alternate forms of reusable software: code templates, schemas (code and design), and abstractions for programming in the small. The paper concludes with an assessment of how these approaches scale to programming in the large.

The next paper, "A Framework and Economic Foundation for Software Reuse" by Bruce Barnes, Tom Durek, Jim Gaffney, and Art Pyster, presents economic models developed by the Software Productivity Consortium to measure and evaluate the cost of reuse. These models are useful in predicting the payoff threshold for amortizing the additional costs of developing reusable software as well as projecting the benefits. The paper also analyzes the five dimensions of reuse: abstraction, adaptation, accessing, integrating and generalization. A parameterized canonical architecture is described as having the ideal properties of a reusable component.

The final paper, "Reusability Comes of Age" by Will Tracz, is the guest editor's introduction to the July 1987 special issue of *IEEE Software* on software reuse tools. All of the papers from this issue are contained in this tutorial (in some form). Besides introducing the papers, Tracz analyzes the attributes of reusable software and the buy/build/reuse decision process by means of an analogy of buying a new/used car. This type of analogy is further applied in the collection of essays, "Confessions of a Used-Program Salesman," that follow. These six vignettes address issues of programming languages, interface design, quality, and programmer culture related to software reuse.

Software Reuse: Motivators and Inhibitors

Will Tracz

Program Analysis and Verification Group[1]

Stanford, California 94305

Abstract

The software engineering community is showing a renewed interest in software reuse. The search for quality and productivity has brought about attempts to apply manufacturing technology to programming. This paper summarizes the motivators and inhibitors of software reuse and analyzes the limited success that it has enjoyed. Technical, organizational, political, psychological, and economic issues related to software reuse are addressed.

1. Introduction

Reusable software software is the technology of the future. Whether it always has been and always will be is the question.

The concept of software reuse has been part of the programming heritage since the origins of the stored program computer EDSAC at the University of Cambridge in 1949. Maurice Wilkes[1] first recognized the need for avoiding the redundant effort in writing scientific subroutines and recommended a library of routines be kept for general use. Until recently, little had been done to extend program reusability beyond this rather simple level. The formidable "software crisis" coupled with impressive improvements in the price-to-processing-power ratio, advances in programming language design, compiler construction, and interactive graphics have forced developers to reevaluate the tradeoffs made in establishing the traditional ad hoc development methodologies and environments used previously. New and better ways are being explored to harness these recent technological advances and to develop an integrated software/hardware system optimized for programmer productivity. Again[2] and again[3] the role of reusable software has been identified and discussed[4,5,6,7,8].

This paper examines the three issues: why the paradigm of reusable software engineering is desirable; why it has not had, to date, the broad sweeping effects envisioned by the programming prophets; and why it has enjoyed, under certain circumstances, limited success. The goal of this paper is to identify, summarize, and analyze the technical, organizational, political, psychological and economic motivators and inhibitors associated with software reuse. By consolidating these factors, a clearer picture of the dependencies and interactions is created. This paper is organized into three sections. The first section elaborates on the two main motivations for reusing software:

- **productivity** and
- **quality**.

The second section[2] addresses the question *"What makes reusing software artifacts (e.g., code, designs, documentation, or test cases) difficult?"* This question is answered from the perspective of a

- **Programmer,**
- **Software Manager,**
- **Computer Scientist,** and
- **Cognitive Psychologist.**

The last section summarizes recent industrial experience in software reuse. The limited success of software reuse for programming-in-the-small is contrasted with the much more publicized Japanese Software Factories accomplishments.

2. Why Reusable Software Should Be

Before one addresses the technical and economic reasons why software should be reused, it is important to gain a perspective on recent advances in the state of the practice. Current software engineering technology has focused on improving workstation performance, generating friendly user interfaces, and integrating environments. Assuming that these goals will be attained in the near future, the key issue becomes *"What is next? How can we find a way to make programmers an order of magnitude more productive?"* Barring any immediate breakthroughs in artificial intelligence, the next frontier appears to be software reuse.

2.1. Advantages of Software Reuse

There are two major reasons for reusing software: **productivity** and **quality**. Systems developed based on reusable software artifacts, in principle, should cost less (partially attributable to a shorter schedule), and contain fewer defects because of the "tried and true" parts it is composed of. Productivity and quality will be individually addressed in the sections that follow.

2.1.1. Productivity

Gains in productivity reduce development costs and schedule. Software reuse increases productivity because

---

[1]The author is an employee of the IBM Federal Systems Division, Owego, NY, participating in the IBM PhD Resident Study Program in the Electrical Engineering Department at Stanford University.

[2]Portions of this section were presented at the Workshop on Future Directions in Computer Architecture and Software, May 5-8, 1986.

Reprinted from *Proceedings of COMPCON S'87*, 1987, pages 358-363.

- Software reuse "amplifies" programming capabilities[9]. The programmer has fewer symbols to write when large portions of the code or design are copied verbatim.

- Software reuse reduces the amount of documentation and testing required.

- A synergistic effect occurs when systems are developed based on reusable components. The system becomes easier to maintain and modify because the software developers are more familiar with the reusable building blocks from which it is constructed and can more rapidly understand the complete system design.

Finally, software development based on reusable building blocks offers opportunities for increased system performance when frequently-used components are migrated into microcode, special hardware, or silicon.

2.1.2. Quality
Improvements in quality from developing software based on reusable components can be attributed to the following characteristics of reused software.

- It is well designed (i.e., designed for reuse).

- It is well documented - according to an established standard.

- It is well tested - certified for reuse. The more software is reused, the greater the probability an error will not be found.

- Its function is well understood and likely to be used appropriately.

One aspect of quality seldom recognized when developing software based on reusable software artifacts is realized when rapid prototyping is used in conjunction with software reuse. Rapid prototyping allows for system concepts and user interfaces to be demonstrated earlier in the development cycle, thus reducing costly rework during later phases.

3. Why Reusable Software Isn't
"What makes reusing software artifacts difficult?" The answers to this question are dependent upon many technical, organizational, political and psychological issues. This section contains a discussion of the inhibitors identified with reusable software presented from four points of view:

- **Programmer**: someone who designs, implements and tests a portion of a software system.

- **Software Manager**: someone who manages a software development project.

- **Computer Scientist**: someone on the leading edge of technology, exploring and developing new techniques for expanding the reusable software engineering paradigm.

- **Cognitive Psychologist**: someone who understands the human thought process, its limitations, and implications for programming.

3.1. A Programmer's Viewpoint
What are some of the reasons why a programmer doesn't use someone else's code or design?

- It is more fun to write it oneself.

- It would imply a sign of weakness not to be able to do it oneself.

- It is not **my** code. This is part of the **NIH** (Not Invented Here) syndrome of making oneself indispensable to assure job security.

- It is easier to write it oneself, then to try to locate it, figure out what it does, and find out if it works. If it has to be modified, then it also might be easier to rewrite it from scratch.

- There was not enough shelf space or disk space to save the last version to reuse.

- There are no tools to help find components or compose a system from the reusable pieces.

- There are no software development methodologies that stress reusing code, let alone reusing a design or a specification.

- There was no consideration by the system analyst, who specified the system, that portions of an existing system could be salvaged and reused.

- There is little emphasis on reusing software taught in academia[10]; in fact, most students don't have any mechanism or motivation to save programs from assignment to assignment, let alone, from course to course.

- The code or artifact in question
  - is not supported. If a bug is found, no one will fix it, or assist in determining the cause.
  - executes too slowly.
  - has parameters of the wrong data type.
  - is too big[3].
  - is written in the wrong language.
  - was written in the right language on a different processor (Is it transportable?)
  - was not developed according to current standards.

The issues raise in this section are both technical and psychological. The technical issues raised focus on the lack of well described, useful, and reliable reusable component libraries and an integrated programming environment available to take advantage of them. On the psychological side, the reluctance of a programmer to re-tool and place a dependence on someone else's work generally inhibits initial acceptance of this approach.

---

[3]The larger an artifact is, the more benefit it is to reuse, but the less likely it is to fit an application[11].

3.2. A Manager's Viewpoint

Managers often make decisions based on more than just technical issues. Some reasons for not adopting a reusable software engineering approach for a software project might be as follows:

- If no tools or components exist, then it will take time and manpower to create the tools and components, and to gain the expertise in their use. Such costs are generally not within the budget of a single project[12].

- If the tools do exist for making programmers more productive, then this will make the project more dependent on fewer personnel. Decreasing the number of experts in a project increases the impact (and risk factor) of loosing an employee due to illness (the Mac truck theory). Finally, any reduction in headcount might be perceived as reducing the empire a manager commands[8].

- If special tools (e.g., application generators, or preprocessors) are used to create a program, then a customer might expect these tools to be delivered along with the product for maintenance purposes.

- If systems are built incorporating proprietary reusable components, how is the proprietary software protected from being plagiarized in delivered systems?

- If a defect appears in a program developed using reused components, who is legally responsible for damages?

- If there are no standards to control what is entered into the components library[13], then time and money must be spent setting and maintaining the standards.

Finally, there are no economic or other type of incentives for creating reusable components[12]. If a contractor delivers a reusable/adaptable piece of software then the chances of follow-on or maintenance work are reduced. Furthermore, technical issues faced by management are sometimes tainted by political considerations or personal aspirations. Nevertheless, a certain amount of experience in budgeting, scheduling, and managing a software project based on a reusable components library is necessary before any confidence can be placed in the methodology.

3.3. A Computer Scientist's Viewpoint

Computer scientists have the luxury of taking a broader perspective when addressing the issue of reusability than programmers faced with existing schedules and budgets. "Used Program Sales and Service" isn't a likely dissertation topic. Balzer[7] has stated that "Code is not reusable." He suggested that instead of the black box, plug compatible approach that is focused on programming **products**, the answer to reusable software lies in analyzing the programming **process**. From this perspective, Horowitz[5] has suggested the following alternative approaches to reusability:

- **Very High Level Languages** (VHLL's) allow specification of problem domain entities and operations directly in the syntax of the language.

Similarly, Problem Oriented Languages (POL's) are a form of VHLL's specifically tailored for a particular problem domain. Reusability is accomplished by reusing the compiler.

- **Application Generators** are software tools that create programs given a parameterized or programmed specification. Reusability is accomplished by reusing the application generator for each new problem.

- **Transformation Systems** require high-level specifications be written describing *what* the software system should do. The specifications are then transformed by a series of pattern-matching expansions into a program[14].

The key concept in each of these three examples focuses on the automated application of reusable components. Each tool recognizes some type of high-level pattern in the problem domain that can be implemented by substituting some (parameterized) code fragments. Certain theoretical limits of the transformational techniques have been investigated.

3.4. A Cognitive Psychologist's Viewpoint

Computer programming is simply one form of problem solving. Understanding the merits of existing programming paradigms from the perspective of cognitive psychology[15] has provided valuable insight in dealing with complexity. Reusable software has been the focus of studies by Soloway[16] and Curtis[17]. A summary of the empirical evidence gathered as it applies to reusable software engineering follows:

- The size of Short Term Memory limits the number $(7+/-2)$[18] of pieces of information one can manipulate consciously at one moment in time. This limit on complexity can be overcome by proper *chunking* or modularization of components, that is, by collecting units of information together into one semantically meaningful piece (or package) (Note: this argument supports information hiding and object-oriented design[19], two paradigms which are useful when creating reusable components).

- Expert (i.e., experienced) programmers develop applications through a recursive mental process[20] of matching pieces of the problem with solution segments with which they are familiar (e.g., plans[21]). Therefore, subconsciously, portions of designs are reused each time a program is written.

- Internal conceptualization of the knowledge base in which program/design segments reside tends to evolve with experience into having a uniform content for all programmers[22]. In other words, experienced programmers tend to think alike and express their solutions in similar forms.

- Programmers cannot reuse something they don't understand. Furthermore, expert programmers follow certain explicit *rules of discourse*[16] regarding naming conventions and programming style[23] which enhance program readability and comprehension. This implies that for something to be reused, it has to be well written, and documented according to an accepted standard.

These observations support the need for a proper programming environment to facilitate the reusable software engineering paradigm. Tools must be available to handle the complexity and assist the programmer in finding and understanding what software components exist. These results also demonstrate the intuitive validity of such an approach.

4. Why Reusable Software Is
Software reuse has met with some limited success. However, Advances in the state of the practice have been slow and sporadic. This section analyzes circumstances under which software has been reused. Two environments will be examined:

1. Programming-in-the-small (i.e., small software projects) and,

2. Software Factories.

4.1. Programming-in-the-Small
A majority of the software developed in the United States is written by individuals or small teams of programmers associated with a single project or product. Software is reused for the following reasons:

- It was written by the person who is reusing it.

- It was written by another person in the project.

- An application is being developed where a previous version or a similar program is available.

- The software is for an function that is
  - well understood,
  - only has a few data types,
  - relies on a stable underlying technology (i.e., I/O), and
  - has standards within the problem domain.

  Scientific subroutines are examples of this type of software.

- It was mandated by the manager to do so.

- It was determined by the developer to be to his advantage, either financially[4], or technically.

Finally, some programmers view developing reusable software as being a chance to become immortal, a chance to put the ego back in programming.

4.2. Software Factories
The Japanese have taken a different approach to programming; instead of software development, they view it as software production. The reasons that they can cite up to an order of magnitude more programming productivity are:

---

[4]At Bell Labs they have the *Thief of the Week* award for the programmer who reuses the most code on a program.

- They have established a critical mass in the number of reusable components and programmers (>1000) available to use and develop them.

- They have taken the separate phases in software development process and assigned them to different organizations within the software factory.

- They have developed an integrated set of tools and rigid standards to support reuse in the software production life cycle. Because of the large numbers of programmers using the tools, their initial development cost can be economically justified.

- Their management is committed to this approach.

- Software reuse is part of their training process. One software factory[24] gives programming exercises each month to all its programmers. These exercises require referencing the library of reusable components in order to be completed with the minimum of effort.

The average programmer productivity in US is **100-500 SLOC/month**[6] of new and reused code. The average programmer productivity in Japanese Software Factory is **500-800 SLOC/month**[25] new code, and **800-3200 SLOC/month** new and reused code.

5. Conclusion
Those who cannot remember the past are condemned to repeat it - *George Santayana*

This paper has described the difficulties faced by programmers and program managers who attempt to reuse software artifacts and the motivation for overcoming them. The limited areas of success have also be discussed. The major issues may be summarized as:

- The primary factors motivating the reuse of software are productivity and quality.

- Most programmers tend to view reusability from the perspective of simply reusing code, whereas reusing other programming artifacts (e.g., designs, specifications, and tests) leads to more productivity. Furthermore, other reusability paradigms (e.g., application generators, translation systems, VHLLs, and POLs) have proven successful[5].

- Meaningful, properly documented, tested, verified and classified reusable components need to be developed before they can be reused.[26,7]

- Expert (i.e., experienced) programmers with an understanding of the problem domain and the contents of a component library are best suited to fully exploit the reusable software engineering paradigm.[16]

- Tools and methodologies are needed to support developing and cataloging reusable components and composing software systems from them.[13]

- A component-based approach introduces real, or perceived staffing risks associated with the increased dependence on a single individual to do the work of many.[8]

- Reusable software development systems cost money, time, and manpower to develop and become proficient at using.

- Software is most likely to be reused if it is geographically close to the originator.

- This feasibility of software reuse has been demonstrated by the Japanese Software Factories partly because of the concentration of programmers (critical mass) that maximizes their return on tool investment.

Wegner's[27] adage "We should stand on each others shoulders, not on each others feet" aptly describes the potential of software reuse. The computer industry is faced with a software crisis, a predicted shortage of programmers and, the fact that software productivity increased only 3-8% a year over the last 30 years[28]. Studies on reuse have shown that

- 40%-60% of all code is reusable from one application to another[9],

- 60% of the design and code on all business applications is reusable[29],

- 75% of program functions are common to more than one program, and

- only 15% of the code found in most programs is unique and novel to a specific application[6].

Software reuse will continue to be a topic of research and technology infusion for the rest of the decade and the decade to come. The factors cited in this paper, once recognized and properly addressed, should assist in making advances in software reuse a reality, and a technology whose time has come.

References

1. Office of Eames, editors, *A Computer Perspective,* Harvard Press, 1973.

2. Druffel, L.E. Redwine, S.T. Riddle, W.E., "The STARS Program: Overview and Rationale", *Computer,* Vol. 16, No. 11, November, 1983, pp. 21-29.

3. Alexandridis, N.A., "Adaptable Software and Hardware: Problems and Solutions", *Computer,* Vol. 19, No. 2, February, 1986, pp. 29-39.

4. Freeman, P., "Reusable Software Engineering: Concepts and Research Directions", *Proceedings of ITT Workshop on Reusability in Programming,* September 7-9 1983.

5. Horowitz, E., and Munson, J.B., "An Expansive View of Reusable Software", *IEEE Transactions on Software Engineering,* Vol. SE-10, No. 5, September, 1984, pp. 477-487.

6. Jones, T.C., "Reusability in Programming: A Survey of the State of the Art", *IEEE Transactions on Software Engineering,* Vol. SE-10, No. 5, September, 1984, pp. 488-493.

7. Standish, T.A., "An Essay on Software Reuse", *IEEE Transactions on Software Engineering,* Vol. SE-10, No. 5, September, 1984, pp. 494-497.

8. Rauch-Hindin, W.B., "Reusable Software", *Electronic Design,* Vol. 31, No. 3, February, 3, 1983, pp. 176-193.

9. Biggerstaff, T.J. and Perlis, A.J., "Forward: Special Issue on Software Reusability", *IEEE Transactions on Software Engineering,* Vol. SE-10, No. 5, September, 1984, pp. 474-476.

10. Denning, P.J., "Throwaway Programs", *Communications of the ACM,* Vol. 24, No. 2, February, 1981, pp. 259-260.

11. Prieto-Diaz, R., *A Software Classification Scheme,* PhD dissertation, University of California, Irvine, 1985.

12. Jones, T. C., *Programming Productivity,* McGraw-Hill Book Company, 1986.

13. Chandersekaran, C.S., and Perriens, M.P., "Towards an Assessment of Software Reusability", *Proceedings of ITT Workshop on Reusability in Programming,* September 7-9 1983.

14. Cheatham, T.E. Jr., "Reusability Through Program Transformations", *IEEE Transactions on Software Engineering,* Vol. SE-10, No. 5, September, 1984, pp. 589-594.

15. Tracz, W.J., "Computer Programming and the Human Thought Process", *Software-Practice and Experience,* Vol. 9, 1979, pp. 127-137.

16. Soloway, E. and Ehrlich, K., "Empirical Studies of Programming Knowledge", *IEEE Transactions on Software Engineering,* Vol. SE-10, No. 5, September, 1984, pp. 595-609.

17. Curtis, B., "Cognitive Issues in Reusability", *Proceedings of ITT Workshop on Reusability in Programming,* September 7-9 1983.

18. Miller, G.A., "The magical number seven plus or minus two: some limits on our capacity to process information", *Psychological Review,* Vol. 63, 1956, pp. 81-97.

19. Parnas, D.L., Clements, P.C., and Weiss, D.M., "Enhancing Reusability with Information Hiding", *Proceedings of ITT Workshop on Reusability in Programming,* September 7-9 1983.

20. Jefferies, R., Turner, A.A, Polson, P.G., and Atwood, M.E., "The Processes Involved in Designing Software", in *Cognitive Skills and Their Acquisition,* Anderson, J.R., ed., Hillsdale, N.J.: Erlbaum, 1981.

21. Soloway, E. and Ehrlich, K., "What Do Programmers Reuse? Theory and Experiment", *Proceedings of ITT Workshop on Reusability in Programming,* September 7-9 1983.

22. McKeihen, K.B., Reiman, J.S., Rueer, H.H., and Hirle, S.C., "Knowledge organization and skill differences in computer programmers", *Psychological Review*, Vol. 13, 1981, pp. 307-325.

23. Kernighan, B. and Plauger, P., *The Elements of Style*, New York: McGraw-Hill, 1978.

24. Tajima, D., and Matsubara, T., "Inside the Japaneses Software Industry", *IEEE Computer*, March, 1984, pp. 34-43.

25. Matsumoto, Y., "Some Experience in Promoting Reusable Software: Presentation in Higher Abstract Levels", *IEEE Transactions on Software Engineering*, Vol. SE-10, No. 5, September, 1984, pp. 502-512.

26. St. Dennis, R. J., Stachour, P., Frankowski, E., Onuegbe, E., "Measurable Characteristics of Reusable Ada Software", *Ada Letters*, Vol. 5, No. 2, March-April, 1986, pp. 41-49.

27. Wegner, P., "Varieties of Reusability", *Proceedings of ITT Workshop on Reusability in Programming*, September 7-9 1983.

28. Boehm, B., *Software Engineering Economics*, Prentice Hall, Englewood Cliffs, NJ, 1981.

29. Lanergan, R.G. and Grasso, C.A., "Software Engineering with Reusable Design and Code", *IEEE Transactions on Software Engineering*, Vol. SE-10, No. 5, September, 1984, pp. 498-501.

CODE REUSABILITY IN THE LARGE VERSUS CODE REUSABILITY IN THE SMALL

Mitchell D. Lubars
Microelectronics and Computer Technology Corp.
3500 West Balcones Center Drive
Austin, TX 78759

An earlier version of this paper appeared in *ACM SIGSOFT Software Engineering Notes*.

ABSTRACT

As a general rule, the goals of software engineering involve the development of techniques for improving software development productivity. It is no surprise, then, that a lot of attention has been focused on facilitating the reuse of program code. However, much of this attention has been directed with only shortsighted and self-supporting goals, and has thus condemned code reuse techniques to limited areas of success. This paper brings to light some of the issues involving code reusability and contrasts the two ends of the reusability spectrum; "code reusability in the large" and "code reusability in the small." Methods for possibly improving code reusability are examined.

INTRODUCTION

Each year, the worldwide software industry produces billions of lines of computer code. However, only a small fraction of this code is ever reused despite the fact that most of the programming problems and functions are fairly common [1]. This sad fact is the result of a number of technical, social, economic, and other problems [2]. In order to understand some of these problems, we will examine and contrast the two ends of the spectrum of code reusability that we refer to as "code reusability in the large" and "code reusability in the small." By focusing on these extremes, we will be able to identify some of the major barriers to solving the code reusability problems and propose some possible solutions.

CODE REUSABILITY IN THE SMALL VERSUS CODE REUSABILITY IN THE LARGE

We first distinguish code reusability in the small from code reusability in the large. Code reusability in the small is the type of reusability performed by a single programmer or a small group of programmers working together on related programs to take advantage of the common aspects of those programs. It frequently involves the lifting of a piece of code from one program, to be directly used in another related program. Most often, code reusability in the small is performed within a group of a organization that is developing those programs to be related products. Typically, such code is highly specialized and application domain-oriented, such as air-tracking software or flight control software. The ability of the organization to reuse such code gives the organization a competitive advantage in the bidding of contracts for similar projects. Thus, the code is considered to be highly proprietary and cannot be made available to other companies with similar software needs. Nevertheless, code reusability in the small has frequently been quite successful in improving software productivity within particular groups of some organizations.

Code reusability in the large has the opposite attitude. The premise here is that someone has developed an implementation for some programming problem and is willing to share it with the world. Such pieces of code are published in journals, placed in libraries, and distributed across networks. They are available for the asking and can be used without permission. For this reason, code reusability in the large can also be referred to as "code sharing". Code in this category tends to be for general types of problem solving algorithms, such as traversal, and sorting techniques. Such pieces of code are often small (compared to reusable code in the small), and offer little competitive advantage to the organization owning sole rights to the code.

It is clear that code reusability in the small is counter productive to the software industry as a whole because it precludes large amounts of potential code reuse, and gives many organizations effective monopolies in certain software sectors. Consider for example, that company X specializes in the construction of air traffic control systems, and company Y specializes in the construction of weapons system software. A request for proposal is distributed, regarding the development of an air defense system, which includes air tracking and weapon system components. Company X bids the contract, knowing that it can reuse a large portion of the air tracking software but must develop new weapon system code. Company Y bids the contract, with the knowledge that it already has most of the weapon system code, but must develop air tracking code. A more benevolent industry-wide approach to code reusability would have permitted the development of the new system, reusing code from both the air tracking and weapon system components. Unfortunately, there are also several practical and legal issues that would make such code reuse difficult, such as various protection laws and government contracting obligations.

On the other hand, the current types of available code for code reusability in the large make only a slight impact possible on overall industry-wide software productivity. This is partly because most large software projects contain only a small fraction of general algorithmic type components, and because such code must often be customized anyway to fit the application. Furthermore, such code is generally small, and the effort to find and incorporate an existing copy of it will often exceed the effort to develop it from scratch. As a consequence, code reusability in the large has only been successful for the most well-defined and commonly used procedures, in the form of standard subroutine libraries.

CODE SELECTION

Perhaps the most significant technical barrier to code reuse is the problem of finding the desired piece of code. There are actually three stages to this problem:

(1) Realizing that the code exists in a relatively usable form i.e., is written in a compatible programming language for the application.

(2) Finding the general location of the code, i.e. finding the correct program, library, or journal.

(3) Finding the particular location and boundaries of the code, i.e. finding the right module, subroutine, or page, and its extent.

The first two steps are not generally problematic with code reusability in the small. Normally, such related programs are written in the same language, and it is clear which programs contain the desired code. The third step is generally the most significant in this case, because often the code is not written to be reusable (liftable). Thus, the bounds of the desired code may not be easily recognized, and there may be numerous interactions between the desired code and the rest of the program. These may be due to the use of global variables, files, and other side effects. Fortunately, the amount of effort required to define the bounds of the reusable code is frequently more than offset by the size and complexity of the reusable code. Therefore, the code reuse is often justified on those terms.

Code can be engineered to be more reusable using several well-understood software engineering practices, such as structured analysis [3,4], structured design [5], and structured programming [6]. These techniques help to reduce the number of interactions within the code. The use of subroutines, modules, and abstract data types also help in the development of reusable pieces. Thorough documentation makes the code more reusable by carefully delineating all lines of communication and identifying all "visible" components. Since the interactions are recorded this way, they don't have to be "rediscovered" later. Unfortunately, code that is a candidate for reuse in the small is often developed under sub-optimal circumstances, such as tight deadlines and changing user specifications. Consequently, good software engineering practices are often overlooked or followed in a non-rigorous manner.

In contrast, there is also a danger that the perceived benefit from reusing code will always outweigh the problems associated with "lifting" the code from the old program. This may in fact not be true if the code interactions between the lifted code and the rest of the program are excessive, so that extreme effort is required by the programmer to "understand" the interactions. Nevertheless, the programmer (or the programmer's manager) may have such an overwhelming desire to "not waste" "liftable" code, that this tradeoff is overlooked, and more effort is expended reusing old program code than rewriting the code from scratch. The degree to which this is a problem often depends on the similarity between the two programs, since greater similarity permits lifting larger blocks of target code, which includes the entire scope of some of the interactions.

The situation is reversed with code reusability in the large. Such pieces of code are generally written with very high modularity, and are frequently well documented. Thus, step three is fairly easy. On the other hand, steps one and two can be significantly more difficult because the programmer may not even know where to begin to look for the desired code or its documentation. The programmer may remember seeing a published algorithm in a recent journal or a subroutine in some utility library (step 1), but not remember the date or name of the journal or the name of the library (step 2). As another example, the programmer may believe that standard techniques exist for solving his type of traversal problem, but not remember coming across any such solutions, or even know a name for the problem.

The inclination of programmers in these cases is to recode program solutions without even trying to find available solutions, even though such solutions may exist in immediately usable form. This is further complicated by the fact, that most such components are fairly small, and the effort to recode them is not that substantial anyway. Once again, the primary situations where code reusability in the large has been successful involve standard subroutine libraries.

Obviously, the way to significantly improve code reusability in the large involves the use of improved cataloging and indexing tools and techniques. The issues here are that the effort to specify the desired components, and the probability of not finding the desired component must both be small enough to justify the programmer's use of the catalog; Otherwise, the programmer is still better off to write the code from scratch. This implies a minimum size and complexity of the cataloged software components, below which the programmer will always perceive that the effort of using the catalog is unjustified. It should be interesting to predict what such a minimum software component would be, although that is beyond the scope of this paper.

USING THE REUSABLE CODE

Once a section of reusable code is identified, it must be carefully spliced into the new program under development. There are two problems associated with this stage.

(1) The proper interaction between the reusable code and the rest of the program must be set up. As in performing an organ transplant, all the vessels and nerves must be made to line up correctly between the transplanted code and the host program.

(2) The reusable code may have to be modified to precisely fit the new application. The code may solve a slightly different case, or may be too general or too specialized as originally coded. In either case, some changes may have to be made before the reusable code is suitable for reuse.

With code reusability in the small, the first problem is similar in magnitude to determining the bounds of the reusable code. The reusable code will often interact with the program in complex ways. The degree of ease in making the connections often reflects the degree to which the new program is similar to the original program. Thus, in general for the more restricted application domains, the easier it is to reuse code.

The second problem also requires less modification when the developed programs are similar. That is, the greater the similarity between programs, the more likely it is that the reusable code will achieve the same function, with the same degree of generality. Thus, with code reusability in the small, both modification problems are of similar magnitude.

The first problem is usually not very serious with code reusability in the large, since such code is generally written modularly with few outside interactions. The required communication is normally well documented, intuitive, and easy to set up. The main problem here is with making the reusable code do precisely what is desired. All too often it seems that the reusable code is too general, too specialized, or just handles the wrong type of data structure. Sometimes, the code handles the boundary conditions or error conditions "wrong", or simply doesn't "fit" in the desired way. Other times, the reusable code can be fit in, but the overall program will be inefficient and considered suitable only as a "prototype."

Sometimes a good deal of modification is required to get the reusable code to precisely perform the desired function. Unfortunately, the programmer trying to reuse the code is almost never the same programmer who wrote the code, and the effort to understand the code in order to modify it is excessive. In these cases, the programmer is more likely to write the code himself, rather than try to understand and modify the reusable code. In fact, even if the effort to modify the code would not be excessive, the programmer may perceive it to be, or the programmer may lack confidence in the original code and simply feel that he could write a "better" version anyway.

Once again, the primary exception to these problems with code reusability in the large involve standardized subroutine libraries. In these cases, the common functions available in the libraries have been well enough understood that their proper use can be "planned" without need for modification. Furthermore, these pieces of reusable code have been developed at the right level of generality so that they directly fit into most of their target programs, and they have been used often enough that there is sufficient confidence in their correctness.

CODE REUSABILITY IN THE BROAD

So far, we have painted a fairly dim picture regarding code reusability. The two ends of the reusability spectrum ("small" vs. "large") have been contrasted, and their problems and strengths have been discussed. One approach that would appear to offer considerable improvement over the two extremes is an intermediate approach that combines the best aspects from both. Such an approach might be called "reusability in the broad".

The characteristics of reusability in the broad are that the pieces of code tend to be somewhat large and complex, application domain-oriented, and contain proprietary code (as in reusability in the small). They also tend to be well documented, modular, and developed using good software-engineering practices (as in reusability in the large). They are cataloged and placed in libraries to become more widely available. Because of the size and complexity of the code and the subsequent benefit of reuse, programmers are more willing to go through the effort of locating the reusable pieces. The effort required to customize the reusable code is potentially reduced due to their well-engineered development and the similarity of requirements due to the use of narrow application domains. Unfortunately, because of the proprietary nature of the code and various legal issues, this type of reusability can not be easily practiced across the software industry, such as through the establishment of a "software clearing house". However, reusability in the broad has been successfully employed within some companies in the form of "software factories" [7] to produce considerable improvements in programmer productivity.

CODE TEMPLATES, SCHEMAS, AND ABSTRACTIONS

There are also other techniques that are available to help with some of the steps involved in making code reusable. These are mostly aimed at making code reusable in a broader range of situations and reducing the effort of customizing reusable code.

As described earlier, the use of modular, well-engineered code makes the code considerably more reusable. However, one of the main problems with the straightforward modular approach occurs when the reused code must be modified in order to perform the precisely desired function. The solution is not always to make the original code more general, because by making it solve a larger class of problems, the code becomes less cohesive, less efficient, and harder to fit into the new program. A more promising solution is to identify the class of problems that a generalized version of the code would solve, and then build a template or abstraction of the code, that can be instantiated to the particular version [8,9,10]. If the template is carefully constructed, and the parameters to the template are clearly documented, then instantiating the template should require significantly less effort than modifying the program code directly.

Once again, in order to make this an acceptable approach, the user must perceive that the effort to locate and instantiate the template be less than the effort to write the code from scratch. This implies a tradeoff between the complexity of the generated code and the complexity of the user's interface to the template. The more complex the generated code, the more likely the user is to use the template. However, the more parameters there are in the template, the less likely the user is to want to use the template.

More complicated code [11] and design [12,13] schemas can be used to increase the complexity of the generated code, without unnecessarily increasing the complexity of the interface to the schema. Through such schemas, relationships between parts of the code can be expressed to reduce the number of required decisions. Hierarchies of schemas can also be set up to represent structural and abstractional relationships that help in locating reusable schemas. These improvements help to maximize the efficiency of schema instantiation and permit more complex pieces of code to be generated with less user input. For example, a schema for a generalized inventory control system could be instantiated in different ways to generate a library system, a car rental system, or a ticketing system. User-supplied requirements would guide the refinement, and much of the detail would be derived from constraints established by the requirements. Typically, such schemas also require a large amount of supporting application domain information.

The main problem with such schemas is that it requires considerable effort to create them so that the potential for code reuse must be very high before their cost can be justified. Also, their use is especially suited for fairly complex pieces of code with lots of interaction, such as is typical with code reusability in the small. Without larger industry-wide support for sharing significant pieces of code, the areas of application for such code and design schema mechanisms may be limited by the economics of the technology.

SCHEMA SELECTION

The problems of locating the desired pieces of reusable code, templates, data abstractions, or schemas are considerable, except in the common forms of code reusability in the small. These have been discussed earlier. The main question is whether solutions can be devised to help the user locate the desired reusable component. There are two aspects to this problem

(1) The user must specify the component that he wants. This specification may not only describe the component, but may also include information on how to instantiate it in the case of templates and schemas.

(2) The user's specification must be used to perform a search of the available reusable components, selecting the best match, and possibly instantiating the component to the desired instance of code.

In order to specify the reusable component, we need to have a commonly agreed upon vocabulary for specifying software components. Except for the most common types of algorithms and data structures, there is no generally agreed upon vocabulary throughout the software industry. This perhaps is our greatest distinction from other engineering disciplines. Various types of formal methods have been proposed for specifying software, but no single formal system is universally accepted. Furthermore, it is frequently as hard or even more difficult to formally specify a piece of software than to actually program it. However, within many application domains there exists a commonly accepted vocabulary for the concepts in that domain. For code and schemas within those domains, that vocabulary can be used to assist in the selection process.

The second problem involves the actual cataloging of reusable software components. The catalog must facilitate the rapid location and instantiation of available software pieces. One aspect of the problem is being able to extract the key information from the specifications to use in selecting software components. It is not at all clear what the crucial identifying properties of software components are, although some progress has been made using various facets (characteristics) of the application domain [14]. Finally, with code and design schemas, it may not be clear which schemas best satisfy the given specifications until the schemas are instantiated. Thus, a lot of trial and error effort may be involved in the schema selection process itself. Automated techniques, however, may help to make this process feasible.

CONCLUDING REMARKS

The two major types of code reusability on the ends of the reuse spectrum have been distinguished; code reusability in the small and code reusability in the large. Each of these types of reusable code differ in a number of key aspects such as size and complexity of the code, application specificity, and problems associated with locating and reusing the code. Several other distinctions were also discussed, such as economic value, perceived utility, and required effort to reuse the code. Code reusability in the small has had limited impact on the overall software industry because of its strongly self-centered orientation. Code reusability in the large has had limited impact because of its qualities of high generality and relatively small complexity, as well as the high degree of difficulty in finding the reusable components. An intermediate point on the reuse spectrum, reusability in the broad, was also discussed that combines several of the benefits of both reusability in the large and reusability in the small. It has been practically realized in the form of software factories that sometimes offer significant improvements in programmer productivity.

Other methods that can be used to improve the applicability of reusable code include the use of templates, schemas, and schema selection strategies. While the use of schemas is best suited for the types of code that are reusable in the small, the limited availability of this type of code makes it likely that many applications will not be able to justify the high initial cost of generating the schemas. Furthermore, there are still numerous technical problems associated with the selection of reusable software schemas. Nevertheless, some classes of applications may be able to achieve improvements through this technology, due to a demand for large numbers of similar programs. Code templates can be used to improve the reusability of some software code that is not suitable for reusability with schemas, but there is a sensitive tradeoff between the complexity of the generated code and the complexity of the template, in terms of their usability.

Realizing greater potential for code reusability may require a major change in attitude in the software industry in order to better merge the qualities of code reusability in the small and large. What would be needed is a willingness of organizations to share their base of complex, reusable software components in order to achieve mutual software product goals. Rather than bidding on their proprietary collections of software, companies would bid on their capability to construct software from generally available reusable components. Such reusable components would be schematized and placed in a large library that would act as a clearing house for reusable software, and royalties would be paid for use of reusable components. Numerous technical and legal barriers, however, still exist before such an approach could be generally realized.

REFERENCES

[1]   Jones, T.C. Reusability in Programming: A Survey of the State of the Art. IEEE Trans. on Soft. Eng. SE-10,5 (Sept. 1984), 488-493.

[2]   Standish, T.A. An Essay on Software Reuse. IEEE Trans. on Soft. Eng. SE-10,5 (Sept. 1984), 494-497.

[3]   DeMarco, T. Structured Analysis and System Specification. Yourdon Inc., New York, 1978.

[4]   Gane, C., and Sarson, T. Structured Systems Analysis: Tools and Techniques. Improved System Technologies, Inc., New York, 1977.

[5]   Yourdon, E., and Constantine, L.L. Structured Design: Fundamentals of a Discipline of Computer Program and Systems Design, Prentice-Hall, Inc., Englewood Cliffs, N.J., 1979.

[6]   Dijkstra, E.W. "Notes on Structured Programming" in Structured Programming, Academic Press, New York, 1972.

[7]   Matsumoto, Y., et. al. SWB System: A Software Factory, in: Hunke, E., Ed., *Software Engineering Environments* (North-Holland, Amsterdam, The Netherlands, 1981), 305-318.

[8]   Litvintchouk, S.D., and Matsumoto, A.S. Design of Ada Systems Yielding Reusable Components: An Approach Using Structured Algebraic Specification. IEEE Trans. on Soft. Eng. SE-10,5 (Sept. 1984), 544-551.

[9]   Dershowitz, N. The Evolution of Programs: Program Abstraction and Instantiation. Proceedings of the Fifth International Conference on Software Engineering, San Diego, CA (March 1981), 79-88.

[10] Goguen, J.A. Parameterized Programming. IEEE Trans. on Soft. Eng. SE-10,5 (Sept. 1984), 528-543.

[11] Rich, C. A Formal Representation for Plans in the Programmer's Apprentice. Proceedings of the Seventh International Joint Conference on Artificial Intelligence, Vancouver, British Columbia (Aug. 1981), 1044-1052.

[12] Lubars, M.D., and Harandi, M.T. Knowledge-Based Software Design Using Design Schemas. Proceedings of the Ninth International Conference on Software Engineering, Monterey, California (March 1987), 253-262.

[13] Harandi, M.T., and Lubars, M.D. A Knowledge-Based Design Aid for Software Systems. Proceedings of SOFTFAIR-II, San Francisco, California. (December 1985), 67-74.

[14] Prieto-Diaz, R., and Freeman, P. Classifying Software for Reusability. IEEE Software 4,1 (January 1987), 6-16.

A Framework and Economic Foundation
for Software Reuse

Bruce Barnes, Thomas Durek, John Gaffney, Arthur Pyster

Software Productivity Consortium
Reston VA 22091
June 1987

Extensive software reuse provides the greatest potential for significant gains in software development productivity. Many forms of reuse exist, each offering different potential productivity gains. Associated with these gains are the costs necessary to produce, maintain, and apply it. A framework for analyzing the various forms of reuse is presented together with an economic model which addresses both their costs and their benefits.

1. The Problem

The biggest gains in software development productivity will come from increased software reuse (Boehm, et al–84 and Brooks–87). This proposition is almost universally accepted based on the obvious notion that it is cheaper to reuse someone else's work than to reinvent it. The natural analog to this situation is in hardware development where extensive reuse at the chip, board, and module levels have been largely responsible for the remarkable speed with which new hardware systems can be produced.

Despite the obvious comparison between hardware and software, a mature marketplace for reusable software components has not yet materialized (Kang and Levy–85). Only a handful of vendors sell them (EVB–87 and PPI–87) in what can only be called a tough market. The problems in achieving such a marketplace can be characterized by the lack of:

1. Well understood and accepted terminology to describe concepts related to reusability equivalent to the existing one for hardware.

2. Tools and techniques which support software reuse.

3. An economic model which explains to software development organizations what the real benefits and costs of software reuse are and which provides a method to analyze their situation.

4. A corporate infrastructure which encourages and rewards reuse.

The Software Productivity Consortium is a consortium owned by 14 U.S. aerospace companies which builds and supports software tools to improve productivity. Its current effort is focused on three major thrusts: *reuse, prototyping*, and *knowledge engineering*. The Consortium has an ongoing program which directly addresses the first three reuse problems and which is trying to understand what is required to solve the fourth problem in the context of its customers.

2. The Dimensions of Software Reuse

There are five independent dimensions to software reuse:

1. level of *process abstraction* of a part

2. methods of *adapting* a part which are supported

3. methods of *organizing and accessing* a set of parts

4. methods of *integrating* a part into a development effort

5. *generality* of a part

Figure 1 shows a variety of parts with different combination of dimensions.

NOTATION CHARACTERISTIC	PROCESS ABSTRACTION	SOFTWARE ORGANIZATION STRUCTURE
USER–ORIENTED NOTATION	REQUIREMENTS SPECIFICATIONS	PARAMETRICALLY CONFIGURABLE DOMAIN ARCHITECTURE e.g. OS, DBMS, etc.
	DESIGN SPECIFICATIONS	APPLICATION GENERATOR
PROGRAMMING LANGUAGE NOTATION	PDL DESCRIPTIONS	GENERIC PACKAGE LIBRARY
	SOURCE CODE	SOURCE–CODE LIBRARY
MACHINE LANGUAGE	EXECUTABLE CODE	OBJECT–CODE LIBRARY

Figure 1: Some Dimensions Of Software Reuse

2.1 Abstraction. *Abstraction* reflects the degree to which the reused part is logically removed from the running implementation on a computer; e.g., a requirements analysis generated to support the process of producing a system is more abstract than a design specification for the same system, which in turn is more abstract than the source code, which is more abstract than the object code. Most of the work in software reuse has centered around code parts because they are the easiest to organize and understand. However, much more of the effort in building a system goes into the earlier requirements and design analysis phases than into coding. Consequently, the potential gain in productivity increases with the level of abstraction of the part

2.2 Adaptation. *Adaptation* is the degree to which the user can customize the part; i.e., modify the part as given to him for reuse. The simplest and one of the most common forms of adaptation is hand modification. This unstructured adaptation method is, of course, very labor intensive and error prone. It requires the developer to understand the details of the part's implementation and decide how that differs from what he really needs. Nevertheless, it is very useful in many cases when more structured adaptation mechanisms are either not available or adequate.

Subprogram parameterization is one of the oldest and certainly the most common form of structured adaptation. Applicable at the code level, it allows a developer to use the same code segment in a number of contexts. This adaptation mechanism is technically well understood and well accepted. Subprograms are usually packaged into libraries based either on the manipulation of a common datatype such as a window, stack, or table, or based on a common area of functionality such as trigonometric functions.

As a method for adapting code, subprogram parameterization handles well the case where the datatypes being manipulated do not vary across uses–just the values in them do. It fails in most languages when the types themselves must be changed. Ada's generic packages extend parameterization to support replacement of the datatypes manipulated by subprograms at compile–time. Note that the Ada generic package concept also raises the level of process abstraction since the part being manipulated is source code, while subroutine parameterization applies to object code.

Still stronger methods of structured adaptation exist. The CAMP Project (McNicholl 86) has defined the notion of a *schematic* part in which the structure of the code itself is altered in well–defined ways through interaction with a library of reusable parts; e.g., in real–time process control systems, matrix manipulation methods are highly customized to the data and application. A process control system implementor could spend weeks hand adapting standard matrix manipulation routines to get needed performance characteristics. Schematic parts for such routines contain the essential algorithms plus mechanisms for restructuring them on user request. This allows the implementor in a matter of hours to step through the same number of alternatives that would take weeks to adapt manually.

2.3 Organization and Access. The method of organizing a collection of reusable parts dramatically influences their real value. You can't use what you can't find. If it is difficult to locate and retrieve a part from among a collection, users will be disinclined to bother. This partially explains why subroutine libraries supplied by hardware vendors are so successful. Operating systems such as unix and vms make it very easy for a programmer to reference a component subroutine within libraries. unix is especially friendly in this regard. On the other hand, large companies have trouble collecting and sharing libraries across projects. Most companies do not have a central repository where a project can deposit a software element for reuse by others. Furthermore, money is not typically allocated to a project to support efforts which facilitate sharing with other projects. Applying Government funds on Government contracts for this purpose is usually illegal. Hence, internally developed reusable libraries are much rarer.

2.4 Integration. There are two major paradigms for *integrating* a reused part into a larger system:

 1.   composition, or direct integration

2.   generation, or indirect integration

2.4.1 Composition. In composition the part itself is used directly as a component of a larger system; e.g., a reused subroutine is linked with other subprograms some of which may also be reused parts, others of which may be newly created. unix is replete with examples of reusable executable parts, namely the tool set accessible from the shell. Numerous books including (Kernighan and Pike 86) explain the paradigm of software development in unix that encourages reuse through shell scripts and piping.

2.4.2 Generation. In generation the reused part is not used directly as a component of the larger system; instead it generates the component part from user supplied parameters. The generated part is then directly integrated into the larger system. A generator is usually restricted to a single well–defined domain such as lexical analysis, table generation, spreadsheet computation, or even to certain types of "higher level" domains such as accounting, banking, and management information systems.

Application generators are so powerful because they are built around a *canonical architecture* for the relevant domain and a domain specific parameterization language. A collection of subroutine libraries by themselves give no guidance on how to compose them to build a particular application. On the other hand, the developer of an application generator has a mental model of how a whole set of applications within a particular domain should be structured. That model is reflected in the canonical architecture.

Narrowing the focus to solve a special class of problems all of which have the same basic structure is one key. The second is developing a domain specific language which allows the user of the generator to express the parameters of the particular application he wants built in a language natural to him. A BNF description given to the parser generator yacc is an example of one such domain specific language.

A single application generator usually reflects a single canonical architecture. It is the domain engineer's view of how systems for that application should be built. All parsers built using yacc have the same basic structure. For example, they all use the same LALR parsing algorithm. Further generalization is possible by doing a more complete domain analysis into *parameterized canonical architectures*. This deeper domain analysis admits that there is a family of compatable architectures for systems in the same domain; e.g., parser generators which use LL as well as LALR methods, or which work in tandem with a lexical analyzer rather than as a subsequent pass, or which use different error recovery schemes.

The advantage of the parameterized canonical architectures is that it allows the tailored construction of application generators to user specified constraints. Instead of attempting to have one monolithic application generator which understands many parsing methods, many interfaces to lexical analyzers, many symbol table organizations, etc., a combination of parametized features can be assembled into an application generator tuned to the user's needs. The process of first constructing a particular application generator from a parameterized canonical architecture and then supplying it parameters to create a specific application is called *synthesis*. Of course, generalized domain analysis is hard but still tractable. The Software Productivity Consortium is currently developing a prototype library support system for reuse of parameterized canonical architectures and synthesis of applications from them.

2.5 Generality. A part which is excellent at a task no one ever does will not be reused. Parts must be *general* to be reused. Generality coupled with well supported adaptation mechanisms allow a part to be applied in a wide context. *Domain knowledge* is the degree to which the visible attributes of a part reflect a specific application domain; e.g., the *curses* subroutine library in unix is used to support the building of applications which manipulate character-oriented terminals. The authors of the library had a specific model of terminals in mind when they developed the package. This model pervades the use of *curses*. "Process control" is a much higher level domain than "terminal displays". A library system that supports parameterized canonical architectures for process control systems written in Ada together with the adaptation techniques mentioned earlier would be quite general and powerful for developers in that domain.

The breadth of applicability of reusable parts is inversely proportional to the degree of domain knowledge embedded within them. A very general math library is applicable in thousands of diverse cases ranging from banking to weather simulation,to cruise missile flight control. On the other hand, an application generator such as lex is useful only for generating lexical analyzers. Even that is more widely applicable than one which generates accounting systems.

On the other hand, the potential gain in productivity within a domain in which the part is applicable varies directly with domain knowledge. One of the author's (Pyster) personal experience indicates that lexical analyzers can be generated in far less than 1% of the time using lex than they can be using standard C libraries on unix. Boehm has estimated that the equivalent of 30,000 lines of code per month are produced by using such standard applications generators as spreadsheet calculators. This probably understates the gain.

3. A Reuse Centered Development Paradigm

Pictured in Figure 2 is the model of software development in which no explicit reuse occurs. It does not detail the particular lifecycle phases (requirements, design, code, ...), instead focusing on the fact that the components which make up the generated product are produced from scratch. Figure 3 shows a revised paradigm in which reusable components and application generators play a key role. Development combines the act of creating new components in the traditional manner with the selection and adaptation of existing parts from libraries and the creation and adaptation of new parts through application generators. Figure 4 shows the particular approach being taken at the Software Productivity Consortium which focuses on domain libraries and application generators.

4. Economics of Software Reuse

The simplest view of reuse fashions a software product to have two types of code, *new* and *old (reused)*. The total cost of delivering the product is the cost of developing new code plus the cost of reusing that old code in the project. As the proportion of reused code, R increases, the potential for greater productivity increases. This will be true whenever the relative cost to reuse code is less than the corresponding cost to develop that same code from scratch.

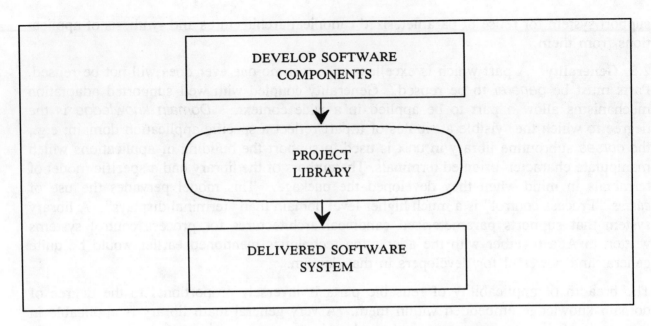

Figure 2: Non-Reuse Software Development Model

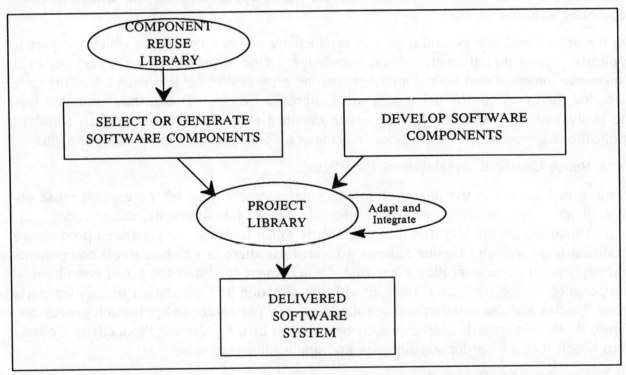

Figure 3: Reusable Component Software Development Model

Suppose b is the relative cost of developing software from reusable parts rather than creating new code, where the cost of developing new code is 1. b is the cost of integrating the reusable parts into the project. The proportion of new code in the product is (1–R). The simplest equation for the relative cost, RC, of the overall software development effort is given by:

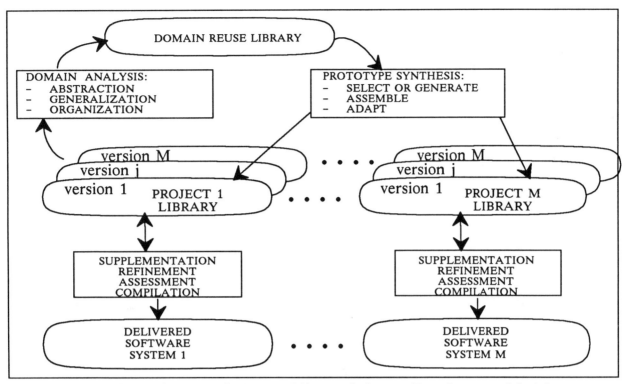

Figure 4: Domain Reuse Library Software Development Model

$$RC = (1-R)1 + Rb = (b-1)R + 1$$

Eq. 1

Further, let the relative productivity, RP = 1/RC be given by:

$$RP = \frac{1}{(b-1)R + 1}$$

Eq. 2

4.1 Reuse Is Free. The simplest model for reuse ignores the cost of establishing and maintaining the library of reusable parts, and assumes that b, the recurring cost of reusing parts, is 0. In this case the development productivity advantage afforded by reuse is:

$$RP = \frac{1}{1 - R}$$

Eq. 3

As the value of b increases the relative productivity advantage of reuse decreases. Figure 5 shows the decline in RP as b increases. The keys to maintaining an economic advantage in reusing software are to minimize b while maximizing the potential for reuse among projects.

In reality the cost of establishing and maintaining the library is significant for any nontrivial collection of reusable parts. That cost will vary with the size and complexity of the library organization, adaptation methods, and other reuse dimensions discussed in Section 2. Es-

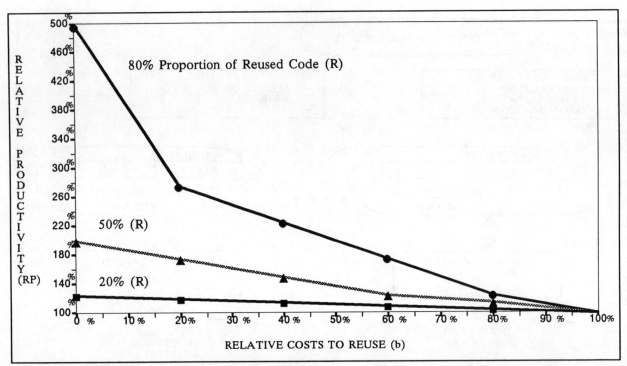

Figure 5: Relative Productivity as a Function of Proportion of Reused Code
and Relative Cost of Reuse

tablishing a subroutine library is a much simpler task than establishing a canonical architecture and support mechanisms for a specialized domain such as process control. The
authors are not aware of any studies which quantify the relative costs for different types of
libraries.

There are two obvious models for creating and maintaining reusable parts. In the first
model a central authority has that task separate from individual project activities. Projects
are library users but not direct contributors. In the second model, a central authority establishes the library and is responsible for administrating and maintaining its structure, but
each project spends some percentage of its effort contributing reusable parts to it. The
central authority remains responsible for the library structure, while projects become primary contributors to the library contents.

The first model offers the advantages of centralization and perhaps the efficiencies of
scale; on the other hand, the actual projects are more likely to understand what parts are
really useful and so produce better quality parts. The latter approach is recommended by
the CAMP project. In practice some combination of the two is likely. In any event, there
will always be central costs associated with managing the reusable parts and procuring
some parts from external sources even if the predominant method of populating libraries is
through contributions from internal projects.

For libraries with "low" valued dimensions such as a C subroutine library, the cost of
creating and maintaining the library structure and administering the library is fairly nomi-
nal. Most of the effort is in developing the reusable parts. As the dimension values
increase, the overhead associated with initially establishing the library could increase significantly and require significantly higher effort to maintain. For example, developing a

parser generator requires a domain analysis which establishes a canonical architecture for parsers plus the creation of a domain specific language which is the input to the generator. This is much harder than just defining a set of subroutines which are deemed "useful" in building parsers. The added structure and domain specific language make that task hard. Furthermore, maintenance of a subroutine library often means simply fixing a bug or adding another module which does something "new" relative to the old subroutine library. Such libraries have so little structure that there is relatively little interaction between parts. Little effort needs to be devoted to understanding the full implications of the change. On the other hand, adding a feature to the domain specific input language of a parser generator requires careful examination and integration. If the initial cost of establishing a library is too great, those costs could swamp the advantages the library offers to projects which apply it. High establishment costs will only be paid by an organization if it is confident enough projects will subsequently use the library to effectively amortize the cost. Even then, if the initial costs are too high, the organization may not be able to allocate funds to build it.

4.2 Tithing Projects for Library Establishment and Maintenance

Consider the model in which a central authority develops and maintains the entire library of size m for D dollars, where m is in whatever units the organization finds convenient such as source lines of code. Projects are users but not contributors. For simplicity suppose the organization values each unit of reusable part equally at D/m dollars and establishes a cost recovery policy of charging D/(mN) dollars to the first N users of that unit. If the cost of producing a reusable unit of code relative to the cost of producing one which is not intended to be reused is E, then RC and RP become:

$$RC = \left(b + \frac{E}{N} - 1 \right) R + 1$$

$$RP = \frac{1}{\left(b + \frac{E}{N} - 1 \right) R + 1}$$

Eq. 4

Let the minimum value of N for reuse to payoff be given as 'N_0'. This the value of N at which RC = 1; it might be termed the *payoff threshold* value. From the expression for RC in Equation 4 we have:

$$1 = \left(b + \frac{E}{N_0} - 1 \right) R + 1$$

Eq. 5

Isolating N_0 produces:

$$N_0 = \frac{E}{1-b}$$

Eq. 6

For example, if E = 1.20 and b = 0.10, the minimum number of reuses of a unit of code which pays for itself is just 1.33. If E were particularly high as would be expected for the more powerful reuse technologies, it would take longer to recover the library overhead; e.g., if E = 4.0, and b = 0.10, then N_0 = 4.44. Unfortunately, there are no empirical studies which the authors are aware of that show typical values of E and b for the various reuse technologies, so it is impossible to really understand what value of N_0 to expect. Empirical studies in this area are needed. When deciding whether to invest in building a library, an organization can use Eq. 6 to determine how many projects must be tithed to recover the original development costs of each library unit. If k is the proportion of the whole library reused by projects on average, it will take N/k projects to recover all overhead costs.

E can be kept small in one of several ways. First, the libraries can be kept small. This is clearly a poor method since that means R will also tend to be small. Assuming b, the cost of integrating reusable code, is relatively small (< 0.15), increasing R pays off handsomely. The second method is to reduce the level of power of the library; e.g., use weaker adaptation methods since construction of lower level libraries is easier. This is also undesireable because decreasing the level of the library also decreases R. Finally, the process of building the library can be better automated, understood, and supported, driving down incidental construction costs. This is obviously the most desirable method.

4.3 Creating Reusable Code within Projects

The model presented in the last section assumes projects reuse parts but never contribute them to the library. Once project contribution is allowed, it is natural to amortize the cost of its development as well. Amortization is over M projects, where M is not necessarily equal to N. For simplicity, suppose the relative cost of creating reusable software within the project is also E. Let the proportion of the code written for contribution in the present software product be Rc. Then the equation for RC becomes:

$$RC = (1-Rc-R) + Rc\,\frac{E}{M} + R\left(\frac{E}{N} + b\right)$$

Eq. 7

Consider several cases:

case i: M=1; Rc+R<1. The present project creates some of its new software for free reuse by other projects. Then

$$RC = (1-Rc-R) + Rc*E + R\left(\frac{E}{N} + b\right)$$

$$= (1+Rc(E-1)) + R\left(\frac{E}{N} + b - 1\right)$$

Eq. 8

case ii: M=N>1; Rc+R<1. The present project contributes some of its new software, the cost to be amortized over it and N-1 other users.

$$RC = (1-Rc-R) + Rc\,\frac{E}{N} + R\left(\frac{E}{N} + b\right)$$

$$= \left(1 + Rc\left(\frac{E}{N} - 1\right)\right) + R\left(\frac{E}{N} + b - 1\right)$$

Eq. 9

case iii: M=N>1, Rc+r=1, Rc=1-R. The present project creates all of its new software to be reusable, contributing it to a library, to be amortized over it and N-1 oher users.

$$RC = (1-R)\,\frac{E}{N} + R\left(\frac{E}{N} + b\right)$$

$$= \frac{E}{N} + Rb$$

Eq. 10

In some sense case *iii* is ideal. All new code in each project potentially helps subsequent projects by contributing to the library. In fact, such as ideal can never be met, so that case *ii* is the most practical.

5. Economic Barriers to Software Reuse

The potential gains to be realized from software reuse will be moderated by technical, organizational, and economic factors. Simpler forms of reuse such as object–code libraries and generic Ada packages are well understood and their application is not significantly hindered by technical barriers. However, both organizational and economic barriers impede increasing the availability of such libraries and packages within large organizations. A central repository and cataloging service is needed. This can be relatively modest in cost. More important is getting an organization to commit to developing and maintaining libraries specifically with reuse in mind. As mentioned earlier, this can be considerably more expensive than developing the components for single use. Project managers typically are not rewarded for such efforts, nor are they allocated money to support such activities.

A revision to government procurement policies to facilitate reuse in software developed under Government contract would potentially offer a high reward to the nation as a whole. Allowing a contractor to charge for the extra costs incurred in developir ʳeusable parts would be handsomely rewarded if those parts could subsequently be dⁱ ᵗ to many government contractors. The cost of building and maintaining the   ʰse- quently be amortized over many government contracts driving down ᶜ contractor dramatically. The government would gain by having a larᶠ parts, driving down the overall cost of contracts.

6. Conclusions

The potential for substantial improvement of software develc the application of reusable software component libraries hᵃ readily accepted as a fundamental principle. However, technical, organizational, and economic factors mitigate much of that potential.

A framework for discussing software reuse has been developed focusing on 5 independent dimensions. Several economic models of software reuse have been presented in the context of that framework. The models make a number of simplifying assumptions. Each set of assumptions reveals new insights into the relative costs and potential benefits of reuse and provides guidance to an organization in structuring itself to support reuse. Many additional models are possible by varying the assumptions further. They await future work.

The costs of both the creation of libraries of reusable components and their application in the creation of new software systems must be considered. In earlier papers on reuse, the cost of creation has been largely ignored. It is especially important to consider these costs as the mechanisms and techniques to support reuse become more complex and as the material being reused becomes more abstract; e.g., when building library systems around either canonical architectures or parameterized canonical architectures. These costs will likely be significantly higher than for simpler reuse approaches, especially now when this industry is immature and tool support is relatively primitive. Empirical studies confirming these models and predictions should be performed. Some are being conducted now at the Software Productivity Consortium. More are required to fully understand the economic implications of software reuse.

7. References

[Boehm, et al 84] B.W. Boehm, M. Penedo, A. Pyster, E.D. Stuckle, R.D. Williams, "An environment for improving software productivity", *Computer*, June 1984.

[Brooks 87] F.P. Brooks, "No silver bullet", *Computer*, April 1987.

[EVB 87] EVB Software Engineering, Inc. *Grace Notes*, 1987.

[Gaffney 83] J.E. Gaffney Jr., "Approaches to Estimating And Controlling Software Costs," *Proceedings of the Computer Performance Group International Conference*, December 1983.

[Kang and Levy 85] K.C. Kang and L.S. Levy, "Software Reuse: What's Behind the Buzzword," AT&T Bell Laboratories, Warren NJ, pp. 20, 1985.

[Kernighan and Pike 86] B. Kernighan and R. Pike, *The Unix Programming Environment*, Prentice-Hall, 1986.

[McNicholl 86] D.G. McNicholl, "Overview and commonality study results," AFATL-TR-85-93, *Common Ada Missle Packages (CAMP)*, McDonnell Douglas Astronautics Co., May, 1986, Vol. I, pg. 74

[PPI 87] Productivity Products International. *Hope with objects*, presentation at the National Conference on Software Productivity, sponsored by the DPMA Education Foundation,

Reusability Comes of Age

Will Tracz
IBM Federal Systems Division/
Stanford University

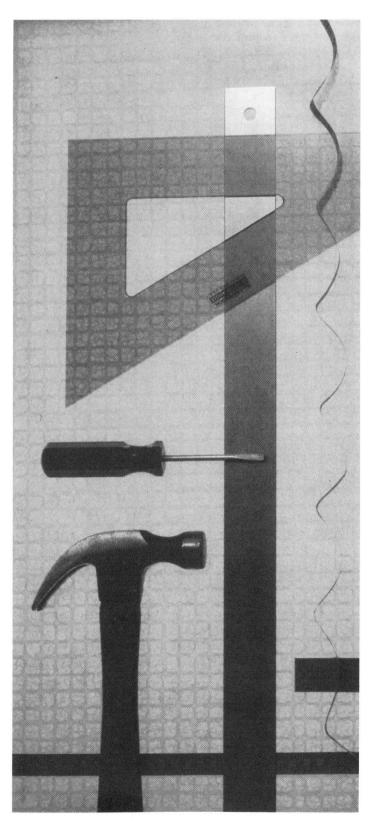

O f the seven articles selected for this special issue of *IEEE Software*, five are accounts of projects that have made the reuse of software components a reality. This focus is deliberate: By showing how it's been done in the real world, we hope to provide some insight and tools to implement reuse in the workplace. The final two articles examine what kind of help programmers need to evaluate and understand software intended for reuse.

For years, I have used an analogy that compares used cars to used programs (*Computer*, April 1983, June 1986, and May 1987). I think this analogy holds for pungent and pragmatic reasons: People are leery about buying a used car for many of the same reasons programmers are reluctant to reuse someone else's work. With this analogy in mind, I offer some of my own insights — as a seasoned veteran of many used-program sales — into the problems of software reuse and what factors have inhibited its acceptance as viable form of software development.

New or used? Before deciding on whether to invest in a new or used car, a prospective buyer should first identify his needs (features, performance, price range). Other factors, like urgency, may constrain the selection process to a vehicle on the lot instead of one ordered from the factory. In any case, the buyer should develop a strategy for evaluating candidates.

The next step is to shop around. Will a potential candidate that looks good on paper really live up to everything a smooth-talking salesman says?

Standard features. The first question that needs to be answered is: Does the vehicle meet the customer's requirements? Some models have options (a convertible roof, four-wheel drive) that enhance their adaptability to future operating environments. But these features may just be extra baggage that interfere with overall performance or add to maintenance costs.

89

Clearly, if a software program meets the customer's basic requirements, then it warrants further consideration. But program options are mixed blessings: On one hand, parameters aid adaptation of the software to future needs; on the other hand, they can result in normal operating inefficiencies and increased maintenance costs.

Mileage. A new or low-mileage used car, in all probability, will require less maintenance than a high-mileage used car. Yet finding a low-mileage car on a used-car lot is cause for suspicion, since most people would not part with it unless it was giving them problems.

But software is unfatiguing, so the higher the mileage (the more users, the more systems it is available on, or the longer it has been in use) the more desirable it is. History has proven that the number of bugs found in software decreases with use, assuming other factors remain the same.

Maintenance record. Knowing the types of repairs made on a vehicle and the quality of the maintenance effort will influence a customer's decision. If serious problems occurred early in the vehicle's life but were properly repaired, they will not weigh as heavily in the selection process.

A customer can readily evaluate the quality of a program by looking at the type, severity, and date of problems found in a piece of software. If many miles have been put on the program since the last change or if the types of updates have been insignificant, the prospective buyer can place more confidence in the product. The customer should avoid a situation where the maintenance record indicates more problems are introduced each time one problem is fixed.

Reputation. If no maintenance record is available, the customer can estimate the reliability of the vehicle by associating it with the overall quality of the manufacturer's vehicles.

Similarly, if a software manufacturer has a track record of delivering quality programs, the customer can place more trust in other programs that manufacturer sells.

Appearance. Kicking the tires and checking the paint job and trim are other ways the customer can gain useful information. Sometimes it pays to have a skilled mechanic perform a close inspection under the hood to determine potential problem areas (temporary repairs or shoddy workmanship).

A software buyer can also tell shoddy workmanship by examining the exterior (the user interface and documentation) of a program. Looking under the hood helps the customer assess certain programming characteristics (naming and commenting conventions) that can indicate the overall maintainability, modifiability, and reliability of the component or product.

Standards. Standard instrumentation and compliance to safety and operating standards (seat belts and emissions control) give customers a feeling of confidence in the product. Standard compliance dispels some of the fears of being stuck with a lemon.

If a piece of software complies with certain standards (in documentation, interface design, and testing), its potential for reuse is increased because of the perceived quality and useability of the software.

Warranty. What happens if something goes wrong? Will the dealer fix the problem or will the customer be left holding the bag?

To establish the credibility and viability of new and used programs and components, the seller should provide both a policy for determining responsibility for error and a mechanism for resolving problems.

If a program does not meet all the customer's requirements, the manufacturer, dealer, or customer is faced with the task of modification. What options are available, and how easily is a program customized? These characteristics play an important role in determining the overall reusability of a program. Finally, the buyer should ask how customization affects the warranty. If things go wrong, the new owner might have difficulty soliciting assistance from the original manufacturer if the program has since been modified.

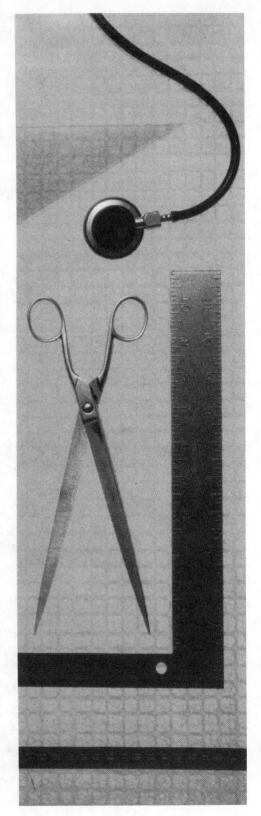

Options. Because customer requirements and tastes vary, a manufacturer provides options to satisfy the customer's needs as closely as possible. Certain options must be installed by the manufacturer; others can be installed by factory-trained mechanics; still others can be installed by the customer. In any case, the risk associated with adding an option decreases as the expertise of the person making the changes increases.

Accessibility. Customers don't want to waste their time driving all around town to find the car that meets their needs. Dealers who advertise a large selection have a better chance of attracting business.

Similarly, the convenience of shopping or getting a program serviced locally is very appealing. The less effort customers have to expend in finding candidates for reuse the more likely they are to buy them.

Price. When buying a new or used car off the lot customers have to pay for whatever options come with the car, whether or not they were on the customer's original list of options.

Programs require investments in both capital and time. Off-the-shelf software is often sold as a package deal. In this case, the customer may be paying for more functions than required and will end up dragging around extra options that they neither need nor have space for. Similarly, the customer has to pay the price for learning how to drive the new software effectively and how to maintain it. These hidden prices, plus the price of failure, must be factored into the buy-or-build decision.

Test drive. The acid test to determine the suitability of a candidate is the test drive. The buyer can experience the true feel for how a car handles under different driving conditions and can project realistically what it would be like to own.

A customer who tries a program on for size can determine if any rough spots exists in the user interface and how the program performs under simulated working conditions (if possible). If the problems are minor, the seller might be to able customize the software before consummating the sale.

Intangible inhibitors. The reputation of used-car salesmen and the products they promote is somewhat negative. Getting stuck with a lemon is a major concern of most used-car customers. This same lack of trust in programming products has been the major inhibitor in advancing software reuse. Unfortunately, because it is often easier to write an incorrect program than to understand a correct program, programmer productivity (which would increase if software developers didn't reinvent the wheel each time) and program quality (which would increase if they used high-quality parts) have not evolved.

Two other reasons may explain why the used-program market originally envisioned by M.D. McIlroy in 1968 has failed to materialize:

1. There are no clearly defined standards, either for developing reusable software or for systems based on reusable software.

2. There are neither large repositories of reusable software and components nor the tools to access and synthesize systems from them.

What will it take to create a successful used-program business?

• Quality parts: Customers should have confidence that what they buy will perform without error.

• Standard interfaces: Customers should be able to use what they buy in a manner that complies with standard operating conventions. Software should be easily integrated into new or existing systems.

• Documentation: Customers should understand what the software they buy does, how they can use it, and how they can modify it if necessary.

• Selection: Customers should have a choice of options available on what they buy.

Nothing is better than cruising along in a high-performance, well-tuned program with complete confidence in the safety of all those who depend on you to get the job done. Unfortunately, the state of the practice today has us lumbering along in a clunker that spends most of its time in the shop undergoing repairs and has the distinct possibility of crashing due to some unforeseen manufacturing defect.

To some the choice is obvious, and to those I say, "Read on!" Your skepticism should be abated by the progress of this issue's authors. The technical foundations from making software reuse a viable alternative to program development have been identified and demonstrated, thus adding credibility to the used-program business. Reuse is not a reality for us all, but the question of whether or not it is — and always will be — the technology of the future has been settled. □

Will Tracz is an advisory programmer for IBM Federal Systems Division, Owego, New York, where, until 1984, he was responsible for the design and development of microcode support software for military and aerospace processors.

During his 12 years at IBM he has also taught classes as a visiting professor at the Rochester Institute of Technology, and was an adjunct professor at Syracuse University.

Tracz is the ACM SIGMicro/IEEE TC-Micro newsletter editor, and past chairman of the 15th Workshop on Microprogramming (Micro-15). He has written over a dozen papers and technical reports on microprogramming, programming languages, and software reusability, including a satirical collection: *Confessions of a Used Program Salesman.*

Tracz received an MS in computer science from Pennsylvania State University, an MS in computer engineering from Syracuse University, and is currently completing work for a PhD at Stanford University.

Confessions of a used program salesman

I am a used program salesman. My profession is probably one of the oldest yet most overlooked in the software industry today. My glory is not in creating shiny new systems, but is often delegated to brushing up an old clunker with a new coat of paint. I was not always a refurbisher of programs; once I aspired to be a great creator of wonderful and complex systems. Fresh out of grad school, I entered the job market ready to apply my expertise to solve all the world's problems. Too soon after accepting my first job I realized the completely inexplicable reluctance of management to unleash the super programmer lurking in a naive and humble employee like myself.

My baptism into the used program business occurred right after my training period. I was assigned to the task of modifying a punch tape program, and I remember the zeal with which I attacked my first "real" program. I also remember, not as pleasantly, how I took two days to recover from the impact of trying to read that "REAL" (wretched would be a better word) code. Talk about a bowl of spaghetti. Being innocent and naive I thought self-modifying code was the exception, not the norm. The comments, what few appeared, were classics like 'DO IT TO IT" and "IN MEMORY OF JIM AND GLEN." But this assignment was just the start, and after many more patch and paste jobs I began to catch on. I soon adopted the strategy of rewriting more and modifying less. I saw the light of modularization and was saved by the hand of documentation. Gradually I budgeted more for program improvement to go along with program modification.

Then, one cold and dark December day I took the bull by the horns and accepted an assignment that was to change my destiny. Instead of producing the delivered program by modifying an existing program, I created a new baseline, applying all my skill and modern programming practice. From then on, I had it made; customers beat a path to my door, knowing that I could produce more and better at a greater speed and for less. My ego was once again properly inflated. I had become the best used program salesman on my block; but that is not the end of my story. There is a moral to be told, a lesson to be learned.

In all seriousness, the used program business is a realistic and practical aspect of the software industry today. Quite simply, we don't "reinvent the wheel" every time we develop new programs. Time and money are our major constraints. Often we are faced with a schedule or budget that forces us to work smarter not harder. Here is where good programming practice pays off.

When systems are properly modularized, documented, and debugged, and have all the other good things done to them, they can be used as basic components of or building blocks for other systems. I learned the merits of modular strength and coupling, not in Comp Sci 406—Introduction to Used Program Sales, but from the school of hard knocks. It is a program modification lesson I have taken to heart, a lesson that has helped me increase my productivity—which, in turn, has increased the productivity of those who use my software.

William J. Tracz
11 Larchmont Road
Owego, NY 13827

Confessions of a used program salesman—an update

Since you last heard from me (see *Computer,* April 1982), something has happened to the used program business. While I was busy basking in that warm glow of success that stemmed from finding a way to not reinvent the wheel each time I had to get a product out the door, it seems that a new lady came into town with an even better bag of tricks.

At first I couldn't quite figure out the exact orientation of the object she was peddling. The banter and hoopla that surrounded this universal elixir of hers was confounded by the reported complexity and sheer immensity of the instructions that came with it. Furthermore, the manufacturer's track record was suspect, although the formula they were using consisted of elements of known therapeutic value. Were they in the right proportions? How easy were they to use? How did they all fit together? I decided to investigate.

I scheduled a rendezvous with her and, I must admit, was a bit taken aback by her massiveness and frills, but "You can't judge a book by its cover," I always say, and, besides, she seemed to have all the right stuff in the places that really mattered. I was most interested in her bag of tricks which, she said, contained objects that I would find of value in perpetuating my trade of selling used programs. What she pulled out were *packages.* Not just ordinary packages, like the kind you get on your birthday where you have to guess what is inside. These packages had an envelope on the top of each one which specified what was inside them. Like a flash, I could see the writing on the wall, but in reality it was her writing on those envelopes that lit the fire. I could use the packages as building blocks without looking inside them by just referencing the envelopes for instructions on how to use what was inside. No more looking under the hood of every used program to see what was inside, and how to use it. I could just keep a file of each of these so-called package specifications around to reference.

I asked her what other kinds of talents she had. She told me she was good at juggling, too. Her bag of tricks had some special packages just tailored for doing two things at once. I was impressed at the thought, since there were many of my used programs I could speed up given a mechanism and facility for concurrency. I could run on two 4-cylinder engines instead of a V8 and keep my customers happy.

After this we were making small talk when I asked her if she had any other classy objects to show. She said there was one other package she hadn't shown. I asked her what type it was. She said it was a do-it-yourself type. That I could make it into any type I wanted and it would perform the same function. At first, I was skeptical. How could there such a generalized routine? But she showed me several instances and I was convinced.

So where does that leave our young hero? What is a gentleman to do? This casual relationship with the lady has turned into a full-fledged courtship. I have fully embraced her way of packaging, and she has taught me to juggle. I am working on a new set of packages to help me in the used program business, and I will keep you posted on how they turn out. I have learned that while you can't always judge a book by its cover, you can pretty well always judge a package by its specification. Ada is, at first look, a complex lady whose reputation has been tarnished by accusations that she is part of the problem, rather than the solution to the software crisis (see "The Emperor's Old Clothes," *CACM,* Vol. 24, No. 2, Feb. 1981). From personal experience, I can honestly say that while she is still a little rough around the edges, she is a welcome partner in the quest for reusable software (the so-called used programs that I purport to sell).

Will Tracz, your friendly used program salesman
Stanford University

Confessions of a used-program salesman— fringe benefits

I have just got to tell you about a strange phenomenon that has been happening in my used-program business. Ever since I have been reusing some special parts to refurbish programs,* my maintenance work has dropped off dramatically. I have had to shift my personnel around down at the body shop by placing more workers in manufacturing and fewer in repair. Quite frankly, it has been a drain financially, since over half my revenue in the past has come from maintenance.

On the bright side, my reputation for delivering defect-free products has increased the number of customers I serve. I don't mind the shift in

workload—and to tell you the truth, my workers don't mind it either—for two reasons. First, manufacturing software with reused parts is a lot more fun than maintaining software. Second, maintenance now requires less effort. It is easier to find bugs because they are almost never in the special parts or building blocks that we have been reusing in each product, but almost always in the glue that holds the parts together. Finally, new products get easier to assemble from these components as we become more familiar with the components. We are constantly salvaging new software pieces to add to our parts warehouse whenever a new program to refurbish comes into the factory. Business is booming. (Now, if I could only figure out a way to recoup my lost maintenance revenue. Actually, I am thinking about going into the parts-distribution business, but I haven't worked out the economic and legal issues yet.)

Seriously, one of the fringe benefits

of software reuse is that the quality of the delivered product is increased. Reusable software components—in particular, components *designed* for reuse—generally have a very low defect rate. Furthermore, with each successful use, a component's confidence factor increases, as does the confidence of the programmer who reuses the component. Indeed, the saying that "one way to eliminate software bugs is by not putting them there in the first place" supports building software from reused parts. Actually, I should make a distinction between "plain parts" (the old subroutine library) and "reusable parts" (highly parameterized generic packages), but that is a topic for another true confession.

Sincerely,
Will Tracz (your friendly
used-program salesman)
Computer Systems Laboratory
Stanford University

---

*For a reference to the composition of programs from Ada packages, see "Confessions of a used-program salesman—an update," *Computer,* Vol. 19, No. 6, June 1986, p. 91.

Confessions of a used-program salesman—excuses

Did you ever reach a point of frustration when you just wanted to scream? Well, the used-program business has had its ups and downs, and lately I've been in a slump. Since I opened my new Parts Department, I have been running into all kinds of problems convincing my old customers to take advantage of these reusable components. My customers always seem to find excuses* for buying a new program instead of investing in some of my well-oiled or refurbished parts. I swear that I've heard every excuse in the book; in fact, I've decided to write them down along with translations of what I think each customer is really saying. The following, then, are the most popular excuses for not reusing software.

1. Only wimps use someone else's software.

Translation: If I were to reuse someone else's software, then I'd be admitting that I couldn't write software myself.

2. Reuse of software destroys the ability to create it.

Translation: It's more fun to do it myself.

3. Introduction of reusable software will eliminate my job.

Translation: As long as I am measured by how many lines of code I write, why should I do something that reduces my perceived productivity?

4. Reusable software cannot be efficient.

Translation: Why should I pay for all the additional baggage that someone else puts in to check software for error conditions and to add extra parameters that I'll never use? Besides, I know a better algorithm anyway.

5. I don't want to be the first.

Translation: Let someone else work out the bugs and pay the start-up cost to create the parts initially.

6. Trying to reuse someone else's software is a waste of my time.

Translation: Why should I pay for someone else's mistakes? The software probably has bugs in it, probably isn't very well documented, and probably won't work for my application. I'll probably spend more time trying to figure out what it does—whether or not it works—and how to modify it than I would writing it myself in the first place.

7. I don't believe that software reusability is a viable concept.

Translation: I am too comfortable developing software the way I've been developing it for the last *n* years. Besides, I've already learned structured programming; isn't that enough?

There are many technical issues associated with making software reuse feasible. Those most often cited include determining what should be reused, how to design for reuse, how to design with reused software, and how to classify, store, and retrieve software components for reuse. However, the bottom line, I have found, is that the most prevalent excuses for not reusing software are nontechnical; they are sociological, psychological, or administrative. What we are faced with is an inherent distrust of another person's software. (What does that say about the general reputation of software quality?)

I often wonder what it will take for us to learn that if we can't do it right the first time, we can always do it over and over...and so the story continues.

Sincerely,
Will Tracz (your friendly
used-program salesman)
Computer Systems Laboratory
Stanford University

---

*I would like to thank Ed Berard of EVB Software Engineering for sharing some of his favorite excuses with me.

Confessions of a used-program salesman—the RISC versus CISC debate

Just when things seemed to be going smoothly, a battle of epic proportions started brewing down at the used-program shop. I never thought we would have a RISC versus CISC debate related to used programs, but as I always say, "If the module has the right parameters, call it." And that really was the crux of the problem. You see, my customers seemed to have gotten a bad case of the WIBNIs (the "Wouldn't It Be Nice Ifs"*). My programmers, eager to please existing customers and attract new ones, started adding new parameters and options to existing software packages and building blocks. At first, this tactic gave the desired results: it increased each module's domain of applicability, thereby increasing its reuse. But pretty soon the advantages of having all these options actually decreased a program's reusability because customers grew unable to comprehend the dependencies and interactions between the options. We had violated two of the Golden Rules of Reusability: (1) Before you can reuse something, you have to know what it does; and (2) before you can reuse something, you have to know how to reuse it.**

Furthermore, the customers were concerned about dragging around all the extra code for the options they didn't use, thus paying for the additional size and function they didn't want or need. More importantly, I realized that these multifaceted, monolithic modules were becoming harder to document and maintain.

This is how the great RISC (Reduced Interface Software Component) versus CISC (Complex Interface Software Component) debate began. Should software subroutines have complex or simple interfaces? The CISC proponents wanted to throw everything, including the kitchen sink, through the one interface, arguing that with intelligent defaults their interfaces were as simple to use as the RISC interfaces. The RISC side pointed out that the overhead from dragging all the extra logic to handle the bells and whistles (which were seldom used anyway) was a needless penalty for the most frequently used operations. They argued that the CISC format could be replaced by a series of RISC operations. The CISC camp countered by pointing out that to achieve the same power as a CISC operation, a RISC implementation would result in more context switches (notorious cycle burners). They observed that, although their operations were slightly slower than the RISC subroutines, they could do more at once because they had more opportunities for parallelism. The RISC side countered that their interface allowed the same parallelism with more flexibility and better user control. The CISC side scored their biggest points when they argued that the RISC approach would fail in a multitasking situation, where multiple threads of control could adversely affect each other through side effects.

Somehow, as I watched this debate, I had the feeling of déjà vu. Personally, I was most interested in the bottom line—what made dollars and sense. I preferred reducing the number of interfaces because there would be less configuration management, and I knew that current optimization technology could take care of the dead code problem.

The conclusion that I came to was that both camps had some valuable points to make. The RISC people were right that the CISC people were not exercising caution in their application of "tail-fin" technology. Instead of increasing the domain of applicability, we were approaching the domain of absurdity. The CISC people were right in trying to provide additional function, but they had missed the opportunity to practice what they preach (modularization). One of the fundamental underlying software principles of reusable software development is factoring: developing a hierarchy of reusable components (each capable of performing a single function) and combining these reusable components through inheritance, instantiation, or simple importation. Factoring breaks a monolithic module into pieces. This practice helps the programmer to compose and maintain a better user interface by hiding the actual implementation one layer down.

We learn by our mistakes, but I wish we didn't have to relearn things so often.

Sincerely,
Will Tracz (your friendly
used-program salesman)
Computer Systems Laboratory
Stanford University

---

*I first encountered this term in Peter Brown's *Starting with Unix* (Addison-Wesley Publishing Company, 1984).

**The first Golden Rule of Reusability is "Before you can reuse something, you have to find it."

My personal profiles of programmer personnel

Programmers span a wide range of attitudes, abilities, experience, and education. Their backgrounds influence their perception and reception of new ideas and tools. This article proposes a scientific scheme for classifying programmer personnel. It is based on my personal, *opun*-minded observations (and years of frustration) from dealing with software users and developers. The recognition of the programmer class or category to which these individuals belong can prove useful in developing tools and documentation, as well as in communicating with them in general.

Programmer classifications. Programmers generally fall (or are pushed or shoved) into one of four classes:

- Novices (New, Overzealous, Very Inquisitive ComputEr Students),
- Wimps* (Well-Intentioned, Mediocre ProgrammerS),
- Pros (Perceivably Reliable, Omnipotent Software Engineers), and
- Prima Donnas (PeRmanently IMmutAble Software Developers Of Notorious Narcissistic Attitude).

(Note: Some programmers have no class, in which case they don't fit in anywhere. Unfortunately, it is beyond the scope of this article to discuss the backgrounds of my relatives.)

Novices. Novices are usually fresh out of school, starry-eyed, and easily motivated. They are very receptive to "playing with" new tools or adopting new development methodologies, since they are still in learning mode. They have very little invested in previous techniques, and have yet to be burned by flakey software and by hideous compiler bugs. They have yet to be christened into the real world and put through the school of hard knocks.

Wimps. A majority, unfortunately, of the professional programmer community falls into this category. Battle scarred and war weary, they are leery of innovation. This group really needs to be sold on the technical merits of any new system or technique (that is, they need to be told what's in it for them). They are comfortable and reasonably productive with their old (possibly antiquated) tools and methodologies. Unless properly motivated or threat-

---

*This classification was inspired by Bill Neugent's "Well Intentioned, but Mediocre People" category, which was discussed in "Preposterous Opinions About Computer Security," SOGSAC Review, Vol. 4, No. 3, Summer 1986.

ened, they will dismiss any efforts to extend their capabilities. The rhetorical question becomes, "Can you teach an old programmer new tricks?"

Pros. These are the technical gurus in any software organization—the people to whom the Novices and Wimps (but not the Prima Donnas) go for assistance. "Working smarter, not harder" is their motto, and they are always receptive to using or abusing any new tool or software system that they can buy, borrow, or steal. Pros do not need to be motivated, since they will rapidly latch onto any technology that they perceive as offering them leverage and enhancing their ability to perform their jobs.

Prima Donnas. Prima Donnas embody the antithesis of egoless programming. They refuse to accept any new tool or technology unless they can get credit for thinking of it themselves. (After all, they are legends in their own minds.) Also, Prima Donnas often lose touch with reality and develop systems that are either incomplete or totally useless to anyone but themselves. Motivating Prima Donnas to step down from their thrones is a management challenge that often boils down to a battle of wills (that is, "You will do it, or else!").

Postscript. Enabling people to make the transition from one software technology to another involves developing new tools, techniques, and associated training methods to facilitate the dissemination, assimilation, and eventual application of advances in the state of the art. The effectiveness of any approach is further enhanced when the backgrounds of the targeted individuals are taken into consideration, and the respective tools, techniques, and training methods are tailored accordingly. The classification scheme for programmer personnel proposed here addresses these issues in a *pung*ent but pragmatic perspective.

William J. Tracz
Computer Systems Laboratory
Stanford University

Confessions of a used-program salesman—programming-in-the-new

OK, it's time to fall on my sword again. Another revelation has just hit me right where it hurts the most—in the wallet. Having gone through the "old school" of programming (assembly language, Fortran, Cobol, and PL/I), I consider myself an experienced, battle-scarred veteran of many programming wars. But, as the result of an opportunity I couldn't refuse, I have spent the last three years retooling at the "new school" of software engineering (Ada, Prolog, and Smalltalk). Now I consider myself a somewhat naive, battle-scared beginner thrust into the front line of new softwars.

Regarding my business of developing and selling reusable programs, I have come to the realization that it is time to switch horses; that my programming-in-the-old mindset has reached its limits of productivity and profitability, and it is time to harness the new (to me) technology and adopt new programming paradigms to the business at hand.

Reuse and programming-in-the-old

As I reminisce about the good old days, I begin to realize that they were the "old days" and that there wasn't really that much "good" about them (other than the fact that my ego was bigger and there was more hair on the top of my head). When people talk about growing pains, the birth of the programming profession gave a new meaning to the word labor. Key punches, and waiting three to four hours for a batch job to turn around (only to find you missed a comma in your JCL) hardly bring back sweet memories. We did the best we could with the coding forms and "flaw charts"* we had for tools. The field was young, and we were having too much to know any better. Besides, we were becoming legends in our own minds—who could argue with success?

Fortran subroutine and assembler language macro libraries were the primary technologies we had to ply our trade of reusable software. (APL and Lisp function libraries had some cute

features that never really seemed to catch on with most mainframe macho machine-code mainliners.) Functional decomposition worked well—most of the time. The only problem with top-down stepwise refinement was that in the used-programming business we needed to work bottom-up to capitalize on our library of subroutines and macros. Working top-down and bottom-up, we sometimes didn't meet in the middle—a somewhat annoying situation. Also, adding more parameters and writing larger macros (later called application generators) only scaled so far until they collapsed under their own complexity. I felt that the used-program business was not evolving, and lacked an adequate technical foundation to build upon.

Programming-in-the-new

Has there been a revolution in the used-programming business, or has software technology just taken the path of least resistance, with the law of the bungle determining the survival of the witless? In my case, I certainly was skeptical that artificial intelligence would ever provide anything to make my job easier. All the hype that I read about expert systems sent me quickly searching for the "del" key. But, upon further examination, I found several really clever ideas lurking in the myths.

Formal methods helped me assert the correctness of my reusable components as well as verify their interfaces. Language features such as user-defined types were abstract at first, but along with certain parameterization capabilities, they were just the type of thing I was looking for. Data abstraction and encapsulation along with information hiding became the basis for developing a collection of reusable components. Finally, programming by difference using hierarchies of types helped localize the common operations and distinguish the unique characteristic of my reusable software.

After wrestling with several new software development mythodologies, I realized that an object-oriented approach suited my top-down and bottom-up design style. Using a layered

approach, I seldom ran into the problem of designs not meeting in the middle. I have always believed that what sets reusable software apart is how it is put together. These new technologies helped me take systems apart and put them back together more easily and with less expense in time and money.

The expert system engineers had provided insight into one tough reuse problem that remained—How does one reuse software artifacts other than just code? In their search for storing knowledge, the AI researchers had tried various representation methods, which along with the sophisticated graphical programming environment provided the missing link in my reuse environment. Now I could capture the design decisions along with the design for future reuse using a Hypertext system. Furthermore, I could track what part of my requirements was satisfied by what part of my design and implemented in what part of my code. If my requirements changed, I could quickly find where the code needed to be changed. There was even some talk about parameterizing the requirements so the changes would automatically filter down to the implementation.

I still wasn't done recycling and adapting expert system technology to program reuse; all the domain analysis techniques easily transferred to identifying and parameterizing new systems.

Time and technology wait for no one, and technical obsolescence can rapidly reduce one's ability to compete in the marketplace. I have switched so I can fight for my market share. Most of the software technologies that I have identified in the previous section have been around at least 10-15 years (object-oriented programming was introduced in 1960). It has just taken this long for the price per MIPS to decrease enough to make the technology attractive for widespread reuse. The bottom line is that it makes cents—dollars and cents—to leverage the new technology.

Will Tracz (your friendly used-program salesman)
Computer Systems Laboratory
Stanford University

*I first encountered this term in David Gries' *The Science of Programming*.

Part 3: State of the Practice

The papers that follow reflect several approaches to software reuse. In general, they focus on one or more of the following topics:

- reusable components
- reusable component libraries
- methodologies for constructing applications with reusable software
- the use of Ada

The state of the practice of software reuse, as characterized by the following papers, is an evolution of the classic subroutine library. The granularity of the components has increased, in most instances, along with the degree of built-in adaptability through parameterization and domain analysis.

Components

Subroutine libraries are (were) the most prevalent (first) form of software reuse. These papers describe how the black-box concept of a subroutine has been expanded to increase its domain of applicability.

The first paper, "Software Reuse through Building Blocks" by Manfred Lenz, Hans Schmid, and Peter Wolf, describes what some might call a meager but highly successful approach to introducing software reuse and modern programming practices into the application domain of systems programming. Starting with an IBM internal language PL/S (a C-like language), the authors have added Ada-like constructs of packages, generics, and exceptions through the use of a custom macro-processor BB/LX. The paper includes a discussion on why this generative approach is superior to the traditional subroutine library approach and also includes a list of the contents in building block library and their documentation requirements.

The focus of the second paper, "Software Engineering with Reusable Parts" by Bets Wald, is an approach being taken by the U.S. Department of Defense to foster the creation of an inventory of accessible, understandable, and useful reusable software components. The paper also describes a data-flow type tool to assist in the composition of systems from these parts.

A Japanese software factory approach to software reuse is described in the next paper entitled "Software Prototyping with Reusable Components" by S. Honiden et al. at Toshiba. Using SPIDER (subroutine package for image data enhancement and recognition), a Prolog-based expert system has been built to assist the nonexpert in selecting, and combining FORTRAN components.

Contrasted with the use-as-is building block approach as described in the M. Lenz et al. paper, the last paper entitled "Frame-Based Software Engineering" by Paul Bassett describes a same-as-except approach. Through the use of a target language independent preprocessor, reusable software components, in the form of frames (similar to macros) are translated into executable source code (which is thrown away). The specification of new applications and modification of old ones centers on one root frame that contains the customizing context information for all context-free frames that are in the resulting frame hierarchy. The language primitives are described in the paper along with a COBOL example.

Software Libraries

The papers in this part describe three approaches to organizing libraries of reusable software components based on

- relational databases
- information retrieval systems
- a faceted retrieval mechanism

In the first paper, "The Reusable Software Library," Bruce Burton et al. describe an integrated environment for software reuse based on their reusable software library (RSL) (a relational database approach). The system includes a natural language query front end, a citation evaluation program (SCORE), and a graphical design and documentation tool (SoftCAD).

The paper describes the functional, administrative, qualitative, and quantitative attributes necessary to catalog and retrieve the reusable components. The last half of the paper discusses the SoftCAD system, a way of entering object-oriented diagrams, and automatically generating Ada PDL.

The next paper, "The Reuse System: Cataloging and Retrieval of Reusable Software" by Susan Arnold, presents additional background information regarding the desireable properties of a repository for reusable software. The emphasis on this approach is on the customization of the user interface and on the mapping of retrieval information into an information retrieval (IR) database.

Another information retrieval approach is described in "An Information System for Software Reuse" by Bill Frakes and Brian Nejmeh. After some preliminary motivational

97

material, the paper focuses on the reuse library built by using CATALOG, an IR system developed at AT&T. The paper concludes with a summary of the user interface and includes the formats of the module and function prologs.

A different classification strategy is proposed by Rèuben Prieto-Dĭaz and Gerry Jones in their paper, "Breathing New Life into Old Software." The Asset Management Program (AMP) at GTE Data Services is based on a faceted classification scheme. AMP consists of several groups that work together to create, maintain, and manage the Asset Library. Besides detailing this organizational structure, the paper describes the faceted classification scheme. This scheme is very powerful and flexible at the cost of preengineering the classification and maintaining a weighted conceptual distance graph to assist in locating assets that are "close" to meeting the specified query. (A weighted conceptual distance graph is a more powerful form of a thesaurus.)

The last paper in this section, "Software Classification as an Aid to Reuse: Initial Use as Part of a Rapid Prototyping System" by Emmanuel Onuegbe, compliments some of the ideas behind the faceted classification scheme described in the previous paper and leads nicely into the research papers found in Part 4 of this tutorial. The essence of the approach described in this paper is to go beyond the syntactical search methods of IR or relational database approaches and base retrieval on the semantics of the components. A SMALL-TALK-like generic hierarchy of "behavioral abstractions," each with one or more implementations is proposed.

Methodologies

The first two papers in this part deal with empirical evidence pertaining to software reuse. The first paper, "Can Programmers Reuse Software?" by Scott Woodfield, David Embley, and David Scott, describes an experiment conducted at Brigham Young University that required students and professionals to decide on how much, if any, effort would be saved by reusing an exisiting module/package. The object of the experiment was to assess people's ability to judge the reusability of objects, the perceived effort to reuse objects, and to deterimine the tools and training that would enhance this process.

The second paper, "Quantitative Studies of Software Reuse" by Rick Selby, describes a study analyzing 25 NASA ground-flight-control software systems written in FORTRAN. The characteristics of the modules most often reused support intuitive notions of what makes software reusable.

Gerry Jones in his paper, "Methodology/Environment Support for Reusability," describes the methodology issues being addressed by GTE in developing a software development model that incorporates software reuse objectives. The methodology effort is one of three areas of focus by the GTE

Labs Research Project. The other two, domain analysis and classification and library support, are described in papers by Rèuben Prieto-Dĭaz found in the Part 4 and the software library subsection of this part.

The next paper, "A Reuse-Based Software Development Methodology" by Kyo Kang of the Software Engineering Institute's Application of Reusable Components Project, describes a modification of the U.S. Department of Defense life-cycle model (Mil-Std 2167A) to take into consideration the existence of reuseable software components.

The STEP (Structured Techniques for Engineering Projects) environment is described in the paper, "Reusability Benefits of a Structure Which Supports a Development Methodology and Environment" by J.M. Perry, J. Roder, and F. Rosene. This language-independent software life-cycle support environment is based on a generic architecture developed by the GTE Government Systems, Communication Systems Division. It supports several forms of reuse (design, component, subsystem, generative) and has a reusable library mechanism.

The final two papers in this part describe some of the contributions of Bertrand Meyer to the field of software reuse. His work in language design and software development methodology is significant, strategic, and insightful. His paper, "Reusability: The Case for Object-Oriented Design," contains a discussion of the technical and nontechnical issues of software reuse, with emphasis on the technical problems that can be overcome with an object-oriented approach.

His second paper, "Eiffel™ Reusability and Reliability," describes an object-oriented programming language designed for developing reusable software components following a "programming by contract" paradigm. The language includes such features as "classes, multiple inheritance, polymorphism, dynamic binding, genericity, strict static type checking and a disciplined exception handling mechanism," along with constructs for specifying assertions and invariants, which are useful in "ensuring program correctness." The Eiffel compiler is a preprocessor that generates portable C-code.

Ada

The programming language Ada has been a focal point of much interest (and funding) in the software reuse arena. The paper by Tracz in Part 1 of this tutorial gives a good perspective on the size and scope of the activity. The first paper in this part, "Reusability Issues and Ada" by Tony Gargaro and Frank Pappas, explores in more detail the use of Ada to develop reusable software components. It contains several examples of how the language and its extensions (Anna) can be used.

The second paper, "The Ada Software Repository and Software Reusability" by Rick Conn, contains an overview of the contents in the Ada Software Repository (ASR) and directions for accessing and acquiring this source of Ada programs and related documents.

Gary Russell's paper, "Experiences Implementing a Reusable Data Structure Component Taxonomy," contains a summary of the "Booch" Taxonomy of reusable software components. The taxonomy is language independent (but it so happens that two Ada versions, EVB and Booch, are commercially available). Of special interest is the appendix to this paper, which contains sample documentation of a software component. The reader should note the "object-oriented" flavor of this documentation as well as its thoroughness.

The final paper in this part, "Reusable Ada Software Guidelines" by Rick St. Dennis, describes research conducted at the Honeywell Corporate Systems Development Division related to writing guidelines for the development of reusable components in Ada. This approach first hypothesized several "qualitative" metacharacteristics of reusable software and then identified several "quantitative" characteristics that could be used to judge whether software met the metacharacteristics. The three metacharacteristics and sixteen characteristics of reusable software then served as the context for the guidelines. Examples of the guidelines and Ada modules written by following the guidelines are provided.

Software Reuse through Building Blocks

Specification, design, and code can all be reused easily if handled as a building block. An IBM group recently developed this concept and applied it to systems programming — with success.

Manfred Lenz, Hans Albrecht Schmid, and Peter F. Wolf
IBM Laboratories

Software reusability has attracted increasing attention over the past few years and is now a major interest. It promises substantial quality and productivity improvements.[1] Practical experience with reuse has been scant, however, and a generally accepted methodological foundation is still lacking.

The terms "software reuse" and "software reusability" are applied to many techniques, methods, and processes. This spectrum includes portability in the classical sense, code-sharing in successive releases, common subsystems, common routines in application families, repeated exploitation of algorithms, and something like building blocks, which our advanced development department is trying to introduce into systems programming at IBM.

Building blocks have characteristics much like electronic chips: Their functionality is encapsulated. They have well-defined interfaces. They require zero-defect quality. And the knowledge of functionality and interfaces (the specifications) is sufficient to use the chip in development.

Because of these traits, designing software with building blocks should become less complex. Compared to the traditional methods of software development, it should lead to better quality, productivity improvement roughly proportional to the reuse rate (not counting the development of the building blocks), and a shorter development cycle.

Our effort has addressed the problems of defining building blocks for existing languages and tools. It also successfuly applied building blocks to real projects.

To allow the implementation of building blocks in the IBM systems programming language PL/S (used for IBM System/370-based systems), our group developed a language extension and a tool called BB/LX. BB/LX supports Ada-like concepts (such as packages, generics, and exception handling) and procedural, functional, and data abstractions. Based on these concepts and tools, we have set up a library of building blocks. This library is oriented toward systems programming. We have validated our overall approach in systems-programming projects in different environments.

EH0278-2/88/0000/0100$01.00 ©1987

IEEE SOFTWARE

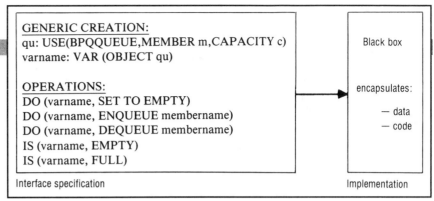

GENERIC CREATION:
qu: USE(BPQQUEUE,MEMBER m,CAPACITY c)
varname: VAR (OBJECT qu)

OPERATIONS:
DO (varname, SET TO EMPTY)
DO (varname, ENQUEUE membername)
DO (varname, DEQUEUE membername)
IS (varname, EMPTY)
IS (varname, FULL)

Black box

encapsulates:

— data
— code

Interface specification   Implementation

Figure 1. Building-block structure example queue.

Characteristics

Building blocks are our units of reusability. They are self-contained modular units according to modern software engineering principles like abstraction, encapsulation, and information hiding. They embody a data abstraction (abstract data type), a functional abstraction, or a procedural abstraction.

Both the processing code and, if applicable, the data representation that implement a building block are encapsulated, so all implementation details are hidden. The user cannot view, access, or modify the code or the data representation.

Structure. The building block's interface is formed by a set of parameterized statements. Generic statements let building blocks be tailored to meet user requirements via generic parameters.

Figure 1 represents these statements. For example, the left of the figure lists statements available to manipulate a queue. The Use statement lets the definition of *qu* (a special type of queue) with generic parameters tailor its contents and size. The Var statement instantiates a specific queue object, *varname*. The Do statements let the queue be set to an empty state; they also queue and dequeue members. And the Is statements return Boolean values on different checks.

These operations are the only way to invoke a building block and exchange information between a building block and the program using it. There are no other interrelationships between a building block and the program (such as global variables and common control blocks). All interdependencies are made explicit through the operations and their parameters.

However, a building block may use subsystem services that create dependencies on its environment. For example, to acquire dynamic storage, different system services are used in IBM operating systems and in IBM subsystems such as VSE, CICS, VM, and MVS.

A building block can be considered a black box. It contains the code and a specification describing how to use it. In addition to these two major parts, a building block contains design, test cases, and other material.

Specification. The specification gives a description of the building block's function and user interface. There may be several building blocks with different implementations of the same specification.

Because a building block's user interface is formed only by operations, the block's specification is given by describing the syntax and semantics of its operations without describing the implementation of the operations.

In addition, the block's implementation characteristics, which may be relevant to its use and are also criteria for its selection, are described abstractly. Examples are space requirements, performance characteristics, and system dependencies. These characteristics form the selection criteria when there are alternative implementations with the same functional behavior available.

The specification has five parts:
• a functional overview;
• a user interface, an operations syntax, and informal operations semantics;
• a formal operations semantics;
• dependencies, characteristics (like space and performance), and design aspects; and
• an example.

There is only one building-block specification for all the different environments in which a building block runs. Only in the dependencies/characteristics area of a specification might minor differences in the system dependencies be described.

The building block's specification completely describes all user interfaces, all dependencies on the building-block environment, and the implementation characteristics. Developers use only the specification during development.

Scope. Building blocks can be used in different IBM System/370 environments. There are IBM operating systems (like MVS, VM, and VSE) and subsystems (like CICS, VTAM, JES-2, JES-3, and Power) or components within these that have unique environments (like conventions and systems services). The systems programming language PL/S shields many such differences; the major exception is calls to system services.

all these environments, we originally tried a pure encapsulation strategy. Each class of system services was encapsulated in an auxiliary building block with a common interface. For example, our building blocks internally call another building block called memory to acquire storage. This building block encapsulates this system dependency so all other building blocks do not have to cope with it. Parameterization by the environment lets the appropriate system service calls be generated.

This encapsulation approach did work very well in several cases. But it proved difficult to add new environments where a service had additional parameters, for which the inner building block can set no reasonable defaults Therefore, they must be specified by the outer building block.

The problem was not extending the interfaces of the inner building block (to offer a new parameter), which would be a minor effort. Rather, the difficulty was that

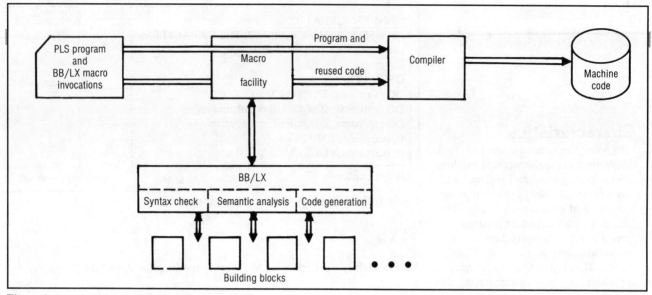

Figure 2. Processing building blocks with BB/LX.

the interfaces of all outer building blocks would have to be extended to let the user pass these new parameters. This is *not* desirable.

Yet we did not want to lose the simplicity of the encapsulated approach for the simpler cases.

Our solution is based on the user-controlled parameterization of a building block with another building block (that provides, for example, system services). All declarations for the other building block are made explicitly in this case. However, as a default for that parameter there is an encapsulated building block. Thus, we kept the simplicity of encapsulation as a default case.

This gives us a high payoff from the development of one building block, since it can be used over a variety of environments — both existing and future ones. Other approaches would have forced us to develop a different version of the reusable component for each environment.

Testing. A building block is tested completely before its actual use. This is possible because no modification of the code is required — or allowed. In addition, a test program can handle the testing easily because a building block is a well-structured and separate entity, because a building block has an accurate, well-defined user interface (only the building-block statements), and because a building block has no other interdependencies with the user program. It is sufficient to call building-block operations from the test program. Usually, no scaffolding and setup of the test environment is required.

For smaller building blocks, thorough

test coverage can be obtained. All relevant data states must be determined from the specifications and, possibly, by inspecting the code (white-box testing). All operations must be applied to all relevant states for a complete test.

When programmers use a building block, they cannot introduce defects into the building-block code. This means that once a building block is free of defects it will remain free of them. Therefore, the quality inherent in building blocks will directly and proportionally improve the quality of the product. Our experience has proven the quality gains to be significant.

Code

Building blocks are implemented in BB/LX and in an associated language processor implemented on the base of the macro facility of the PL/S systems-programming language. BB/LX provides a standardized language framework for the operations forming the building blocks' interfaces. It was modeled after Ada's primary reusability feature: generic packages and private types. We added several features that we found to be important in our practical systems programming environments.

The PL/S compile step is preceded (automatically) by a macro-processing step. Macros reside in a library, from which they are retrieved for processing by the macro facility. Both BB/LX and the building blocks are stored as macros in different libraries. (Figure 2 gives an overview on the processing of building blocks by BB/LX and its use of the macro facility.)

BB/LX is invoked by a building-block operation (really a macro invocation) and interprets it using the building block (macro) code. As a result, code is generated into the user program as an in-line expansion of the operation or as call statements to external procedures. (By using the building-block macro in the external procedure, the abstract type definitions can be made visible to the procedures.)

BB/LX checks the syntax of building-block operations as invoked by the user, stores and maintains generic parameters for building blocks, provides a mechanism like Ada's Private mechanism (to implement abstract data types), and performs static semantics analysis.

Design rationale. BB/LX follows the model of Ada's generic packages with Private parts for the implementation of abstract data types under the principle of information hiding. We found that something like the Ada library system was essential because it can bind code entities to programs without seeing the internals of the bound entities and because it can support the binding with as much syntax and semantics checking as possible.

In our environment, there are two library systems: link libraries, which contain output from compilation or assembly in a relocatable form, and macro libraries, which contain macros and pieces of source code to be generated into the user code.

Our project started with an approach to reusability based on link libraries. Code entities to be reused were PL/S procedures compiled individually with a self-contained scope of variables. An abstract data type was implemented according to

Denert's approach.[2] Each procedure had multiple entries (one for each abstract data-type operation) and a common part in which a data representation was declared for the abstract type.

This approach proved unsatisfactory because:

• It required a procedure call overhead (even for trivial operations) that was too high for people to accept reuse.

• Parameters that were by their very nature generic had to be repeated on each and every operation invocation, making interfaces very complex and cumbersome.

• The complete absence of compiler support to check the correctness of calls to the procedures (or procedure entries) was a never-ending cause of frustration for reusers.

We thus abandoned the link-library-based approach in favor of the macro-library-based approach, which evolved into BB/LX.

In the macro-based approach, the performance problem is solved through in-line generation of reusable code. Support of generic parameterization is the domain of macro processing, anyway, so we could program into BB/LX the syntax-checking and the static semantics of building-block use with fairly standard techniques.

Building block reuse. BB/LX statements follow the form of high-level language statements, except for idiosyncrasies imposed by the macro language itself. For example, each macro invocation begins with a question mark (not shown in the examples below) and the user must specify the instance name with each operation or function as a macro label (also omitted in the examples).

Each program that wants to reuse a building block begins with an invocation of the With statement, which functions like the Ada With clause. The invocation also specifies the operating system environment, whose services are used when required (like for storage allocation). For example,

    WITH (bpqset1) ENVIRONMENT
    (MVS);

In this example statement, bpqset1 is the name of the building block, a set imple-

mentation. MVS is the name of the environment in which the program will run.

Generic parameters may be specified with the Use statement. (The Use statement does not correspond to the Use clause of the Ada Context clause.) For example,

    myset: USE (bpqset1, element 12 bytes,
        capacity 100 elements)
    EXCEPTION (myproblem);

This statement instantiates the set bpqset1 and customizes it to hold no more than 100 elements of 12 bytes each (it defines an abstract data type). This data type, or generic instance of the set, is called myset. In Ada this function would be accom-

---

We abandoned the link-library-based approach in favor of the macro-library-based approach, which evolved into BB/LX.

---

plished through a generic instantiation of the form

    PACKAGE myset IS NEW bpqset1
    (element_bytes = > 12,
        capacity = > 100);

A variable of an abstract type (of type myset here) is declared through the Var statement

    DECLARE s : VAR (OBJECT myset);;

This statement declares the variable s to be of the type myset, and the generic parameter Object specifies that the storage for the variable will be allocated from static program storage. The Var statement allows the declaration of access variables (as in Ada) by specifying the generic parameter Access. This means that the storage for the variable p in the following statement will be acquired and allocated by dynamic storage management:

    DECLARE p : VAR (ACCESS myset);;

This is an example of an area where BB/LX is better than Ada for reusability. A user must specify only the generic Object or Access parameter in the Var statement to select static or dynamic storage alloca-

tion; all other calls of building-block statements are identical. In an Ada program, this causes larger differences.

What corresponds to the allocator in Ada

    p : = NEW myset;

is expressed in BB/LX through the Make Ready statement:

    MAKE (p READY);

The Make statement with the Ready parameter allocates dynamic storage for the variable p (since it was declared an Access variable in the Var statement) and initializes the variables (both Object and Access).

Building-block operations are invoked through the Do statement. For example,

    DO (s, insert element x);

inserts element x in set s, where Insert is the operation name.

Or, if the operation is syntactically a function, you might write the statement

    IF IS (s, empty); THEN . . .

This statement tests if set s is empty, where Empty is a parameter denoting the function to be performed. The Empty function is defined to return a Boolean value. (If Then is the language If statement, in which the building-block operation is invoked to return a Boolean value.)

BB/LX (unlike Ada) has specific constructs to support iterators. For example,

    BEGIN ITERATION (s, for all elements
    x);
        . . .
        . . .
    END ITERATION;

Within the iteration loop, one element of set s becomes available after the other in the variable x in some undetermined order.

BB/LX supports exception handlers like Ada does. A building block may have more than one associated exception handler. An exception handler can be related to an abstract type (like an instance of a building block) as shown in the Use statement example above or to specific operations in Do statements. Thus, exception handlers can be very global or very specific, as required. The following is an example of an exception handler:

```
BEGIN Exception (myproblem);
  ON (space unavailable);
    . . . PL/S and/or BB/LX statements
    to handle the "space unavailable"
    error
  ON ( . . . etc. . . . );
    . . .
  ON OTHERS;
    . . . code to handle all exceptions
    not named specifically
END Exception;
```

BB/LX lets you parameterize building blocks with building blocks of a predefined type, which in Ada would amount to parameterizing packages with packages (but Ada cannot do this). This parameterization is expressed through a For clause on the Use statement (to determine which building-block instantiation to use as an argument in a parameter position) and through a For clause on the Var statement (to determine which abstract type variable of the argument building block implements the parameterized building block).

Library

Using the building-block reuse technology, we are setting up a library of building blocks primarily for reuse in systems programming. In other areas like applications programming, some experience is available in building libraries of reusable elements.[3] We do not know of such work in the general systems-programming area. Experience seems to be available only in special areas like compiler construction.

General systems domain. Because the reusable elements in this domain were not known, we had to determine the established concepts and techniques to form reusable building blocks.

First, a clear understanding of the domain was required. We used two sources: practical project experience and current practice. We decided to divide the domain of systems programming into a domain of general systems programming and into specific subdomains that had concepts not found in other domains. Each subdomain (for example, operating systems and data-communication systems) may again be divided into smaller subdomains.

The general systems domain covers all elements that are reusable in the overall context of systems programming, from the development of operating systems and subsystems (like database management and data-communication systems) to compiler construction.

We focused on general systems programming for two reasons: The chances for an element of this domain being reused are much higher than for elements of the subdomains. The subdomain knowledge and skill reside with the development organizations responsible for products in these areas, so it would be difficult to gather knowledge of the different subdomains. Therefore, our approach is to leave the responsibility for developing subdomain-specific building blocks with the respective development organizations. Our group supports them as required.

Classes. In the general systems domain, there are several building-block classes: abstract data types, procedural building blocks, and building blocks implementing

---

Reuse classification criteria

There are three important aspects of reusability: the abstraction level, customization methods, and reusability conditions.

Abstraction level. A main criterion for classifying reuse approaches is the abstraction level at which reuse occurs. Starting with the concrete units, we can distinguish reuse of code and test cases, of design, of specifications, and (quite abstractly) of concepts.[1]

Reusing design means using a design written in a different environment. This might be a different piece of software into which the reused design is incorporated. It might be a different hardware base or different performance constraints under which the design will run. Different code can be derived from the same design.

Reusing specifications has similar characteristics. However, different design and different code may be derived from the same specification.

Reusing code has very tangible benefits ("this saves me writing so many lines of code on my own"), so it seems more readily accepted by an average programmer. However, the danger is that reuse of code is planned for only at coding time, not before. This causes problems because decisions as important as whether to reuse code should be made during design, not later.

It is also very difficult to find pieces of code that can be reused without change. Code usually contains many dependencies on its environment, such as when global variables like control blocks are used. Furthermore, too many representational details are reflected in the code.

This has been confirmed by an experience we had at an early stage of our project, when we tried (with little success) to identify pieces of reusable code in the VSE operating system and some of its subsystems. We concluded that reusable parts should be developed for reuse from the outset.

Reuse on the specification or design level offers benefits that complement those of reuse on the code level. Specifications and design do not yet contain detailed representational decisions and, therefore, their potential for reuse is greater. Further, reusing specification or design necessarily occurs early in the development cycle — and this is the right time to consider reuse.

We developed the concept of building blocks to combine reuse on the code and on the specification/design level to realize the benefits of both.

Customization methods. Another criterion for classifying approaches to reuse is how a reusable part is customized and tailored to meet the new requirements.[2] (The word "user" refers to the programmer/designer who includes a reusable part into the program, *not* to an end user of the program.)
Methods are:
• No tailoring at all.
• Adaptation after the fact. This means manual modification of the reusable part's internals. Consequently, the user requires detailed knowledge of those internals.

---

functions like conversion and sorting and functions like time and date editing.

Abstract data types encompass data and all operations that access and modify these data. All data are kept in main memory. A further classification into variants is, for example: Are they bounded or unbounded (do they have a maximum number of elements that must be specified as a generic parameter?)? Are all elements the same length, or is the length variable?

Other criteria, like storage management and concurrency aspects, do not create a need for additional variants. For storage management, BB/LX has several facilities. For more complex cases, we provide special building blocks for storage management, and free-space management is handled uniformly for unbounded building blocks. Concurrency management is usually done outside the building blocks with facilities provided by the system environment. Variants of an abstract data type may have different implementations of the same building-block specification.

Our library contains typical abstract-data-type building blocks, like stack, queue, chain, list, table, map, and sequence. Moreover, there are building blocks for storage management and allocation. On the average, there are 10 to 20 operations available on each building block.

Procedural building blocks include message handlers, command parsers, and input checkers. Typically, the number of operations available on each building block is much smaller than on the abstract data types.

Contents. When this article was written, our library contained 16 abstract data types, four procedural building blocks, and three functional-abstraction building blocks. We continue to add to this library. For some abstract data types, there are two variants or implementations available. The block sizes range between a hundred and a few thousand lines of code, the average being less than a thousand lines of code.

Our experience is that abstract data types are not as predominant in actual project use as we expected them to be. Indeed, procedural and functional building blocks were just as important as abstract data types in our project environment. This appears to be true because, in existing components, data are stored very frequently in control blocks. When you enhance and extend these components, it is often more natural to use the existing control blocks than to introduce abstract data types to store additional data. In new components, it was easier to identify abstract data types for reuse — especially when projects used software engineering techniques and a design language.[4]

A building block has 10 to 20 functions. It provides at least the same number of system environments and storage allocation possibilities. It can also be tailored via the generic parameters. Hence, a building block is a very abstract and nonspecific reusable component.

Compare building blocks to the reuse of less abstract, less tailorable, and more environment-specific reusable functions.[5]

• Modification by completing templates or skeletons. This is easier and safer than adaptation after the fact. However, there is a danger of introducing errors into the reusable part through defective modifications.

• Generic parameterization of reusable parts. This method guarantees that modifications cannot impair the correctness of the modified part.

For quality reasons, we selected generic parameterization for our reuse technology. A drawback is that all modifications must be planned in advance. This is not easy, and it requires experience. It also requires more effort to be invested in the creation of reusable parts. However, we believe this effort to be worthwhile, and our practical experience seems to confirm our opinion.

Reusability conditions. When an application domain has reached a certain degree of maturity, common abstractions and concepts become apparent.[2] These common concepts constitute the entities to be reused. If a part does not represent a concept in the specific domain, it is bound to be not reusable.

When common concepts are not known beforehand, a domain analysis is required to identify them.[3] In our domain (systems programming), many common techniques and concepts have been established by computer science and practical experience.

Our approach is to draw on both sources to identify reusable entities. From computer science, we take concepts like specific abstract data types and storage-administration, sorting, and scanning algorithms. With program development departments, we verify if implementations of these concepts are actually required in our environment. On the other hand, we solicit requests for reusable entities from project requirements and investigate if they represent generally acknowledged concepts.

Even when a concept of a domain has been identified and implemented as a part, it is not necessarily accepted as reusable by its intended users. Several conditions (compare, for example McCain[4]) must be fulfilled before a part qualifies as reusable. It must represent a good modularization with well-selected and usable interfaces. It must also provide the right degree of functionality (functional completeness without excessive generality).

In short, it must result from good software engineering practices as well as exhibit reusability-specific characteristics.

References

1. P. Freeman, "Reusable Software Engineering: Concepts and Research Directions," *Proc. Workshop Reusability in Programming*, ITT, Stratford, Conn., 1983, pp. 2-16.
2. T.A. Standish, "Software Reuse," *Proc. Workshop Reusability in Programming*, ITT, Stratford, Conn., 1983, pp. 45-49.
3. J.M. Neighbors, "The Draco Approach to Constructing Software from Reusable Components," *Proc. Workshop Reusability in Programming*, ITT, Stratford, Conn., 1983, pp. 167-178.
4. R. McCain, "A Software Development Methodology for Reusable Components," *Proc. Hawaii Int'l Conf. System Sciences*, CS Press, Los Alamitos, Calif., 1985.

More than a hundred simple reusable functions or components would have to be developed and stored in a library to provide the same functional offering that *one* building block does.

We strongly favor building blocks over the elementary reusable functions because of the advantages for both users and developers. For both, handling fewer components is easier. Furthermore, users get a consistent set of the functions that they may require, and they need not collect them. Because in-line code is generated only for building-block functions actually used, there is not even memory overhead. Moreover, developers spend less effort maintaining and extending one component than they would for a hundred.

Effect on development

While building-block technology is worthwhile, it does require extra investment at the beginning of the design process to realize its benefits later.

Reuse requires specific extensions to the usual development process for reusing building blocks. Programmers are not the only development people affected. For example, departments that build and integrate product drivers must set up a library structure for storing and using building blocks.

A program-design process that is oriented to reusing building blocks (or any other reusable elements) is never a pure top-down process. Instead, it is a combination of top-down and bottom-up steps.

Design with reuse. Initially, a top-down step is appropriate to refine the task to a detail level that comes near the function level where building blocks could be used. This refinement step determines which elements are wanted and which functions and characteristics they should have. As a parallel action the developer searches — as a bottom-up step — the building-block library for candidates that fulfill the requirements.

The available building blocks will not usually match the elements exactly. But for some elements, there may be building blocks that come quite close, although they do not fit exactly. Developers must consider carefully whether to
• use existing building blocks (and save

development and testing effort) by modifying the top-down design to allow the use of existing building blocks (bottom-up),
• develop new building blocks if the new functions have general applicability, or
• develop the functions conventionally.

No further refinement is required for any part of the design represented by building blocks because this refinement was performed when the building blocks were developed.

Overall process with reuse. This process is related to the framework of the IBM Process Architecture.[6] During component-level design (conventionally called high-level design), program developers must review the available building blocks and determine the candidate building blocks for this component. This must be done now — not later — because a different module structure might be derived by using available building blocks than by developing your own code. On the other hand, this review need not be done at the earlier product-level design stage because our building blocks are not larger than a few thousand lines of code, so the availability of building blocks will hardly influence the decomposition of a product into components.

During module-level (low-level) design, program developers must decide which candidate building blocks to use. They will design the module down to the interfaces of the selected building blocks. No further refinement is required for the building-block functions because the design is a part of the building block itself. The building-block specifications may be included in the design, or they may be referenced. Reusing building blocks saves specification and design effort and represents an implicit reuse of design and specification.

The inspections during each development step are also affected. Two items are added: a check if available building blocks are being used and a check if new code should be written as building blocks.

At coding, developers code BB/LX calls to building-block operations in their source code for new or changed modules. No coding for the building blocks themselves is required because the code is part of a building block. The building-block

code will be fetched automatically from a building-block macro library at program

Unit-test times done by program development can be smaller than traditional test times when building blocks are used because the blocks are already tested.

Ownership, distribution, and maintenance. Each component of IBM operating systems and subsystems is owned by separate development groups, possibly at different locations. Some components have their own release cycle and their own change team for maintenance. We had to solve some organizational problems to introduce reusability to this environment. The main problems were:
• Which component owns a building block when the building block is reused by several components? Should the building-block code be owned and maintained independently by each component using it, or by the component using it first, or by no component at all?
• How can future enhancements of a building block be implemented and timed independently of a component's release cycle?
• How can the building blocks be made available for each component and processed by the local driver-build functions using different integration libraries and processes?
• The organizational structure of maintenance (a change team per component) runs the risk of that of implementing multiple fixes for the same error in a building block when it is reused by different components. How can we avoid multiple building-block versions caused by maintenance? How can we prevent a cross-component building block from being converted to a component-specific piece of code during its lifetime?

Our solutions to these problems were to have a single development group own each building block that is a candidate for cross-component reuse, to introduce a central distribution process from a one building-block library for all cross-component building blocks, and to have a single maintenance group responsible for each cross-component building block.

By having a single group responsible for maintenance, we expect considerable maintenance-cost reductions. This means that using building blocks will provide savings over the entire life cycle, not just for the design or coding phase.

Practical experiences

In addition to small experimental exercises, we have completed two product-development projects:

• A component of a small product extending a major teleprocessing subsystem. The component was about 7000 lines of new code with interfaces embedded in the subsystem.

• Products in a release of the IBM VSE operating system that provided enhancements or extensions to existing products in a medium-size effort.

Two other projects are under way:

• A small-to-medium component of the IBM MVS operating system that is a new development with interfaces to existing products.

• Another release of the VSE operating system with characteristics similar to the first one.

Technology validation. In all the development projects, the building-block reuse technology proved adequate, although some significant enhancements of BB/LX were necessary.

Many enhancements supported requirements related to systems programming, including

• adjustments for module reentrancy (and the resulting storage allocation schemes),

• provision for connections between user code and building-block code (in-line, linked procedures, and separate load modules/phases), and

• support for different storage allocation methods (user-provided, static, and dynamic).

Other enhancements added functionality to the reused entities and to how they interact, thus allowing generic tailoring facilities to functions and procedures and allowing building blocks to be parameterized with building blocks (letting unbounded data types build on several blocking and storage-allocating building blocks). The rest of the enhancements made the system easier to use.

Method acceptance. To introduce the reuse of building blocks to real projects, we decided to convince the technical people of its technical merits, create a positive management attitude, and provide the building blocks at no cost. Thus, the projects had a tangible advantage (by saving design and coding effort), which compensated for the cost of learning a new approach and the risks associated with a new technology.

On the other hand, our strategy was also to develop building blocks based on development-project requirements, and not to create a large library of building blocks without having a practical application of these building blocks. This let us make sure that no investment was made in

---

To introduce building blocks to real projects, we decided to convince technical people of its technical merits, create a positive management attitude, and provide the blocks for free.

---

building blocks that never found a practical application.

The investment in a building block (which may be up to 100 percent higher than just developing the required code) will usually pay off with the building block's second use.

We first taught project members the techniques for about half a day. The project participants then identified candidate building blocks with our help. When the candidate building blocks were not available in our library, we decided if it was worthwhile to create a new building block. If the block would be generally reusable, we created it. This method proved very satisfactory.

Still, we met a lot of resistance with the first project. That resistance was voiced in two forms: variations of the "not invented here" syndrome and performance concerns.

When the reuse methodology stabilized — and when the success and the good quality results from the first project became known — technical people became

willing to try the new technology. By briefing management on the results of the first project, we could create a positive management attitude that encouraged broader use.

Practical aspects — confidence in the quality of the building blocks, in our promises of fast maintenance, and in the quality of our support when problems arose — played an equally important role in acceptance as the merits of the new reuse technology did.

Standardizing the building block interfaces and their use in development also contributed much to their acceptance. This became evident when existing modules (with different interfaces) were brought into the form of building blocks and were then more easily accepted for reuse than before.

We found that the more programming skill developers had and the more remote their software layer was from the target hardware, the more easily they accepted reusable building-block technology.

One problem, however, is that even though most of our developers have education in software engineering, their design is closely tied to domain-specific abstractions. Furthermore, the granularity of their abstractions is too coarse to identify more than a few potentially reusable abstractions. So we still had to help identify the building blocks. After that, applying the building blocks was very easy and was done without our support. The eventual availability of a comprehensive library of building blocks, reuse experience, and education should alter these thinking patterns.

Identification. Identifying and developing new building blocks proceeded in cooperation between the development groups and our group. This cooperation was very intensive at the beginning, but it became looser and looser as developers acquired more experience.

In the first project, a member of the reusability team participated in the project design with the objectives of shaping the design in terms of many abstractions (preferably data abstractions) and of identifying those that have a potential for reuse. That project resulted in a high ratio (around 50 percent) of code implemented by building blocks compared to the total code. The high reuse rate was achieved by including as many domain-specific building blocks (like teleprocessing and networking) as general-systems building blocks.

In later projects the cooperation became looser: First, we asked project developers to identify and propose building blocks. When the response was not sufficient, we did informal design reviews to identify potential building blocks. Then we defined the interfaces of the identified building blocks so they would be generally reusable. The proposals from the development projects usually covered just the functions required in their special environment.

Overall, the cooperation was less intensive but broader. Also, our intention was not to include domain-specific building blocks. As a result, just a few building blocks were used per project. This resulted, of course, in lower reuse rates.

Reuse effects. The reuse rate may be calculated relative to the project's (or subproject's) total code. Most frequently, building blocks were used only in a few subprojects (for resource or technical reasons). For example, a subproject for new hardware support with small and scattered changes to existing programs does not lend itself to the use of building blocks.

The subprojects where building blocks were used varied between extensions of existing programs (these extensions were larger than 1000 lines of code) to new program systems with about 10,000 to 20,000 lines of code. For subprojects, the reuse rates were about 50 percent; for projects, they were between 10 percent and 25 percent.

The building blocks also showed good quality. In one project, the building-block code's quality (number of errors per lines of code) was about nine times better during the function test and 4.5 times better during the component and system test than the non-building-block's code.

In the other completed project, the results are even better: No errors in the building blocks were found during the entire test cycle. We estimate the building blocks would have had about 40 errors if their quality had been the same as that of the product they were used in.

Our current interest is — besides enhancing the building-block reuse technology and enlarging the library — providing more automated support for all reuse-related activities in the development process. We are doing this by developing an interactive reuse environment that extends the conventional development environment by all typical reuse functions.

Identifying building blocks from a library plays an important role, but there are other functions that have the same importance (like selective on-line access to building-block specifications and related development support functions, distribution, tracking, and maintenance). Moreover, we are acquiring experience with expert systems that will select and identify building blocks. □

Acknowledgments

This article is based partly on an IBM internal technical report that was written by Hans Albrecht Schmid, Karl-Hans Holder, Manfred Lenz, and Konrad Theobald. We thank Holder and Theobald for their contribution. Also, we acknowledge the work of Michael Ostmeyer, who is responsible for a lot of the project's early success. In addition, we are grateful to all other members of the project team, in particular to Ursula Braun, Bengt Schulze-Wenck and Thomas Wappler, without whom this effort could not have been accomplished. The careful review of this article by Bengt Schulze-Wenck and by the referees deserves special thanks since it contributed much to improving its readability and clarity.

References

1. E. Horowitz and J.B. Munson, "An Expansive View of Reusable Software," *Proc. Workshop Reusability in Programming*, ITT, Stratford, Conn., 1983, pp. 250-262.
2. E. Denert, "Software-Modularisierung [Software Modularization]," *Informatik-Spektrum*, 1979, pp. 204-218.
3. R.G. Lanergan and C.A. Grasso, "Software Engineering with Reusable Designs and Code, *Proc. Workshop Reusability in Programming*, ITT, Stratford, Conn., 1983, pp. 224-227.
4. M.B. Carpenter and H.K. Hallman, "Quality Emphasis at IBM's Software Engineering Institute," *IBM Systems J.*, No. 2, 1985, pp. 121-133.
5. R. Prieto-Diaz and P. Freeman, "Classifying Software for Reusability," *IEEE Software*, Jan. 1987, pp. 6-16.
6. R.A. Radice et al., "Programming Process Architecture," *IBM Systems J.*, No. 2, 1985, pp. 79-90.

Manfred Lenz is a staff programmer at the IBM Data Systems Division Laboratory in Boeblingen, West Germany, as a member of the Advanced Programming Dept. He was responsible for designing and developing components of the IBM VSE operating system. He now works on software reuse.

Hans Albrecht Schmid is manager of the Advanced Development Dept. at IBM Data Systems Division Laboratory in Boeblingen, West Germany. He has been on the faculty of several universities, including the University of Karlsruhe and the University of Toronto. His main research interests are software engineering and reuse.

Schmid received a doctorate in computer science from the University of Karlsruhe, a diploma in electrical engineering from the University of Stuttgart, and a diploma in computer science from the Institut National Polytechnique of Grenoble, France.

Peter F. Wolf is an advisory programmer at IBM Program Product Development Center in Sindelfingen, West Germany. He has been involved in many compiler and operating-systems component projects, and has concentrated on reusability and software-engineering issues in recent years.

Wolf received a diploma in nuclear physics from the University of Hamburg.

Lenz and Schmid can be contacted at Advanced Development Dept., IBM Laboratories, Schoenaicher Str. 220, D-7030 Boeblingen, West Germany. Wolf can be reached at IBM Program Product Development Center, Schwertstr. 58-60, D-7032 Sindelfingen, West Germany.

SOFTWARE ENGINEERING WITH REUSABLE PARTS

Elizabeth E. Wald*

Naval Research Laboratory

Abstract

Unnecessary redevelopment of software is being attacked through DOD-mandated socio-legal reforms, software parts inventory activities, and the development of tools for system building. The ACOS/ECOS methodology will facilitate the composition of new signal processing systems from reusable software parts.

Introduction

We would not retain a software engineer who designed, coded, tested and documented a new sine routine every time a new system required that mathematical function; we would expect instead that a library function would be reused. Yet we tolerate and even expect that more demanding functions will be redeveloped in each new system.

Human progress has resulted from one generation building upon the successes and failures of previous generations. In most fields of engineering, practitioners follow standard models, and deviate from a standard practice only when the project at hand imposes a special requirement. When software designers address a new project or a major upgrade, however, the dominant practice is to begin anew, or at best, to focus only on the prior experience of the immediate team of players. The result is a proliferation of "unique" software that is functionally identical. This duplication includes not only code, but also design, test programs, data and instrumentation, and maintenance.

This paper addresses both the socio-legal causes of this practice, and the parts inventory and tool development activities that are required to permit its avoidance. Examples will be given of DOD initiatives designed to reduce these unnecessary redevelopments.

----

* Head, Software/Systems Development Branch, Acoustics Division, Naval Research Laboratory, Washington DC 20375-5000. Former Technical Director, DOD STARS Applications Area.

Socio-legal Causes

Our educational systems have taught us to be inventors; an academic paper too closely related to another causes expulsion of the submitter upon conviction of plagiarism. Engineers like to leave their signature on the world by creating complete new systems, and their managers may have a contract type that confuses added cost with added value. Other managers may sincerely fear legal or ethical liability for errors, Trojan Horses or time bombs which could be introduced into their systems if they attempted to reuse software that was not developed under their supervision.

A counter to the academic demand for originality is the revolution brought on by the personal computer (PC). The PC marketplace is teaching people to reuse existing software packages. The vast majority of PC users perform no programming and still get their job done.

Furthermore, the academic and industrial research communities have been helpful in teaching us about information hiding, separation of concerns, and other modularization techniques that make software reuse more possible.

Finally, the DOD, concerned about the costs in time, money and reliability of present practices, has embarked on an effort to reform them. The Ada** language has been mandated as the standard language to be used across the Department of Defense (DOD) application areas for mission-critical systems. Although DOD has attempted standardization before, e.g. on Algol-58 dialects, without complete success, this time there is international, inter-company, inter-academic-institution, and inter-service DOD momentum behind the movement. Chances for success are greater than ever before. Ada implementations provide new opportunities for incorporation of additional software engineering practices.

** Ada is a registered trademark of the DOD Ada Joint Project Office.

The Software Technology for Adaptable, Reliable Software (STARS) Project, the Software Engineering Institute (SEI) and the Ada Joint Project Office are all efforts initiated by the Office of the Secretary of Defense (OSD). The goals for these initiatives are to serve as a major stimulus to reduce the amount of time from the availability of technology, to its insertion in mission-critical programs (the current value is 17 years); to mechanize certification of standard Ada compiler implementations; and to focus on solutions (preferably automated) to long-festering software and concomitant system development and maintenance problems. A primary theme within both the STARS and SEI OSD initiatives is the maximization of reuse of system parts.

Parts Inventory Activities

We must leverage on reusable parts for building future systems. Parts that can be reused across varying applications will have maximum benefit; those reusable within a single application area, e.g. avionics, are also useful as corporate or DOD project office resources. Reusable parts must be accessible, understandable and useful.

Accessibility involves both recognition of the functional requirement and the identification of components that can perform the function. It is trivial to recognize that the mathematical operation of sine can be accomplished by the library routine labeled 'sine', but as recently as a decade ago not every programmer recognized that the management of i/o conversations between operators and command/control systems could be performed by components labeled 'compiler parser' provided that the parser was suitably table driven. It is not clear that current practices of cross indexing attributes of parts is sufficiently robust to attack this problem. The availability of massively parallel processors, e.g the Connection Machine, promises the ability to search and associate parts descriptions that have not had a subjective indexing processing imposed on them.

Understandability involves documentation sufficiently transparent to permit the engineer to decide whether the component can serve the required function. It is not trivial to document a component well enough to permit a stranger to decide whether the component will be effective for an entirely new mission. Is a list-processing interpreter useful for graphics? Before answering too hastily consider the origins of LOGO and its principal application today! The challenge is in deciding how to form a question with sufficient precision that a part browser can find a functional fit to the need.

Usability involves not only precision in the statement of a component's inputs, outputs, assumptions, etc. but also in the statement of its behavior under unusual circumstances. It may involve legal issues, not only of ownership but also of liability. Usability requires certifiability. To the consumer, excellence is not necessarily paramount in reusing a part. However, the user must be given some measure of expectation; if he has used it before, his expectation is very well known. The ability to gain an expectation of merit from automated examination tools should be an early consideration of an organization directed to adopt reusable technology.

Among the projects begun by STARS are a series of government/industry conferences that are generating a Reusability Guide, the Common Ada Missile Parts (CAMP) project, and the Ada Based Integrated Combat System (ABICS). These projects are evolving library definitions, inter-library interactions, and part descriptions and implementations, and will be coordinated with findings in the signal processing community to determine where parts can be used across application domains.

Tool Development Activities

Besides a change in the socio-legal climate and vigorous inventory activities, greater reuse of software parts will require the development of tools to automate the routine aspects of the composition of new systems from old parts. What follows is a case history of the development of a framework for the development of signal processing systems.

Background

Inspired by Dennis[1], the Naval Research Laboratory (NRL) has developed a flow-graph specification[2] from the model of Karp and Miller[3]. The early NRL effort was referred to as the ASP Common Operational Software (ACOS), where ASP refers to the Navy's standard Advanced Signal Processor, AN/UYS-1. The implementation on the ASP was abandoned after completion of a proof-of-principle, because of cost and the need to focus on the next generation machine. The specification, however, was mandated by the Naval Sea Systems Command (PMS-412) in its Request for Proposals for the development of the Enhanced Modular Signal Processor (EMSP), AN/UYS-2, to assure that competing vendors would produce an efficient system for building future signal processing applications. The same basic specification is configuration controlled under the EMSP Project (now called ECOS/ACOS), and retains the same goals:

(1) To relieve the application programmer from concerns about the hardware architecture, thus allowing transportability between hardware systems;

(2) To relieve the programmer from routine rebuilding of functions (termed primitives) through library access to standard parts, e.g. Fourier Transforms, filters, etc.; and

(3) To relieve the programmer from details of algorithms (until detailed inspection is requested) through focus on the environment where they are to be used.

Techniques

Systems are specified in terms of a directed data-flow graph. A node, as user-specified, consists of input and output queues and an underlying primitive that provides a transformation function (transforming input data to output information); sub-graphs can also be nodes with the restriction that no graph can be a subgraph of itself either directly or indirectly. In a directed graph, each directed edge represents a first-in first-out (FIFO) queue that carries data from its predecessor node to its successor node. Each node executes at run-time when a pre-specified number of data points are available on each of its input queues, i.e. the function cannot operate until all of the data it requires is available. Upon completion of execution, data is removed from the input queues and data as a function of the node's primitive is placed on the output queue(s).

The graph writer is given the ability to specify execution parameters, which control node operation. For input queues, these include: threshold (exceeding the specified amount signals signal queue readiness to trigger node operation - all inputs to a single node have to reported readiness to allow execution), read amount (the amount of data that the primitive requires at execution time), offset (the place where the read is to begin is specified by the first element on the queue), and a consume (the amount of data that is to be removed from the queue, once the execution is complete). For output queues, an execution parameter called a valve is provided. This latter parameter is taken into consideration at node execution time. The valve determines whether or not the data produced by the primitive is transmitted to the associated output queue. Each of the node execution parameters, except threshold, can be computed at each node execution, thereby giving considerable flexibility.

Graph variables can be specified as input and/or output for any number of nodes to define buffers for storage of data to be accessed by several nodes. Node execution parameters do not apply to graph variables, but graph variables may be used to compute the values of node execution parameters.

Often in the environment, or as a consequence of an operational scenario, it is desirable to monitor and control graphs that are in execution. For example, an operator may wish to change to a new filter profile, requiring the introduction of a new set of coefficients, to change center frequency of a vernier filter, to reconfigure the topology of processing graphs, or to stop sub-graphs. These and other capabilities are controlled in the command programs, programs written in Ada. Allowed command program accesses to graphs are: starting and stopping graphs, connection of queues to and from graphs, reading and writing graph variables, starting and stopping I/O channels, adding or awaiting data on a queue or creation/termination of other command programs.

User Perspective

The application development scenario is as follows. The system designer sits at a graphic entry terminal and specifies nodes by function name and predecessor/successor relationships. If the information is in the library, the parameters are filled in automatically with the user giving approval before proceeding. If the primitive is unknown, the node and its execution parameters must be entered by the designer. The context of the specification is retained as well as the specific node. Once the entire system is built, several levels of translation take place: from the picture to an internal textual form, from the textual form to a High Order Language (Ada), and then Ada to the object code for the system where the application is to run. The translations are performed automatically giving the user notice only when a problem that cannot be resolved is encountered. The multiple translation steps are partitioned to allow easy porting to new development processors and execution environments.

Status

The design and execution facilities are being implemented for the Navy's next generation signal processor, the EMSP, by AT&T. Recently, efforts have begun to implement the functionality for the ASP computer, the current Navy standard signal processor. ASP application developers will have early access to the methodology, and resultant designs can transition to the EMSP as the application exceeds the ASP hardware resources or logistic support span.

To make the techniques commercially available, the methodology is being implemented for execution on the Digital Equipment Company VAX computer (Hughes Ground Systems, contract support). Many documents[4] are available on this project now, and the VAX execution system will be available for release by summer 1987. We anticipate usage of the VAX run-time system as a facility for functional prototyping of applications (albeit execution speed is a limiting factor, particularly for signal processing and real-time system designs), and for exploration of the utility of the methodology for applications where data sets are large, static bodies (sometimes distributed) and there is a high percentage of logical switch points vs mathematical computation (e.g. command, control, communication and intelligence applications).

Basic research is being targeted towards a more direct-execution hardware architecture and advanced algorithms that would be needed to keep power and hardware footprints to an absolute minimum. A modular approach to signal processing was developed by the United Kingdom Admiralty Research Establishment by Curtis[5]. This approach, Control Ordered Sonar Hardware (COSH), uses a small set of programmable hardware modules to perform the major sonar-processing primitives, thus providing a static hardware implementation.

Basic research is being performed by NRL on analysis of graph specifications. Preliminary work shows that a number of errors and computational bottlenecks can be determined prior to execution and that significant economies through overhead reduction can be attained by pre- determination of execution strategies. Continued work is needed to reduce the time it takes to do the analysis, to address the effects of dynamic hardware outage to pre-execution predictions, and to encorporate the effects of differing hardware architectures.

Primary graphics-entry to date has been through Control Data Corporation's commercially-available IBM/PC CAD/CAM product SCALD. Although it is keystroke intensive, it is adequate to support the development of the rest of the system. More sophisticated man/machine interfaces being pursued by AT&T, TRW, Brown University and others can be retrofitted.

In the future the knowledge-based augmentation for application system building and effective debug feedbacks from an execution system will be integrated to allow a builder to interact at the highest possible graph level of his interest.

Conclusion

Reduction of unnecessary software redevelopment requires vigorous action to change the socio-legal climate, to provide inventories of reusable parts and their descriptions, and to develop tools to facilitate the composition of systems from reusable parts. It is necessary to design the complex systems of the future at a level above that of High-Order Languages (e.g. Fortran, Ada ...). Only in this way

can humans receive computer assistance in envisioning the connectivity of system parts and analyzing and optimizing their interaction. Once we achieve a structured framework for system design, we can embellish it with additional automated aids to include knowledge-based assistants and sophisticated measurement aids. None of this will be effective however unless we do a good job in building and certifying usable, reusable parts.

References

[1] Dennis, J.B., "First version of a data flow procedure language," MIT Laboratory for Computer Science, MIT/LCS/TM-61, May 1975.

[2] "EMSP/ASP Common Operational Support Software Methodology Specification", V 3.0, 31 May 1984. (Requests may be sent to R.S. Stevens, Code 5155, Naval Research Laboratory, Washington, DC 20375-5000.)

[3] Karp, R.M. and Miller, R.E., "Properties of a Model for Parallel Computations: Determinancy, Termination, Queueing", SIAM J. Appl. Math., 14:6, 1390-1411.

[4] VAX Implementation Specifications (Requests for documentation my be sent to D. Kaplan, Code 5155, Naval Research Laboratory, Washington DC 20375-5000.)

[5] Curtis, T.E., "A Modular Approach to Signal Processing", Proc. Real-time General-Purpose, High-Speed Signal Processing Systems for Underwater Research, SACLANT ASW Research Centre, La Spezia, Italy, 1979.

Software Prototyping with Reusable Components

SHINICHI HONIDEN,* NAOMICHI SUEDA,* AKIRA HOSHI,*
NAOSHI UCHIHIRA*, and KAZUO MIKAME*

Reprinted with permission from *Journal of Information Processing*, Volume
9, Number 3, 1986, pages 123-129. Copyright ©1986 by Japan Publishers
Trading Company, Ltd. All rights reserved.

Recently, a prototyping method has attracted attention as a software specification method. Though many methods have been proposed, no standard method has been established. This paper proposes a prototyping method with reusable components based on knowledge engineering. This method provides support to even non-expert personnel in selecting and combining individual software components to satisfy their requirements rapidly. The proposed method is realized by an expert system, which consists of a component inference part, a parameter inference part, and an execution part. The component inference part selects the appropriate components to satisfy a user's requirement, and to determine the purpose of combining components. The parameter inference part combines parameters based on logical attribute and physical attribute. The execution part activates and carries out the roles indicated in the combined components. As an application example, an image processing expert system is described.

1. Introduction

Prototyping, as a software specification method, has recently come to be highly regarded. Various prototyping methods have been proposed, such as the existing programming language method [1], a program generator method wherein the field of application is limited [2], software reuse method [3], and the executable requirement specification language method [4]. Among them, the executable requirement specification language method is more applicable to various areas than other methods. However, suitable executable requirement specification languages have not yet been fully developed, and prototyping systems based upon them are not available. In other words, in order to develop general purpose prototyping systems, such as the executable requirement specification language, many problems remain to be resolved. Therefore, the practical approach involves developing an application-oriented prototyping system.

Using a software library is one known method for application-oriented prototyping system, because a user can construct a prototype rapidly with only knowledge about the library. However, it is hard for a user who doesn't have that knowledge (such a person is called a non-expert in this paper) to use the library. To recognize this method as a prototyping method exactly, the method must include functions which allow even a non-expert to use the library easily.

This paper describes an expert system which provides support to non-experts in selecting and combining individual software components stored in the software library.

As an application example, an image processing expert system is described. When the technology used for image processing is reviewed from the standpoint of pre-processing in two-dimensional image processing, established methods have been readily available in various areas. Many software packages for that purpose have been developed and used. Among them is SPIDER (Subroutine Package for Image Data Enhancement and Recognition) [6]. SPIDER consists of approximately 350 subroutine packages, which cover various processing areas, such as orthogonal transformation, emphasis and smoothing of image-data. They are described in FORTRAN.

Engineers engaged in image processing must choose appropriate software components among the group of subroutines (components) and develop programs to combine such components. To obviate such troublesome jobs, facilities have been requested which automatically combine, execute, and verify necessary components without programming and which generate and register the resultant combination as a new component.

In short, the requirements are:

*Each component should be used without programming.

*A combination of components should be automatically generated.

To satisfy these requirements, the image processing expert system was studied and developed.

2. Software Reuse Based on Knowledge Engineering

The proposed method involves software prototyping with reusable components. The software reusability rate has been increasing in various applications, and software reuse contributes to higher software produc-

*Systems & Software Engineering Division, Toshiba Corporation, 1-1-1, Shibaura, Minato-ku, Tokyo 105, Japan.

tivity. If software can be treated as components, the components can be reused, easily modified, and easily understood with better reliability and maintainability. Many problems, however, must be solved to realize the idea. In order to stock and reuse software components, internal and external specifications for each component must be clearly defined. Also, environments where the components can be easily utilized must be provided. The authors defined the environment, in which each component can be easily used, as the one which satisfies the following criteria:

(1) Each needed component should be searched easily.

(2) Components searched for and found should be easily combined.

(3) The resultant combination should be immediately executable.

This environment provides ways to construct a prototype rapidly.

There are two software reuse methods,

(1) Customize general component to satisfy the user's requirement, that is, modify the internal structure in the component (called a white-box approach in this paper).

(2) Use components without modifying the internal structure (called a black-box approach in this paper). The white-box approach is applicable to various areas and has high flexibility. However, the user must have knowledge about internal structure, and computerization is very difficult. The black-box approach is applied to only a limited domain, but automatic selection and combination is possible with knowledge about only external structure such as function and interface.

This paper describes a black-box approach. A typical example of the black-box approach is using a software library. That is, components stored in the library are used without modifying the internal structure. Many software libraries have been presented. However, it is hard for the library user to select and combine reusable components. It takes non-experts, who don't have knowledge about the library, much time to select and combine the components. To solve this problem, the authors developed an expert system for the education and assistance of non-expert users.

The presented expert system consists of:

(1) Component inference part

(2) Parameter inference part

(3) Execution part

The component inference part selects the appropriate components to satisfy a user's requirement, and determines the purpose of combining components. The parameter inference part combines parameters based on physical attribute, logical attribute and the purpose of combining components. The execution part activates and carries out the roles indicated in the combined components.

3. Image Processing Expert System

The image processing expert system consists of a component inference part, a parameter inference part, and an image processing execution part, as shown in Fig. 1.

3.1 Component Inference Part

This section explains component inference for user's requirements and dealing with the purpose of combining components. Its general idea is that, when a user requests processings, the system should automatically select appropriate software components.

The component inference part is realized by an expert system. An expert system consists of knowledge-base and inference engine. Knowledge representation and inference mechanism are described in the following.

3.1.1 Knowledge Representation

There are two knowledge categories, knowledge about components and knowledge about state.

The knowledge structure about the components is divided into the following categories:

(a) Meta inference (ex. for process A-process is a set of components-, processes a1, a2, a3, or a4, a5, a6 are performed).

(b) Effects on the state (ex. when process a1 is performed, state changes).

(c) Relationship between before and after processing (ex. process a1 should be performed prior to process a2).

The knowledge structure can be described using the

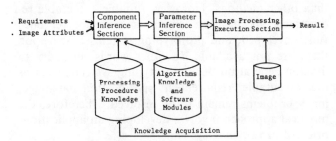

Fig. 1 Image processing expert system.

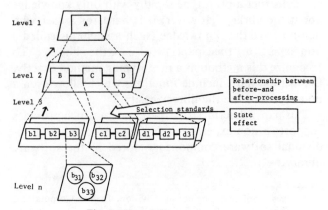

Fig. 2 Knowledge structure.

hierarchical structure shown in Fig. 2. The examples are as follow;

A: Segmentation, B: Binarization, b1: Histogram, b2: Threshold selection, b3: Binarization, b31: Single thresholding, b32: Double thresholding
This knowledge is not systematic, it is stored in fragments, and may correspond with, be inferred from, or be related to the state when the knowledge is used.

```
Rule No.: rule 21
Process request part:
Condition part: IF
              (state a and
               state b or
               state c) or
              (state d and
               state e and
               state f )
Execution part: THEN
              (component E and
               component F and
               component G)
Effect part: (state h and
               state i and
               state j and
               state k)
Parameter combination part:
              (e2 in E=f1 in F)
              (f2 in F=g1 in G)
```

Fig. 3   An example of knowledge about component.

```
Noise frame
Features
  Shape       : Circle, point, line and band
  Color       : Monochrome
  Size        : Minute and small
  Uniformity : Yes or No
Range
  Shape       : Optional
  Color       : Optional
  Size        : Optional
Effects
  Visibility  : Hard to see
  Supplement : If the density is high, this density will affect optional
               processing.
```

Fig. 4   Representation example of image attribute.

Knowledge about a component is the rule which consists of rule number, process request part, condition part, execution part, effect part, and process result state. An example is shown in Fig. 3.

Knowledge about the state is closely related to the application. Here, "state" means "image attribute" in image processing. The structure and representation for the image attribute are given in Fig. 4. The specialist, to whom the image to be processed is given, should understand:

(i)   Overall image
(ii)   Target conditions
(iii)   Relationship with the background
(iv)   Noise, Strain, Diffusion

Examples of such knowledge about image attribute are as follow.

*Background is in an area other than the target area.

*Background is often a large area with the same features.

*Background is often composed of two or more textures.

3.1.2   Inference Mechanism

The inference mechanism to select the software component makes non-deterministic inferences. It adopts a forward inference method, in which the inference is made under an assumption that "if the given states are a, b, c, . . . , perform processes A, B and C." This mechanism is shown in Fig. 5. Levels 2, 3 and n in Fig. 5 correspond to the processing component knowledge levels 2, 3 and n given in Fig. 2, respectively. The mechanism unifies the fact list with the condition rule. After unifications, the fact list is updated by the changed state.

3.1.3   Rule for User's Intention Regarding Parameter Combination

As mentioned in 3.1.1, in order to select the components, the rule shown in Fig. 3 is used. For example, components E, F, G are selected in Fig. 3. Knowledge

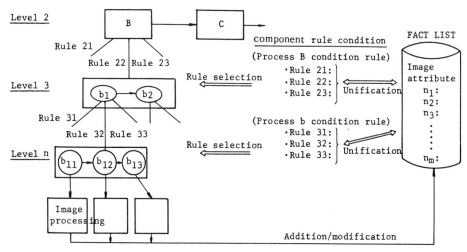

Fig. 5   Inference Process.

about the combination of parameters is also described in this rule. This rule shows that parameter e2 in component *E* is related to parameter f1 in component *F*.

3.2 Parameter Inference Part

This section explains parameter inference mechanism. Parameter inference means parameter matching among selected components in the component inference part.

It would be ideal for users if combination among components could be performed without any user assistance. To determine the relationship between components, the information shown in Fig. 6 is generally used.

Each parameter has three attributes, physical attribute, logical attribute and the purpose of combining components. An example of physical attribute is shown in Fig. 7. The logical attribute means the attribute heuristically determined, i.e., some intention, such as "Let's assign such and such a role to this parameter" is kept in mind. The authors consider that the probability of making right choices by automatic combination could be improved by introduction of the logical attribute. When the logical attribute concept is introduced, and as long as one to one correspondence between one logical attribute specified by a parameter and the other logical attribute by another parameter is retained, the character matching method is satisfactory. However, meanings of parameters do not correspond on a one to one basis. The example shown in Fig. 8 indicates this situation. In this example, the logical attribute for parameter "RHST" of the component "HIST1" is defined as "Histogram data" and that for parameter "DATA" of "THDS" is defined as "percent data". If a simple character matching is applied to this particular example, these attributes to not match and cannot be combined. To solve this problem, the inference mechanism based on the defined attribute is required.

The information regarding "purpose of combining

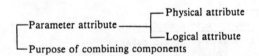

Fig. 6   Relationship between components.

* Input/output made: Input, output, input/output, . . .
* Dimension
* Element size of dimension: Constant, depending on other parameters, . . .
* Input type: Keyboard input, constant, operation between other parameters, . . .
* Input value range

Fig. 7   An example of physical attribute.

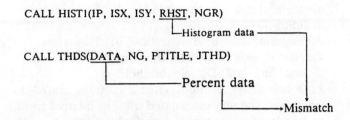

CALL HIST1(IP, ISX, ISY, RHST, NGR)
└─ Histogram data ─
CALL THDS(DATA, NG, PTITLE, JTHD)
└─── Percent data
→ Mismatch

Fig. 8   An example of parameter mismatch.

components" is also indispensable for automatic combination. This can be shown in the following example.
CALL STAS (A, MEAN, MAX, MIN, STDEV)
CALL DIVCIR (B C)
The average value (MEAN), maximum value (MAX), minimum value (MIN), and standard deviation (STDEV) for distribution A are obtained by "CALL STAS" first. Then, value B is divided by a constant value C by "CALL DIVCIR." At this time, the value of B can be related to the value of MEAN, MAX, MIN, or STDEV. Only the user knows the right selection. Therefore, knowledge about the purpose of combining components is required to combine such components automatically. This knowledge is involved in component knowledge described in 3.1.

3.2.1   Component Attribute Knowledge

The attribute structure for each component is organized as shown in Fig. 9. An individual component and its parameters make up an individual frame. Each logical attribute definition also takes the form of the frame. Each frame inherits necessary information from upper-level frames.

3.2.2   Rules of Combination

The component combination inference is the backward inference method and it is a non-deterministic method. The rules used for combination consists of rules for selection, rules for evaluation, and rules for determination.

(1)   Rules for Selection
The selection based on the logical attribute is inferred by interpreting the meaning of each parameter using the upper-level concepts. However, if a structure of knowledge to define the logical attribute includes extremely abstract upper-level concepts, matching of some components at some level does not have any practical sense. For example, it is easily understood that a structure such as (histogram data) (percent data) . . . (numerical values) does not have any practical sense, even if components are related to each other, based on the numerical values concept. To avoid such a case, care has been taken to determine a way to furnish knowledge regarding the definition of logical attributes. Also, the concept of logical distance (the number of inheritance links) has been incorporated to quantify the discussion. Thus, the difference in logical distance can be checked, after the logical attribute between

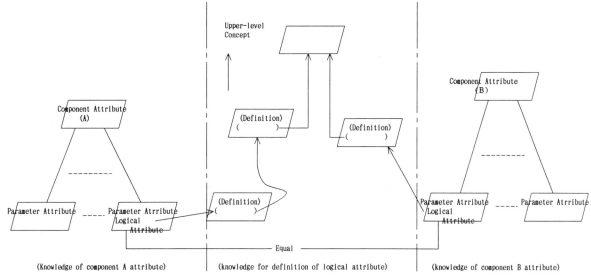

Fig. 9 Attribute structure.

parameters is matched.

(2) Rule for Evaluation and Determination

Candidates selected using the rules for selection are finally determined. For the parameters to be related, the physical distance is calculated based on the positional relationship (order of candidates in the coded program) of the candidates to be related. The index wherein parameter "a" will be related to parameter "b" is calculated, as shown below.

$f(a, b) = \alpha 1 *$ (logical distance between "a" and "b") $+$
$\qquad \alpha 2 *$ (physical distance between "a" and "b")
$\qquad \alpha 1$ and $\alpha 2$ are weighting coefficients.

The $f(a, x)$ having the smallest value is selected, using the determination rules:

Determination (a, x):- comparison $(f(a, x) < f(a, y))$.

For the parameter inference part, Fig. 10 shows an example of a Prolog fact statement which is component attribute knowledge, while Figs. 11 and 12 show examples of Prolog statements, for selection rules and evaluation rules, respectively. Figure 13 shows the system flow for the image processing expert system, which selects components needed by the user, relates to parameters for each component, generates a new component, and then registers them the library and the component attribute data.

```
s_rule1(*x):-mode(*x, input).
s_rule1(*x):-mode(*x, input-output).
s_rule2(*x, *y):-front(*x, *y).
s_rule3(*x):-dimension(*x, *a),
          dimension(*y, *b),
          equal(*a, *b).
s_rule25(*x, *y):-semantics(*x, *a),
          semantics(*y, *b),
          equal(*a, *b).
relation(*a, *b):-s_rule1(*a),
          s_rule2(*a, *b),
          s_rule3(*b),
          s_rule25(*a, *b).
```

```
IF
    Input/Output mode of *a is input or input-output
        AND
    *b is set before *a
        AND
    Dimension of *a is equal to dimension of *b
        AND
    Logical attribute of *a is equal to logical attribute of
*b
THEN
    *a is related to *b
```

```
class(histl).
parameter(histl, ip, isx, isy, rhst, ngr).
class(ip).
ako(ip, histl).
mode(ip, input).
dimension(ip, 2, para, isx, para, isy).
class(isx).
ako(isx, isx. d).
class(isy).
ako(isy, isy. d).
class(rhst).
ako(rhst, histl).
ako(rhst, histogram-data).
mode(rhst, output).
```

Fig. 10 An example of knowledge expressions.

Fig. 11 An example of a rule expression (selection rule).

117

```
function(*a, *b, *f):-logical__length(*a, *b, *ll),
            physical__length(*a, *b, *pl),
            multiply(*ll, alph1, *x),
            multiply(*pl, alph2, *y),
            add(*x, *y, *f).
determination(*a, *x):-function(*a, *x, *xf),
               function(*a, *y, *yf),
               less(*xf, *yf).
```

Fig. 12 An example of rules expression(evaluation and determination).

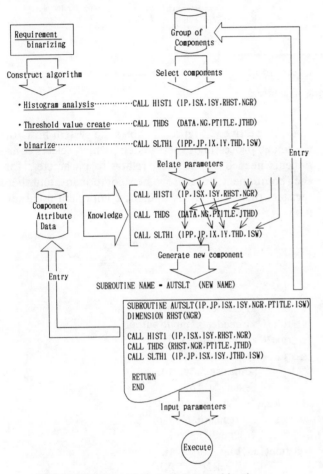

Fig. 13 Outline of component combination.

3.3 Execution Part

The execution part generates the executable format from combined components and activates and carries out the rules indicated in the components. The user's load for preparing execution environment is decreased, that is, additional codings for execution, such as parameter input routine and declaration, are generated automatically. The execution part processes the image data after obtaining necessary information through a conversation with the user.

3.4 Effects

The system has been verified with approximately 300 rules and approximately 70 software components. When processing is performed by a non-expert in image processing, about one hour is required to perform the steps from the introductory explanation to processing. System capability depends on the completeness of the knowledge base. Especially the rules for user's intention regarding parameter combination contributes to the system capability. These rules have two categories, the one beween components to be appeared in each knowledge about component and the one between components not to be appeared. Current knowledge bases do not have the latter rule. Therefore, when the combination fails, knowledge about the library is required. On the other hand, achievement of a target image depends on the component execution. Component functions are the subject of image processing technology, which should be further improved. As described previously, at present, the operator's load in the derivation of image processing procedures is markedly decreased.

5. Conclusion

A new method for use in software prototyping with reusable components is proposed. This method provides support to even non-experts, to enable them to select and combine the reusable components stored in a library rapidly. This method is realized by an expert system. As an application example, the image processing expert system is described. Currently, $\alpha 1$ and $\alpha 2$ in determination rules are set as 0.35 and 0.65, respectively, in the image processing expert system. However, to obtain better determination, $\alpha 1$ and $\alpha 2$ must be improved by practical use.

A problem to be studied in the future concerns the fact that the time required for inference will increase in proportion to the complexity of the inference procedure, when the number of components is increased and the associated quantity of the knowledge is increased.

This method can be applied to various applications. In this method, for the component inference part, there are two knowledge categories, knowledge about components and knowledge about state. The former knowledge is independent on applications, but the latter knowledge depends on the particular application. On the other hand, the knowledge used in the parameter inference part is independent from the application.

Acknowledgement

The authors would like to thank Akira Ito and Masahiko Arai, Systems & Software Engineering Division of Toshiba Corporation, for their valuable comments.

References

1. DUNCAN, A. G. Prototyping in ADA: Case Study, *ACM Sigsoft Eng*. Notes, **7**, 5 (1982), 54–60.
2. BARSTOW, D. Automatic Programming System to Support Experimental Science, *Proc. 6th ICSE* (1982), 360–366.
3. JONES, T. G. Reusability in Programming: A Survey of the state of the art, *IEEE Trans. Software Eng*. **10**, 5 (1984), 488–493.
4. BALZER, R. M. et al. Operational Specification as Basis for Rapid Prototyping, *ACM Sigsoft Software Eng. Notes*, **7**, 5 (1982), 3–16.
5. TAMURA, H., Sakaue, K. Three kinds of knowledge for building Digital-Image-Analysis expert system, Paper of Technical group AL83–49, *IECE Japan* (1983), 27–40.
6. TAMURA, H. et al. SPIDER USER'S MANUAL.
7. MIKAME, K. et al. Knowledge Engineering Application in Image Processing, *Proc. Graphics Interface* '85 (1985), 435–441.

(Received September 9, 1985; revised September 2, 1986)

Frame-Based Software Engineering

Paul G. Bassett, Netron, Inc.

One of reusability's main problems is how to easily modify available components. This frame-based approach handles the problem.

It is ironic that software — the very engine of our high-tech, automated society — is such a low-tech cottage industry. While no civil engineer would dream of designing a bridge from scratch (and few would cross the bridge if it were), software is routinely designed that way.

Craftsman programmers still build programs character by character, obliviously reinventing similar wheels over and over again. When they do notice, it often takes more work to separate and recustomize the common parts than to rewrite them from scratch. And, although less than 10 percent of a typical Cobol program is non-reusable or worth maintaining,[1] 100 percent of the program's code is maintained.

Reuse concepts play a key role in several issues: productivity, maintainability, portability, quality, and standards. Reusability can be applied to each major stage of the software life cycle: analysis and design, construction and testing, maintenance, and new releases.

The simplest possible notion of reusability is use-as-is. Obviously, if the shoe fits, wear it. Beneath most software problems, however, are too many ill-fitting shoes. Such problems are manifest in the use of subroutines, structured programming, programming languages, and code generators.[2,3]

The notion of same-as-except ("*A* is the same as *B* except. . . . ") is a needed generalization of use-as-is.

In design, the more we can take for granted about the basic features and functions of a system, the more we can concentrate on its unique aspects. Unfortunately, use-as-is is impossible at the system-design level or we would have nothing to design. Nor can we simply add and subtract components. Too many things must be modified in unforeseen ways.

Program construction can benefit from fixed, use-as-is text components. But again, people must be able at construction time to tailor the original component to their needs. These modifications are made at construction time so we do not pay unnecessary overhead in time or space at runtime. Moreover, programs often can be generated largely from declarative specifications (such as screen and report definitions).

But patching generated code prevents reuse of the generator (within the same program) on pain of destroying the patches already made. (Many commercial generators, recognizing this problem, attempt to overcome it by providing user exits; but this approach is also fraught with use-as-is difficulties.)

At execution time, use-as-is is both trivial and vital. Programs and subroutines get reused by simply invoking them as is. The less we need to vary things at runtime, the faster and simpler our code will run because runtime variables and parameters create complexity and overheads. Minimizing such complexities and overheads is why we need variability during design, construction, and maintenance.

Maintenance is by far the most expensive part of the life cycle, yet it too is a process of reusing modules (across time rather than across applications). Changing cir-cumstances force software to be modified in unforeseen ways, much as happens during design. Same-as-except can close the loop, making maintenance a process of design refinement and giving real meaning to the word "cycle" in the software life cycle.

Frames usefully formalize same-as-except and provide a basis for a rigorous software-engineering discipline. Generally speaking, a frame is any fixed theme plus the means to accommodate unforeseen variations on that theme.

For example, how many seconds of unique melody are contained in a typical song? Composers have fixed, frame-like patterns for repeating the themes with variations in words, harmonies, instruments, and the like.

Also consider manufacturing: In about 20 minutes you can order a new car that is as unique as your fingerprints. In principle, every car on the assembly line can be one of a kind. How can they be made in high volume and quality at reasonable cost? When you tour an automobile plant, the first thing you notice is that every car on the line looks the same. Of course, you are looking at the frames. The unique results are obtained from the combinatorial explosion of options that can be bolted, sprayed, and welded onto the frame. And because the frame is engineered for such options, hundreds of millions of dollars can be invested in automatic assembly equipment such as robot welders.

Programs are variations on themes that recur again and again. A software-engineering frame is a model solution to a class of related programming problems containing predefined engineering change points.

What are model solutions to related programming problems? When we speak informally about data entry or spectral analysis or matrix inversion, we are not referring to specific programs; we are referring to infinite classes of programs, each class sharing common properties among its members. Frames let you formalize what you mean by those properties so the computer can create custom program instances automatically. Where does the custom code come from? Other frames.

A Cobol implementation

The definition of frame makes no reference to any language. Frames can apply the same-as-except notion to any language (including documentation). While the language places no intrinsic constraints on frame engineering, the types of applications written in that language induce characteristic frame sets. Over the past 10 years, extensive Cobol frame experience has been accumulated (as have some with Lisp[4] and Ada[5]). Cobol applications are an excellent source of potential gains because the scope for reusability is immense.

For example, Noma Industries, Ltd., a Toronto-based diversified group of manufacturing concerns and Netron's parent company, has developed and installed more than 20 million lines of custom Cobol in thousands of programs, forming scores of different applications. We accomplished this over the past five years with a staff that has grown from six to 15 people. Moreover, some four million lines are being added or replaced each year.

The programs are composed from 30 input/output frames, 38 application-oriented frames, about 400 data-view frames (defining more than 10,000 data fields), screen and report frame generators, and one custom specification frame per program. The specification frames contain less than four percent of the total Cobol.

Of pivotal importance are the specification frames. Each program corresponds to one specification frame, which is the root of a frame hierarchy. The specification frame controls the hierarchy's composition of the program and stores all its custom aspects. Specification frames typically contain less than 10 percent of a program's source code — and specification frames are the only Cobol frames for which application developers are ever responsible.

Specification frames are created from template specification frames. A template defines a default frame composition for an application domain and provides all the important options, with explanations to guide the choices. The two-dimensional hierarchy of options is flattened into a linear list. The application engineer, unaware of the underlying tree structure, customizes a renamed copy of the template. The resulting specification frame, with the underlying frames, is processed automatically (including a compile and link) to produce an executable load module.

While the specification frame is unique to a single program (not reused), more than 90 percent of the program is constructed from frames that are reused or generic. A frame tree stratifies contexts, with generic or context-free frames (such as I/O) at or near the leaves and with custom or context-sensitive frames at or near the root.

One type of engineering change point in the frames is Break. Breaks are slots that can receive frame text from any parent frame in the hierarchy, including the specification frame. (When several parent frames try to fill the same Break, the one in the hierarchy that is at or closest to the specification frame takes precedence.)

Breaks can be located anywhere that code changes are anticipated but not specifically known in advance. Breaks are also associated with defaults, which will be used as part of the resulting program unless overridden by some parent frame.

A good technique to engineer code for such changes is to let the structured programming code units be the defaults. A good structured decomposition yields the appropriate graininess levels where change is possible.

Another type of predefined engineering change point is Select: It stores predefined variations on an algorithmic theme. For example, a date-conversion frame might map dates from one format to another. By setting the appropriate Select parameter in the specification frame (or some other parent frame), any map can be selected and constructed using a mixture of code common to every map and code unique to each format.

Select is also used to protect programs against incompatible upgrades to generic frames: Frame version symbols are used to control frame upgrades and rewrites. Select chooses the correct version according to the one locked into the specification frame at creation (when its template was copied). Any obsolete frame code that predates the frame's use of a version symbol is put into Otherwise clauses of the Selects.

(The Otherwise clause is exercised when no other Select clauses are selected.)

Obsolete frame parts can also be split into a separate file. While logically still part of the frame, they are effectively archived, so programmers don't have to wade through them when reading the frame. The archived parts are still available to old programs that are still dependent on those parts.

Text symbols, such as file names, record names, and picture-clause elements, that tend to change from program to program

---

You should always apply standards when appropriate and never when inappropriate.

---

can be defined generically. The Replace command will instantiate a specific value for the symbol wherever it occurs within the subtree rooted in the frame containing the Replace.

Because Cobol is not block-structured (so code must be separated into its various divisions and sections), the Group command is used to logically tag the code in each frame. After the frames have been spliced together, there is an automatic sort that satisfies the divisional needs of the Cobol compiler.

Frames are also handy for defining generic record structures and user data views. A typical Cobol program may deal with several files having similar but different structures. By defining record structures generically, it becomes easy to create multiple instances of such structures in one program, avoiding name clashes and the like.

Another important engineering issue is fine-tuning and optimizing code that was generated from declarative notations, such as screen and report definitions. By generating frames, rather than raw source code, such generators can now be reused throughout the program's life cycle without fear of destroying previous customizations. The specification frame keeps the custom code permanently factored for easy maintenance and retuning.[2]

Frames embody an interesting notion of "standard": You should always apply a standard whenever appropriate and never when inappropriate. But if a standard can be applied automatically on a same-as-except basis, it becomes the path of least resistance in getting the job done. Frames provide an engineering basis for this. By storing exceptions in custom frames that are separated from the standard frames, you can concentrate on needed exceptions while taking for granted the great bulk of details that are still standard.

Hence, frames do more than reuse code. They facilitate the design, manufacture, and maintenance of software. In design, a generic frame is a rigorous, parameterized analysis of a problem domain. A library of such frames constitutes an inventory of standard designs, a same-as-except basis for defining new applications.

Construction is an automated manufacturing process where frames play the role of standard subassemblies. Engineering specifications — in the form of screen and report definitions, relational data frames, and fine-tuning specification frames — are *translated* into executable code. (Conventional manufacturing requires specifications to be *transduced* from abstract to physical form, an intrinsically more complex problem.)

Rapid prototyping[6] also plays a new and important role because prototypes can be evolved into production-quality versions rather than being scrapped. There are more engineering degrees of freedom available to a software frame than to physical frames; for example, it is just as easy to subtract software functionality as it is to add it. (Try subtracting the back seat from an automobile frame.)

Debugging and maintenance efforts are reduced tenfold because there is a tenth of the usual source code to maintain. Also, rather than tracing a bug from its symptoms through a tortuous inference chain to its diagnosis, you simply read the specification frame with the symptoms in mind. The robustness of the underlying frames makes it very likely that the bug is localized to the one-shot, custom code. Moreover, all and nothing but the one-shot code is in the specification frame rather than being scattered in the nooks and crannies of the whole program.

Maintenance always takes place on the specifications, never on the resulting source code, so effort becomes proportional to the novelty of the application, not to the number of lines of source code. Logically, maintenance disappears as an activity distinct from the refinement process that produced the software in the first place.

Portability is a special case of same-as-except reusability. We handled portability this way in our software-engineering system partly by writing system tools with the system itself. The tools operate in a variety of computer hardware (IBM, Digital Equipment Corp., and Wang) and operating system environments. One set of specifications is enough to manufacture application software that will run with equivalent functionality on any of these machines.

Frame formalization

When implementing an actual frame system to be used with a particular language, you may want to change the details of the frame syntax to suit that language's style.

General frame semantics. Figure 1 shows the frame syntax. To be understood, the syntax should be read in the context of the frame semantics.

In the artificial intelligence literature[7,8] the word "frame" is associated with decomposition of wholes into parts. Here, frames are applied to the inverse problem: composition of parts into wholes. As an operator, a frame contains the glue necessary to compose and adapt the information in frames below it in a hierarchy. As an operand, it contains information to be adapted by frames above it in the hierarchy. The result is text in some target language not described here. Typically, the text is a compilable program, but could just as well be documentation or another frame. Frames are a form of macros.[9,10]

Starting with some root frame, its Text is evaluated from left to right. All Texts are a mixture of Commands embedded in some target text, such text being simply output as is. Commands handle the variations and exceptions and are always delimited by a pair of braces ({ }). The root frame is always the most specific (context-sensitive) frame. Frames lower in the hierarchy are progressively more generic (context-free).

Vital to the frame concept are the scoping and evaluation properties of parameters. (To avoid confusion between variables used by frames during program construction and variables used by programs at runtime, I shall call frame variables parameters.)

An undefined parameter, V, becomes defined by executing an assignment to it. If V is defined, *no* assignment to V in any direct or indirect descendant frame can be executed. In effect, *all assignments are defaults*, subject to overrides from more specific context frames. V becomes undefined by exiting the frame in which V is defined.

However, if frame A calls frame B with a list of executed assignments, parameters thus assigned become undefined on exit from B, rather than A, because each time A calls B a different subset of defaults may need to be executed in the tree of frames rooted in B.

These scoping rules allow the relatively context-sensitive frame A to directly modulate any relatively context-free frame in the subtree rooted in frame A — context optimizations can be factored (localized) to maximize reusability.

There are three ways to evaluate parameters. The : prefix means evaluate and convert into target-language text, and ; means do not evaluate. Thus, evaluation can take place at each assignment, at each reference, or at neither. Evaluation-at-assignment propagates target text to all frames in the subtree rooted in the first reference, while evaluation-at-reference

```
Frame_Set    ::= +(Frame)
Frame        ::= { Name Text }
Text         ::= +[Commands, $]
Commands     ::= { +[Frame_Call, Parm_Name, ((Expr, +({, })) ),
                   Assign, Group Select, Loop, Comments] }
Frame_Call   ::= Name_Ref [$] { +[Assign] }
Parm_Name    ::= (;, :) Name_Ref
Name_Ref     ::= +(Name, ( Expr ))
Name         ::= +(letter, digit, underscore)

Expr         ::= Term +[(+, -) Term]
Term         ::= Factor +[(*, /) Factor]
Factor       ::= (Parm_Name, +(digit), ( Expr ))

Assign       ::= Parm_Name = +[((Expr, +({, })) ), { Text }]
Group        ::= @ Name_Ref
Select       ::= ? Name_Ref +(Bool_Expr { Text }) .
Loop         ::= # (+(Name_Ref), = Name_Ref Expr) { Text }
Comments     ::= % +($) %

Bool_Expr    ::= Bool_Term +[| Bool_Term]
Bool_Term    ::= Bool_Fac +[& Bool_Fac]
Bool_Fac     ::= (Reln (Expr, { Text }), (~) ( Bool_Expr ))
Reln         ::= (<, >, =, <>, <=, =>)
```

Figure 1. Frame syntax. The modified Backus-Naur form (, ,) means choose one syntax option from the list. [, ,] means the list is optional. +() means choose one or more from the list. +[] means choose zero or more. $ means any literal text symbol. Terminal symbols are in reverse-video display. The delimiters { and } should be seldom used in the target language (because they are less easy to generate), and they must be distinct from the other symbols in the syntax of the commands.

propagates frame Text. Such Text is treated as part of the referencing frames. Text can be output completely unevaluated, when frames construct other frames (see example 3 in the box on pp. 14-15).

Breaks as described in the Cobol implementation correspond to evaluate-at-reference parameters (these are also called slots in the AI literature on frames). Replaceable symbols correspond to evaluate-at-assignment parameters.

Because frames must often reference frames and parameters whose specific names are not known when the frame is written (for example, when a static or prewritten frame must reference generated frames), such names can themselves be constructed from parameters.

Detailed frame semantics. For each major syntactic construct, an explanation of the meaning is provided, followed by an instance of its use.

Frame_Call: Name_Ref { }

This command invokes the frame whose name is determined by evaluating Name_Ref. Name_Ref is an expression that must evaluate to the name of a frame in Frame_Set (see Name_Ref semantics below). Recursive calls, direct or indirect, are not permitted. Frames can have hundreds of parameters, even though very few are typically altered at each invocation. Thus values are passed by overriding assignments to defaulted parameters rather than by positional correspondences between actual and formal arguments. Intermediate context frames can be used to constrain highly parameterized (very generic) frames.

The list of assignments — if executed (if not overridden in some parent frame) — cause the assigned parameters to be undefined on exit from the called frame. $ lets frames containing independent information be linked together at the same context level. If $ is present, then the Text of the called frame is processed as if it were part of the calling frame (it is not treated as a descendant frame).

For example,

MERGE $ { ;P1 = {a}. :P4 = (;Num + 1) {:A}. }

calls the Merge frame at the same level,

passing values for parameters P1 and P4 (presumably P2 and P3 exist with default values).

Evaluate-on-assignment:
:Name_Ref =

If Name_Ref has not been assigned in a parent frame, it is assigned a list of zero or more *evaluated* Expr expressions and Texts, not including the delimiters (parentheses and braces). No text is output. (If Name_Ref has been assigned in a parent frame, this assignment is ignored.) By enclosing delimiters { and } in parentheses, these symbols are treated as ordinary symbols, not delimiters of Commands (see example 3 in the box on pp. 14-15).

Because frames must often reference other frames whose names they don't know, such names can be constructed from parameters.

For example, in

:P4 = (;Num + 1) {:A}.

P4 is assigned a two-element list. The first element is the value of Num added to 1, and the second element is the evaluated value of *A*.

Reference-as-is Parm_Name:
;Name_Ref

This outputs Name_Ref's current list element for further use *as is*. If Name_Ref is not defined, or if Name_Ref is a zero-element list, its value is null and nothing is output. If Name_Ref is a one-element list, it is output as is. If it is a multielement list, ;Name_Ref must occur inside the scope of a loop command that declares it — otherwise it is an error.

For example,

;P4

Assuming P4 was assigned as :P4 above and that it is referenced in its declaring loop, the first time through the loop, the first element of P4 will be output for further use as is; the second time, the second value of P4 will be output as is.

Assignment-as-is: ;Name_Ref =

If Name_Ref has not been assigned in a parent frame, it is assigned a list of zero or more *un*evaluated Expr expressions and Texts, not including the delimiters. No text is output. (If Name_Ref has been assigned in a parent frame, this assignment is ignored.) As with : assignments, { and } can be stored as ordinary symbols. But, so unevaluated expressions and texts can be scanned efficiently, the frame processor simply increments one for each { and decrements one for each } until the count equals zero.

For example, in

;P4 = (;Num + 1) {:A}.

P4 is assigned a two-element list. The first element is the expression ;Num + 1, and the second element is the text :A.

Evaluate-on-reference Parm_Name:
:Name_Ref

This *evaluates* Name_Ref's current list element and outputs the literal for further use. If the element has been evaluated at assignment, the literal is simply output because the combination is redundant. If Name_Ref is not defined, or if Name_Ref is a zero-element list, its value is null and nothing is output. If Name_Ref is a one-element list, its evaluated text is output. If it is a multielement list, Name_Ref must occur inside the scope of a Loop command that declares it — otherwise it is an error.

For example,

:P4

Assuming P4 was assigned as ;P4 was above and that it is referenced in its declaring loop, the first time through the loop, the expression ;Num + 1 will be evaluated and then output for further use; the second time through, the value of *A* will be evaluated and then output.

Constructing names: Name_Ref

Name_Ref is a rule for constructing a parameter name or frame name. The rule evaluates Expr expressions and concatenates the resulting character strings (not including the delimiting parentheses). The constructed name must be a letter followed by zero or more letters, numerals, and underscores, or else it is an error.

For example,

ABC (;Num + 1)_23

Assuming Num's value is −1, the name of the parameter or frame is ABC0_23.

Group: @;Name_Ref

The order in which the text is output may differ from the order required by whatever consumes the output text (such as a compiler). This command invisibly tags all subsequently output text with Name_Ref's value until another group command is executed. After the root frame exits, the entire output is sorted, using the tags as the sort key. (The tags are then discarded.)

For example,

@;Generics

tags all subsequently output text (until the next group command) with the value of the parameter called Generics. Presumably the sort code assigned to Generics will cause all generic functions in an Ada frame hierarchy to be brought together in the required order for the resulting Ada program.

Select: ?

This operation assumes that ;Name_Ref is on the left of every relational operator in every Bool_Expr. The first (if any) true Bool_Expr selects the corresponding Text to be evaluated. If the last Bool_Expr is = ;Name_Ref, where both Name_Refs evaluate to the same parameter, it functions as an Otherwise clause.

For example,

? ;Matrix = {Regular} {text1}
      = {Sparse} {text2} .

will process text1 if the value of Matrix equals Regular; it will process text2 if the value of Matrix equals Sparse. If Matrix equals neither, nothing will be processed.

Loop: #

This operation is valuable when code generators and variably iterated texts are required. If a set of + (Name_Ref)s is declared, the loop is controlled by the Name_Ref with the most elements (this could change due to assignments in Text). Each time Text is iterated, each Name_Ref reference in Text accesses its next list element. The last element of each Name_Ref is reused, if necessary, until the loop terminates. Name_Refs with zero elements

Examples

The following examples are meant only to illustrate the use of the commands. Realistic frames are usually larger than space permits here. Generic frames usually carry more functionality than is used in any particular instance. Thus it is possible for the resulting code to be smaller than the frames themselves.

Example 1. Two frames combine to generate a list of range checks.

A. Here is IF_STM, a generic or reusable frame:

```
{IF_STM { # VRBL MIN MAX      { :ERR = (;ERR+1).
  IF NAME_{VRBL} IS LESS THAN {;MIN} OR NAME_{;VRBL} IS GREATER THAN {;MAX}
    THEN PERFORM ERROR_{;ERR}.
                              }}}
```

B. SPECIFY_IFS is a custom frame that uses the IF_STM frame created above:

```
{SPECIFY_IFS {IF_STM {   ;VRBL = {A} {B} {C}.
                         ;MIN  = {15} {57} {1000}.
                         ;MAX  = {30} {60} {1500}.
                      }}}
```

Assuming a suitable implementation convention for breaking output text into lines, the result of invoking SPECIFY_IFS is

```
IF NAME_A IS LESS THAN 15 OR NAME_A IS GREATER THAN 30
    THEN PERFORM ERROR_1.
IF NAME_B IS LESS THAN 57 OR NAME_B IS GREATER THAN 60
    THEN PERFORM ERROR_2.
IF NAME_C IS LESS THAN 1000 OR NAME_C IS GREATER THAN 1500
    THEN PERFORM ERROR_3.
```

Example 2: This three-part example illustrates how a problem context can be stratified into three levels (generic, intermediate, and specific) to facilitate multiple contexts of use.

A. Shown below is a "toy" routine, RIGHT_TO_BLANK, for scanning text, followed by a generic frame, SCAN, whose frame parameters default to the RIGHT_TO_BLANK version. The target language is Pascal-like. Program comments are prefixed by dashes (—) and continue to the end of the line.

```
RIGHT_TO_BLANK(p: INTEGER) RETURN INTEGER:
— Scan TEXT to the RIGHT, starting at position p, until
— a BLANK is found. Return the first BLANK position found.
— Failure to find a BLANK is detected.

j: INTEGER;
BEGIN j := p;
      WHILE NOT (j GT 80 OR TEXT(j) EQ BLANK)
        DO j := j + 1;
      IF j GT 80 THEN
        RETURN p−1
      ELSE RETURN j;
END FUNCTION RIGHT_TO_BLANK
```

Notice in SCAN that PAST_LIMIT is evaluated on assignment and FAILURE is evaluated on reference (part C below explains why).

```
{SCAN  {;DIRECTION  = {RIGHT}.  ;NOT  =. ;CHAR = {BLANK}.
        ;VAR_NAME   = {TEXT}.      ;LGTH = {30}.
        :PAST_LIMIT = {{? ;DIRECTION   = {LEFT} {LT 1}
                                       = {RIGHT} {GT {;LGTH}}.}.}.}
```

```
— Scan {;VAR_NAME} to the {;DIRECTION}, starting at position p, until
— a {;CHAR} is {;NOT} found. Return the first {;NOT;CHAR} position found.
— Failure to find a {;NOT;CHAR} is detected.
```

```
    j: INTEGER;
    BEGIN j := p;
        WHILE NOT (j {;PAST_LIMIT} OR {;VAR_NAME}(j) {;NOT} EQ {;CHAR})
          DO j := j {? ;DIRECTION = {LEFT} { − } = {RIGHT} { + }.} 1;
        IF j {;PAST_LIMIT} THEN
          {;FAILURE = {RETURN p − 1}. :FAILURE}
        ELSE RETURN j;
    END FUNCTION {;DIRECTION}_TO_{;NOT;CHAR}
}
```

B. Here we see an intermediate context frame that makes some assumptions about a class of usage for the SCAN frame.

```
{SCAN_FUNCTIONS {%Create four variations of scanning functions. User frames
        may assign VAR_NAME, LGTH, FAILURE, RIGHT-JUSTIFIED.%
    %Left-to-right until blank:%        SCAN{}
    %Left-to-right until nonblank:%   SCAN{;NOT = {NOT}.}
    %Right-to-left until nonblank:%   SCAN{;DIRECTION = {LEFT}. ;NOT= {NOT}.}
    %Right-to-left until blank (this rare case is provided only when asked)%
        ? ;RIGHT-JUSTIFIED = {YES} {{SCAN{;DIRECTION = {LEFT}.}}}.} }
```

C. Now a context-specific frame, NAME_SWITCH, is provided that uses the frame tree developed in part B. You are left to determine that the resulting source code, when executed, will extract the surname from the beginning of the input and place it behind the given names.

Controlling when evaluation occurs is important:

• FAILURE is evaluated several times, a different variation produced each time because of parameters assigned *after* FAILURE is assigned as a default override. (This explains why evaluate-on-reference is important, as part A mentions.)

• LGTH modulates every context except the intermediate context frame, SCAN_FUNCTIONS.

• RIGHT-JUSTIFIED's null default modulates the intermediate context appropriately.

```
{NAME_SWITCH {;LGTH = {30}.}
DECLARE:
    SUR-NAME-FIRST, GIVEN-NAMES-FIRST: STRING(1..{;LGTH}) := {;LGTH}" ";
    LENGTH-SUR, LENGTH-GIVEN, START-OF-GIVEN: INTEGER;

BEGIN
    READ(SUR-NAME-FIRST);
    LENGTH-SUR     := RIGHT_TO_BLANK(1) − 1;   GET LENGTH OF SUR NAME
    START-OF-GIVEN := RIGHT_TO_NONBLANK(LENGTH-SUR + 1);
    LENGTH-GIVEN   := LEFT_TO_NONBLANK({;LGTH}) − START-OF-GIVEN + 1;

    GIVEN-NAMES-FIRST(1, LENGTH-GIVEN)
                  := SUR-NAME-FIRST(START-OF-GIVEN, LENGTH-GIVEN);
    GIVEN-NAMES-FIRST(LENGTH-GIVEN +)
                  := SUR-NAME-FIRST(1, LENGTH-SUR);

    WRITE(GIVEN-NAMES-FIRST);
END

{SCAN_FUNCTIONS{   ;VAR_NAME    = {SUR-NAME-FIRST}.
              {   ;FAILURE     = GIVEN-NAMES-FIRST(1,{;LGTH}) := "BAD
                                 {;DIRECTION}-TO-{;NOT:CHAR} SCAN.";}. }}}
```

Example 3. As an interesting stunt, CLONE is a self-reproducing frame (the format highlights the self-encoding, not a desire to reproduce the blanks). To appreciate this solution, try solving it in other languages!

```
{    CLONE   {       ;DNA =    {
{({ )}} CLONE {({ )}   ;DNA =   {({ )   ;DNA ( )}}.    :DNA {( }})}
                                     } .    :DNA     }}
```

CLONE does two things: (1) It assigns an unevaluated string to the parameter DNA, then (2) it evaluates DNA: DNA's text is output as is except for what is inside the command delimiters. {({)} has the net effect of outputting a {. {({ ;DNA (})} outputs a { followed by the value of DNA, *unevaluated*, followed by a }. In other words, the infinite regress of self-encodings is avoided.

are permitted (implying zero iterations). The = ;Name_Ref option lets Name_Ref be assigned the loop counter value at the beginning of each iteration. The value is preserved on loop exit.

If = ;Name_Ref Expr is declared, the loop is iterated Expr times (Expr must evaluate to a nonnegative integer). Each time Text is iterated, Name_Ref is incremented, from 1 to Expr, and the value is preserved on loop exit. If Text contains loops, no declared Name_Ref can be declared for those loops.

For example,

```
# P1 P2 = ;TOT { Text }
```

Assume P1 has five elements and P2 has seven elements. The frame processor acts as if P1 is extended to seven elements with the last two elements having the same value as the fifth element. Text will be processed seven times, and during iteration i, the value of Tot will be i and each reference to P1 or P2 will cause element i to be processed (used as is if ; is prefixed or evaluated if : is prefixed).

Comments: % . . . %

These are delimited by a pair of percent symbols and can be placed anywhere a Command is permitted. They are ignored by the frame processor.

For example,

```
% This is a comment.%
```

Expressions.

Bool_Expr is a Boolean combination of terms using , for the Or operator, & for the And operator, and − () for the Not operator. Similarly, Expr is an arithmetic combination of terms using + , − , *, and / as the usual operators. If these operators are present, both operands of each operator must evaluate to integers, or an error results.

For example,

```
:A & − (:B , :C)
```

If A, B, and C are true, false, and false, respectively, the value of the Boolean expression is true.

The operation

```
(35 + 7) * 2
```

results in 84.

function is a map from a domain to a range. Mathematics has traditionally focused on the properties of functions. As representations of functions, algorithms have additional properties — time and space — that are irrelevant to the study of functions. Recent work in mathematics, such as automata and complexity theory, is helping us understand these properties. Programs are representations of algorithms that carry still more properties: ease of construction and modification. Studying these properties involves the formalization of software engineering.

We need a mathematics of software engineering. Because software is still new, mathematics has not gotten around to the formal study of program properties not found in algorithms and functions. The frame technique is an empirical example of a construction system that makes precise some fuzzy issues about ease of construction and modification. Frame hierarchies embody the notion of context stratification. They also provide a consistent way to reconcile inconsistent information structures: generic frames that must be blended but not at the expense of their reusability or the efficiency of the resulting program.

Can a calculus of frames be developed? How about correctness-preserving transformations? Can canonical or normal forms be found that minimize redundancy while maximizing reusability (the dual of relational database normal forms)?

Frame-based software engineering clearly works well. The bonus is that it provides grist for some interesting mills in both mathematics and computer science. ☐

References

1. Judith Drake, "Software Manufacturing: A Case Study," tech. report, Netron, Inc., Toronto, 1983.

2. Paul G. Bassett, "Brittle Software: A Programming Paradox," *J. Information Syst. Management*, July 1987.

3. Paul G. Bassett, "Design Principles for Software Manufacturing Tools," *Proc. ACM Conf. Fifth-Generation Challenge*, ACM, New York, 1984.

4. Larry Jones, "A Frame-Based Regression Test Synthesizer for VAX/VMS," tech. report, Digital Equipment Corp., Nashua, N.H., June 1985.

5. Paul G. Bassett, "Frames and Ada: A Reusability Analysis," tech. report, Netron, Inc., Toronto, 1985.

6. *Proc. Rapid Prototyping Workshop*, University of Maryland, Columbia, Md., 1982.

7. Marvin Minsky, "A Framework for Representing Knowledge," in *Psychology of Computer Vision*, P. Winston, ed., McGraw-Hill, New York, 1975, pp. 211-277.

8. Richard Fikes and T. Kehler, "The Role of Frame-Based Representation in Reasoning," *Comm. ACM*, Sept. 1985, pp. 904-941.

9. *Cobol/MP Macro Facility Reference Manual Version 9*, Applied Data Research, Princeton, N.J., 1979.

10. Calvin N. Mooers, quoted in *Computer Lib*, Theodor H. Nelson, Hugo's Book Service, Chicago, 1974, pp. 18-21.

Paul G. Bassett is vice president of research at Netron, Inc. Netron markets the Netron/CAP Development Center, an integrated set of software engineering tools based on Bassett's frame technology. Before cofounding Netron, Bassett was an assistant professor of computer science at York University in Toronto. Previously, he worked as a systems engineer at IBM and headed the real-time patient-monitoring project at Toronto's Hospital for Sick Children.

Bassett received BS degrees in mathematics, physics, and chemistry and an MS in computer science from the University of Toronto. He is a member of ACM, AAAI, CSCI, and SMA.

Bassett can be contacted at Netron, Inc., 99 St. Regis Crescent N., Downsview, Ont. M3J 1Y9, Canada.

The Reusable Software Library

Bruce A. Burton, Rhonda Wienk Aragon, Stephen A. Bailey,
Kenneth D. Koehler, and Lauren A. Mayes
Intermetrics, Inc.

The RSL couples a passive database with interactive design tools to make reuse an integral part of the software development process.

As the demand for cost-effective software rises, reuse becomes increasingly important as a potential solution to low programmer productivity. To investigate this potential solution and to promote reuse, Intermetrics has developed the Reusable Software Library.

This prototype system caters to Ada, which supports software reuse through its package and generic features. However, the RSL also accepts and supports reusable software written in other languages.

The RSL's software classification scheme and its database of software attributes have been designed to ease the selection of reusable components. More important, the RSL's tools help software developers find and evaluate components that meet their requirements. These library tools have been integrated with software design tools, making reuse a natural extension of the design process. Still more tools automate the work of the librarian, who must enter the components' attributes into the database and maintain the RSL.

Design phases

We defined a long-term, phased development plan to produce a library suitable for large software development projects. Rather than define an elaborate reuse library to be implemented in a single step, our plan is to prototype the system in parts so that we can evaluate the feasibility, utility, and potential of the design as the prototype is developed.

Table 1 is an overview of the seven phases in our approach; a more complete overview has been published elsewhere.[1] The phases progress from a small prototype library system to a fully functional, geographically distributed system. First we focused on developing a software catalog with tools for component evaluation and reuse-oriented design. Three phases are complete; the fourth is under way.

Table 1.
The RSL's phased development plan.

Phase	Activity
1. Analysis and requirements	— identify characteristics of previous software libraries — identify classification scheme
2. Develop initial Reusable Software Library	— design and implement prototype library — catalog initial holdings — provide capability for component evaluation
3. Develop initial reuse-oriented design tool	— develop interface to the library — provide support for object-oriented design tool — support inclusion of reuse components into top-level design — support automatic generation of Ada PDL
4. Integrate subsystems of the Reusable Software Library	— develop uniform user interface — migrate all subsystems of the Reusable Software Library to a common window-oriented workstation
5. Add additional functionality to the Reusable Software Library	— add tools to support component entry
6. Distribute Reusable Software Library	— provide the capability of accessing the database from multiple machines across a single company — provide support for multiple databases within a single company
7. Formulate a Reusable Software Library for use by multiple companies	— develop a Reusable Software Library which can be tailored for the needs of many companies

Architecture

As Figure 1 shows, the RSL comprises the RSL database and four subsystems

(1) Library Management,
(2) User Query,
(3) Software Component Retrieval and Evaluation (Score), and
(4) Software Computer-Aided Design (SoftCAD).

The database. The foundation of the RSL is the database which stores the attributes of every reusable software component in the RSL. All information in the database is accessible to each of the RSL's subsystems, but, to protect the database, only the Library Management subsystem has tools that can modify the database contents.

Several types of software components can be entered into the RSL, including functions, procedures, packages, and programs. These components may be written in any language. We emphasize Ada over other languages because many of Intermetrics' applications are Ada-related, and because Ada's generic packages show great promise for reuse — they are natural candidates for entry into the RSL.

Although Ada supports reusability, many factors in addition to the programming language must be evaluated before a component can be declared reusable and therefore qualified for entry in the RSL database. This judgment must be made by the RSL librarian after analyzing the component's structure, functionality, complexity, level of testing, quality of documentation, and other issues that affect software reusability.

Life cycle. We made the RSL prototype an integral part of the software development life cycle, and we expect a significant improvement in the software development process. Figure 2 shows a traditional software development life cycle; Figure 3 illustrates how our RSL prototype and other related tools have been integrated into the life cycle. The result is a more automated, reliable, and productive method for developing Ada software.

Using SoftCAD, a designer may specify the top-level design of a system by generating object-oriented graphs and Ada program design language. The Ada PDL may

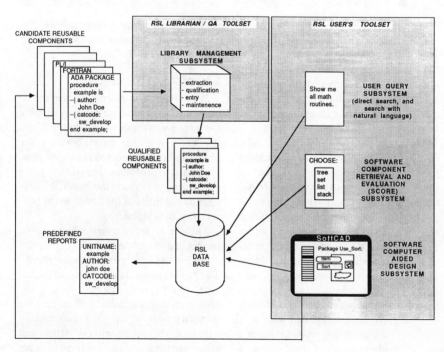

Figure 1. Overview of the RSL prototype.

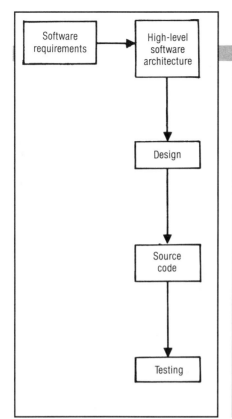

Figure 2. The traditional software development life cycle.

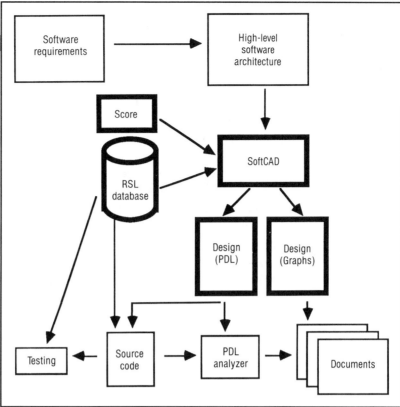

Figure 3. Integration of the RSL with the software development life cycle.

then be used as a template to produce the detailed design and, ultimately, the source code. Software documents are automatically generated by processing the PDL or source code with an Ada-based PDL analyzer such as Intermetrics' Byron PDL analyzer.[2]

Reusable components may be accessed during both the design and coding phases. Because quality assurance requires that each component have satisfied some level of documented testing as a condition for entry into the library, the time and cost associated with software verification should be reduced, provided major changes are not made to the reused code. In general, the savings realized during verification will reflect the level of the test requirements and the rigor of the enforcement when evaluating the components for entry into the library.

Library Management

The Library Management subsystem provides a set of tools to help the RSL librarian and quality-assurance personnel populate and maintain a software library.

The functions of the Library Management subsystem are to extract reuse information from design or source code files, to assure the quality of the candidate components, to enter the qualified components

into the RSL database, and to maintain the RSL.

The Library Management subsystem includes tools to insure efficient operation, including

- automated data collection,
- standardized data entries,
- continuity and consistency of reuse information across the life cycle,

---

> *The foundation of the RSL is the database of attributes of every reusable software component in the RSL.*

- completeness and reasonableness of reuse information, and
- examination of reuse information.

Automatic extraction. A program was developed on the VAX 11/750 that automatically scans PDL and source code files and extracts specially labeled reuse comment statements. We defined several types of reuse comments as attributes of the reusable components, and we gave each type a different label to correspond to the attribute (for example, the comment labeled Overview contains a description of

the component's function).

With this extraction program, the attributes of a candidate component are automatically retrieved from properly commented PDL and source code files. This data can then be reviewed for possible entry into the RSL database. The list of labels and corresponding attributes is presented in Table 2.

Selecting the software attributes to extract is really a subset of a larger question: What information should be retrieved about a particular entry? The list of storable elements seems to be highly influenced by the size of the library (number of software units stored) and the degree of cooperation (or potential antagonism) among the users of the library.

Our initial list was based on an ultimate system, one with multiple sites, multiple organizations, and multiple usage types. We came up with more than 60 attributes that could affect the suitability of an entry. This list was far too large for the prototype, so we examined the context in which the prototype would operate and filtered the list down to the attributes shown in Table 2. Only the most relevant information is stored in the library, but other information, such as calling conventions and parameters, is available from the source code.

131

Table 2.
Software attributes extracted from reusable components.

Attributes	Description
UNITNAME	The unitname is the name of the procedure, package, or subroutine.
CATEGORY CODE	The catcode is a predefined code that describes the functionality of the component.
MACHINE	The machine signifies the computer on which the component was programmed.
COMPILER	The compiler signifies the compiler used during development of the component.
KEYWORDS	Keywords are programmer-defined words that describe the functionality of the component.
AUTHOR	The author is the person who wrote the component.
DATE CREATED	The date created is the date the component was completed.
LAST UPDATE	The last update is the date the component was last updated.
VERSION	The version is the version number of the component.
REQUIREMENTS	The requires field contains information about any special requirements of the component (eg. other components that must be available).
OVERVIEW	the overview of the component contains a brief textual description of the component.
ERRORS	The errors field contains information about any error handling or exceptions raised in the component.
ALGORITHM	The algorithm field contains the algorithm used in the design of the component.
DOCUMENTATION AND TESTING	The documentation and testing field contains a description of available documentation about the component and a description of test cases.

Request	Response	Action
I need a stak package.	by "stak" do you mean "stack"? ┌ Current series of requests: ┐ I need a stack package.	The unitnames and overviews of all stack packages are displayed.
Only display those that implement garbage collection	┌ Current series of requests: ┐ I need a stack package. Only display those which implement garbage collection.	The above search is pruned so that only those stacks that are managed are displayed.
When were they written, and what version are they?	┌ Current series of requests: ┐ I need a stack package. Only display those that implement garbage collection. When were they written, and what version are they?	In addition to unitnames and overviews, the dates and version numbers of the packages from the previous search are displayed.

Figure 4. A typical natural-language query session.

Classification. The RSL's software classification strategy was based upon the combination of two alternate mechanisms.

The first mechanism is the assignment of a hierarchical category code to each component added to the library. A category code specifies the type of the component and its relationship to other components. Sample categories include common math functions, data structures, and sort and search routines. This scheme's concept is similar to the one used by *Computing Reviews*[3] and the IMSL library.[4]

The second mechanism permits up to five descriptive keywords for each component. These keywords are not associated with the category codes, allow for overlapping topics (because packages do not

> **As expected, the natural-language front end was significantly easier to use than the database query language. It was also significantly slower.**

always conveniently fall into strict tree classifications), and can grow with the project's needs (without reprogramming and without an all-knowing database administrator).

Validation and maintenance. The program that enters a component's attributes into the RSL database automatically performs limited validation of some attributes, but a quality-assurance expert (or team) must manually review each component for accuracy before the attributes can be entered into the database. A librarian is also required to enter additional information, determined by the category code of the software component. This additional information consists of both functional and qualitative data and is later used by the Score subsystem.

Maintenance of the RSL is done via a menu-driven program that lets the RSL librarian edit and delete components, add new category codes, and adjust any validation parameters.

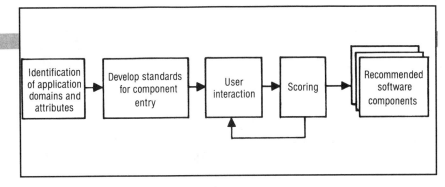

Figure 5. Overview of the Score evaluation process.

User Query

The User Query subsystem provides a menu-driven interface to search for components with specific attributes and to generate reports about their attributes. The search can be targeted on a particular attribute (author, unit name, category code). Or the search can be expressed in English with the RSL's natural-language feature ("Show me all math packages.") Figure 4 illustrates some typical requests and responses.

The RSL user may generate any one of several types of reports on the attributes of components retrieved from the database. The information contained in these reports ranges from a minimal amount of data to a comprehensive list of all data contained in the component's database record.

Although the user's interaction with the natural-language system has not been fully explored, we have observed both advantages and disadvantages in the natural-language front end.

As expected, the natural-language front end was significantly easier to use than the database query language supplied with our database management system. However, it was also significantly slower. Initial figures show a performance penalty that ranged from a factor of five for relatively simple queries to a factor of ten for fairly complex queries. With more research, this approach can probably be developed into a more viable alternative to the traditional database query language.

Score

Previous selection methods have required that the user manually evaluate the software components retrieved from the RSL. But, as the software library grows, a user may be confronted with an extensive list of software components, all of which might suit their applications. Users may be discouraged from using the library if they are overwhelmed by the prospect of manually evaluating and comparing all components in the list. A method to help the user choose among similar components is critical.

Score was developed to alleviate this task. It selects and evaluates reusable components based on the designer's responses to questions about his software require-

ments. Score helps the user select the most appropriate software to reuse by identifying components that perform the functions requested by the user and comparing their attributes to other requirements. Score then presents the user with an ordered list of recommended components.

Figure 5 illustrates the approach we have implemented in the Score subsystem to evaluate the closeness of fit between the user's software needs and the software components in the library.

Component evaluation. Central to Score's evaluation process is the identification of software application domains, because application domains determine which functional and qualitative attributes are most significant when examining components for reuse.

Functional attributes describe what the software component does and how it is implemented. Qualitative attributes provide objective and subjective metrics that rate the quality of software components. Objective metrics include line counts and complexity measurements. Subjective metrics include readability, program structure, programming style, documentation, and testing.

For Score to accurately evaluate components against the user's software requirements, it is mandatory that all components be rated against the same yardsticks. Standard metrics must be established for each qualitative attribute, and guidelines must be defined for uniform grading practices. Consistent quality ratings are especially important for the subjective metrics.

When the user invokes Score, he is prompted to specify the required application domain and to indicate the importance of each attribute that Score considers when evaluating components in this domain. Based on this information, Score searches the library for candidate components, evaluates them against the user's requirements, and rates them according to a scoring algorithm.

A similar method for evaluating components was developed by Prieto-Diaz and Freeman.[5] Their approach uses fuzzy logic, with user experience serving as a modifier to evaluate similar components. Our approach differs in that we let users explicitly describe the relative importance of software attributes.

Score session. Figure 6 illustrates a user's abridged session with Score. After the user is asked some preliminary questions to determine what type of component is needed, the Score "barometers" are displayed on the screen. Using a mouse to click on the arrows beneath each barometer, the user may raise or lower the barometer levels to reflect the relative importance of the software attributes to the application.

In the second Score screen, the user has indicated that the component's operations, its programming language, the level of testing, the quality of its overview and external documentation, and its set type (for example, multiset) are especially important.

Score then generates additional questions based on the barometer levels. After these questions are answered, a list of components is presented in the order of their suitability. The user may now choose to end the session or to reset the barometers. Resetting the barometers will result in a reordering of applicable components. Upon exiting the Score system the user is returned to the RSL main menu, where he can generate a report of the ordered components.

Score's assessment. The utility and accuracy of Score have not been completely assessed. Preliminary findings show that the Score concept is quite useful in evaluating alternative software components and in helping the user select one of the recommended components.

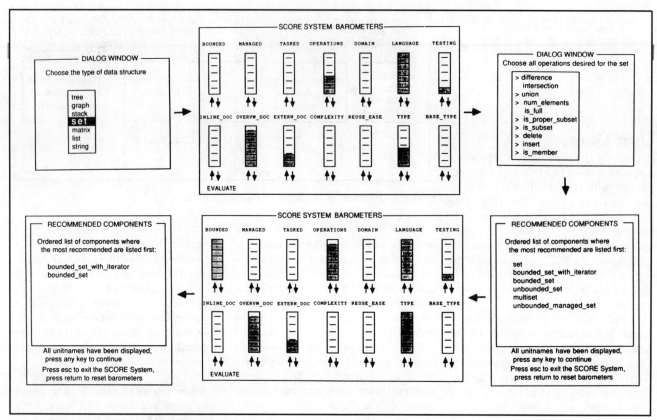

Figure 6. A user's abridged session with Score.

The interactive nature of Score facilitates an iterative, what-if process. After receiving a recommended list of components from Score, the user may adjust the barometer levels of the software attributes to reflect any reassessment of their relative importance. In this way the user can quickly obtain reordered lists of recommended components and determine their relative strengths and weaknesses.

Although Score represents a potentially powerful concept in software reuse, it is not without its shortcomings. One of the difficulties with the concept is that the software attributes mentioned above must be evaluated by people trained in software engineering techniques, and their evaluation methods must be rigorously defined to maintain consistent ratings throughout the library.

The Score system has been implemented for software components belonging to the data-structure class. Because the attributes for this class of components are well-defined in the literature, determining the type of questions was not as difficult as it might be in more complex software domains.

Several enhancements have been identified that could significantly improve the quality of Score's software recommendations. A thesaurus would help define relationships between similar attributes, improving both component evaluation

and entry. Defining uniform interfaces (for example, parameters) for components in an application domain would facilitate both manual and automated component comparison and evaluation. It would also be helpful to have an expanded selection criteria to include more information about the environment where the needed component will be used. This information could include the application area, a list of other components being reused, and a list of other components being custom-designed for the application.

SoftCAD

SoftCAD is a graphical design and documentation tool that has been integrated with the RSL prototype to aid the user in the high-level design of software systems. With SoftCAD, a designer can develop an architecture design by drawing object-oriented design diagrams[6] that are interpreted by SoftCAD and automatically translated into Ada PDL.

Because SoftCAD has been integrated with the RSL database, components retrieved from the RSL can be used in a SoftCAD design, and new components written as a result of a SoftCAD design can be entered into the RSL.

Before beginning a session with Soft-CAD, the designer would draft a rough, object-oriented design. This design should be flexible enough so the designer can eas-

ily reuse software components that closely match the needs of the proposed system. This rough design is formalized by using SoftCAD to include appropriate components from the RSL in the design.

Figure 7 depicts the sequence of events that occur when adding a reusable component to SoftCAD's graphic design. The first SoftCAD screen shows the top-level menu and the contents of the current design session. When the designer invokes the design option from this menu, he is immediately presented with the Soft-CAD/RSL screen to remind him that the RSL is at his fingertips.

SoftCAD lets the designer search for reusable components in two ways. If the component's domain is known, the component's category code can be specified. On the other hand, if the desired function is known, but the application domain is not known, the designer may choose to search by keywords that describe the component's function (up to five keywords may be specified). The designer may also search for a component by specifying a category code and keywords.

The user is free to continue with the design while the RSL conducts its search for components with matching category codes or keywords. Each time SoftCAD returns to the top-level menu, it checks to see if the search for components has been completed.

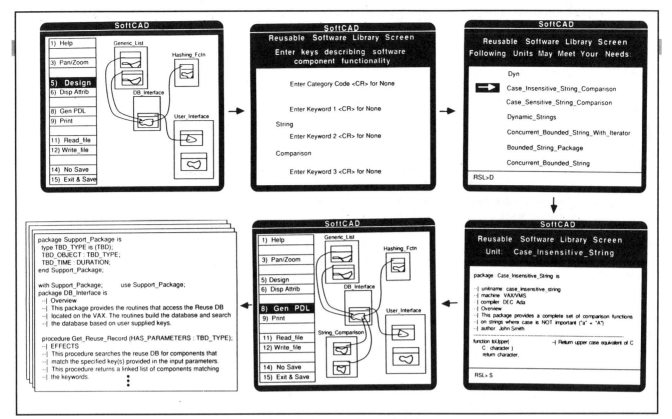

Figure 7. Integration of the RSL with SoftCAD makes reuse a natural part of design.

The third SoftCAD/RSL screen shows the results of an RSL search. The designer may display and browse through any component listed. The fourth SoftCAD/RSL screen shows SoftCAD's on-line browsing capability. The designer can scroll through the component's source code listing to determine if the component satisfies his needs. If it does, he may include the component in his design; if it doesn't, he may return to the previous screen and select another component to browse.

The fifth SoftCAD screen shows the graphical design after a string comparison package from the RSL has been included. To include a package, the designer must specify a location on the screen for the package and draw the needed subroutines to specify which of the package's functions are required. Then he may draw lines to indicate the visibility and the invocations of the package's subroutines.

The final screen in Figure 7 shows the Ada PDL generated by SoftCAD as the result of a graphical design session. Reused components can optionally be included in the PDL listing. A reused component is usually included if the designer planned to modify the component to meet unsatisfied requirements. If the component is not included in the listing, in-line comments are added to the PDL stating the component's name and where a machine-processable form of it can be found.

Enhancements

Several aspects of the RSL require work to achieve the final system presented in the phased development plan. As the system evolves, the RSL will be integrated with a Configuration Management tool that will maintain information on the frequency and success of reusing components from the library. The Configuration Management tool will also help manage different versions of the same component.

While the subsystems that comprise the RSL prototype logically represent a single system, the RSL is distributed across two computers, an IBM PC and a VAX 11/750. This distribution was dictated because the off-the-shelf software used to develop the RSL ran on these two computers. To enhance the user interface and improve its speed and efficiency, all software is being hosted on the IBM PC and a common-window operating environment is being introduced to more tightly integrate the separate components of the system.

SoftCAD will be enhanced to prompt for reuse comments when PDL code is written for a new, reusable component. The reuse information for this component may then be added to the RSL. SoftCAD will also be modified to generate an object-oriented design diagram from an existing component.

We are also examining various ways to distribute the library across different computer systems. Thus, the RSL will provide more efficient and reliable access.

Other possible tools are being contemplated to help create reuse comments for the design and source code files, and to help the RSL librarians enter components into the database. To help determine the category code that applies to a new component, a tool could be designed to recommend or select a category code based on the component's characteristics. A reuse-oriented editor could provide a template for entering reuse comments, and the editor could also verify some comments' compliance with standards. Based on a component's category code, additional automated assistance could be provided to prompt the designer for the functional and qualitative software attributes needed by the Score program. New software metrics are under examination to help standardize the evaluation of components. Well-defined metrics that accurately measure qualitative characteristics of components are essential to provide a dependable component evaluation and retrieval system.

Most important, RSL users will be solicited for comments on how to improve the system to meet their needs. Software reuse will not be advanced by a system unless it is easy to use and unless it provides services needed by its users.

The lessons learned from our efforts fall into two areas: those that involve the reuse of software components in general and those that are specifically related to the development, collection, evaluation, and cataloging of reusable components in the RSL.

Management involvement. In general, we have learned that management must be actively involved in the reuse effort. Recently, Intermetrics' management emphasized software reuse in the development of test and analysis tools written in Ada and designed to support Ada software development.

As a result, more than 33 percent of the delivered code was composed of reused packages. On the negative side, several tools initially exhibited poor performance due to the general nature of the reused packages. Tool performance was substantially improved when we used a performance analyzer and tailored the code for the new application.[7]

A significant outcome of this software development project is that management was able to achieve greater productivity by viewing software development as the production of a long-lived corporate asset rather than as an effort required to pro-

duce the current deliverable.[8]

Prototype lessons. The lessons learned while constructing and using the prototype can be grouped into three classes: standardization, domain analysis, and integration.

Although we have been able to standardize the types of reuse information (like attributes) required to document components in a reusable software library, the information submitted to the library for some attributes must also conform to some standards. Standard techniques (subjective and objective metrics) are also needed to help system librarians rate all components' qualitative attributes on an equal basis. Such standards are absolutely essential for the Score subsystem to be effective.

The ability of automated tools to evaluate candidate components depends on a thorough analysis of the application domains for the components that will populate the library. We used domain analysis to design Score for a limited domain — data structures — of reusable components, and we achieved significant success in identifying and solving several problems associated with component evaluation and selection. More analysis,

however, would certainly result in a system with greater scope and utility for a wider variety of application domains.

But perhaps the most important lesson we learned was the value of the RSL when integrated with other design tools. When we combined the passive RSL with active design tools like SoftCAD, we created a system that can be used in design and implementation. In addition, the separation of the single RSL software catalog into multiple databases of smaller size containing project-specific reusable components should greatly enhance the RSL's performance.

Although problems exist with software reuse, there are significant benefits. Recent experience in the development of Ada software has shown that reuse can increase productivity if the proper tools are available, and if sufficient thought is given to how packages are to be reused.

The Ada language and associated methodologies have helped to promote reuse. But they are not sufficient by themselves. Management's commitment and desire to improve productivity, when coupled with a comprehensive reuse methodology and a proper set of tools, offer substantial promise for improvement. □

References

1. B.A. Burton and M.D. Broido, "A Phased Approach to Ada Package Reuse," STARS Workshop on Software Reuse, Naval Research Laboratory, Washington, DC., April 1985.
2. Michael Gordon, "The Byron Program Development Language," *Journal of Pascal and Ada*, May/June 1983, pp.24-28.
3. "Introduction to the CR Classification System," *Computing Reviews*, Jan. 1985, pp. 45-57.
4. *Reference Manual of the International Mathematical & Statistics Libraries*, IMSL,

Fall 1976.
5. Ruben Prieto-Diaz and Peter Freeman, "Classifying Software for Reusability," *IEEE Software*, Jan. 1987, pp. 6-16.
6. G. Booch, *Software Engineering with Ada*, Benjamin/Cummings Publishing, Menlo Park, Calif., 1983.
7. R.L. Rathgeber, *Technical Report on Ada Test and Analysis Tools, Intermetrics, Huntington Beach, Calif., Jan. 1986.*
8. P. Wegner, "Capital-Intensive Software Technology," *IEEE Software*, July 1984, pp. 7-45.

Bruce A. Burton is the manger of the software technology department at Intermetrics, Inc. and a part-time computer science teacher at Chapman College in Orange, California. His responsibilities include the identification and application of software technologies for aerospace software systems.

His primary research interests are in software reuse for computer-aided software engineering and in real-time system development.

Burton received the MS in information and computer science and the PhD in physical chemistry from the University of California at Irvine in 1982 and 1981, respectively. He is a member the Computer Society of the IEEE and ACM.

Rhonda Wienk Aragon is a software engineer in the aerospace system group's software technology department at Intermetrics. Her interests include software reuse and database management and design.

She received the BS in computer science from Chapman College and is a member of IEEE and ACM.

Kenneth Koehler is a systems engineer with the aerospace systems group at Intermetrics. His interests include software reusability and its application to the space station's software support environment.

He received the BS and MS in aerospace engineering from the University of Cincinnati.

Stephen A. Bailey is a software engineer in the aerospace system group's software technology department at Intermetrics. His interests include computer-aided software engineering tools, distributed computing, and communications.

He received the BS in computer science from Chapman College and is currently studying for the MS at Chapman. He is a member of the Computer Society of the IEEE and ACM.

Lauren Mayes is a software engineer in the aerospace systems group's software technology department at Intermetrics. Her interests include software reuse, design and development tools, and quality metrics.

She received the BS in information and computer science from the University of California at Irvine. She is a member of the Computer Society of the IEEE and ACM.

Questions about this article can be addressed to the authors at Intermetrics, Inc., 5312 Bolsa Ave., Huntington Beach, CA 92649; (714) 891-4631.

THE REUSE SYSTEM:
CATALOGING AND RETRIEVAL OF REUSABLE SOFTWARE

Susan P. Arnold * - Stephen L. Stepoway **

* Texas Instruments Inc., Plano, TX
** Southern Methodist University, Dallas, TX

ABSTRACT

Only a small percentage of software in any given application area is unique or innovative. The remaining generic software could be reused to reduce the overall cost of producing software. The REUsing Software Efficiently (REUSE) system was defined to help software engineers catalog and retrieve existing software information. The REUSE system provides a customizable, menu driven front-end to information retrieval (IR) systems. A software organization uses keywords to build a hierarchical system of menus which reflect their specific standards and methodologies. These menus and keywords provide consistent classification of contributed software and are used to construct information retrieval queries. The REUSE system also maintains a thesaurus to reduce terminology differences within the user community.

INTRODUCTION

As the demand for new software applications increases, so does the cost associated with their development. Three reasons for the constant rise in software costs have been identified as: (1) new software systems are more complex, (2) qualified software professionals are in demand, and (3) current software development tools and methodologies are not advancing our ability to create software.

One specific area being studied in relation to increasing the effectiveness of software development is the reuse of software. By using previously proven ideas and software, the design, coding, and unit test phases could all be significantly shortened. Prototyping could also become more advantageous, in relation to both time and money.

The different approaches to reusable software can be separated into two fundamental categories: (1) active and (2) passive. [3] The active methods involve components which are executed to generate target systems. These generators are reused whenever they are executed. Since the general problem of program synthesis is very difficult, most of these systems must be specially tailored for a specific application area. Therefore, their effective user base is restricted.

The passive methods are not as elaborate. A major objective for these reuse approaches is the creation of software libraries containing generic, reusable software components, which are combined to produce new target systems. A major problem with this approach is that individual users must be aware of existing components, know where they are, and how to use them.

Many software organizations are hesitant to invest the time and money needed to convert new ideas into usable development tools. If a reusability system is to be used and accepted by industry, it must provide the needed reuse capabilities; but must not disrupt the accepted development cycle.

The passive reusability approach can be used to integrate existing software and software libraries without substantial rework. Most industries today have an abundance of existing software which must be maintained. The ability to include this existing software into the reusability system is important, thus only the passive approaches are applicable.

Another advantage of the passive reuse approach is that the existing software development life cycle remains basically intact. The basic software development methodology and existing tools would still be used and new formal specification languages would not be required.

An obvious problem associated with passive reusability is the absence of a system for cataloging and retrieving existing, reusable software. Current technology can be used to achieve this goal.

Most software designers and developers are not fully aware of what software is actually available for their use. By systematically cataloging, in one location, information concerning existing software components a portion of this problem is solved.

Purpose

The primary purpose of the REUsing Software Efficiently (REUSE) system is to encourage the use of existing software by providing a cataloging and retrieval system for reusable software components.

Three major considerations must be addressed throughout the definition process: (1) customization capabilities, (2) the ability to integrate existing software, and (3) flexibility in handling a wide variety of users and software.

The ability to customize a system continually to meet the changing needs of a software organization is a necessity. Too many existing software tools have not been used to their full potential because they do not accurately reflect the current methodologies and standards of an organization, or have become obsolete as methodologies and standards change.

The ability to integrate existing software into the REUSE system without modifications eliminates the need for costly alterations and/or the prospect of abandoning expensive, existing software.

The REUSE system must be flexible enough to handle a wide variety of information and diverse user groups. The system must respect the individual needs and personalities of the users by providing an easy-to-use user interface which offers a variety of options for manipulating the stored information. Since no two users, or organizations, are alike; the ability to customize the REUSE system is necessary.

Software Environment and User Base

The methodology and standards followed by an organization represent a collaboration between software engineers and configuration management with some input from a cross section of the development staff. It is this unique, and possibly changing, philosophy which must be captured when customizing the REUSE system.

Reprinted from *Proceedings of COMPCON S'87*, 1987, pages 376-379.

EH0278-2/88/0000/0138$01.00 ©1987

138

Overview

The overall functionality of the REUSE system consists of two major user capabilities: (1) customization and (2) cataloging and retrieval. These features and the various relationships within the REUSE system are illustrated in Figure 1.

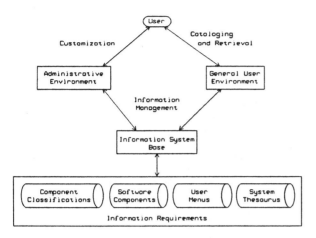

Fig. 1. Block Diagram of REUSE System

INFORMATION REQUIREMENTS

The information needs of the REUSE system are logically divided into four areas: (1) component classifications, (2) user menus, (3) software components, and (4) a system thesaurus.

Component Classifications

A set of four predefined component classifications should be adequate for the initial use of this system and most subsequent uses. These predefined classifications are: (1) template, (2) module, (3) package, and (4) program.

Template A template is the most general and user dependent of the component classes. A template is a representative model of a program, module, algorithm, or data type structure. Examples of components classified as templates include: generic sort and search algorithms, program structures associated with report generators and inventory control systems, and standard spreadsheet and organizational forms.

Module A module is a single, separable unit which is responsible for a specific function or task; typically an individual macro, data structure, or procedure source and/or object code. Examples of module components include: simple error recovery in a compiler, macros for detecting empty and full stack conditions, and a simple linked list structure.

Package A package represents a related collection of module components, usually contained in a single object library, that perform a specific task. Examples of packages include: low level file input and output, pattern matching, and mathematical functions.

Program A program is an executable entity which performs a specified function or possibly multiple functions. A program is generally user independent, although a user may be required to supply input and/or output information or options. Examples of programs include: text editors, spelling checkers, and document formatters.

Software Components

There are two major categories of information maintained for each component entry: (1) required and (2) free-form. Through these two information types, the REUSE system is able to provide a certain degree of consistency while also allowing users the flexibility of self expression. The overall purpose of the required information fields is to provide uniformity among component entries throughout the system. The required information is subdivided into two categories: global

and specific. Global information is common to all component classifications (e.g., component name and author). Specific information is associated with one or more of the component types, but not all of them (e.g., specifying a language processor to be used may be appropriate for modules and packages, but not for templates and programs).

It is impossible for anyone to anticipate what information different users consider necessary. The free-form information area allows the users to express what they feel is important, but which may not fit into the predefined menus.

As software becomes obsolete, it will be necessary to remove it from the software component structure. This will prevent the reuse of out-of-date software as well as reduce the size of the software component structure.

User Menus

A system of user menus is used within the REUSE system for cataloging and retrieving software component information. Each user menu consists of a list of keywords, which are defined to reflect the special needs of the software organization.

The number of user menus required is directly related to the number of defined component classifications. As new component types are added, new user menus must be created.

System Thesaurus

The REUSE system uses a system thesaurus when attempting to resolve terminology differences among various members of the user base and during the retrieval process to help eliminate any ambiguities or terminology differences between the stored information and the user's query. This information could also be used as an integral part of a user help facility during cataloging.

The system thesaurus stores a dictionary of words and phrases along with their associated synonyms. The primary words stored in this structure include all of the menu keywords and other non-keywords which are considered common or important to the overall organization.

INFORMATION SYSTEM BASE

In keeping with the overall philosophy of the REUSE system, existing information system abilities and concepts should be utilized. The storage and retrieval mechanisms required by the REUSE system are available today.

Selecting an Appropriate Information System

Current technology offers many alternatives in the area of information systems. Several of these systems include: (1) information retrieval (IR) systems, (2) data base management systems (DBMS), (3) management information systems (MIS), (4) decision support systems (DSS), and (5) question-answering (QA) systems. [7]

The information system is needed for low level support and for basic storage and retrieval capabilities. The additional processing capabilities available within the MIS, DSS and QA systems are not needed since the REUSE system itself will provide any additional processing.

Another major consideration is the type of data to be processed. The information processed by the REUSE system is textual in nature. IR systems specialize in processing textual information while most of the other systems handle factual data.

Based on these considerations, the IR system has been selected as a base for the REUSE system. The general storage structure and the indexing and query negotiation processes of the IR system remain unaltered. The REUSE system simply interfaces with the IR system as a individual user.

Mapping the REUSE System into an IR System

Each entry in an IR system is identified as a single document. In turn each document consists of individual words which may or may not be divided into separate paragraphs and sentences. In order to utilize the capabilities of an IR system, the software component information within the REUSE system must conform to this structure.

Most commercially available IR systems use an inverted file structure for organizing data items. [7] This storage approach provides rapid access to individually stored items. Enhanced versions of these indexes include additional word location information. In some cases, this information specifies exact term location by document, paragraph, sentence, and word. [7] By storing such precise locations, textual relationships between specified words can be determined without extensive string searches.

The enhanced version of the inverted index helps to eliminate two distinct problems within the REUSE system. The first concerns the use of phrases, as well as single words, for retrieval. The REUSE system must be able to specify both words and phrases in query requests to the IR system. By using the stored word locations, simple numeric comparisons can be used to identify adjacent words instead of relying on expensive, time consuming textual searches.

The second problem eliminated by the enhanced indexes is the mapping of the structured data of the REUSE system into the free-form, textual format of the IR system. Component classifications, user menus, and the system thesaurus can be managed in a relatively straightforward manner. Software component information provides a greater challenge.

Component Classifications and User Menus

User menus can be stored as a single document within the IR system. To properly identify each user menu and to enumerate the defined component types, the first paragraph of each document should consist of the component classification associated with that specific menu. Both component types and user menus can be accessed using this method. A specific component type exists only if it appears in the first paragraph of a stored document (i.e., a defined user menu).

System Thesaurus

System thesaurus entries consist of a primary word and a list of synonyms. This type of structured data can be handled in one of two methods: (1) the entire thesaurus is represented as a single document with each paragraph describing a single word entry, or (2) each word entry represents a single document. Either of these methods can be easily implemented and used within the REUSE system, the ultimate choice depends on the performance of the IR system in each of these situations. Using either method, both primary words and synonyms can be easily accessed and any pair of words which occur in the same paragraph or document, respectively, are considered to be synonymous.

Software Components

The software component entries are slightly more complex. They involve a combination of both structured and free-form data. An entire software component entry should be stored as a single textual document within the IR system.

Structured information consists of a specific keyword along with an associated response field. It is important that the relationships between keywords and responses are preserved while cataloging and retrieving software component information. The REUSE system must be able to request data from the IR system based on these relationships. By storing each keyword along with its response field as an individual paragraph within a total document, the special association between keywords and response fields can be maintained. To determine whether a word is used in the response field of a specific keyword, both the keyword and the specific word must appear in the same paragraph of the same document. The REUSE system must be able to construct and submit queries which search for words within a single paragraph as well as within a single document.

Obviously, the free-form information does not need to be manipulated for storage within the IR system. Therefore, the free-form information associated with a software component is also stored as a single paragraph within the overall document.

ADMINISTRATIVE ENVIRONMENT

These procedures are associated with the customization of this system to the specific needs of a given organization and are performed by the system administrator. This definition process not only provides for the initial setup of the system, but also for the changes and expansions which are inevitable in any organization.

There are four distinct functions which are the responsibility of the administrator: (1) creating user menus, (2) updating these menus, (3) updating the system thesaurus, and (4) adding a new component classification along with its menu.

Create New User Menus

Creating the various user menus must take place before any other function of this system. Once the administrator has defined the menu system, other functions within the administrative environment may be executed.

The system of menus, defined by the administrator, represents the required information related to each component entry and consists of a global menu along with additional specific menus. These menus correspond to the defined component classifications.

The first user menu defined is the global keyword menu which is used for all component entries, regardless of classification. The system prompts the administrator for the global information, which consists of keywords and their related synonyms.

The other appropriate menu structures are created and initialized through this same process. The system thesaurus is also updated to reflect the addition of the new keywords and their related synonyms.

Update an Existing User Menu

The REUSE system must allow existing menu structures to be modified. It may become necessary to make these changes so that the menu system will better reflect the overall needs of the organization.

Once the menu structure has been identified, two distinct actions are available: (1) adding a new menu keyword, and related synonyms; and (2) deleting an existing menu keyword along with its synonyms.

The addition of a menu keyword, and any associated synonyms, is similar to the initial menu creation task described above. The new menu keyword along with all of its synonyms are also added to the system thesaurus.

To delete an existing menu keyword, the administrator identifies the specific keyword to be deleted and the keyword is removed from the appropriate user menu structure, but the keyword and its synonyms remain in the thesaurus for future use. By leaving all defined keywords and their synonyms in the system thesaurus, existing software component entries are not affected.

Update System Thesaurus

It may be necessary, from time to time, to explicitly update the system thesaurus. New keywords are added automatically when menus are updated, but non-keywords may need to be added or deleted, or the synonym list of an existing word modified.

In adding a non-keyword, or adding a synonym to an existing word, the system must verify that the word to be added is not already in the thesaurus. Non-keywords may freely be deleted, but keywords are never removed, as stated earlier. Synonyms many also be freely deleted from the thesaurus.

Add New Component Classification

The final, and most infrequent, of the administrative procedures allows for the expansion of the component classification list. Since they form the basis for the user menus and stored data, the number of component types may never be reduced.

The administrator must first identify the new component type. The new component type must be checked against the existing component classifications to prevent repetitions and conflicts.

At this point, the administrator must define the specific keywords which will make up the user menu for this new component type. This procedure is similar to creating the initial user menus.

GENERAL USER ENVIRONMENT

The general user procedures are associated with the cataloging and retrieval of software components. All of these tasks may be performed on a day-to-day basis by the general users of the REUSE system.

There are four basic functions that the general user must be able to perform: (1) inserting a new component entry, (2) updating an existing component entry, (3) deleting an existing component entry, and (4) searching for existing component entries.

Insert a New Component Entry

When inserting a new component entry into the REUSE system, the user specifies both the required and free-form information associated with the software component. The displayed user menu templates are constructed from information stored in the various user menu structures. Any free-form information may be entered in any format which is convenient for the user.

The first user menu displayed is associated with the global information. This menu is used for all component entries regardless of the specific component classification.

Once the global data have been entered, the user must specify the component classification of the new entry, and the appropriate user menu is displayed. The user must now enter the component specific information. When all of the required information has been entered, the user is prompted for the free-form information. This data section represents all of the information that the user feels is necessary, but not specifically requested by the displayed user menus.

Update an Existing Component Entry

Although all information entered by the user is verified before it is cataloged by the information system, some modifications may still be necessary. Therefore, the REUSE system must also allow existing component information to be changed.

Before any changes can be made to a component entry, that entry must be located and retrieved from the software component storage area. The retrieval process involves prompting the user for any known information via the appropriate user menus.

If no component entries are retrieved, the user must supply additional information and another query is constructed. When more than one entry is returned, the user must examine the retrieved entries and identify the component entry to be modified. The updated component entry replaces the previously stored information associated with this particular component.

Delete an Existing Component Entry

As software becomes obsolete or as errors are detected, a software organization may no longer want to reuse it. The REUSE system must allow component entries to be removed from the software component storage area.

Before a component entry can be deleted, it must be located and precisely identified. This process is handled in the same manner as locating an entry for modification.

Search for Existing Component Entries

The ability to search for existing software components is the core of the REUSE system. A catalog of reusable software components is useless if that stored information cannot be accessed.

The user must specify all known information through the appropriate user menus and through additional, free-form words and phrases. This data, along with the system thesaurus, is used to format an appropriate information system query.

CONCLUSIONS

Taking advantage of reusable software, either through an active or passive system, can increase overall software productivity. The benefits to be gained from this approach affect the total software life cycle. Both time and money can be saved by using previously proven ideas and software.

The passive reuse approach has several distinct advantages: (1) existing software can be integrated without major rework, (2) it easily accommodates diverse user groups and application areas, and (3) it can be incorporated into an existing methodology without major modifications. The full potential of this reuse approach can only be realized when cataloging and retrieval of existing software is available.

Two separate facilities would be provided by the REUSE system: (1) customization and (2) cataloging and retrieval. The unique needs and responsibilities of both the users and the software organization must be reflected in these two capabilities.

The customization procedures allow the software organization to establish user menus which represent its individual standards and methodologies. The ability to modify these menus provides an additional degree of flexibility to mirror the ever changing philosophies of an organization.

This same system of menus provides a consistent base for cataloging and retrieving reusable software components. Reusable software information can be recorded and accessed in a uniform manner.

The REUSE system represents an initial attempt at solving the problem of cataloging and retrieving reusable software information.

LIST OF REFERENCES

[1] Arnold, Susan P., "The REUSE System: Cataloging and Retrieval of Reusable Software." Masters thesis, Southern Methodist University, 1985.

[2] Arnold, Susan P. and Stepoway, Stephen L., "The REUSE System: Cataloging and Retrieval of Reusable Software." Technical report 86-CSE-22, Southern Methodist University, 1986.

[3] Biggerstaff, Ted J. and Perlis, Alan J. Foreword. IEEE Trans. Software Eng. SE-10 (September 1984), 474-477.

[4] Horowitz, Ellis and Munson, John B. "An Expansive View of Reusable Software." IEEE Trans. Software Eng. SE-10 (September 1984), 477-487.

[5] Jones, T. Capers. "Reusability in Programming: A Survey of the State of the Art." IEEE Trans. Software Eng. SE-10 (September 1984), 488-494.

[6] Kidd, E.R. "Programming in ITT." Electr. Commun. 57 (1983), 276-283.

[7] Salton, Gerard and McGill, Michael, J. Introduction to Modern Information Retrieval. McGraw-Hill, New York, 1983.

[8] Standish, Thomas A. "An Essay on Software Reuse." IEEE Trans. Software Eng. SE-10 (September 1984), 494-497.

[9] Wasserman, Anthony I. and Gutz, Steven. "The Future of Programming." Commun. ACM 25 (March 1982), 196-206.

[10] Weinberg, Gerald M. The Psychology of Computer Programming. Van Nostrand Reinhold, New York, 1971.

An Information System for Software Reuse

W. B. Frakes
B. A. Nejmeh

AT&T Bell Laboratories
Holmdel, New Jersey 07733

ABSTRACT

A fundamental problem in software reuse is the lack of tools to locate potential code for reuse. In this paper we argue that information retrieval (IR) systems have the power and flexibility to ameliorate this problem. We then discuss the issue of database design, and show the viability of our approach using the CATALOG information retrieval system. The paper concludes by considering trends in IR research and development likely to improve IR systems as tools for reuse.

KEYWORDS

SOFTWARE REUSE, INFORMATION RETRIEVAL, INDEXING, DATABASES

1. Introduction

There is widespread need for safe, verifiable, efficient, and reliable software that can be delivered in a timely manner. Software reuse can contribute to this goal by increasing programmer productivity and software quality. Jones [1] reports productivity increases in the 50% range for projects with high levels of reuse.

Unfortunately, the amount of software reuse currently done is quite small. DeMarco [2] estimates that in the average software development environment only about five percent of code is reused.

A fundamental problem in software reuse is the lack of tools to locate potential code for reuse. In this paper we argue that information retrieval (IR) systems have the power and flexibility to ameliorate this problem. We then discuss the issue of database design, and show the viability of our approach using the CATALOG information retrieval system [3] [4]. We conclude with a discussion of current research in IR that is likely to improve IR systems as tools for managing software reuse.

2. Motivation for Software Reuse

The search for effective methods of promoting software reuse has a strong economic basis. The demand for software continues to rise sharply and the gap between the supply and demand for software continues to grow [5] Thus, effective means of promoting software reuse have become of paramount importance to the software engineering community.

Software reliability has also become a problem of increasing importance as real-time applications of computers emerge in (for example) financial arenas, the military, and the medical profession. In these domains there is a critical need for software to operate without failure over long periods of time, so as not to cause significant economic loss or endanger human life. Reliability is also important because maintenance now accounts for the largest portion of system costs [6], and more reliable software should be cheaper to maintain. One potential means of increasing software reliability is through the use of existing software, because reusable software components have presumably been rigorously tested and verified.

3. Factors hindering software reuse

A fundamental problem with software production in the US is that a new software system is typically constructed "from scratch" [7]. This is unfortunate because studies have shown that much of the code in a system is functionally identical to previously written code. For example, the Missile systems Division of Raytheon Company observed that 40-60% of code was repeated in more than one application [8].

The desirability of software reuse is contingent on the *value* and *feasibility* of reusing a particular type of software product [9]. The value of software reuse refers to whether it is more cost effective, in terms of time, money, or personnel, to reuse software as opposed to developing it from scratch each time it is needed. Since software reuse has its own costs, e.g. location, classification, documentation, and storage, the reuse of software is not always valuable. The *feasibility* of software reuse relates to the ease with which software can be effectively reused. *Feasibility* is dependent on the facilities provided by a software development environment, and the ease with which reusable software candidates can be identified.

Frequently, software is not reused because the *value* of reusing software is low and the *feasibility* of reuse is minimal. The factors affecting the *value* and *feasibility* of software reuse can be classified as follows:

- Differences in software development environments - if there are differences in programming languages or operating systems, the value and feasibility of reuse can be reduced because of excessive translation or porting costs.

- Reuse support environment - if the retrieval and specification of software components are not automated, the amount of time required to locate reusable software increases greatly. If potentially reusable software components cannot be located, retrieved, and reviewed effectively, reuse is neither feasible nor valuable.

- How software modules are designed and implemented - Software modules should be designed with little dependency on global variables, types, and constants. Likewise, software should be designed to avoid hardware, compiler, and operating system dependencies. A number of recent papers argue that the object oriented paradigm supports the development of more easily reusable modules [10] [11] For example, since object oriented languages such as C++ [12] allow overloading of function names, it becomes easier to write generic routines that will handle arguments with different data types. Finally, software should be implemented in accord with the programming standards and conventions established by the development organization.

4. The Need for Support Tools in Reuse Support Environments

The Japanese have been extremely successful in promoting and encouraging software reuse. Japanese software factories have cited reuse factors of 85 percent [13]. Moreover, the Japanese stress the use of keyword searching of software module abstracts to promote reuse [5].

Both the Japanese, and software researchers in the US, have argued that to effectively promote reuse we must learn how to organize, index, describe, and reference software components effectively. Standish [5] argues that "... a system of software components could be organized and indexed by conventional techniques for indexing papers in the computer science literature, and that by having each component in a software library an effective means of locating reusable software will be established."

In addition, the Hughes Aircraft Company recently studied 19 software development methodologies to evaluate their usefulness with respect to promoting software reuse. In this study Hughes Aircraft concluded that "no methodology for large-scale software development provides a reliable storage and retrieval mechanism for a code-level library." [14] Finally, Horowitz [7] states that "... there are no tools to catalog, refine, and compose [software] components in an efficient manner."

In short, there is strong support for the belief that to effectively promote software reuse we must develop tools to aid in the process of locating software components that are candidates for reuse. Such a tool must provide the user with an effective means of indexing, searching, retrieving, and reviewing software components. In the following sections of the paper we describe a tool to meet this need.

5. Types of Interactive Information Systems

Many different types of systems for handling information are currently in use. These systems have different underlying models and capabilities. Perhaps the best known type of system is the database management system (DBMS) [15]. DBMS are widely used for storing, managing, and retrieving highly structured information such as parts lists, personnel files, etc. Retrieval from these systems is deterministic. For example, if a query is put to a DBMS asking for records of all employees in Kansas City who make more than $35,000, the system will retrieve all and only those records matching the query criteria.

While DBMS are powerful, they are usually limited in their ability to handle data that is not highly structured, such as text or source code. Current systems for handling this kind of data are information retrieval (IR) systems. [16] [17] Originally developed to manage the literature of the natural sciences, IR systems incorporate many techniques for storing and retrieving unstructured data. These techniques, such as boolean queries and partial string matching are discussed below.

Because IR systems are capable of handling unstructured data, they can be used to store and retrieve products produced throughout the software lifecycle such as feasibility documents, requirements documents, design documents, code, test cases, test documents, methodology documents, maintenance documents, quality information, etc. This is not to say that the problems of designing databases to hold these documents, and assuring their quality are not difficult. IR systems do, however, offer a powerful and flexible means of coping with these problems.

As a demonstration of the use of IR Systems for software reuse, we built a small database of software modules using CATALOG, an IR system developed at AT&T. These modules were from SUPER [18], a system built at Bell Laboratories for interactive reliability analysis. The information used to index these modules was taken from the descriptive headers required of each module in the SUPER system. The text from these headers was passed to CATALOG which placed the words from the text in inverted files. Searches in this database could then be made via CATALOG's menu or command driven search interfaces as described below.

5.1 How Should Reusable Components Be Indexed?

There are two ways of indexing documents (e.g., code modules) for use with an IR system. The first way is to use a *natural language or free text* approach, which is the approach taken took with the SUPER modules. Here, terms used to index and search for documents are taken directly from the documents themselves. Lancaster and Fayen [19], point out that use of a controlled vocabulary is more expensive than use of an uncontrolled vocabulary since human indexers are required, and that use of controlled vocabularies generally requires the use of professional searchers. Specifically, they state that, *The use of a somewhat artificial controlled vocabulary, where conventions must be learned, along with the need to input search statements as boolean algebraic queries, may be a very definite barrier to the effective use of on-line bibliographic systems by the searcher who is not an information specialist.*

These statements strongly contradict recent claims in an article on reuse [20], which states that the development of controlled vocabularies for indexing software is a prerequisite for effective software reuse. Given the above considerations, the use of controlled vocabularies may increase the costs of reuse, and impede the location of of code by programmers or other non-professional searchers.

6. The CATALOG Information Retrieval System

CATALOG is an information retrieval system designed to allow end users to create, maintain, and search databases containing both formatted records, such as are typically found in DBMS, and unformatted records, such as text, which most DBMS handle poorly. It has been used within AT&T for such tasks as document management, marketing information management and distribution, in LATTIS, the AT&T IS library system [21], and in Video Data Locator, a

CATALOG application that allows retrieval of both text and color images.

CATALOG features a database generator which assists users in setting up databases, an interactive tool for creating, modifying, adding, and deleting records, and a search interface with a menu driven mode for novice users, and a command driven mode for expert users. The search interface allows full boolean combinations of search terms and sets of retrieved records, and sophisticated partial term matching techniques such as automatic stemming, and phonetic matching. CATALOG databases are built using B-Trees, providing rapid search and retrieval capabilities.

CATALOG was written in the C programming language, and currently runs under UNIX, and MS-DOS. CATALOG was originally developed on a VAX 11-780, and has since been ported to the 3B2, 3B5, and 3B20, the IBM PC, the AT&T PC6300, and the PC7300.

6.1 Searching using CATALOG

CATALOG will allow the complete source code for a module to be entered into the system providing full source searchable databases. It is also possible to enter only source code module surrogates, for example the information in the header such as title, author, and description. These surrogates are then available as primary searchable records, and the full records are available as secondary records for viewing and printing. Both record size and database size are unlimited.

Searching is carried out using inverted indexes containing every significant word in a database. Nonsignificant words, e.g. *a, an, the, is,* are those that appear in a stoplist defined by the database administrator. CATALOG creates sets of records in response to user queries. These sets can then be combined using boolean operators to form new sets. The display of these sets shows the query used to create the list, and the number of records that match the query.

6.2 Queries

In novice mode, CATALOG prompts for queries with the phrase "Look for:". In response, a query or command (described below) may be entered. For example the query:

Look for: *sorting routines*

will cause CATALOG to attempt to find records that contain the terms "sorting" and "routines", and their variants as described below.

CATALOG provides for full boolean search specification through menu selection. It is also possible, though not necessary, to specify boolean logic in a query. For example,

Look for: *((sorting and routines) or quicksort) not heapsort*

This query will retrieve source code records about sorting routines or quicksort, which are not about heapsort.

To find records relevant to a query, CATALOG will take the words in the query one at a time, and try to find other words in the database which might be related. If it finds any possibly related words, CATALOG will present its guesses to the user for selection. For the query term "sorting" for example, CATALOG might respond as follows:

```
Search Term: sorting

        Term                              Occurrences
    1.  sort                                  15
    2.  sorting                                1
    3.  sorts                                  3

Which terms (0 = none, CR = all) :
```

Users select the terms they want by entering their numbers.

The "related word" feature can be suppressed by putting the character "\" at the end of an entered word, in which case the index is searched for an exact match. The "related word" feature can also be suppressed by putting wild card characters into an entered word. Two wild card characters are available. The character "*" stands for zero or more occurrences of any character, and the character "?" stands for a single arbitrary character.

CATALOG also provides the ability to match on phonetic variants of a query term. This feature is most easily illustrated with human names. If a field has been marked for phonetic searching, the phonetic match routine will relate such names as "Kahn", "Cohen", "Cohn", etc. The phonetic match is invoked by appending the character "#" to a search term.

6.3 List Display

When a user has made his choices for all the words in the query, a list such as the following is formed.

```
Lists  (& indicates a stemmed term)          records

    a) (software)                               26
    b) (sorting and algorithms)                  9
    c) (system& and call&)                       3
```

This display indicates that three searches have been done, and that the last search formed list "c" which contains three records. These three records are related to both the concept "system" (i.e., the records contain one or more words related to the word stem "system") and the concept "call" (i.e., the records contain one or more words related to the word stem "call").

6.4 Main Menu Display

The main menu in CATALOG allows users to exit the system, access help messages, go back to the "Look for:" prompt, and perform operations on record lists. By selecting appropriate items from this menu, users can manipulate the system to give desired results such as:

- Creating new lists of records, e.g. software modules, from old lists
- Removing lists
- Displaying and printing records
- Sorting lists
- Placing records in files
- Restricted field searching
- Restricted field display
- Restricted date searching

7. A Software Template Design to Promote Reuse

The extent to which IR technology will promote software reuse is directly related to the quality and accuracy of the information in its software database. That is, poor descriptions of code capability and functionality will decrease the probability that the code will be located for potential reuse during the search process. Likewise, lack of information about how to call a function, the side-effects of the function, and the environmental requirements of the function also increase the overhead associated with its reuse. We now propose a template for the descriptive information that should be maintained for each module and function in the code base to increase the ease with which it can be reused.

Throughout this section we will use the terms *module* and *function*. For our purposes, a module is a file consisting of one or more functions. A function is as defined in the C programming language. We now describe the contents of module and function prologues which we believe will increase the probability that the code appearing in the module is located as a candidate for reuse whenever possible. Likewise, we believe that the information contained in each template will reduce the amount of time required to interface into an existing function and assure that it is performing the necessary operations without harmful side-effects.

Our basic premise is that every module and function must begin with a prologue. The contents of the prologue for each case will now be described.

7.1 Module Prologue

The following fields are suggested for a module prologue.

- Module: the name of the module.

- Abstract: a concise and short (less than 10 line) synopsis of the module.

- Description: a concise description of what the functions contained in the file do. This description should be written with an understanding that generic inquiries into the source data base will be matched on the prose appearing in this section of the file.

- Supporting Documents: References to supporting requirements or design documents should be given here.

- Size: Number of functions in module, number of lines of code in module, and object code size for each machine the module runs on.

- Contents: List the functions appearing in the file in the order in which they appear, with a brief description of each function.

- Data: List the global data defined in the file with a brief description of each data item.

- Environmental Requirements: List the hardware and software that the module requires (i.e. certain kinds of hardware, compilers, software libraries, operating systems, tools databases, etc.) to function properly.

- Documentation Quality: State the comment-to-code ratio for the module and the documentation standards used for the module.

- Portability: List the machines the module will run on.

- Programming Standards: List the programming standards document used in the module.

- Time in Use: State the amount of time the module has been used prior to being added to the reuse data base.

- Reuse Statistics: List each project that has used all or part of the module, how the module was used, when the module was used, and the person who used the module.

- Reuse Reviews: Comments from others that have reused all or part of the module. comments should be related to the performance, functionality, modifiability, testability, and understandability of the module.

7.2 Function Prologue

The following format is recommended for a function prologue.

- Function: the name of the function.

- Author: name, location, and phone number of developer who wrote the function.

- Date: date the function was written

- Abstract: a concise and short (less than 5 line) synopsis of the function.

- Description: a concise overview of the function in terms of the processing it performs. In addition, the input, output, and transformational processing performed by the function should be described.

- Keywords: Useful and pertinent keywords that can be used for quick searches.

- Size: Number of lines of code in function and object code size for each machine the function runs on.

- Complexity: Number of acyclic execution paths through function, number of logical conditions in the function, and any other complexity metrics available for the function.

- Performance: Execution times required by function for different data sets.

- Inspection: State whether or not the function has been inspected or reviewed.

- Testing: Specify the types of testing that have been done on the function (unit test, integration test, system test), the statement or branch coverage achieved on the function and the location of test suites for the function (if available).

- Usage: List the #include files necessary to call the function.

- Parameters: The parameters passed to the function with a description of each parameter should appear here. For pointer parameters, the object pointed to should be discussed. Finally, if the value of any parameter is changed by the function, the modification should be described.

- Externals: All of the global variables referenced in the function, along with how their values are modified should be described here.

- Macros: List the macros used by the function.

- Returns: The value returned by the function should be described here. The function should be declared "void" if it does not return a value.

- Calls: List the functions called by this function along with the modules in which the called functions appear.

- Called By: List the functions and their corresponding files which call this function.

- Modifications: For each change to the file, list the following information: Date, Author of Change, Description of Change, Reason for Change. The contents of this field is taken directly from the modification history maintained by the version control system in use.

7.3 Quality Control on Reuse Data Base

The motivation for software reuse is to increase software productivity and quality. However, reusing modules that are not of high quality could dramatically decrease software productivity and quality. Thus, an important issue in reuse is the quality control of the modules in the reuse data base.

The information stored in the template for each modules could be used to control the quality of the modules in the data base. Minimally, every field in the template should contain be complete. In addition, certain standards should be met concerning the content of several fields. An example of such standards follows:

- Support Documents - references to design documents used to implement the module should be included in the template.

- Data - there should be no dependency on data that appears external of the module.

- Documentation Quality - the comment-to-code ratio should be no less than 1.

- Portability - the module should have been demonstrated to run correctly on several different machines.

- Programming Standards - the module should adhere to existing coding standards.

- Time in Use - the module should have been used in one or more systems that have been released to the field for a period of three months.

- Reuse Statistics - the extent to which the module has been successfully reused by others is perhaps the best indicator of module quality. However, it may take some time for modules newly added to the reuse library to be used by others.

- Reuse Reviews - favorable reviews from those that have used the module is a good indication that the module is of high quality.

- Complexity - overly complex modules may not be easy to modify or maintain.

- Inspection - the module should have been inspected.

- Testing - the modules should have been thoroughly tested at the unit level with statement coverage of 100% and a branch coverage of at least 80%.

8. Future Directions

There are many difficult problems to be solved if IR systems are to be used effectively for software reuse, some of which we have already discussed. The requirements definition and design phases of a project are often the most difficult, and certainly have the greatest possibility for negatively affecting system costs and quality.

The ability to reuse products from earlier parts of the software lifecycle such as requirements and design documents is, therefore, highly desirable, but it is unclear at this point how this should be done. IR systems can certainly be used to locate all or parts of these documents which might at least serve as a guide to subsequent system developers. More ambitious efforts, involving the integration of all or parts of existing requirements and design documents into new systems, will probably have to await better formalisms for representing the documents themselves, the system as a whole, and the system design process.

Certain areas of IR research are likely to improve IR systems as tools for managing software reuse. Despite extensive research on IR systems, improvements have been slow in coming, and the systems in practical use today are similar to those in use in the 1960's. Improvements have in general been caused by better computing environments rather than advances in IR research per se. However the use of user feedback [22] has given experimental improvements in retrieval performance, as has the use of extended boolean models [23].

A major practical problem in IR is the management of very large databases. Databases in existence today have already pushed the limits of magnetic disk storage, and these databases are growing exponentially. Storage of the source code and documentation for projects in large corporations will also result in very large databases. Optical storage technology offers the ability to store gigabytes of information on a single optical disk, thus offering a solution to this problem. Current optical disk technology is write once, however multiwrite technology will probably be available within the next two years.

As IR databases become larger and larger, it becomes difficult to search and retrieve records quickly. To address this problem, specialized hardware to perform IR operations has been built [24] [25]. Such hardware promises to provide searching speeds for full text of millions of characters per second. Specialized hardware is also needed to speed up certain IR operations such as stemming and set processing that are bottlenecks in current systems.

A central problem of IR has been how to represent the meaning of text or other records in a way comprehensible to a computer. The knowledge representation techniques used in AI systems [26] offer promise in this direction. Oddy [27] has used a semantic net approach to document representation, production rules have been used to create an intelligent thesaurus [28], and natural language systems have been used to extract and formalize the information in medical documents [29].

Taking these newer technologies together, it appears probable that future IR systems for software reuse will have capabilities for massive storage in the gigabyte range, and specialized hardware for text searching, and set combination. Such systems will allow better semantic representation of records, and will provide intelligent interfaces that will guide users in system use. Other probable developments in IR technology can be found in Fox [30].

9. Conclusion

We have argued that reuse is crucial if we are to deliver efficient, reliable, and maintainable software in a timely manner. The lack of adequate tools to organize, search, and retrieve reusable modules has impeded reuse. IR systems have been proposed as the technology of choice for managing code reuse; and the CATALOG system has been used to demonstrate the feasibility of this approach. We have concluded by discussing important trends in IR research and development likely to improve IR systems as tools for reuse.

Acknowledgements

A number of people have contributed to this work in various ways. Bill Leighton and Siroos Aftshar used CATALOG to build a database of software modules at AT&T Information Systems. Their experience pointed out both the potential of using CATALOG for reuse, and the difficulties of designing a database for reuse. Chris Fox and Stew Crawford reviewed earlier versions of this manuscript, and offered many valuable suggestions.

REFERENCES

1. Jones, Capers, *Programming Productivity*, New York, McGraw-Hill Book Company, 1986.

2. DeMarco, T., Lister, T. *Controlling Software Projects: Management, Measurement, and Evaluation*, Seminar Notes, New York, Atlantic Systems Guild Inc., 1984.

3. Frakes, W.B. "Term Conflation for Information Retrieval", in VanRijsbergen C.J. Ed. *Research and Development in Information Retrieval* Cambridge: Cambridge University Press, 1984.

4. Frakes, W.B., Leighton W.J., "The Catalog Information Management System", *Proceedings of Symposium on Workstations in the Future Computing Environment* , AT&T Bell Laboratories , Naperville Il., 1985.

5. Standish, T., "An Essay on Software Reuse", *IEEE Transactions on Software Engineering*, Vol. SE-10, Sept. 1984.

6. Boehm, Barry, *Software Engineering Economics*, Prentice-Hall, Englewood Cliffs N.J., 1981.

7. Horowitz, E. and Munson, J. "An Expansive View of Software Reuse", *IEEE Transactions on Software Engineering*, Vol. SE-10, Sept. 1984.

8. Frank, W.L., "What Limits to Software Gains", *Computerworld*, pp. 65-70, May 4, 1984.

9. Grabow, P., "Software Reuse, Where Are We Going?", *IEEE COMPSAC85*, Oct. 9-11, 1985, pp.202.

10. Cox, Brad J., *Object Oriented Programming*, Reading Mass: Addison-Wesley, 1986.

11. Meyer, B., "Reusability: The Case for Object Oriented Design", *IEEE Software*, v.4, no. 2, March 1987.

12. Stroustrup, B., *The C++ Reference Manual*, Reading Mass: Addison-Wesley, 1986.

13. McNamara, D. "Japanese Software Factories", presentation at Computer Science Colloquium, University of California, Irvine, May 1983.

14. Huang, C., "Reusable Software Implementation Technology : A Review of the Current Practice", *IEEE COMPSAC85*, Oct. 9-11, 1985, pp.207.

15. Date, C. J., *An Introduction to Database Systems*, 3rd Ed. Reading, Mass., Addison Wesley, 1981.

16. Lancaster F. W. and Fayen, E. G. *Information Retrieval On-Line*, Los Angeles, Melville Publishing Co., 1973.

17. Salton G. and McGill M. *Introduction to Modern Information Retrieval*, New York, McGraw-Hill, 1983.

18. Crocker, S.L., Frakes, W.B., Leon, R.V., Tortorella, M., "SUPER: System Used for Prediction and Evaluation of Reliability", Paper read at IEEE Conference on Reliability of Computer Controlled Telecommunications Systems, 1985, at Val David, Canada.

19. Lancaster, F. W. and Fayen, E. G. *Information Retrieval On-Line*, Los Angeles, Melville Publishing Co., 1973.

20. Prieto-Diaz, R., and Freeman, P., "Classifying Software for Reusability", *IEEE Software*, v.4, no.1, January, 1987.

21. Frakes, W.B., "LATTIS: A Corporate Library and Information System for the UNIX Environment", *Proceedings of the National Online Conference*, 1986.

22. Rocchio, J. J., "Relevance Feedback in Information Retrieval" in *The SMART Retrieval System - Experiments in Automatic Document Processing*, G. Salton Editor, Prentice-Hall Inc., Englewood Cliffs N.J., 1971, Chapter 14.

23. Salton, G., Fox, E., Wu, H., "Extended Boolean Information Retrieval", *Communications of the ACM*, 26(11): pp. 1022-1036, Nov, 1983.

24. *Proceedings of the Fourth Workshop on Computer Architecture for Nonnumeric Processing*, Syracuse, N.Y. 1979.

25. Hollaar, L.A., "The Utah Text Retrieval Project -- A Status Report", in VanRijsbergen C.J. Ed. *Research and Development in Information Retrieval* Cambridge: Cambridge University Press, 1984.

26. Winston, Patrick Henry, *Artificial Intelligence* 2nd Ed., Reading Mass., 1984.

27. Oddy, R. N., "Information Retrieval Through Man-Machine Dialogue", *Journal of Documentation*, 33. 1-14(1977).

28. McCune, B. et. al. "RUBRIC: A System for Rule Based Information Retrieval", *IEEE Transactions of Software Engineering*, 1985.

29. Sager, Naomi, "Information Structures in Texts of a Sublanguage", *Proceedings of 44th ASIS Annual Meeting*, Washington D.C., October 1981.

30. Fox, Christopher and Zappert, F., "Future Generation Information Systems", To appear in the *Journal of the American Society for Information Science*.

BREATHING NEW LIFE
into Old Software

Ruben Prieto-Diaz/Gerald A. Jones, GTE Laboratories

Software re-usability improves the productivity and quality of software development. By using existing software components to develop new applications, overall development costs and the time needed to bring a new product to market are reduced. Moreover, software quality is improved because components that already have been tested and proven effective are incorporated into new systems.

In well-established disciplines, like civil engineering or electrical engineering, reusability is a standard part of development. Electrical engineers, for example, consult component catalogs continuously during the design process to check what available part best fits the design constraints. In many cases, the original design requirements are modified to take advantage of existing components.

In software engineering, however, reusability has not been as widely practiced. This can be attributed to the generally accepted belief that it is not as difficult to customize software as to customize material objects. But this attitude is quickly changing as the complexity and cost associated with software development continue to grow. Today, many organizations view software reusability as an indispensable technology that must be developed to ensure future competitiveness.

It is estimated that, in some application domains, only 15 percent of all software is unique and specific to a single application. The remaining 85 percent is common, generic and potentially reusable across applications (1). In commercial data processing, Raytheon has reported reusability figures of 60 percent and greater (2). In process control applications, Toshiba has reported productivity increases of 14 percent every year for five years by applying a 'software factory' approach that emphasizes software reusability (3). Such figures indicate the tremendous potential for software reusability.

REUSABILITY — APPROACHES AND ISSUES

There is a great variety of possible approaches to software reusability. The two primary approaches are the "building block" approach and the "generative" approach. The building block approach emphasizes the creation of new software from existing components retrieved from a reusability library. In the generative approach, reusable components are built into a tool (such as an application generator) and much of the work of selecting, customizing, and composing the components is automated.

Reusable building blocks can span all levels of software, including specification, design, and code. They may range in size from complete subsystems down to individual modules or fragments. Both application-specific components and general purpose components are important. Some components can be reused "as-is" while others may have to be customized for each application.

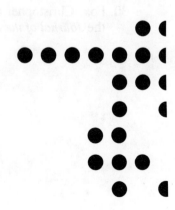

Category	Issue	Examples
Technical	Domain Analysis	component identification/standardization
	Methodology	design "for"/"with" reusability
	Environment	integrated tool support
	Library	component classification/retrieval
	Transformation	component customization
	Language	abstraction/encapsulation mechanisms
Management	Organizational	establish/support project independent reusability group
	Motivational	abolish "not-invented-here" syndrome; employee training/incentives
	Financial	accept up-front costs

Figure 1. There are many important issues—technical and managerial—related to implementing a successful software reusability program within an organization. A few key examples are listed above.

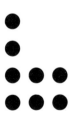
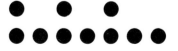

There is no single best approach. Rather, a combination of approaches, dependent on an organization's individual needs, should be applied to provide the greatest impact.

There is much that can be done now to improve software reusability and the future holds promise of even greater gains. Yet there are many important issues that must be resolved in order to realize these gains. Figure 1 lists some of the key technical issues that must be researched to provide these improvements and also lists important management issues related to putting the technology into practice.

SOFTWARE ASSET MANAGEMENT

GTE Data Services (GTEDS) is a subsidiary of GTE with responsibility for providing computer-based services to GTE Telephone Companies worldwide. As such, GTEDS is one of the largest developers of software within the Corporation.

GTEDS management has recognized the important role of reusability in improving the productivity and quality of new information products. Accordingly, GTEDS established the Asset Management Program (AMP) in 1986.

The Asset Management Program's aim is to create, maintain and make available a collection of reusable assets. A reusable asset in this context is defined as any facility that can be reused in the process of producing software. The program's emphasis is on reusable software components.

Figure 2 provides an overall view of how the Asset Management Program is structured. Overseeing the activities of the AMP is the *asset management group*. This group is responsible for setting the policies on asset acquisition and distribution, for managing the program budget, and for promoting asset use.

Central to the AMP is the creation of an asset library, consisting of an *asset shelf* (containing the assets) and an *asset catalog* (containing asset descriptions).

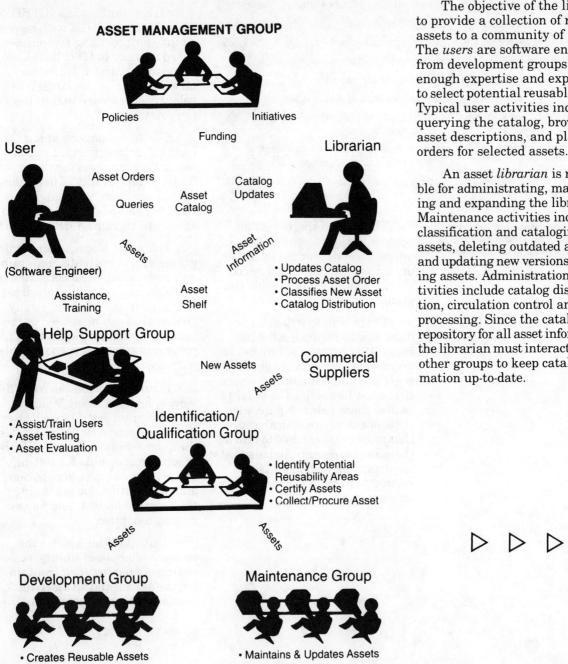

ASSET MANAGEMENT GROUP

Policies

Initiatives

Funding

User

Asset Orders

Queries

Asset Catalog

Librarian

Catalog Updates

Assets

Asset Information

(Software Engineer)

Assistance, Training

Asset Shelf

• Updates Catalog
• Process Asset Order
• Classifies New Asset
• Catalog Distribution

Help Support Group

New Assets

Commercial Suppliers

Assets

Identification/ Qualification Group

• Assist/Train Users
• Asset Testing
• Asset Evaluation

• Identify Potential Reusability Areas
• Certify Assets
• Collect/Procure Asset

Assets

Assets

Development Group

Maintenance Group

• Creates Reusable Assets

• Maintains & Updates Assets

Figure 2. The objective of the Asset Management Program is to create, maintain and make available a collection of reusable software.

The objective of the library is to provide a collection of reusable assets to a community of users. The *users* are software engineers from development groups with enough expertise and experience to select potential reusable assets. Typical user activities include querying the catalog, browsing asset descriptions, and placing orders for selected assets.

An asset *librarian* is responsible for administrating, maintaining and expanding the library. Maintenance activities include classification and cataloging new assets, deleting outdated assets and updating new versions of existing assets. Administration activities include catalog distribution, circulation control and order processing. Since the catalog is the repository for all asset information, the librarian must interact with all other groups to keep catalog information up-to-date.

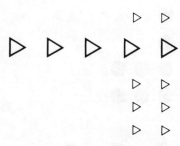

An *identification and qualification group* has responsibility for building the asset shelf. This group identifies and certifies new assets. Existing and new projects must be analyzed with respect to their application domain to determine which software components have high potential for reusability. The group also collects existing assets and certifies them for inclusion in the library.

Development and maintenance groups consist of software development teams. These groups produce assets as assigned by the identification and qualification group or they submit existing components that they think will qualify as reusable assets. Often the same group that submits an asset will be in charge of maintaining the asset.

Thus far, approximately 200 reusable assets have been collected and catalogued from existing projects as part of the Asset Management Program. Work currently is under way to expand this number to 1,000 within the next two years. A printed catalog of assets already is available to users, and an automated library system is nearing completion.

CLASSIFYING SOFTWARE FOR REUSABILITY

Research in software classification conducted at GTE Laboratories supports the GTEDS Asset Management Program. Effective use of an asset library system depends on an appropriate classification scheme to organize the collection.

Classification is the act of grouping like things together. All members of a group (or class) share at least one characteristic that members of other classes do not possess. Classification displays the relationships among classes of things.

The result is a network or structure of relationships. A classification scheme is a tool for the production of systematic order based on a controlled and structured index vocabulary. This index vocabulary is called the classification schedule. It consists of the set of names or symbols representing concepts or classes, listed in systematic order, to display relationships between classes (4).

Two types of classification schemes are used in library science—enumerative and faceted. The traditional, enumerative method postulates a universe of knowledge divided into successively narrower classes. These classes include all the possible subclasses and compounded classes arranged in hierarchial relationships. The Dewey Decimal system is a typical example of an enumerative hierarchy with a branching factor of 10 where all possible classes are predefined and listed in a ready-made classification schedule.

The faceted approach, proposed by Ranganathan in 1939 and used by many libraries in India and Europe, relies not on the breakdown of the universe, but on the building up or synthesizing from the subject of particular documents.

Through this method, subject statements are analyzed into their component elemental classes, and these classes are listed in the schedule. Their generic relationships are the only relationships displayed. When the classifier, using such a scheme, has to express a compound class, this is accomplished by assembling its elemental classes. This process is called synthesis. The arranged groups of elemental classes making up the scheme are called facets. Facets are considered the perspectives, viewpoints or dimensions of a particular domain.

In library science, the classification process consists of selecting from a classification schedule the class that best describes or represents the title to be entered into the library. In the Dewey Decimal system, for example, the title *Structured Systems Programming* would be classified by choosing the predefined class from the hierarchical structure that best describes the title. Figure 3 provides a partial listing of the Dewey Decimal system hierarchy for this example.

An inherent problem with enumerative schemes is traversing the hierarchical tree to find the appropriate class. In the example, the librarian could have ended the traversal in any of the following classes: system analysis (001.61), software (001.642 5), systems (003), systems analysis (620.72) or systems construction (620.73).

Therefore, it is critically important in this type of classification scheme that the librarian have expertise in both the classification scheme and the subject matter of the title. Selecting the most appropriate class is a difficult task because more than one class may be applicable. To compensate for such ambiguity cross references are established, but cross referencing is a cumbersome and error-prone process.

Figure 3. This partial listing of the Dewey Decimal system hierarchy shows the typical problem with enumerative schemes. A title such as *Structured Systems Programming* may not neatly fall into one of the predefined classes.

Faceted classification, on the other hand, is more straightforward. To classify a title, a term is selected from each facet to best describe the concepts in the title. Figure 4 illustrates a partial listing of a hypothetical faceted scheme for the example. For the title *Structured Systems Programming*, 'systems' was chosen from the entities facet, and 'programming' from the activity facet. This results in a synthesized class called systems/programming. In this way, the faceted approach enables a class to be tailored specifically to the subject. By contrast, an enumerative scheme forces the librarian to choose from a collection of standard classes.

... entities	activity ...
1. programs	1. programming
2. designs	2. design
3. systems	3. evaluation
4. structures	4. analysis
.	.
.	.
.	.

Figure 4. This partial listing of a hypothetical faceted scheme contrasts with the hierarchy scheme. For the title *Structured Systems Programming*, a new class (systems/programming) would be synthesized from the existing facets.

FACETS					
function	objects	medium	system-type	functional-area	setting
add	arguments	array	assembler	accounts-payable	advertising
append	arrays	buffer	code-generation	accounts-receivable	aircraft-manufacture
close	backspaces	cards	code-optimization	analysis-structural	appliance-store
compare	blanks	disk	compiler	auditing	association
complement	buffers	file	DB-management	batch-job-control	auto-repair
compress	characters	keyboard	expression-evaluator	billing	barbershop
create	descriptors	line	file-handler	bookkeeping	broadcast-station
decode	digits	list	hierarchical-DB	budgeting	cable-station
delete	directories	mouse	hybrid-DB	capacity-planning	car-dealer
divide	expressions	printer	interpreter	CAD	catalog-sales
evaluate	files	screen	lexical-analyzer	cost-accounting	cemetery
exchange	functions	sensor	line-editor	cost-control	circulation
expand	instructions	stack	matrix-inverter	customer-information	classified-ads
format	integers	table	pattern-matcher	DB-analysis	cleaning
input	lines	tape	predictive-parsing	DB-design	clothing-store
insert	lists	tree	relational-DB	DB-management	composition
join	macros		retriever	modeling	computer-store
measure	pages		scheduler		
modify					
move					

Figure 5. A partial listing of a faceted classification schedule for a collection of small, general purpose software components.

Figure 5 provides an example of a faceted classification scheme for reusable software components. The example provides a partial listing of a preliminary faceted classification schedule used for a collection of 200 small, general purpose software components (5). Six facets were identified. The first three—function, objects and medium—describe program functionality. The last three—system type, functional area and setting—describe the program environment. To classify a component using this scheme, the librarian selects the term under each facet that best describes the component.

The faceted approach offers a very attractive method for classifying reusable software. In addition to tailoring classifications to the specific subject, facets may be ordered by their relevance to the users of the collection. For example, the classification scheme for *Structured Systems Programming* could list 'activity' as the first facet and 'entities' as the second. The resulting classification, programming/systems, then emphasizes the activity facet. This feature enhances search and retrieval performance when used to organize a database.

Another important feature enables terms to be ordered within each facet according to how closely related they are to each other. This feature allows one to find similar items in a collection, something essential for reusability.

Typically, "linear ordering" is used to identify related terms within a facet. In this method, two closely related terms are listed next to each other while nonrelated terms are listed far apart from each other.

This idea has been extended to provide an even more precise measurement of similarity among terms. Every term in a facet is related to one or more general terms or supertypes by means of a weighted conceptual distance graph. (See Figure 6.)

The conceptual distance graph provides a more objective measurement of conceptual closeness among terms than can be achieved by a linear list. If no match of a description can be made during the initial retrieval process, the conceptual graph provides the user with other closely related terms. These terms can be used to generate queries for retrieving closely related components.

Such a feature is key to establishing a successful library system for reusable software because it is unlikely that a user will find a single component that satisfies all specifications. Instead, the user may find several candidates that partially satisfy the specifications. Being able to retrieve a group of components closely related to the original specifications is a great aid to the user.

Figure 6. A weighted conceptual distance graph to show the closeness between related terms. For example, the term *measure* is closer (more similar) to *add* (distance 6) than to *move* (distance 16).

A faceted scheme also provides expandability and flexibility. In a faceted scheme, new classes can be easily added as new terms under the appropriate facet. By contrast, in an enumerative scheme, adding a new class generates several new cross references from related classes. Working with such a predefined hierarchy would be especially difficult in technologies experiencing rapid growth, such as computers.

In summary, the faceted approach is the most flexible and precise scheme for large, continuously expanding collections such as reusable software components.

THE ASSET LIBRARY SYSTEM

A prototype asset library system based on faceted classification is currently being developed to support the GTEDS Asset Management Program. The faceted classification scheme uses five facets: Functional Area, Action, Object, Language and Hardware.

The Functional Area is the general functional name (e.g., keyboard interface or file handler) for the area in which the component resides. Action and Object are the lower level verb/noun descriptions of the function performed by the components (e.g., format/reports or convert/dates). An individual component may have multiple action/object descriptors. The Language facet indicates the programming language used to write the software component, and the Hardware facet indicates the machine environment for the component (e.g., IBM Mainframe, PC or Tandem).

As a group, these facets provide users with several different perspectives from which they can search for reusable software.

Figure 7 provides an overall data flow diagram for the library system. The system contains three external interfaces—the user, the librarian and the asset manager.

The user places requests in the form of queries to the *query and retrieve subsystem* and obtains descriptors of assets that satisfy the request. Figure 8 illustrates the system interface for the user to create a query.

During the query process, the user is assisted by various vocabulary tables which contain valid terms organized in a faceted classification. A thesaurus is used for each facet to resolve semantic ambiguities during query construction.

Closeness metrics for terms in the system vocabulary are used by the query and retrieve subsystem to provide the user with descriptors of components similar to the original request. The user also can have the system rank the descriptors by their degree of reusability. The ranking is based on reusability-related metrics such as component size, complexity and documentation quality. If satisfied, the user may then invoke the *order asset subsystem* to obtain an asset from the asset shelf.

The query and retrieve subsystem keeps a detailed log of all user activities in the usage data files. Off line analysis of these files, through the *analyze usage subsystem*, provide the librarian and asset manager with essential feedback for customizing and tuning the system.

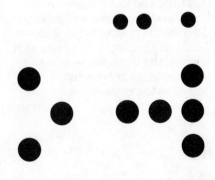

All classification schemes must be customized for a particular environment so that it satisfies user needs. Customization is achieved by integrating the users' terminology in the vocabulary and by analyzing the semantics of terms used to form the queries. This analysis also provides data for tuning the conceptual distance graphs and the ranking system.

The librarian analyzes the usage reports generated by the analyze usage subsystem and collects data from the environment to customize and tune the library system. The librarian has a specialized interface to access all database tables (i.e., asset catalog, classification schedules, thesauri, conceptual graphs and ranking functions).

The role of the asset manager is to coordinate the steady operation of the system by providing the required assets and user information, and by observing the effectiveness of system operation.

System specifications and high-level design of the library system were jointly developed by GTE Laboratories and GTE Data Services (GTEDS). GTEDS is implementing a version of the system on an IBM mainframe while GTE Laboratories implements a version on an IBM personal computer. The initial system release emphasizes the query and retrieve functions and the gathering of system usage data. Data from this release will be used in future releases to extend functionality and tune the system.

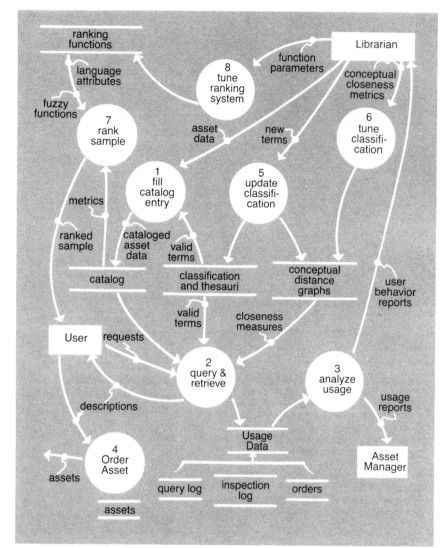

FUTURE DIRECTIONS

Research into software classification and library support is only one aspect of GTE Laboratories' work in software reusability. Two other areas of current research involve domain analysis and methodology/environment support for reusability.

Figure 7. The dataflow diagram for the asset library system shows the major functionality of the system to support the user, the librarian, and the asset manager.

```
QUERY                   —ASSET LIBRARY SYSTEM—

Please enter values for each of the search fields below
(use ? for field help, * for wild-card):

Functional-Area  ____
Action           ____
Object           ____
Hardware         ____
Language         ____

In addition you may specify other arbitrary keywords for textual
searching. Separate the words with commas.

Keywords  ____

F1    F2    F3    F4    F5    F6    F7    F8    F9    F10
Help         Retrieve                                 Return
```

Figure 8. To query the asset library system, the user can either enter terms directly or interact with system vocabulary tables to help in forming the query. In addition, the system allows users to specify arbitrary keywords for textual searching of component text descriptions. After the query is formed, the catalog is searched to retrieve asset descriptors that match (or are similar to) the query. The user can then broaden or narrow his query to alter the search.

Domain analysis is important to reusability for two reasons. First, to produce meaningful terms and an effective thesaurus, the domain for the vocabulary must be analyzed. This means that objects, operations and their relationships must be identified in a particular domain before names and semantics can be created that users will understand.

The second reason domain analysis is important to reusability is that it forms the basis for creating reusable components. Instead of building an ad-hoc collection of software components, components should be built that encapsulate common objects and operations identified by domain analysis. Such an approach substantially increases the reusability potential of a software collection.

Methodology/environment support is also crucially important. Unless reusability is made a standard part of software development methodology and is supported by an integrated development environment, reusability will remain the exception, instead of the norm.

Current focus is on methodology/environment support for the front end of the software development process (i.e., specification and design). This is where the most potential of significant impact for reusability exists. Accordingly, GTE Laboratories is researching ways of reusing specifications and designs as a natural part of the development process.

REFERENCES

1. T.C. Jones, **Reusability in Programming: A Survey of the State of the Art,** IEEE Transactions on Software Engineering, Vol. SE-10, No. 5, pp. 488-493 (September 1984).

2. R. Lanergan and C. Grasso, **Software Engineering with Reusable Design and Code,** IEEE Transactions on Software Engineering, Vol SE-10, No. 5, pp. 498-501 (September 1984).

3. Y. Matsumoto, et. al., **SWB System: A Software Factory,** Software Engineering Environments (H. Hunke, editor), North-Holland, pp. 305-318 (1981).

4. R. Prieto-Diaz **Classifying Software for Reusability,** IEEE Software, Vol. 4, No. 1, pp. 6-16 (January 1987).

5. R. Prieto-Diaz and P. Freeman, **A Software Classification Scheme,** Ph.D. Dissertation, Department of Information and Computer Science, University of California, Irving CA (1985).

Software Classification

SOFTWARE CLASSIFICATION AS AN AID TO REUSE: INITIAL USE AS PART OF A RAPID PROTOTYPING SYSTEM(1)

Emmanuel O. Onuegbe

Honeywell Corporate Systems Development Division
1000 Boone Avenue North
Golden Valley, MN, 55427.
Phone (612) 541-6819

Abstract

A classification scheme for software parts that are archived for reuse in a software base is described in this paper. This classification scheme derives from the object-oriented paradigm which groups objects based on shared semantics. Also described, is the design of an associated browsing tool. The entire apparatus for software reuse is part of the RAPIER (RAPid Prototyping to Identify End User Requirements) system being developed by Honeywell's Corporate Systems Deveopment Division's Computer Sciences Center.

1 INTRODUCTION

The ease of locating a potentially reusable software part is a motivation for the user who wants to search for, and reuse such a part. Many of today's software repositories, for example the Ada(1) SIMTEL repository on ARPANET, are not easy to use especially if the user is not familiar with the names of the software parts they contain, and cannot guess portions of some of the keywords needed to retrieve the part. Modern database management systems especially, relational databases, allow the user to retrieve candidate software parts through the use of associative queries. Modules are described by simply putting some values in database attributes (for example name-of-author, function, timestamp, or where_used). This classification, flexible as it has become, is based on the syntax of values in database attributes rather than on semantics.

The classification of objects in modern object-oriented programming systems such as SMALLTALK [GOLDBERG83] is more meaningful than database classifications in the sense that the system has generic hierarchies of objects that have been built up, based on semantics. But, outside of the small set of predefined objects which the original implementors of the system have provided, these small object-oriented systems do not provide mechanisms for continual update to the software base.

In our work on a system for rapid prototyping, there is need to construct the software from a library of reusable Ada components that are stored in a large software base. Because new software is continually inserted into the software base, some of the software may possess the same behavior. Also, a librarian or database administrator can delete any of the components at any time (for example, a piece of software could be too slow, or unreliable). In order for future users to trust it, such an archival library must incorporate a methodology for guaranteeing the correctness of the classifications. In the short-term, a manual method of verification, such as software audits, may suffice; in the long-term, however, a

(1) This research was funded in part by contract No. N00014-85-C-0666 from the Office of Naval Research.

(1) Ada is a registered trademark of the U.S Department of Defence, AJPO.

mechanized approach such as mechanical theorem proving should be incorporated into the software base management system (SBMS). An object-oriented classification scheme for a large, shared software base, has been formalized for use in the RAPIER system; there is also a phased approach to its implementation. An accompanying browsing tool, with which a user with little or no previous knowledge of the system can peruse the contents of the software base, has also been designed.

In the rest of this paper, there is a description of the RAPIER system and a background of the software classification problem. Then the clasification scheme and the design of an associated browsing tool are pesented. There is also a summary and a discussion of implementation approaches.

2 BACKGROUND

2.1 THE RAPIER SYSTEM

The RAPIER system is designed as a vehicle for investigating computer system and software requirements for embedded computer systems. The system is targeted towards two types of users. One user is the prototype developer who is an expert in computer systems engineering and works with the prototyping system to investigate user requirements for some critical portions of a system under specification. The other user is the domain expert, who is not always developing computer systems (for example the procurement specialist), but who must use the system in order to address critical portions of a requirements document. For these two users, the ease-of-use of the system is important. Since the RAPIER is intended for generating prototypes that could be disposed of rather than for incremental development of systems, it is important that prototypes be generated quickly and cheaply.

One way to generate prototypes quickly and cheaply is to reuse software components -- designs and code. The other way is to generate the code automatically. Our goal in RAPIER is to reuse what software components are available and to generate code for those portions of the specification that cannot be implemented by reusing existing components. The subject of this paper is software reuse and, specifically, the classification of software.

2.2 SOFTWARE CLASSIFICATION

A classification scheme that models user perceptions of module functions is critical to the success of the SBMS. Previous classification schemes stress loose groupings of software parts

by their functions. For example, all mathematical functions could belong to one group while logic functions get grouped separately. Keywords and partial string searches have been helpful in retrieving modules so long as the user knows or can guess some portion of the module's name.

The use of modern database management systems, especially relational databases, enables a user to retrieve a class of software components through associative queries [YEH84, AMANO84]. For example a user can retrieve all mathematical functions that were written by a named author before a specified date so long as those attributes exist in a database. The names of the modules that meet the query specifications are then used during software construction.

Even though relational systems are a major improvement over the older cataloguing schemes, the structural properties as well as the semantics of software modules are hard to describe using relations. Improvements in the modelling power of databases, especially the semantic models, as well as advances in object-oriented programming, provide the impetus for more powerful classification methodologies.

2.2.1 Semantic Model_ing and Object-oriented Classification

Semantic modelling has grown out of the programming language, database, and artificial intelligence communities in order to improve the semantic expressiveness of databases and other information repositories. The following semantic modelling concepts are useful in the SBMS.

i. Generalization Hierarchies. A generalization hierarchy is one in which types and subtypes are defined. A type is defined by a set of attributes; all objects possessing those attributes are grouped together. A subtype is a specialization within a type. This well-known notion of taxonomies was incorporated into data modelling in [SMITH77]. Figure 1 illustrates a generalization hierarchy for computers. MICRO, MINI, MAINFRAME, SUPERCOMPUTER, are each subtyes within the type of COMPUTER. Similarly, WORKSTATION, HOME COMPUTER, and PERSONAL COMPUTER are each subtypes within the type of MICRO. In a similar fashion, a behavioral hierarchy for software parts can be modelled in an SBMS that directly supports generalization hierarchies.

ii. Composition Graphs. A software part may be a composite that references or is made up of other software parts, which in turn may reference or include other software parts, possibly recursively. For example, in the Symbolics Flavor System [SYMBOLICS84], a flavor is an object type and each flavor has a name and a set of methods (a method is an implementation of the response to the set of messages that an object understands). Bottom-up object-oriented programming using the flavor system begins with a collection of reusable flavors (objects); new flavors are built by combining more primitive ones. Eventually, one obtains the appropriate objects to solve the problem at hand. The Flavor Examiner on the Symbolics provides the means by which the user traverses this composition graph in order to find potentially reusable objects.

2.2.2 Building Prototypes With Reusable Objects

The concept of an object as a named computational entity with an identifiable behavior is central to object-oriented programming. An object's behavior is its reaction to the set of messages it "understands," where a message is a request to initiate processing or provide information, and "understanding" means possessing a defined response. Messages are akin to conventional procedure calls with the distinction that the sender has no idea how the receiver implements its request. Inside the receiver, messages are handled by directing further messages to other objects, and or by performing activities [RENTCH82]. Procedure calls are commands to carry out specific algorithms, while messages are requests to accomplish some activity by whatever algorithm is appropriate, where the object receiving the message decides what is appropriate. Similar objects (i.e. objects exhibiting some of the same behavior) constitute a class. The same abstraction mechanisms discussed for databases are used to organize objects into a class hierarchy.

A typical example is the Flavor System on the Symbolics 3600 LISP machine. A flavor is essentially an object type; every flavor has a name and a set of methods. A method is an implementation of the response to one of the messages an object understands. A flavor is similar to an Ada(1) generic unit in many respects. An instantiation of a flavor receives requests for services called messages and may also respond to those messages. A message has a name and appropriate parameters.

Object-oriented programming can be carried out top-down or bottom-up. Top-down object-oriented programming comprises the following activities[BOOCH83]:

o Define an informal strategy for solving the problem at hand,

o Identify the objects (nouns) in the informal strategy,

o Identify each objects operations (verbs) in the informal strategy,

o Define each object's interface: -- the services and information it offers to other objects,

o Implement each of the objects

o Implement the informal strategy as a program that uses these objects

o In this case, an implementation is developed for each object needed.

Bottom-up object-oriented programming begins with a collection of reusable software objects such as the SMALLTALK system objects, the collection of flavors on the Symbolics, or a user's personal library. These objects are well-documented, are usually reliable, and the system is usually well-organized. Objects for the problem at hand are built up by combining more primitive (system or user-defined) objects. Eventually, the system contains the appropriate objects to solve the problem at hand. Bottom-up object oriented-programming is a natural way to exploit a software repository's resources.

3 THE CLASSIFICATION SCHEME IN RAPIER

3.1 BEHAVIOR ABSTRACTION

The classification scheme discusssed here is called The Behavior Abstraction Classification Scheme, (BACS). BACS builds generic hierarchies out of a set of functional specifications. This is similar to the SMALLTALK object hierarchy. In the RAPIER however, each behavior class is a formally specified abstract object. For each such abstract object, there can be more than one alternative implementation. Discriminants are then used to restrict retrieval whenever the user needs a specific implementation. The task of verifying that a software part does indeed implement a given abstract object is the task of a theorem prover, or the human librarian, or software auditors.

The following terms used in this paper are now defined in the context of RAPIER and Behavior Abstraction.

Definition 1. A behavior is the state change caused by an object's response to one of the requests it understands.

Definition 2. A catalogue is the set of behaviors that can be attributed to the components in the software base. In RAPIER's SBMS, a catalogue can be organized into a generic object hierarchy.

Definition 3. An object is a set of related messages. Each object type is unique - for example "table manager," "window," "mouse" or "calendar". For each object type, there is always a distinguished object, the abstract object; for each such object, there may be more than one other object, each of which implements the abstract object.

Definition 4. A message is a pair <object, request> where object is the name of an object and request is the name of one of the object's behaviors.

Definition 5. Behavior Abstraction is the functional specification of objects and their arrangement into generic behavior hierarchies in SBMS.

Definition 6. Delayed binding is the binding of a concrete object to an abstract object. Delayed binding is similar to the retrieval of data in response to a query. When Behavior Abstraction is fully implemented, abstract messages rather than implementation names will be used in PSDL. The right implementation will be retrieved when the PSDL description is submitted to the SBMS.

Definition 7. Inheritance is the acquisition of attributes, state values, and functional behavior by an object from other object(s).

3.2 RULES OF THUMB

The emphasis is on building domain-specific libraries in order to simplify the initial RAPIER and to help us gain experience. Classification in RAPIER is a bottom-up process; a human librarian reads the functional specifications of the various software parts and decides which generic object classes should be created. It is the librarian's responsibility to group implementations of an abstract object together. The librarian also builds a generic hierarchy of the abstract objects. Also, for the composition graph, the librarian would have to read the implementations in order to identify the call or "with" chain of the Ada code. (This is a tedious process!) Follow-on work includes automating this process by building interfaces between the SBMS and syntax-directed editors or other parser-like tools.

The following rules guide the classification.

Rule 1: An abstract object B is said to be a subtype of another abstract object A, iff B inherits some or all of of A's messages. Each hierarchy of abstract objects constitutes a partial ordering; the discipline of Behavior Abstraction involves the construction of such partial orders.

Rule 2: An implementation is said to belong to a behavior category (abstract object) iff there exists a homomorphic mapping between the implementation's specification and that of the abstract object. A theorem prover can be used to enforce this [GUTTAG78], otherwise the human librarian would have to make that judgement.

4 IMPLEMENTATION

We intend to use the RAPIER system to leverage the front-end of the life-cycle of embedded computer systems software development. It is, however, impractical to realize a production quality RAPIER system in which Behavior Abstraction is mechanized. One reason is that the technology for processing functional specifications has yet to mature. We are currently prototyping the concept of Behavior Abstraction using an advanced object-based computing environment and powerful LISP machines. Our prototyping exercise is proceeding in two phases.

4.1 PHASE 1 - MANUAL CLASSIFICATION

In prototyping the concept of Behavior Abstraction, we are adopting a proprietary object-oriented DBMS for the SBMS. The user interacts with the SBMS through the query/browse interface. The external schema that the user sees is modeled using concepts from the array theoretic model [MORE81, JENKINS86, ONUEGBE86]. In array theory, objects are described in terms of their components; such a hierarchic description makes it easy for a user of the browser to navigate the data structures.

4.1.1 The SBMS Schema

The schema of SBMS is a very simple one. The object ABSTRACT OBJECT along with its subtypes (same as subcategories in Figure 2) serve to represent a generic hierarchy in the system. IMPLEMENTATION object along with the attribute "components" constitute a composition graph. The object INTERFACE represents the interface imported or exported by the various modules. Its attributes include names of importers and exporters and the input and output parameters among others. These structures for representing the generic object hierarchies support our clasification scheme. Some of the attributes of the objects described above are shown in Figure 2

The behaviors of software parts will be formalized. The array IMPLEMENTATION is the list of all implementations of an abstract object. The attributes of IMPLEMENTATION include id, name, toolstamp, version number, author, and other arrays which help the user navigate the composition graph (immediate component, immediate dependent, and so forth). The discriminants consist of those extra specifications that make the implementation different from the generic functional specs. Such discriminants include specifications concerning the environment, performance, reliability, and so forth. For Phase 1, the discriminants are being captured as database values (in order to support queries); eventually, however, they may be formally specified as well.

The implementions being classified are Ada packages written according to the guidelines suggested in [ST. DENNIS86].

4.1.2 Browsing

Browsing in SBMS consists of navigation and probing [MOTRO84] through the generic hierarchy of abstract objects and the composition graph of their implementations. As soon as the browser is invoked for use in RAPIER, three major contexts are established as shown in Figure 3a. The first is the context for ABSTRACT OBJECT, the second is the context for IMPLEMENTATION, and the third is for INTERFACE. As a user browses through the hierarchy of functional specifications, data is displayed in a window as shown in Figure 3b. In order to display data concerning a particular implementation, the user would have to pick on the name of a particular implementation in the ABSTRACT OBJECT context. In order to display information concerning a particular interface, the user has to pick on one from the IMPLEMENTATION context.

The windows described in Figure 3a and 3b are used for illustrating the concepts only. In practice, browsing in RAPIER is within the larger context of the Construction Environment, so the windows do not appear exactly as shown in the figures.

In order for a naive user to browse quickly through or to update the database, the browser has features such as:

(1) Editing Capability. This allows the user to directly modify data that is displayed on the screen much in the same way as one modifies text in an editing buffer. Commands to enable the user to save the buffer, undo previous updates, or apply a specified modification to more than one object should be provided. We recommended that the update rights be reserved for the librarian (or the group of individuals performing that function) in order to avoid possible chaotic updates.

Scrolling of the data on the screen will also enable the user to "hop" around until information that is of interest is found. Some of the editing capability discussed here are already available in some of today's form-based query interfaces.

(2) Query Modifications. This feature enables the user to recall a previous query, modify such query, and reexecute it. For instance, if a user issued a query, "FIND ALL MODULES WRITTEN BEFORE 1980", and modified it to, "FIND ALL MODULES WRITTEN BEFORE 1975", the immediate effect would be to probably lessen the number of module names in the buffer. If the user changes 1975 to 1982, then the number of tuples could be larger than for the two earlier forms of the query.

(3) Context Switching. Two kinds of context switching are useful. The first kind is analogous to the use of buffers in a text editor. It should be possible to issue more than one query, direct the results of each query to a different buffer and manipulate the buffers as needed.

To summarize, browsing in SBMS consists of navigation and probing of a generic object hierarchy and a composition graph structure created by the dependencies among software parts. In Phase 1 implementation of Behavior Abstraction, a human librarian loads the database manually.

4.2 PHASE 2 - SEMI-AUTOMATIC UPDATES

We noted earlier that the composition graph of the SBMS is very tedious to update. Phase 2 implementation consists of interfacing the SBMS with an Ada syntax-directed editor so that the relationships among components can be automatically updated. Also, a stand alone tool which uses the symbol table of a compilation to update the database should be available after Phase 2.

The choice of the appropriate node in the generic behavior hierarchy in which to classify the part is still a manual process though.

5 CONCLUSION

Archival libraries must support a systematic way to insert and delete software parts as well as support different implementations of a given behavior. The concept of Behavior Abstraction, for classifying reusable parts in a software base, has been presented. The implementation of this concept will foster trust in future archival libraries. We have stressed the importance of the concept rather than its mechanization, though such mechanization will go a long way to making the job of the librarian or software auditors less error-prone.

After building and consolidating a domain-specific library, we will experiment with object-oriented programming using reusable specifications. The browser will guide the user through the catalogue, the user will incorporate abstract objects into the PSDL, and the binding of implementation to specification occurs only when the PSDL(1) is submitted to be processed.

5 ACKNOWLEDGEMENT

I would like to thank Dr. Elaine Frankowski who leads the RAPIER system effort at Honeywell for the lengthy discussions we had concerning software classification, and Dr. James Richardson who read and critiqued an earlier version of the Behavior Abstraction Classification Scheme.

BIBLIOGRAPHY

[YEH84]   Raymond T. Yeh, Nicholas Roussopoulos. "Management of Reusable Software" IEEE Compcon, Arlington, Virginia September 16-20, 1984, Page 311-320.

[SMITH77] John M. Smith, Diane C. P. Smith "Database Abstraction: Aggregation and Generalization" ACM Trans. on Database Systems Vol. 2, No. 2, 1977.

[ONUEGBE86] Emmanuel O. Onuegbe, "Database Management System Requirements For A Software Engineering Environment," To appear in the Proceedings of 3rd Intl. Conference on Data Engineering, Los Angeles, California, Feb. 1987.

[GOLDBERG83] A. Goldberg, and D. Robson, "SMALLTALK-80: The Language and Its Implementation", Addison-Wesley, Reading, Mass., 1983.

[SYMBOLICS84] Symbolics 3600 Series User's Manual, LISP FLAVORS, Vol. 3B, 1984, Symbolics Inc, Cambridge, Mass.

[ST. DENNIS86] Richard St. Dennis "A Guidebook for Writing Reusable Source CodeAda" Honeywell CSC, Bloomington, MN 55420

[AMANO84] Amano, K., et al "An Approach Toward Integrated Algorithm Information System", Information Systems, Vol. 9, No. 3/4 1984.

[RENTCH82] Tom Rentch, "Object-oriented Programming," ACM SIGPLAN Notices, Vol. 17, No. 9, September 1982.

[RAPIER86]   RaPIER Project Final Scientific Report, RaPIER Project (Contract No. N00014-85-C-0666) Honeywell Computer Sciences Center, Golden Valley, MN March 1986

[BOOCH83] Grady Booch, "Object-oriented Design," Tutorial On Software Design Techniques (P. Freeman and A. Wasserman, editors), fourth edition (Catalogue Number EHO205-5), IEEE Computer Society Press, 1983.

[GUTTAG78] John V. Guttag, Ellis Horowitz, "Abstract Data Types and Software Validation" CACM Vol. 21, No. 12., December 1978, pp 1048 - 1064.

[MORE81] Trenchard More, "Notes On Diagrams, Logic and Operations of Array Theory," Tech. Report G320 - 2137, IBM Cambridge Scientific Center, Cambridge Mass., 1981.

[JENKINS86] Micheal A. Jenkins, Janice I. Glasgow, Carl D. McCrosky, "Programming Styles in Nial" IEEE Software, January 1986.

[MOTRO84] Amilhai Motro, "Browsing in A Loosely Structured Database," Proceedings, Annual Meeting of ACM SIGMOD, Vol. 14, No. 2, May 18 - 21, 1984.

BIOGRAPHY

Emmanuel O. Onuegbe is a Principal Research Scientist at the Corporate Systems Development Division of Honeywell Inc. at Golden Valley, Minnesota. He is currently involved in research and development in Engineering Data Management Systems, Software Engineering and Rapid Prototyping. Prior to that, he worked on the Distributed Database Testbed System at Honeywell's Computer Sciences Center in Bloomington, Minnesota. During that time, he developed and published query optimization algorithms and also contributed to the design and development of a functional software engineering environment. Mr. Emmanuel Onuegbe holds a BSc. degree in Computer and Information Science from Kansas State University and a Master of Science degree in Computer Science from the University of Minnesota.

---

(1) PSDL: Prototype Specification and Design Language is being built by an independent contractor.

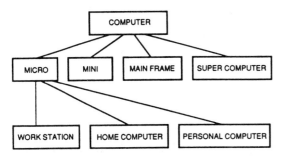

Figure 1: A Generalization Hierarchy for Computer

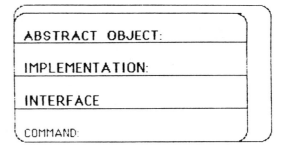

Figure 3a: Browsing Contexts

```
ABSTRACT OBJECT:

id:
author:
timestamp:
immediate subcategory:
immediate supercategory:
all subcategory:
all supercategory:
functional specs:
implementation:
-
-
-
-

IMPLEMENTATION

id:
name:
type:  (PACKAGE | SUBPROGRAM | TASK)
tool stamp:
immediate component:
immediate dependent:
all component:
all dependent:
discriminants (if package):
version:
timestamp:
author:
imported interface:
/* implementation specific specifications */
exported interface:
-
-
-

INTERFACE          (especially package specs)

id:
name:
specification:         /* implementation specific */
immediate exporter:
immediate importer:
all exporter:
all importer:
timestamp:
toolstamp:
version:
-
-
-
```

Figure 2: Array Model Implementation of Behavior Abstraction Data Structures

Figure 3b: Browsing Contexts Showing the Implementation Choices for a Table Manager

Can Programmers Reuse Software?

An experiment asked programmers untrained in reuse to evaluate component reusability. They did poorly. Are reusability's promises hollow? Or are there some answers?

Scott N. Woodfield, David W. Embley, and Del T. Scott
Brigham Young University

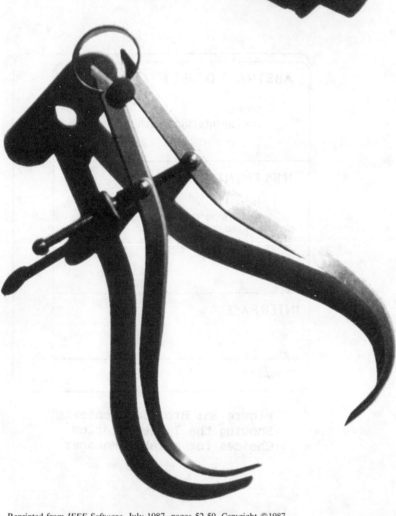

Software reusability has long held out the unrealized promise of increased productivity. Researchers have predicted the development of certified software components available for easy incorporation in new systems, and they have presupposed that by the 1990s many software engineers would be more like computer designers determining gross system structure and connections and relying heavily on prefabricated software components.[1] Indeed, where software reuse has been encouraged and practiced, managers report satisfaction and success,[2] and as much as a 35- to 85-percent improvement in productivity can be realized.[3]

Despite the promise and flurry of activity, software is rarely reused in practice. Tracz identifies and discusses several technical, organizational, political, and psychological barriers to software reuse.[4] He observed that the barriers are not insurmountable, but to surmount them

• useful and certified components must be made available,

• tools and methods to support both creation and use of component libraries must be developed, and

• money, time, and personnel must be expended to develop software reuse systems and train users to become proficient with them.

EH0278-2/88/0000/0168$01.00 ©1987

From the perspective of a software production staff, profitability depends largely on component availability and on easily locating components, assessing their applicability, and incorporating them into the software system being developed. Because we can do little initially about component availability, and because we consider component incorporation an important issue — but one that is mute unless relevant components can be found and their applicability properly assessed[4,5] — we focus on these issues. Locating software components and assessing their applicability are both based on the same issue: They both compare a specification of what is required with a candidate component in a software-reuse library.

To better understand the process of comparing specified and required components, we conducted an experiment to test if programmers could accurately assess component reusability. We gave 51 software developers 21 treatments in which they were asked whether they would reuse an existing abstract data type to meet an abstract-data-type specification.

The results show that there is considerable confusion. Software-development personnel untrained in reuse cannot assess the worth of reusing a candidate abstract data type to satisfy the implementation requirements of a specified abstract data type. Their decisions were also influenced by some unimportant features — and were *not* influenced by other important ones.

Focus and hypotheses

We restricted our investigation to libraries whose software components are abstract data types and assumed an environment where programmers do object-oriented design and development. We chose to investigate abstract-data-type libraries rather than function libraries because we believe that more resources can be saved per unit resource invested when searching for and reusing an abstract data type than when searching for and reusing a single function.[5,6]

Researchers exploring an unknown area in computer science often rely exclusively on introspection when trying to study issues and answer important questions about human-computer interaction. Unfortunately, as Moran said, a "designer, relying on an egocentric, 'folk psychology' has no way to gauge his intuitions; and intuitions about complex psychological behavior (even about one's own behavior) can be remarkably deceptive."[7]

To avoid these pitfalls, we should gather at least some empirical evidence to help guide the design. Although a single experiment cannot provide all the information needed, much can be gleaned from a well-designed experiment, especially if the experiment is conducted early in the design stage when, because of folk psychology, it is easy to start building a system modeled on invalid assumptions.

We investigated abstract-data-type libraries rather than function libraries because abstract data types can save more resources per unit.

In our experiment we posed four questions:

1. Given an abstract-data-type requirements specification, do subjects properly assess the worth of reusing a candidate abstract data type?

Because the people tested were untrained in software reuse and were given no guidelines or assistance in assessing the worth of reusing a component, we hypothesized that they would be unable to appropriately compare a specification with a candidate software component. We also hypothesized that they would be inconsistent among themselves in their assessments. The responses to this question should establish the degree of need for education and software tools.

2. What features best explain how subjects assess the worth of reusing a candidate abstract data type for a given abstract-data-type requirements specification?

Features we expected to be of interest were missing domain specifications and operations, extraneous domain specifications and operations, implied modifica- tions, and size. If the subjects overlooked important features, that would show that users must be trained to consider these overlooked features and tools must be designed to bring these features to the users' attention. If the subjects based decisions on questionable features, that would show what features users should be warned to ignore.

3. Based on performance and demographics, do distinguishable groups of subjects exist?

Because the subjects all have about the same expertise in software design and development, we hypothesized that no distinguishable groups should exist. If distinguishable groups did exist, we must determine whether different sets of instructional material and software tools should be developed to meet the differing needs.

4. Can a threshold value be predicted that discriminates between acceptance and rejection of a candidate abstract data type for a given abstract-data-type requirements specification?

We hypothesized that a threshold value exists and that training, experience, and the availability and use of software tools may alter the threshold value. A threshold and the knowledge of its value, along with a proper understanding of the important features, would give us a starting point for developing a system that could automatically assess the worth of reusing a candidate component for a specification. Automatic assessment would give us a way to measure algorithmically how closely a candidate component matches a specification, thus giving us an initial means of automatically finding candidate components in a library.

The experiment

To test these hypotheses, we conducted an exploratory experiment that simulated an environment where someone knowledgeable about abstract data types worked in a software design and development project that required abstract data types. We assumed that if time and effort could be saved, the person would rather reuse an abstract data type than create one from scratch. Thus, the basic measurement in the experiment was the person's perception of time saved. By varying the circumstances under which a person might decide to reuse a candidate abstract data type and by measuring how much time a person thought might be saved, we hoped to answer our questions.

The subjects. Fifty-one people participated in the experiment. Twenty-five were from three local industries (Hercules, Word Perfect, and Novell). The other 26 were senior and graduate students taking various software engineering classes at Brigham Young University. All the subjects were familiar with abstract data types and had created programs using the concept.

Although the subjects were not picked randomly from the general population of knowledgeable abstract-data-type users, they are representative of both industrial and academic environments and have a wide range of practical experience.

Experimental design. We designed an exploratory experiment to investigate the influence of four factors on subjects' perceptions of time saved:

• the percent of the specified abstract data type's domain definition that must be added to the candidate abstract data type,

• the percent of the candidate abstract data type's domain definition that could be deleted,

• the percent of the specified abstract data type's operations that must be added, and

• the percent of the candidate abstract data type's operations that could be deleted.

In an exploratory experiment the number of levels should be minimized, and their values should be chosen to create a distribution of responses about each factor level. The results of a pilot study indicated that there would be a good distribution of results at about the 20-percent and 50-percent addition/deletion levels.

We designed 16 treatments to cover the four factors; each factor had two levels. To make our experiment more representative of reality, we added four treatment combinations. These treatments held the addition/deletion levels for domains at zero and provided combinations of the addition/deletion levels for the two operation factors. To investigate nonlinearity, we added a center point. Thus, the experiment contained 21 treatments ($2^4 + 4 + 1$).

Our study shared a problem common to experimental designs in social science and clinical studies: the need to control subjects' differences. To minimize this problem, each person should take all the treatments. Because subjects' responses may be affected by treatment order, each subject received an instrument containing a different randomized sequence of treatments.

Instrument. Figure 1 shows part of treatment 9. It consists of a specified abstract data type (Specification 9 in the figure) and a candidate abstract data type (Data Abstraction 9), both given in the same format. The first part of both the specification and data abstraction was a

---

```
SPECIFICATION 9
    room addition

Components of room addition:
    height
    length
    width
    .
    .
    .

Operations on room addition:
    COMPUTE_VOLUME_OF(room) -> volume
        calculate the total air space of the room
    ESTIMATE_CARPET_COSTS(room,price_per_yard) -> dollars
        estimate the cost of carpet for the room given the cost per yard


DATA ABTRACTION 9
    room addition

Components of room addition:
    height
    length
    width
    .
    .
    .

Operations on room addition:
    COMPUTE_VOLUME_OF(room) -> volume
        calculate the total air space of the room
    ESTIMATE_AIR_CONDITIONING_NEEDS(room,climate)
                    -> air_conditioning_capacity
        estimate the number of tons of air conditioning needed to cool room in summer
    .
    .
    .

Would you reuse this data abstraction to meet the given specification? (circle one) YES NO

If YES, what percent of the estimated creation time do you think you will spend
modifying the code (circle one)

0%   10%   20%   30%   40%   50%   60%   70%   80%   90%   100%
```

Figure 1. Sample treatment.

brief domain definition containing a list of components of the abstract data type's domain. The second part of both contained a list of operations defined at a very high level by giving only input and output parameters and brief English descriptions. In all but a few cases each instance fit on one page.

As the figure shows, the subjects were asked two questions for each treatment. First, they were asked if they would reuse the candidate abstract data type to create an abstract data type for the specification. Second, if they answered yes, they were asked to estimate the amount of time it would take to modify the candidate abstract data type to meet the specified abstract data type. This response was to be a percent of the estimated time it would take to create the specified abstract data type from scratch.

Measures. The experiment yielded two types of measures: the subject's responses and quantitative measures on the instrument itself. With 51 subjects, 21 treatments, and two questions, there were 2142 data values for responses.

To fill out the subject-response table completely, a 100-percent value was automatically recorded for all negative responses. The 100-percent value for a negative response means that if an abstract data type is written from scratch, it requires all (100 percent) of the creation time to produce the abstract data type.

A 100-percent response for yes is also possible and means that the person believes it would take the same amount of time either way and that the person chose to reuse the candidate abstract data type.

The person may also believe that it might actually take longer to create the specified abstract data type by reusing the candidate abstract data type, but in this case the response should simply be no. We did not request percents for negative responses because we thought that this might confuse many of the subjects and because it is not clear how much above 100 percent people might estimate.

There are several quantitative measures on the instrument itself. In addition to the designed-in percentage of additions and deletions, the amount of modification necessary is also important — but it is eas-

ily overlooked. In general, changes to the domain constituents often imply changes to operations. Although we did not design specific amounts of modification into the instrument, we could measure the amount of modification induced.

We were also interested in the absolute number of operators to be added. We thought that people might consider deletions and domain additions to be insignificant because these changes are relatively simple compared to adding a new operation.

We also thought that the treatment size might influence people. The treatment size

---

Effort estimation has long been a problem in software engineering. Most managers use lines-of-code estimates. We used software-science estimates because our projects were small.

---

varied from one domain constituent to 10 and from four operations to 32.

Because one of our major objectives was to determine whether people could properly assess the worth of reusing a candidate abstract data type, we needed an estimate of the creation time percentage required to reuse each candidate abstract data type to produce the specified abstract data type. The cost of having each person write the necessary code for all abstract data types in the experiment was estimated to be more than 100 hours per person (much too expensive).

Effort estimation has long been a problem in software engineering. When required, software-production managers have relied most often on lines-of-code estimates.[8] Software science is another technique that can be used.[9] Although software-science estimations appear to be unreliable when applied to large projects, empirical evidence shows that for relatively small functions — like those operators in the treatments of our experiment — this technique is acceptable.

The lines-of-code technique is based on

an estimation formula of the form $time = a(\text{LOC})^b$. Basili cites references showing that for several different studies b is close to one and that for small functions it can be taken to be one.[8] We counted lines of code for each operation to be added or modified after having written it in pseudocode.

The software-science technique assumes that the time it would take to implement the function can be estimated from a function specification and knowledge of the implementation language. The formula is $time = ((V^*)^3/\lambda^2)/S$, where λ is a language-level constant, S is the Stroud constant, and $V^* = (2 + \eta_2{}^*)\log_2(2 + \eta_2{}^*)$ is the potential volume and depends only on $\eta_2{}^*$, which is the number of input/output operands for the operation. Once the specification for an operation is given, the number of input/output operands is easily obtained.

Both the software-science estimations and the lines-of-code estimations are sensitive to their multiplicative constants, λ, S, and a. For our analysis, these constants do not affect the results because the constants cancel out when the ratio of estimated efforts is computed.

We obtained the lines-of-code and software-science metrics for our treatments by computing an abstract-data-type modification effort with one of the metrics and dividing by the estimated creation effort derived with the same metric. There were two types of abstract-data-type modification efforts calculated. One was based on the effort needed to create the new operations to be added to an abstract data type, and the other (and more sophisticated) effort estimator also included the effort needed to modify operations. For our purposes the effort needed to modify an operation was assumed to be equal to the creation effort raised to the ⅔ power.[10]

We used both lines-of-code and software-science metrics because one or both may be imperfect. To determine if the two measures were consistent, we computed the means, standard deviations, correlation coefficient, and coefficient of determination for all treatments. The software-science mean and standard deviation are 46.27 and 29.06. The lines-of-code mean and standard deviation are 46.59 and 23.89. The correlation coefficient is 0.91 and the correlation of determination is 0.83. We also considered the differences between pairs of lines-of-code and software-science estimators and found that the mean difference is − 0.32 percent and that the standard deviation of the differences is 12.41.

Statistically, we cannot show that the means or variances are different. From this evidence and from personal evaluation, we are confident that the estimators, when used together, reasonably predict how much effort is required to modify an abstract data type for reuse.

Results

After testing our subjects and determining our metrics, we found the following results.

Worth assessment. Our first working hypothesis was that effort estimations for modifying a candidate abstract data type to satisfy the requirements of a specified abstract data type would be close to the actual effort needed to modify the candidate abstract data type. Because determining the actual amount of effort was beyond our capability to measure accurately, we decided to estimate the actual modification effort associated with each treatment by the average of the software-science and lines-of-code measures.

Our hypothesis thus became that effort estimations for modifying a candidate abstract data type to satisfy the requirements of a specified abstract data type would be close to the software-science/lines-of-code estimate.

One method of measuring closeness is to compare the mean of an effort estimation with the expected value derived from software science/lines of code. Although this let us determine if a person is close to the average, it indicated nothing about whether we could expect a person to be close for a given situation. For example, a person might give wild estimates, but the person's average might still be quite close to the expected value derived from software-science/lines-of-code measures. We were interested not only in whether the average was good but whether every estimate was fairly accurate. Therefore, we wanted not only the mean of the effort

estimations to be close to the expected value for each treatment, but we also wanted the variances of the estimates to be small.

Initial observations indicated that the people underestimated the amount of effort needed to modify a candidate abstract data type for reuse and that their estimates varied highly. On average, the people were 15.35 percent low and had a standard deviation of 28.15.

Believing that people were generally low and highly variant, we chose to test two stronger hypotheses: (1) that at least one person's effort estimations over the 21 treatments is consistently close to the software-science/lines-of-code estimates and (2) that there exists at least one question for which the 51 people consistently give an effort estimation close to the software-science/lines-of-code estimate.

Although size should not have been a significant factor, we found that it influenced people unnecessarily.

To test the two hypothesis, we used a goodness-of-fit test based on the chi-squared distribution,[6] χ^2. We let the α level be 0.001, which means we will accept a factor as being significant only if there is a one-in-a-thousand chance we could be wrong. We chose this α level, instead of the usual 0.05, because of the study's exploratory nature — we wanted to identify only the large factors of practical importance.

We can reject the first hypothesis at $\alpha = 0.001$ ($X^2 = 127 > \chi^2_{(0.999, 20)} = 45.3$) and conclude that the best person's estimates are not consistently close to the software-science/lines-of-code estimate. These results imply that the best person (and therefore all people) could not accurately estimate the effort needed to modify a candidate abstract data type for reuse.

We can reject the second hypothesis $\alpha = 0.001$ ($X^2 = 454 > \chi^2_{(0.999, 50)} = 86.7$) and conclude that the estimates were not consistently close to the software-science/lines-of-code estimate for the best question. These results imply that for the

best question (and therefore for all questions) the people could not make accurate estimates.

Significant factors. We applied analysis of variance, covariance analysis, and regression techniques to determine which factors best explain the results. The factors of interest were the effects of person variability, answering yes or no, question variability, treatment size as measured in characters and entities, and different types of effort estimation. We analyzed these factors by constructing different models and determining if the factors of the model are statistically and practically significant.

The basic model includes factors for person variability, for decisions about whether to reuse the candidate abstract data type, and for question variability. The first two factors, person variability and yes/no decisions, are nuisance factors, factors of little interest that account for a lot of the overall variability. If ignored, they give a false representation of the unexplained variability. Because each factor explains a certain percent of remaining variance, their order is important, and because we must account for any correlation that the nuisance factors have with the primary factors, the nuisance factors should be put in the model first.

For the basic model, the question variability is the most important factor. We did not consider percent of operation addition and deletion, percent of subdomain addition and deletion, and other correlated values individually because the question-variability factor contains all this information. Thus, we have an overall test to determine whether any of these individual factors or combinations of these factors is important.

The statistics here are based on an analysis of variance of the data. While not perfect, probability plots of the residuals make us confident of the results produced by the analysis of variance. Table 1 shows the results for the basic model. This model accounts for 74.4 percent of the variance. Because the F value for the questions factor (18.86) is greater than the F statistic (2.27), we rejected the hypothesis that all the questions are identical. Hence, some of the individual factors — percent of operation addition and deletion, percent of

Table 1.
Basic model results, $\alpha = 0.001$.

Factor	% variance explained	F statistic	df	F value
Subjects	12.1	9.44	50,988	1.75
Yes/no	52.6	2050.00	1,998	10.83
Questions	9.7	18.86	20,998	2.27

Table 2.
Effect of size, analysis 1, $\alpha = 0.001$.

Factor	% variance explained	F statistic	df	F value
Subjects	12.1	9.44	50,988	1.75
Yes/no	52.6	2049.95	1,998	10.83
Character size	3.6	35.62	4,998	4.62
Entity size	0.8	8.16	4,998	4.62
Question	5.2	16.89	12,998	2.74

Table 3.
Effect of size, analysis 2, $\alpha = 0.001$.

Factor	% variance explained	F statistic	df	F value
Subjects	12.1	9.44	50,988	1.75
Yes/no	52.6	2049.95	1,998	10.83
Entity size	4.3	42.35	4,998	4.62
Character size	0.1	1.29	4,998	4.62
Question	5.2	16.89	12,998	2.74

subdomain addition and deletion, and other correlated values — are significant.

We thought the size of a particular treatment might cause people to change their estimates of the abstract-data-type modification effort. But although the experiment was designed so size should not have been significant, we found that people responded differently to treatments that differed only in size.

We analyzed two types of size metrics: entity size and character size. Entity size is the number of subdomains and operations in the specification and candidate abstract data types. Character size is the number of characters in the domain and operation descriptions of the specification and candidate abstract data types.

We analyzed these two size metrics by including them in the model as nuisance factors; they were introduced as the third and fourth factors in the model. Because order is important, we ran two analyses. The first analysis used character size as the third factor and entity size as the fourth factor. In the second run, the positions were reversed. Tables 2 and 3 show the results.

These results show that, regardless of order, the number of entities in a treatment is significant. Character size, when introduced after entity size, is not significant, even at the 0.1 α level ($F = 1.96$). This implies that entity size can explain character size, but character size cannot account for all the variance due to entity size. We therefore concluded that size is a significant factor and can be represented by the number of entities in a treatment.

We then investigated how people measured effort to determine what factors are best correlated with people's effort estimations. We had three hypotheses:

1. People used the absolute number of subdomains and operations that must be added, deleted, or modified to estimate effort. We call this the absolute-entities measure.

2. People measured the percent of subdomains and operations that needed to be added, deleted, or modified. We call this the relative-entities measure.

3. People estimated the true modification effort in hours and divided by the estimated creation effort. We call this the true-effort-estimation measure. This last measure is our lines-of-code/software-science estimate.

To evaluate these three measures, we made three analyses. Each analysis added one of the measures as the fourth factor to the model (after subjects, yes/no, and entity size); the other two effort measures were not included. The questions factor was retained and became the fifth factor, letting us determine if the new factor explained some of the question variability.

Table 4 shows the results. Unlike the previous tables, Table 4 summarizes the three analyses. Each row in the table shows only the results for the fourth factor in each of the five-factor models. These results show that all three measures are significant but that the relative-entities measure is best. Further analysis showed that the relative-entities measure accounts for most of the variability of the absolute-entities and true-effort-estimation measures.

We believe that people evaluated the effort to modify an abstract data type primarily as the ratio of affected entities to total specified entities. Unfortunately, the true-effort-estimation — which we believe they should have used — seemed to be the least important.

Having concluded that the relative-entities measure is important, we then decomposed it into its five components: subdomain addition, subdomain deletion, operation addition, operation deletion, and operation modification. These are the factors we originally wanted to investigate.

We examined different orderings of the factors in the model and observed that they all lead to the same conclusions. Table 5 presents the results for one of the orderings. These results show that the most influential factor was the percent of operations that must be added to a candidate abstract data type to make it meet a specification. All other factors are unimportant.

Although we expected the addition and deletion of subdomains to be overlooked, we had hoped that the percent of operations to be modified would have been significant.

Distinguishable groups. To determine if subject groupings affected performance, we analyzed the demographics using clus-

Table 4.
Comparison of three effort estimators, $\alpha = 0.001$.

Factor	% total variance explained	% question variance explained	F statistic	fd	F value
Absolute entities	6.3	65.0	61.32	4,998	4.62
Relative entities	7.3	75.5	71.22	4,998	4.62
True effort estimation	4.9	50.6	95.36	2,998	6.91

Table 5.
Analysis of relative-entities measure, $\alpha = 0.001$.

Factor	% total variance explained	% question variance explained	F statistic	fd	F value
Subject	12.10	—	9.44	50,998	1.75
Yes/no	52.60	—	2049.95	1,998	10.83
Entity size	4.30	—	42.35	4,998	4.62
Subdomains added	0.02	0.40	0.90	1,998	10.83
Subdomains deleted	0.00	confounded			
Operations added	4.00	75.50	156.88	1,998	10.83
Operations deleted	0.05	0.99	2.05	1,998	10.83
Operations modified	0.001	0.02	0.06	1,998	10.83
Questions	1.20	23.10	3.99	12,998	2.74

ter analysis. Statistically, there were two (perhaps three) groups.[6] One group contained four people who had significantly more work experience, but these four did not behave measurably differently than the other 47 people. Except for this group, we were unable to give a rational explanation for any other cluster.

Threshold value. Finally, we investigated the relationship between the estimated effort to modify a candidate abstract data type for reuse and the decision to reuse the abstract data type. We were interested in a threshold effort-estimation value that could be used to determine if a person would reuse a candidate abstract data type.

Logic indicates that the modification effort should be less than or equal to the effort needed to create the specified abstract data type. Because the modification-estimation effort was measured as a percent of the creation effort, the threshold value should be 100 percent or less.

Because of the experimental design, we could not determine an exact threshold value from unadjusted responses. If we used unadjusted values, about half the responses should be no and half the responses should be yes. Our experiment

concentrated on abstract data types likely to be reused. Also, there was no real relation between negative answers and estimated modification effort because all negative responses were explicitly assigned a modification effort of 100 percent. These problems could be overcome if we analyzed the adjusted responses.

Of the 805 yes responses, none had an adjusted-modification-effort estimation greater than 63.5 percent. Also, none of the 265 no responses had an adjusted-modification-effort estimation less than 73.5 percent. From this evidence, we think that the threshold value is about 70 percent for software-developer populations similar to ours.

If the worth of reusing an abstract data type could accurately be assessed, we would expect a person to reuse an abstract data type even if only a few percent of the creation effort could be saved. The 70-percent threshold value suggests that the people made decisions based not only on possible effort saved, but also on an assessment of risk. The large variance in responses suggests that the people were not sure of their effort estimations. To protect themselves from undue risk, it appears that most people will only reuse an abstract data type if they can save more than 30 percent of the effort.

Our experiment supports these conclusions:
• Software-development personnel untrained in software reuse cannot assess the worth of reusing a candidate abstract data type to satisfy the implementation requirements of a specified abstract data type. Assuming that the expected effort determined by our software-science/lines-of-code measure is a reasonable estimate of expected effort, no person accurately estimated the expected effort for all candidate/specified abstract-data-type pairs, and there was no pair for which all people gave an accurate estimate. The data shows that subject responses were highly variable and generally low when compared to software-science/lines-of-code measures.

• Software-development personnel untrained in software reuse are influenced by some unimportant features and are not influenced by some important ones. People were influenced by the size of the candidate abstract data type and by the percent of additional operations required. People were not influenced by the percent of operators to be modified nor by estimates of effort based on software science and lines of code. Size, per se, is unimportant, and percentage of operator addition is less important than percentage of operator modification and reasonably accurate estimates of actual effort.

• For people similar to our subjects, demographics are not likely to affect performance. In our experiment, no identifiable groups of people performed differently than the other people.

• For people similar to our subjects, the data suggests that if the effort to reuse a candidate abstract data type is perceived to be less than 70 percent of the effort to create an abstract data type from scratch, the candidate abstract data type would be chosen for reuse. The threshold is less than 100 percent, and after adjustment for people who were consistently higher or lower than the average, the data indicates that the threshold is close to 70 percent.

Some directions for future research are clear. Because users cannot properly assess the worth of reusing a candidate abstract data type to satisfy the requirements of a specified abstract data type, we must provide enough help to avert the bad experiences users are certain to have if left solely to their own resources. User assistance can be provided through educa-

tion and software tools that summarize appropriate information.

The data shows that untrained users tend to consider size an important feature on which to base decisions about reusability. They shouldn't. On the other hand, users fail to estimate modification effort in any form — and, instead of estimating the amount of time to add operations, they only considered the percent of operations to be added. While the latter factor is a crude estimate of effort, we should be able to do better. Users should be taught to ignore unimportant features and to properly evaluate important ones.

Furthermore, an initial set of tools should concentrate on providing accurate information for informed decision-making. As an initial information set, we suggest the number and percent of operations that must be added and modified. Eventually, the tool should be enhanced to help estimate abstract-data-type creation and modification effort. Before building tools for abstract-data-type reusability, however, we will carry out further controlled experiments to get the data necessary to help us proceed with confidence. □

Scott N. Woodfield is an associate professor of computer science at Brigham Young University. Before joining Brigham Young, he was faculty member at Arizona State University. His research interests include software reusability and metrics.

Woodfield received a PhD in computer science from Purdue University. He is a member of IEEE and ACM.

David W. Embley is a professor of computer science at Brigham Young University. Before joining Brigham Young, he was a faculty member at the University of Nebraska. His research interests include database query languages, object-oriented systems, and software reusability.

Embley received a PhD in computer science from the University of Illinois. He is a member of ACM.

References

1. A.I. Wasserman and S. Gutz, "The Future of Programming," *Comm. ACM*, March 1982, pp. 196-206.

2. R.G. Lanergan and C.A. Grasso, "Software Engineering with Reusable Design and Code," *Trans. Software Engineering*, Sept. 1984, pp. 498-501.

3. T.C. Jones, "Reusability in Programming: A Survey of the State of the Art," *Trans. Software Engineering*, Sept. 1984, pp. 499-493.

4. W.J. Tracz, "Why Reusable Software Isn't," tech. report, Electrical Engineering Dept., Stanford Univ., Stanford, Calif., 1986.

5. D.W. Embley and S.N. Woodfield, "A Knowledge Structure for Reusing Abstract Data Types," *Proc. Ninth Int'l Software Engineering Conf.*, CS Press, Los Alamitos, Calif., 1987, pp. 360-368.

6. D.W. Embley, D.T. Scott, and S.N. Woodfield, "An Exploratory Experiment Directed Toward Unraveling the Problems of Software Reusability," Tech. Report BYU-CS-87-4, Computer Science Dept., Brigham Young Univ., Provo, Utah, 1987.

7. T.P. Moran, "An Applied Psychology of the User," *ACM Computing Surveys*, March 1981, pp. 1-11.

8. V.R. Basili, "Resource Models," in *Tutorial on Models and Metrics for Software Management and Engineering*, V.R. Basili, ed., CS Press, Los Alamitos, Calif., 1980, pp. 4-9.

9. M.H. Halstead, *Elements of Software Science*, North Holland, New York, 1977.

10. S.M. Thebaut, "The Saturation Effect in Large-Scale Software Development: Its Impact and Control," PhD dissertation, Computer Science Dept., Purdue Univ., West Lafayette, Ind., 1983.

Del T. Scott is an associate professor of statistics at Brigham Young University. He is also a consultant on the development of the Statistics Dept.'s computer facilities. He has developed statistical programs for linear models.

Scott received a BS and MS from Brigham Young University and a PhD from Pennsylvania State University, all in statistics. He is a member of ASA, the Royal Statistical Society, and the Biometric Society.

Embley and Woodfield can be reached at Computer Science Dept., Brigham Young University, Provo, UT 84602. Scott can be contacted at 244 TMCB, Brigham Young University, Provo, UT 84602.

Empirically Analyzing Software Reuse in a Production Environment[1]

Richard W. Selby

Department of Information and Computer Science
University of California
Irvine, California 92717
U.S.A.

ABSTRACT

Reusing software may be the catalyst that helps the software community achieve large improvements in software productivity and quality. There are several motivations for desiring software reuse, including gains in productivity by avoiding redevelopment and gains in quality by incorporating components whose reliability has already been established. The purpose of this study is to characterize software reuse empirically by investigating one development environment that actively reuses software. Twenty-five software systems ranging from 3000 to 112,000 source lines have been selected for analysis from a NASA production environment. The amount of software either reused or modified from previous systems averages 32% per project in this environment. Non-parametric statistical models are applied to examine 46 development variables across the 7188 software modules in the systems. The analysis focuses on the characterization of software reuse at the project, module design, and module implementation levels. Four classes of modules are characterized: (a) modules reused without revision, (b) modules reused with slight revision (< 25% changes), (c) modules reused with major revision (≥ 25% changes), and (d) newly developed modules. The modules reused without revision tended to be small and well documented with simple interfaces and little input-output processing. Those modules tended to be "terminal nodes" in the projects' module invocation hierarchies and their incorporation required relatively little development effort.

1 Introduction

There is a growing recognition that reuse of software can contribute to quality and productivity improvement in software development and maintenance. Several entities associated with software are candidates for reuse:

- the reuse of processes by which software is created and manipulated [Ost87];

- the reuse of technical personnel across projects [Mey87];

- the reuse of design objects [Boo86];

- the reuse of design histories [Nei84]; and

- the reuse of subroutine implementations [Con86]; among others.

Proposed ideas for software reusability have been embodied in various approaches [KG87]. One approach has been through software generation, such as report generators, complier-compilers, and language-based editors (e.g., [Rep83] [HN86]). Another approach has been through the use of object-oriented programming languages, such as Smalltalk-80 [GR83], Flavors [Can80], Loops [BS82], CommonLoops [BKK*86], Ceyx [Hul84], C++ [Str86], Eiffel [Mey87], Object Pascal [Tes85], and Simula [Bea73]. A third approach has been through the use of subroutine libraries or catalogs (e.g., [Con86]). Some hybrid approaches have also been proposed, such as the MELD system which is intended to combine the advantages of object-oriented programming and software generation [KG87].

The purpose of this paper is to provide a basis for insights into approaches for supporting software reuse. One method for learning about how software can be reused is to study development organizations that actively reuse software. Therefore, the focus of this paper is to examine empirical data from one particular software development site that reuses software effectively. Twenty-five software projects of moderate to large size have been selected from a NASA software production environment for this study. The amount of software either reused or modified from previous systems averages 32% per project in this environment (details are given in Table 1).

Given the attractive payoff of reusing software, there have been several efforts undertaken to discuss the topic of reusability (e.g., [BP84] [Big83] [Tra87b] [BP]). Some

[1]This work was supported in part by the National Aeronautics and Space Administration under grant NSG–5123; the National Science Foundation under grant CCR–8704311 with cooperation from the Defense Advanced Research Projects Agency under Arpa order 6108, program code 7T10; and the National Science Foundation under grant DCR–8521398.

recent articles in the literature have intended to capture the state-of-the-practice in software reusability [Tra87a] and future research directions for reusability [BR87].

2 Overview

The objective for this study is to characterize software reuse across several projects in a large software production environment. This analysis is intended to address questions such as the following.

- How much software is being reused in production environments?

- How does project size affect the amount of software reused or modified from previous systems?

- Is there more reuse in recent projects than in earlier projects, due to the greater availability of preexisting software?

- How can different classes of software modules be characterized: reuse without revision, reuse with slight revision, reuse with major revision, and new development?

- How do module design attributes, such as interfaces and calling relationships, affect the amount of software reuse?

- How do module implementation attributes, such as size and control flow information, affect the amount of software reuse?

- How does the extent of software reuse (e.g., complete reuse, slight modification, major modification) affect software development effort?

The next two sections describe the software development environment examined and the method of data collection and analysis. The following sections present the data analysis that characterizes software reuse at the project level, the module design level, and the module implementation level.

3 The Software Environment

Twenty-five moderate and large size software systems have been selected from a NASA software production environment for this study [BZM*77] [CMP*82] [SEL82] [Sel]. The software is ground support software for unmanned spacecraft control. These systems ranged in size from 3000 to 112,000 lines of Fortran source code. They took between 5 and 140 person-months to develop over a period of 5 to 25 months. The staff size ranged from 4 to 23 persons per project. There were from 22 to 853 *modules* in each system. The term *modules* is used to refer to the subroutines, utility functions, main programs, macros, and block data in the systems. Table 1 char-

acterizes the projects according to chronology, size, and distribution of module origin.

4 Data Collection and Analysis Method

A variety of information was collected about each of the software projects and their constituent modules. Modules were classified into four categories based on their degree of reuse from previous systems. The four categories were:

1. Complete reuse without revision

2. Reuse with slight revision ($< 25\%$ changes)

3. Reuse with major revision ($\geq 25\%$ changes)

4. Complete new development

A static analysis program called SAP was employed to gather various statistics – for example, the number of module parameters and number of module versions – for the projects, module designs, and module implementations [DT82]. A set of data collection forms was used by development personnel to record the amount of effort spent during the various development phases [CMP*82]. The development effort analyzed in the study spanned design specification through acceptance testing. The methods applied for validation of the data were described in earlier work [BSP83] [BW84].

The preliminary analysis and scanning of the empirical data was done with scatter plots and histograms. The preliminary analysis showed that several of the dependent variables, such as development effort per source line, were not normally distributed in this environment (which is consistent with earlier studies [CPM85] [CCA86]). Therefore, the primary method for further analysis was through non-parametric analysis of variance (ANOVA) models using ranked data [Sch59]. Analysis of variance models enable the assessment of the potential contributions of a wide range of factors simultaneously. The specific factors considered are outlined below. Such models also enable the interactions of the factors to be detected, not only their individual contributions. Forty-six dependent variables were analyzed by the models; the variables are described under the relevant data interpretation sections (Section 5, 6, 7, or 8). The results are interpreted in Section 9.

4.1 Project Analysis

For the analysis of the projects, the following factors were considered in a non-parametric analysis of variance model at the levels given. Note that the classifications given below (e.g., "larger" vs. "smaller" project) are relative and pertain to the particular environment examined. These factors were selected since studies have indicated the importance of project size and date in the analysis of soft-

Table 1: Origin of modules by project date, project size, and individual project.

Project date	Project size	Project ID#	Percentage (%) of modules**				Number of modules
			New	Major revision	Slight revision	Complete reuse	
Earlier	Larger	P1	90.07	.	6.51	3.42	292
		P2	68.47	8.24	6.25	17.05	352
		P3	63.76	4.62	24.27	7.35	585
		P4	18.12	6.12	7.29	68.47	425
		P5	67.92	1.10	5.01	25.98	639
		P6	66.51	12.56	12.87	8.06	645
		P7	67.06	6.80	12.90	13.25	853
		P8	98.56	0.48	.	0.96	418
	Smaller	P9	60.87	.	13.04	26.09	23
		P10	92.86	.	2.38	4.76	42
		P11	54.46	6.93	14.85	23.76	101
		P12	91.15	2.65	.	6.19	113
		P13	79.73	5.41	12.16	2.70	74
Later	Larger	P14	48.51	8.01	16.48	27.00	437
		P15	55.41	5.18	15.09	24.32	444
		P16	75.59	0.39	.	24.02	254
		P17	76.57	3.53	15.37	4.53	397
		P18	91.37	2.40	6.24	.	417
	Smaller	P19	59.39	0.61	16.36	23.64	165
		P20	66.20	.	.	33.80	71
		P21	27.27	.	.	72.73	22
		P22	87.40	.	.	12.60	246
		P23	100.00	.	.	.	28
		P24	77.89	.	2.11	20.00	95
		P25	38.00	2.00	32.00	28.00	50
All			68.07	4.58	10.27	17.08	7188

** A period (.) means 0%.

ware development data [Bro75] [WF77] [Boe81] [Bro81] [VCW*84].

1. Project size
   - Larger (over 20,000 source lines)
   - Smaller (under 20,000 source lines)

2. Project start date
   - Earlier (prior to September 1979)
   - Later (within or after September 1979)

3. Interaction between project size and project start date

4.2 Module Design and Implementation Analysis

For the analysis of the module designs and implementations, the following factors were considered in a nonparametric analysis of variance model at the levels given. As above, the classifications given below are relative and specific for the particular environment. These factors were selected since the focus of this analysis is on module origin and since studies have indicated the importance of module size and individual project differences in the analysis of software development data [Bro75] [WF77] [Boe81] [Bro81] [BSP83] [VCW*84].

1. Module origin
   - Complete reuse without revision
   - Reuse with slight revision ($< 25\%$ changes)
   - Reuse with major revision ($\geq 25\%$ changes)
   - Complete new development

2. Module size
   - Larger (over 140 source lines)
   - Smaller (equal to or less than 140 source lines)

3. Individual Project containing the module
   - One level for each of the individual projects

4. Interaction of module origin with module size

The results presented in this paper focus on the statistically significant differences in the dependent variables

Figure 1: Origin of modules in the 25 projects. Projects are sorted according to the percentage of their modules reused without revision. There is one index for each project: the higher the percentage of modules reused without revision, the higher the index. (These project indexes have no relation to the project ID#'s in Table 1.)

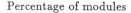

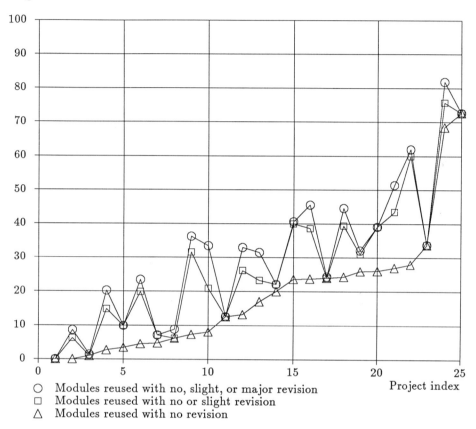

○ Modules reused with no, slight, or major revision
□ Modules reused with no or slight revision
△ Modules reused with no revision

due to the effect of module origin.

5   Characterizing Software Reuse at the Project Level

Table 1 presents the distribution of the origin of modules according to project date, project size, and individual project. Of the 7188 total modules, 17.1% were reused without modification from previous systems, 10.3% were reused with slight modification, and 4.6% were reused with major modification. Hence, approximately one-third (31.9%) of the modules in this environment were either reused or modified from previous projects. The amount of reuse varied across the projects: in project P4 81.9% of the modules were either reused or modified, while in project P23 0% of the modules were either reused or modified. Figure 1 graphically depicts the percentage of modules reused or modified in the projects.

Several different perspectives were analyzed in order to characterize the type of reuse across the projects. The analysis of variance model described in Section 4.1 was applied to determine statistically significant differences in the projects according to several dependent variables. They included the following measures for each project:

the number of modules reused without revision,

the number of modules reused with slight revision,

the number of modules reused with major revision,

the number of modules newly developed,

the number of modules reused with either no or slight revision,

the number of modules reused with either slight or major revision,

the number of modules reused with either no, slight, or major revision, and

the percentages of a project's modules in each of these seven categories.

Projects of larger size had a higher number of modules in each of these seven categories of reuse (statistically significant at $\alpha < .02$, $\alpha < .002$, $\alpha < .0002$, $\alpha < .0001$, α

Figure 2: Project size versus the percentage of project modules that were reused with either no, slight, or major revision.

Percentage of modules

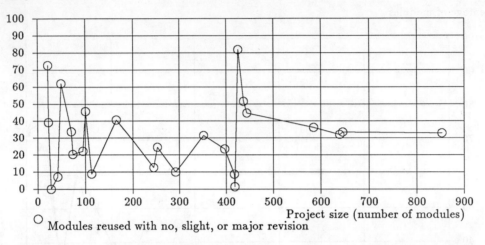

○ Modules reused with no, slight, or major revision

$< .0006$, $\alpha < .0004$, $\alpha < .0003$, respectively). This result is not surprising since other studies have observed that the number of modules in a software project tends to be related to the size of the project [WF77] [Boe81]. Given that there were a different number of modules in each of the projects, another interpretation examines the percentage of modules in each of the categories listed above. Projects of larger size had a higher percentage of modules that were reused with major revision ($\alpha < .02$). However, project size had no statistically significant effect on any of the other percentages of module reuse ($\alpha > .05$). Figure 2 displays the relationship between project size, in terms of number of modules, and the amount of reuse. When the project start date was considered, it had no significant effect on any of the 14 measures listed above — neither the actual numbers nor the percentages of modules reused ($\alpha > .05$ for all).

The data analysis at the project level does not seem to differentiate cleanly among the projects. This may be due to the variation in functionality and development factors that tends to occur across individual projects. The next step in the data analysis characterizes software reuse at finer levels of granularity: the module design level and the module implementation level.

6 Characterizing Module Level Data

6.1 Modules Analyzed

Of the 7188 modules appearing in Table 1, 2954 modules were Fortran subroutines with complete data collected on their development. The remainder of the modules were either: (a) not Fortran subroutines (e.g., they were assembler macros, utility functions, main programs, block data); (b) Fortran subroutines with incomplete development effort data; or (c) Fortran subroutines that have not yet been analyzed with the SAP static analysis tool mentioned in Section 4. The distribution of the 2954 modules according to module origin is given in Table 2. The overall distribution profile is similar to the one in Table 1. The module level analysis in this section and Sections 7 and 8 is based on applying the analysis of variance model from Section 4.2 to data from these 2954 modules.

6.2 Module Size and Development Effort

The size and development effort of the modules analyzed provide an initial characterization of them. Table 3a dis-

Table 2: Origin of modules for those Fortran subroutines with complete data collected on their development.

| Distribution of | Module origin | | | | |
	New	Major revision	Slight revision	Complete reuse	All
Number	1629	205	300	820	2954
Percentage	55.15	6.94	10.16	27.76	100

Table 3: Module attributes that characterize the classes of module origin: size and development effort. Overall differences for the three attributes are statistically significant at: $\alpha < .0001$; $\alpha < .0001$; and $\alpha < .0001$; respectively. Number of modules in each category is: 1629, 205, 300, 820, and 2954, respectively.

Module attribute			Class of software modules				All modules
Factor	Metric	Statistic	New development	Major revision	Slight revision	Complete reuse	All modules
a) Final implementation size	Source lines	Mean	226.7	324.1	192.8	146.2	207.7
		Std. dev.	158.1	221.3	125.7	152.3	165.5
		Median	185.0	262.0	164.5	92.0	165.0
b) Total development effort	Tenths of human hours	Mean	213.5	193.6	86.2	5.8	141.5
		Std. dev.	378.0	284.8	144.6	28.0	308.5
		Median	110.0	100.0	60.0	0.0	60.0
c) Total development effort	Tenths of human hours per source line	Mean	1.089	0.758	0.601	0.047	0.727
		Std. dev.	3.575	1.976	1.861	0.207	2.808
		Median	0.616	0.421	0.345	0.000	0.346

plays the module averages for final implementation size in source lines. The modules reused with extensive revision were the largest, and the newly developed modules were the second largest; those reused with slight revision were the third largest, and those completely reused without revision were the smallest (simultaneous $\alpha < .05$). This comparison among the module origins and all of those comparisons that follow were rejected by using Tukey's multiple comparisons test[CC50]. Table 3b displays the module averages for total development effort. Modules that were either newly developed or extensively revised had the most development effort, while slightly revised modules had the second most and those completely reused had the least (simultaneous $\alpha < .05$). (In general, the discussion will focus on only those pairwise comparisons of module origins that were statistically significant. For example, there was no statistically significant difference in development effort when newly developed modules and extensively revised modules were compared.) The development effort for an extensively revised, slightly revised, or completely reused module is the effort spent on an existing module to modify and/or evaluate it for a current project; the effort required for its original development is not included. Although some of the completely reused modules required a design inspection or some testing, 696 (84.9%) of them required zero hours of development effort.

Studies in general have indicated that module attributes, such as effort and various static measures, tend to correlate with module size [Boe81]. In particular, an earlier study showed this relationship to be true for data from this environment [BSP83]. Therefore, the subsequent analysis uses only module attributes that have been normalized by the final module implementation size measured in source lines. Table 3c displays the module averages for total development effort per source line. Newly developed modules had the most effort per source line, modules extensively or slightly revised had the second

most, and completely reused modules had the least (simultaneous $\alpha < .05$).

7 Characterizing Software Reuse at the Module Design Level

Several researchers have advocated the merits of software reuse at the design level (e.g., [KG87] [BR87]). Software design information tends to be applicable across a variety of problems, while specific implementations tend to embody information customized to individual circumstances. This section focuses on the characterization of software reuse at the module design level. Several aspects of software design are considered:

- the interfaces that a module has with other system modules;

- the interfaces that other system modules have with a module;

- the interfaces that a module has with human users;

- the documentation describing the functionality of a module; and

- the effort spent in designing a module.

7.1 A Module's Interfaces with Other Modules

Two interpretations are considered for capturing the interfaces between a given module and other modules. The first interpretation is the number of calls that a module makes to other system modules, where utility functions are not counted since they are relatively low level. The second interpretation is the total number of calls that a module makes just to utility functions. These two views

Table 4: Module design attributes that characterize the classes of module origin: interfaces among modules and utility functions. In the first attribute ('a'), calls to utility functions are not counted. Overall differences for the three attributes are statistically significant at: $\alpha <$ .0001; $\alpha <$ .0001; and $\alpha <$ .0001; respectively. Number of modules in each category is: 1629, 205, 300, 820, and 2954, respectively.

Module attribute			Class of software modules				All modules
Factor	Metric	Statistic	New devel-opment	Major revision	Slight revision	Com-plete reuse	
a) Interface with other sys-tem modules	Module calls per source line	Mean	0.0315	0.0353	0.0307	0.0186	0.0281
		Std. dev.	0.0329	0.0303	0.0384	0.0375	0.0352
		Median	0.0246	0.0283	0.0204	0.0000	0.0195
b) Interface with utility functions	Utility func-tion calls per source line	Mean	0.0146	0.0142	0.0144	0.0328	0.0196
		Std. dev.	0.0317	0.0230	0.0266	0.0810	0.0505
		Median	0.0000	0.0040	0.0000	0.0055	0.0000
c) Interface provided to other modules	Input-output parameters per source line	Mean	0.096	0.118	0.103	0.081	0.094
		Std. dev.	0.063	0.072	0.090	0.084	0.073
		Median	0.086	0.104	0.088	0.066	0.083

are intended to capture the amount of potential interaction that a module has with other system modules and with support modules, respectively. These are two forms of module "fan-out." Tables 4a and 4b present these two interpretations. Extensively revised modules had the most calls to other system modules, newly developed or slightly revised modules had the second most, and completely reused ones had the fewest (Table 4a; simultaneous $\alpha <$ .05). Completely reused modules had more calls to utility functions than did either newly developed or slightly revised modules (Table 4b; simultaneous $\alpha <$ .05).

7.2 The Interfaces Other System Modules have with a Module

A straightforward measure is considered for characterizing the interface between other system modules and a given module. The measure is the number of input and output parameters in a module, including any global data referenced. Table 4c displays the module averages for the number of input and output parameters. Modules that were extensively revised had the most parameters, those that were either newly developed or slightly revised had the second most, and those that were completely reused had the fewest (simultaneous $\alpha <$ .05).

Table 5: Module design attributes that characterize the classes of module origin: interface with users, documentation, and design effort. Overall differences for the three attributes are statistically significant at: $\alpha <$ .0001; $\alpha <$ .0001; and $\alpha <$ .0001; respectively. Number of modules in each category for the first two attributes ('a' and 'b') is: 1629, 205, 300, 820, and 2954, respectively. Number of modules in each category for the third attribute ('c') is: 1629, 205, 300, 124, and 2258, respectively (since 696 completely reused modules had zero hours development effort).

Module attribute			Class of software modules				All modules
Factor	Metric	Statistic	New devel-opment	Major revision	Slight revision	Com-plete reuse	
a) Interface with human users	Read and write statements per source line	Mean	0.0178	0.0156	0.0187	0.0058	0.0144
		Std. dev.	0.0213	0.0163	0.0189	0.0134	0.0196
		Median	0.0120	0.0106	0.0141	0.0000	0.0072
b) Documen-tation	Comments per source line	Mean	0.546	0.524	0.543	0.585	0.555
		Std. dev.	0.141	0.128	0.146	0.197	0.159
		Median	0.554	0.538	0.565	0.621	0.566
c) Design effort	% of develop-ment effort spent in design	Mean	19.8	15.7	12.3	14.6	18.1
		Std. dev.	24.7	24.6	22.2	30.3	24.9
		Median	9.5	0.0	0.0	0.0	5.4

Table 6: Module implementation attributes that characterize the classes of module origin: changes and implementation style. Overall differences for the first and third attributes ('a' and 'c') are statistically significant at: $\alpha < .0001$; and $\alpha < .0001$; respectively. The overall difference for the second attribute ('b') is not statistically significant: $\alpha > .05$. Number of modules in each category is: 1629, 205, 300, 820, and 2954, respectively.

Module attribute			Class of software modules				All modules
Factor	Metric	Statistic	New development	Major revision	Slight revision	Complete reuse	
a) Changes	Changes	Mean	0.0481	0.0280	0.0305	0.0228	0.0379
	per	Std. dev.	0.0944	0.0287	0.0375	0.0377	0.0751
	source line	Median	0.0262	0.0209	0.0222	0.0130	0.0217
b) Implementation	Cyclomatic	Mean	0.0795	0.0902	0.0882	0.0806	0.0814
tation	complexity per	Std. dev.	0.0512	0.0475	0.0554	0.0696	0.0572
style	source line	Median	0.0709	0.0849	0.0827	0.0645	0.0710
c) Implementation	Assignment	Mean	0.111	0.134	0.117	0.141	0.121
tation	statements per	Std. dev.	0.080	0.087	0.089	0.123	0.096
style	source line	Median	0.099	0.123	0.098	0.118	0.105

7.3 A Module's Interfaces with Human Users

Modules have interfaces not only with other modules, but also with human users. One perspective of a module's interface with humans is captured by the number of its input and output statements, which is the number of reads and writes. Table 5a presents the module averages for read and write statements. The modules that were completely reused had the fewest read and write statements (simultaneous $\alpha < .05$).

7.4 The Documentation of a Module's Functionality

In the environment being examined, a description of the intended functionality of a module is recorded in English. This description is included with the final implementation of a module as a set of comments. One may argue that a lengthy description enables a clear understanding of a module's functionality. One may also argue that a lengthy description indicates a complicated specification that may be difficult to understand or implement. An approximation for a module's ratio of commentary to functionality is the number of comments per source line in the final implementation. The distribution across module origin for this measure is given in Table 5b. Modules that were completely reused had a higher commentary to source line ratio than did all other modules (simultaneous $\alpha < .05$).

7.5 Module Design Effort

Table 5c displays the average percentage of module development effort spent in module design. Modules that were newly developed had a higher percentage of effort

spent in module design than did all other modules (simultaneous $\alpha < .05$).

8 Characterizing Software Reuse at the Module Implementation Level

This section focuses on the characterization of software reuse at the module implementation level. Several aspects of software implementation are considered:

- the changes in a module;
- the control flow structure in a module; and
- the assignment statements ("non-control flow structure") in a module.

8.1 Module Changes

Table 6a displays a simple measure of the evolution that a module undergoes: its number of changes. Newly developed modules had the most changes, modules reused with extensive or slight revision had the second most, and modules completely reused had the fewest (simultaneous $\alpha < .05$).

8.2 Module Control Flow

One characteristic of an implementation for a module is its control flow structure. The cyclomatic complexity metric is based on the control flow graph for a module and has provided the foundations for various software testing methods [McC76]. Table 6b gives the module averages for cyclomatic complexity divided by the number of source lines. The overall difference is not statistically

Figure 3: Summary of 10 module attributes for modules reused without revision. There were 820 modules reused without revision and 2954 total modules (except for the design effort attribute where there were 124 and 2258 modules, respectively). For example interpretations of this plot, consider the following. A value of –20% for some attribute (e.g., size) means that 30% (= –20% + 50%) of the modules reused without revision had size above the median size value for all classes of modules. A value of +10% for some attribute (e.g., documentation) means that 60% (= 10% + 50%) of the modules reused without revision had documentation above the median documentation level for all classes of modules. If modules reused without revision were representative of all classes of modules in terms of some attribute, then it is likely that the attribute would be very close to 0% on this plot; this would mean that close to 50% of the reused modules are above and close to 50% of the reused modules are below the median for all module classes. The median value for an attribute is the value that is less than 50% of the attribute values and greater than 50% of the attribute values.

Percentage of modules above median value for all modules (minus 50%)

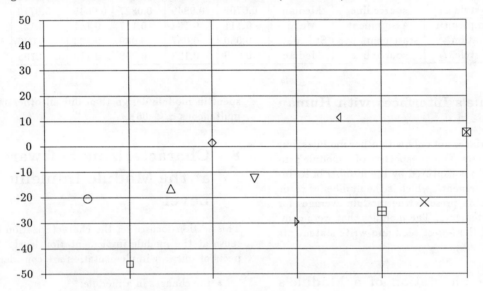

○   Size (source lines)
□   Effort (total development effort per source line)
△   Interface with other system modules (module calls per source line)
◇   Interface with utility functions (utility function calls per source line)
▽   Interface provided to other modules (input-output parameters per source line)
▷   Interface with human users (read and write statements per source line)
◁   Documentation (comments per source line)
⊞   Design effort (percentage of development effort spent in design)
×   Changes (changes per source line)
⊠   Implementation style (assignment statements per source line)

significant ($\alpha > .05$). However, an earlier study in this environment has indicated that cyclomatic complexity per executable statement is the lowest for completely reused modules [CCA86].

8.3   Module Assignment Statements

One aspect of the "non-control flow structure" in a module is its assignment statements. Table 6c gives the module averages for the number of assignment statements divided by the number of source lines. Modules that were either completely reused or extensively revised had

a higher number of assignment statements than did newly developed modules (simultaneous $\alpha < .05$).

9   Interpretations and Conclusions

Reusing software may be the catalyst that helps the software community achieve large improvements in software productivity and quality. The goal of frequent software reuse, however, continues to challenge the software community. There are several motivations for desiring software reuse, including gains in productivity by avoiding

Figure 4: Summary of 10 module attributes for modules reused with slight revision ($<$ 25% changes). There were 300 modules reused with slight revision and 2954 total modules. For example interpretations of this plot, see the caption for Figure 3.

Percentage of modules above median value for all modules (minus 50%)

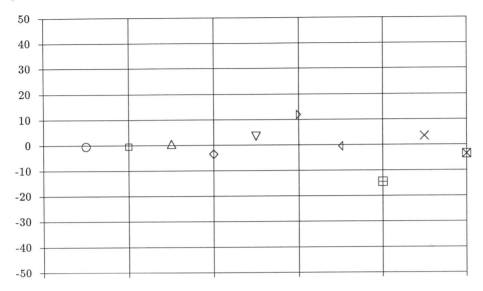

○ Size (source lines)
□ Effort (total development effort per source line)
△ Interface with other system modules (module calls per source line)
◇ Interface with utility functions (utility function calls per source line)
▽ Interface provided to other modules (input-output parameters per source line)
▷ Interface with human users (read and write statements per source line)
◁ Documentation (comments per source line)
⊞ Design effort (percentage of development effort spent in design)
✕ Changes (changes per source line)
⊠ Implementation style (assignment statements per source line)

redevelopment and gains in quality by incorporating components whose reliability has already been established. The approach presented in this study has been to provide insights through empirical analysis of an environment that actively reuses software. Twenty-five software systems ranging from 3000 to 112,000 source lines were selected for analysis from a NASA production environment. The amount of software either reused or modified from previous systems averages 32% per project in this environment. Non-parametric analysis of variance models were applied to examine a wide range of development variables across the software modules in the systems. The analysis has focused on the characterization of software reuse at the project, module design, and module implementation levels.

9.1 Summary of Empirical Results

Classes of Modules Figures 3, 4, 5, and 6 summarize the characterization of module attributes for the four module classes:

- modules reused without revision,
- modules reused with slight revision ($<$ 25% changes),
- modules reused with major revision ($\geq$ 25% changes), and
- newly developed modules, respectively.

Module Design Level A summary of the characterization of software reuse at the module design level in the environment is as follows. When compared to modules that were either newly developed, extensively revised, or slightly revised, modules that were completely reused without revision had

- less interaction with other system modules, in terms of the number of module calls per source line;
- simpler interfaces, in terms of the number of input-output parameters per source line;

Figure 5: Summary of 10 module attributes for modules reused with major revision ($\geq 25\%$ changes). There were 205 modules reused with major revision and 2954 total modules. For example interpretations of this plot, see the caption for Figure 3.

Percentage of modules above median value for all modules (minus 50%)

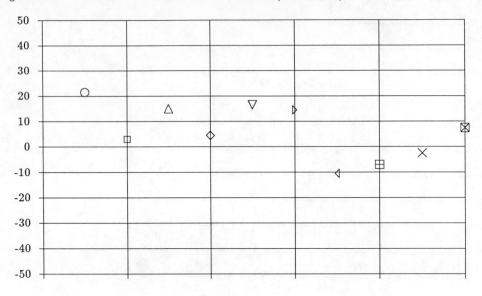

○   Size (source lines)
□   Effort (total development effort per source line)
△   Interface with other system modules (module calls per source line)
◇   Interface with utility functions (utility function calls per source line)
▽   Interface provided to other modules (input-output parameters per source line)
▷   Interface with human users (read and write statements per source line)
◁   Documentation (comments per source line)
⊞   Design effort (percentage of development effort spent in design)
×   Changes (changes per source line)
⊠   Implementation style (assignment statements per source line)

- less interaction with human users, in terms of the number of read-write statements per source line; and

- higher ratios of commentary to eventual implementation size, in terms of the number of comments per source line.

When compared to newly developed modules, modules that were completely reused without revision had

- more interaction with utility functions, in terms of the number of utility function calls per source line; and

- a lower percentage of development effort spent in design.

Module Implementation Level   A summary of the characterization of software reuse at the module implementation level in the environment is as follows. When compared to modules that were either newly developed,

extensively revised, or slightly revised, modules that were completely reused without revision had

- smaller size, in terms of the number of source lines;

- less total development effort, in terms of the number of either total development hours or total development hours per source line; and

- fewer changes, in terms of the number of versions per source line.

When compared to newly developed modules, modules that were completely reused without revision had

- more assignment statements, in terms of the number of assignment statements per source line.

Project Level   The project level analysis indicated that projects of larger size had

- a higher percentage of modules that were reused with major revision.

Figure 6: Summary of 10 module attributes for modules newly developed. There were 1629 modules newly developed and 2954 total modules. For example interpretations of this plot, see the caption for Figure 3.

Percentage of modules above median value for all modules (minus 50%)

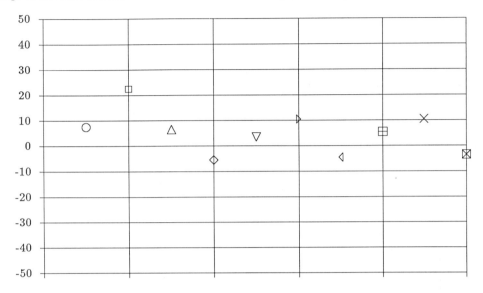

○ Size (source lines)
□ Effort (total development effort per source line)
△ Interface with other system modules (module calls per source line)
◇ Interface with utility functions (utility function calls per source line)
▽ Interface provided to other modules (input-output parameters per source line)
▷ Interface with human users (read and write statements per source line)
◁ Documentation (comments per source line)
⊞ Design effort (percentage of development effort spent in design)
✕ Changes (changes per source line)
⊠ Implementation style (assignment statements per source line)

9.2   Interpretations

The empirical results from this study suggest several trends for the specific environment examined. Completely reused modules tended to be small, well-documented modules with simple interfaces and little input-output processing. There is an indication that the completely reused modules tended to be "terminal nodes" in the projects' module invocation hierarchies. This is because the completely reused modules had less interaction with other systems modules but more interaction with utility functions, when compared to newly developed modules. The completely reused modules required little development effort or changes. Considering the development effort that was expended, a lower proportion was spent in design activities. This is because the design of a module from scratch requires the creation and evaluation of a new design, while the complete reuse of a module may require only a walkthrough of an existing design. There is a hint that the completely reused modules had implementations of a sequential — as opposed to branching — nature, because of their higher proportion of assignment statements. When the developers were working on large projects, they may have been even more motivated than usual to reuse modules because of the project scale. Consequently, a higher percentage of modules on those projects ended up with extensive revisions.

Several statistically significant relationships have been outlined in this paper. For example, modules reused without revision had fewer input-output parameters. Does this result suggest that reused modules just happened to have simpler interfaces or that the simpler interfaces led to the reuse of the modules? There is a certain circularity in the reasoning that needs to be considered before concluding the causality of effects (e.g., simpler interfaces caused the modules to be reused). In some cases the causes and effects may not be cleanly separable from one another and from the other factors affecting the projects in the environment.

Reusing software is a natural process for the developers in this environment. The reuse is by developer choice, not management directive. This willingness to reuse indicates that the developers are convinced of its payoffs.

Also, there is relatively low turnover of development personnel. Although the projects vary in functionality, the overall problem domain — ground support software for unmanned spacecraft control — has an established set of algorithms and processing methods. Therefore, several factors about this environment aid their ability to reuse software.

Developers in this environment do not have automated tools to assist in the reuse process. Developers simply use their own experience and knowledge to accomplish software reuse. They are able to do so because of the low personnel turnover and established problem domain. An open question is how such an environment would be impacted by automated systems intended to catalyze the reuse process. The development of such a system is one of my current research projects.

9.3 Future Work

This paper has discussed an initial set of results from an empirical study of one environment — further interpretation of the data is underway. This work is intended to provide implications that span a variety of software development areas:

- lifecycle models incorporating reuse,

- reuse methodologies, and

- tools to support reuse.

A continuing theme in this work is to analyze more than just the reuse of source code, including in particular, information that relates to software reuse at the design level.

Further analysis of software reuse in the projects is in progress. An expanded set of project and module attributes is being examined, including information about software errors that occurred during development. There is also some recently acquired project data about reuse in a second development organization. The continued analysis is intended to yield further information about the development, organization, and identification of reusable software objects.

References

[Bea73]   G. Birstwistle and et al. *Simula Begin*. Studentliteratur and Auerbach Publishers, Berlin, 1973.

[Big83]   T. Biggerstaff, editor. *Proceedings of the Workshop on Reusability in Programming*. ITT, Shelton, Conn., 1983.

[BKK*86]   D. Bobrow, K. Kahn, G. Kiczales, L. Masinter, M. Stefik, and F. Zdybel. Commonloops: merging lisp and object-oriented programming. In *OOPSLA 86: Object Oriented Programming Systems, Languages, and Applications*, pages 17–29, 1986.

[Boe81]   B. W. Boehm. *Software Engineering Economics*. Prentice-Hall, Englewood Cliffs, NJ, 1981.

[Boo86]   G. Booch. Object-oriented development. *IEEE Transactions on Software Engineering*, SE-12(2):211–221, February 1986.

[BP]   T. Biggerstaff and A. Perlis, editors. *Software Reusability*. Addison-Wesley, Reading, Mass. (in press).

[BP84]   T. Biggerstaff and A. Perlis, editors. *IEEE Transactions on Software Engineering*. SE-10(5), Special Issue on Software Reusability, September 1984.

[BR87]   T. Biggerstaff and C. Richter. Reusability framework, assessment, and directions. *IEEE Software*, 4(2):41–49, March 1987.

[Bro75]   F. P. Brooks. *The Mythical Man-Month*. Addison-Wesley Publishing Co., Reading, MA, 1975.

[Bro81]   W. D. Brooks. Software technology payoff: some statistical evidence. *Journal of Systems and Software*, 2:3–9, 1981.

[BS82]   D. G. Bobrow and M. J. Stefik. *Loops: An Objected-Oriented Programming System for Interlisp*. Technical Report, Xerox PARC, Palo Alto, California, 1982.

[BSP83]   V. R. Basili, R. W. Selby, and T. Y. Phillips. Metric analysis and data validation across fortran projects. *IEEE Transactions on Software Engineering*, SE-9(6):652–663, Nov. 1983.

[BW84]   V. R. Basili and D. M. Weiss. A methodology for collecting valid software engineering data. *IEEE Transactions on Software Engineering*, SE-10(6):728–738, Nov. 1984.

[BZM*77]   V. R. Basili, M. V. Zelkowitz, F. E. McGarry, Jr. R. W. Reiter, W. F. Truszkowski, and D. L. Weiss. *The Software Engineering Laboratory*. Technical Report SEL-77-001, Software Engineering Laboratory, NASA/Goddard Space Flight Center, Greenbelt, MD, May 1977.

[Can80]   J. I. Cannon. *Flavors*. Technical Report, MIT Artificial Intelligence Laboratory, Cambridge, Mass, 1980.

[CC50]   W. G. Cochran and G. M. Cox. *Experimen-*

tal Designs. John Wiley & Sons, New York, 1950.

[CCA86]   D. N. Card, V. E. Church, and W. W. Agresti. An empirical study of software design practices. *IEEE Transactions on Software Engineering*, SE-12(2):264–271, February 1986.

[CMP*82]   D. N. Card, F. E. McGarry, J. Page, S. Eslinger, and V. R. Basili. *The Software Engineering Laboratory.* Technical Report SEL-81-104, Software Engineering Laboratory, NASA/Goddard Space Flight Center, Greenbelt, MD, Feb. 1982.

[Con86]   R. Conn. An overview of the dod ada software repository. *Dr. Dobbs Journal*, 60–61,86–91, February 1986.

[CPM85]   D. N. Card, G. T. Page, and F. E. McGarry. Criteria for software modularization. In *Proceedings of the Eighth International Conference on Software Engineering*, pages 372–377, London, August 28-30, 1985.

[DT82]   W. J Decker and W. A. Taylor. *FORTRAN Static Source Code Analyzer Program (SAP) User's Guide (Revision 1).* Technical Report SEL-78-102, Software Engineering Laboratory, NASA/Goddard Space Flight Center, Greenbelt, MD, May 1982.

[GR83]   A. Goldberg and D. Robson. *Smalltalk-80: The Language and its Implementation.* Addison-Wesley, Reading, Mass., 1983.

[HN86]   A. N. Habermann and D. Notkin. Gandalf: software development environments. *IEEE Transactions on Software Engineering*, SE-12(12), December 1986.

[Hul84]   J.-H. Hulot. *Ceyx, Version 15:1 – Une Initiation.* Technical Report 44, INRIA, France, 1984.

[KG87]   G. E. Kaiser and D. Garlan. Melding software systems from reusable building blocks. *IEEE Software*, 4(4):17–24, July 1987.

[McC76]   T. J. McCabe. A complexity measure. *IEEE Transactions on Software Engineering*, SE-2(4):308–320, Dec. 1976.

[Mey87]   B. Meyer. Reusability: the case for object-oriented design. *IEEE Software*, 4(2):50–64, March 1987.

[Nei84]   J. Neighbors. The Draco approach to constructing software from reusable components. *IEEE Transactions on Software Engineering*, SE-10(5):564–573, September 1984.

[Ost87]   L. J. Osterweil. Software processes are software too. In *Proceedings of the Ninth International Conference on Software Engineering*, pages 2–13, Monterey, CA, March 30 – April 2, 1987.

[Rep83]   T. Reps. *Generating Language-Based Environments.* M.I.T. Press, Cambridge, Mass., 1983.

[Sch59]   H. Scheffe. *The Analysis of Variance.* John Wiley & Sons, New York, 1959.

[Sel]   R. W. Selby. Quantitative studies of software reuse. In T. Biggerstaff and A. Perlis, editors, *Software Reusability*, Addison-Wesley, Reading, Mass. (in press).

[SEL82]   SEL. *Annotated Bibliography of Software Engineering Laboratory (SEL)Literature.* Technical Report SEL-82-006, Software Engineering Laboratory, NASA/Goddard Space Flight Center, Greenbelt, MD, Nov. 1982.

[Str86]   B. Stroustrup. *The C++ Programming Language.* Addison-Wesley, Menlo Park, California, 1986.

[Tes85]   L. Tesler. Object pascal report. *Structured Language World*, 1985.

[Tra87a]   W. Tracz. Ada reusability efforts: a survey of the state of the practice. In *Proceedings of the Fifth National Conference on Ada Technology*, Arlington, VA, March 1987.

[Tra87b]   W. Tracz, editor. *IEEE Software.* 4(4), Special Issue on Software Reusability, July 1987.

[VCW*84]   J. Vosburgh, B. Curtis, R. Wolverton, B. Albert, H. Malec, S. Hoben, and Y. Liu. Productivity factors and programming environments. In *Proceedings of the Seventh International Conference on Software Engineering*, pages 143–152, Orlando, FL, 1984.

[WF77]   C. E. Walston and C. P. Felix. A method of programming measurement and estimation. *IBM Systems J.*, 16(1):54–73, 1977.

METHODOLOGY/ENVIRONMENT SUPPORT FOR REUSABILITY

Gerald Jones
GTE Laboratories, Inc.
40 Sylvan Rd.
Waltham, MA 02254

INTRODUCTION

Our research project in software reusability at GTE Labs currently has three areas of focus: classification/library support for reusability, domain analysis, and methodology/environment support for reusability. A separate position paper has been submitted by Ruben Prieto describing some of our work in the first two areas; in this paper, we present our initial thoughts on the key issues in the methodology/environment area, though we have not yet begun detailed research in this area.

In order to realize substantial reusability, it is necessary to incorporate a reusability emphasis into all phases of a software development methodology and then provide environmental support for this methodology. The goal must be a methodology and environment in which reusing software is the natural, easy, standard way of developing software. If reusing software is not the standard or involves considerable extra work then it will remain the exception rather than the norm.

SCOPE OF REUSABILITY

Software reusability is a very broad area and involves many issues (both managerial and technical) and allows many different approaches. The two major categories of approaches to reusability are the building block approach and the generative approach [BIG87]. The building block approach emphasizes the creation of new software from existing components retrieved from a reusability library. In the generative approach, reusable components are built into a tool (such as an application generator) or a language, and much of the work of selecting, customizing, and composing the components is automated.

In a sense, the building block approach is more fundamental because it is not possible to develop an application generator, for example, for a domain until the basic building blocks for that domain are well enough understood so that they can be incorporated into such a tool. And the basic building blocks in a domain will not be understood until there is considerable experience in building applications from standard building blocks. The generative approach is a natural extension of the building block approach and has the potential of much greater payoff.

There are many varieties of software building blocks that can and should be exploited for reuse:

- all levels of the software, including specification, design, and code;

- all sizes of components from individual fragments to complete subsystems;

- both application-specific and general-purpose components;

- both off-the-shelf components (no modification needed) and adaptive components (must be customized).

Our view is that there is no single best approach. Rather, a combination of approaches, dependent on an organization's individual needs, should be applied to provide the greatest impact.

METHODOLOGY ISSUES

Figure 1 shows an overall view of a reusability library supporting the software development process. It emphasizes the diversity of components that populate the library, and that reusability should impact the software process thru all phases of development. The general paradigm is to explicitly or implicity (through the environment) ask the library which components are available that may be usable or customizable at the various levels of development. The use of a set of design templates may be automated thru the use of a design tool, whereas an explicit library search of code fragments may be used at a lower level.

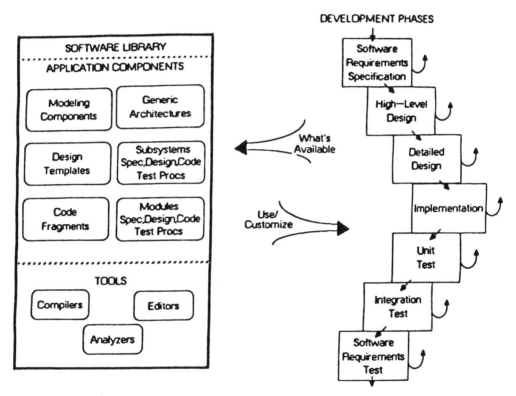

Figure 1: Reusability Library to Support Software Development Process

Reusability must be incorporated into all phases of the software development methodology in order to maximize the potential gain. Some of the key issues are:

- a careful domain analysis of the application domain(s) in order to identify the basic objects/operations within the domain and to provide a generic domain model for applications within the domain;

- using the domain model and possibly a collection of modeling components during the specification phase;

- using a generic software architecture and standard design templates during the high-level design phase;

- including a bottom-up component in the design methodology (what parts are available for helping build this application?);

- designing for future reusability (issues of abstraction, encapsulation, documentation);

- maintaining connections between specification, design, code, test levels so that, for example, a design that is reused can easily lead to code reuse and test case reuse;

- a project-independent reusability group to monitor project reviews and promote reusability;

- standardization of methodology, environment, languages as much as possible.

In addition there are many crucial management issues related to emphasizing and promoting reusability (e.g. training, incentives).

We are particularly interested in design-level reusability. The use of generic architectures and design templates (e.g. task idioms in the AdaGraph tool) need to be better exploited. The object-oriented concepts of abstraction, inheritance, and encapsulation need to be exploited further at the design level. The link between design information and requirements at one end and code at the other end needs to more complete. The bottom-up component of design needs to be better understood; for example, considering alternative designs based on the availability of parts. The SARA methodology [PEN79] is a good starting point. These are some of the areas that we plan for our research focus.

ENVIRONMENT ISSUES

The environment must support the development methodology so that the reusable paradigm is enforced and is the natural, easy mode of development. The Smalltalk environment with its class browser is a good example of making it easier to find and reuse components.

Our work has touched two areas related to environment support for reusability. One is the development of a library system based on faceted software classification [PRI87a,PRI87b] for cataloging and retrieving collections of software components. A major impediment to reusability in many organizations is the difficulty in finding components even though they do exist and are appropriate for reuse.

The classification scheme forces the development of a standard vocabulary for an organization and its application domains, and that in itself is a big help in finding existing software components. The faceted approach has several advantages over other classification schemes in terms of flexibility, expandability, and precision. The library system has been used in several GTE organizations for promoting existing collections of code level components.

The second area of work related to environments is a summary of general reusability requirements for a data model for software environments. Another GTE Labs project is researching such a data model [KUO87]. The key requirements are:

- the ability to represent a wide variety of software information structures, since a reusability library may contain components of many varieties;

- the ability to represent abstract, generic software information structures;

- the ability to to support component transformation operations from reusable abstractions to concrete implementations;

- the ability to support component composition operations;

- the ability to relate documentation and classification information to the software components.

The data model being researched in the GTE Labs environment project seemed to support these requirements very well and we are planning to design a library-based design environment on top of their generic environment model.

CONCLUSIONS

This paper has briefly described some of our current work and thoughts for future work in the area of methodology and environment support for reusability. This is a new area of focus for us, but we believe it is of central importance to realizing a successful reusability program within an organization.

REFERENCES

[BIG87] Biggerstaff, T. and C. Richter, "Reusability Framework, Assessment, and Directions," **IEEE Software**, Vol. 4, No. 2, March 1987, pp. 41-49.

[KUO87] Kuo, J. and H. Tu, "Prototyping a Software Information Base for Software Environments," to be presented at COMPSAC 87, Tokyo, October 1987.

[PEN79] Penedo, M. and D. Berry, "The Use of a Module Interconnection Language in the SARA System Design Methodology," **Proceedings of 4th International Conference on Software Engineering**, Munich, September 1979, pp. 294-307.

[PRI87a] Prieto-Diaz, R. and P. Freeman, "Classifying Software for Reusability," **IEEE Software**, Vol. 4, No. 1, January 1987, pp. 6-16.

[PRI87b] Prieto-Diaz, R. and G. Jones, "Breathing New Life Into Old Software," **GTE Journal**, Vol. 1, No. 1, June 1987, pp. 22-31.

A Reuse-Based Software Development Methodology[1]

Kyo C. Kang

Software Engineering Institute

Carnegie-Mellon University

Pittsburgh, PA 15213

Abstract

Software has been reused in the applications development ever since programming started. However, the practices have mostly been ad hoc, and the potential benefits of reuse have never been fully realized nor understood. Most of the available software development methodologies do not identify reuse activities explicitly. The Application of Reusable Software Components Project of the Software Engineering Institute is developing a reuse-based software development methodology, and the current direction and the progress of the methodology work are discussed in this paper.

The methodology is based on the life cycle model in [DOD87] with refinement of each phase to identify reuse activities. The reuse activities that are common across the life cycle phases are identified as: 1) understanding the problem and identifying a solution structure based on the reusable components, 2) reconfiguring the solution structure to improve reuse at the next phase, 3) acquiring, instantiating, and/or modifying existing reusable components, and 4) integrating the reused and any newly developed components into the products for the phase. These activities are used as the base model for defining the specific activities at each phase of the life cycle.

The methodology, when completed, will be used in an application redevelopment experiment and then will be improved based on our experience.

1 Introduction

Software reuse is not a new development concept; for instance, we have been reusing software libraries for decades. However, reuse has mostly been limited to code reuse and has generally been practiced in an ad hoc way, and the impacts of reuse on software development and the potential benefits and risks of reusing other life cycle products (e.g., requirements, design) have not been fully understood.

The Application of Reusable Software Components Project of the Software Engineering Institute is planning to conduct a reuse experiment through redevelopment of an existing system. Through the experiment we want to gain experience with available reuse technology, measure and understand the impact of software reuse on products and the development process, understand what and how we can reuse at each phase of the life cycle, and collect and accumulate data for evaluating technologies in the future.

One of the tasks identified for the experiment is the development of a reuse-based software development methodology. This paper discusses the current direction and the progress of the methodology development task.

---

[1]The Software Engineering Institute is a federally funded research and development center sponsored by the Department of Defense under contract to Carnegie-Mellon University. This paper is approved for public release.

2 A Reuse Activity Model

The purpose of the methodology task is to identify the development activities and to define the order in which the identified activities are to be carried out during the software development. The methodology is based on the life cycle model defined in [DOD87] and follows the guidance of [STARS86]. The methodology is not yet complete. By applying the methodology during the experiment, we want to understand what and how we reuse; based on our experience, we will improve the methodology.

The methodology refines the life cycle model in [DOD87] by identifying reuse activities applicable to each phase. ([DOD87] identifies the life cycle phases as: system concepts development, system requirements analysis, software requirements analysis, preliminary design, detailed design, coding and unit testing, software component integration and testing, and system integration and testing.) In refining each phase, a generic reuse activity model is used as the base model. The generic model is discussed in this section.

Reuse is an act of synthesizing a solution to a problem based on predefined solutions to subproblems. The reuse activity is divided into four major steps performed at each phase in preparation for the next phase. These steps are:

1. Understanding the problem and identifying a solution structure based on the predefined components,

2. Reconfiguring the solution structure to improve the possibility of using predefined components available at the next phase,

3. Acquiring, instantiating, and modifying predefined components, and

4. Integrating the components into the products for this phase.

The major tasks under the first step are to understand the problem to solve, build up the knowledge of the predefined solutions, and apply the knowledge in structuring the problem in terms of the subproblems to which solutions already exist.

Once a solution structure is identified based on the predefined components available at a given phase, the next step is to reconfigure the solution in order to optimize reuse both at the current phase and the next phase. Doing so requires identifying experts of the next phase activity who will review the proposed solution, identify candidate components available at the next phase, and evaluate the reusability of the candidate components. Based on the potential reuse at the next phase as well as at the current phase, an optimal solution structure is to be identified. We anticipate that the first two steps would be iterated a number of times.

The major output from the first two steps are a solution structure and a reuse plan for the next phase. The third step includes tasks of making components identified in the solution structure ready for integration. These tasks include acquiring reusable components, modifying and/or instantiating reusable components, and developing the components that cannot be acquired or for which modification is not economic. Finally, the completed components are integrated into the product(s) required for the phase. The products are subjected to a formal review before being released to the next phase.

The next section shows how this generic reuse model can be applied to the software requirements phase.

3 Software Requirements Analysis

The major activities at the software requirements analysis phase, as defined in [DOD87], are:

1. Preparing the software requirements specification (SRS) and the interface requirements specifications (IRS) for each computer software configuration item (CSCI) identified at the

previous phase (the system requirements analysis phase),

2. Test planning, in which qualification requirements are defined for each CSCI, and

3. Software specification review (SSR), in which the SRS and IRS are evaluated for their conformance to the predefined criteria.

Of these activities, the activity of preparing the SRS and IRS is refined in this section based on the generic reuse model defined in the previous section.

The major inputs to this phase are the system segment specification (SSS), the preliminary interface requirements specification (PIRS), and the preliminary software requirements specifications (PSRS). The first step to develop SRS and IRS is to study the input documents (SSS, PIRS, and PSRS) and understand the high-level requirements, and then to review the reusable requirements identified in the requirements reuse plan, which is produced at the system requirements analysis phase. (We believe that system structures similar to the system under development and the specifications of the objects, functions, interfaces, etc. defined for each structure are reusable components at this phase.)

Based on a reusable structure(s) (if any), a new structure for the target system is created, and reusable components are identified and reviewed. Domain experts are identified, and they review and evaluate the proposed structure and reusable software components. Based on their evaluation results and recommendations, the structure is modified if the modified structure results in an improved solution (for example, a solution that will result in higher productivity or quality). These activities (studying the SSS, PIRS, and PSRS; examining the reusable requirements; creating or modifying the structure; and evaluating the structure against reusable software) are repeated until an "optimal" structure is obtained.

For example, the functional structure of an inventory control system might provide a good framework for developing the functional structure of a library system since both systems maintain information about the components (parts in the case of an inventory system, and books in the case of a library system), inventory status, back orders, customer, etc. The objects that are handled by the two systems are different, but the processing requirements can be quite similar.

Once a structure is identified, the components that come from outside the project must be acquired, the components that need to be modified or refined must be processed accordingly, and components that cannot be acquired or that are too expensive to modify must be defined. These pieces are combined to create the requirements documents (SRS and IRS).

The generic reuse model has been applied in refining the other phases of the life cycle in much the same way as it is applied for the requirements analysis phase. We are currently analyzing the methodology to identify the activities particular to each phase.

4 Expected Results

By applying the methodology under the controlled conditions of an experiment, we will evaluate the methodology to identify and quantify the benefits and risks of a reuse-based approach. We will also characterize the reusable components and the development process.

Our understanding will help to define the requirements for a high-productivity software engineering environment that is based on reuse. This new technology will mature through experimentation, evaluation, and improvement.

5 References

[DOD87] Defense System Software Development, Military Standard DOD-STD-2167A (Draft), April 1, 1987.

[STARS86] "STARS Reusability Guidebook V4.0," STARS Application Workshop, NRL, San Diego, CA, September 1986.

Reusability Benefits of
a Structure which Supports
a Development Methodology and Environment

J.M.Perry, J.Roder, F.Rosene
GTE Government Systems
Waltham, MA 02254
and
GTE Government Systems
Communication Systems Division
77 A Street
Needham, Massachusetts 02194

Introduction

A primary goal for software engineering is the continued transition of software development to an engineering discipline through the improvement of tools, methods, methodologies and, more fundamentally, of structures necessary for controlling complexity. Structures provide organization for the software system and the software artifacts produced, as well as, for the management, control, and measurement of software processes. Structures include those provided by the software engineering methods and methodology and those which result from well developed and understood application domain models. Structures are most effectively utilized when they are supported by tools and an environment and by languages with compatible or complementary programming structures. Structures which have been shown to be successful, on the basis of extensive experience, have the corollary effect of promoting software reuse.

The tenet of this position paper is that such structures are necessary for substantive software reuse. To support this position, this paper briefly describes the STEP environment to illustrate a structure which serves as the model for the software system, as well as the model for the development process. The generic architecture is the integrating structure for the tools and languages used in the STEP environment. The generic architecture provides the foundation for several different forms of reuse, including architectural reuse, component reuse, subsystem reuse, and reusable libraries.

Motivational Discussion

MCCR(mission critical computer resource) systems are large, software intensive systems, which are characterized by features for real time processing, concurrency, distribution of data and processes, extensive intra- and inter-system communication, scheduling, event handling, extensive error handling, complex storage management, recovery, and user interaction, as well as special features which depend on the application domain.

A fundamental assumption of our position is that software reuse, especially in the context of MCCR applications, will have lower cost and greater benefit if it is based upon the same fundamental structures which also provide the foundation for the development methodology and which also serve as the integrating concept for methods, tool support, language and application domain features. Such structures can be the foundation for more substantive reuse.

Concepts and objects which support the development of MCCR systems derive from the programming language, the environment, and application domain. For example, current programming languages support modularization and encapsulation, and some directly support object-oriented design, all of which help control the complexity of system interaction and communication. Development environments provide programming-in-the-large support. For example, they can provide a structure which extends that of the module units of the programming language, or for example, they can support tasking, if it is not supported by the programming language, or if the tasking model embodied in the programming language is not appropriate for the application. Understanding of and experience with the application domain can provide the more unique concepts needed to satisfy special system requirements. For example, an application dependent model can provide for event handling, for recovery, or special processing. Thus, the construction of MCCR systems can utilize concepts and objects from the programming language, from the environment, or application domain, itself. Ideally, such concepts and objects should be embodied in the language or the environment in order to systematize their application. Practically, not all concepts and objects can be or should be incorporated into a programming language or development environment. As concepts and objects, both application independent and application dependent, are identified and defined, they are potentially reusable. Those which are sufficiently general, can be supported by the environment or language. A difficulty, in fact one which is often not even recognized, is the optimum balance of language, environment, and application concepts and objects in the design of a language, environment, or a system. As programming languages become conceptually richer and more powerful, and as experience in particular application domains continues to evolve, environment issues will become even more important in this balance. Maintaining this balance and integration of concepts and objects will require environment structures which extend programming languages, provide the foundation for necessary environmental support, and model the application domain, as well. An approach to reuse which is integral to a methodology and environment and which is based on these structures has greater potential for enabling and promoting software reuse.

Background

STEP, Structured Techniques for Engineering Projects, is a language independent software life-cycle support environment based on a generic architecture. STEP has been in use at GTE Government Systems for the development of a variety of real time applications, including air traffic simulation, command communications, and control. STEP is currently in use and is evolving to incorporate the latest advances in software engineering technology.

STEP is an extension of Phoenix(1976), a machine-aided software development methodology for reducing the costs and risks of software development and maintenance, and for improving software quality. Phoenix sought to achieve these goals by the automation of labor-intensive tasks, by producing systems based on a proven architecture, and by enforcing design and development standards. Users of

Phoenix included system designers, software designers, software managers, configuration control, and quality assurance personnel. The machine-aids of Phoenix consisted of an executive program, a collection of processors, and a data base. The executive received commands from interactive users and invoked command procedures. A' command procedure verified user and access rights and in turn invoked a processor which carried out the task of the command. The command procedure then updated design, management, or configuration data relevant to the task carried out. Processors enforced standards, supported documentation, quality assurance and configuration control. A unique processor of Phoenix was an analyzer which checked the design and implementation of a software component for adherence to architectural and coding standards. While perhaps somewhat limited in comparison to today's tools, these early machine-aids were state-of-the-art for the 1970's and some have evolved to take advantage of current technology. Machine-aids were planned for testing, simulation, prototyping, scheduling and estimating, but were never developed for Phoenix.

In several ways, Phoenix was ahead of its time. First, it "provided a means of taking advantage of techniques and implementations developed on preceding projects rather than continually reinventing the wheel". Second, it produced systems based on a proven architecture, such that the systems are "similar in so many ways that a person familiar with any one system can readily familiarize himself with another."

As a proof of concept, Phoenix was a success. However, implemented using a data base language, performance was limited. In addition, limitations of user friendliness, production quality of the tools , and the lack of wide agreement on standards, prevented Phoenix from becoming a practical, widely-used environment.

STEP I which followed Phoenix addressed some of these limitations. STEP I was implemented on several host time-shared computers, had improved tools and language support, was adopted as the standard development environment for one of the GTE divisions, and has been in use since 1979. Although more efficient that Phoenix, STEP I was limited with respect to meeting increasing demands more user friendliness and for more performance efficiency for ever larger projects.

STEP II is the recent extension of STEP. It is a distributed workstation based environment with high performance efficiency, growth capacity for the largest projects, and a high resolution graphic user interface.

The STEP Structure - the Generic Architecture

The central integrating concept of STEP is a generic design structure, called the generic architecture. The generic architecture describes the constituent components and their relationships, both static and dynamic, which comprise a system. This structure consists of a five level hierarchy. The levels are termed program, class, subprogram, module, and segment. The levels encompass data as well as procedural components. A component of the hierarchy is an abstraction of its descendant lower components and is implemented by combining these subcomponents according to the rules of an implementation language and system conventions. This hierarchy is also the logical specification of the software artifacts data base of the STEP environment.

Allowed interactions between components are specified as access rules and rules for transfer of control. These rules are enforced by the environment.

At the operating level, each subprogram is realized as a task. In MCCR applications, these become distributed concurrent tasks. Task communication is specified by rules and controlled by a generic executive which also provides other services, including storage management and recovery.

Structural Basis for Software Reuse

The STEP structure supports a variety of different forms of software reuse. First, it supports architectural or design reuse, since every system built using STEP will have the same architecture. Second, it supports component reuse by identifying types of components and standardizing on the interfaces between them. Third, STEP supports subsystem reuse by making its own communication, scheduling, event handling, storage management, recovery, and user-interface subsystems available for the application itself. Since the application has the same structure, that is, a similar architecture (the same generic architecture) and adheres to the same rules, subsystems are more readily reused in the application. Four, STEP supports a form of generative reuse, in the sense of generation as the automatic construction of software using available elements. In this case, the elements are components and generation is their integration during the software build process. Fifth, STEP supports the application of reusable libraries by providing a structure, data base, and mechanisms for storing, retrieving, relating, controlling, and integrating components. Moreover, this support for reusable libraries does not treat them apart from the design process but treats them as a natural corollary of the environment and generic architecture.

Conclusion

This position paper assumes that the primary goal of introducing structure into the software engineering process and products has the corollary effect of naturally promoting software reusability. The proper structure enables and encourages a variety of forms of reuse and integrates them in a natural way into the system development process.

This position is illustrated by a brief description of STEP and its generic architecture. This integrating structure has evolved from its implementation in Phoenix in the early 1970's, to STEP I in the late and early 1980's, to the current implementation in STEP II.

*"Neither ever
quite the same,
nor ever
quite another"*

Reusability: The Case for Object-Oriented Design

Bertrand Meyer, Interactive Software Engineering

Simply being more organized will not make the reuse problem go away. The issues are technical, not managerial. The answers lie in object-oriented design.

"Why isn't software more like hardware? Why must every new development start from scratch? There should be catalogs of software modules, as there are catalogs of VLSI devices: When we build a new system, we should be ordering components from these catalogs and combining them, rather that reinventing the wheel every time. We would write less software, and perhaps do a better job at that which we do develop. Then wouldn't the problems everyone laments — the high costs, the overruns, the lack of reliability — just go away? Why isn't it so?"

If you are a software developer or manager you have probably heard such remarks before. Perhaps you have uttered them yourself.

The repetitive nature of computer programming is indeed striking. Over and over again, programmers weave a number of basic patterns: sorting, searching, reading, writing, comparing, traversing, allocating, synchronizing. . . Experienced programmers know well the feeling of *déjà vu* that is so characteristic of their trade.

Attempts have been made to measure this phenomenon; one estimate is that less than 15 percent of new code serves an original purpose.[1]

A way to assess this situation less quantitatively but perhaps closer to home is to answer the following question honestly, again assuming you develop software or direct people who do. Consider the problem of table searching: An element of some kind, say x, is given with a set of similar elements, t; the program is to determine if x appears in t. The question is: How many times in the last six months did you or people working for you write some program fragment for table searching?

Chances are the answer will be one or more. But what is really remarkable is that, most likely, the fragment or fragments will have been written at the lowest reasonable level of abstraction — as code instead of by calling existing routines.

Yet table searching is one of the best researched areas of computer science. Excellent books describe the fundamental algorithms — it would seem nobody should need to code a searching algorithm in standard cases anymore. After all, electronic engineers don't design standard inverters, they buy them.

This article addresses this fundamental goal of software engineering, reusability, and a companion requirement, extendibility (the ease with which software can be modified to reflect changes in specifications). Progress in one of these areas usually advances the aims of the other as well, so when we discuss reusability, we will be adding *in petto*, ". . .and extendibility."

Our main thesis is that object-oriented design is the most promising technique now known for attaining the goals of extendability and reusability.

Ni tout à fait la même. . .

Why isn't reuse more common? Some of the reasons are nontechnical:

• Economic incentives tend to work against reusability. If you, as a contractor, deliver software that is too general and too reusable, you won't get the next job — your client won't need a next job!

• The famous not-invented-here complex also works against reusability.

• Reusable software must be retrievable, which means we need libraries of reusable modules and good database searching tools so client programmers can find appropriate modules easily. (Some terminology: A client of a module M is any module relying on M; a client programmer is a person who writes a client module; an implementer of M is the programmer who writes M.)

In the US, the STARS project is an effort that aims, among other things, to overcome such obstacles.

Tip of the iceberg. In my opinion, these issues are only the tip of the iceberg; the main roadblocks are technical. Reuse is limited because designing reusable software is hard. This article elaborates on what makes it so hard and should dispel any naive hope that software problems would just go away if we were more organized in filing program units.

Let's take a closer look at the repetitive nature of software development. Programmers do tend to do the same kinds of things time and time again, but they are not *exactly* the same things. If they were, the solution would be easy, at least on paper; but in practice, so many details may change as to render moot any simple-minded attempt at capturing commonality.

Such is the software engineer's plight: time and time again composing a new variation that elaborates on the same basic themes: "neither ever quite the same, nor ever quite another. . ."*

Take table searching again. True, the general form of the code is going to look the same each time: Start at some position in the table t; explore the table from that position, checking if the element found at the current position is the one being sought; if not, move to another position. The process terminates either when the element has been found or when all positions of interest in the table have been unsuccessfully probed.

This paradigm applies to all standard cases of data representation (unsorted or sorted array, unsorted or sorted linked list, sequential file, binary tree, B-tree, hash table, etc.). It may be expressed more precisely as a program schema:

```
Search(x : ELEMENT, t :
TABLE_OF_ELEMENT)
return boolean is
    --Look for element x in table t
pos: POSITION
begin
    pos:= INITIAL_POSITION (x,t);
    while not EXHAUSTED (pos,t)
    and then not FOUND (pos,x,t) do
        pos := NEXT (pos,x,t);
    end;
```

* Et qui n'est chaque fois ni tout à fait la même. Ni tout à fait une autre. . .: And [she] who from one [dream] to the next is neither ever quite the same, nor ever quite another. . . — Gérard de Nerval.

```
    return not EXHAUSTED (pos,t)
end -- Search
```

Too many variants. The difficulty in coming up with a general software element for searching is apparent: Even though the pattern is fixed, the amount of variable information is considerable. Details that may change include the type of table elements (ELEMENT), how the initial position is selected (INITIAL_POSITION), how the algorithm proceeds from one position to the next (NEXT), and all the types and routines in uppercase, which will admit a different refinement for each variant of the algorithm.

Not only is it hard to implement a general-purpose searching module, it is almost as hard to *specify* such a module so that client modules could rely on it without knowing the implementation.

Beyond the basic problem of factoring out the parts that are common to all implementations of table searching, an even tougher challenge is to capture the commonality within some conceptual subset. For example, an implementation using sequential search in arrays is very similar to one based on sequential linked lists; the code will differ only by small (yet crucial) details, shown in Table 1.

Within each group of implementations (all sequential tables, for example), there are similarities. If we really want to write carefully organized libraries of reusable software elements, we must be able to use commonalities at all levels of abstraction.

All these issues are purely technical; solving all the managerial and economical obstacles to reusability that one hears about in executives' meetings will not help a bit here.

Routines

Work on reusability has followed several approaches (see the box on p. 54). The classical technique is to build libraries of routines (we use the word "routine" to cover what is variously called procedure, function, subroutine, or subprogram). Each routine in the library implements a well-defined operation. This approach has been quite successful in scientific computation — excellent libraries exist for numerical applications.

Table 1.
Implementation variants for sequential search.

	Sequential array	Linked list	Sequential file
Start search at first position	$i := 1$	$l := first$	rewind
Move to next position	$i := l + 1$	$l := l.next$	read
Test for table exhausted	$i >$ size	$l =$ null	end_ of_ file

Indeed, the routine-library approach seems to work well in areas where a set of individual problems can be identified, provided the following limitations hold:

• Every instance of each problem should be identifiable with a small set of parameters.

• The individual problems should be clearly distinct. Any significant commonality that might exist cannot be put to good use, except by reusing some of the design.

• No complex data structures should be involved because they would have to be distributed among the routines and the conceptual autonomy of modules would be lost.

The table-searching example may be used to show the limitations of this approach. We can either write a single routine or a set of routines, each corresponding to a specific case.

A single routine will have many parameters and will probably be structured like a gigantic set of case instructions. Its complexity and inefficiency will make it unusable. Worse, the addition of any new case will mean modification and recompilation of the whole routine.

A set of routines will be large and contain many routines that look very similar (like the searching routines for sequential arrays and sequential linked lists). But there is no simple way for the implementers to use this similarity. Client programmers will have to find their way through a maze of routines.

Modular languages

Languages like Modula-2 and Ada offer a first step toward a solution. These languages use the notion of module (the Ada term is package), providing a higher level structuring facility than the routine. A module may contain more than one routine, together with declarations of types, constants, and variables. A module may thus be devoted to an entire data structure and its associated operations.

This approach is rooted in the theory of data abstraction, but its basic concepts may be illustrated simply with our table-searching example.

A table-searching routine isn't worth very much by itself; it must be complemented by routines that create and delete tables and insert and delete elements, all governed by a certain representation of the table, given by a type declaration. These routines and the type declaration are closely connected logically, so they might as well be part of the same syntactic unit. Such units are basically what modular languages offer.

This is a significant improvement: We can now keep under one roof a set of related routines that pertain to a specific implementation of a data abstraction. For example, the module for a binary search tree of integers (INT_BINARY_TREE) will contain the declaration of a type intbintree and routines Create, Search, Insert, and so on. The client code might look like:

```
x : integer; b : boolean; p :
INT_BINARY_TREE.intbintree;
INT_BINARY_TREE.Create (t);
INT_BINARY_TREE.Insert (x,b) ;
b := INT_BINARY_TREE.Search(x,p)
```

(Here I use the Ada dot notation: *A.f* means "feature *f*, such as a type or routine, from module *A*." In Ada and other languages, simpler notations are available when a client repeatedly uses features from a given module.)

For reusability, these techniques are useful but limited. They are useful because encapsulating groups of related features helps implementers (in gathering features) as well as clients (in retrieving features), and all of this favors reusability. But they

are limited because they do not reduce significantly the amount of software that needs to be written. Specifically, they don't offer any new clue as to how to capture common features.

Overloading and genericity

A further improvement is overloading, as provided in Algol 68 and Ada. Overloading means attaching more than one meaning to a name, such as the name of an operation.

For example, when different representations of tables are each defined by a separate type declaration, you would use overloading to give the same name, say Search, to all associated search procedures. In this way, a search operation will always be invoked as $b :=$ Search (x,t), regardless of the implementation chosen for t and the type of table elements.

Overloading works well in a strictly typed language where the compiler has enough type information about x and t to choose the right version of search.

A companion technique is genericity, provided in Ada and Clu. Genericity allows a module to be defined with generic parameters that represent types. Instances of the module are then produced by supplying different types as actual parameters. This is a definite aid to reusability because just one generic module is defined, instead of a group of modules that differ only in the types of objects they manipulate.

For example, instead of having an INT_BINARY_TREE module, a REAL_BINARY_TREE module, and so on, you could define a single generic BINARY_TREE [*T*] module. Any actual type (INTEGER, REAL, etc.) could correspond to the formal generic parameter *T*. The search routine can be defined in the generic module to act on an argument x of type *T*. Then every instance of the module automatically has its own version of search.

In summary, overloading and genericity each offer something toward reuse:

• with overloading, the client programmer may write the same code when using different implementations of the same data

203

abstraction, as provided by different modules;

• with genericity, the implementer may write a single module for all instances of the same implementation of a data abstraction, applied to various types of objects.

These techniques are interesting advancements in reusability. But they do not go far enough. Roughly speaking, they do not provide enough flexibility and they force programmers to decide too much too soon.

Not enough flexibility. They are not flexible enough because they cannot capture fine grains of commonality between groups of implementations of the same general data abstraction. This is because there are only two levels of modules: generic modules, which are parameterized and thus open to variation, but not directly usable; and fully instantiated modules, which are directly usable but not open to refinement. Thus we cannot describe a complex hierarchy of representations that have different levels of parameterizations.

Too much too soon. Neither technique allows a client to use various implementations of a data abstraction (say the table) without knowing which implementation is used in each instance.

On one hand, each generic module refers to a single, explicitly specified instance of that module. Overloading, on the other hand, is essentially a syntactic facility that relieves the programmer of having to invent names for different implementations; the burden is placed on the compiler instead. Nevertheless, each invocation of an overloaded operation name, say Search(x,t), refers to a specific version of the operation — and both the client programmer and compiler know which version that is.

Client programmers do not actually need to know how each version is implemented, since Ada and Modula-2 modules are used by clients through an interface that lists the available routines, independent of their implementation. But they do need to decide explicitly which version is used. For example, if your modules use various kinds of tables, you don't have to know how to implement hash tables,

indexed sequential files, and the like — but you must say which representation you want each time you use a table operation.

True representation-independence only happens when a client can write the invocation Search(x,t) and mean, "look for x in t using the appropriate algorithm for whatever kind of table and element x and t happen to be at the time the invocation is executed."

This degree of flexibility, essential for the construction of reusable software elements, can only be achieved with object-oriented design.

Object-oriented design

This fashionable term has been somewhat overused in recent years. The definition used here is fairly dogmatic. Object-oriented design is viewed as a *software decomposition technique*. An overview of some object-oriented languages is given in the box on p. 59.

Object-oriented design may be defined as a technique which, unlike classical (functional) design, bases the modular decomposition of a software system on the classes of objects the system manipulates, not on the functions the system performs. Classical approaches like functional top-down design (even, to a large extent, dataflow analysis methods) require designers to first ask what the system does. Object-oriented design avoids such questions as long as possible, in fact until the system actually is run. Why?

The top-down functional approach is probably adequate if the program you are writing solves a fixed problem once and for all. But the picture changes when you take a long-term view, for what the system will do in its first release is probably going to be a little different from what you think it will do at requirements time, and *very* different from what it will do five years later, if it survives that long.

However, the categories of objects on which the system acts will probably be more or less the same. An operating system will always work on devices, memories,

processing units, communication channels, and so on; a document processing system will always work on documents, chapters, sections, paragraphs, and so on.

Thus it is wiser in the long term to rely on categories of objects as a basis for decomposition, but (and this is an important but) only if these categories are viewed at a sufficiently high level of abstraction. This is where abstract data types come in.*

Abstract data types

If we use the physical structure of objects as the basis for decomposition, we won't go very far toward protecting our software's structure against requirement changes. In fact, we will probably be worse off than we would be with functional design. A study by Lientz and Swanson,[3] quoted by Boehm,[4] shows that 17.5 percent of the cost of software maintenance stems from changes in programs that reflect changes in data formats. This emphasizes the need to separate the programs from the physical structure of the objects they handle.

Abstract data types provide a remarkable solution to this problem. An abstract data type describes a class of objects through the external properties of these objects instead of their computer representation. More precisely, an abstract data type is a class of objects characterized by the operations available on them and the abstract properties of these operations.

It turns out that abstract data types, which provide an excellent basis for software specification, are also useful at the design and implementation stage. In fact, they are essential to the object-oriented approach, and enable us to refine the definition of object-oriented design: Object-oriented design is the construction of software systems as structured collections of abstract data-type implementations.

An important aspect of the object-oriented method is that it actually identifies modules with implementations of

---

* One other design method that does emphasize the motto "look at the data before you look at the functions" is Jackson's method.[2] However, a comparative analysis of Jackson's method and object-oriented design falls beyond the scope of this article.

abstract data types. It is not only that modules *comprise* these implementations (as in Ada and Modula-2, and in Fortran-77, thanks to multiple-entry subroutines); a single program structure *is* both a module and a type. Such a dual-purpose structure was dubbed a "class" by the creators of the pioneer object-oriented language, Simula 67.

Two words should be emphasized in the above definition. The first is "implementation": A module of an object-oriented program is not an abstract data type, but one implementation of an abstract data type. However, the details of the implementation are not normally available to the rest of the world, which only sees the official specification of the abstract data type.

The second is "structured." Collections of classes may indeed be structured using two different relations: client and inheritance. Figure 1 illustrates these two relations. The client relation is represented by horizontal double arrows; inheritance by a single, vertical arrow.

Class *A* is said to be a client of *B* if *A* contains a declaration of the form *bb: B*. (In this and all other object-oriented examples, I use the notations and terminology of the object-oriented language Eiffel. See the box on p. 60 for more about Eiffel.)

In this case, *A* may manipulate *bb* only through the features defined in the specification of *B*. Features comprise both attributes (data items associated with objects of type *B*) and routines (operations for accessing or changing these objects). In Eiffel, features are applied through dot notation, as in *bb.x*, *bb.f (u,w,x)*.

As an example, consider a client class *X* of class BINARY_SEARCH_TREE that implements a specific form of tables. Client *X* may contain elements of the form:

```
bb:BINARY_SEARCH_TREE;
    -- declare bb as binary search tree
bb.Create;
    -- allocate table (routine call)
bb.insert (x);
    -- insert x into bb (routine call)
y:= bb.size ;
    -- (attribute access)
```

The second relation between classes, inheritance, is fundamental to true object-oriented languages. For example, our BINARY_SEARCH_TREE class may be defined as an heir (possibly indirect) to a class TABLE that describes the general properties of tables, independent of the representation.

A class *C* defined as an heir to a class *A* has all the features of *A*, to which it may add its own. Descendants of a class include its heirs, the heirs of its heirs, and so on. The relationship between *C* and *A* may be defined from the viewpoint of both the module and the type.

From the module perspective, inheritance allows the programmer to take an existing world (class *A*) and plunge it as a whole into a new world, *C*, which will inherit all its properties and add its own. In *multiple* inheritance, as present in Eiffel, more than one world may be used to define a new one.

From the type perspective, *C* is considered a special case of *A*: Any object of type *C* may also be interpreted as an object of type *A*. In particular, a variable of type *A* may be assigned an object of type *C*, although the reverse is not true, at least in a statically typed language like Eiffel. This

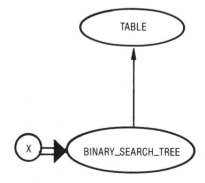

Figure 1. The client and inheritance relations in abstract data types. The client is represented by a horizontal double arrow; inheritance by a single, vertical arrow.

also holds in the case of multiple inheritance, as Figure 2 shows. This property is extremely important because it allows program entities to take different forms at runtime. The relation between *C* and *A* is an instance of the so-called Is-a relation (every lily *is a* flower; every binary search tree *is a* table).

The powerful combination of object-oriented design and these two relations — client and inheritance — is a key element in achieving extendibility and reusability.

An illustrative example

A new example, a full-screen entry system, will help contrast the object-oriented approach with classical functional decomposition. The example, a common data processing problem, should be interesting on its own: The problem is to write an interactive application that guides the user with full-screen panels at each stage.

The problem. Interactive sessions for such systems go through a series of states, each with a well-defined general pattern: A panel is displayed with questions for the user; the user supplies the required answer; the answer is checked for consistency (questions are asked until an acceptable answer is supplied); and the answer is processed somehow (a database is updated, for example). Part of the user's answer is a choice of the next steps; the system translates the user's choice into a transition to another state, and the same process is applied in the new state.

Figure 3 shows a panel for an imaginary airline reservation system. The screen shown is toward the end of a step; the user's answers are in italics.

The process begins in some initial state and ends whenever any among a set of final states is reached. A transition graph, like that in Figure 4, shows the overall structure of a session — the possible states and the transitions between them. The edges of the graph are labeled by numbers that correspond to the user's possible choices for the next step.

Our mission is to come up with a design and implementation for such applications that have as much generality and flexibility as possible.

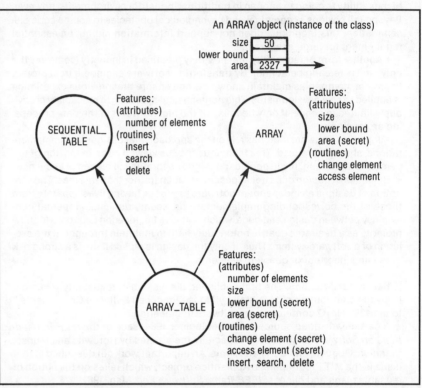

Figure 2. Multiple inheritance. In Eiffel, more than one world can be used to define a new world, which will inherit all the properies and add its own.

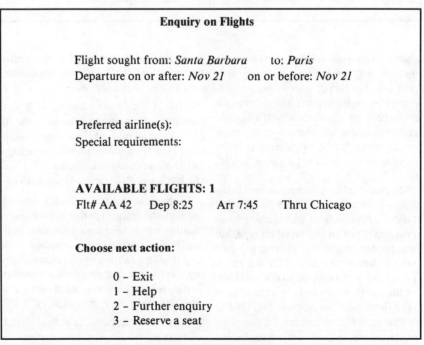

Figure 3. A panel for an interactive airline reservation system. The screen shown is toward the end of a step; the user's answers are in italics.

A simple-minded solution. We'll begin with a straightforward, unsophisticated program scheme. This version is made of a number of blocks, one for each state of the system: $B_{Enquiry}$, $B_{Reservation}$, $B_{Cancellation}$, and so on. A typical block looks like:

```
B_Enquiry:
    output "enquiry on flights" panel;
    repeat
        read user's answers and choice C for
        next step ;
        if error in answer then
        output appropriate message
    end until not error in answer end;
    process answer;
```

```
case C in
    C_0:goto Exit,
    C_1:goto B_help,
    C_2:goto B_Reservation,
    ...
end
```

(And similarly for each state.)

This structure will do the job, but of course there is much to criticize. The numerous goto instructions give it that famous spaghetti bowl look. This may be viewed as a cosmetic issue, solved by restructuring the program to eliminate jumps. But that would miss the point.

The problem is deeper. This program is bad not just because it has a lot of explicit branch instructions, but because the physical form of the problem has been wired into it. The branching structure of the program reflects exactly the transition structure of the graph in Figure 4.

This it terrible from a reusability and extendability standpoint. In real-world data-entry systems, the graph of Figure 4 might be quite complex — one study mentions examples with 300 different states.[5]

It is highly unlikely that the transition structure of such a system will be right the first time it is designed. Even after the first version is working, users will inevitably request new transitions, shortcuts, or help states. The prospect of modifying the whole program structure (not just program elements — the overall organization) for any one change is horrendous.

To improve on this solution we must separate the graph structure from the traversal algorithm. This seems appropriate because the structure depends on the particular interactive application (airline reservation), while its traversal is generic. As a side benefit, a functional decomposition will also remove the heretical gotos.

A procedural, "top-down" solution. We may encapsulate the graph structure in a two-argument function, Transition, such that Transition(s,c) is the state obtained when the user chooses c on leaving state s.

We use the word "function" in a mathematical sense: Transition may be represented either by a function in the programming sense (a routine that returns a value) or by a data structure, such as an array. The first solution may be preferable for readability because the transitions will appear in the program code itself. The second is better for flexibility because it is easier to change a data structure than a program. We can afford to postpone this decision.

The function transition is not sufficient to describe the transition graph. We must also define the state, initial, that begins the traversal and a Boolean-valued function is-final(s) that determines when a state is final. Initial and final states are treated dissymmetrically; while it is reasonable to

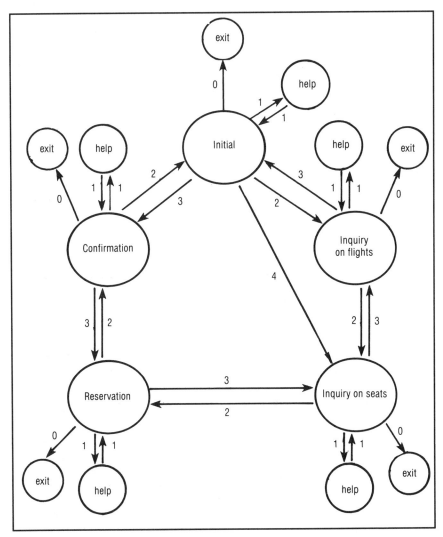

Figure 4. A state transition graph for an interactive application. The edges of the graph are labeled by numbers that correspond to the user's possible choices for the next step.

IEEE SOFTWARE

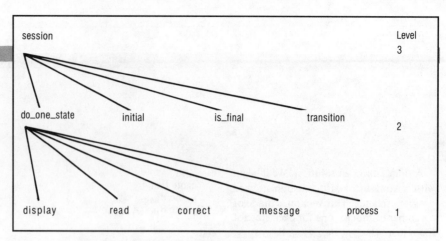

Figure 5. An orthodox, functional architecture for an interactive application. The "top," or main program, is the routine Session.

expect the dialog to always begin in the same state, we cannot expect it to always end in the same state.

Figure 5 shows the orthodox, functional architecture derived from this solution. As the top-down method teaches, this system has a "top," or main program. What else could it be but the routine that describes how to execute a complete interactive session?

This routine may be written to emphasize application-independence. Assume that a suitable representation is found for states (type STATE) and for the user's choice after each state (CHOICE):

```
session is
    -- execute a complete session of
    -- the interactive system
    current: STATE ; next: CHOICE
begin
    current := initial ;
    repeat
        do_one_state (current, next) ;
    -- the value of next is returned by routine
    -- do_one_state
        current := transition (current, next)
    until is_final (current) end
end -- session
```

This procedure does not show direct dependency upon any interactive application. To describe such an application, we must provide three of the elements on level two in Figure 5: a transition function (routine or data structure), an initial state, and an is_final predicate.

To complete the design, we refine the do_one_state routine, which describes the actions to be performed in each state. The body of this routine is essentially an abstracted form of the blocks in our spaghetti version:

```
do_one_state (in s : STATE ; out c : CHOICE) is
    --execute the actions associated with
    --state s,
    --returning into c the user's choice
    --for the next state
    a: ANSWER ; ok: BOOLEAN ;
begin
    repeat
        display(s) ; read(s,a) ;
        ok := correct(s,a) ;
        if not ok then message(s,a) end
    until ok end ;
    process (s,a) ; c := next_choice (a)
end -- do_one_state
```

For the remaining routines, we can only give a specification, because the implementations depend on the details of the appli-

cation and its various states: display(s) outputs the panel associated with state s; read(s,a) reads the user's answer to state s into a; correct(s,a) returns true if and only if a is an acceptable answer; if it is, process(s,a) processes answer a; if it isn't, message(s,a) outputs the relevant error message.

Type ANSWER is left unspecified. A value of this type, say a, globally represents the input entered by the user in a given state, including the user's choice of the next step, next_choice(a).

Data transmission. Is this solution satisfactory? Not from the standpoint of reusability.

True, we did separate what is generic and what is specific to a particular application, but this does not buy much flexibility. The main problem is the system's data transmission structure. Consider the functionalities (types of arguments and results) of the routines:

```
do_one_state: (in s: STATE ; out c: CHOICE)
display: (in s: STATE)
read: (in s: STATE ; out a: ANSWER)
correct: (in s: STATE ; a: ANSWER):
BOOLEAN
message: (in s: STATE, a: ANSWER)
process: (in s: STATE, a: ANSWER)
```

All these routines share the state s as a parameter, coming from the top module Session (where it is known as Current). The flow of data, illustrated in Figure 6, shows that (as a conservative economist might say) there's far too much state intervention. As a result, all the above routines must perform some form of case discrimination on s:

```
case s of
    State₁:....,
    ...................,
    Stateₙ:....,
end
```

This implies long, complex code (a problem which could be solved with further decomposition) and (more annoying) it means that every routine must deal with, and thus know about, all possible states of the application. This makes it very difficult to implement extensions. Adding a new state, for example, entails modifications throughout. Such a situation is all too common in software development. System evolution becomes a nightmare as simple changes touch off a complex chain reaction in the system.

The situation is even worse than it appears. It would seem desirable to profit from the similar aspects of these types of interactive applications by storing the common parts in library routines. But this is unrealistic in the solution above: On top of the explicit parameters, all routines have an implicit one — the application itself, airline reservations.

A general-purpose version of display, for example, should know about all states of all possible applications in a given environment! The function transition should contain the transition graph for all applications. This is clearly impossible.

The law of inversion. What is wrong? Figure 6 exposes the flaw: there is too much data transmission in the software architecture. The remedy, which leads directly to object-oriented design, may be expressed by the following law: If there is too much data transmission in your routines, then put your routines into your data.

Instead of building modules around operations (session, do_one_state) and distributing data structures between the resulting routines, object-oriented design does the reverse. It uses the most important data structures as the basis for modularization and attaches each routine to the data structure to which it applies most closely.

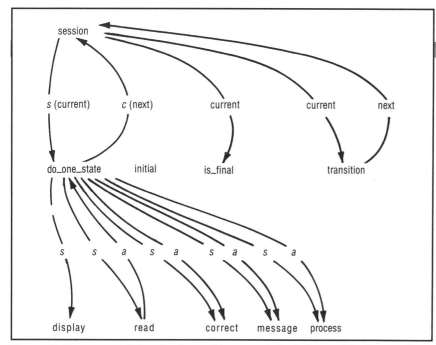

Figure 6. Data transmission in the architecture derived from with the top-down approach.

This law of inversion is the key to turning a functional decomposition into an object-oriented design: reverse the viewpoint and attach the routines to the data structures. To programmers trained in functional approaches, this is as revolutionary as making the Sun orbit Earth.

Of course, it's best to design in an object-oriented fashion from the beginning. However, the process of moving from a functional decomposition to an object-oriented structure is itself interesting. How do we find the most important data structures, around which modules are to be built?

Data transmission provides a clue. The data structures that are constantly transmitted between routines must be important, mustn't they?

Here the first candidate is obvious, the state (current, s). So our object-oriented solution will include a class STATE to implement the corresponding abstract data type. Among the features of a state are the five routines of level one in Figure 5 that describe the operations performed in a state (display, read, message, correct, and process), and the routine do_one_state without the state parameter.

In Eiffel notation, the class STATE may be written:

```
class STATE export
    next_choice, display, read, correct,
    message, process, do_one_state
feature
    user_answer: ANSWER ;
    next_choice: INTEGER ;
    do_one_state is
        do
            ...body of the routine...
```

```
        end;
    display is ... ;
    read is... ;
    correct: BOOLEAN is... ;
    message: is... ;
    process is... ;
end -- class STATE
```

The features of the class include two attributes, next_choice and user_answer, and six routines. Routines are divided into functions, which return a result (like correct, which returns a Boolean value) and procedures, which don't.

The export clause is used for information hiding: In a client class containing a declaration *s: STATE*, a feature application *s.f* is only correct if *f* is one of the features listed in the clause. Here all features are exported, except for user_answer, which is accessible by STATE routines but not by the outside world. A nonexported feature is said to be secret. As before, we assume that type ANSWER is declared elsewhere, now as a class. Values that represent exit choices are coded as integers.

Unlike its counterpart in a functional decomposition, each routine has no explicit STATE parameter. The state to which routines apply reappears in calls made by clients:

```
s: STATE; b:BOOLEAN;
choicecode: INTEGER;
s.do_one_state ; s.read ;
b := s.correct ;
choicecode := s.next_choice;
etc.
```

We have also replaced the ANSWER parameter in level-one routines with the secret

attribute user_answer. Information hiding is the motive — client code doesn't need to look at answers except through the interface provided by the exported features.

Inheritance and deferred features. There's a problem, however. How can we write the class STATE without knowing the properties of a specific state? Routine do_one_state and attribute next_choice are the same for all states, but display is not.

Inheritance is the key to this problem. At the STATE level we know (1) all details of routine do_one_state, (2) the attribute next_choice; (3) the fact that routines like display must exist and (4) what their functionalities are.

So we write the class and define these partially known routines as *deferred*. This means that, while any actual state must have them, their details are postponed to descendant classes that describe specific states. (The notion of deferred routines come from Simula 67, where they are called "virtual.") Thus the class is written:

```
class STATE export
    next_choice, display, read, correct,
    message, process, do_one_state

feature
    user_answer: ANSWER ;
        -- secret attribute
    next_choice: INTEGER ;

    do_one_state is
        -- execute the actions associated
        -- with the current state
        -- and assign to next_choice the
        -- user's choice for the next state
    local
        ok: BOOLEAN
    do
        from
            ok:= false
        until
            ok
        loop
            display ; read ; ok := correct ;
            if not ok then
                message
            end
        end ; -- loop
        process
    ensure
        correct
    end; -- do_one_state

    display is
        -- display the panel associated
        -- with current state
```

```
deferred
end ; -- display
read is
    -- return the user's answer
    -- into user_answer
    -- and the user's next choice
    -- into next_choice
    deferred
    end ; -- read

correct: BOOLEAN is
    -- return true if and only if
    -- user_answer is
    -- a correct answer
    deferred
    end; -- correct

message is
    -- output the error message
    -- associated with user_answer
    require
        not correct
    deferred
    end ; -- message

process is
    -- process user_answer
    require
        correct
    deferred
    end -- process
end -- class STATE
```

Note the syntax of the Eiffel loop, with initialization in the from clause and the exit test in the until clause. This is equivalent to a while loop, with an exit test rather than a continuation test.

Also note the require clauses that appear at the beginning of routines message and process. These clauses introduce preconditions that must be obeyed whenever a routine is called. Similarly, a postcondition, introduced by the keyword ensure, may be associated with a routine. Preconditions and postconditions express the precise effect of a routine. They can also be monitored at runtime for debugging and control.

The class just described does not by itself describe any actual states — it expresses the pattern common to all states. Specific states are defined by descendants of STATE. It is incumbent on these descendants to provide actual implementations of the deferred routines, such as:

```
class ENQUIRY_ON_FLIGHTS export....
inherit
        STATE
feature
    display is
        do
            ...specific display procedure...
        end ;
        ...and similarly for read, correct,
            message, and process...
end -- class ENQUIRY_ON_FLIGHTS
```

Several important comments are in order:

• We have succeeded in separating — at the exact grain of detail required — the elements common to all states from those specific to individual states. Common elements are concentrated in STATE and need not be redeclared in descendants of STATE like ENQUIRY_ON_FLIGHTS.

• If s is an object of type STATE and d an object of type DS, where DS is a descendant of STATE, the assignment $s := d$ is permitted and d is acceptable whenever an element of type STATE is required. For example, the array Transition introduced below to represent the transition graph of an application may be declared of type STATE and filled with elements of descendant types.

• This goes beyond Ada-style separation of interface and implementation. First, an Ada interface may contain only bodiless routines; it corresponds to a class where all routines are deferred. In Eiffel, however, you may freely combine nondeferred and deferred routines in the same class. Even more important, Eiffel allows any number of descendant types of STATE to coexist in the same application, whereas Ada allows at most one implementation per interface. This openness of classes (a class may always be extended by new descendants) is a fundamental advantage of object-oriented languages over the closed modules of such languages as Ada and Modula-2.

• The presence of preconditions and postconditions in Eiffel maintains the conceptual integrity of a system. Just as a deferred routine must be defined in descendant classes, so must we define the constraints such a definition must observe. This is why a precondition and postcondition may be associated with a routine even in a deferred declaration. These conditions are then binding on any actual definition of the routine in a descendant of the original class. The technique is paramount in

---

Object-oriented languages.

Other languages implement the concept of object-oriented programming with inheritance and would allow solutions to our airline reservation system example, in a manner similar to the one given here in Eiffel.

These include Simula, the father of all object-oriented language, object-oriented expressions of C such as Objective C and C++, and an extension of Pascal, Object Pascal. These four languages, however, support only single inheritance. Other object-oriented languages include Smalltalk and extensions of Lisp such as Loops, Flavors, and Ceyx. The Clu language shares some of the properties of these languages, but does not offer inheritance.

In recent years, many languages have been added to the above list, mostly for exploratory programming and artificial intelligence purposes.

Bibliography
Birstwistle, G., et al., *Simula Begin*, Studentliteratur and Auerbach Publishers, Berlin, 1973.
Bobrow, D.G, and M.J. Sefik, "Loops: An Object-Oriented Programming System for Interlisp," Xerox PARC, Palo Alto, Calif., 1982.
Booch, G., "Object-Oriented Software Development," *IEEE Trans. Software Eng.*, Feb. 1986, pp. 211-221.
Cannon, J.I., "Flavors," MIT Artificial Intelligence Lab, Cambridge, Mass., 1980.
Cox, B., *Object-Oriented Programming: An Evolutionary Approach*, Addison-Wesley, Reading, Mass., 1986.
Goldberg, A., and D. Robson, *Smalltalk-80: The Language and Its Implementation*, Addison-Wesley, Reading, Mass., 1983.
Hulot J.-H., "Ceyx, Version 15: 1 — Une Initiation," Tech. Report 44, INRIA, Paris, 1984.
Liskov, et al., *Clu Reference Manual*, Springer Verlag, Berlin-New York, 1981.
Stroustrup, B., *The C++ Programming Language*, Addison-Wesely, Menlo Park, Calif., 1986.
Tesler, L., "Object Pascal Report," *Structured Language World*, 1985.

using Eiffel as design language: A design module will be written as a class with deferred routines, whose effects are characterized by pre- and postconditions.

A complete system. The final step in our example is to adapt the routine that was at the top of the functional decomposition: session. But we should be a little wiser by now.

The top of the top-down method is mythical. Most real systems have no such thing, especially if the top is meant to be a routine — *the* function of the system. Large software systems perform many functions, all equally important. Again, the abstract data type approach is more appropriate because it considers the system as an abstract entity capable of rendering many services.

In this case the obvious candidate is the notion of application: a specific interactive system like the airline reservation system.

It makes sense to associate with this concept a full-fledged abstract data type that will yield a class, say INTERACTIVE_APPLICATION, at the design and implementation stages. For, although INTERACTIVE_APPLICATION will include as one of its features the routine session describing the execution of an applicaton, there are other things we may want to do with an application, all of which may be added incrementally to class APPLICATION.

By renouncing the notion of "main program" and seeing session as just one feature of the class INTERACTIVE_APPLICATION, we have added considerable flexibility.

The class is given in Figure 7. Its principal features include the remaining elements at levels two and three in Figure 5. The following implementations decisions have been made:

• The transition function is represented by a two-dimensional array, Transition, of size $n \times m$, where n is the number of states

and m the number of possible exit choices.

• States are numbered 1 to n. An auxiliary, one-dimensional array, associated_state, yields the state corresponding to any integer.

• The number of the initial state is set by the routine Choose_initial and kept in the attribute Initial_number. The convention for final states is a transition to pseudo-state 0; normal states have positive numbers.

The class includes a Create procedure that will be executed on object initialization. As in most object-oriented languages, objects are created dynamically. If a is declared of type C, the instruction a.Create creates an object of type C and associates it with a.

The Create procedure and its parameters makes it possible to execute specific initialization actions on creation, instead of initializing the new object with standard default values.

The procedure Create of class INTERACTIVE_APPLICATION itself uses the Create procedures of library classes ARRAY and ARRAY2, which allocate arrays dynamically within the bounds given as parameters. For example, a two-dimensional array may be created by a.Create $(1,25, 1,10)$.

Classes ARRAY and ARRAY2 also include features Entry and Enter for array access and modification. Other features of an array are its bounds, upper and lower for a one-dimensional array, and so on.

These classes are declared as ARRAY[T] and ARRAY2[T], an example of Eiffel classes with generic parameters, in this case the type of array elements. Many fundamental classes in the Eiffel library (lists, trees, stacks) are generic. With Eiffel a programmer can combine genericity with inheritance in a type-safe manner.[6]

Class INTERACTIVE_APPLICATION uses Eiffel assertions, an aspect of the language designed to emphasize correctness and reliability. Assertions express formal properties of program elements. They may appear in preconditions and postconditions, the loop invariants, and the class invariants.

Such constructs are used primarily to ensure correct program designs and to document the correctness of arguments, but they may also be used as checks at run-time. More profoundly, assertions (especially pre- and postconditions and class invariants) bring the formal properties of abstract data types back into classes.

An interactive application will be represented by an entity, air_reservation, declared of type INTERACTIVE_APPLICATION and initialized by

air_reservation.Create (number_of_states, number_of_possible_choices)

The states of the application must be defined separately as entities, declared of descendants STATE, and created. Each state s is assigned a number i:

air_reservation.enter_state(s,i)

One state, i_0, is chosen as the initial:

air_reservation.choose_initial(i_0)

Each successive transition (from state number sn to state number tn, with label l) is entered by:

air_reservation.enter_transition(sn,tn,l)

This includes exits, for which tn is 0. The application may now be executed by air_reservation.session.

The same routines can by used during system evolution to add a new state, a new transition, and so on. The class may be extended, of course (either by itself or through descendants).

Multiple inheritance. This example exposes many of the principles in Eiffel, except the concept of multiple inheritance. A previous article on the same example[7,8] relied on Simula 67, which supports only single inheritance. Multiple inheritance is another concept that is essential to a practical use of object-oriented design and programming.

Multiple inheritance makes it possible to define a class as heir to more than one other class, thus combining the features of several previously defined environments. Multiple inheritance would be essential, for example, to implement a satisfactory solution to the table-management problem, detailed in the box on p. 62.

```
classINTERACTIVE_APPLICATION export
   session, first_number, enter_state,
   choose_initial, enter_transition, ...
feature
   transition: ARRAY2 [STATE] ; associated_state: ARRAY [STATE] ;
   -- secret attributes
   first_number; INTEGER ;
   Create (n,m:INTEGER) is
   -- allocate application with n states and m possible choices
      do
         transition.Create (1,n,1,m) ;
         associated_state.Create (1,n)
      end; -- Create

   session is -- execute application
      local
         st: STATE ; st_number: INTEGER ;
      do
         from
            st_number:=first_number ;
         invariant
            0 ≤ next; next ≤ n
         until st_number = 0 loop
            st:=associated_state.entry(st_number) ;
            st.do_one_state ;
            st_number:=transition.entry(st_number, st.next_choice)
         end -- loop
      end; -- session

   enter_state (s: STATE ; number: INTEGER) is
   -- enter state s with index number
      require
         1 ≤ number;
         number ≤ associated_state.upper
      do
         associated_state.enter (number,s)
      end; -- enter_state

   choose_initial (number: INTEGER) is
   -- define state number number as the initial state
      require
         1 ≤ number;
         number ≤ associated_state.upper
      do
         first_number:=number
      end; -- choose_initial
   enter_transition (source: INTEGER ; target:INTEGER ; label: INTEGER) is
   -- enter transition labeled "label" from state number source
   -- to state number target
      require
         1 ≤ source; source ≤ associated_state.upper ;
         0 ≤ target; target ≤ associated_state upper ;
         1 ≤ label; label ≤ transition.upper2 ;
      do
         transition.enter (source, label, target)
      end -- enter_transistion

...other features...

invariant
   0 ≤ st_number ; st_number ≤ n ;
   transition.upper1 = associated_state.upper ;
end -- class INTERACTIVE_APPLICATION
```

Figure 7. The class INTERACTIVE_APPLICATION.

A table-searching module

It is impossible to give, in one article, a satisfactory solution to the problem of designing a general-purpose table-searching module. But we can outline how Eiffel would be applied to that case.

First, it is obvious that we are talking not about a table-searching module, but about a module for table management. In fact, we're talking just about the table as an abstract data type with operations such as search, insert, delete, and so on.

As with STATE, the most general notion of table will be represented by a class with deferred routines. The various kinds of tables are descendants of this class. To obtain them, an in-depth analysis of the notion of table and its possible implementations is required. Such an analysis and the associated design and implementation effort are a considerable endeavor, especially as you realize that there is not a single notion of table, but a network of related notions.

The inheritance mechanism can help express the structure of this network and capture differences and similarities at the exact grain of detail required. For example, we may have a descendant of TABLE, SEQUENTIAL_TABLE, that covers tables stored sequentially in arrays, linked lists, or files, with a version of the function search (x):

```
from
    restart
until
    off_limits or else current_value = x
invariant
    - - x does not appear in the table before current postion
loop
    move_forth
end ;
if off_limits ...(etc.)
```

The structure is similar to that of STATE, where the essential routine do_one_state was not deferred, but was expressed in terms of other deferred routines. In this case, search is not deferred but uses deferred routines for which the descendants of TABLE must provide implementations.

What's remarkable is that an entity t declared of type TABLE may dynamically refer to an object of any descendant type of TABLE; however the call t.search(x) may be written without any knowledge of what kind of table implementation t will actually be at runtime.

This approach captures — at the exact grain of detail required — the commonality within a family of implementations of the same data abstractions. A family will consist of a header class (SEQUENTIAL_TABLE) and specific descendants (ARRAY_TABLE).

The inheritance graph may span more than one level. Features common to all members of the family (like Search for sequential tables) are concentrated at the header level and shared; features unique to various members are deferred in the header and expanded on in the individual members. The diagram below illustrates this inheritance structure.

Both genericity and multiple inheritance are essential to this problem's solution: All table classes take the type of table elements as a generic parameter, and several will combine two or more parent classes (BINARY_SEARCH_TREE from both BINARY_TREE and TABLE).

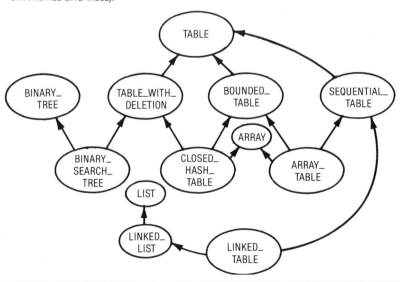

Even in the previous example, multiple inheritance is not far away — if we had defined a data abstraction WINDOW to describe screen panels, some descendants of STATE might inherit from this class, too.

In lieu of conclusion

This article has promoted the view that, if one accepts that reusability is essential to better software quality, the object-oriented approach — defined as the construction of software systems as structured collections of abstract data type implementations — provides a promising set of solutions.

One epithet this approach certainly does not deserve is "top-down." It is puzzling to see this adjective used almost universally as a synonym for "good." Top-down design may be an effective method for developing individual algorithms and routines. But applying it at the system level is inappropriate unless the system can be characterized by a single, frozen, top-level function, a case that is rare in practice.

> *One epithet this approach certainly does not deserve is "top-down."*

More importantly, top-down design goes against the key factor of software reusability because it promotes one-of-a-kind developments, rather than general-pupose, combinable software elements.

It is surprising to see top-down design built in as an essential requirement in the US Dept. of Defense directive MIL-STD-2167, which by the sheer power of its sponsor is bound to have a serious (and, we fear, negative) influence for years to come.

Of course, the bottom-up method promoted here does not mean that system design should start at the lowest possible level. What it implies is construction of systems by reusing and combining existing software. This is a bootstrapping approach in which software elements are progressively combined into more and more ambitious systems.

As a consequence of this approach, there is no notion of main program in Eiffel. Classes are meant to be developed separately. Integrating those classes into an Eiffel "system" is the last, and least binding, decision.

A system is a set of classes with one distinguishing element, the root. The only role of the root is to initiate the execution of the system (by creating an object of the root type and executing its create procedure). A system has no existence as Eiffel construct; it is simply a particular assembly of classes.

Such an approach is viable only if there are adequate facilities to produce flexible software elements and combine them effectively. The concepts of object-oriented design with multiple inheritance and genericity provide such facilities.

Design and implementation are essentially the same activity: constructing software to satisfy a certain specification. The only difference is the level of abstraction — during design certain details may be left unspecified, but in an implementation everything should be expressed in full. However, the process of filling in the details should be continuous, from system architecture to working program. Language constructs such as deferred features are particularly helpful in this process. Software development is made much smoother when you use a language that encompasses

database of components.

As evidence of the limitations of the "managerial" approach to reusability, consider the relations that exist between these components, such as specialization (a hash table is a specialized table, a B-tree is a specialized tree). If an object-oriented language is used, they can be expressed directly by inheritance and recorded within the components themselves. But if the language does not provide direct support for expressing this relation, the information must be entered explicitly into the database, separate from the components.

Give your poor, your huddled projects a decent technical environment in the first place. Then worry about whether you are managing them properly.

Object-oriented design means more than just putting data types into modules; the inheritance concept is essential. This requires an object-oriented language. As structured programming showed a few years ago, you can attempt to implement new methodological concepts without a language that directly supports them — but it will never be quite as good as the real thing: using the right language to implement the right concepts.

Another aspect of the approach promoted here is that it tends to blur the distinction between design and implementation. While this distinction may be unavoidable today, it is undesirable because it tends to introduce an artificial discontinuity in software construction.

the traditional area of design and implementation, but that is no more difficult to master than conventional programming languages. Such is the aim of Eiffel.

We do not propose, however, to remove the boundary between design and implementation, on the one hand, and system specification on the other. These activities are of a different nature: specification states problems, design and implementation solve them. (A companion effort, the specification method M,[9] applies similar concepts to formal, nonexecutable specifications.)

One more fundamental theme has been guiding this discussion: the idea that today the essential problems of software engineering are *technical* problems.

Not everybody agrees. There is a large and influential school of thought that sees management, organization, and economic issues as the biggest obstacles to progress in software development. Programming aspects, in this view, are less important. This view is evidenced in many discussions of reusability that consider technical issues, such as the choice of programming language, as less important for reusability than such things as an easily accessible

This immediately raises some difficult issues: how to provide an adequate user interface, check the consistency of the relation information, and maintain the integrity of this information as components are updated. Advanced project-management techniques are required to solve these issues. This is a typical example of an organizational solution to a technical problem, with the resulting complexity and loss of effectiveness.

Overemphasis on management issues is premature. While it is indeed true that many software projects are plagued with management problems, focusing on these problems first confuses the symptom with cause. It's like expecting better hospital management to solve the public hygiene problem 10 years before Pasteur came along!

Give your poor, your huddled projects a decent technical environment in the first place. *Then* worry about whether you are managing them properly. ☐

Acknowledgments

The comments and suggestions made by the referees, those who agreed with the article's thesis and those who didn't, were much appreciated. The influence of Simula 67, the first object-oriented language and still one of the best, is gratefully acknowledged.

References

1. T.C. Jones, "Reusability in Programming: A Survey of the State of the Art," *IEEE Trans. Software Eng.* Sept. 1984, pp. 488-494.

2. M.A. Jackson, *System Development*, Prentice-Hall, Englewood Cliffs, N.J., 1983.

3. B.P. Lientz and E.B. Swanson, "Software Maintenance: A User/Management Tug of War," *Data Management*, April 1979, pp. 26-30.

4. B.W. Boehm, "Software Engineering — As It Is," *Proc. Fourth Int'l Conf. Software Eng.*, CS Press, Los Alamitos, Calif., Sept. 1979, pp. 11-21.

5. B. Dwyer, "A User-Friendly Algorithm," *Comm. ACM*, Sept. 1981, pp. 556-561.

6. B. Meyer, "Genericity versus Inheritance," *Proc. ACM Conf. Object-Oriented Programming Syst, Languages, and Applications*, ACM, New York, pp. 391-405 (revised version to appear in *J. Pascal, Ada, and Modula-2*).

7. B. Meyer, "Vers un Environnement Conversationnel à Deux Dimensions," *Journées BIGRE*, Grenoble, France, Jan. 1982, pp. 27-39.

8. B. Meyer, "Towards a Two-Dimensional Programming Environment," *Proc. 1982 European Conf. Integrated Computer Syst.*, P. Degano and R. Sandewall, eds., North Holland, Amsterdam, 1983, pp. 167-179.

9. B. Meyer, "M: A System Description Method," Tech. Report TRCS 85-15, Computer Science Dept., University of California, Santa Barbara, May 1985.

Bertrand Meyer is president of Interactive Software Engineering, Inc., a Santa Barbara, California, company specializing in tools and education for improving software quality. The Eiffel environment is one of Interactive's products.

From 1983 to 1986, he was a visiting associate professor at the University of California, Santa Barbara. Previously, he was division head at Electricité de France. He is a member of AFCET, the Computer Society of the IEEE, and ACM. He has engineering degrees from Polytechnique and Suptélécom, an MS from Stanford University, and the Dr. Sc. from the University of Nancy, France.

EIFFEL:
REUSABILITY
AND RELIABILITY

Bertrand Meyer

Interactive Software Engineering Inc.

270 Storke Road Suite 7
Goleta, CA 93117 (USA)
(805) 685-1006 - Fax (805) 685-6869

ABSTRACT

This article is a general introduction to the **Eiffel** language and environment, which applies the concepts of object-oriented design and programming to the construction of high-quality software.

As a language, Eiffel provides a range of features for the construction of reusable and reliable software components: classes, multiple inheritance, polymorphism and dynamic binding, genericity, strict static type checking, a disciplined exception mechanism, systematic use of assertions, invariants and other constructs for ensuring program correctness.

Eiffel is implemented by compilation through C, ensuring wide portability. On option, a stand-alone C package, movable to any machine supporting C, will be generated from the text of an Eiffel system. However the language itself is an original design and has no relation to C.

The environment ensures separate compilation of Eiffel classes; it also takes care of configuration management, automatically triggering re-compilation of modified classes without programmer intervention. The tools of the environment include facilities for automatic documentation (producing a class interface description from class texts), an interactive debugger, a system for graphical design and exploration of class hierarchies, an optimizing postprocessor and other facilities.

The environment also includes a library of reusable software components (classes) covering fundamental data structures and algorithms as well as bit-map graphics.

1 Introduction

Eiffel is a language and environment intended for the design and implementation of quality software in production environments. The language is based on the principles of object-oriented design, augmented by features enhancing correctness, extendibility and efficiency; the environment, currently available on Unix, includes a library of reusable classes and tools for such tasks as automatic configuration management, documentation and debugging.

Beyond the language and environment aspects, Eiffel promotes a method of software construction by combination of reusable and flexible modules.

The present note is a general introduction to Eiffel. More detailed information [12, 15, 11, 7, 8] is available. A recent book [16] explores the issues and techniques of object-oriented design and programming and is based for a large part on the Eiffel approach.

2 Design principles

Software quality is a tradeoff between many factors [10]. In the current state of the software industry, some of these factors appear worth a particular effort. One is *reusability*, or the ability to produce software components that may be used in many different applications; observation of programmers shows that many of the same program patterns frequently recur, but that actual reuse of program modules is much less widespread than it ought to be. Another important factor is *extendibility*: although software is supposed to be "soft", it is notoriously hard to modify software systems, especially large ones.

As compared to other quality factors, reusability and extendibility play a special role: satisfying them means having *less* software to write and thus, presumably, more time to devote to the other goals (such as efficiency, ease of use etc.). Thus it may pay off in the long run to concentrate on these two factors, and they were indeed paramount in the design of Eiffel.

Other design goals also played a significant part. Helping programmers ensure *correctness* and *robustness* of their software is of course a prime concern. *Portability* was one of the requirements on the implementation. Finally, *efficiency* cannot be neglected in a tool that is aimed at practical, medium- to large-scale developments.

3 Object-oriented design

To achieve reusability and extendibility, the principles of object-oriented design seem to provide the best known technical answer to date. This introduction is not the place to discuss these principles in depth. We shall simply offer a definition: Object-oriented design is **the construction of software systems as structured collections of abstract data type implementations**. The following points are worth noting in this definition:

- The emphasis is on structuring a system around the classes of objects it manipulates rather than the functions it performs on them, and on reusing whole data structures, together with the associated operations, rather than isolated routines.

- Objects are described as instances of abstract data types – that is to say, data structures known from an official interface rather than through their representation.

- The basic modular unit, called the class, describes one implementation of an abstract data type (or, in the case of "deferred" classes, studied below, a set of possible implementations of the same abstract data type).

- The word *collection* reflects how classes should be designed: as units which are interesting and useful on their own, independently of the systems to which they belong, and may be reused by many different systems. Software construction is viewed as the assembly of existing classes, not as a top-down process starting from scratch.

- Finally, the word *structured* reflects the existence of important relationships between classes, particularly the **multiple inheritance** relation.

Following Simula 67 [1], several object-oriented languages have appeared in recent years, such as Smalltalk [5], extensions of Pascal such as Object Pascal [19], of C such as Objective C [4] or C++ [18], of Lisp such as Loops [2], Flavors [17] and Ceyx [6]. Eiffel shares some properties of these languages but goes beyond them in many respects, by offering multiple inheritance (which, of the systems quoted, is only available in recent versions of Smalltalk, in the AT&T research version of C++, and in the Lisp extensions), generic classes, static type checking (whereas most existing languages are either untyped or offer dynamic checking only) and facilities for redefinition and renaming (see below). Furthermore, Eiffel is unique among object-oriented languages in providing strong support for software reliability through its techniques for expressing and checking formal program properties (assertions, invariants), a new approach to safe exception handling, and a solution to the problem of name clashes in multiple inheritance. Finally the language comes with an important library of reusable software components, and a programming environment geared towards the development of sizable software in production environments.

Eiffel as a language includes more than presented in this introduction, but not *much* more; it is a small language, comparable in size (by such a measure as the number of keywords) to Pascal. It was meant to be a member of the class of languages which programmers can master entirely – as opposed to languages of which most programmers know only a subset. Yet it is appropriate for the development of industrial software systems, as has by now been shown by a number of full-scale projects in various companies including our own.

4 Classes

A class, it was said above, represents an implementation of an abstract data type, that is to say a set of run-time objects characterized by the operations available on them (the same for all instances of a given class), and the properties of these operations. These objects are called the **instances** of the class. Classes and objects should not be confused: "class" is a compile-time notion, whereas objects only exist at run-time. This is similar to the difference that exists in classical programming between a program and one execution of that program.

A simple example is a class *ACCOUNT* describing bank accounts. Before we show the class, we first describe how it would be used by another class, say *X*.

To use *ACCOUNT*, class *X* may introduce an entity and declare it of this type:

acc1: ACCOUNT

The term "entity" is preferred here to "variable" as it denotes a more general notion. An entity declared of a class type, such as *acc1*, may at any time during execution refer to an object; as Eiffel is a typed language, this object must be an instance of *ACCOUNT* (or, as we shall see below, of a "descendant class" of *ACCOUNT*). An entity which does not refer to any object is said to be void.

By default (at initialization) entities are void; objects must be created explicitly, by an instruction

acc1.Create

which associates *acc1* with the newly created object. *Create* is a predefined "feature" of the language.

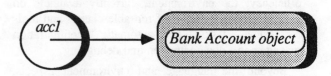

Figure 1: Entity and associated object

Once *acc1* has been associated with an object, the features defined in class *ACCOUNT* may be applied to it. Examples are:

acc1.open ("John");
acc1.deposit (5000);

if *acc1.may_withdraw (3000)* **then**
    acc1.withdraw (3000)
end*;*
print (acc1.balance)

All feature applications use the dot notation: *entity_name.feature_name*. There are two kinds of features: **routines** (as *open*, *deposit*, *may_withdraw* or *withdraw*), that is to say operations; and **attributes**, that is to say data items associated with instances of the class.

Routines are further divided into procedures (actions, which do not return a value) and functions (which return a value). Here *may_withdraw* is a function with an integer parameter, returning a boolean result; the other three routines invoked are procedures.

The above extract of class *X* does not show whether, in class *ACCOUNT*, *balance* is an attribute or a function without parameters. This ambiguity is intentional. A class such as *X*, said to be a **client** of *ACCOUNT*, does not need to know how a balance is obtained: it could be stored as attribute of every account object, or re-computed by a function, whenever requested, from other attributes such as the list of previous deposits and withdrawals. Deciding on one of these implementations is the business of class *ACCOUNT*, not anybody else's. This is important because such decisions are often reversed over the lifetime of a project; so it is essential to protect clients against the effects of these changes.

Here now is a first sketch of how class *ACCOUNT* itself might look. Line segments beginning with -- are comments.

```
class ACCOUNT export
    open, deposit, may_withdraw,
    withdraw, balance, owner
feature
    balance: INTEGER ;

    minimum_balance: INTEGER is 1000 ;

    owner: STRING ;

    open (who: STRING) is
            -- Assign the account to owner who
        do
            owner := who
        end ; -- open

    add (sum: INTEGER) is
            -- Add sum to the balance
            -- (Secret procedure)
        do
            balance := balance+sum
        end ; -- deposit

    deposit (sum: INTEGER) is
            -- Deposit sum into the account
        do
            add (sum)
        end ; -- deposit

    withdraw (sum: INTEGER) is
            -- Withdraw sum from the account
        do
            add (-sum)
        end ; -- withdraw

    may_withdraw (sum: INTEGER): BOOLEAN is
            -- Is it permitted to withdraw sum
            -- from the account?
        do
            Result := (balance >= minimum_balance)
        end ; -- deposit
end -- class ACCOUNT
```

This class includes two clauses: **feature**, which describes the features of the class, and **export**, which lists the names of features available to clients of the class. Non-exported features are said to be secret. Here procedure *add* is secret, so that *acc1.add (–3000)* would be illegal in *X*. Attribute *minimum_balance* is also secret.

Let us examine the features in sequence. Routines are distinguished from attributes by a clause of the form **is**...**do**...**end**. Thus *balance* is in fact an attribute. The clause **is** *1000* introduces *minimum_balance* as a constant attribute, which will not occupy any physical space in objects of the class. Non-constant attributes such as *balance* do use space for each object of the class; they are similar to components of a record in Pascal.

Attributes *balance* and *minimum_balance* are declared of type *INTEGER*. Eiffel is strongly typed: every entity is declared of a certain type. A type is either simple, that is to say one of *INTEGER*, *REAL*, *CHARACTER* and *BOOLEAN*, or a class. Arrays and strings belong to the second category; they are described by predefined system classes, *ARRAY* and *STRING*, treated exactly as user-defined classes with one exception: a special notation, as in *"John"*, is available to denote literal string constants.

Automatic initialization is ensured by the language definition, so that the initial *balance* of an account object will be zero after a *Create*. Numeric attributes are initialized to zero, booleans to false, characters to the null character; those of class types are initially void.

The other five features are straightforward routines. The first four are procedures, the last one (*may_withdraw*) a function returning a boolean value; note that the special variable *Result* denotes the function result. It is initialized on function entry to the default value of the appropriate type, as defined above.

To properly understand the routines, it is necessary to remember that in an object-oriented languages any operation is relative to a certain object. In an external client invoking the operation, this object is specified by writing the corresponding entity on the left of the dot, as *acc1* in *acc1.open ("John")*. Within the class, however, the "current" instance to which operations apply usually remains implicit, so that unqualified references, such as *owner* in procedure *open* or *add* in *deposit*, mean "the *owner* attribute or *add* routine relative to the current instance". The special variable *Current* may be used, if needed, to explicitly denote this object. Thus the unqualified occurrences of *add* appearing in the above class are equivalent to *Current.add*.

In summary, this simple example shows the basic structuring mechanism of the language, the class. A class describes a data structure, accessible to clients through an official interface comprising some of the class features. Features are implemented as attributes or routines; the implementation of exported features may rely on other, secret ones.

5 Assertions

Classes are defined as abstract data type implementations. What defines an abstract data type, however, is not just the available operations, but also the formal properties of these operations, which do not appear in the above example.

Eiffel enables and encourages programmers to express formal properties of classes by writing **assertions**, which may in particular appear in the following positions:

• routine **preconditions** express conditions that must be satisfied whenever a routine is called. For example withdrawal might only be permitted if it keeps the account's balance on or above the minimum. Preconditions are introduced by the keyword **require**.

• Routine **postconditions**, introduced by the keyword **ensure**, express conditions that are guaranteed to be true on routine return (if the precondition was satisfied on entry).

• Class **invariants** must be satisfied by objects of the class at all times, or more precisely after object creation and after any call to a routine of the class. They are described in the **invariant** clause of the class and represent general consistency constraints that are imposed on all routines of the class.

Assertions (which as far as I know are not supported by any other object-oriented language) are one of the language traits that reflect the concern for correctness mentioned at the beginning of this article. Remarkable as object-oriented techniques are for producing extendible and reusable components, they are of little interest unless we can convince ourselves that these components are also correct and robust.

The *ACCOUNT* class may be rewritten with appropriate assertions:

class *ACCOUNT* **export** ... (as before)
feature
... Attributes as before:
...*balance, minimum_balance, owner*

open ... -- as before ;

add ... -- as before ;

deposit (sum: INTEGER) **is**
    -- Deposit *sum* into the account
  require
    sum >= 0
  do
    add (sum)
  ensure
    balance = **old** *balance + sum*
  end ; -- *deposit*

withdraw (sum: INTEGER) **is**
    -- Withdraw *sum* from the account
  require
    sum >= 0 ;
    sum <= balance – minimum_balance
  do
    add (–sum)
  ensure
    balance = **old** *balance – sum*
  end ; -- *withdraw*

may_withdraw ... -- as before

Create (initial: INTEGER) **is**
  require
    initial >= minimum_balance
  do
    balance := initial
  end -- *Create*

invariant
  balance >= minimum_balance
end -- class *ACCOUNT*

The **old**... notation may be used in an **ensure** clause, with a self-explanatory meaning.

This class now includes a specific *Create* procedure, as needed when the default initializations are not sufficient. Under the previous scheme, an account was created by, say, *acc1.Create*. Because of the initialization rules, *balance* is then zero and the invariant is violated. If a different initialization is required, possibly requiring (as here) client-supplied arguments, the class should include a procedure called *Create*. The effect of

acc1.Create (5500)

is to allocate the object (as in the default *Create*) and to call the procedure called *Create* in the class, with the given argument. This call is correct as it satisfies the precondition and ensures the invariant. (Procedure *Create*, when provided, is recognized as special; it is automatically exported and should not be included in the **export** clause.)

Syntactically, assertions are boolean expressions, with a few extensions (like the **old** notation). The semicolon (see the precondition to *withdraw*) is equivalent to an "and", but permits individual identification of the components, useful for producing informative error messages when assertions are checked at run-time.

Assertions may be indeed be monitored at run-time; since such monitoring may penalize the performance, it is enabled on option, class by class. (For each class, two levels of monitoring are possible: preconditions only or all assertions). This provides a powerful debugging tool, in particular because the classes of the Basic Eiffel Library, which are widely used in Eiffel programming, are protected by carefully written assertions. A violated assertion will trigger an exception, as described below; unless the programmer has written an appropriate exception handler, the exception will cause an error message and termination.

Independently of any run-time checking, however, assertions are powerful tools for documenting correctness arguments: they serve to make explicit the assumptions on which programmers rely when they write program fragments that they believe are correct. Writing assertions, in particular preconditions and postconditions, amounts to spelling out the terms of the **contract** that controls the relationship between a routine and its callers. The precondition binds the callers; the postcondition binds the routine. This metaphor of *programming as contracting* (see [13]) is a general and fruitful paradigm. Inheritance, as we shall see, extends it by introducing subcontracting.

6 Exceptions

Whenever there is a contract, the risk exists that the contract may be broken. This is where exceptions come in. (Other references [16, 13, 14] describes the Eiffel exception mechanism in more detail.)

An exception may arise from one of several causes. When assertions are monitored, an assertion violation will raise an exception. Another cause is the occurrence of a hardware-triggered abnormal signal, arising for example from arithmetic overflow or a failure to find the memory needed for allocating an object.

Unless a routine has made specific provision to handle exceptions, it will **fail** if an exception arises during its execution. Failure of a routine is a third cause of exception: a routine that fails triggers an exception in its caller.

A routine may, however, handle an exception through a **rescue** clause. This optional clause attempts to "patch things up" by bringing the current instance to a stable state (one satisfying the class invariant). Then it can terminate in either of two ways:

- The rescue clause may execute a **retry** instruction. This will cause the routine to restart its execution from the beginning, attempting again to fulfil the routine's contract, usually through another strategy. This assumes that the instructions of the rescue clause, before the **retry**, have attempted to correct the cause of the exception.

- If the rescue clause does not end with **retry**, then the routine fails: it returns to its caller, immediately signaling an exception. (The caller's rescue clause will be executed according to the same rules.)

Note that a routine with no rescue clause is considered to have an empty rescue clause, so that any exception occurring during the execution of the routine will cause the routine to fail immediately.

The principle underlying this approach is that **a routine must either succeed or fail**: either it fulfils its contract, or it doesn't; in the latter case it must notify its caller by triggering an exception.

This should be contrasted with the Ada exception mechanism, which does not rely on any notion of contract. This encourages writing routines that will fail to achieve their purpose but fail to notify the caller because the exception is handled locally. Such examples, which may even be found in Ada textbooks (see example quoted in [13]), violate the above principle by involving routines that neither succeed (they didn't fulfil their job) nor fail (the caller is not notified and continues its execution on the false assumption that the call was normally completed). This is the reason why the Ada mechanism is so dangerous. Also note that the **retry** instruction can only be implemented in Ada using intricate control structures: **goto** instructions and multi-level loop exits [13].

An example of the Eiffel exception mechanism is a routine *attempt_transmission* that transmits a message over a phone line. The actual transmission is performed by a routine *transmit*; once started, however, *transmit* may abruptly fail, triggering an exception, if the line is disconnected. Routine *attempt_transmission* tries the transmission at most 5 times; before returning to its caller, it sets a boolean attribute *successful* to **true** or **false** depending on the outcome. Here is the text of the routine:

```
attempt_transmission (message: STRING) is
    -- Attempt transmission of message,
    -- at most 5 times.
    -- Set successful accordingly.
local
    failures: INTEGER
do
    if failures < 5 then
        transmit (message);
        successful := true
    else
        successful := false
    end
rescue
    failures := failures + 1;
    retry
end; -- attempt_transmission
```

Note that the integer local variable *failures* is initialized to zero on routine entry.

This example shows one of the key reasons for the simplicity of the mechanism: the rescue clause never attempts to achieve the original intent of the routine; this is the sole responsibility of the normal body (the **do** clause). The only role of the rescue clause is to "patch things up" and either fail or retry.

This disciplined exception mechanism is, we believe, essential for practicing programmers, who need a protection against unexpected events, but cannot be expected to sacrifice safety and simplicity, as in Ada, to pay for this protection.

7 Generic classes

Building software components (classes) as implementations of abstract data types yields systems with a solid architecture but does not in itself suffice to ensure reusability and extendibility. This section and the next two describe Eiffel techniques for making the components as general and flexible as possible.

The first technique is genericity, which exists under different forms in Ada and CLU but is more new to object-oriented language. Classes may have generic parameters representing types. The following examples come from the Basic Eiffel Library:

ARRAY [T]
LIST [T]
LINKED_LIST [T]

They respectively describe one-dimensional arrays, general lists (without commitment as to a specific representation) and lists in linked representation. Each has a formal generic parameter *T* representing an arbitrary type. To actually use these classes, you provide actual generic parameters, which may be either simple or class types, as in the following declarations:

il: LIST [INTEGER];
aa: ARRAY [ACCOUNT];
aal: LIST [ARRAY [ACCOUNT]] --etc.

An earlier article [15] discussed the role of genericity in comparison to inheritance and explained their combination in Eiffel, especially in the context of strict type checking. An important component of the solution, required to guarantee type consistency, is the notion of "declaration by association". [15, 16, 12].

8 Multiple inheritance

Multiple inheritance is a key technique for reusability. The basic idea is simple: when defining a new class, it is often fruitful to introduce it by combination and specialization of existing classes rather than as a new entity defined from scratch.

The following simple example, from the Basic Library, is typical. *LIST*, as indicated, describes lists of any representation. One possible representation for lists with a fixed number of elements uses an array. Such a class will be defined by combination of *LIST* and *ARRAY*, as follows:

```
class FIXED_LIST [T] export ...
inherit
    LIST [T];
    ARRAY [T]
feature
    ... Specific features of fixed-size lists ...
end -- class FIXED_LIST
```

The **inherit**... clause lists all the "parents" of the new class, which is said to be their "heir". (The "ancestors" of a class include the class itself, its parents, grandparents etc.; the reverse term is "descendant".) Declaring *FIXED_LIST* as shown ensures that all the features and properties of lists and arrays are applicable to fixed lists as well.

Another example is extracted from a windowing system based on a class *WINDOW*. Windows have **graphical** features: a height, a width, a position etc., with associated routines to scale windows, move them and so on. The system permits windows to be nested, so that a window also has **hierarchical** features: access to subwindows and the parent window, adding a subwindow, deleting a subwindow, attaching to another parent and so on. Rather than writing a complex class that would contain specific implementations for all of these features, it is much preferable to inherit all hierarchical features from *TREE* (one of a number of classes in the Basic Eiffel Library describing tree implementations), and all graphical features from a class *RECTANGLE*.

Multiple inheritance yields remarkable economies of programming effort and has a profound effect on the software development process. Users have repeatedly told us that it is one of the key benefits of programming with Eiffel.

The very power of the mechanism demands adequate means to keep it under control. In Eiffel, no name conflict is permitted between inherited features. Since name conflicts inevitably arise in practice, especially for software components contributed by independent developers, the language provides a technique to remove them: **renaming**, as in

    class *C* **export**... **inherit**
      A **rename** *x* **as** *x1*, *y* **as** *y1*;
      B **rename** *x* **as** *x2*, *y* **as** *y2*
    feature...

Here the **inherit** clause would be illegal without renaming, since the example assumes that both *A* and *B* have features named *x* and *y*.

Renaming also serves to provide more appropriate feature names in descendants. For example, class *WINDOW*, as mentioned above, inherits from *TREE* routines such as *insert_subtree*. For clients of *WINDOW*, however, this is not an appropriate name. A client of *WINDOW* (such as a class used in the implementation of a multiple-windowing text editor) needs coherent window terminology, and shouldn't be concerned with the inheritance structure that led to the implementation of the class. So it is appropriate to rename *insert_subtree* as *add_subwindow* in the inheritance clause of *WINDOW*.

To further ensure that the multiple inheritance mechanism is not misused, the invariants of all parent classes automatically apply to a newly defined class. Thus classes may not be combined if their invariants are incompatible.

9 Polymorphism

One important aspect of inheritance is that it enables the definition of flexible program entities that may refer to objects of various forms at run-time (hence the name "polymorphic").

This possibility is one of the distinctive features of object-oriented languages. In Eiffel, it is reconciled with static typing. The underlying language convention is simple: an assignment of the form $a := b$ is permitted not only if a and b are of the same type, but more generally if a and b are of class types A and B such that B is a descendant of A.

This corresponds to the intuitive idea that a value of a more specialized type may be assigned to an entity of a less specialized type – but not the reverse. (As an analogy, consider the fact that if I request vegetables, getting green vegetables is fine, but if I ask for green vegetables, receiving a dish labeled just "vegetables" is not acceptable, as it could include, say, carrots.)

What makes this possibility particularly powerful is the complementary facility: **feature redefinition**. A feature of a class may be redefined in any descendant class; the type of the redefined feature (if an attribute or a function) may be redefined as a descendant type of the original feature, and, in the case of a routine, its body may also be replaced by a new one.

Assume for example that a class *POLYGON*, describing polygons, has among its features an array of points representing the vertices and a function *perimeter* returning a real result, the perimeter of the current polygon, obtained by summing the successive distances between vertices. An heir of *POLYGON* may be:

class *RECTANGLE* **export** ... **inherit**
  POLYGON **redefine** *perimeter*
feature
  -- Specific features of rectangles, such as:
  side1: REAL; side2: REAL;

  perimeter: REAL **is**
    -- Rectangle-specific version
  do
    *Result := 2 * (side1 + side2)*
  end; -- *perimeter*
  ... other *RECTANGLE* features ...

Here it is appropriate to redefine *perimeter* for rectangles as there is a simpler and more efficient algorithm. Note the explicit **redefine** subclause (which would come after the **rename** if present).

Other descendants of *POLYGON* may also have their own redefinitions of *perimeter*. The version to use in any call is determined by the run-time form of the parameter. Consider the following class fragment:

p: POLYGON; r: RECTANGLE;
... p.Create; r.Create; ...
if *c* **then** *p := r* **end**;
print (p.perimeter)

The assignment *p := r* is valid because of the above rule. If condition *c* is false, *p* will refer to an object of type *POLYGON* when *p.perimeter* is evaluated, so the polygon algorithm will be used; in the opposite case, however, *p* will dynamically refer to a rectangle, so that the redefined version of the feature will be applied. This possibility is known as **dynamic binding**. We shall see below that it is implemented in Eiffel without negative effects on run-time performance.

Dynamic binding provides a high degree of flexibility and generality. The remarkable advantage for clients is the ability to request an operation (here the computation of a figure's perimeter) without knowing what version of the operation will be selected; the selection only occurs at run-time. This is essential in large systems, where many variants of operations may be available, and each component of the system needs to be protected against variant changes in other components.

There is no equivalent to this possibility in non-object-oriented languages. Note for example that discrimination on records with variants, as permitted by Pascal or Ada, is of a much more restrictive nature, as the list of variants of a record type is fixed: any extension may invalidate existing code. In contrast, inheritance is open and incremental: an existing class may always be given a new heir (with new and/or redefined features) without itself being changed. This facility is of great importance in software development, an activity which (whether by design or circumstance) is invariably incremental.

Neither do the generic and overloading facilities of Ada offer the kind of polymorphism shown here, as they do not support a programming style in which a client module may issue a request meaning: ''compute the perimeter of *p*, using the algorithm appropriate for whatever form *p* happens to have when the request is executed''.

This mechanism is more disciplined in Eiffel than in most other object-oriented languages. First, feature redefinition, as seen above, is explicit. Second, because the language is typed, the compiler may always check statically whether a feature

application *a.f* is correct; in contrast, languages such as Smalltalk and its descendants (such as Objective-C) defer checks until run-time and hope for the best: if an object "sends a message" to another (Smalltalk terminology for calling a routine), one just expects that the class of the receiving object, or one of its ancestor classes, will happen to include an appropriate "method" (Smalltalk term for routine); if not, a run-time error will occur. Such errors may not happen during the execution of a correctly compiled Eiffel system.

A further disadvantage of the Smalltalk approach is that it may imply costly run-time searches, as a requested method may not be defined in the class of the receiving object but inherited from a possibly remote ancestor.

Another tool for controlling the power of the redefinition mechanism is provided in Eiffel by assertions. If no precautions are taken, redefinition may be dangerous: how can a client be sure that evaluation of *p.perimeter* will not in some cases return, say, the area? One way to maintain the semantic consistency of routines throughout their redefinitions is to use preconditions and postconditions, which are binding on redefinitions. More precisely, any redefined version must satisfy a weaker or equal precondition and ensure a stronger or equal postcondition than in the original. Thus, by making the semantic constraints explicit, routine writers may limit the amount of freedom granted to eventual redefiners.

These rules should be understood in light of the contracting metaphor introduced above. Redefinition and dynamic binding introduce sub-contracting: *POLYGON*, for example, sub-contracts the implementation of *perimeter* to *RECTANGLE* when applied to any entity that refers at run-time to a rectangle object. An honest sub-contractor is bound by the contract accepted by the prime contractor: it may not impose stronger requirements on the clients (but may accept more general requests, hence the possibility for the precondition to be weaker); and it must achieve at least as much as promised by the original contractor (but may achieve more, hence the possibility for the postcondition to be stronger).

10 Deferred classes

An important extension of the inheritance mechanism is provided by deferred classes. A deferred class is a class which contains at least one deferred routine; a routine is declared as deferred to express that implementations of the routine will only be provided in descendants. For example, a system used by the Department of Motor Vehicles to register vehicles could include a class of the form

deferred class *VEHICLE* **export**
    dues_paid, valid_plate, register, ...
feature
    dues_paid (year: INTEGER): BOOLEAN **is**

      ...
    end*; -- dues_paid*

    valid_plate (year: INTEGER): BOOLEAN **is**

      ...
    end*; -- valid_plate*

    register (year: INTEGER) **is**
      -- Register vehicle for year
    require
      dues_paid (year)
    deferred
    ensure
      valid_plate (year)
    end*; -- register*
    ... Other features ...
end *-- class VEHICLE*

This example assumes that no single registration algorithm applies to all kinds of vehicle; passenger cars, motorcycles, trucks etc. are all registered differently. But the same precondition and postcondition apply in all cases. The solution is to treat *register* as a deferred routine, making *VEHICLE* a deferred class. Effective versions of the routine are given in of class *VEHICLE*, such as *CAR* or *TRUCK*. They are similar to redefined versions of a routine; only here there is no effective definition in the original class, only a specification in the form of a deferred routine.

Deferred classes describe a group of implementations of an abstract data type rather than just a single implementation. A deferred class may not be instantiated: *v.Create* is illegal if *v* is an entity declared of type *VEHICLE*. But such an entity may be assigned a reference to an instance of a non-deferred descendant of *VEHICLE*. For example, assuming *CAR* and *TRUCK* provide effective definitions for all deferred routines of *VEHICLE*, the following will be correct:

    v: VEHICLE; c: CAR; t: TRUCK;
    ...
    c. Create (...); t.Create (...);
    ...
    if *"some test"* **then** *v := c* **else** *v := t* **end***;*
    v.register (1988)

The mechanisms of polymorphism and dynamic binding are fully exploited here: depending on the outcome of "some test", *v* will be treated as a car or a truck, and the appropriate registration algorithm will be applied. Note that "some test" may depend on some event whose outcome is impossible to predict until run-time, for example the user clicking with the mouse to select one among several vehicle icons displayed on the screen.

Deferred classes are particularly useful for the application of Eiffel as high-level design language. The first version of a module, obtained at the global design stage, may be a deferred class, which will later be refined into one or more effective (non-deferred) classes. Particularly important for this application is the possibility to associate a precondition and a postcondition to a routine even though it is deferred (as with routine *register* above), and an invariant to a class even though it is a deferred class. This enables the designer to attach a precise semantics to a module at the design stage, long before any implementation is provided.

The combination of deferred classes and assertions makes Eiffel a more appropriate tool for high-level design than existing "PDLs" (Program Design Languages). Common PDLs offer no facility comparable to Eiffel assertions for describing the semantics of routines independently of their implementations. (The only significant exception seems to be Anna [9], but this is a research tool rather than a practical product.) The further benefit with Eiffel, of course, is that it is not just a design language, but can be efficiently executed as well, so that that no conceptual gap is introduced between design and programming.

This concludes the overview of the language. As it is well known that a programming language is in practice no better than its implementation, we now describe the Eiffel environment.

11 The implementation

The Eiffel implementation runs on various versions of Unix (System V, 4.2BSD, Xenix); we have ported it to more than 20 different machine architectures. The compiler uses C as intermediate language, making Eiffel potentially portable to any environment supporting C, although we have limited ourselves so far to Unix environments. (Vax-VMS is under way.)

As the above discussion should suffice to show, Eiffel is in no way an extension of C; C is only used as implementation vehicle and had no influence on the language design. Other compilation techniques are possible, but the use of a widely available assembly language such as C as intermediate code has obvious portability advantages.

Great care has been taken to provide efficient compilation and execution, so that the environment would support the development of serious software. The following points are particularly worth noting.

• Redefinition and dynamic binding imply that a qualified routine reference, say *p.perimeter*, may have many different interpretations depending on the value of *p* at run-time. A run-time search for the appropriate routine, as implemented in many systems, carries a heavy performance penalty. The maximum search length grows with the depth of the inheritance graph, putting reusability (which tends to increase this depth) and extendibility (which promotes redefinition) at odds with efficiency. With multiple inheritance, run-time search becomes hopeless: a complete graph of ancestor classes, not just a linear list, would have to be searched at run-time.

In contrast, the Eiffel implementation always finds the appropriate routine in constant time, with only a small penalty over a standard procedure call, and no significant space overhead. This result was difficult to achieve, but essential in light of the previous discussion. Regardless of the amount of redefinition and polymorphism in your system, *a.f* always takes the same (small) time.

• There is almost never any code duplication. Again this was difficult to achieve with multiple inheritance and genericity: multiple inheritance as included in recent versions of Smalltalk [3] requires duplication of code for parent classes other than the first, to avoid run-time search; most Ada implementations also duplicate code for every instance of a generic module. In Eiffel, code is only duplicated in a special case, "repeated" inheritance with renaming, not described here.

• The run-time system handles object creation and memory de-allocation. It includes an incremental garbage collector, implemented as a coroutine which steals only negligible time from application programs. Although not available in all object-oriented environments, automatic garbage collection is an essential component of the approach; object-oriented applications, which typically create many objects, should not be polluted with complex, error-prone memory

management code. Garbage collection may be turned off (for example during initialization); the collector coroutine may also be explicitly activated for a certain time at points where the programmer knows some CPU time is available (for example while awaiting user input in an interactive application).

• Compilation is performed on a class-by-class basis, so that large systems can be changed and extended incrementally. The Eiffel to C translation time is usually about half of the time for the next step, C to machine code.

One more property of the implementation deserves a mention: its **openness**. Eiffel classes are meant to be interfaced with code written in other languages. This concern is reflected in the language by the optional **external** clause which, in a routine declaration, lists external subprograms used by the routine. For example, a square root routine might rely on an external function, as follows:

sqrt (x: REAL, eps: REAL): REAL **is**
   -- Square root of *x* with precision *eps*
require
   x >= 0 ; eps > 0
external
   csqrt (x: REAL, eps: REAL): REAL
     name "*sqrt*" **language** "*C*"
do
   Result := csqrt (x, eps)
ensure
   abs (Result ^ 2 – x) <= eps
end -- *sqrt*

The optional **name...** subclause caters to the various naming conventions of other languages.

This mechanism makes it possible to use external routines without impacting the conceptual consistency of the Eiffel classes. Note in particular how the C function *sqrt* is granted a more dignified status as Eiffel routine with the addition of a precondition and a postcondition.

This facility is essential in view of the design objectives listed in section 2: an environment promoting reusability should enable reuse of software written prior to its introduction, not just of future software to be developed with it. Beyond this remark, the "external" construct lies at the basis of one of the applications of Eiffel: as an integrating mechanism for components written in other languages. An example might be scientific software: although numerical programs will benefit just as much as others from such structuring mechanisms as classes, multiple inheritance, genericity, export controls, assertions etc., programmers may prefer to code the actual bodies of numerical routines in a language specifically designed for this purpose, and package them cleanly in Eiffel classes.

12 The environment

The construction of systems in Eiffel is supported by a set of development tools.

Most important are the facilities for automatic configuration management integrated in the compilation command **es** (for Eiffel System). When a class C is compiled, the system automatically looks for all classes on which C depends directly or indirectly (as client or heir), and re-compiles those whose compiled versions are obsolete. Unix programmers will recognize this facility as giving the power of Make, but there is a fundamental difference: instead of having to manually describe the dependencies between modules, a tedious and error-prone process, the Eiffel programmer lets **es** take care of analyzing these dependencies automatically.

This problem is far from trivial because dependency relations are complex (a class may be, say, a client of one of its descendants) and, in the case of the client relation, may involve cycles. But our solution completely frees programmers from having to keep track of changed modules to maintain the consistency of their systems. The algorithm avoids many unneeded recompilations by detecting the case in which a class has been modified but its interface has not changed, so that clients need not be recompiled. This has proved very important in practice, preventing a chain reaction of re-compilations in a large system when a feature implementation is changed in a low-level class.

The environment also contains debugging tools: tools for run-time checking of assertions; a tracer; a full-screen source-level debugger, which lets programmers do their debugging in terms of object and classes (in contrast with to a traditional, function-oriented debugger), and enables them to explore the object structure at run-time.

A documentation tool, **short**, produces a summary version of a class showing the interface as available to clients: the exported features only and, in the case of routines, only the header, precondition and postcondition. The manual for the Basic Eiffel Library [7] is an example of Eiffel documentation produced almost entirely from output generated by **short**. Such documentation is essentially obtained

"for free" and, even more importantly, is guaranteed to be consistent with the documented software, as it is extracted from it. This should be contrasted with classical approaches, where software and documentation are viewed as separate products.

A postprocessor integrated in **es** performs optional optimizations on the generated C code: removal of unneeded routines; simplification of calls to non-polymorphic routines; in-line expansion of routine calls satisfying appropriate criteria. These optimizations are essential to allow programmers to enjoy the elegant and highly modular programming style favored by Eiffel without paying an unacceptable performance overhead.

The postprocessor is also responsible for another important function of the environment: the generation of a stand-alone **C package** from an Eiffel system. The resulting package comes complete with its Make file and a copy of the run-time system (garbage collector etc.). It may be ported to any environment supporting C. This facility is particularly interesting for developers who use Eiffel to design and implement their software but deliver it to their customers in C form: Eiffel need not be available on the target environments.

Finally the environment includes the Basic Eiffel Library, a repertoire of classes covering many of the most important data structures and algorithms of everyday programming. Use of the library is one of the elements that give Eiffel programming its distinctive flavor, enabling programmers to think and write in terms of lists, trees, stacks, hash tables etc. rather than arrays, pointers, flags and the like.

The library also contains a set of graphical classes, based on the MIT X Windows systems, which enable users to manipulate windows, menus, geometrical figures and other graphical objects.

A recent development based on this library is the "Eiffel-Good" system (Graphics for Object-Oriented Design), which supports the graphical design and exploration of class hierarchies, with automatic generation of class skeletons.

13 Conclusion

Our most important debts to are to Simula 67, Ada (for the syntax only) and Alphard. Among the new contributions are, from the language standpoint, the safe treatment of multiple inheritance through renaming, the combination between genericity and inheritance, disciplined polymorphism by explicit redefinition, the assertion mechanism and its combination with inheritance, a clean interface with external routines, the introduction of full static typing into an object-oriented language, and the disciplined approach to exception handling based on the notion of contract. From the implementation viewpoint, a number of our solutions are also original: constant-time feature access, separate compilation with automatic recompilation, coroutine garbage collection, support for object-oriented debugging and documentation, support for the preparation of portable software packages.

More generally, we think that Eiffel is the first language to combine the powerful ideas of object-oriented languages with the modern concepts of software engineering; these results have been made available to practicing software developers in an environment offering the facilities that are required to develop serious software.

1. Graham Birtwistle, Ole-Johan Dahl, Bjorn Myrhaug, and Kristen Nygaard, *Simula Begin*, Studentliteratur and Auerbach Publishers, 1973.

2. Daniel G. Bobrow and Mark J. Stefik, *LOOPS: an Object-Oriented Programming System for Interlisp*, Xerox PARC, 1982.

3. Alan H. Borning and Daniel H. H. Ingalls, "Multiple Inheritance in Smalltalk-80," in *Proceedings of AAAI-82*, pp. 234-237, 1982.

4. Brad J. Cox, *Object-Oriented Programming: An Evolutionary Approach*, Addison-Wesley, Reading (Mass.), 1986.

5. Adele Goldberg and David Robson, *Smalltalk-80: The Language and its Implementation*, Addison-Wesley, Reading (Mass.), 1983.

6. Jean-Marie Hullot, "Ceyx, Version 15: I - une Initiation," Rapport Technique no. 44, INRIA, Rocquencourt, Eté 1984.

7. Interactive Software Engineering, Inc., "Eiffel Library Manual," Technical Report TR-EI-7/LI, 1986.

8. Interactive Software Engineering, Inc., "Eiffel User's Manual," Technical Report TR-EI-5/UM, 1986.

9. David Luckham and Friedrich W. von Henke, "An Overview of Anna, a Specification Language for Ada," *IEEE Software*, vol. 2, no. 2, pp. 9-22, March 1985.

10. James McCall, (Ed.) *Factors in Software Quality*, General Electric, 1977.

11. Bertrand Meyer, "Reusability: the Case for Object-Oriented Design," *IEEE Software*, vol. 4, no. 2 , pp. 50-64, March 1987.

12. Bertrand Meyer, "Eiffel: A Language and Environment for Software Engineering," *The Journal of Systems and Software*, 1988. To appear.

13. Bertrand Meyer, "Programming as Contracting," Submitted for publication, 1988.

14. Bertrand Meyer, "Eiffel Complements 1: Disciplined Exceptions," Submitted for publication, 1988.

15. Bertrand Meyer, "Genericity, static type checking, and inheritance," *The Journal of Pascal, Ada and Modula-2*, 1988. To appear (Revised version of paper in OOPSLA conference, Portland, Oregon, ACM SIGPLAN Notices, September 1986, pp. 391-405).

16. Bertrand Meyer, *Object-Oriented Software Construction*, Prentice-Hall, 1988.

17. David A. Moon, "Object-Oriented Programming with Flavors," in *OOPSLA '86 Conference Proceedings, Portland (Oreg.), Sept. 29-Oct. 2, 1986*, pp. 1-8, 1986. (Published as *SIGPLAN Notices*, 21, 11, Nov. 1986.)

18. Bjarne Stroustrup, *The C++ Programming Language*, Addison-Wesley, Menlo Park (Calif.), 1986.

19. Larry Tesler, "Object Pascal Report," *Structured Language World*, vol. 9, no. 3, 1985.

Trademarks: Unix (AT&T Bell Laboratories); Ada (AJPO); Objective C (Productivity Products International); Smalltalk (Xerox); Eiffel, Cépage (Interactive Software Engineering, Inc.).

Reusability Issues and Ada

Reprinted from *IEEE Software,* July 1987, pages 43-51. Copyright ©1987 by the Institute of Electrical and Electronics Engineers, Inc. All rights reserved.

**Anthony Gargaro,
Computer Sciences Corp.
T.L. (Frank) Pappas, * Intermetrics**

How do you write reusable code when your methodology doesn't address reusability? These guidelines developed by a major defense contractor may help.

One of the expected benefits of writing applications in Ada is the ability to reuse parts of the software in different applications and execution environments.

To do this, reuse must be a consideration during both design and implementation. However, many software development methodologies don't require reusable designs, so in the near term reusability may be restricted to what is achievable through proficiency in Ada. In other words, the programmer must have knowledge of both the language features that facilitate part reuse and the features that compromise part reuse.

While work has been undertaken in the reuse of Ada parts,[1] that work usually has assumed that reusability is a requirement in the design of the part and that the functional performance of the part would not inherently impede its reuse. For example, the CAMP[2] and EVB[3] initiatives comprise parts that are carefully designed for reuse. Similarly, informal guidelines[4] proposed for the reuse of Ada parts emphasize the need to design for reuse.

This article, however, focuses on writing reusable parts for applications like mission-critical computer resource software that are expected to exploit the full capabilities of the language but that may not have been explicitly designed for reuse.

*This work was done while Pappas was at Computer Sciences Corp.

```
        Table : array (1 .. Max_Table_Elements) of Element_Type;
        . . .
        function Binary_Search (Element: in Element_Type) return Natural is

        Left_End_Point  : Natural : = 1;
        Right_End_Point : Natural : = Max_Table_Elements;
        Mid_Point       : Positive;

    begin

        while Left_End_Point <= Right_End_Point loop
            Mid_Point : = (Left_End_Point + Right_End_Point) / 2;
            if Element < Table (Mid_Point) then
                Right_End_Point : = Mid_Point - 1;
            elsif Table (Mid_Point) < Element then
                Left_End_Point : = Mid_Point + 1;
            else
                return Mid_Point;
            end if;
        end loop;
        return 0;

    end Binary_Search;
```

Figure 1. A binary search function with weak reusability.

Reusability in MCCR applications

Reports about MCCR systems that use Ada have focused on evaluating the adequacy of the language in meeting system performance requirements. They have not considered the reuse of the software among different applications and execution environments.

However, these reports indicate that, in the initial transition to Ada, rigid performance requirements may require the use of Ada constructs that are explicitly and implicitly dependent on the target execution environment. Furthermore, the most common requirements for real-time, embedded MCCR applications (interrupt control, cyclic execution, critical and predictable timing, storage control, and flexible scheduling) conflict with the goal of developing reusable software parts.

This conflict is exacerbated by programming practices that favor techniques that produce code for target execution environments with limited processing resources. These practices reduce the opportunity for reusing the code, and so it is unlikely that MCCR applications resulting from such practices will have a legacy of reusable code.

To foster reusability of parts for MCCR software, applications should be

• independent of the characteristics of a particular target execution environment and

• composed of parts that are independent of their enclosing context.

Ada has features that can help achieve both objectives. Its comprehensive support for modern software construction principles such as abstraction, composition, encapsulation, and instantiation provides a framework for writing applications composed of reusable parts. In addition, Ada provides a model for program execution that removes many application requirements on specialized services provided by the target execution environment.

Based on this, we propose three criteria to follow when writing reusable code. To be reusable, a program must:

• be transportable,

• have an orthogonal (context-independent) composition, and

• be independent of the Ada runtime system.

Because MCCR applications may not be specifically designed for reusability, parts of the programs may meet these criteria in different degrees. A part whose potential for reuse is low is *weakly reusable*; a part whose potential for reuse is high is *strongly reusable*. These are the extremes of reusability.

We expect parts that are weakly reusable to require source modifications and to have limited application; strongly reusable parts should require no source modifications and be widely applicable. Pragmatic issues of interface or performance may prevent a strongly reusable part from fulfilling its high reuse potential. For example, a generic-intensive component may require too many parameters — it may sacrifice flexibility for generality.

An *effectively reusable* part has a high pragmatic potential for reuse. In practice, weak reusability should be avoided, strong reusability sought, and effective reusability obtained.

Transportability

Developers must meet this first criterion to establish confidence in the reusability of a program's parts in different target execution environments.

When the entire program is to be reused, the distinction between transportability and reusability is determined by how well the execution satisfies the application requirements. In this context, the execution behavior of a transportable program among different target environments is equivalent but not necessarily identical.[5] For example, the processing capacity of the target environment and the compiling system may change a program's execution within the semantic domain of the Ada standard, providing the change is not the result of an explicit feature or option specified in the program because this would violate the transportability criterion.

Others have written guidelines for writing transportable Ada programs,[6,7] so we will limit this discussion to the latter two criteria.

Orthogonality

When we say that a program's composition is orthogonal, we mean that its parts are independent of their enclosing context. For example, a subprogram that depends on entities in an enclosing subprogram or package is dependent on that context. The more a part depends on its context, the less potential it has for reuse because more of the context must be transported with it. Conversely, the less a part depends on its context, the more potential it has for reuse because less of the context must be transported with it.

When coupled with programming for flexibility, context independence will yield effectively reusable, if not strongly reusable, parts.

Composition orthogonality is not an issue in program transportability because the entire context of each program part is transported to the new execution environment. It becomes an issue only when a part is extracted from its context. An exception

```
generic
    type Element_Type is limited private;
    type Index_Type    is (<>);
    type Table_Type    is array (Index_Type range <>) of Element_Type;

    with function "<" (Left, Right : Element_Type) return Boolean is <>;
    with function "=" (Left, Right : Element_Type) return Boolean is <>;
package Binary_Search_Package_Template is

    function Binary_Search (Table: Table_Type; Element: Element_Type) return Index_Type;

    Not_Found     : exception;
    Context_Error : exception;

end Binary_Search_Package_Template;
```

Figure 2. A generic binary search function with strong reusability.

is a program whose main subprogram has parameters. Here, the dependency is on the execution context, not the application context, so the issue is still transportability, not reusability.

An example. Search and sort subprograms are one source of classical reusability issues. A definitive case study on writing reusable Ada parts for sorting has been performed.[8] Therefore, we will use a binary search function to illustrate the effect of composition orthogonality on a part's degree of reusability. Our intent is not to provide the definitive work on writing Ada parts for searching but to illustrate some issues in writing reusable parts in Ada.

Figure 1 shows a typical binary search function. Its many context dependencies make it weakly reusable. This part can only be reused in a new context that provides

(1) a number named Max_Table_Elements,

(2) a type named Element_Type, and

(3) an array named Table with the structure shown.

If these entity names or the array structure are not appropriate in the new context, the part must be modified.

In addition to these dependencies, this function also depends on the array index subtype being a subtype of Positive. This dependency is explicit in the calculations of the midpoint and the left and right end points, and implicit in the use of zero to indicate that the element is not found in Table. This dependency is implicit in the use of Natural as the function subtype. Natural extends Positive by one value, zero, allowing Natural to serve a dual purpose: return the array index on a successful search and indicate failure on an unsuccessful search. Finally, there is a context dependency on the names Positive and Natural, namely, that they are not hidden in the new context.

Figure 2, on the other hand, shows a strongly reusable binary search function. Here, the function has been encapsulated in a generic package. The use of generic formal parameters has removed most context dependencies.

This version is flexible and general, and provides a template for building instances

```
    --PRI: Pulse Repetition Interval

    type PRI_Type is delta . . . range . . .; --a fixed point type
    type Emitter_Description_Type is
        record
            PRI_Part : PRI_Type;
            . . .
        end record;

    type Emitter_Range_Type is range 1 .. Max_Emitters;
    type Emitter_List_Type is array (Emitter_Range_Type range <>)
                             of Emitter_Description_Type;

    Known_Threat_List : Emitter_List_Type (1 .. Number_Of_Known_Threats);

    Emitter_Description : Emitter_Description_Type;
(a)

    function Equals (Left, Right : Emitter_Description_Type) return Boolean is
    begin
        return Left.PRI_Part = Right.PRI_Part;
    end Equals;

    function Less_Than (Left, Right : Emitter_Description_Type) return Boolean is
    begin
        return Left.PRI_Part < Right.PRI_Part;
    end Less_Than;
(b)

    package Known_Threat_Search_Package is new
        Binary_Search_Package_Template
           (Element_Type  => Emitter_Description_Type,
            Index_Type    => Emitter_Range_Type,
            Table_Type    => Emitter_List_Type,
            "<"           => Less_Than,
            "="           => Equals);
(c)

    begin
        Index : = Known_Threat_Search_Package.Binary_Search
                    (Table   => Known_Threat_List,
                     Element => Emitter_Description);
        --take actions if known threat found
    exception
        when Known_Threat_Search_Package.Not_Found =>
        --take actions if known threat not found
    end;
    --continue processing
(d)
```

Figure 3. Creating an instance by tiling in template slots. Given the table in (a) and the functions in (b), an instance called Known_Threat_Search_Package is created in (c), and the paradigm in (d) would be used to search for a known threat.

```
package body Binary_Search_Package_Template is

    function Mid_Point_Of (Table: Table_Type) return Index_Type is
    begin
        return Index_Type'Val (Index_Type'Pos (Table'First) + Table'Length/2);
    end Mid_Point_Of;
    pragma INLINE (Mid_Point_Of);

    function More_Than_Two_Elements_In (Table: Table_Type) return Boolean is
    begin
        return Table'Length > 2;
    end More_Than_Two_Elements_In;
    pragma INLINE (More_Than_Two_Elements_In);

    function Predecessor (Index : Index_Type) return Index_Type is
    begin
        return Index_Type'Pred (Index);
    end Predecessor;
    pragma INLINE (Predecessor);

    function Successor (Index: Index_Type) return Index_Type is
    begin
        return Index_Type'Succ (Index);
    end Successor;
    pragma INLINE (Successor);

    function Binary_Search (Table: Table_Type; Element: Element_Type) return Index_Type
        is separate;

begin

    --ensure that 'Length can always be evaluated for objects in Table_Type

    Context_Validation:
        begin
            if Index_Type'Pos (Index_Type'First) <= Index_Type'Pos (Index_Type'Last) then
            if abs (Index_Type'Pos (Index_Type'First) − Index_Type'Pos (Index_Type'Last))
                    >0
            and then Index_Type'Pos (Index_Type'First) < 0 then
            if abs (Index_Type'Pos (Index_Type'First) − Index_Type'Pos (Index_Type'Last))
                    + 1 > 0 then
                    null;
                end if;
            end if;
            end if;
        exception
            when Constraint_Error | Numeric_Error =>
            raise Context_Error;
        end Context_Validation;

end Binary_Search_Package_Template;
```

Figure 4. Context validation for the generic binary search function with strong reusability.

of binary search packages. Each instance provides a function, Binary_Search, and two exceptions, Not_Found and Context_Error. The exception Not_Found signals the condition element not in table. The exception Context_Error signals that the instance is used in a context inconsistent with the view held by the author of the part.

The generic parameters of the template are slots the user fills in when creating an instance of the generic binary search package. Slots for the element type, index type, and array type define a table, and " < " and " = " define the functions used in the search.

Figure 3 shows an example of creating an instance called Known_Threat_Search_Package by filling in the slots in the generic binary search function in Figure 2. Dependencies on the context are specifically called out when the template is instantiated. The paradigm to search for a known threat is shown in Figure 3d.

Readability. However, removing context dependencies can create difficulties, as the package body in Figure 4 illustrates. Four auxiliary functions have been added to the Binary_Search function to improve readability. Such functions frequently will be needed when context dependencies are

removed because the necessary introduction of attributes can make a readable expression unreadable. Auxiliary functions should be easily understood and should be named to improve clarity.

This generic package provides generality because it encompasses all possible generalizations of the binary search that do not change its function or algorithm. It provides flexibility because it passes the array as a parameter to the function. Flexibility is also provided in the specification of the equality operator, " = ", and the comparison operator, " < ". If a definition of " = " or " < " exists in the context of the instantiation, that function need not be mentioned in the instantiation.

Consider the complex expression

```
Index_Type'Val (Index_Type'Pos
(Table'First) + Table'Length/2)
```

hidden in the function Mid_Point_Of. This lets us use

```
Mid_Point : = Mid_Point_Of (Table
(Left_End_Point .. Right_End_Point));
```

in Figure 5 instead of

```
Mid_Point : = Index_Type'Val
(Index_Type'Pos (Table (Left_End_Point
.. Right_End_Point)'First) + Table
(Left_End_Point ..
Right_End_Point)'Length/2)
```

Attributes have also been added to the function in Figure 4.

Attributes 'Val and 'Pos were introduced to accommodate the index subtype of the array, Index_Type. This subtype is an arbitrary, discrete type for which arithmetic is not defined. These attributes allow the arithmetic to be performed in Universal_Integer.

The attributes 'First and 'Length were introduced to accommodate a Table whose bounds have positions — Index_Type'Pos (Table'First) and Index_Type'Pos (Table'Last) — that are large integers. For example, if the index subtype of Table has the range 32_000 .. 32_100, then an implementation may perform the original midpoint computation of (32_000 + 32_100)/2. However, if System.Max_Int = 32_767, then some implementations may raise either a Constraint_Error or a Numeric_Error.

The revised midpoint computation is written to accommodate these latter

```
separate(Binary_Search_Package_Template)
function Binary_Search (Table: Table_Type; Element: Element_Type) return Index_Type is

    Left_End_Point    : Index_Type : = Table'First;
    Right_End_Point : Index_Type : = Table'Last;
    Mid_Point          : Index_Type;

begin
    if Table'Length = 0 then
        raise Not_Found;
    else
        while More_Than_Two_Elements_In ((Table (Left_End_Point..Right_End_Point))) loop
            Mid_Point : = Mid_Point_Of (Table (Left_End_Point..Right_End_Point));
            if Element < Table (Mid_Point) then
                Right_End_Point : = Predecessor (Mid_Point);
            elsif Table (Mid_Point) < Element then
                Left_End_Point : = Successor (Mid_Point);
            else
                return Mid_Point;
            end if;
        end loop;
        if Element = Table (Left_End_Point) then
            return Left_End_Point;
        elsif Left_End_Point /= Right_End_Point and then Element =
                Table (Right_End_Point) then
            return Right_End_Point;
        else
            raise Not_Found;
        end if;
    end if;
end Binary_Search;
```

Figure 5. A generic binary search function with strong reusability.

implementations. Note that the midpoints calculated are not necessarily the same as in the original version in Figure 2.

We don't discuss readability in detail here, but it is an important issue in reusability because a part that is difficult to read will probably not be reused. To balance readability and performance, the Inline pragma has been specified for the auxiliary functions in Figure 5 to advise the compiler that calls to these functions should be expanded in-line, if possible, rather than generated as subprogram calls. While the advice given by a pragma can be ignored by an implementation, many production-quality Ada compilers will support the Inline pragma in simple cases. The use of this pragma is justified here because without it the overhead of the subprogram calls would dominate each loop iteration in certain instantiations.

In Figure 4, the auxiliary functions and Inline pragma serve as compile-time macros with the advantage that the consistency between the macro specification and invocation is validated during compilation of the part.

> *Readability is an important issue in reusability because a part that is difficult to read will probably not be reused.*

Context validation. An important concept in parts reusability is *context validation*, which minimizes reuse of a part in an inappropriate context. The statements of the package body in Figure 4 illustrate context validation. For example, the generic binary search function is based on the assumption that Table'Length can always be computed for any Table argument. However, if the result exceeds System.Max_Int, then Table'Length need not be computable. The sequence in Figure 4 validates the computability of Table'Length, raising the Context_Error exception if the validation fails. The exception can be raised during elaboration of an instantiation of the package body and would be detected in the early stages of testing.

Context validation must accommodate special situations that may falsely signal an incorrect context. For example, the context validation of Figure 4 contains the expression

abs Index_Type'Pos(Index_Type'First) − Index_Type'Pos(Index_Type'Last)

It may seem that the expression could be written as

(Index_Type'Pos(Index_Type'Last) − Index_Type'Pos(Index_Type'First))

but the two expressions may not be equivalent in a two's-complement architecture. Consider a 16-bit architecture for which Integer'First = − 32_768, and suppose the Integer subtype

subtype Negative is Integer range Integer'First .. − 1;
has been specified for Index. Then the first expression is equivalent to

abs (− 32_768 − (− 1))

and the second expression is equivalent to

(− 1 − (− 32_768))

Evaluation of the second expression may well raise Numeric_Error because 32_768 may not be a valid Integer value

returned by the unary minus operation. The use of the short-circuit control form and then ensures that optimizations performed by the compiler do not eliminate the critical evaluation of

abs (Index_Type'Pos (Index_Type'First) - Index_Type'Pos (Index_Type'Last))

Without this, a compiler might optimize the context validation to evaluate Index_Type'Pos(Index_Type'First) < 0 first and bypass the critical evaluation if the result is false. The short-circuit control form ensures that the evaluation occurs in the desired order.

The body of the generic binary search, shown in Figure 5, is quite different from the nongeneric version in Figure 2. It has been written to minimize Element_Type comparisons. For example, it uses the short-circuit control form and then in case the user-supplied "<" and "=" functions are expensive (if they use hashing, for example).

In the nongeneric version, there was no problem if Right_End_Point took on the value 0 or Left_End_Point took on the value Max_Table_Elements + 1. However, in the generic version no analogous values exist in Index_Type, so the algorithm must be modified. In particular, no

```
generic

    type Element_Type is limited private;
    type Index_type      is (<>);
    type Table_type      is array (Index_Type range <>) of Element_Type;

    with function "<" (Left, Right : Element_Type) return Boolean is <>;

    --| for all X, Y, Z: Element_Type =>
    --|    not X< X,
    --|    X<Y and Y<Z-> X<Z,
    --|    X<Y xor Y<X xor X=Y;

    --   These annotations constrain the generic actual parameter specified
    --      for "<" to be a strict linear ordering
    --

    with function "=" (Left, Right : Element_Type) return Boolean is <>;

    --
    --   Annotations for "=" are predefined in Anna to ensure that
    --      the usual mathematical properties of equality hold.
    --

    package Binary_Search_Package_Template is

    --: function Ordered (Table: Table_Type) return Boolean;

    --| where
    --|    return for all I, J: Table'Range =>
    --|                      I <J -> Table (I) < Table (J);

    function Binary_Search (Table: Table_Type; Element: Element_Type)
                            return Index_Type;

    --| where Ordered (Table),
    --|    return Index: Index_Type => Table (Index) = Element,
    --|    for all Index: Table'Range => Element /= Table (Index) =>
    --|       raise Not_Found;

    Not_Found : exception;

    end Binary_Search_Package_Template;
```

Figure 6. Context validation using formal comments.

value of Index_Type can be used to indicate that an element is not found, so the exception Not_Found is introduced to signal this condition.

There are reasons other than performance for which an effectively reusable software part would be preferred over a strongly reusable one.

Consider, for example, a generic subprogram that implements a numerical algorithm that requires a real type. The real type is a generic formal parameter of the generic subprogram. If only standard mathematical operations are required for this type, then a private type can be used as the generic real type because the subprogram can use either fixed- or floating-point types in an instantiation. The mathematical operations would be generic formal function parameters — with appropriate defaults — to the generic subprogram.

However, if accuracy demands you use either fixed-point or floating-point attributes, two versions of the generic subpro-

gram are needed because the attributes for floating-point types differ from those of fixed-point types. This example illustrates the difference between effective reusability and strong reusability: Both versions are effectively reusable but neither is strongly reusable.

A single, strongly reusable version could accommodate both fixed- and floating-point types by using a private type for the real type and adding several generic formal subprograms as generic parameters. But instead of providing any real benefit, these subprograms would simply isolate floating- and fixed-point attribute dependencies, perform type conversions, and so on. While this version might satisfy the strong reusability notion of this article, in reality users would not be likely to use a part that requires generic actual parameters merely to comply with Ada's rules. Therefore, the two effectively reusable parts are preferred over the single, strongly reusable part.

Dynamic context validation. Our generic binary search function is still flawed from a strong reusability viewpoint. We have made three assumptions that seem reasonable:
- the generic actual function parameter for "=" satisfies the usual properties of equality,
- the generic actual function parameter for "<" satisfies the usual properties of a comparison operator (a strict linear ordering), and
- the actual parameter to Table is sorted with respect to "<".

> *There are reasons other than performance to prefer an effectively reusable part over a strongly reusable part.*

But, while these are reasonable assumptions, they may not hold. For example, consider the function Truth, which always returns the value True and the function Flip_Flop, a Boolean state function that negates its current state and returns the new value. If either function is supplied for "=" or "<", Table will not be sorted with respect to "<".

Ada requires only that the parameter profile (number of parameters, type, mode, and position) and result profile (return type) of each function be consistent with the parameter and result profiles of the corresponding generic, formal subprogram parameter. Even if reasonable functions are specified, there is no guarantee that the actual parameter to Table will be sorted with respect to "<".

The assumptions are also context dependencies, but they are dynamic in nature as opposed to the earlier examples (other than the computability of Table'Length), which were static. Neither Ada nor any other widely used, general-purpose language provides features for detecting and validating dynamic context dependencies.

One way to detect and validate dynamic context dependencies is to include formal comments. As an example of formal com-

```
                    --Task controlling read/write access to shared variable
                    task body RW_Control is
                      . . .
                    select
                    --Activate new reader if no writer is waiting
                       when Start_Write 'Count = 0 =>
                          accept Start_Read;
                          Active_Readers : = Active_Readers + 1;
                    or
                    --Active writer if no active readers
                       when Active_Readers = 0 =>
                          accept Start_Write;
                          accept Stop_Write;
                    or
                    --Wait for active reader to complete
                          accept Stop_Read;
                          Active_Readers : = Active_Readers - 1;
                          if Active_Readers = 0 then
                    --Activate and serialize waiting writers
                               while Start_Write'Count > 0 loop
                    -- > > > Implicit dependency on stability of 'Count
                               accept Start_Write;
                               accept Stop_Write;
                             end loop;
                          end if;
                    or
                       terminate;
                    end select;
                      . . .
                    end RW_Control;

                  --procedure called by writer tasks
                    . . .
                    select
                       RW_Control.Start_Write;
                    --Update shared variable with actual parameter from call
                    or
                       delay Write_Time_Limit;
                       RW_Control.Start_Write;
                    --Update shared variable to indicate that the writer was late
                    end select;
```

Figure 7. An implicit runtime system dependency.

ments used to validate dynamic context dependencies we use Annotated Ada (Anna),[9] since it stays within the spirit of Ada.

Figure 6 shows an Anna version of the generic binary search function in Figure 2. (The Context_Error exception has been removed to simplify the discussion.)

The formal comments (Anna annotations) are embedded as Ada comments that start with --| and --:. The annotations for "<" illustrate how to specify that the generic actual parameter for "<" must satisfy a reasonable notion of comparison (the axioms of a strict linear order). The annotations for Binary_ Search specify that Table must be ordered with respect to "<". Moreover, the latter annotations specify that

• the function completes normally when Element is in Table,

• if the function completes normally, the value returned is the index of Element in Table, and

• the exception Not_Found is raised when Element is not in Table.

The Boolean function Ordered, used in the subprogram annotations, illustrates the use of an Anna virtual function. The annotations for the virtual function describe its behavior as yielding True exactly when Table is ordered with respect to "<".

An Anna processor can transform the Anna generic version into a compilable Ada version in which annotations and virtual functions have been translated into Ada text. This allows context validation to be performed during testing without including context validation code directly in the part.

For example, the context validation for Table'Length could be specified in Anna rather than in Ada. This is an important consideration for MCCR programs that have stringent start-up-time requirements. For such programs, context validation as illustrated in Figure 4 may have an unacceptable impact on performance.

RTS dependencies

We will illustrate the potential for dependency on the Ada runtime system (RTS) to affect reuse in real-time MCCR applications with a specific example — dependency on a particular implementa-

tion of task scheduling.

This dependency does not necessarily prevent the program from being transportable, even when the dependency is not satisfied in the new execution environment. However, it does mean that successful reuse of the part that includes the dependency cannot be guaranteed.

Our example is contrived to expedite a straightforward discussion — this code represents neither a recommended use of the language nor a dependency that cannot be mitigated in some other way. It originated in a revision to a program from the Ada Fair benchmark suite.

The original program included packages designed to control access to a shared variable as a means of evaluating the integrity of the task scheduler. In the revised version, the access-control task had been modified to service concurrent reader and writer tasks, and the access protocol is biased in favor of writer tasks to simulate real-time updating of the shared variable. The shared variable is of a composite type

and may be read concurrently by more than one task, providing no task has been granted write access. Furthermore, writing must be serialized and outstanding writes should be serviced before a task is granted read access.

Figure 7 shows the two code fragments. The first fragment is the select statement, enclosed by the task that grants read/write access. The second fragment is the timed entry statement, enclosed by the procedure that is called by the writer tasks. The dependency is associated with the use of the 'Count attribute in the iteration scheme of the while loop that is designed to service all outstanding write requests before a new read request is accepted.

The *Ada Reference Manual* cautions against the use of the 'Count attribute because its value is not stable. In this case, sufficient stability is required only to ensure that the Start_Write entry queue is not decremented before accepting the Start_Write entry. This depends on a class of first-in, first-out task scheduling that

```
generic
   type Element_Type is limited private;
   type Index_Type     is (<>);
   type Table_Type     is array (Index_Type ) of Element_Type;

   with function "< =" (Left, Right : Element_Type) return Boolean is <>;
   with function "=" (Left, Right : Element_Type) return Boolean is <>;
package Binary_Search_Package_Template is

   function Binary_Search (Table: Table_Type; Element: Element_Type) return Index_Type;

   Not_Found      : exception;
   Context_Error : exception;

end Binary_Search_Package_Template;

package body Binary_Search_Package_Template is

   type Integer_Index_Type is range 1 .. 1000;

   function " +" (Left: Index_Type; Right: Integer_Index_Type) return Index_Type is
   begin
      return Index_Type'Val (Index_Type'Pos (Left) + Right);
   end "+";

   function Binary_Search (Table: Table_Type; Element: Element_Type) return Index_Type
      is separate;

begin

   --ensure that Index_Type has exactly 1000 values

   Context_Validation:
      begin
         if abs (Index_Type'Pos (Index_Type'First) - Index_Type'Pos (Index_Type'Last))
            + 1 /= 1000 then
         raise Context_Error;
      end if;
      exception
         when Constraint_Error | Numeric_Error | Context_Error =>
            raise Context_Error;
      end Context_Validation;

end Binary_Search_Package_Template;
```

Figure 8. Context validation in a distributed, generic binary search package.

Efficiency versus reusability

Parts that are effectively reusable or strongly reusable are consistent with good programming style, so ideally all program parts should be written this way. In reality, this is not likely to occur because MCCR performance issues may dictate otherwise. The strong reusability of a part may have to be compromised in favor of increased performance.

For example, performance considerations and program tuning may favor the distributed binary search in Figures 8 and 9 over the strongly reusable binary search in Figure 5. The difference in performance between these versions may be significant. Statistics for binary searches, similar to those of the nondistributed and distributed versions, show that a million searches of a 1000-element integer array required 3.8

Parts that are effectively or strongly reusable are consistent with good programming, so ideally all parts should be written this way. In reality, this is not likely.

prevents interruption of control task execution until task rescheduling is required.

The dependency requires that expiration of the delay does not result in runtime action (mainly changing the state of the delayed writer task) until the executing task is blocked and a new task has to be executed.

This dependency does not preclude successful execution in a different environment where task scheduling is not guaranteed to maintain the stability of the value of the 'Count attribute. For instance, an RTS that implements a preemptive class of task scheduling may result in the value being decremented after the evaluation of the while loop but before accepting the Start_Write entry. However, because of the Start_Write entry statement following the expired delay, the number of queued requests remains the same. Consequently, program transportability is achieved — the execution is functionally equivalent in both environments.

When this implicit dependency is not clearly stipulated, the control task may be mistakenly considered to be strongly reusable on the basis of its transportability. But an attempt to reuse the control task with a different procedure for writer tasks can have unacceptable execution behavior in an execution environment that does not guarantee the stability of the 'Count attribute.

A simple change to the timed entry statement that removes the Start_Write following the delay can cause the entry queue count to reach zero. The control task is now forced to wait unexpectedly at the Start_Write, resulting in a disruption of performance because the reader tasks are dependent on a write request for execution. This is contrary to the guard specification of the enclosing select statement. In the worst case, when no further writes are requested, the control task is blocked indefinitely.

minutes in the former, but only 50 seconds in the latter.

The distributed version is created by completely unfolding the loop of the nondistributed version and by replacing "<" with "< =". Unfolding the loop requires specific bounds on Table. The example assumes that a table with 1000 elements is required and context validation ensures that this requirement is satisfied.

The distributed version may be weakly reusable, but it might still be strongly reusable at the program-generator level. To prepare the distributed version manually would be error-prone, as would extending an existing version to provide increased functionality. A program generator, supplied with a template for the distributed version, could generate the correct number of if statements and the appropriate bounds for a Table whose size is specified when the program generator is invoked.

IEEE SOFTWARE

Composition orthogonality and independence from the implementation freedom of the Ada RTS are practical criteria to use when developing rules for writing reusable parts in the transition of MCCR applications to Ada.

We have developed a preliminary set of guidelines based on these reusability criteria.[10] These guidelines have been introduced on a trial basis by Computer Sciences Corp., a major defense contractor, for all MCCR applications that use Ada. □

Acknowledgments

We are pleased to acknowledge the constructive commentary by the referees on the original version of this article. In particular, we are grateful to Geoffrey Mendal for identifying several flaws in the original version.

References

1. W. Tracz, "Ada Reusability Efforts: A Survey of the State of the Practice," *Proc. Washington Ada Symposium*, Washington, D.C., 1987.

2. D.G. McNicholl et al., *Common Ada Missile Packages (CAMP)*, Tech. Report AFATL-TR-85-93, McDonnell Douglas Astronautics Co., St. Louis, May 1986.

3. *GRACE (Generic Reusable Ada Components for Engineering)*, EVB Software Engineering, Inc., Frederick, Md.

4. C. Braun and J. Goodenough, "Ada Reusability Guidelines," Tech. Report TR-3285-2-208/2, SofTech, Inc., Waltham, Mass., 1985.

5. *Ada Reusability Study*, Tech. Report SP-IRD 9, Computer Sciences Corp., Moorestown, N.J., 1986.

6. J. Nissen and P. Wallis, *Portability and Style in Ada*, Cambridge University Press, New York, 1984.

7. F. Pappas, "Ada Portability Guidelines," Tech. Report ESD-TR-85-141, SofTech, Inc., Waltham, Mass., 1985.

8. G. Mendal, "Designing for Ada Reuse: A Case Study," *Proc. Second Int'l Conf. Ada Applications and Environments*, CS Press, Los Alamitos, Calif., 1986, pp. 33-42.

9. D. Luckham and F.W. von Henke, "An Overview of Anna, A Specification Language for Ada," *IEEE Software*, March 1985, pp. 9-22.

10. *Ada Reusability Handbook*, Tech. Report SP-IRD 11, Computer Sciences Corp., Moorestown, N.J., 1987.

```
separate (Binary_Search_Package_Template)
function Binary_Search (Table: Table_Type; Element: Element_Type) return Index_Type is

   Left_End_Point: Index_Type;

begin
   if Element <= Table (Index_Type'First + 511) then
      Left_End_Point : = Index_Type'First;
   else
      Left_End_Point : = Index_Type'First + (1000 - 512);
   end if;
   if Table (Left_End_Point + 256) <= Element then
      Left_End_Point : = Left_End_Point + 256;
   end if;
   if Table (Left_End_Point + 128) <= Element then
      Left_End_Point : = Left_End_Point + 128;
   end if;
   if Table (Left_End_Point + 64) <= Element then
      Left_End_Point : = Left_End_Point + 64;
   end if;
   if Table (Left_End_Point + 32) <= Element then
      Left_End_Point : = Left_End_Point + 32;
   end if;
   if Table (Left_End_Point + 16) <= Element then
      Left_End_Point : = Left_End_Point + 16;
   end if;
   if Table (Left_End_Point + 8) <= Element then
      Left_End_Point : = Left_End_Point + 8;
   end if;
   if Table (Left_End_Point + 4) <= Element then
      Left_End_Point : = Left_End_Point + 4;
   end if;
   if Table (Left_End_Point + 2) <= Element then
      Left_End_Point : = Left_End_Point + 2;
   end if;
   if Table (Left_End_Point + 1) <= Element then
      Left_End_Point : = Left_End_Point + 1;
   end if;
   if Table (Left_End_Point) = Element then
      return Left_End_Point;
   else
      raise Not_Found;
   end if;
end Binary_Search;
```

Figure 9. Distributed, generic binary search subprogram.

Anthony Gargaro is a lead scientist at Computer Sciences Corp., where he specializes in applying Ada to real-time, embedded defense systems. He recently served as chair of ACM SIGAda and on the Department of Defense's Ada Board. In 1983 he received the DoD Distinguished Service Award for contributions to the Ada program.

Gargaro received a degree in numerical analysis and statistics from Brunel College, U.K. He holds the ICCP CDP and CCP. He is a member of the ACM SIG Board and the British Computer Society.

Frank Pappas is a senior computer scientist at Intermetrics. He was formerly with Computer Sciences Corp, where he participated in the work reported in this article. His interests include the implementation and application of programming languages. Involved in the Ada effort since 1983, he coauthored the *SofTech/U.S. Army Ada Training Curriculum* and has performed many investigations into using Ada effectively.

Gargaro can be reached at Computer Sciences Corp., 304 W. Rte. 38, PO Box N, Moorestown, NJ 08057. Pappas can be reached at Intermetrics, 607 Louis Dr., Warminster, PA 18974.

The Ada Software Repository and Software Reusability

Richard Conn

Maintainer of the Ada Software Repository
2700 Bowline Court
Maineville, OH 45039
Phone: 513/583-4786

Abstract

The Ada Software Repository (ASR) is a collection of Ada programs, software components, information files, and educational material that resides on the computer known as SIMTEL20 on the Defense Data Network (DDN), a world-wide network of computer networks supported by the US Department of Defense. This repository has been accessible to any host computer on the DDN since November 26, 1984, and is available to any member of the Ada community in the United States and its allies.

The Ada Software Repository (ASR) is a free source of Ada programs and information. It serves two roles: to promote the exchange and use of Ada programs (including reusable software components) and to promote Ada education (by providing information on items of interest to the Ada community and by providing examples of working, useful Ada programs). There are 40M bytes of source code, documentation, and information files in the ASR.

The Defense Data Network

The Defense Data Network is a network of over 400 computer networks that supports electronic mail and file transfer between the White House, the Pentagon, major DoD commands, many corporations doing business with the DoD, and many universities in the United States. Several computers on the DDN also act as gateways for the transfer of electronic mail between the DDN and other computer networks, such as CSNET, BITNET, and USENET. The DDN is managed by the Defense Communications Agency.

The operation of the ASR is oriented around the Defense Data Network. Two major networks on the DDN are the MILNET, which supports the operational side of the DoD (including the Ada Software Repository), and the ARPANET, which is a research network (and the original network on which today's DDN is based). Many networks owned by with government organizations and major universities are a part of the DDN.

The DDN represents an enormous resource which supports electronic mail, the sharing of information via file transfer, and the sharing of resources ranging from CRAY supercomputers to IC fabrication facilities. Each computer on each network of the DDN uses the DoD standard communications protocol, TCP/IP, and each computer can access the Ada Software Repository. The MILNET alone contains over 140 VAX computers (VAX 11/750 and larger) as well as a wide variety of other computers, and the MILNET interfaces with over 40 distinct operating systems.

Overview of the ASR

The Ada Software Repository is divided into several subdirectories which are organized by topic (see Figure 1). Some of the topics are educational information, software development (including tools such as Ada pretty printers and standards checkers), reusable software components, project management, graphics, benchmarks, CAIS (Common APSE Interface Set), communications (including message handling and protocols like TCP/IP), and data base management.

Three subdirectories contain documentation files of interest to the Ada community. These are GENERAL, the general information directory, EDUCATION, a directory containing information on subjects of "lessons learned" and educational resources such as textbooks, and POINTERS, a directory containing pointers to sources of information outside the ASR.

GENERAL contains documentation on the use of the ASR, a listing of all subdirectories with a brief description of each, information on communications protocols such as KERMIT and XMODEM, instructions on how to access the ADA-SW electronic mailing list, and information on how to acquire magnetic tapes of the ASR.

EDUCATION contains listings of Ada text books, a glossary of Ada terms, discussions on object-oriented design with Ada, notes on common programming errors encountered by Ada programmers, reports from experiments on interfacing Ada with other languages, and technical reports containing programming productivity and valuable "lessons learned" data from projects which were done using Ada.

POINTERS contains information on the Ada-oriented resources on the ADA20 host computer on the DDN, a list of validated Ada compilers, information on DoD Directives and individual service (Army, Navy, Air Force) policies on the use of Ada, information on the Ada Evaluation and Verification effort, and information and addresses of vendors working on Ada compilers.

The ANSI-LRM subdirectory contains a complete copy of MIL-STD-1815A, the Ada Language Reference Manual. Files indicating errors found throughout the LRM are included.

The WIS-ADA-TOOLS subdirectory provides detailed information on all software submitted by the WIS program office to the ASR. In support of the Ada effort, the WIS (WWMCCS Information System, where WWMCCS stands for World Wide Military Command and Control System) program office in conjunction with NOSC (the Naval Oceans Systems Center) funded the development of many useful tools written in Ada. Several purposes of this project were to determine the feasibility of Ada, to analyze the Ada language and determine what drawbacks and limitations it may have, and to obtain productivity and "lessons learned" data on projects which are implemented using Ada. Over $7M went into this project, and, having achieved its purpose, the WIS program office made the non-proprietary and non-sensitive software developed under this project available to the public through the ASR. Figure 2 gives a partial listing of the 57 WIS/NOSC tools along with cost data and other metrics. In interpreting this data, an Ada statement is counted by a terminating semicolon, and a line is counted by a terminating carriage return/line feed.

The other subdirectories in the ASR make up by far the largest part of the ASR. They contain software grouped by subject area. Some of the subject areas include AI, benchmarks, reusable software components, cross-reference tools, management tools, math libraries, Ada pretty printers, simulation programs, and Ada style and programming standards checkers, to name a few.

Figure 1 shows a snapshot of the ASR which was taken on December 31, 1986. This figure is presented without explanation of the directory names. The reader is referred to the documents identified later in this paper for a further explanation of the ASR and its organization.

Key to the operation of the ASR is the ADA-SW electronic mailing list. ADA-SW is used to inform ASR users of new software submissions, releases of new information files and newsletters, bug reported on ASR software, and other items of interest. ADA-SW also provides a mechanism for users of the ASR to communicate with the people maintaining the ASR and other users of the ASR.

Acquiring Files from the ASR

There are three mechanisms for acquiring software directly from the Ada Software Repository. Users of DDN hosts are able to scan the directories of the repository and transfer files to their hosts by employing the File Transfer Protocol (FTP) program. People able to communicate with the DDN via electronic mail may access the ASR by means of the Archive Server, an electronic mail handler that can receive requests for files via electronic mail and then mail the files to the requestor. Finally, a tape distribution facility is provided by people at White Sands Missile Range.

ADA-SW

Users with an electronic mail interface to the DDN may subscribe to the ADA-SW electronic mailing list; send a request via electronic mail to:

ADA-SW-REQUEST@SIMTEL20.ARPA

After a user has been entered into the repository's mailing list, he will receive a welcome message which includes introductory information on how to access the repository and how to use FTP to copy files from the repository to his DDN host computer.

Tape Distribution

Tape copies of the files in PD:<ADA.*> on 9 Track, 1600 BPI tapes in TOPS-20 DUMPER, TOPS-10 INTERCHANGE, and UNIX TAR formats are available. Send three 2400-foot tapes, a stamped, self-addressed mailing label, and a short, informal cover letter stating that you would like a copy of this collection and specifying the format. The tapes will be made at the convenience of the personnel at White Sands and mailed back to you. There is no charge for this service.

White Sands cannot accept cash, checks, money orders, or purchase orders. Include return postage in stamps and send your tapes to:

Commander
US Army White Sands Missile Range
STEWS-IM-CM-S (Bldg. 362, F. Wancho)
White Sands Missile Range,
    New Mexico 88002-5072

Queries on the status of a particular tape may be addressed via electronic mail to
    WANCHO@SIMTEL20.ARPA.

Documentation on the ASR

Documentation available to the ASR user community includes:

1. The Ada Software Repository Master Index, a 428-page loose-leaf book which details the contents of the ASR,

2. The Ada Software Repository and the Defense Data Network: A Resource Handbook, a paperback which contains user-oriented information on the Defense Data Network and its resources, including the Ada Software Repository and other repositories on the Defense Data Network,

3. The Ada Software Repository Newsletter, a monthly publication which contains information on new submissions to the Ada Software Repository and items of interest to the ASR users, and

4. AHELP and the Online Documentation of the ASR, a data base and a group of programs which allow a user to interactively query

the data base in order to locate items.

The Ada Software Repository Master Index[1] contains details on all items of software and information in the Ada Software Repository. It is a living document, provided in loose-leaf form to facilitate updating as the ASR grows.

The Ada Software Repository and the Defense Data Network: A Resource Handbook[2] is a reference book for users of the Defense Data Network and the Ada Software Repository in particular. It compliments the Master Index, providing details on the operation and use of the Defense Data Network as well as the ASR and other resources available on the DDN.

Ada Software Repository Newsletters[3] are published monthly; they are available in the directory PD:<ADA.NEWS> and by subscription. The newsletters provide information of interest to users of the Ada Software Repository, including information on new submissions during the previous month.

The directory PD:<ADA.ONLINE-DOC> contains a data base which details the contents of the Ada Software Repository and programs written in Ada which may be used to interactively query this data base. The data base is updated as changes are made to the ASR, so it always contains information on an up-to-the-minute basis. Documentation on compiling and using the support programs (AHELP) is included.

Software Reusability

The usage of the ASR is monitored in a variety of ways, including an automatic count of the number of accesses made to each file in the ASR. Figure 3 lists the 30 most popular files in the ASR as of 30 December 1986, where popularity is measured by the number of times the files have been accessed. Of these 30 files, 17 are from reusable

software components libraries (10 are the source code to reusable software components and 7 are the prologue documentation files on reusable software components).

In order for software reusability to be effective, the cost (in terms of time and manpower) required to reuse code from a library must be less than the cost of creating new code. The cost of software reuse is derived from (1) the cost of searching the library and selecting the most desirable candidates, (2) the cost of reading the documentation and the code of the candidate components and gaining a working understanding of them, and (3) the cost of adapting one or more of the candidates to fit the particular need. The reader is referred to the Prieto-Diaz/Freeman article[4] for an excellent discussion of this topic.

Software reusability has been an issue with the users of the ASR and other software repositories on SIMTEL20. Over the years, several ideas associated with the effective reuse of software have emerged, including (1) the application of effective configuration management (CM) and information retrieval (IR) schemes, (2) the use of a taxonomy to provide keywords by which to categorize items in the library, (3) the use of an integrated documentation system to generate both online data bases (which are searched by software tools) and hardcopy documentation from a common documentation data base, and (4) the adoption of a mechanism to automate the selection of several candidates from the library which satisfy some or all of the requirements of the application.

Effective CM and IR Schemes

Once the software library reaches a significant size, it is usually necessary to establish a formal configuration management scheme to maintain the library. DoD-STD-2167, MICR 80009[6] provides several good ideas which include the application of a software librarian through which all software is entered into the library, a formal mechanism for the processing of software problem reports (SPRs) and software development change requests (SDCRs), and formal problem review procedures. Each of the nine repositories on SIMTEL20 are maintained by a key individual who acts as a software librarian.

CM can become a very time-consuming, manpower-intensive task as the library grows. Consideration should be given to the automation of this process, and, if automation is done, the implementation of an effective interactive information retrieval (IR) system is also desirable. The IR system should be able to support the software librarian, detailing and tracking the information contained in the unit development folders (see DoD-STD-2167) for the modules, and it should also support the users of the library by providing an effective keyword search mechanism.

Taxonomy

The development of a taxonomy, which is a list keywords and their meanings as they apply to the systematic classification of elements in the library, may become instrumental as the library grows. The taxonomy would provide the keywords to be used in searching for modules in either the IR system or a hardcopy document (via its index). Two taxonomies, one developed by the National Bureau of Standards and the other under development by the Software Engineering Institute, are applicable to the Ada community.

Integrated Documentation

Documentation on a software library may be presented in two basic formats: (1) online documentation which is accessed interactively via a computer and (2) hardcopy. Each form has its advantages, and both forms are desirable.

The ASR is supported by a central data base and toolset which generates (1) an online data base that the users may access and query interactively and (2) hardcopy documents that can be printed and updated with a minimum of effort. The online data base and tools written in Ada to access this data base are provided to the users through the <ADA.ONLINE-DOC> directory. The hardcopy is available in loose-leaf book form with an extensive table of contents and index[1].

Due to the nature of the online and hardcopy mediums, it may not be desired to present exactly the same information in both. The online system, for example, may present short summaries not larger than one screen and references to the hardcopy documentation. Provision may also be made in the support software of the online system to print details of modules under review and allow the user to read the hardcopy offline at his leasure.

Candidate Selection

A simple keyword-only search is the minimum requirement for interactive IR on a computer system, but it is desirable for the search mechanism to also allow for the development of boolean expressions to detail the desired attributes of the modules. For example, searches may be done for modules which meet criteria like:

(linear_search OR binary_search)
AND
(68000_assembly_language OR Ada)

"Close" as well as exact matching against the user's criteria may also be employed in the IR search mechanism. This is also a candidate for the application of artificial intelligence techniques (such as heuristic analysis).

Closing

The Ada Software Repository (ASR) is a collection of Ada programs, software components, information files, and educational material that resides on the SIMTEL20 host computer on the Defense Data Network (DDN). The ASR is available to any member of the Ada community in the United States and its allies.

The purpose of this paper is to bring the Ada Software Repository to the attention of potential new users and to provide a number of pointers for further information. Ideas for effective software reuse are also discussed.

The first step a new user should take is to read the ASR newsletters. These newsletters are available for free from the ASR itself and for a minor subscription fee. Back issues are available. Two books which document the ASR and its use are described in the References.

References

1. Conn, Richard. The Ada Software Repository Master Index, 1986, Echelon, Inc., 885 N. San Antonio Road, Los Altos, CA 94022, 415/948-3820, 428 pp, $49.95.

2. Conn, Richard. The Ada Software Repository and the Defense Data Network: A Resource Handbook, 1987, New York Zoetrope, Inc., 838 Broadway, New York, NY 10003, 800/242-7546, $16.95.

3. Conn, Richard (newsletter editor). Ada Software Repository Newsletters, 1986-1987, Echelon, Inc., 885 N. San Antonio Road, Los Altos, CA 94022, 415/948-3820, $16.00/year.

4. Prieto-Diaz, Ruben, and Freeman, Peter, "Classifying Software for Reusability," IEEE Software, Volume 4, Number 1, January 1987.

5. United States Department of Defense, DoD-STD-2167.

6. United States Department of Defense, DoD-STD-2167, MICR 80009: Software Configuration Management.

About the Author

Richard Conn has been a fan of Ada for over six years. He was involved in the the proposal evaluation effort for Ada (then DoD-1) in 1979 when he was working for the Army's Satellite Communications Agency at Fort Monmouth, NJ, and he has worked on many Ada-oriented projects in the areas of satellite communications and applied research (specifically, the WIS tools) since then. Rick is currently involved in an R&D project which investigates the use of Ada in the design of embedded aircraft engine control software.

Rick is the founder of the Ada Software Repository and is active in maintaining it and the ADA-SW electronic mailing list. He is the author of two books on the Ada Software Repository and the Defense Data Network and also acts as editor of the Ada Software Repository Newsletter.

Rick holds a Bachelor of Science degree in Computer Science from Rose-Hulman Institute of Technology in Terre Haute, Indiana, and a Master of Science degree in Computer Science from the University of Illinois in Urbana.

Figure 1: Snapshot of the Ada Software Repository, 31 Dec 1986

Directory	---- Source Code ---- Byte Count	Line Count	--- Documentation --- Byte Count	Line Count
PD:<ADA.ADA-SQL>	1117750	30503	248404	6038
PD:<ADA.AI>	250984	7326	321559	10354
PD:<ADA.ANSI-LRM>	0	0	1201050	46091
PD:<ADA.BENCHMARKS>	302163	13431	56750	1236
PD:<ADA.CAIS>	1719047	50360	10742	216
PD:<ADA.CAIS-TOOLS>	152675	4442	7140	132
PD:<ADA.COMPILATION-ORDER>	359990	8147	86428	2790
PD:<ADA.COMPONENTS>	2038727	63217	141214	2966
PD:<ADA.CROSS-REFERENCE>	23786	695	4457	99
PD:<ADA.DBMS>	81285	2345	5314	116
PD:<ADA.DDN>	1959099	52150	135474	3426
PD:<ADA.DEBUGGER>	889057	23052	512159	15927
PD:<ADA.EDITORS>	1615008	36463	219584	5802
PD:<ADA.EDUCATION>	0	0	366103	8698
PD:<ADA.EXTERNAL-TOOLS>	92404	3396	47265	1301
PD:<ADA.FORMGEN>	318402	9788	152458	7965
PD:<ADA.GENERAL>	11904	333	361635	7969
PD:<ADA.GKS>	1991575	55737	273777	9884
PD:<ADA.MANAGEMENT-TOOLS>	1347705	38114	643121	26054
PD:<ADA.MATH>	1226925	38096	1595731	75515
PD:<ADA.MENU>	453562	10861	297293	8046
PD:<ADA.MESSAGE-HANDLING>	977501	25714	222916	5983
PD:<ADA.METRICS>	2940672	81611	419416	14150
PD:<ADA.NEWS>	0	0	306204	6927
PD:<ADA.ONLINE-DOC>	63360	2260	225751	6654
PD:<ADA.PAGER>	98378	3566	28338	1267
PD:<ADA.PDL>	1963068	51631	1120314	22759
PD:<ADA.POINTERS>	0	0	267527	5176
PD:<ADA.PRETTY-PRINTERS>	1037841	20866	99222	3063
PD:<ADA.SIMULATION>	337803	10346	170261	6615
PD:<ADA.SPELLER>	893957	60483	466092	46028
PD:<ADA.STARTER-KIT>	0	0	522	11
PD:<ADA.STUBBER>	81309	1808	5754	131
PD:<ADA.STYLE>	2021624	48628	212703	7262
PD:<ADA.TOOLS>	1320403	41278	397188	33374
PD:<ADA.VIRTERM>	312797	8887	642761	17479
PD:<ADA.WIS-ADA-TOOLS>	0	0	350390	7016

Totals	---- Source Code ---- Byte Count	Line Count	--- Documentation --- Byte Count	Line Count
Column Totals -->	28000761	805534	11623017	424520

	Byte Count	Line Count
Grand Total -->	39623778	1230054

Figure 2: WIS/NOSC Toolset
(Note: Most, But Not All, is in the ASR At This Time)

N	TOOL	ADA STATEMENTS	LINES	COMMENTS	COST(K)
1	VIRTUAL TERMINAL	2421	6300	590	85
2	SPELLING CHECKER	2743	9458	2626	77
3	STYLE CHECKER (TI)	3189	9762	2013	100
4	FORMS GENERATOR (TI)	2869	8307	1707	112
5	COMBINE_FILES	419	889	109	0
6	COMMAND INTERPRETER	577	1045	93	0
7	SOURCE FORMATTER	1322	3318	1163	0
8	STUBBER	707	1795	600	0
9	COMPILE BENCHMARKS	4464	6880	2037	0
10	GMHF	4300	12519	5016	49
...					
39	REQUIREMENTS TRACE	1484	9176	2179	73
40	DATA DICTIONARY	1903	8283	2200	54
46	SYMBOLIC DEBUGGER	3640	44577	12746	262
47	TEXT EDITOR	7237	28871	9574	56
48	TEXT FORMATTER	4902	10461	2426	32
49	GKS THROUGH 2c	21215	95436	28658	1115
50	COMPLEXITY MEASURES	5051	23307	4559	45
51	PROPAGATION PREDICT	9138	20240	7017	54
52	STANDARD ADA/RDBMS	3513	7131	80	140
54	AI PACKAGES	2219	5523	1167	142
55	GRAPHIC ADA DESIGNER	8103	23986	6462	284
56	COBOL/FORTRAN TO ADA	29393	125045	10347	1630
57	SAVE	4071	9829	1381	47

SUMMARY

```
TOTAL COST    (KILOBUCKS)        =    $ 7187.0
AVERAGE COST (KILOBUCKS)         =    $  163.3
   --  "Zero cost" code excluded
LOWEST COST [MANPOWER (COCOMO)] (KILOBUCKS)
                                 =    $    3.0
HIGHEST COST [COBOL/FORTRAN TO ADA] (KILOBUCKS)
                                 =    $ 1630.0


TOTAL ADA STATEMENTS             =    212562.0
AVERAGE STATEMENTS PER TOOL      =      3729.2
AVERAGE COST PER STATEMENT       =    $   39.10
   --  "Zero cost" code excluded
LOWEST COST/STATEMENT [PROPAGATION PREDICT]
                                 =    $    5.91
HIGHEST COST/STATEMENT [TEST/ANALYZER TOOL]
                                 =    $   86.51


TOTAL LINES                      =    715054.0
AVERAGE COST PER LINE            =    $   10.65
   --  "Zero cost" code excluded
LOWEST COST/LINE [COMPLEXITY MEASURES]
                                 =    $    1.93
HIGHEST COST/LINE [AI PACKAGES]  =    $   25.71
```

Figure 3: 30 Most Popular Files in the Ada Software Repository
as of Tuesday, 30 Dec 1986

name	# refs	rate/month
<ADA.COMPONENTS>LIST.ADA.2	352	13
<ADA.GENERAL>KERMIT.DOC.1	297	11
<ADA.EDUCATION>TITR.DOC.1	290	14
<ADA.COMPONENTS>SAFEIO.ADA.2	288	11
<ADA.COMPONENTS>LIMPRIOR.ADA.2	285	11
<ADA.COMPONENTS>VDT100.SRC.1	284	11
<ADA.COMPONENTS>LIST.PRO.2	283	11
<ADA.BENCHMARKS>BENCH.DOC.1	280	17
<ADA.AI>EXPERT.ADA.1	277	21
<ADA.COMPONENTS>SAFEIO.PRO.2	275	10
<ADA.COMPONENTS>ABSTRACT.SRC.1	273	15
<ADA.COMPONENTS>PRIOR.ADA.2	272	10
<ADA.COMPONENTS>QSORT.SRC.1	271	11
<ADA.COMPONENTS>DSTR1.ADA.1	271	13
<ADA.AI>EXPERT.PRO.1	269	20
<ADA.COMPONENTS>VDT100.PRO.1	267	11
<ADA.COMPONENTS>LIMPRIOR.PRO.2	266	10
<ADA.GKS>GKSUSER.DOC.1	262	15
<ADA.GENERAL>KERMICRO.DOC.1	262	9
<ADA.EDUCATION>ADA1FOR.DOC.1	262	12
<ADA.PRETTY-PRINTERS>PRET.SRC.1	259	14
<ADA.COMPONENTS>CAS2.ADA.2	258	11
<ADA.EDUCATION>OBJECT.DOC.2	257	11
<ADA.COMPONENTS>PRIOR.PRO.2	256	10
<ADA.GKS>GKS.PRO.1	255	15
<ADA.COMPONENTS>PARSER.PRO.1	255	14
<ADA.COMPONENTS>CAS2.PRO.1	255	11
<ADA.GENERAL>COPYRITE.DOC.1	254	10
<ADA.COMPONENTS>DSTR1.PRO.1	254	12
<ADA.AI>EXPERT.DAT.1	254	19

Explanation of Directory Names, File Names, and File Types:
Directory names are enclosed in <>; <ADA.GKS> is the GKS subdirectory
under the ADA main directory.

File names are of the form NAME.TYPE.VERS; CAS2.PRO.1 has a name of
CAS2, a type of PRO, and a version number of 1.

File types have the following meanings:
ADA - Ada source code
DAT - data file
DOC - documentation (text)
PRO - prologue file (each item of software has a prologue file
which identifies the author, host and target compilers and
operating systems, keywords, and abstracts)
SRC - source file created and manipulated by the PAGER program;
SRC files contain one or more component files which may be
extracted by the PAGER program (like a library file)

Experiences Implementing a Reusable Data Structure Component Taxonomy

Gary Russell

EVB Software Engineering, Inc.

Abstract

EVB Software Engineering Inc. has developed a library of reusable software components. This paper attempts to relay some of the experiences encountered during the development of these reusable components. Sections of a sample component are shown.

Introduction

One potential method to improve software productivity is *reusable software*. (We define reusability as *the extent to which a module can be used in multiple applications* [1]. This definition does not address how much of the software, if any, may be modified for different applications.) Programmer productivity is greatly enhanced whenever reusable designs and code are used. T. Capers Jones states that "it is significant that all of the enterprises reporting productivity rates in excess of 20,000 delivered source code statements per programmer-year, make use of reusable designs and reusable code in order to achieve those high levels."[2] The U.S. industry standard for productivity is approximately 3,600 source code lines per programmer-year. In Japan, where the use of reusable software is more widely practiced, the industry standard is approximately 24,000 source code lines per programmer-year[3].

Studies show that as much as 75% of the software in the existing systems studied have common functions[4]. This means that if we can identify the common functions and either save the existing software or create highly reusable software components designed for reusability, then as much as 75% or more of future systems will already be developed and partially tested.

In July 1985, EVB Software Engineering Inc. began a project to produce reusable software components. All components were developed according to a data structures taxonomy developed by Grady Booch of Rational Inc[5]. (and modified at EVB to incorporate additional technology). At present, we have developed 275 reusable components (see appendix A for portions of a sample component) with each component containing between 400 and 1,000 physical lines of Ada® source code. All components have between 40 and 120 pages of documentation and were designed using Object Oriented Design (OOD)[6]. Each component was designed on an Apple MacIntosh computer and then downloaded to a computer with a validated Ada compiler for testing.

All of the reusable components were developed with an emphasis on incorporating many software engineering goals. For instance, each component must be highly reliable, be easily understood by all readers, be modifiable with a minimum amount of effort, be 100% portable, be designed for reusability, and use efficient (but understandable by component users) algorithms.

The purpose of this paper is to relate some of the technical experiences we encountered during the development of EVB's reusable components. Some of the non-technical issues will also be briefly mentioned. Although an entire book might be written on the technical information encountered, only the more interesting topics will be mentioned.

Technical Issues

The Taxonomy

The software components developed at EVB are families of generic Ada packages[1]. Each family implements a different data structure (i.e., stacks, queues, graphs, singly-linked lists). The taxonomy describes not the functional behavior of the component, but rather the time and space behavior of the component. For example, if a list component describes a list whose maximum number of elements is fixed at declaration time (i.e., it describes the component's space behavior), the component is referred to as a bounded list. If there is no fixed maximum number of elements established at declaration time, the component is referred to as an unbounded list.

To describe the time and space behavior of each component, Booch developed a subtaxonomy called "forms". During the development of EVB's component, the subtaxonomy was modified slightly to include additional technology. The forms that Booch identified include :

- Bounded,
- Unbounded,
- Iterator,
- Managed,
- Unmanaged,
- Controlled,
- Concurrent (EVB has renamed this form to Protected),
- Guarded,
- Multiple,
- Priority (Not included in EVB's taxonomy), and
- Balking (Not included in EVB's taxonomy)

EVB has also added the additional forms Object, Multi-Guarded and Limited. Many of the preceding forms can be combined. For example, one can have an Object, Multiple, Managed, Unbounded, Iterator Circular Doubly-Linked List. For a complete description of the taxonomy, see reference 7.

One of the primary differences between Booch's taxonomy and EVB's modified taxonomy is in the area of parallel components, that is components that operate in an environment containing multiple tasks. Booch's taxonomy only supports parallel components on an operation basis (protection is associated with the generic package and not with the objects declared using the package). In addition to operation based concurrency, EVB's modified taxonomy supports concurrency based on objects declared using the type exported by the generic package. For example, an object protected component sequentializes accesses to

Reprinted from Proceedings of the *Fifth Annual Joint Conference on Ada Technology and Washington Ada Symposium*, 1987, pages 8-18. Copyright ©1987 by G. Russell. All rights reserved.

each object declared using the type exported by the generic package. An operation protected (concurrent in Booch's taxonomy) component however, sequentializes the operations for the package. There is more overhead associated with an object protected component, but there is more truly concurrent processing.

Component Design

We decided to design and implement all components using **Object Oriented Design** (OOD has been modified considerably since we first started the project and is now known as **Object Oriented Development**. See references 8, 9, and 10 for descriptions of this development methodology). OOD provides an established method of generating each component with easily understandable and modifiable documentation. OOD identifies the abstract objects at a given level of abstraction in a system and the appropriate operations for each object. If OOD is used correctly, then the component solution will have a strong resemblance to the real world problem. The component is therefore using the same terminology as the real world problem, and is understandable and easy to modify.

Selecting Operations

The operations for each abstraction are chosen based on three criteria; **primitive, complete,** and **sufficient**[11]. A primitive operation is an operation that cannot be implemented without access to the underlying implementation of the object (exported private/limited private type). For instance, the operations Pop and Push in a stack package (see Appendix A) are considered to be primitive operations, since each operation must have access to implementation of the stack. Sufficient means that a minimum number of operations are provided for the user. Sufficient operations would include not only primitive operations, but operations which are not absolutely primitive. The operation Peek in the stack package is an example of an operation which is not absolutely primitive. Peek may be built using the Copy and Pop operations and thus does not need to know the underlying implementation of the stack object. Complete means that all aspects of the abstract behavior of the abstraction are captured. This means for example, that we *should not* create a stack component that only has a Push operation, and not a Pop operation.

Compilers and Portability

All components were developed with the intention of each component being 100 per cent portable, and thus more reusable. All machine dependent features such as input/output (except in the test program) and Ada LRM chapter 13 were not used. Nearly all of the components have been successfully compiled and executed on at least two different validated Ada compilers with no changes required (We used six different validated Ada compilers during development). The remainder of the components have been successfully run on one validated Ada compiler.

We anticipate no portability problems with any of the components, however there have been errors discovered in some validated Ada compilers. During the development of many components, we discovered a number of compiler errors. These errors ranged from internal errors that stopped the compiler, to run-time errors when executing a component test program. A majority of these errors seem to be associated with Ada's generic packages and tasking. Compiler vendors

were informed of each error and many errors have already been corrected.

Layers of Abstraction

There were several approaches that might have been used to develop our reusable components. One approach would have been to develop each component without using any previously developed components. This approach is attractive since efficient algorithms can be used (i.e. the package has complete access to all data structure information). However, since the entire software is included in a single component, the source code may be more complex, and is therefore harder to understand and maintain.

We chose to implement EVB's reusable components using **layers of abstractions** (Dijkstra was one of the first to introduce this concept[12]). This method involves building abstractions on top of (or using) previously developed abstractions. For instance, the unbounded stack components are built using unbounded singly-linked list components. This method is attractive because stack components are not as complex and are easier to understand. Stack components, though, are coupled to singly-linked list components. If modifications are made to the interface of a singly-linked list component, then the corresponding stack component must be modified.

This coupling is tolerable, however, since many of the changes will be made to the body of the singly-linked list component and will not affect the stack component's specification. Other layers of abstractions include the following :

Form of Abstraction	Lower level abstraction
All Sets	Balanced Binary Search Tree
All Multisets	Balanced Binary Search Tree
All Ring Structures	Circular Doubly-Linked List
Unbounded Queues	Singly-Linked List
Unbounded Strings	Singly-Linked List
Unbounded Deques	Singly-Linked List
Unbounded Maps	Balanced Binary Search Tree
Bounded Maps	Undirected Graph
Bounded Priority Queues	Heap
Iterator Directed Graphs	Stack and Queue
Iterator Undirected Graphs	Stack and Queue

In addition, all parallel components are built using the corresponding sequential components.

Testing Reusable Components

Reusable software components must be subjected to a rigorous testing methodology to ensure that the largest number of errors will be found in each component. Components may be used in many diverse environments where reliability is of paramount concern and where component developers have little knowledge of the types of applications and the reasons each component will be used. For instance, reusable components might be used in applications such as banking systems, missile guidance systems, oil exploration, home computers, etc.

Since all of EVB's components are written in Ada and use generic packages which export private (or limited private) types, testing techniques are different than the well documented techniques used for applications written in other languages (FORTRAN, COBOL, Pascal, etc.). There may be state information either stored inside of the package body or that is associated with an object declared of the exported private type in the user's application . In either case, the state information is hidden from a tester and cannot be observed except either through exported **selector** operations (selector operations are operations which return *only* state information of an object and *do not modify* the object's state information[13]), added output statements which display the state information on the terminal screen, or using a run-time debugger.

There are negative issues associated with each method of observing hidden state information. Selector operations are an excellent method, except not all state information may be observed through sectors (i.e. there were no selector operations to observe the free-list associated with each managed component) and a tester must trust the results of the selector. Adding output statements will allow testers to observe all state information but requires the tester to modify the source code. Most testing methodologies should state that any change to the software would require regression testing. Changing the source code also takes a considerable amount of time to modify the software and to recompile the system. A debugger can be a useful tool for quick debugging by developers, but should be used with caution by testers. Debuggers may have errors which will obscure the test case results and affect critical timing results. Debuggers may also be limited in the amount of state information that may be observed. In most instances, the selector operations approach was used in the testing of our reusable components.

Three basic testing techniques were used to generate test cases for all developed reusable components with some additional test cases for parallel components. The black box techniques include boundary value analysis and equivalence class partioning[14]. Basis path testing was also used as a white box technique[15]. Selector and selective iterator operations were tested first, since these operations do not change state information and could then be used to test **constructor** and constructive iterator operations (operations which may change state information of an object).

User Interfaces

It is extremely important for reusable components to have well-defined user interfaces (i.e. package specifications)[16,17]. Unless efficiency becomes an issue, the users of reusable components should only observe component specifications and not their corresponding bodies. All necessary information for the use of the component should be available in the specification (If the component is a package, then the private section *should be* separated from the rest of the specification, and does *not* need to be distributed to users). Each operation should supply enough comments for users to know the function of the operation (we used informal annotation although a formal annotation might have been used (i.e., ANNA)), if there are any special considerations when using this operation, and if there are any exceptions that might be raised during execution.

We have attempted to make the specifications for all components within an abstraction (i.e. stacks, queues, graphs) as similar as possible. Similar specifications will allow users to easily modify their applications if a different form of an abstraction is required. For example, a user may need to limit the maximum number of elements for an abstraction, and thus replace an unbounded component with a bounded component.

Private vs. Limited Private Types

There are several considerations and tradeoffs when determining which types to include in the generic specification for each reusable component. The following is a template for a potential reusable data structure component.

```
generic

    type Element is private ; -- or limited private
    -- this type will be inserted into the Abstraction

    ... -- operations and objects needed by this package

package Form_Of_Abstraction is

    type Abstraction is limited private ;
        -- or just private, or visible

    ... -- declaration of operations for this abstraction

private

    ... -- implementation of type Abstraction

end Form_Of_Abstraction ;
```

Type Element may be either private or limited private. If type Element is of type private, then it will not match any limited private types. This will *not allow* users to directly instantiate the generic package Form_Of_Abstraction with a limited private type. The user must instead access the limited private type with a pointer. Pointers may require an extra burden on the user and may increase the complexity of the user's code. This situation might easily occur if systems are built using layers of abstraction. For instance, we might need to push queue objects onto a stack.

Another consideration in making type Element private is the pre-defined equality operator. If the generic package Form_Of_Abstraction is instantiated with a record for type Element, then the equality operator probably will not be correct. There are several solutions to this problem. The user of the generic may redefine the equality operator. Redefining the equality operator, however, is not easy and does require work by the user. Another solution might include the user supplying the equality operator

```
with function Is_Equal(Left  : in Element ;
                       Right : in Element) return Boolean;
```

as an extra generic parameter. The generic package itself might then redefine the supplied generic parameter Is_Equal to "=" in order to increase the package understandability.

If type Element is changed to being limited private, then additional generic parameters must be added. The additional generic parameters would include the assignment and equality operator. This solution requires minimal work by the user. This issue and additional issues are being evaluated for potential improvement modifications to the components.

Type Abstraction may also be of type private, limited private or totally visible. All **managed** components (a managed component maintains a free-list of unused nodes rather than relying on the system to maintain storage) require the type Abstraction to be limited private because of the potential for structural sharing in the ability to perform garbage collection. If the assignment operator (limited private prevents the assignment operator from being visible) is available to users of managed components, then two objects may structurally share the same elements. When elements are then deleted and inserted, the abstraction may become corrupted because of dangling references into the free-list.

Sequentializing Operations

Object protected reusable components presented a problem that was initially difficult to solve. Since all parallel component are built in layers of abstraction (where the parallel component is built on top of the corresponding sequential component), most operations will lock the object with a semaphore (in order to mutually exclude this object from other operations, until the operation has completed), invoke the underlying sequential operation, and then unlock the object so that other tasks may use the object. The problem with this method occurs when more than one object needs to be locked, before the sequential operation is invoked. If for instance, there are two tasks trying to invoke the Copy operation,

```
procedure Copy (Source      : in     Stack ;
                Destination :    out Stack) is
begin -- Copy

   Semaphore.Lock
      (This_Semaphore => Source.Resource)  ;
   Semaphore.Lock
      (This_Semaphore => Destination.Resource) ;
   Sequential.Copy (Source      => Source,
                    Destination => Destination) ;
   Semaphore.Unlock
      (This_Semaphore => Source.Resource) ;
   Semaphore.Unlock
      (This_Semaphore => Destination.Resource) ;

end Copy ;
```

First User Task

```
Copy (Source      => First_Stack,
      Destination => Second_Stack) ;
```

Second User Task

```
Copy (Source      => Second_Stack,
      Destination => First_Stack) ;
```

a deadlock situation may occur (this situation can also occur when only one user is involved). Our solution to this problem included adding a task with entry points corresponding to all operations with more than one object as a parameter. The Copy operations would then rendezvous with this sequentializing task. The solution reduced the amount of parallelism in the component (operations with more than one object as a parameter cannot be executed in parallel), but eliminated the possibility of a deadlock situation, and thus made the component more reliable.

Non-Technical Issues

A great number of non-technical issues have been encountered during the development of EVB's reusable components. One large issue is the education problem associated with reusability and software engineering in general. Much established technology is not widely used or known in industry. For instance, a great number of software developers have a difficult time comprehending common data structure other than

stacks, queues and linked lists. Some of the more difficult to implement data structures, such as balanced binary search trees (BST), are extremely useful and easy to understand from the abstraction point of view. However BSTs are not typically used. Some managers are even avoiding the education issues, and it is difficult to convince them that they need to change the way business is conducted.

Another non-technical issue is the legal rights that are associated with reusable software. Reusable software should be sold in source code format, since the user needs to minimally observe the specification (and in many instances the corresponding bodies). The legal rights to reusable software are difficult to maintain after reusable software leaves the development company. A copyright notice in each piece of software may not be enough. The government, for instance, requires that an additional restricted rights legend be inserted into each piece of software. Many of the legal issues are just now starting to be understood and tested in the courts.

Future Issues

There are many issues that are being evaluated for improvement to the EVB's developed components and for future additional components. These issues include expanding the testing methodology to include proofs of correctness and additional parallel testing, modifying the component development methodology to include recent technology advances, modifying components to increase their reuse, evaluating the taxonomy to determine which components are used the most, and expanding the component library to include additional taxonomies.

Appendix A

Sections of a sample component

All sections of the Bounded_Stack component are included except the test program and bibliography.

1   Defining the Problem

1.1   Stating the Problem

Create a generic bounded stack package.

1.2   Analysis and Clarifications of the Givens

1. The following is a definition of a *linear list* : "A *linear list* is a set of $n >= 0$ nodes X[1], X[2], ..., X[n] whose structural properties essentially involve only the linear (one-dimensional) relative positions of the nodes: the facts that, if $n >= 0$, X[1] is the first node; when $1 < k < n$, the k th node X[k] is preceded by X[k - 1] and followed by X[k + 1]; and X[n] is the last node." (See [Knuth, 1973].)

2. A **stack** is defined to be "a linear list for which all insertions and deletions (and usually all accesses) are made at one end of the list" ([Knuth, 1973]). This end is usually called the

top of the stack. Notice that the above definition *implicitly* states the Last-In-First-Out (LIFO) property of a stack.

3. By **bounded**, we mean that the *maximum length* of a given stack does not change. Thus, a user of this generic must specify the desired length of a stack when the stack object is declared.

4. The stack abstraction must be **sufficient**, **complete**, and **primitive**. *Sufficient* means that a sufficient variety of operations are provided to allow the user of the abstraction to implement what is needed. *Complete* means that all aspects of the abstract behavior of the abstraction are captured. *Primitive* means that only those operations that could not be implemented effectively without access to the underlying implementation are provided.

5. The following operations (meeting the tradeoffs of the criteria defined above) are defined inside the stack package: push down an element onto a stack, pop up an element off a stack, check whether a stack is empty or full, find out how many elements are currently in a given stack, find out the top element in the stack, peek at the n th element below the top (where $1 <= n <= current number of elements in the stack$), clear a given stack (i.e., create an empty stack), test two stacks for equality, and copy one stack to another.

6. If a given stack is *empty* and the user tries to *pop* an element off the stack, an exception (**Underflow**) will be raised.

7. **Overflow** will be raised if a user tries to *push* an element onto a full stack.

8. **Element_Not_Found** will be raised if a user tries to *peek* at a non-existent element or tries to find out the top element in an empty stack.

9. We are not concerned with what types of elements are put on the stack. As many kinds of elements as possible should be allowed.

2 Developing an Informal Strategy

A user will be able to push an element onto a stack, pop an element off a stack, find out whether a stack is empty, find out whether a stack is full, determine the number of elements in a stack, find out the top element in a stack, peek at an element in a stack, and clear a stack. The user will also be provided with a means to test two stacks for equality and a means of copying the contents of one stack to another.

3 Formalizing the Strategy

3.1 Identifying the Objects of Interest

3.1.1 Identifying Objects and Types

A <u>user</u> will be able to push an <u>element</u> onto a <u>stack</u>, pop an <u>element</u> off a <u>stack</u>, find out whether a <u>stack</u> is empty, find out whether a <u>stack</u> is full, determine the number of <u>elements</u> in a <u>stack</u>, find out the <u>top element</u> in a <u>stack</u>, peek at an <u>element</u> in a <u>stack</u>, and clear a <u>stack</u>. The <u>user</u> will also be provided with a means to test two <u>stacks</u> for equality and a means of copying the contents of one <u>stack</u> to another.

Objects	Space	Identifier
user	Problem	
element	Solution	Element
stack	Solution	Stack
top element	Solution	(=Element)

3.1.2 Associating Attributes with the Objects and Types of Interest

Element

-- is an abstract type

-- can be copied

-- can be tested to see if it is equal to another element

Stack

-- defines an abstract type

-- its fixed maximum length does not change

-- can be empty

-- can be full

-- can contain up to some user-defined maximum number of items

-- elements in a stack are pushed on to the top of the stack, or popped from the top of the stack, but all insertions and deletions are from that end only.

-- The Last element In is the First element Out (LIFO)

3.2 Identifying the Operations of Interest

3.2.1 Identifying Operations

A user **will be able** to **push** an element onto a stack, **pop** an element off a stack, **find out whether** a stack is **empty**, **find out whether** a stack is full, **determine the** number of elements in a stack, **find out** the top element in a stack, **peek** at an element in a stack, and **clear a stack.** The user **will also be provided** with a means **to test** two stacks **for equality** and a means of **copying the** contents of one stack to another.

Operations	Space	Objects	Identifier
will be able	Problem		
push an element onto a stack	Solution	Stack	Push
pop an element off a stack	Solution	Stack	Pop
find out whether ... is empty	Solution	Stack	Is_Empty
find out whether ... is full	Solution	Stack	Is_Full
determine number of elements	Solution	Stack Number_Of_Elements	
find out the top element in a stack	Solution	Stack	Top_Of
peek at an element in a stack	Solution	Stack	Peek
clear a stack	Solution	Stack	Clear
will also be provided	Problem		
to test two stacks for equality	Solution	Stack	"="
copying the contents of one stack to another	Solution	Stack	Copy

3.2.2 Associating Attributes with the Operations of Interest

Push

-- Is a constructor

-- puts a given element onto the top of a given stack

-- raises an exception (**Overflow**) if a user tries to push an element onto a full stack

Pop

-- Is a constructor

-- pops the top element off a given stack

-- raises an exception (**Underflow**) if a user tries to pop an element off an empty stack

Is_Empty

-- Is a selector

-- has a true value if the given stack is empty; false otherwise

Is_Full

-- Is a selector

-- has a true value if the given stack is full; false otherwise

Number_Of_Elements

-- Is a selector

-- is the current number of elements in a given stack

Top_Of

-- Is a selector

-- allows a user to look at the content of the top of a given stack, i.e., the top element in a given stack

-- raises an exception (**Element_Not_Found**) if the stack is empty

Peek

-- Is a selector

-- allows a user to look at the nth element in a given stack (including the top)

-- raises an exception (**Element_Not_Found**) if a user tries to peek at a non existent element (e.g., there are currently 5 elements in a stack and a user tries to peek at the 8th element)

Clear

-- Is a constructor

-- initialize stack to empty stack

"="

-- Is a selector

-- returns true if two stacks are equal

-- two stacks are equal if the following conditions are all true :

1. the *current number of elements* in both stacks are equal, and

2. the *values of the corresponding elements* in both stacks are equal

Copy

-- Is a constructor

-- copy one entire stack to another

-- will raise an exception (**Overflow**) if the destination stack has an upper bound that is smaller than the number of elements in the source stack

3.2.3 Grouping Operations, Objects, and Types

Stack

Push

Pop

Is_Empty

Is_Full

Number_Of_Elements

Top_Of

Peek

Clear

"="

Copy

Elements

«none» (is part of the interface data to the other program units. See [EVB, 1985] page 3-38 # 3.)

3.3 Defining the Interfaces

3.3.1 Formal Description of the Visible Interfaces

The **generic** package Bounded_Stack *contains*:

the **generic** formal parameter: Element,

the **type** Stack,

and the following *operations*:

Push
Pop
Is_Empty
Is_Full

Number_Of_Elements
Top_Of
Peek
Clear
"="
Copy,

and the following *exceptions*:

Underflow
Overflow
Element_Not_Found

3.3.2 Analysis and Clarifications of High-Level Design Decisions

1. The generic formal type parameter Element will be of type **private** to satisfy the criteria set down in the Analysis and Clarifications for the Givens (1.2) number 9 and the fact that assignment of Elements will be needed in order to put things onto the stack.

3.3.3 Graphic Annotation of the Visible Interfaces

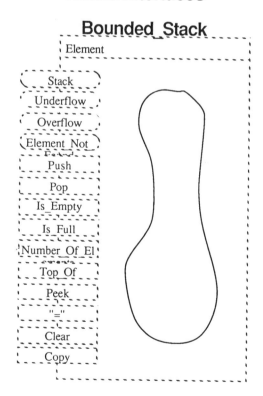

3.4 Implementing the Solution

3.4.1 Implementing the Operation Interfaces

```
generic

  type Element is private ;
    -- Element is the type of object that will be put on the stack

package Bounded_Stack is
  -----------------------------------------------------------------
  -- This generic bounded stack package provides stack manipulation
  -- operations necessary for most applications where stack data
  -- structure is needed. In building this package, we were striving
  -- for the following:  operations provided in this package must
  -- be primitive and complete and sufficient.
  --
  -- A primitive operation is an operation which can NOT be
  -- implemented effectively WITHOUT knowing the underlying
  -- representation of a particular object (in this case our
  -- object is STACK). By complete we mean that a user will find
  -- that the following operations will be the ONLY operations
  -- needed to manipulate a bounded stack in almost any application.
  -- Whenever necessary, a user will be able to build other
  -- operations based only on the operations provided in this package.
  --
  -- Written by Johan Margono, reviewed by (in alphabetical order):
  -- B.D. Balfour, E.V. Berard, G.E. Russell
  --
  -- Author      Revision    Date        Reason
  -- ------      --------    ----         ------
  -- J. Margono    1.0       8 Jul 1985
  -- J. Margono    2.0       19 Mar 1986  "type Stack (Length : ..." is
  --                                      changed to "type Stack
  --                                      (Maximum_Length : ..." to be
  --                                      consistent with our naming
  --                                      convention
  -- J. Margono    3.0       5 Jun 1986   "Natural" in Peek should hav
  --                                      been "Positive"
  --
  -- Copyright EVB Software Engineering, Inc. 1986
  --
  -- RESTRICTED RIGHTS LEGEND
  -- Use, duplication or disclosure is subject to restrictions
  -- as stated in the accompanying documentation
  --
  -----------------------------------------------------------------

  type Stack (Maximum_Length : Positive) is limited private ;

  procedure Push (This_Element   : in      Element ;
                  Into_This_Stack : in out Stack) ;
    --
    -- push This_Element onto the top of Into_This_Stack;
    -- exception Overflow will be raised if Into_This_Stack is full
    --

  procedure Pop (Top_Element   :     out Element ;
                 Off_This_Stack : in out Stack) ;
    --
    -- pop Top_Element off Off_This_Stack;
    -- exception Underflow will be raised if Off_This_Stack is empty
    --

  function Is_Empty (This_Stack : in Stack) return Boolean ;
    --
    -- returns true if This_Stack is empty; false otherwise
    --

  function Is_Full (This_Stack : in Stack) return Boolean ;
    --
    -- returns true if This_Stack is full; false otherwise
    --

  function Number_Of_Elements (In_This_Stack : in Stack) return Natural ;
    --
    -- returns the current number of elements in In_This_Stack;
    -- error is returned if In_This_Stack is empty
    --

  function Top_Of (This_Stack : in Stack) return Element ;
    --
    -- returns the top element in This_Stack;
    -- exception Element_Not_Found is raised if This_Stack is empty
    --

  function Peek (At_Element    : in Positive ;
                 In_This_Stack : in Stack) return Element ;
    --
    -- returns the nth element in In_This_Stack 1 <= n <= length
    -- (n is equal to At_Element). If At_Element is greater than the
    -- current number of elements in In_This_Stack, the exception
    -- Element_Not_Found will be raised (note : Element_Not_Found will
    -- also be raised if In_This_Stack is empty)
    --

  procedure Clear (This_Stack : in out Stack) ;
    --
    -- makes This_Stack an empty stack
    --

  function "=" (Left  : in Stack ; Right  : in Stack) return Boolean ;
    --
    -- returns true if :
    --   1. number of elements in Left is equal to number of elements
    --      in Right, AND
    --   2. values of elements in Left is equal to values of elements
    --      in Right (i.e., in corresponding slots);
    -- false otherwise
    --

  procedure Copy (This_Stack : in      Stack ;
                  Into        :     out Stack) ;
    --
    -- copy the contents of one stack into another stack (Into);
    -- will raise Overflow if the destination stack (Into) has
    -- length that is smaller than the number of elements in the
    -- source stack (This_Stack)
    --
```

```
  Underflow        : exception ;
    -- raised if a user tries to pop an element off an empty stack

  Overflow         : exception ;
    -- raised if a user tries to push an element onto a full stack

  Element_Not_Found  : exception ;
    -- raised if a user tries to find the top of an empty stack
    -- or Peek at an empty stack or peek at non-existent element

private

  Empty_Stack_Index : constant := 0 ;

  type Contents_Of_Stack is array (Positive range <>) of Element ;

  type Stack (Maximum_Length : Positive) is record
    Top      : Natural := Empty_Stack_Index ;
    Contents : Contents_Of_Stack (1 .. Maximum_Length) ;
  end record ;
    -- Stack is initially Empty (i.e., Top = Empty_Stack_Index)

end Bounded_Stack ;
```

3.4.2 Stepwise Refinement of the Highest-Level Program Unit

```
package body Bounded_Stack is
  -----------------------------------------------------------------
  -- This generic bounded stack package provides stack manipulation
  -- operations necessary for most applications where stack data
  -- structure is needed. In building this package, we were striving
  -- for the following:  operations provided in this package must
  -- be primitive and complete and sufficient.
  --
  -- A primitive operation is an operation which can NOT be
  -- implemented effectively WITHOUT knowing the underlying
  -- representation of a particular object (in this case our
  -- object is STACK). By complete we mean that a user will find
  -- that the following operations will be the ONLY operations
  -- needed to manipulate a bounded stack in almost any application.
  -- Whenever necessary, a user will be able to build other
  -- operations based only on the operations provided in this package.
  --
  -- Written by Johan Margono, reviewed by (in alphabetical order):
  -- B.D. Balfour, E.V. Berard, G.E. Russell
  --
  -- Author      Revision    Date        Reason
  -- ------      --------    ----         ------
  -- J. Margono    1.0       8 Jul 1985
  -- J. Margono    2.0       5 Jun 1986   "Natural" in Peek should have
  --                                      been "Positive"
  --
  -- Copyright EVB Software Engineering, Inc. 1986
  --
  -- RESTRICTED RIGHTS LEGEND
  -- Use, duplication or disclosure is subject to restrictions
  -- as stated in the accompanying documentation
  --
  -----------------------------------------------------------------

  procedure Push (This_Element    : in      Element ;
                  Into_This_Stack : in out Stack) is separate ;
    --
    -- push This_Element onto the top of Into_This_Stack;
    -- exception Overflow will be raised if Into_This_Stack is full
    --

  procedure Pop (Top_Element   :     out Element ;
                 Off_This_Stack : in out Stack) is separate ;
    --
    -- pop Top_Element off Off_This_Stack;
    -- exception Underflow will be raised if Off_This_Stack is empty
    --

  function Is_Empty (This_Stack : in Stack) return Boolean is separate ;
    --
    -- returns true if This_Stack is empty; false otherwise
    --

  function Is_Full (This_Stack : in Stack) return Boolean is separate ;
    --
    -- returns true if This_Stack is full; false otherwise
    --

  function Number_Of_Elements (In_This_Stack : in Stack)
                   return Natural is separate ;
    --
    -- returns the current number of elements in In_This_Stack;
    -- zero is returned if In_This_Stack is empty
    --

  function Top_Of (This_Stack : in Stack) return Element is separate ;
    --
    -- returns the top element in This_Stack;
    -- exception Element_Not_Found is raised if This_Stack is empty
    --

  function Peek (At_Element    : in Positive ;
                 In_This_Stack : in Stack) return Element is separate;
    --
    -- returns the nth element below the top element in In_This_Stack
    -- (n is equal to At_Element). If At_Element is greater than the
    -- current number of elements in In_This_Stack minus one, exception
    -- Element_Not_Found will be raised (note : Element_Not_Found will
    -- also be raised if In_This_Stack is empty)
    --

  procedure Clear (This_Stack : in out Stack) is separate ;
    --
    -- set This_Stack to be the same as an empty stack
    --
```

```ada
      --
   function "=" (Left  : in Stack ; Right : in Stack) return Boolean is
   --------------------------------------------------------------------
      --
      -- returns true if :
      --    1. number of elements in Left is equal to number of elements
      --       in Right, AND
      --    2. values of elements in Left is equal to values of elements
      --       in Right (i.e., in corresponding slots);
      -- false otherwise
      --
      -- NOTE: This function is included in the body of the package (as
      --       opposed to being implemented as a subunit) because,
      --       according to section 10.1, paragraph 3 of the Ada
      --       Language Reference Manual, "The designator of a
      --       separately compiled subprogram (whether a library unit
      --       or a subunit) must be an identifier."
      --
      -- Written by Johan Margono, reviewed by (in alphabetical order):
      -- B.D. Balfour, E.V. Berard, G.E. Russell
      --
      -- Author        Revision        Date           Reason
      -- ------        --------        -----          ------
      -- J. Margono    1.0             8 Jul 1985
      -- B. Balfour    2.0             20 Feb 1986    removed restriction
      --                                              that stacks must
      --                                              have the same lengt
      --
      -- Copyright EVB Software Engineering, Inc. 1986
      --
      -- RESTRICTED RIGHTS LEGEND
      -- Use, duplication or disclosure is subject to restrictions
      -- as stated in the accompanying documentation
      --
   --------------------------------------------------------------------
   begin -- "="

      return Left.Contents(1 .. Left.Top) = Right.Contents(1 .. Right.Top) ;

   end "=" ;

   procedure Copy (This_Stack : in      Stack ;
                   Into       :     out Stack) is separate;
      --
      -- copy the contents of This_Stack into another stack (Into);
      -- will raise Overflow if the destination stack (Into) has
      -- length that is smaller than the number of elements in the
      -- source stack (This_Stack)
      --

end Bounded_Stack ;

separate (Bounded_Stack)
procedure Push (This_Element   : in     Element ;
                Into_This_Stack : in out Stack) is
--------------------------------------------------------------------
   --
   -- push This_Element onto the top of Into_This_Stack;
   -- exception Overflow will be raised if Into_This_Stack is full
   --
   -- Written by Johan Margono, reviewed by (in alphabetical order):
   -- B.D. Balfour, E.V. Berard, G.E. Russell
   --
   -- Author        Revision        Date           Reason
   -- ------        --------        -----          ------
   -- J. Margono    1.0             8 Jul 1985
   --
   -- Copyright EVB Software Engineering, Inc. 1986
   --
   -- RESTRICTED RIGHTS LEGEND
   -- Use, duplication or disclosure is subject to restrictions
   -- as stated in the accompanying documentation
   --
--------------------------------------------------------------------
begin -- Push

   if Into_This_Stack.Top = Into_This_Stack.Maximum_Length then

      raise Overflow ;

   else

      Into_This_Stack.Top := Into_This_Stack.Top + 1 ;
      Into_This_Stack.Contents(Into_This_Stack.Top) := This_Element ;

   end if ;

end Push ;

separate (Bounded_Stack)
procedure Pop (Top_Element   :    out Element ;
               Off_This_Stack : in out Stack) is
--------------------------------------------------------------------
   --
   -- pop Top_Element off Off_This_Stack;
   -- exception Underflow will be raised if Off_This_Stack is empty
   --
   -- Written by Johan Margono, reviewed by (in alphabetical order):
   -- B.D. Balfour, E.V. Berard, G.E. Russell
   --
   -- Author        Revision        Date           Reason
   -- ------        --------        -----          ------
   -- J. Margono    1.0             8 Jul 1985
   --
   -- Copyright EVB Software Engineering, Inc. 1986
   --
   -- RESTRICTED RIGHTS LEGEND
   -- Use, duplication or disclosure is subject to restrictions
   -- as stated in the accompanying documentation
   --
--------------------------------------------------------------------
begin -- Pop

   if Off_This_Stack.Top = Empty_Stack_Index then

      raise Underflow ;

   else

      Top_Element := Top_Of (This_Stack => Off_This_Stack) ;
      Off_This_Stack.Top := Off_This_Stack.Top - 1 ;

   end if ;

end Pop ;
```

```ada
separate (Bounded_Stack)
function Is_Empty (This_Stack : in Stack) return Boolean is
--------------------------------------------------------------------
   --
   -- returns true if This_Stack is empty; false otherwise
   --
   -- Written by Johan Margono, reviewed by (in alphabetical order):
   -- B.D. Balfour, E.V. Berard, G.E. Russell
   --
   -- Author        Revision        Date           Reason
   -- ------        --------        -----          ------
   -- J. Margono    1.0             8 Jul 1985
   --
   -- Copyright EVB Software Engineering, Inc. 1986
   --
   -- RESTRICTED RIGHTS LEGEND
   -- Use, duplication or disclosure is subject to restrictions
   -- as stated in the accompanying documentation
   --
--------------------------------------------------------------------
begin -- Is_Empty

   return This_Stack.Top = Empty_Stack_Index ;

end Is_Empty ;

separate (Bounded_Stack)
function Is_Full (This_Stack : in Stack) return Boolean is
--------------------------------------------------------------------
   --
   -- returns true if This_Stack is full; false otherwise
   --
   -- Written by Johan Margono, reviewed by (in alphabetical order):
   -- B.D. Balfour, E.V. Berard, G.E. Russell
   --
   -- Author        Revision        Date           Reason
   -- ------        --------        -----          ------
   -- J. Margono    1.0             8 Jul 1985
   --
   -- Copyright EVB Software Engineering, Inc. 1986
   --
   -- RESTRICTED RIGHTS LEGEND
   -- Use, duplication or disclosure is subject to restrictions
   -- as stated in the accompanying documentation
   --
--------------------------------------------------------------------
begin -- Is_Full

   -- check if top of stack is equal to length of stack
   return This_Stack.Top = This_Stack.Maximum_Length ;

end Is_Full ;

separate (Bounded_Stack)
function Number_Of_Elements (In_This_Stack : in Stack) return Natural is
--------------------------------------------------------------------
   --
   -- returns the current number of elements in In_This_Stack;
   -- zero is returned if In_This_Stack is empty
   --
   -- Written by Johan Margono, reviewed by (in alphabetical order):
   -- B.D. Balfour, E.V. Berard, G.E. Russell
   --
   -- Author        Revision        Date           Reason
   -- ------        --------        -----          ------
   -- J. Margono    1.0             8 Jul 1985
   --
   -- Copyright EVB Software Engineering, Inc. 1986
   --
   -- RESTRICTED RIGHTS LEGEND
   -- Use, duplication or disclosure is subject to restrictions
   -- as stated in the accompanying documentation
   --
--------------------------------------------------------------------
begin -- Number_Of_Elements

   return In_This_Stack.Top ;

end Number_Of_Elements ;

separate (Bounded_Stack)
function Top_Of (This_Stack : in Stack) return Element is
--------------------------------------------------------------------
   --
   -- returns the top element in This_Stack;
   -- exception Element_Not_Found is raised if This_Stack is empty
   --
   -- Written by Johan Margono, reviewed by (in alphabetical order):
   -- B.D. Balfour, E.V. Berard, G.E. Russell
   --
   -- Author        Revision  Date        Reason
   -- ------        --------  -----       ------
   -- J. Margono    1.0       8 Jul 1985
   -- J. Margono    2.0       19 Mar 1985  Constraint_Error will not
   --                                      be raised if pragma SUPPRESS
   --                                      is used
   --
   -- Copyright EVB Software Engineering, Inc. 1986
   --
   -- RESTRICTED RIGHTS LEGEND
   -- Use, duplication or disclosure is subject to restrictions
   -- as stated in the accompanying documentation
   --
--------------------------------------------------------------------
begin -- Top_Of

   if This_Stack.Top = Empty_Stack_Index then

      raise Element_Not_Found ;

   else

      return This_Stack.Contents(This_Stack.Top) ;

   end if ;

end Top_Of ;

separate (Bounded_Stack)
function Peek (At_Element   : in Positive ;
               In_This_Stack : in Stack) return Element is
--------------------------------------------------------------------
   --
   -- returns the nth element below the top element in In_This_Stack
   -- (n is equal to At_Element). If At_Element is greater than the
   -- current number of elements in In_This_Stack, exception
   -- Element_Not_Found will be raised (note : Element_Not_Found will
   -- also be raised if In_This_Stack is empty)
   --
   -- Written by Johan Margono, reviewed by (in alphabetical order):
```

```
--  B.D. Balfour, E.V. Berard, G.E. Russell
--
-- Author        Revision    Date        Reason
--  ------        --------    ----        ------
-- J. Margono     1.0         8 Jul 1985
-- J. Margono     2.0         19 Mar 1985  Constraint Error will not
--                                         be raised if pragma SUPPRESS
--                                         is used
-- J. Margono     3.0         5 Jun 1986   "Natural" in Peek should have
--                                         been "Positive"
--
-- Copyright EVB Software Engineering, Inc. 1986
--
-- RESTRICTED RIGHTS LEGEND
-- Use, duplication or disclosure is subject to restrictions
-- as stated in the accompanying documentation
--  ----------------------------------------------------------
begin -- Peek

    if At_Element > In_This_Stack.Top then

        raise Element_Not_Found ;

    else

        return In_This_Stack.Contents(In_This_Stack.Top - At_Element + 1) ;

    end if ;

end Peek ;

separate (Bounded_Stack)
procedure Clear (This_Stack : in out Stack) is
--  ----------------------------------------------------------
--
-- set This Stack to be an empty stack
-- this is the same as if all elements had been popped off.
--
-- Written by Johan Margono, reviewed by (in alphabetical order):
-- B.D. Balfour, E.V. Berard, G.E. Russell
--
-- Author        Revision    Date        Reason
--  ------        --------    ----        ------
-- J. Margono     1.0         8 Jul 1985
--
-- Copyright EVB Software Engineering, Inc. 1986
--
-- RESTRICTED RIGHTS LEGEND
-- Use, duplication or disclosure is subject to restrictions
-- as stated in the accompanying documentation
--
--  ----------------------------------------------------------
begin -- Clear

    -- re-assign stack top
    This_Stack.Top := Empty_Stack_Index ;

end Clear ;

separate (Bounded_Stack)
procedure Copy (This_Stack : in      Stack ;
                Into       :    out Stack) is
--  ----------------------------------------------------------
--
-- copy the contents of This_Stack into Into;
-- will raise Overflow if the destination stack (Into) has
-- length that is smaller than the number of elements in the
-- source stack (This_Stack)
--
-- Written by Johan Margono, reviewed by (in alphabetical order):
-- B.D. Balfour, E.V. Berard, G.E. Russell
--
-- Author        Revision    Date        Reason
--  ------        --------    ----        ------
-- J. Margono     1.0         8 Jul 1985
--
-- Copyright EVB Software Engineering, Inc. 1986
--
-- RESTRICTED RIGHTS LEGEND
-- Use, duplication or disclosure is subject to restrictions
-- as stated in the accompanying documentation
--  ----------------------------------------------------------
begin -- Copy

    if This_Stack.Top > Into.Maximum_Length then

        raise Overflow;

    else    -- there is enough room to put the contents of
            -- This_Stack into Into

        Into.Top := This_Stack.Top;

        Into.Contents(1 .. This_Stack.Top) :=
            This_Stack.Contents(1 .. This_Stack.Top);

    end if;

end Copy ;
```

Bibliography

1. *IEEE Standard Glossary of Software Engineering Teminology*, The Institute of Electrical and Electronics, Inc., New York, N.Y., 1983.

2. T. Capers Jones, *Programmer Productivity*, McGraw-Hill Book Company, New York, N.Y., 1986, pp. 151-156.

3. Ware Myers, "*An Assessment of the Competiveness of the United States Software Industry*", IEEE Computer, IEEE Computer Society, New York, New York, March 1985, pp. 81-92.

4. T. Capers Jones, *Reusability in Programming: A Survey of the State of the Art*, IEEE Software Engineering, New York, The Institue of Electrical and Electronics Engineers, Inc., 1984, pp. 488-494.

5. Grady Booch, *Software Components With Ada*, Benjamin/Cummings, Menlo Park, California, 1987.

6. Grady Booch, *Software Engineering with Ada*, Menlo Park, California, Benjamin/Cummings Publishing Company, Inc., 1983.

7. Ed Berard and Johan Margono, *A Modified Booch's Taxonomy for Ada Generic Data Structure Components and Their Implementation*, paper to be presented at Ada Europe conference, May, 1987.

8. *An Object Oriented Design Handbook for Ada Software*, EVB Software Engineering Inc., Frederick, Maryland, 1985.

9. Grady Booch, "*Object Oriented Design*," IEEE Tutorial on Software Design Techniques, Fourth Edition, P. Freeman and A.I. Wasserman, Editors, IEEE Computer Society Press, IEEE Catalog No. EH0205-5, IEEE-CS Order No. 514, pp. 420-436.

10. Grady Booch, "*Object Oriented Development*", IEEE Transactions on Software Engineering, Vol. SE-12, No. 2, February 1986, pp. 211-221.

11. *An Object Oriented Design Handbook for Ada Software*, EVB Software Engineering Inc., Frederick, Maryland, 1985.

12. E.W. Dijikstra, "*The Structure of the "The" - Multiprogramming System*", Writings of the Revolution, Yourdon Inc., New York, N.Y., 1982, pp. 89-98.

13. Grady Booch, *Software Components With Ada*, Benjamin/Cummings, Menlo Park, California, 1987.

14. Glenford J. Myers, *Software Reliability*, John Wiley & Sons, New York, N. Y., 1976.

15. Thomas McCabe, "*A Complexity Measure*", Structured Testing IEEE Tutorial, IEEE Computer Society, Los Angelas, California, pp. 3-15, 1983.

16. R. St. Dennis, et al., *Measurable Characteristics of Resuable Ada Software*, Ada Letters, Vol VI, No. 2, March-April 1986, pp. 41-50.

17. Standish, Thomas A., *An Essay on Software Reuse*, IEEE Software Engineering, New York, The Institue of Electrical and Electronics Engineers, Inc., 1984, pp. 494-497.

REUSABLE ADA (R) SOFTWARE GUIDELINES

Richard J. St. Dennis
Honeywell, Inc.
Corporate Systems Development Division
Golden Valley, Minnesota

Abstract

Software reuse is key to significant gains in programmer productivity. However, to achieve its full potential, guidelines for writing reusable software must exist and be followed. While language independent, measurable characteristics of reusable software can be the basis for these guidelines, the guidelines themselves should be language-specific. This paper describes ongoing research at the Honeywell Corporate Systems Development Division (CSDD) to define a set of characteristics of reusable software as well as guidelines for implementing them in the Ada language.

1 INTRODUCTION

Both software production costs and the amount of new software produced annually are skyrocketing. In 1980, the U.S. Department of Defense (DoD) spent over $3 billion on software. By 1990, their expenses are expected to grow to $30 billion/year [6]. If current development trends continue, future costs will be increased even more by unreliable software, software delivered late, and continuing maintenance problems.

Today's software needs outpace our ability to produce it, as shown by the backlogs in MIS departments nationwide, and needs are growing each year [15]. There is and will continue to be a serious shortage of qualified programmers to meet these needs. We feel that a key to significant gains in programmer productivity lies in the area of software reuse.

To date, no adequate characterization of what makes software reusable exists. It is quite common to read unmeasurable, qualitative admonitions as to what makes software reusable and/or specific examples of software that is claimed to be reusable. However, these admonitions (or "metacharacteristics") and software examples are not enough. Measurable characteristics of reusable software are needed as well as specific guidelines to implement them in source code. Only through use of these characteristics and guidelines can the full potential of reusability be achieved.

The Honeywell RaPIER (Rapid Prototyping to Identify End-user Requirements) project has developed Version 1.1 of "A Guidebook For Writing Reusable Source Code in Ada (R)" [16], [13]. This guidebook contains three reusability metacharacteristics, fifteen measurable, language-independent characteristics that realize the metacharacteristics, and 63 guidelines for implementing these characteristics in Ada source code. Guidebook chapters are organized to follow the Ada Language Reference Manual [17]. Version 1.1 of the guidebook contains eight selected chapters (out of fourteen) covering all Ada program units, program structure, compilation issues, and visibility rules. Example Ada modules that were written following the guidelines are also provided. This guidebook provides the RaPIER project with a basis to begin writing reusable Ada software parts to be used in its prototyping system.

This paper outlines the approach to achieving reusability we prescribe in our guidebook. We list our reusability metacharacteristics, characteristics, highlight one characteristic, and provide guidelines supporting this characteristic. We also provide examples of Ada modules written following the guidelines, conclusions, and discuss plans for future work.

Ada is a registered trademark of the U.S. Government (AJPO)

This work was supported in part by the Office of Naval Research under contract number N00014-85-C-0666.

Reprinted from *Proceedings of the Twentieth Annual Hawaii International Conference on System Sciences,* 1987, pages 513-520. Copyright ©1987. Reprinted by permission of Hawaii International Conference on System Sciences.

2 OUR APPROACH TO ACHIEVING REUSABILITY

Our approach to reusing source code centers around reusable components, written as Ada packages, classified for both browsing and retrieval, and residing in a library or software base [13]. We believe that the features of the Ada language combined with a set of software design and coding guidelines supporting characteristics of reusable software will enable creation and reuse of software in a manner not possible with most other languages and systems. * These guidelines will constrain how Ada software is written for the sake of reusability.

Companion work at Honeywell CSDD and International Software Systems, Inc. (ISSI) is also addressing the organization and composition principles that will provide a framework for reuse of components. This work involves classification of reusable components according to behavior, program composition using an adaptation of the operational paradigm for program design, and a high-level Prototype System Description Language (PSDL) for composing programs of components drawn from a software base [13], [7].

3 REUSABILITY METACHARACTERISTICS

We propose these metacharacteristics of reusable software:

(1) Candidate software for reuse must be able to be found.

Findable software must comprise both code and specification. At a minimum, the specification tells users what a software part does, thus allowing them to decide whether it meets their functional needs. A specification may describe attributes of the software part such as author, hardware dependencies, execution time on a particular configuration, and so forth, which further assist users in deciding what software is appropriate.

The apparatus for storing and managing software contributes greatly to its findability. That apparatus includes a software base management system and intelligent schemes for classifying software so that searches into the software base are successful without being unnecessarily long.

It must be significantly less costly to find software and reuse it than to recreate it.

Both the specifications and the apparatus for managing the reusable software must support relatively low (human and machine) overhead for storing software and searching for it.

(2) Once found, software must be understood enough to be reused.

This requirement involves both the software part's specification and, if its code is to be modified, the way in which it is coded. ** There are judgments to be made about what attributes of a software part re-users need to know in order to decide whether the software meets their needs.

If the software is to be modified, it must be engineered so that re-users can examine the code and make changes that do not introduce errors or unwanted side effects.

(3) Once found and understood, it must be feasible to reuse the software.

Software that can be reused

● is built for reuse - constructed under the constraint that it will be reused.

● is fit for reuse (i.e., is a "plug-compatible" part) - composable with other code in such a way that it neither interferes with that other code nor allows itself to be interfered with.

● displays conceptual clarity or appropriateness - presents a useful abstraction (such as a table, a database, a sensor or a stack) at an "appropriate" level.

Each of the software characteristics listed in Section 4 is a means of achieving one (or some) of these metacharacteristics. Figure 1 relates each of the proposed characteristics to the metacharacteristics it promotes.

4 REUSABILITY CHARACTERISTICS

4.1 CRITERIA FOR CHARACTERISTICS

The reusability metacharacteristics in Section 3 are qualitative "good practice" admonitions. In general, they are not measurable or achievable without further guidance. In contrast, the characteristics listed in this section are measurable or judgable qualities that software should possess

---

* These features include packages, separate compilation and checking across program units, separate specifications and bodies for program units, information hiding constructs, generics, and strong typing.

** Ideally, a user would only need to look at a specification to decide to reuse a software part. However, this may not always be sufficient, at least in the near term.

in order to meet the metacharacteristics. We have proposed characteristics that are <u>statically</u> measurable or judgable today or will be measurable/judgable once we have more experience with reusable software.

The characteristics listed below are also reuse-specific; using them will produce software that is designed and coded <u>a priori</u> for reuse. "Good" software engineering practices will contribute to reuse but will not specifically make software reusable.

We expect that domain or application specificity will be a major factor in enabling software reuse [4], [11]. However, just as all software intended for reuse must be built using good software engineering practices, it must be built using application neutral basic reusability guidelines in addition to application specific guidelines. The characteristics listed below are those underlying guidelines for reusability across application areas.

4.2 LIST OF CHARACTERISTICS

In [16], we posit the following 15 language-independent characteristics of reusable software:

(1) Interface is both syntactically and semantically clear [14].

(2) Interface is written at appropriate (abstract) level.

(3) Component does not interfere with its environment.

(4) Component is designed as object-oriented; that is, packaged as typed data with procedures and functions which act on that data.

(5) Actions based on function results are made at the next level up.

(6) Component incorporates scaffolding for use during "building phase."

(7) Separate the information needed to use software, its specification, from the details of its implementation, its body.

(8) Component exhibits high cohesion/low coupling [1].

(9) Component and interface are written to be readable by persons other than the author.

(10) Component is written with the right balance between generality and specificity [10].

(11) Component is accompanied by sufficient documentation to make it findable.

(12) Component can be used without change or with only minor modifications.

(13) Insulate a component from host/target dependencies and assumptions about its environment; Isolate a component from format and content of information passed through it which it does not use.

(14) Component is standardized in the areas of invoking, controlling, terminating its function [8], error-handling, communication and structure [9].

(15) Components should be written to exploit domain of applicability [12]; components should constitute the right abstraction and modularity for the application.

Figure 1 relates each of the proposed characteristics to the metacharacteristics it promotes.

4.3 ONE CHARACTERISTIC IN DETAIL

For the purposes of this paper, we highlight reusability characteristic # 4: Component is designed as object-oriented; that is, packaged as typed data with procedures and functions which act on that data. For a further explanation of the other characteristics, refer to [16].

An object orientation to code involves mapping of "solutions" to our human view of the "problems" the software is trying to solve [2]. Our human view involves objects, attributes of these objects, and operations on objects expressed in a noun/verb sense in English. An object orientation to software aids understandability since solutions to problems are expressed in our "human terms."

Reusable software should act on objects explicitly. What we are advocating here is a clear definition and method of "acting" on objects. All actions or operations on objects should be defined as subprograms (or their equivalent) with the objects as parameters. Furthermore, the objects or at least their types should be "packaged" as close to the definition of the operations on them as possible. Ideally, they should be packaged together to ease location, reference, and use. To promote reusability it is better not to use global data that is changed implicitly by routines to which it is visible but to pass the data to routines as parameters making it explicit that (1) these routines are actors/operators on the data and (2) this is just how this data will be treated (e.g., as input only, as a constant, and so forth).

We define operations on data in context as implementations of behaviors that characterize objects, the objects being defined by the set of all behaviors associated with them [13].

Characteristic	Metacharacteristics

Character-istic	1:findable	2:understand-able	3a: built	3b:fit	3c:conceptually sound
1		*		o	
2		o			*
3		o		*	
4	o	o	o		*
5		*		o	
6			*		
7		o	o		*
8		o		*	
9		*		o	
10		o			*
11	*	o	o		
12			o	*	
13		o	o	*	
14			o	*	
15		o			*

(KEY: * = major metcharacteristic supported;
o = other metcharacteristics supported)

Figure 1: Reusability Characteristics Realize the Metacharacteristics

5 REUSABILITY GUIDELINES

In this section we provide seven Ada-specific guidelines from [16] that support the previously detailed reusability characteristic (#4) pertaining to object-oriented software. Several of these guidelines draw upon well understood good programming practices in Ada. In that sense they are not new. However, we present them in terms of reusability and the characteristics previously described. This is new and is their real benefit. We provide all the guidelines in [16] in the same way written in chapters that directly correspond to the Ada Language Reference Manual [17]. More information can be found in [5] concerning use of an object-oriented paradigm to build reusable Ada software.

5.1 CONTEXT FOR GUIDELINES

To provide a context for the guidelines, we first discuss our overall view of reusable software parts. There are, in general, two kinds of reusable software parts - directly reusable parts and indirectly reusable parts. Directly reusable parts are those whose behavior or effect is catalogued, that is, "advertised" in the catalog * of reusable software that developers use to determine what software parts are available for reuse. Directly reusable parts are what developers search for and choose. Indirectly reusable parts support directly reusable parts; they provide the environment, the ancillary defi-

nitions and data that the directly reusable parts need in order to perform correctly. In the ideal case, indirectly reusable parts are incorporated into the program under construction automatically by a software base management system.

Reusable parts, as defined by reusability characteristic #4, should be objects. As abstractions, objects have properties (data) and allowable operations on this data. The Ada package should be the realization or concrete implementation of the object abstraction. Types and data objects/variables implement data; subprograms/tasks implement operations. Packages bundle these things up nicely.

5.2 SAMPLE GUIDELINES

The following guidelines taken from [16] prescribe how to write reusable Ada software satisfying an object-oriented paradigm. Their numbers (e.g., G10-1, etc.) are exactly those used in [16] and correspond to chapters in the Ada Language Reference Manual [17]. For example, G10-1 is a guideline corresponding to Chapter 10: Program Structure and Compilation Issues. Guidelines G10-1, G10-2, and G10-3 provide a specific scheme for writing reusable Ada software in terms of Ada compilation units. Guidelines G6-2, G6-3, G7-2, and G9-2 support this scheme for Ada subprograms, packages, and tasks. We encourage use of generic subprograms and packages in compliance with these guidelines. Further details on the use of generics are found in [16].

* A catalog can be an automated software repository's classification scheme, a list of component names and descriptions on paper, or even a rumor the developer hears from a colleague down the hall.

G10-1: Use library unit package specifications as the encapsulation mechanism for directly reusable software (i.e., data and operations on the data).

Library unit packages are our "unit of reusability" with package specifications as the standard unit for directly reusable software parts. It is the specifications of operations on data as well as data contained in these packages that are directly reusable. These operations are in effect interfaces to reusable objects.

G10-2: Only "first level" nested non-package entities in library unit package specifications form the basis for "catalogued" directly reusable objects/software.

Ada packages can be nested to any level allowed by a compiler implementation, and nesting can be used as desired for implementing reusable components. However, for ease of "cataloging" there should be a practical limit to the level of nesting of packages that encapsulate reusable software. G10-2 simply states that only first-level data and specifications for operations on data form the basis for reusable software and are "catalogued." Data and operations within nested packages are not catalogued as reusable even though they are accessible to client programs according to the Ada language definition. Nesting can easily complicate the environment or context for reusable software. For example, nesting provides an environment for declaration order, information hiding, and visibility rules which is hard to reuse and to understand, and in which operations and data are hard to classify. Classifying only entities that are visible at the first level as reusable operations on data in context will avoid this complication.

G10-3: Use secondary unit package bodies, package specifications containing only data, and subunits corresponding to first-level package body nested stubs as the encapsulation mechanism for indirectly reusable software.

This guideline, along with G10-1, states that all reusable Ada software should be written in terms of packages. In particular, subprograms (with the exception of main subprograms) and tasks should be written either directly within the declarative parts of library unit packages or in that context through the use of body stubs. In Ada, main programs must not be contained in packages. However, we do not treat them as reusable. It is the library unit packages they reference that are reusable. Secondary unit (library unit) package bodies are indirectly reusable. Subprograms and tasks in the context of secondary unit packages (e.g., package bodies) are indirectly reusable. Library unit package specifications containing

only data are indirectly reusable as well.

G6-2: All reusable subprograms except a main program must be written within a library unit package.

In view of guidelines G10-1 and G10-3 reusable subprograms must be written in packages. These packages and their contents are the reusable software in a software repository; they are "glued" together by a main program which is invoked from the environment. If this gluing is automatic or easily specifiable in a very high-level-language, main programs do not have to be kept in a repository. It is the reusable parts that they glue together that are important. However, if a main program glues together a "system" which can be viewed as a potential component of other systems, then that program should be put in a package which will be catalogued as directly reusable software and should be called from "another main program".

G6-3: Use subprogram declarations to specify interfaces to reusable objects. Use subprogram bodies to implement these interfaces and properties of the objects.

The interfaces to reusable objects specified in subprogram declarations comprise a name, parameters of particular types and modes, and return types for functions. Subprogram bodies contain the executable code for reusable objects. This code performs useful work. We are saying that the use of both subprogram declarations and bodies is important. The only exception to this guideline is a main program callable from the environment rather than by other software. In this case, a body alone is sufficient. This guideline is related to G7-2 prescribing that package specifications implement interfaces to object abstractions and their bodies implement specific details of these abstractions.

G7-2: Use package specifications to specify the interface to object abstractions; use package bodies to encapsulate implementation-specific details of these abstractions not needed by client software.

Simply stated, decide what object abstraction a package should implement, decide what the interface to this abstraction should be, and implement these as visible specifications for operations on data in the public part of a package specification. Decide what the implementation structure of the abstraction should be and implement this and all other details in the private part of the package specification and a corresponding package body. This separation benefits the package itself and its environment. The less "connection" a package has with the outside world (e.g., the smaller the visible part of a package specification), the lower its coupling with other modules. Once modules in a package's environment begin to depend on particular visible entities that really should have been hidden, the package becomes less and less insulated from its environment.

There are two strategies for providing abstractions as reusable objects [3]. These are: (1) using packages to implement abstract data types and (2) using packages to implement abstract state machines. The strategy selected depends on the intended use of the reusable objects. Abstract data types provide the basis for multiple "public" reusable objects with common operations on the objects. Abstract state machines provide single, sharable, "private" reusable objects and operations on these objects.

G9-2:   Use task declarations to specify interfaces to reusable objects. Use task bodies to implement these interfaces and properties of the objects.

This guideline is similar to guideline G6-3. For tasks, as compared to subprograms, interfaces are concerned not only with parameter passing but also with synchronization. While subprograms can optionally have a separate declaration and body, tasks must have both declarations and bodies. Tasks and their entries, just as subprograms, should be treated as interfaces to reusable objects.

6 EXAMPLE ADA MODULES

The example Ada modules below are taken from the design of a reusable software repository developed at Honeywell CSDD. This repository supports retrieval, submission, and maintenance of categories of inventory items stored in a database management system. Its user interface is menu oriented. Specifically, the modules below are major portions of (1) a generic package specification for the repository Menu_Manager, (2) a package body for the repository Menu_Manager, and (3) a procedure subunit for one of package Menu_Manager's nested subprograms, Create_Initial_Menu. The object abstraction implemented in this package is a menu and associated menu_stack with operations including Create_Initial_Menu, Display_Menu, Process_Menu_Response, and Log_Menu_Use. When instantiated, package Menu_Manager implements an "abstract state machine" in that it contains a nonexportable stack of menus in its body.

In the examples, package specification Menu_Manager and the type and procedure declarations contained in its visible part are directly reusable. Its private part type declarations are indirectly reusable. Package body Menu_Manager is indirectly reusable as is its nested data declara-

tions and subprograms. The subunit for procedure Create_Initial_Menu is indirectly reusable even though it is compiled separately.

These example modules are provided primarily to illustrate use of our "object-oriented" guidelines to write reusable Ada software. The modules also illustrate other guidelines contained in [16] most noticably, those pertaining to a standard form for reusable software parts.

```
**********************************************************************
*                    EXAMPLE: MODULE 1                            *
**********************************************************************
with DATABASE_INTERFACE;
generic

   type MENU_IDENT is range <>;
   type MENU_ITEM is range <>;
   MENU_STACK_SIZE: in NATURAL := 31;
   MENU_FILESYS_PATH_LENGTH: in NATURAL := 100;

package MENU_MANAGER is

-- Revision History: Created 2/20/86   P. Stachour

-- Purpose:
--   Explanation: Provide data structures for and operations on
--                menu objects.  Generic to allow compile-time
--                allocation of minimal-storage for menus for
--                limited-storage systems.  Includes builtin
--                menu-stack for efficiency in redisplays.
--                Designed to be used as a general menu-manager
--                in multiple application areas.
--   Keywords:    menu, menu_manager

-- Generic Parameter Description:
--   MENU_IDENT      : Integer type used for identifying individual menus.
--   MENU_ITEM       : Integer type used for identifying choices in menu.
--   MENU_STACK_SIZE : Value controlling size of menu stack and its storage.
--   MENU_FILESYS
--         PATH_LENGTH: Value specializing file name-length for a system.

-- Associated Documentation: Design for Honeywell Reusable Software Repository

-- Diagnostics:
   MENU_MANAGEMENT_ERROR : exception;

-- Packages: None

-- Data Declarations:
--   Types:   None
--   Objects: None

-- Operations:
     Subprograms:
----------------------------------------------------------------------

procedure CREATE_INITIAL_MENU
   (M_NUMBER : out MENU_IDENT);

-- Purpose:
--   Explanation: Create initial repository menu.
--   Keywords:    initial_menu, create_initial_menu

-- Parameter Description:
-- M_NUMBER : Menu number associated with initial menu.

-- Associated Documentation: same as above
----------------------------------------------------------------------
procedure DISPLAY_MENU
   (M_NUMBER : in MENU_IDENT);

-- Purpose:
--   Explanation: Displays specific menu.
--   Keywords:    display_menu

-- Parameter Description:
-- M_NUMBER : Number of menu.

-- Associated Documentation : same as above
----------------------------------------------------------------------
procedure PROCESS_MENU_RESPONSE
   (M_NUMBER           : in out MENU_IDENT;
    MENU_ITEM_SELECTED : in MENU_ITEM;
    EXIT_MENU_LOOP     : out BOOLEAN);

-- Purpose:
--   Explanation: Process response specified by menu selection.
--                This processing may involve a call to DISPLAY_MENU
--                and ACCEPT_MENU_RESPONSE and a recursive call
--                to PROCESS_MENU_RESPONSE.
--   Keywords:    menu_response, process_menu_response.

-- Parameter Description:
```

```
   -- M_NUMBER          : Which menu to process or to show next if changed.
   -- MENU_ITEM_SELECTED : Specific item from menu selected.
   -- EXIT_MENU_LOOP    : Indication to exit menu system.

      -- Associated Documentation:  same as above
------------------------------------------------------------------------
.   -- Other operations on MENU-oriented parameters.
.
--  Tasks:
    task LOG_MENU_USE is

      -- Purpose:
      -- Explanation: Record usage of menus.
      -- Keywords:    log, log_menu_use, log_usage.

      -- Entries:
          entry OPEN_LOG (LOG_ID : in out STRING);   -- Open menu log
                                                     -- named LOG_ID;
                                                     -- Note: LOG_ID == ""
                                                     -- => prompt, == " "
                                                     -- => standard-log
              ...

          entry CLOSE_LOG (LOG_ID : in STRING);      -- Close menu log
                                                     -- named LOG_ID;
                                                     -- See note above.
      -- Associated Documentation:  same as above

      end LOG_MENU_USE;
------------------------------------------------------------------------
-- Private:

    private
    ...

end MENU_MANAGER;


****************************************************************
*                  EXAMPLE: MODULE 2                          *
****************************************************************

  with INVENTORY_ITEM, CATEGORY, USER, TEXT_IO;
  with USER_STATE, BULLETIN_BOARD, COMMAND_PROCESSOR, FILE_SYSTEM,
       SYSTEM_SUPPLIED_UTILITIES;
  package body MENU_MANAGER is

    -- Revision History: Created 02/21/86  P. Stachour
    -- Purpose:
    --   Explanation: Provide data structures for and operations on
    --                menu objects.
    --   Keywords:    menu, menu_manager

    -- Associated Documentation: Design for Honeywell Reusable Software
    --                           Repository.
    -- Assumptions/Resources Required: None
    -- Side Effects: None
    -- Diagnostics: None
    -- Packages: None
    -- Data Declarations:
    --   Types:
         type MENU  -- Large variant record managed by this package;

           is ...   -- includes all choices for particular menu.
         type MENU_STORAGE is array(MENU_IDENT) of MENU;
         type MENU_STACK_ELEMENT is
           record
             MENU_POINTER       : MENU_IDENT;
             MENU_FILESYS_LOCATION : STRING (1..MENU_FILESYS_PATH_LENGTH);
           end record;
    --   Objects:
         MENU_STACK       : array (1..MENU_STACK_SIZE) of MENU_STACK_ELEMENT;
         MENU_STACK_INDEX : NATURAL := 0;
    -- Operations:
    --   Subprograms:
         procedure CREATE_INITIAL_MENU
           (M_NUMBER : out MENU_IDENT) is separate;
         procedure DISPLAY_MENU
           (M_NUMBER : in MENU_IDENT) is separate;
         procedure PROCESS_MENU_RESPONSE
           (M_NUMBER       : in out MENU_IDENT;
            MENU_ITEM_SELECTED : in  MENU_ITEM;
            EXIT_MENU_LOOP    : out BOOLEAN) is separate;
         procedure READ_IN_MENU ...
         procedure PUT_MENU_ON_MENU_STACK ...
    .
    .   -- Other operations on MENU-oriented parameters.
    .
    --  Tasks:
         task body LOG_MENU_USE is separate;
    -- Initialization:

  begin

  exception
    when others =>
      raise MENU_MANAGEMENT_ERROR;

  end MENU_MANAGER;
```

```
****************************************************************
*                  EXAMPLE: MODULE 3                          *
****************************************************************

separate (MENU_MANAGER)
procedure CREATE_INITIAL_MENU
   (M_NUMBER : out MENU_IDENT) is

  -- Revision History:  Created 2/21/86  P. Stachour
  -- Purpose:
  --   Explanation:  Creates initial menu by reading data for it from
  --                 a host file and placing it on the MENU_MANAGER MENU_STACK.
  --   Keywords:     initial_menu, create_initial_menu
  -- Associated Documentation: Design for Honeywell Reusable Software Repository
  -- Parameter Description:
  -- M_NUMBER : Number of menu created.

  -- Assumptions/Resources Required: None
  -- Side Effects:  None
  -- Diagnostics: None
  -- Packages:  None
  -- Data Declarations:
  --   Types:  None
  --   Objects:

       FILE_DESIGNATOR : FILE_SYSTEM.FILE_NAME := "DRAO:[SOURCE]INITIAL.MNU";

  -- Operations:
  --   Subprograms: None
  --   Tasks: None
  -- Algorithm:

  begin  -- CREATE_INITIAL_MENU

    -- read from host file, create menu, and place on MENU_STACK;
    -- set M_NUMBER to reference the menu just read in
    M_NUMBER := READ_IN_MENU( FILE_DESIGNATOR );
    PUT_MENU_ON_MENU_STACK( M_NUMBER );

    exception

      when others =>

        raise MENU_MANAGEMENT_ERROR;

  end CREATE_INITIAL_MENU;
```

7 CONCLUSIONS/ FUTURE WORK

We feel that our work to define reusable Ada
software guidelines is of significant benefit to
the RaPIER project and to anyone who wants to
write reusable Ada source code. We have tied our
guidelines to measurable reusability characteristics which support commonly-accepted reusability
metacharacteristics. We have organized our guidebook [16] around chapters of the Ada Language
Reference Manual [17] for easy reference by Ada
programmers.

In the upcoming year we plan to complete the
remaining chapters of our reusability guidebook
and refine/add to the Ada examples it provides.
We intend for the guidebook to be an indepth
technical reference on Ada source code
reusability. Guidelines from the guidebook will
be used to construct reusable software components
for RaPIER's software base management system.
These components will be written for a particular
application domain. This will allow us to investigate the effect of application domain on
reusability. We also plan to circulate the guidebook for review. Feedback we receive from RaPIER
prototyping experiments and the guidebook review
will enable us to evaluate our reusability characteristics and guidelines and refine them accordingly.

In later years, we hope to develop measures and
supporting tools for the reusability guidebook

characteristics and implement/experiment with software base classification schemes tailored to guidebook characteristics and guidelines.

8 ACKNOWLEDGEMENTS

I would like to thank a number of people from Honeywell CSDD who assisted me in preparing this paper: Elaine Frankowski, who gave me the original idea for the paper, Jacklyn Lipscomb for her technical editing, and Paul Stachour for the example Ada modules appearing in Section 6.

BIBLIOGRAPHY

1. G. D. Bergland. "A Guided Tour of Program Design Methodologies," IEEE Computer, Vol. 14 No. 10, October 1981, pp. 13-37.

2. Grady Booch. "Object-oriented Design," Tutorial on Software Design Techniques. Ed. P. Freeman and A. Wasserman, 4th edition (Catalog Number EHO205-5), IEEE Computer Society Press, 1983.

3. Grady Booch. "ACM SIGAda Tutorial: Ada Methodologies," ACM SIGAda Meeting, July 30, 1985.

4. Elaine N. Frankowski, Christine M. Anderson. "Design/Integration Panel Report," Proceedings of the STARS Reusability Workshop, April 1985.

5. Elaine N. Frankowski. "Why Programs Built From Reusable Software Should Be Single Paradigm," Proceedings, STARS Applications Systems and Reusability Workshop, to appear (March 1986).

6. Ellis Horowitz, John B. Munson. "An Expansive View of Reusable Software," IEEE Transactions on Software Engineering, Vol. SE-10, No. 5, September 1984, pp. 477-487.

7. International Software Systems, Inc.. "PSDL: Prototype System Description Language," ISSI Technical Report, unnumbered, January 30, 1986.

8. T. Capers Jones. "Reusability in Programming: A Survey of the State of the Art," IEEE Transactions on Software Engineering, Vol. SE-10 No. 5, September 1984, pp. 488-494.

9. Robert G. Lanergan, Charles A. Grasso. "Software Engineering with Reusable Designs and Code," IEEE Trans. on Software Engineering, Vol. SE-10, No. 5, September 1984, pp. 498-501.

10. Yoshihiro Matsumoto. "Some Experiences in Promoting Reusable Software: Presentation in Higher Abstract Levels," IEEE Transactions on Software Engineering, Vol. SE-10 No. 5, September 1984, pp. 502-513.

11. Daniel G. McNicholl, Constance Palmer, et. al.. "Common Ada (R) Missile Packages (CAMP): Final Report For Period September 1984 - September 1985," Vols. I-III, McDonnell Douglas Astronautics Company, St. Louis, MO, May 1986.

12. James M. Neighbors. "The Draco Approach to Constructing Software from Reusable Components," IEEE Transactions on Software Engineering, Vol. SE-10 No. 5, September 1984, pp. 564-574.

13. RaPIER Project. "Final Scientific Report: RaPIER Project (Contract No. N00014-85-C-0666)," Honeywell Computer Sciences Center, Golden Valley, MN, March 1986.

14. Thomas A. Standish. "An Essay on Software Reuse," IEEE Transactions on Software Engineering, Vol. SE-10 No. 5, September 1984, pp. 494-497.

15. STARS. Software Technology for Adaptable, Reliable Systems (STARS) Program Strategy, U. S. Department of Defense, April 1983.

16. Richard St. Dennis. "A Guidebook for Writing Reusable Source Code in Ada(R): Version 1.1," Honeywell Computer Sciences Center Technical Report, CSC-86-3:8213, Honeywell Computer Sciences Center, 1000 Boone Avenue, Minneapolis MN 55427, May 1986.

17. United States Department of Defense. Reference Manual for the Ada Language: ANSI/MIL-STD-1815A, United States Department of Defense, January 1983.

BIOGRAPHY

Mr. St. Dennis is currently a Principal Research Scientist at the Honeywell Corporate Systems Development Division (CSDD), Golden Valley, MN. At Honeywell, his responsibilities have included principal investigator on the Software Development Environments (SDE) Program and lead for the Ada reusability task of the RaPIER (Rapid Prototyping To Identify End-User Requirements) Program. Prior to his work at Honeywell, Mr. St. Dennis held the position of Senior Software Engineer at Sperry Corporation, Defense Products Group, St. Paul, MN.

Mr. St. Dennis holds a BA in mathematics/physics from Hamline University, St. Paul, MN and is a candidate for an MS degree in applied mathematics/computer science at the University of Minnesota. He is a member of Phi Beta Kappa, Phi Kappa Phi, ACM, and SIGAda.

Part 4: Research

Reusing small code segments in the form of subroutines or modules has long been the most prevalent form of software reuse. Research efforts have been directed toward the reuse of other software artifacts such as designs and specifications as well as the knowledge as to what design and implementation decisions were made.

The papers in this part look upstream in the software development life cycle, and the tools and technology that will help to capture and incorporate more software development knowledge and artifacts for reuse are discussed. Many of the approaches are also based on integrated workstation environments, which include high resolution bit-mapped graphics devices. The use of graphics to represent the relationships between knowledge/information and to help users search for components to reuse is part of the emerging technology being applied to software reuse. There is also a trickle-down effect of artificial intelligence/expert system technology that is making its way into software engineering through the area of software reuse. Automatic program synthesis (taking specifications and automatically generating executable source code) has long been a goal for many researchers in the field of artificial intelligence. The representation of knowledge and the organization of components for reuse are key issues shared by researchers in program synthesis and reuse.

The first paper in this section, "Melding Software Systems from Reusable Building Blocks" by Gail Kaiser and David Garlan, describes a system that combines the power of subroutine libraries, software generators, and object-oriented languages without their inherit limitations of language dependence, inflexibility, and need for well-defined application domains. By introducing language-independent building blocks called *features,* with declarative programming constructs called *action equations,* systems composed of classes can be translated to efficient implementations in a conventional programming language such as C or Ada.

The second paper, "Wide-Spectrum Support for Software Reusability" by Mitch Lubars, serves both as an introduction to the ROSE (reusable software elements) project at MCC and as a pointer to the existing technologies upon which it is based. Wide-spectrum reuse refers to the application of software reuse in all phases of the software life cycle. Lubars' paper describes the framework necessary to have software specifications and requirements be transformed into executable code by having captured domain knowledge and reusable abstract designs, algorithms, data types, and implementations.

In the next paper "Design to Redesign," Gerhard Fischer, Andreas Lemke, and Christian Rathke, introduce a software

reuse environment (Objtalk) based on a Smalltalk-type user interface with a Franz Lisp extension. They present the rational for an "intelligent" design environment and describe the tools that are in place to assist the user in learning the system, locating, and understanding how to combine and modify the building blocks.

An expanded version of this paper, "Cognitive View of Reuse and Redesign," can be found in the July 1987 issue of *IEEE Software.*

In the paper "PARIS: A System for Reusing Partially Interpreted Schemas," Charles Richter, S. Katz, and K. The address several strategic issues in their approach to software reusability. A schema is a code skeleton. Associated with a schema is a list of pre- and post-conditions/assertions, applicability conditions and invariant assertions, and some keywords regarding the domain, mathematical properties, and specification operators. A Boyer-Moore Theorem Prover is used to match schema to problem description specifications in an iterative manner.

Neil Iscoe, in his paper "Domain-Specific Reuse: An Object-Oriented and Knowledge-Based Approach," describes a model for mapping requirements specifications into executable code. A tool that, given a requirement specification, generates possible composition of primitive operations through the use of rewrite rules is also presented. The process model includes an object editor, a data flow and control flow editor, and a rule system editor.

The next paper, "A Knowledge Structure for Reusing Abstract Data Types" by David Embley and Scott Woodfield, raises an important issue justifying the creation of libraries of abstract data types (also known as classes in Smalltalk, or Modules in Modula-2) rather than functions. History shows that the most successful form of reuse has been mathematical subroutine libraries or operating system I/O utilities. These groups of subroutines address the same form of data (reals/characters) and the same data structures (arrays/files). By building on this real-world observation (one of the principles of object-oriented design), the task of locating and understanding the components for reuse is simplified. This paper also highlights the importance of separating context from content. Their approach is to create descriptors of ADTs (abstract data types) that may have several implementations and then to link ADTs together by a list of relations. These relations, which form part of the knowledge base, are closeness, generalization, specialization, generic-of, aggregation, classification, and depends on.

Larry Latour in "SEE: An Automated Tool to Facilitate Reuse in ADA Project Development" describes a tool that assists a programmer or system designer program by analogy. SEEGraph is a network database for capturing the knowledge about analogous designs and programs together with hierarchies of procedural and data abstractions and interconnection structures. This semantic network can then be browsed to gather insight into what can be reused.

The paper, "Mechanisms for Extending the Applicability of Reusable Components" by Bob Arnold et al., describes a transformation system being developed at SPC. As in the Embley and Woodfield paper, context is separated from content, and user-supplied context information for new applications automatically retailors existing components, thus assisting in development and maintenance.

Ira Baxter's research, as described in the next paper "Reusing Design Histories via Transformation Systems," focuses on capturing and reusing the sequence of decisions that transpire when a programmer translates a formal requirement specification into an actual implementation. Derivation history replay systems exist that allow some automated program synthesis using these rewrite/transformation rules, but when changes are made to the specification, it often results in the complete replay/retransformation of the complete derivation. Baxter's approach is to anlayze the change to minimize its impact on the derivation by reasoning about the commutivity between the transformations used.

A powerful method for using algebraic specification techniques to describe parameterized abstract data objects in the functional programming language OBJ2 is presented in the next paper, "Parameterized Programming in OBJ2" by Kokichi Futatsugi, Joseph Goguen, Jose Mesenguer, and Koji Okada. The paper elaborates on the parameterization and composition mechanisms in the language, which is based on order-sorted algebra. Besides having nice mathematical properties, the language's modularization constructs (theories, views, and objects) provide an intuitively appealing formalism to software reuse. Several examples are included to demonstrate the language's features.

Domain analysis is the subject of much interest in the reuse community. Reuben Prieto-Diaz, in his paper "Domain Analysis for Reusability," analyzes two approaches (Raytheon/NEC and CAMP) and two proposed approaches to domain analysis and then describes a three-phased process being applied at GTE. The library science classification technique known as literary warrant is cited as an example of a process similar to domain analysis.

The final paper in this section, "The Domain-Oriented Software Life Cycle: Towards an Extended Process Model for Reusability" by Mark Simos, includes two significant contributions. First, the syntax and semantics analysis and generation system (SSAGS), an application-specific language (ASL) generation tool, is described. The author argues that this generative approach costs the same as a custom-coded application but results in a more maintainable and error-free program. The second portion of the paper describes the merits of modifying the traditional waterfall software life-cyle model to incorporate software reuse.

Melding Software Systems from Reusable Building Blocks

Reprinted from *IEEE Software*, July 1987, pages 17-24. Copyright ©1987 by The Institute of Electrical and Electronics Engineers, Inc. All rights reserved.

Gail E. Kaiser, Columbia University
David Garlan, Carnegie Mellon University

This declarative language takes the best features from the three most popular reusability approaches, but overcomes their flaws. It supports language independence, component composition, and tailoring.

Current approaches to software reuse have not lived up to reusability's potential to dramatically improve software productivity and maintainability.

The shortcomings of the three most popular approaches are discussed in the box on p. 15. The primary deficiency of these approaches is that they tightly couple reusable components to their original context. Either the reusable components are written in one language and cannot easily be reused in another language or they implement a specific abstract data type and/or function and cannot easily be converted into the subtly different requirements of another application — or even the original application when it is repaired or enhanced. Furthermore, the options for tailoring a reusable component are determined when the component is written and cannot easily be expanded to meet unanticipated needs.

To realize the potential of large-scale software reusability, three characteristics are required:

• Language independence, to avoid early implementation decisions. Of course, every notation is a "language," but it is best to avoid concrete representations and control structures until actual reuse, when the most efficient solutions can be chosen.

• Composition of components, to build large software systems to meet complex requirements. Procedural invocation of separately developed components works to some extent, but it does not promote reuse of large-scale components.

• Flexibility, to expand reusability beyond the capabilities and applications anticipated by the original implementor. Most approaches require that the complete set of tailoring options be defined when the reusable component is created. These options are not always sufficient.

EH0278-2/88/0000/0267$01.00 ©1987

We have developed a new approach to reusable software that has these three characteristics. The basis of this approach is Meld,* a declarative language that can be translated to an efficient implementation in a conventional programming language.

An entire software system can be written in Meld and then translated to the desired programming language. System maintenance is done with the Meld representation rather than the implementation language. Or an individual component can be written and maintained in Meld, and its translation integrated into an application written in a conventional language. Thus, old code can be combined with components written in Meld.

Overview of Meld

Meld is an object-oriented language in that it supports the encapsulation of data and operations as objects defined by classes and the inheritance of separately defined data and operations from ancestor classes. In the context of object-oriented languages, such data are called instance variables and such operations are methods.

But Meld has two essential aspects that set it apart from other object-oriented languages, *features* and *action equations*.

Features. Features are reusable building blocks. Like Ada packages, their interfaces are separate from the implementation. A feature bundles a collection of interrelated classes in its implementation. The interface exports a subset of these classes and a subset of their methods.

In effect, a feature is a reusable unit larger than a subroutine, on approximately the same scale as an Ada package, that permits the reuse of the glue among subroutines (methods) and, in fact, among abstract data types (classes). A generic feature is similar to a generic package because the interface can be instantiated according to the requirements of the desired application.

Moreover, unlike Ada packages, features have the flexibility of classes. A feature's interface imports a group of features, making the classes exported by these features available within its implementation. There, an imported class can be merged, either with a locally defined class or with another imported class.

Merging has the effect of inheritance: One class inherits (reuses) all the facilities already defined for another class and can augment and replace any subset of these facilities.

Action equations. Unlike classes, however, features can combine, as well as augment and replace, inherited methods. This is accomplished by writing methods as action equations. Action equations should not be confused with mathematical equations. They were developed to extend attribute grammars for semantics processing of programming environments.[1]

Action equations define (1) the relationships that must hold among objects and among parts of objects and (2) the dynamic interaction among objects and between objects and external agents (such as users, the operating system, and utilities).

When classes merge, separately inherited methods can be combined by assigning them the same selector (the same method name). Because methods define relationships and dynamic interactions in the abstract — as action equations — rather than by a sequence of statements, the behavior of the methods is combined implicitly. The resulting composite behavior does not depend on any sequential ordering of the methods.

Implementation. Meld is implemented by translating each feature into a conventional programming language and by a special runtime environment that supports execution of systems built from features. We derived the implementation algorithms from previous work on software generation, specifically language-based editors, where performance as good as handcoded editors has been achieved.

This implementation technique ensures language independence and portability because all existing features can be produced in a new implementation language or executed on a new architecture simply by reimplementing the translator and runtime support.

Thus, Meld combines the advantages of libraries, software generation, and object-oriented programming — without assuming the limitations of these approaches.

However, there are certain important issues in software reusability we did not address. Meld is no better than the widely used approaches at helping programmers determine if a particular component is suitable for reuse in a particular application. Meld also does not address the separate problem of categorizing and retrieving reusable components, but we are working on this, using a conceptual clustering approach derived from research in artificial intelligence.

An extended example

The important aspects of Meld can be illustrated with an extended example.

Memory manager. Suppose a programmer wants to implement a facility for loading and storing arbitrary entities to disk. Traditionally, he might modify the entities themselves to support memory management. Or he might add the facility directly to the runtime support of the programming language, perhaps as a generic package.

Neither approach promotes reusability. In the first case, memory management is specific to the entities. In the second case, the memory manager is reusable only in the sense that a text editor or a compiler is: I use it today on one file, you use it tomorrow on another file. This memory manager cannot be tailored to the particular needs of the application.

However, with Meld the programmer constructs a reusable building block that can be incorporated into any system that requires memory management.

The Memory Manager describes the world as seen from a simple memory manager's point of view. The world consists of a collection of memory-managed entities grouped under a memory-managed root. Each memory-managed entity has a unique identifier, a disk location, a designation of whether it is loaded in core or not, and a time stamp representing the most recent access to it.

---

*The dictionary definition of "meld" is "melt plus weld," or "to merge." Meld also stands for Multiple Elucidations of Language Descriptions, which was suggested by David Barstow.

The information about each memory-managed entity is always maintained in core; the actual content of the entity is what the memory manager loads and stores. The memory manager loads the content of an entity when it is first accessed. When primary memory is nearly full, entities are stored according to a least-recently-used policy.

Figure 1 shows the classes for a generic memory manager. This description is encapsulated into a feature, which has a name, an interface, and an implementation.

Interface. The interface lists the classes exported by the feature in its exports clause and lists the other features that are imported in its imports clause.

In this case, the ROOT and ENTITY classes are exported. Any exported instance variables are listed in the brackets following the class name; only the listed components are accessible outside the feature. The instance variables of ENTITY are entirely hidden, but the maxentities variable of ROOT is available to other features that import the memory-manager feature. This is more powerful than information hiding in Ada, where either all or none of the fields of a record are exported.

Implementation. The implementation part defines two classes, ROOT and ENTITY, followed by the instance variables and their types. The action equations that describe the behavior of the root and memory-managed entities are given in Figures 2 and 3, respectively.

The ENTITY class represents the entities managed by the memory manager. It defines four instance variables — unique-id, incore, lastuse, and diskid — that contain obvious information. Each instance variable is typed; strong typing is enforced. enforced.

The ENTITY class represents only the stub for an entity — there are no instance variables representing the content of the memory-managed entity. Instance variables that do represent the content are added when the Memory Manager feature is merged with one or more other features that provide entities that require memory management.

The ROOT class defines the memory-

What's wrong with the popular approaches

Three approaches to software reusability have achieved widespread use: subroutine libraries, software generation, and object-oriented programming.

None has achieved marked gains in productivity outside of a small set of application areas, but all treat reusability as part of the design rather than an afterthought of the implementation. It is rarely feasible to decompose an existing software system into reusable components that can be then used to construct other systems. Reusability must be engineered from the start.

Subroutine libraries. Libraries have had a significant effect on the production of mathematical software systems, as well as string manipulation and I/O, but they are not sufficient to achieve a large-scale improvement in software productivity and maintenance.

An individual subroutine is too small and the glue necessary to make many subroutines work together is too large. Small size makes subroutines more amenable to reuse than larger units, since they tend to be relatively simple and context-free, but only a small amount of code is actually reused by each subroutine call.

Libraries are written in a particular programming language, so decisions about primitive data types, constructors for structured data types, and subroutine linkages have already been made.

Subroutines are written with all the details filled in, so it is not possible to change the number or types of the parameters or to pick out part of the algorithm encapsulated in the subroutine without a proliferation of library versions or hand-copying of reused code.

Ada packages extend subroutine libraries, expanding the size of the reusable unit and encapsulating some of the glue among subroutines, so the glue can also be reused. Generic packages permit the types of selected parameters to be specified by the application, but do not support changing the number of parameters and do not help the programmer in specializing algorithms. Ada packages are better than subroutines when it comes to maintenance, since the Ada Programming Support Environment supports version control.

Code skeletons also extend subroutine libraries. They consist of many subroutines, or even many packages, making even more of the glue reusable. Code skeletons are barren, however: Instead of supplying the glue, the programmer must supply the contents. If the data structures and algorithms are not included in the skeleton, they must be provided by the programmer; if either is included, opportunities for reuse are restricted to those planned by the original implementor.

Software generators. Applied successfully to report generators, compiler-compilers and language-based editors, software generation meets the criterion of language independence. The generator can be changed to produce software in a different implementation language without significantly affecting existing input specifications.

Software generation produces code several orders of magnitude larger than the specification, but a new generator can be developed only after the application area is relatively well-understood and standardized — and standardization cannot keep pace with new applications.

It is difficult to combine the output produced by different generators, and large-scale patches to the generated code abandon the advantages of generation for later maintenance.

Object-oriented languages. This approach supports great flexibility in defining and composing reusable components. New classes inherit the facilities of specified existing classes, and a class may augment or replace any subset of the inherited data structures and operations.

In addition to augmenting and replacing, however, it is often necessary to combine distinct operations provided by different reusable components. Some object-oriented languages permit a collection of operations to be combined by sequencing — calling each one individually in some prespecified order — but with no support for conditional choice or interleaving.

Object-oriented programming languages imply particular decisions regarding the implementations of data types and operations, drastically limiting, a priori, the contexts in which a class can be reused.

```
Feature Memory Manager

Interface:

    Exports ROOT[maxentitites], ENTITY[]
    Imports Time, DiskIO

Implementation:

    Class ROOT :: = curid: integer
                    maxentities: integer
                    inuse: integer
                    diskid: DISK-ID
                    allentities: set of ENTITY
                              key uniqueid
                    loaded ordered set of ENTITY
                              key uniqueid
                              ordered low by lastuse

    Class ENTITY :: = uniqueid: integer
                      incore: boolean
                      lastuse: TIMESTAMP
                      diskid: DISK-ID

    End Feature Memory Manager
```

Figure 1. The Memory Manager feature. Meld keywords are underlined, :: = and : are special symbols defined by Meld, and built-in classes are in bold italic.

managed root, which has six instance variables. The most interesting are allentities and loaded.

The allentities instance variable is a set of objects, each an instance of the ENTITY class. In Meld, the semantics of the set constructor guarantee uniqueness and support access according to a key, in this case the uniqueid instance variable of each object. Allentities represents the stubs of all memory-managed entities, both those that have been loaded in core and those that have not.

The loaded instance variable is an ordered set of objects. An ordered set works like a set, except that the objects are automatically ordered according to the value of a particular instance variable (in this case, lastuse). One behavior implemented by the action equations is to maintain loaded as only those memory-managed entities that are currently in core.

Action equations. The behavior of the generic memory manager is implemented by associating methods with the ROOT and ENTITY classes.

ROOT methods. In Figure 2, the first method for ROOT is inuse := Length(loaded). This is an individual equation that states that the inuse instance variable is equal to the length of the table of loaded entities. This method is a *constraint*, and does not have to be activated by a message sent to the ROOT object. Instead, it always constrains the instance variable on the left to have the value denoted by the expression on the right.

The semantics of Meld constraints are unidirectional: Whenever the length of loaded changes, the inuse variable is automatically updated, but not vice versa. The purpose of a constraint is to establish an invariant for all objects defined by the class.

The second constraint in Figure 2, Default maxentities := 100, defines maxentities as maintaining the constant value 100. Because this equation is preceded by the keyword default, it can be overridden by another action equation that also sets the value of maxentities.

The next two constraints illustrate the use of a new mechanism, *views*.[2] A view is a collection of objects that all satisfy some property, where the specification of the property is given by a *pattern*. Views and patterns support associative retrieval with respect to the entire database of objects.

Here, the allentities instance variable is defined to maintain the view is(ENTITY) (all instances of class ENTITY). The loaded instance variable is defined to maintain the view is(ENTITY) and incore (the subset of memory-managed entities whose incore variable is set to true).

The most remarkable property of a view is that its membership is dynamically adjusted as objects are added, deleted, and

```
Class ROOT :: = . . .

    Methods:
    inuse : = Length(loaded)
    Default maxentities : = 100
    allentities : = View: is(ENTITY)
    loaded : = View: is(ENTITY) and incore

    CREATE() -->

        curid : = 1
        diskid : = NewDiskID()

    NEWOBJECT() -->

        curid : = curid + 1

    EXIT() -->

        Send STORE To loaded[all]

    If inuse = > maxentities
    Then Send STORE To loaded[1]
```

Figure 2. Methods for a memory-managed ROOT. The --> symbol separates the method selector and formal parameters from its local variables (not shown in this example) and body. The [] symbols enclose an integer or keyword that selects one or more elements of a collection, and "all" refers to each element of a collection.

IEEE SOFTWARE

modified in the system.

These four methods differ from methods in most object-oriented languages because none has a selector (a name). These methods are not triggered by the receipt of a message. They are *permanently* active, and are evaluated as necessary, according to the dependencies between their inputs and outputs.

When an input to a constraint changes in value, the constraint is automatically reevaluated to produce a new output. For obvious reasons, there must not be any circularities among the inputs and outputs of permanently active methods. Circularities can be detected with an (unfortunately) computationally expensive method developed for attribute grammars.

The next three methods in Figure 2 are closer to traditional object-oriented languages. In each case, one or more action equations is attached to a selector, the name of a method. A message can be sent to an object by the runtime support or by another method, similar to the message passing of object-oriented languages. Messages may have parameters, although no parameters are required for this example. The equations attached to a particular method are evaluated only when the object receives the corresponding message.

A message is sent implicitly to an object whenever any of a collection of primitive operations is performed on the object. The primitive operations that imply messages include Create, Delete, Access, Update, Enter, and Exit. A method for one object can also send a message to another object using a send equation: (Send < message > To < destination(s) >).

When a new memory-managed root is created, Create is sent to the root, causing the corresponding method to be evaluated. This method consists of two assignments, diskid : = NewDiskID() and curid : = 1. One sets diskid to the value of the function NewDiskID (imported from the DiskIO feature) and the other initializes curid to 1. Although listed in sequence, they may be evaluated in either order because they don't depend on each other. The semantics of action equations requires equations to be evaluated in arbitrary order unless the input of one equation depends on the output of another.

These assignments differ from con-

straints in that they are evaluated only when their message is received. In particular, they are not reevaluated when their arguments change. If they were reevaluated, the second equation would reevaluate itself forever since NewDiskID returns a different value on each invocation.

Exit is another primitive operation. When the system terminates, the Exit message is sent implicitly to all objects. The Exit method for the memory-managed root, Send STORE To loaded[all], sends Store to every entity in the loaded table, saving entities that are in core on disk. The Store message is not a primitive operation; it is defined as the selector of a method in the Memory Manager.

The Newobject message is also defined by the implementor. This is sent by a new entity whenever one is created. Its single equation, curid : = curid + 1, increments curid to produce the next unique identifier.

The last method associated with the ROOT class is a conditional (If < Boolean expression > Then < action equation(s) > Else < action equation(s) >), which checks if a certain condition is true and activates the corresponding equations.

In this case, If inuse > = maxentities Then Send STORE To loaded[1], the conditional checks if the system has loaded too many entities into core and, if so, sends Store as needed to store the least recently accessed entities on disk. Since the conditional is not attached to a selector and is therefore a constraint, this activity is repeated as necessary to keep the number of loaded entities less than (or transiently equal to) the value of maxentities.

ENTITY methods. Figure 3 shows the methods for the ENTITY class. Each method is attached to a selector.

The Access method requests the current memory-managed entity into core by sending the Load message if its stub indicates that it is not already there (the stub of every memory-managed entity is always maintained in core as part of the table defined by ROOT). It also updates the entity's time stamp each time it is accessed.

The Create method initializes the instance variables of a new memory-managed entity and informs the root that a new entity has been created and assigned a unique identifier.

```
Class ENTITY :: = . . .

    Methods:

    ACCESS() -->

        If not incore
        Then Send LOAD To self
        lastuse : = Now()

    CREATE() -->

        diskid : = Undefined
        uniqueid : = ROOT.curid
        Send NEWOBJECT To ROOT

    DELETE() -->

        If diskid < > Undefined
        Then diskid : = FreeDiskID (diskid)

    LOAD() -->

        If not incore
        then Print("Could not load.")
        incore : = Load(diskid)

    STORE() -->

        If diskid = Undefined
        Then diskid : = NewDiskID()
        incore : = not Store(diskid)
        If incore
        Then Print ("Could not store.")
```

Figure 3. Methods for a memory-managed ENTITY.

The Delete method performs bookkeeping that frees any disk space previously allocated to the deleted entity.

The Load method loads the current memory-managed entity from disk and updates its stub to indicate that it is now available in primary memory.

The Store method assigns disk space, if not already done, and stores the entity at the required location.

Module Interconnection Language. Figure 4 shows a simple feature, a module interconnection language.

A module consists of an implementation, plus information such as lists of imports and exports. Modules are organized into collections called projects.

The full description of this environment should also contain an associated operational part (for example, methods to check interfaces between modules), but we do not show that here.

The MIL feature is reusable. The MOD-

```
Feature Module Interconnection Language

Interface:

    Exports all
    Imports Programming Language

Implementation:

    Class PROJECT :: = name: identifier
                       modules: seq of MODULE

    Class MODULE :: = name: identifier
                      imports: seq of identifier
                      exports: seq of SIGNATURE
                      components:
                          IMPLEMENTATION


End Feature Module Interconnection Language
```

Figure 4. The Module Interconnection Language feature.

ULE class can be tailored to the desired language by importing a Programming Language feature that defines the SIGNATURE and IMPLEMENTATION classes. In the case of Ada, which defines its own module construct, the MODULE class might be merged with an imported PACKAGE class.

Merging. Continuing with the example, the Memory Manager and MIL features are combined in a small system. In this system, the memory manager will manage the modules and their implementations.

Figure 5 illustrates how we use Meld to do this. We establish a connection between the ROOT and PROJECT classes on one hand, and between the ENTITY, MODULE, and IMPLEMENTATION classes on the other.

A feature may combine a group of imported features. In this case, the Programming-in-the-Large feature imports both Memory Manager and MIL, and certain classes from these two features are merged in the implementation.

For example, when the ROOT class is merged with the PROJECT class, each instance of the *renamed* PROJECT class has all the instance variables from both the

PROJECT class of the MIL feature and the ROOT class of the Memory Manager feature.

However, the only instance variable from the ROOT class that can actually be accessed here is maxentities, since it is the only instance variable exported by Memory Manager. A new action equation overrides its default value of 100 and changes the constant value of maxentities to 200, so the memory manager now maintains at most 200 entities in core. Overriding default methods and constraints makes it easy to tailor features to a wide variety of applications.

The programming-in-the-large feature operates as follows. When a human user tries to read the text of a module, the primitive operation Access is received by the module, which then activates any action equations that are part of the Access method for the MODULE class.

In this case, the only equations are those that were inherited from the ENTITY class in Figure 3. These equations update lastuse to the current time and check if the incore instance variable has the value true. If not, the Load message is sent to self, meaning the module. This has the effect of loading the content of the accessed entity. If there are now too many entities in core, the least recently used entity is stored on disk.

A real system would probably merge many such features, as listed in Figure 6.

Implementation

Three early versions of Meld have been implemented.

The first, the Representation Description Language, barely resembles Meld except that it uses the same notation for instance variables. RDL development began in 1981 as part of the Display-Oriented Structure Editor[3] system and has been used for rapid prototyping of several small systems at Carnegie Mellon University and Siemens Research and Technology Laboratories.

The second, Genie, is much closer to Meld. It has the notion of features, then called views, but applied them only to support display mechanisms. Genie was used in 1985 to implement the MacGnome[4] educational programming environment for Pascal, which is expected to be released

```
Feature Programming in the Large

Interface:

    Exports: . . .
    Imports: Module Interconnection Language,
             Memory Manager

Implementation:

    Merges ROOT, PROJECT as PROJECT
           ENTITY, MODULE as MODULE
           ENTITY, IMPLEMENTATION as IMPLEMENTATION

    Class PROJECT :: = maxentities: integer

    Methods:
       maxentities : = 200

End Feature Programming in the Large
```

Figure 5. The Programming-in-the-Large feature.

```
Feature A Larger System

Interface:

    Exports: . . .
    Imports: Module Interconnection Language, Memory Manager,
             Compilation Unit, Documentation Facility,
             My Error Handler, . . .

Implementation:

    . . .

End Feature A Larger System
```

Figure 6. A larger system.

by Apple Computer as a commercial product.

The most recent implementation, Mercury, was completed in February 1987. Mercury supports constraints but not messages and methods, using parallel algorithms in a distributed environment.[5,6] Mercury has been used to implement demonstration-quality, multiple-user programming environments for small subsets of Modula-2 and Ada.

RDL was originally implemented in extended Pascal on the Perq operating system, was ported to Accent in 1982 and to C on Sun 3.0 (essentially Berkeley Unix) in 1985. Genie was implemented in a different extension of Pascal for the Macintosh. Mercury, written in C, was implemented by modifying the Cornell Synthesizer Generator[7] and runs on Digital Equipment Corp. VAX 750s under Unix 4.3 BSD on a 10M-baud Ethernet.

We are now designing a fourth implementation that will support all of Meld as presented here. The implementation has four parts: an environment for developing and maintaining Meld features, a translator for the structural components of classes and features, a translator for action equations, and runtime support.

The environment is itself described in Meld and will be implemented through a bootstrapping procedure. This environment provides mechanisms for choosing particular concrete representations (for example, for collections) and control structures (for example, sequential versus parallel equation evaluation) appropriate to the implementation language and the reusing application. It also supports evolution of features using techniques previously demonstrated in TransformGen,[8] which automates updates to existing objects when their definitions are modified.

The translator for the structural components is responsible for generating object definitions in a conventional programming language. An object in a Meld system is a synthesis of one or more classes, perhaps defined in different features. The classes themselves are not actually combined in the translation; instead, the physical representation of each object consists of several facets, where each facet corresponds to one of the classes. This is

necessary because only some facets of an object may be active at any time; this was seen in the memory-manager example, where the stub for an object could be loaded and manipulated independently of its content.

It is easy to translate individual classes into the corresponding data types in conventional programming languages. For example, in Pascal each facet would be represented by a record, where each field in the record is a component or a pointer to a component (depending on the type of

the component). The difficulty arises in maintaining the connections and consistency among the various facets of the same object. This is handled by generating new constraints that update the instance variables of one facet in response to changes in another.

Unlike the sets of instance variables, the methods for a merged class are combined in the translator for action equations. A local dependency graph is constructed to represent the action equations attached to the same selector. The nodes in the graph represent equations, and the edges represent the dependencies among the inputs and outputs of the equations. The local dependency graph is also constructed for

> To the popular reuse approaches Meld adds the unique concept of combining both data and operations.

constraints — those action equations (for the same synthesized type) that are not attached to a selector. These dependency graphs are used by the runtime support to determine the evaluation order for active equations.

The translation of action equations also involves translating each individual action equation into a procedure that performs the activities in the equation. The procedures take advantage of the facilities provided by the implementation language, as well as the primitives provided by the runtime support.

The runtime support provides all the necessary primitives for creating, deleting, and accessing objects, as well as for interacting with users, the file system, and the operating system. It sends messages corresponding to these primitives as necessary; for example, the Access message is sent to an object whenever the object is accessed. It also provides primitives to send the new messages defined in the Meld description and manages a queue of pending messages.

The most important job of the runtime support is to order the evaluation of active action equations. This is done using an adaptation of Reps' incremental attribute evaluation algorithm,[9] which was developed to generate language-based editors from attribute grammars. The basic idea is that the local dependency graphs are combined into a composite dependency graph at runtime to reflect the actual connections among objects. Only the graphs for the current message, plus the graphs for constraints, are considered in the composition. A topological sort of the composite graph determines the order in which equations are evaluated. This algorithm is linear in the number of affected objects, and is thus optimal.

Meld meets the three criteria essential to large-scale reuse and is superior to the widely accepted approaches to software reusability. The notation abstracts away the details of any particular programming language, although almost any language is suitable for implementation. Meld supports composition of components through imports and merging and tailoring through renaming and overriding equations.

Meld, then, blends the package library, software generation, and object-oriented programming approaches to reusability and solves most of the problems of these three approaches.

From the package library approach came relatively large-scale modular units — features — that enforce information hiding. From software generation came the idea of a declarative notation that can be translated into an efficient implementation in a conventional programming language. From object-oriented programming came the concepts of inheritance and of encapsulating behavior with data structures.

To these approaches Meld adds the unique concept of combining *both* data and operations. Other object-oriented languages merge data structures, in the sense of creating objects with private memory for the instance variables defined by each ancestor class. But no other notation supports combination of algorithms on the basis of dependencies.

Software reuse will lead to large productivity gains only when it becomes practical to combine separately developed algorithms more flexibly than procedure invocation. Meld represents the first step in this direction. □

Acknowledgments

Yael Cycowicz, Dannie Durand, Charlie Krueger, Josephine Micallef, David Miller, Benjamin Pierce, Calton Pu, and anonymous referees made useful criticisms and suggestions about earlier versions of this article. Bob Schwanke at Siemens RTL, members of the Gandalf project at Carnegie Mellon University and students in the Programming Languages and Translators 1 course at Columbia University have written several features in Meld and discovered certain problems that have since been solved.

We also thank Nico Habermann and Mark Tucker for motivating our interest in reusable software. Meld is an outgrowth of both authors' work on Gandalf.[10]

This article is an expansion of "Composing Software Systems from Reusable Building Blocks," which appears in pp. 536-545 of *Proc. 20th Hawaii Int'l Conf. System Sciences*, (Computer Society Press, Los Alamitos, Calif., 1987).

Kaiser is supported in part by grants from AT&T Foundation, Siemens Research and Technology Laboratories, and New York State Center for Advanced Technology, and in part by a DEC faculty award. Garlan is supported in part by the U.S. Army, Software Technology Development Division of CECOM COMM/ADP, Fort Monmouth, N.J. and in part by ZTI-SOF of Siemens Corp., Munich, West Germany.

References

1. Gail E. Kaiser, "Generation of Run-Time Environments," *SIGPlan 86 Symp. Compiler Construction*, ACM, New York, 1986, pp. 51-57.

2. David Garlan, "Views for Tools in Integrated Environments," *Proc. IFIP WG 2.4 Int'l Workshop Advanced Programming Environments*, Springer Verlag, Berlin, 1986, pp. 341-343.

3. Peter H. Feiler and Gail E. Kaiser, "Display-Oriented Structure Manipulation in a Multi-Purpose System," *Proc. Seventh Int'l Computer Software and Applications Conf.*, CS Press, Los Alamitos, Calif., 1983, pp. 40-48.

4. Ravinder Chandhok et al., "Structure Editing-Based Programming Environments: The GNOME Approach," *Nat'l Computer Conference 85*, AFIPS, Reston, Va., 1985, pp. 359-370.

5. Simon M. Kaplan and Gail E. Kaiser, "Incremental Attribute Evaluation in Distributed Language-Based Environments," *Proc. Fifth SIGACT-SIGOPS Symp. Principles Distributed Computing*, ACM, New York, 1986, pp. 121-130.

6. Gail E. Kaiser and Simon M. Kaplan, "Reliability in Distributed Programming Environments," *Proc. Sixth Symp. Reliability Distributed Software and Database Systems*, CS Press, Los Alamitos, Calif., pp. 45-55.

7. Thomas Reps and Tim Teitelbaum, "The Synthesizer Generator," *Proc. SIGSoft/SIGPlan Software Engineering Symp. Practical Software Development Environments*, ACM, New York, 1984, pp. 41-48.

8. David Garlan, Charles W. Krueger, and Barbara J. Staudt, "A Structural Approach to the Maintenance of Structure-Oriented Environments," *Proc. Second SIGSoft/SIGPlan Software Engineering Symp. Practical Software Development Environments*, ACM, New York, 1986, pp. 160-170.

9. Thomas Reps, Tim Teitelbaum, and Alan Demers, "Incremental Context-Dependent Analysis for Language-Based Editors," *ACM Trans. Programming Languages and Systems*, July 1983, pp. 449-477.

10. A.N. Habermann and D. Notkin, "Gandalf: Software Development Environments," *IEEE Trans. Software Engineering*, Dec. 1986, pp. 1117-1127.

Gail Kaiser is an assistant professor of computer science at Columbia University, where she received a DEC Faculty Award. Her research interests are software reusability, object-oriented languages, programming environments, evolution of large software systems, application of artificial intelligence technology to software development and maintenance, and distributed systems.

Kaiser received the PhD in computer science from Carnegie Mellon University, where she was a Hertz Fellow.

David Garlan recently received the PhD in computer science from Carnegie Mellon University, where he has been an active member of the Gandalf and Gnome projects. His thesis, *Views for Tools in Integrated Environments*, addresses the problem of building tools for highly integrated environments.

His research interests include tool integration, software development environments, reusable software, functional programming languages, educational programming environments, and object-oriented systems and languages.

Questions about this article can be addressed to Kaiser at Columbia University, Computer Science Depart., New York, NY 10027; CSnet kaiser@cs.columbia.edu.

Wide–Spectrum Support for Software Reusability

Mitchell D. Lubars

Microelectronics and Computer Technology Corp.
3500 West Balcones Center Drive, Austin, TX 78759

Introduction

The reuse of existing software components can considerably improve productivity in the software development process. Opportunity is available for reuse throughout the process, from the initial conception of requirements and specifications to the final generation, integration, and testing of executable code. Some of the types of reusable components include domain–related knowledge [1], requirements [14], abstract designs [10], abstract algorithms [17], design and program transformations [12], programming cliches [18], program objects [6], and code [7]. Frequently, strong relationships exist between the various types of software components, such as between requirements and designs, design objects and algorithms, and data types and their implementations. This makes it feasible to automatically select some reusable components based on the selection of others. By assembling the various types of reusable artifacts into a special reuse library that encodes the relationships, integrated support can be provided for selecting and incorporating reusable components throughout the software process. This provides a "wide spectrum" approach to the problem of software reusability and offers a considerable gain due to leveraging reuse very far upstream in the software development process [2].

Most of the recent work in reuse technology has not focused on its wide–spectrum aspects, although some efforts have addressed part of the spectrum. For example systems have been constructed for the refinement and transformation of specifications into designs using various types of refinement [9] and transformation rules [12], the construction of implementations from abstract algorithms [17], and the rule–based construction of effective implementations from executable specifications [16]. This paper proposes that a variety of reusable software artifacts be assembled to support a wide–spectrum reuse methodology. Several of these types of artifacts are described in the following sections, and the relationships between these artifacts are pointed out to illustrate how those artifacts and relationships help to achieve the objectives of wide–spectrum reuse. As a simple example of the approach, the operation of a prototypical reuse system (ROSE) is described that integrates various aspects of requirements, high level design, algorithm, and implementation reuse. ROSE (Reuse of Software Elements) demonstrates how user requirements and specifications can be used to select abstract designs, which in turn can guide the selection of reusable algorithm and data type implementations for generating executable code.

Reuse of Requirements and Domain–Related Information

The formulation of requirements and specifications often requires a thorough understanding of one or more particular application domains. These involve an understanding of the objects in that domain, an understanding of relationships between those objects, and a knowledge of appropriate ways for processing those domain objects. Empirical studies have demonstrated that this is a rare type of expertise that is costly to acquire [4] and may account for large variations in the performance of software engineers [3]. There is considerable payoff in being able to reuse this type of domain–related information. Similarly, Barstow has argued that domain knowledge plays an essential role in the construction of usable program synthesis tools [1].

Various types of representations can be utilized to assist in reusing domain knowledge. These include a domain vocabulary with the concepts arranged in class hierarchies, attributes describing object features, and descriptions of applicable operations [10], requirements cliches [14], and domain–specific specification languages and transformation rules [12]. In DRACO [12], this engineering of domain knowledge is term *Domain Analysis*.

The encoding of domain–knowledge into reusable structures accomplishes four important upstream reuse objectives that also contribute to the wide–spectrum orientation. To illustrate these points, examples are drawn from the domain of *student records*.

1. **Feature–based Selection.** It assists in the selection of domain objects and associated software components from descriptions of their known features [10,13]. For example, a *structure* for recording *achievement information* about *people attending school* might be interpreted as a specification for student records.

2. **Constraint–based Analysis.** It provides the ability to critique and analyze [5,14] user requirements and specifications, based on domain–oriented dependencies and relationships. For example, students and student records are typically associated with various characteristics and components, such as records of their class grades, grade point averages, and address information. These set up expectations that can be checked for and used while acquiring the specifications.

3. **Domain–driven Completion.** The incorporation of reusable structures permits a system to fill in missing requirements and specifications in order to guarantee completeness [8]. The ability of a system to do this reduces the user's burden of having to consider all the minor details that are easily filled in from the context of the task and the domain. For example, if the user wants a list of student records to be sorted, he needn't specify that the sorted list of student records contains the same set of records as the unsorted list, or that the representation of both lists are the same. Similarly, if the user requests a list of failing students, domain information can be used to provide a definition of failing rather than requiring that the user specify it.

4. **Domain–driven Refinement.** Relationships, constraints, and applicable operations can be used to pick appropriate refinements to more detailed specifications and designs [10,12]. For example, known information about a set of student records, such as cardinality and record structure, can be used to pick the most appropriate algorithm for sorting the set of student records. Similarly, a request to send letters to failing students can be used to pick the most appropriate letter formatting routine and combine it with the right letter body and header information to generate student failure letters.

Reuse of Abstract Designs

At an abstract level, many classes of software designs contain significant similarities. For example, warehousing systems, ticketing systems, and reservations systems are all quite similar to the general category of inventory control systems. In each case, there are objects that are requested by customers, checked for availability, assigned, and distributed. The similarity can be further extended to resource allocation problems and to certain components of distributed systems. Such relationships between the designs of related problem domains can be described in terms of abstract design families and a hierarchy of family relationships. Design schemas [10] are one useful way to represent such relationships that provide the capability of high level design reuse.

The ways in which the component pieces of an abstract design are refined depends more on the properties of the actual application area than on the abstract design. Furthermore, there are frequently relationships between the refinement of the various component pieces. For example, the allocation strategy for a resource may influence the way in which resource requests are serviced (in order to prevent deadlock or assure fairness). As another example, a divide–and–conquer strategy may be viewed as the combination decompose–solve–compose, where the decompose and compose operations are intimately related [15]. These relationships (constraints) must be encoded into design schemas to assure that the components of the design are refined in compatible ways.

The use of abstract design schemas provides the design reuse potential, and the encoded relationships assures that the schemas are only applied when appropriate. Information for determining the relationships is derived from the user requirements and the reusable domain information. For example, establishing that a particular resource is a library book places restrictions on how that resource can be allocated, assigned (checked out), and eventually returned. This information can be used to select the most appropriate sub–designs for those components. On the other hand, if the resource is a disk drive then we might choose very different sub–designs for those components. The point is that the design can be automatically tailored from the initial requirements and reusable abstract design schemas, as part of the wide–spectrum approach.

Reuse of Algorithms, Data Types, and Representations

In many cases algorithms can be formulated independently of the data objects that they operate on. These types of solutions are considered polymorphic [11], since they can be applied to objects of a variety of different types. Some examples of these include sort and graph traversal algorithms, and the head and tail functions on lists. The actual data objects that the algorithms are applied to can be determined independently from other user requirements and relationships. The use of such polymorphic representations can increase the reuse potential of the algorithms considerably. This is especially true when the abstract algorithms are represented in a language independent form [17].

Abstract algorithms can be selected as a consequence of the refinement of abstract designs. For example, some of the components of design schemas may refer to specific abstract algorithms, such as a quicksort or postorder tree traversal. Other design components may refer to classes of algorithms, and rules can be used to select the most appropriate algorithm, based on available design constraints. For example, if the class is a table lookup and the table is of moderate size, use binary search. If the table is quite large, then a hash table search might be more appropriate. Note that in this case, the algorithm selection introduces a new design constraint that may affect other parts of the design, namely that the table lookup keys are hashed. That constraint is propagated to other affected portions of the design through the higher level design schema.

The types of the data objects that the abstract algorithms are applied to can be chosen by reusable design schemas, stated in user requirements and specifications, or inferred from domain knowledge, inference rules, and reusable abstract data type descriptions. For example, if a user specifies a program that prepares letters for failing students, a student record structure might be automatically selected with integer components for student id, string components for name and address, and additional components for recording the class grades and GPA. In addition, domain knowledge might be used to decide that the collection of student records and letters be organized as a *list*. Each of these types can themselves be viewed as reusable abstract objects. Definitions for more complex types, such as symbol table and tree are also possible.

The reusability of the data types is enhanced by factoring out issues regarding their representation [17]. For example, the list of student records may be represented as a file, an array, or a linked list. These representations can be collected into a separate set of reusable artifacts. Once again, the selection of the most appropriate data representation can be made from the application of inference rules, domain knowledge, user requirements and specifications, and design schema constraints. For example, if the list of student records is large and resides on external storage, then the best representation of the list may be as a file with some form of indexed access. Implementations for the data type operations can then be selected from the representation library and added to the abstract algorithms to give concrete implementations. These reuse aspects permit the wide–spectrum approach to be carried down to the level of providing executable code.

ROSE

ROSE (Reuse of Software Elements) is being constructed to demonstrate the utility of wide–spectrum reuse techniques. It is based on the concepts of two smaller scope reuse projects, IDeA [8], for addressing domain–knowledge, requirements, and abstract design reuse, and Software Templates [17], for addressing algorithm, data type and representation reuse.

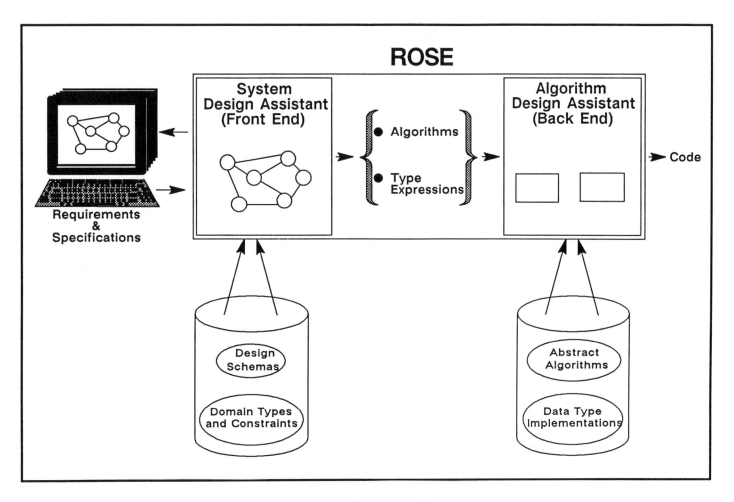

Figure 1. The components of Rose.

ROSE's front–end (see Figure 1) interacts with a user to elicit high level functional specifications of a desired system, in terms of dataflow transformations. The user's description of the input and output data objects and functional description is interpreted to identify the appropriate data and functional components in ROSE's reuse library. ROSE accomplishes this with the assistance of its descriptions of domain objects, attributes, and associated design schemas. Finally, one or more design schemas are selected as the starting point of the system design, from the design component library. ROSE then refines that design with the assistance of refinement rules, additional user–provided information and reusable domain–information to generate a very detailed dataflow design of the system. At that point, the lowest level functional components in the design correspond to abstract algorithms and the data objects correspond to domain–oriented data types.

ROSE converts the domain–oriented data type descriptions to more fundamental data types with the use of additional rules and schema–based information. The same information is used in a similar way to choose representations for those data types. The back–end of ROSE then combines the abstract algorithms, data types, and representations to generate concrete instances of those algorithms. In addition, a language discipline is chosen so that ROSE can generate executable code in a variety of high level languages, such as Pascal or "C". Thus, ROSE's approach is to interpret high level user requirements and specifications, and generate executable code by combining a wide–spectrum of reusable software components. This distinguishes it from other existing reuse systems. ROSE currently runs on a Sun 3 graphics workstations and is being used to investigate the solution of wide–spectrum reusability problems and issues.

Summary

Wide–spectrum reusability takes advantage of reusable software artifacts throughout the software development process. One significant advantage of this approach is that many of the decisions made in the far upstream portion of the process can be used to select reusable components throughout the process. This provides considerable leverage by making it possible to automate a large part of the selection and integration of reusable components. Some of the types of reusable components in a wide spectrum approach include various types of domain knowledge, abstract designs, abstract algorithms, transformation and refinement rules, data types, data objects, data representations, and implementations. ROSE was presented as a prototypical wide spectrum reuse system that interprets high level user specifications in order to produce detailed designs that are combined with abstract algorithms, data types and representations to generate an executable program.

Acknowledgements

Many of the ideas in this paper have been inspired through discussions with Dennis Volpano, Ted Biggerstaff, and other members of our design information group. I gratefully acknowledge their contribution and helpful comments during the preparation of this paper.

REFERENCES

1. D.R. Barstow. *Domain–Specific Automatic Programming.* **IEEE Trans. on Software Eng.** (Nov. 1984) vol. SE–10, no. 11, pp. 1321–1336.

2. T. Biggerstaff and C. Richter. *Reusability Framework, Assessment, and Directions.* **IEEE Software.** (March 1987) vol. 4, no. 3, pp. 41–49.

3. B. Curtis. *Substantiating Programmer Variability.* **Proceedings of the IEEE** (July 1981) vol. 69, no. 7, pp. 846.

4. B. Curtis, H. Krasner, V. Shen, N. Iscoe. *On Building Software Process Models Under the Lamppost.* **Proceedings of the Ninth International Conference on Software Engineering.** (March 1987) pp. 96–103.

5. S. Fickas. *Automating the Analysis Process: An Example.* **Proceedings of the Fourth International Workshop on Software Specification and Design.** (April 1987) pp. 58–67.

6. A. Goldberg and D. Robson. **SMALLTALK–80: The Language and its Implementation**. Reading, MA, 1983.

7. T.C. Jones. *Reusability in Programming: A Survey of the State of the Art.* **IEEE Trans. on Software Eng.** (Sept. 1984) vol. SE–10, no. 5, pp. 488–493.

8. M.D. Lubars. *A Knowledge–Based Design Aid for the Construction of Software Systems.* Ph.D. Thesis, Report No. UIUCDCS–R–86–1304, Department of Computer Science, University of Illinois, Urbana, IL (Jan. 1987).

9. M.D. Lubars and M.T. Harandi. *Intelligent Support for Software Specification and Design.* **IEEE Expert** (1986) vol. 1, no. 4, pp. 33–41.

10. M.D. Lubars and M.T. Harandi. *Knowledge–Based Software Design Using Design Schemas.* **Proceedings of the Ninth International Conference on Software Engineering** (March 1987) pp. 253–262.

11. R. Milner. *A Theory of Type Polymorphism in Programming.* **Journal of Computer and System Sciences.** (1978) vol. 17, pp. 348–375.

12. J.M. Neighbors. *The Draco Approach to Constructing Software from Reusable Components.* **IEEE Trans. on Software Eng.** (Sept. 1984) vol. SE–10, no. 5, pp 564–574.

13. R. Prieto-Diaz and P. Freeman. *Classifying Software for Reusability.* **IEEE Software** (Jan. 1987) vol. 4, no. 1, pp. 6–16.

14. C. Rich, R.C. Waters, and H.B. Reubenstein. *Toward a Requirements Apprentice.* **Proceedings of the Fourth International Workshop on Software Specification and Design** (April 1987) pp. 79–86.

15. D.R. Smith. *Top–Down Synthesis of Divide–and–Conquer Algorithms.* **Artificial Intelligence.** (1985) vol. 27, pp. 43–96.

16. D.R. Smith, G.B. Kotik, and S.J. Westfold. *Research on Knowledge–Based Software Environments at Kestrel Institute.* **IEEE Trans. on Software Eng.** (Nov. 1985) vol. SE–11, no. 11, pp. 1278–1295.

17. D.M. Volpano and R.B. Kieburtz. *Software Templates.* **Proceedings of the Eighth International Conference on Software Engineering** (1985) pp. 55–60.

18. R.C. Waters. *The Programmer's Apprentice: Knowledge Based Program Editing.* **IEEE Trans. on Software Eng.** (Jan. 1982) vol. SE–8, no. 1, pp. 1–12.

FROM DESIGN TO REDESIGN

Gerhard Fischer, Andreas C. Lemke, Christian Rathke

Department of Computer Science and Institute of Cognitive Science
University of Colorado, Campus Box 430
Boulder, CO 80309

"From Design to Redesign" by G. Fischer, A.C. Lemke, and C. Rathke from *Proceedings of the Ninth International Conference on Software Engineering,* 1987, pages 369–376. Copyright 1987, Association for Computing Machinery, Inc., reprinted by premission.

ABSTRACT

Software Engineering environments have to support design methodologies whose main activity is not the generation of new independent programs, but the maintenance, integration, modification and explanation of existing ones. Especially for software systems in ill-structured problem domains where detailed specifications are not available (like Artificial Intelligence and Human-Computer Communication), incremental, evolutionary redesign has to be efficiently supported.

To achieve this goal we have designed and constructed an object-oriented, knowledge-based user interface construction kit and a large number of associated tools and intelligent support systems to be able to exploit this kit effectively. Answers to the "user interface design question" are given by providing appropriate building blocks that suggest the way user interfaces should be built. The object-oriented system architecture provides great flexibility, enhances the reusability of many building blocks, and supports redesign. Because existing objects can be used either directly or with minor modifications, the designer can base a new user interface on standard and well-tested components.

1. Introduction

Human-computer communication and knowledge-based systems are two research domains consisting mostly of ill-structured problems. In these domains it is seldom possible to provide a precise specification of intent; and without this specification, correctness is in general not a meaningful question. The main difficulty is not "correct" implementation of given specifications, but development of specifications that lead to effective solutions corresponding to real needs. In [Fischer, Schneider 84] we argued that life cycle models are inadequate for ill-structured problems and should be replaced by incremental design and a rapid prototyping methodology based on a communication model. Construction kits and support tools that allow the exploration of alternatives can considerably enhance this approach.

Redesign is a methodology which achieves that the prototyping process is *rapid* and it allows us to explore design alternatives for a problem. In addition, it supports that existing systems can be adapted to new requirements and can be tailored to special needs of individual users and user communities. Our redesign methodology is based on a construction kit (see Figure 2-1) which provides as building blocks the abstractions expected to be relevant for exploring the design space. In the domain of human-computer communication and user interfaces, primitives such as windows, menus, icons and editors are the basis for specific applications. Over the last six years we have designed, implemented and continuously enhanced a system for this domain called WLISP [Fabian 86, Boecker, Fabian, Lemke

85][*]. WLISP's flexibility as a construction kit is provided by its object-oriented architecture. It contains a large amount of knowledge about the design of user interfaces. Additional knowledge is represented in support systems that guide the design process and critique intermediate results.

An especially interesting feature of WLISP is that it is one of the few systems implemented in a time sharing environment. It is currently running in FranzLisp and ObjTalk [Rathke 86] on VAX systems using powerful terminals and is not restricted to high performance personal computers. This environment provided both the necessity and the opportunity for implementing a distributed architecture between terminal and main frame.

From a designer's viewpoint, WLISP provides a visually based, interactive programming environment [Barstow, Shrobe, Sandewall 84]. WLISP has been an everyday operational environment at a number of institutions within universities and research organizations for several years. WLISP has served the designers of user interface software as well as the end-users.

Figure 1-1 describes our vision of the architecture of an intelligent design environment. This architecture is based on the belief that the "intelligence" of a complex tool must contribute to its ease of use. Truly

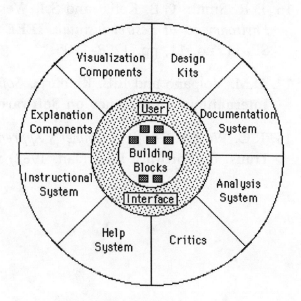

Figure 1-1: Architecture of a design environment

---

[*] The system was named WLISP because its development began 8 years ago with the goal of providing a window-based programming environment for LISP.

Reviewed and recommended by:

David R. Barstow and William E. Riddle

intelligent and knowledgeable humans, such as good teachers, use a substantial part of their knowledge to explain their expertise to others. In the same way, the ''intelligence'' of a computer system should be used to provide effective communication. We have built prototypical systems in many areas of the outer circle: documentation systems [Fischer, Schneider 84], help systems [Fischer, Lemke, Schwab 85], critics [Fischer 87], and visualization tools [Boecker, Fischer, Nieper 86].

In the following sections we illustrate the redesign process with a case study, describe the WLISP system and a prototypical design support tool (TRIKIT) and evaluate the strengths and weaknesses of our approach. In the last section we briefly describe ideas for future developments.

2. From Design to Redesign

Many large software systems are built as in Figure 2-1-a; a monolithic system is completely implemented in a general purpose programming language. Although these systems are usually structured in some way, this structure is oriented only towards the original specification of the problem. To overcome the difficulty of redesign that has been experienced with these systems, the design of one (or more) intermediate levels of abstractions must be an integral part of the software process (Figure 2-1-b). This strategy allows for both easy *redesign* by modifying the original design (Figure 2-1-c) and *reuse* by recombining the intermediate abstractions to form a different system (Figure 2-1-d).

Software Engineering environments of the future have to support design methodologies whose main activity is not the generation of new, independent programs, but the integration, modification, and explanation of existing ones [Winograd 79]. Just as one relies on already established theorems in a new mathematical proof, new systems should be built as much as possible using existing parts. In order to do so, the designer must understand the functioning of these parts. An important question concerns the level of understanding necessary for successful redesign: exactly how much does the user have to understand? Our methodologies (differential programming and programming by specialization [Kay 84] based on our object-oriented knowledge representation language ObjTalk; see Section

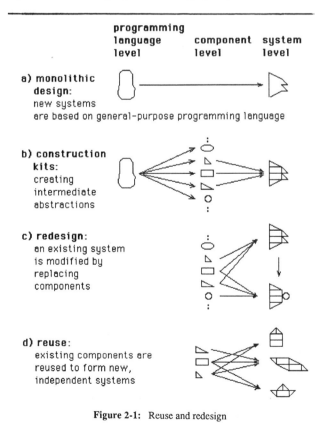

Figure 2-1: Reuse and redesign

3.2) and support tools (e.g., the BROWSER; see Section 4.1) are steps in the direction of making it easier to modify an existing system than to create a new one. Inheritance is important for redesign because it enables objects that are almost like other objects to be created easily with a few incremental changes. Inheritance reduces the need to specify redundant information and simplifies updating and modification by allowing information to be entered and changed in one place.

A construction kit with a large number of generally useful building blocks provides a good basis for redesign. Simon [Simon 81] demonstrates that the evolution of a complex system proceeds much faster if stable intermediate parts exist. The abstractions, represented in WLISP by more than 200 ObjTalk classes, comprise stable intermediate parts for development of user interfaces. The large number of classes in WLISP is a mixed blessing. The advantage is that in all likelihood a building block or set of building blocks that either fits our needs or comes close to doing so already exists and has already been used and tested. The disadvantage is that they are useless unless the designer knows that they are available. Informal experiments [Fischer 87] indicate that the following problems prevent designers from successfully exploiting the potential of high functionality systems:

- designers do not know about the existence of needed objects (either building blocks or tools);
- designers do not know how to access objects;
- designers do not know when to use these objects;
- designers do not understand the results objects produce for them;
- designers cannot combine, adapt and modify an object for their specific needs.

Unless we are able to solve these problems, designers will constantly reinvent the wheel instead of taking advantage of already existing tools.

3. Description of WLISP

Our ideas, models and theories about the design of human-computer interfaces have become operational with the development of WLISP. The structure of the WLISP system defines a way of looking at and dealing with user interfaces. For users it provides a consistent world in which they can transfer interaction techniques among applications. For designers it provides a set of basic building blocks from which they can choose in designing a specific application.

3.1. A User's View

As a whole, WLISP can be described as a world with which the user interacts by screen manipulation. The system is *reactive* in the sense that each object on the screen exhibits a certain type of behavior. Actions that change the common world of user and system can be invoked either by the system (e.g., by updating some information about the state of an application) or by the user (e.g., by selecting some command from a menu). The designer using WLISP or the user of a specific application system deals with *screen objects* such as windows, icons, menus and buttons (see Figure 3-1), that are manipulated using the mouse as a pointing device. Many screen objects are independent of specific applications and serve as basic building blocks for different applications.

The user's view, which, depending on the task, is either that of a software engineer or an end-user is shown in a typical screen image of WLISP Figure 3-1:

- At the top of the screen some **status information** is shown. It is is updated continually by the underlying UNIX operating system. The status line displays time, load average, and number of users and tells about incoming and pending mail.
- A LISP interpreter is running in the **toplevel** window. Currently it displays the ObjTalk-Definition of a character object. On the right-hand side of the **toplevel** window a **static menu** is visible.
- Different systems can be activated by selecting the appropriate icon from the **Catalog**. The **Catalog** tells users which systems are available.

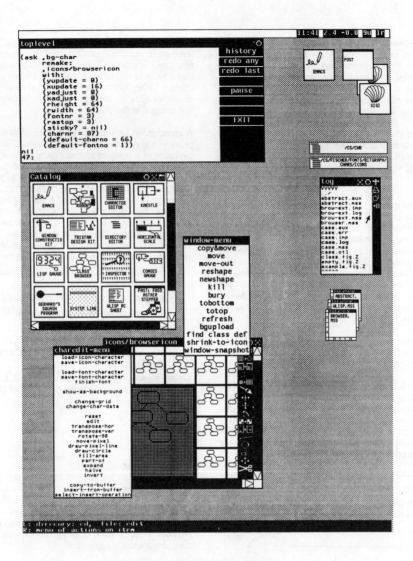

Figure 3-1: The user's view of WLISP

- At the bottom of the screen a **Character-Editor** window is shown that supports the definition of icons. All icons on the screen have been defined with the Character-Editor.

- A **window-menu** is associated with each window. It contains the basic operations on windows. Pressing a mouse button inside a window activates a pop-up menu with operations for the application itself. In the **Character-Editor** this menu displays operations to manipulate the pixel image of the character object.

- Some of these operations are also accessible through **buttons** on the right margin. Menus and buttons are alternative ways to perform the same operations.

- The **directory-editor** window gives access to the UNIX file system. It contains files of a certain directory.

- The **Catalog** and the **Character-Editor** windows have scroll bars on their right and lower sides. Windows in general show only a rectangular part of some larger region. Scrolling means to move this region below the window.

- Windows can be shrunk to icons when they are not needed. Some of them are shown on the right side. Icons are visual reminders of systems, functions and windows. They are organized in **clusters** that determines their spatial layout.

- In the **mouse-documentation-window** at the bottom of the screen information about mouse actions is displayed. As the user moves the mouse over windows, buttons or icons, this information is updated.

The association of applications with windows allows for an arbitrary number of applications to run at the same time. The user has direct access to each of them. WLISP provides a means for their integration.

3.2. A Designer's View

The components of WLISP are implemented in ObjTalk, an *object-oriented knowledge representation language* [Rathke 86]. Control is expressed in terms of a *message passing among objects* [Hewitt 77]. Objects *behave* based on the *interpretation of messages* and their *internal state*.

Objects are organized in *classes*. Objects of the same class - the *instances* of that class - have the same methods and slots and show the same type of behavior. Classes are arranged in hierarchies. They share the properties (i.e., methods and slots) of their parent classes. In this way properties are *inherited* by classes. All classes together form an *inheritance hierarchy* with a special class at the root called OBJECT. The fundamental properties of all objects are defined in OBJECT. They can be modified or extended in any of its subclasses.

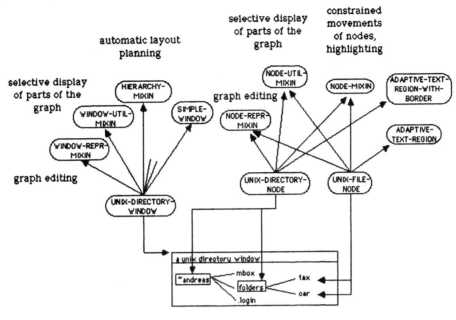

Figure 3-3: The TRISTAN classes

All components of WLISP are organized in inheritance hierarchies of classes. Classes describe screen objects such as windows or menus and components of screen objects such as borders, titles and buttons.

The design, development and use of WLISP have shown that the object-oriented architecture together with well established components and building blocks are extremely useful for the design of user interfaces. WLISP classes provide a set of abstractions on which the designer can rely. Existing systems like menus, icons, the directory editor, the character-editor, and the catalog serve as examples for the construction new user interfaces. The object-oriented architecture supports the reuse of components and building blocks.

Four categories of WLISP system classes can be identified:

1. **Basic system classes.** These classes describe rectangular areas on the screen such as regions, borders and titles. They are combined to construct output windows, text windows or dialogue windows. Superwindows act on subscreens, which can contain multiple subwindows. The inheritance hierarchy of the basic system classes is shown in Figure 3-2.

2. **Basic components of the user interface construction kit.** These classes form the application-independent parts of the user interface. Menus, icons, buttons, scroll bars, etc. inherit properties from the basic system classes. Parts of them can also be used as building blocks for application systems.

3. **Advanced components of the user interface construction kit.** TRISTAN [Nieper 85] is an example of a complex component providing high-level abstractions for displaying and editing graph structures through direct manipulation.

   Figure 3-3 shows the elements of TRISTAN as applied to a graphic UNIX directory editor. TRISTAN is independent of the particular node representation. It assumes only that the node representation is a subclass of the `simple-display-region` window class.

4. **Application systems.** Application systems use the components of the interface construction kit in different ways. Menus, icons, buttons or dialogue windows can be used directly within an application system. Other classes serve as a source from which properties are inherited. Applications usually define their own classes that incorporate the existing functionality by inheritance.

The reuse of WLISP system classes by means of inheritance and combination is supported by the object-oriented architecture:

- The creation of subclasses of existing classes allows the designer to create new objects that differ from existing objects in some desired aspects (e.g., different methods for some messages, additional slots) but that inherit almost all of the functionality of their ancestors.

- The use of predefined components is not an all-or-nothing decision. If the component has one undesired property, this component need not be completely abandoned. Even if the behavior of a superclass is to a very large extent undesired, it can still be used by shadowing all but the useful properties.

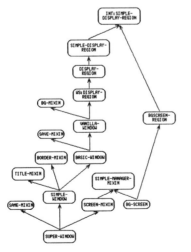

Figure 3-2: The basic window classes

285

- Subclasses are not modified, independent copies of their super-classes. They benefit from any augmentations of their super-classes.
- Extensions can be done on different levels of the hierarchy, thereby affecting selected classes of objects.
- Like other object-oriented languages, ObjTalk supports dynamic modification of classes. Slots can be added without recompilation of other software. This not only makes rapid prototyping easier but also supports modifications by the end user.
- Each method can be a hook for modifying behavior. Methods can be augmented by adding procedures to be executed before, after, or instead of existing methods.

These architectural principles support new programming methodologies such as differential programming and programming by specialization and analogy, which is crucial to a redesign approach to system development.

4. A Case Study in Redesign

In this section we describe a prototypical task, the redesign of the interface to the ObjTalk Browser [Rathke 86] and how problems in redesigning this interface were solved by exploiting the architectural properties of WLISP.

4.1. The ObjTalk BROWSER

To accomplish our main goal, which is to facilitate the redesign of software and avoid building it from scratch, information retrieval tools for reusable software components like ObjTalk classes have become an absolute necessity. Browsers have become increasingly valuable for understanding and changing systems. They displace program listings because they present a program as a multidimensional structure being generated and filtered dynamically. In SMALLTALK [Goldberg 84], the browser is the main interface to the system and is used both for finding and analyzing existing pieces of software and for modifying and creating new software. It replaces the file system and the editor of conventional systems. The interaction style is one of moving and searching through an information space rather than directly accessing the space through names or descriptions.

The WLISP BROWSER displays the inheritance structure of a system. The interconnections between the system and the components it inherits from can be analyzed in more detail by selecting a component and looking at its slot descriptions, defaults, triggers, and methods (Figure 4-1).

The BROWSER exhibits some of the more advanced interface characteristics provided by WLISP. The main window is divided into several subwindows whose relationship is automatically maintained by WLISP and displayed in paned windows. Inside the *Classes Window* ObjTalk classes can be visualized by icons and are connected by arrows to show the superclass relationship. Selecting a class icon causes the other BROWSER windows to be filled with slots, methods, subclasses and instances of that class. This feature is implemented using the constraint mechanism of ObjTalk.

4.2. Description of the Redesign Process

The BROWSER had undergone several redesigns before it took its current shape. In an earlier development stage classes were represented as items of a scrollable menu (Figure 4-2). We describe the process of redesigning the menu-based BROWSER to show iconic representations for ObjTalk classes instead.

The Task. Instead of classes being visualized by strings in a scrollable menu, we would like to display classes as icons that are connected by arrows to show the superclass relationship. Everything else should stay unchanged, especially the dependencies between the selected class and the contents of the other windows.

The Redesign. The class of the window to be replaced (BROWSER-CLASSES-MENU) has two superclasses (Figure 4-3): BROWSER-SELECTION-MIXIN and CLASSES-MENU. BROWSER-SELECTION-MIXIN provides BROWSER-CLASSES-MENU with the application-dependent knowledge. It describes how the consequences of a class selection are propagated to the other BROWSER windows. CLASSES-MENU provides BROWSER-CLASSES-MENU with the knowledge for scrolling and menu selection. The redesign consists of

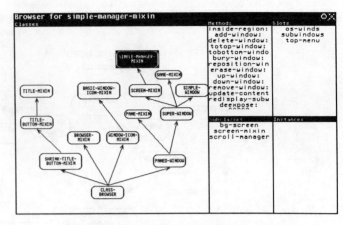

Figure 4-1: The BROWSER with windows to show the class hierarchy, methods, slots, instances and subclasses of a selected class

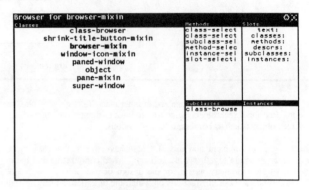

Figure 4-2: The original BROWSER

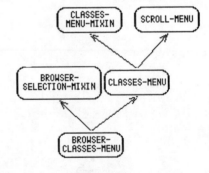

Figure 4-3: The inheritance hierarchy of BROWSER-CLASSES-MENU

replacing this class by a new one, thereby maintaining the important interactive properties of selecting, adding and deleting classes.

In order to find out about the desired properties of the new class we take a closer look at the definition of BROWSER-CLASSES-MENU (Figure 4-3):

SCROLL-MENU is combined with CLASSES-MENU-MIXIN to form the CLASSES-MENU class. Windows of this class are able to display classes as strings. BROWSER-CLASSES-MENU is constructed by mixing BROWSER-SELECTION-MIXIN in with CLASSES-MENU.

In BROWSER-SELECTION-MIXIN the dependencies between the selected class and the other BROWSER windows are represented: Whenever a class is selected, the contents of these windows will be updated to display methods, slots, subclasses and instances of the selected class. Because this functionality is not to be changed, we can use BROWSER-SELECTION-MIXIN without any modifications.

Instead of SCROLL-MENU we use SIMPLE-WINDOW as the basis for the new window. Simple windows provide the basic window capabilities of graphical windows in which icons can be placed and lines can be drawn. It sets up a coordinate system with its origin at the lower left corner. Scrolling the contents of a simple window is interpreted as moving the origin of the graphic coordinate system. CLASSES-MENU-MIXIN is replaced by a new mixin class (CLASS-NET-WINDOW-MIXIN) that specifies methods for selection, addition and deletion of classes. These operations are different from the ones in the preexisting implementation because they now have to display, add and delete icons and connect them by arrows (Figure 4-4).

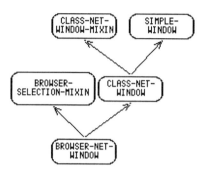

Figure 4-4: The inheritance hierarchy of BROWSER-NET-WINDOW

The implementation of the functionality for CLASS-NET-WINDOW-MIXIN would be a difficult task if there were no support for manipulating icons that contain text and that are connected by lines. Icons are an integrated part of the WLISP system. There are components that deal with text manipulation within icons (e.g., hyphenation and adjustment to the horizontal and vertical center), borders of various shapes and selection feedback. Also, the capability of connecting icons by arrows is supplied by a number of classes from WLISP's net package.

As the final step, the new class CLASS-NET-WINDOW-MIXIN is combined with SIMPLE-WINDOW to form CLASS-NET-WINDOW. Together with BROWSER-SELECTION-MIXIN the final BROWSER-NET-WINDOW is constructed (Figure 4-4).

5. Intelligent Support Tools for Reuse and Redesign
In addition to suitable languages and system architectures, support systems are necessary to enhance reuse and redesign processes. Rich computing environments contain at least hundreds of components that can be combined in many different ways. The existence of a component alone does not guarantee that it is readily available and that its usefulness is apparent. Therefore, support tools are needed that have knowledge about the structure of systems and about the use of existing facilities, that aid in making design decisions, carry out low level details, analyze or criticize intermediate versions, and visualize their structure. We will call these support tools *design kits*.

In this section we describe TRIKIT as an example of this type of systems (for a detailed description see [Fischer, Lemke 87]). TRIKIT supports design and redesign of network displays and editors. With its knowledge of this task domain it can aid the designer by automatically offering interesting design choices, selecting appropriate components, and combining them to make a functioning system. The designer needs much less knowledge and is able to produce higher quality results in shorter time.

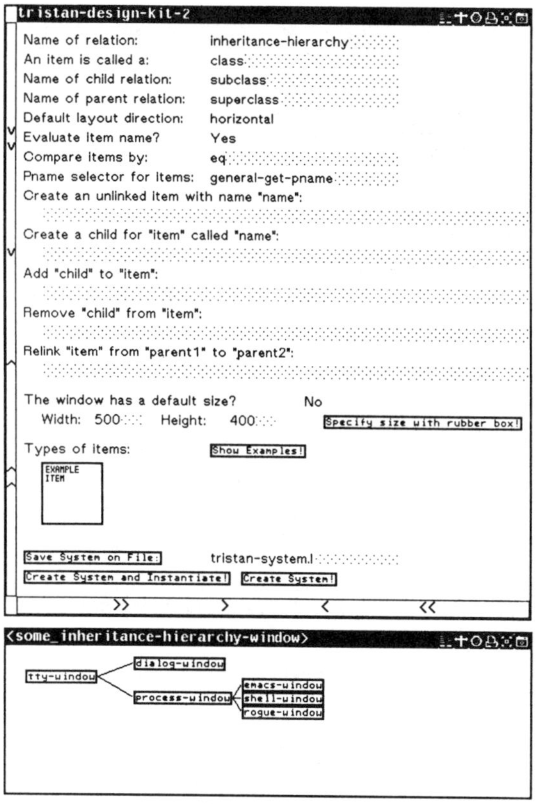

Figure 5-1: Initial state of the main form and an inheritance hierarchy window generated from it

The display and modification of hierarchical and network structures is a common problem in application systems including those that deal with structures of databases, directory trees, inheritance hierarchies, or dependency graphs are examples. TRISTAN, the user interface component described in Section 3.2, is a large set of object-oriented construction components that is applicable to many different types of graphical representations. We have used it to graphically display UNIX file system hierarchies, inheritance networks in object-oriented languages, and dependency relationships between rules in rule-based expert systems.

TRIKIT is a design kit for combining the TRISTAN components with a specific application. It presents itself to the user as a collection of interaction sheets as shown in Figures 5-1 (top window) and 5-2. On these interaction sheets the designer specifies the interface to the application. The designer specifies in terms of the application what it means to create and delete a node or to insert and remove a link. Here the designer chooses the desired graphical representation for the nodes of the graph and controls the creation of the user interface. This design process is carried out above the code level. TRIKIT hides from the designer program code that is generated when the network editor is created or modified.

Initially, the form is filled in with an example application - an ObjTalk inheritance hierarchy viewer; the window at the bottom of Figure 5-1 shows an instance. This allows users to familiarize themselves with TRIKIT and to modify parameters and explore their significance. The system supports redesign by providing designers with prototypical solutions and allowing them to take advantage of as much previous work and knowledge as possible.

Designers using TRIKIT need to know very little about the TRISTAN component. However, they do need to fill in code to access the application, for example, to retrieve the nodes of the graph, or to signal events that changed it. In addition to the specification of the application interface, many options of TRIKIT can be controlled. The representation of different types of nodes of the graph (different fonts, sizes, the use of pictorial representations) or

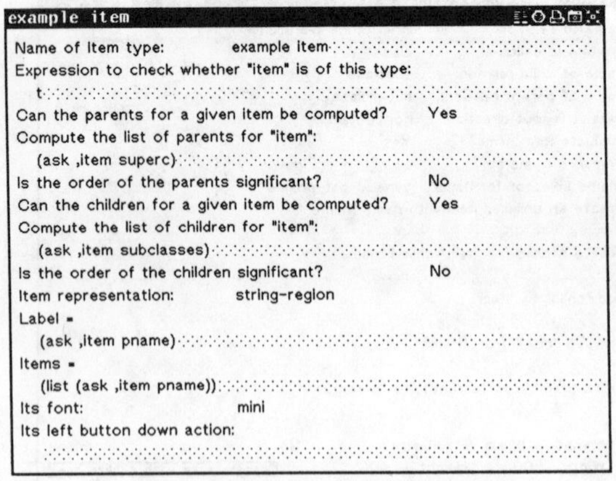

Figure 5-2: Initial state of the node form describing properties of individual nodes.

the layout direction (horizontal or vertical) can be adjusted to an individual application. Although the design space is limited by the available options in the forms, it is still possible to use this system to create a prototype to be further refined on a lower level (ObjTalk).

We have preferred a form-based specification over a specification language because form-based specification does not require the user to learn a language in order to be able to use the tool. An alternative that we will explore further is a direct manipulation interface [Hutchins, Hollan, Norman 86]. However, the abstract nature of many parameters (e.g., access functions for nodes, layout direction, distinguishing characteristics of node types) may make a direct manipulation interface infeasible.

6. The Evolutionary Development of Wlisp

The development of the WLISP system itself has been an incremental evolutionary process in which redesign has played a crucial role. It began many years ago with the implementation of a window system, and new interface components have been added incrementally. Ideas for further development and enhancement originated from the following sources:

- Systems constructed with an existing version of WLISP led to the development of new features that were at first built from scratch, quite often by different persons. Subsequently, the general usability of these features was recognized, and new, general components were built and integrated into WLISP.

- There was a strong interplay between the development of new applications and the recognition of the shortcoming of the available construction blocks and tools. For example, there was a long-felt need for superwindows and paned windows. Many applications resulted in special solutions until our understanding was good enough to develop them as general classes.

- Other developments of similar systems were carefully analyzed (e.g., the SMALLTalk system, the MacIntosh, the LISP machines, expert system shells like KEE, ART and LOOPS).

We believe that this evolutionary process has led to a set of abstractions, represented as classes in an inheritance network, that represent "tools of thought" for the designer and a "weak theory" of user interfaces. Using the current kit guarantees the development of reasonable interfaces with modest efforts and supports a redesign methodology.

Even today, the inheritance lattice of WLISP components is not static. Changes such as moving classes up in the lattice or isolating certain characteristics in separate mixins to increase the amount of shared information, reflect our growing understanding of the hierarchical structure and decomposition of a problem domain. The development of WLISP demonstrates that ill-structured problem domains, such as user interface and AI programming [Fischer, Schneider 84], require the coevolution of specification and implementation to achieve adequate and useful solutions [Swartout, Balzer 82].

7. Evaluation

Observing designers in dealing with complex software systems, one can see that they do not engage in redesign processes (even if they would like the system to behave differently) because redesign is not supported well enough. The effort to change a system or to explore design alternatives is too expensive in most software production environments. Our experience with our systems and tools makes us believe that if the cost of making changes is cheap enough, designers will start to experiment thereby gaining experience and insight leading to better designs. The existence of editors and formatting systems has shown that the willingness of writers to modify existing solutions increases.

Reuse and redesign processes in our environment are supported by WLISP and tools like the browser and TRIKIT. The reaction of designers using these tools has been largely positive, and a large number of complex systems with different user interfaces have been built (e.g., the NEWTON-Interface [Rathke 87]). The increased willingness to redesign has led to the construction of systems which fit an environment of needs. We feel very strongly that the specification of graphical, dynamic interfaces with a static, linear description language has severe limitations. Interfaces have a feel and an aesthetic quality that have to be experienced and that cannot be derived formally from specification languages. We were able to study empirically the consequences of specific design choices. Systems that make use of WLISP's abstractions are relatively easy to modify, maintain and adapt to changing needs. The object-oriented architecture provides a much greater flexibility and range of application than traditional subroutine libraries, which have failed as tools for redesign and reuse, because they are filled with specific implementations [Balzer, Cheatham, Green 83].

We are, however, aware of problems that remain to be solved. As described in Section 2, knowing about the existence of components is not trivial, especially as the number of available components is growing. In Section 4 it remains unclear how the components for building CLASS-NET-WINDOW-MIXIN have been determined. One can only search for something if one knows that something like it might exist.

If one has found a potentially useful component, one has to determine how it has to be used and combined with the other components. One has to understand its functionality and its properties. Design kits such as TRIKIT are an attempt at solving this problem. The problem of understanding, however, remains. The fields of TRIKIT's forms use a certain terminology, which not everybody is familiar with. The design space that is supported by TRIKIT must be extended to make it a more generally applicable tool.

We need more *active* tools or agents that have sufficient self-knowledge to offer their services. Our active help system [Fischer, Lemke, Schwab 85] and our critic [Fischer 87] are other steps in the direction of filling this need.

8. Conclusions

To cope with the ever-increasing complexity of designing, constructing, maintaining and enhancing software products, we have to replace discipline (by the software engineer) with better tools. A formalized, computer-assisted software paradigm must supersede the current informal, person-based software paradigm.

We believe that we have made an important step towards this goal. The classes of WLISP reflect our understanding of how to decompose the domain of modern user interfaces. WLISP contains many building blocks allowing existing software to be reused and supporting design by redesign. Intelligent support tools guide the user in selecting among the numerous building blocks. Part of the knowledge about required or useful combinations about these components can be represented within WLISP itself. In further development stages of WLISP we will formalize the experts' knowledge about the use of components in ObjTalk *meta-classes*. Meta-classes allow the representation of structural and behavioral properties of classes. For instance, the ObjTalk classes that describe *paned windows* (Figure 4-1) are instances of a special meta-class WPANE that automatically supplies its instances with a required set of superclasses.

Design for Redesign is a promising methodology for keeping software "soft" and preventing it from becoming ossified and brittle with age. Modification within our methodology is not automated, but it is greatly facilitated. Redesign of software is similar to interior design of buildings, where contexts and boundaries are given: in our case contexts and boundaries are provided by the components of the construction kit. Made with this approach, incremental improvements will be cheap enough that software engineers can experiment with alternative implementations, thereby gaining experience and insight leading to better designs.

Acknowledgments

The authors would like to thank their former colleagues on the project INFORM at the University of Stuttgart and their current colleagues and students in the research group "Knowledge-based Systems and Human-Computer Communication" at the University of Colorado, Boulder, who all contributed to making WLISP a usable, enjoyable and productive computational environment which allows us to explore new methodologies like redesigning and reusing software.

The research was supported by: grant No. N00014-85-K-0842 from the Office of Naval Research, grant No. DE-FG02-84ER1328 from the Department of Energy, the German Ministry for Research and Technology, and Triumph Adler Corporation, Nuernberg.

References

[Balzer, Cheatham, Green 83]
R. Balzer, T.E. Cheatham, C. Green, *Software Technology in the 1990's: Using a New Paradigm*, Computer, 1983.

[Barstow, Shrobe, Sandewall 84]
D.R. Barstow, H.E. Shrobe, E. Sandewall, *Interactive Programming Environments*, McGraw-Hill Book Company, New York, 1984.

[Boecker, Fabian, Lemke 85]
H.-D. Boecker, F. Fabian Jr., A.C. Lemke, *WLisp: A Window Based Programming Environment for FranzLisp*, Proceedings of the First Pan Pacific Computer Conference, The Australian Computer Society, Melbourne, Australia, September 1985, pp. 580-595.

[Boecker, Fischer, Nieper 86]
H.-D. Boecker, G. Fischer, H. Nieper, *The Enhancement of Understanding through Visual Representations*, Human Factors in Computing Systems, CHI'86 Conference Proceedings (Boston, MA), ACM, New York, April 1986, pp. 44-50.

[Fabian 86]
F. Fabian, *Fenster- und Menuesysteme in der MCK*, in G. Fischer, R. Gunzenhaeuser (eds.), *Methoden und Werkzeuge zur Gestaltung benutzergerechter Computersysteme*, Walter de Gruyter, Berlin - New York, Mensch-Computer-Kommunikation Vol. 1, 1986, pp. 101-119, ch. V.

[Fischer 87]
G. Fischer, *A Critic for LISP*, Technical Report, University of Colorado, Boulder, 1987.

[Fischer, Lemke 87]
G. Fischer, A.C. Lemke, *Design Kits: Steps Toward Human Problem-Domain Communication*, Paper submitted to 'Human-Computer Interaction - Special Issue on User Interfaces to Expert Systems', University of Colorado, Boulder, 1987.

[Fischer, Lemke, Schwab 85]
G. Fischer, A.C. Lemke, T. Schwab, *Knowledge-Based Help Systems*, Human Factors in Computing Systems, CHI'85 Conference Proceedings (San Francisco, CA), ACM, New York, April 1985, pp. 161-167.

[Fischer, Schneider 84]
G. Fischer, M. Schneider, *Knowledge-Based Communication Processes in Software Engineering*, Proceedings of the 7th International Conference on Software Engineering, Orlando, Florida, March 1984, pp. 358-368.

[Goldberg 84]
A. Goldberg, *Smalltalk-80, The Interactive Programming Environment*, Addison-Wesley Publishing Company, Reading, MA, 1984.

[Hewitt 77]
C. Hewitt, *Viewing Control Structures as Patterns of Passing Messages*, Artificial Intelligence Journal, Vol. 8, 1977, pp. 323-364.

[Hutchins, Hollan, Norman 86]
E.L. Hutchins, J.D. Hollan, D.A. Norman, *Direct Manipulation Interfaces*, in D.A. Norman, S.W. Draper (eds.), *User Centered System Design, New Perspectives on Human-Computer Interaction*, Lawrence Erlbaum Associates, Inc., Hillsdale, NJ, 1986, pp. 87-124, ch. 5.

[Kay 84]
A. Kay, *Computer Software*, Scientific American, Vol. 251, No. 3, September 1984, pp. 52-59.

[Nieper 85]
H. Nieper, *TRISTAN: A Generic Display and Editing System for Hierarchical Structures*, Technical Report, Department of Computer Science, University of Colorado, Boulder, 1985.

[Rathke 86]
C. Rathke, *ObjTalk: Repraesentation von Wissen in einer objektorientierten Sprache*, PhD Dissertation, Universitaet Stuttgart, Fakultaet fuer Mathematik und Informatik, 1986.

[Rathke 87]
C. Rathke, *Human-Computer Communication Meets Software Engineering*, Proceedings of the 9th International Conference on Software Engineering, IEEE, March 1987.

[Simon 81]
H.A. Simon, *The Sciences of the Artificial*, The MIT Press, Cambridge, MA, 1981.

[Swartout, Balzer 82]
W.R. Swartout, R. Balzer, *On the Inevitable Intertwining of Specification and Implementation*, Communications of the ACM, Vol. 25, No. 7, July 1982, pp. 438-439.

[Winograd 79]
T. Winograd, *Beyond Programming Languages*, Communications of the ACM, Vol. 22, No. 7, July 1979, pp. 391-401.

PARIS: A System for Reusing Partially Interpreted Schemas

SHMUEL KATZ[1], CHARLES A. RICHTER, and KHE-SING THE

MCC Software Technology Program

Austin, Texas 78759

Abstract. This paper describes PARIS, an implemented system that facilitates the reuse of partially interpreted schemas. A schema is a program and specification with abstract, or uninterpreted, entities. Different interpretations of those entities will produce different programs. The PARIS System maintains a library of such schemas and provides an interactive mechanism to interpret a schema into a useful program by means of partially automated matching and verification procedures.

Key words and phrases: partially interpreted schemas, reusability, abstract programs, specification and verification, distributed programming, matching problems to specifications, applying automatic theorem proving.

1   Introduction

As the number of large and complicated software systems keeps growing, there is a trend in software development processes towards reusability as applied in other engineering disciplines: a large system consists of a hierarchy of building blocks, and similar components should be reusable once invented. A more concrete objective of reusability in software design is to be able to capture the designer's experience in an artifact, such that building a software component doesn't have to start from scratch over and over again.

The reusability issue (see, e.g. [2]) is particularly significant for distributed software because of the difficulty of inventing correct distributed algorithms. It is desirable to have a system that can store clever and correct algorithms once they are created, and then retrieve them later when they are needed in a design process. This is the primary motivation for building our prototype of a system to formalize and automate the reuse of software components.

The prototype discussed in this paper is a LISP [9] implementation of the software reusability concept described in the article "Partially Interpreted Schemas for CSP Programming" by Baruch and Katz [1]. We chose the name of this system, PARIS, as an acronym of that article's title[2]. This initial prototype provides a partial implementation of the proposed system; it is subject to improvements and refinements before it can serve as a fully practical tool for software designers. Its primary objective is to help us, the implementors, understand some of the difficulties which arise in translating theory to a running system. This is necessary both in order to refine and improve the theory, and to identify ways of overcoming the implementation problems inherent in that theory.

A *partially interpreted schema* is a program that has some portions of it remaining abstract or undefined. These abstract entities can be either program sections or non-program entities such as functions, domains, or variables. For different interpretations of abstract entities in the schema, the results will be different programs performing different functions. In other words, many programs have an identical program skeleton, even though each program behaves differently depending on what "components" are inserted into the skeleton.

Described in greater detail in [8], our system maintains a library of partially interpreted schemas, each of which is stored along with assertions about its applicability and results. When a user presents a problem statement (i.e. description of requirements from a program), the system will search through the library for a possible candidate schema which could potentially satisfy the user's problem statement. If a candidate is found, then its abstract entities must be replaced by concrete entities. The replacement of *non-program* abstract entities can be done in two different manners, as will be explained in Section

---

[1] On leave from the Computer Science Dept., The Technion, Haifa, Israel

---

[2] PARIS also happens to be the name of a city in Texas, the state where MCC is located.

Reviewed and recommended by:

Mark Dowson

2.3. After all abstract entities in the schema have been correctly interpreted, the resulting program is presented to the user.

2 The PARIS System

2.1 Definitions

A partially interpreted program *schema* is syntactically a program or independent module in some programming language, but contains abstract entities such as abstract functions, predicates, constant symbols, unspecified domains or unrealized program parts, each represented by free variables in the *abstract entities set*.

Each schema is accompanied by its *specification*, which includes

1. *Applicability conditions*, defining the restrictions on and requirements for using the schema. They are all assertions involving the required input to the schema, and all other non-program abstract entities of the schema (e.g., restrictions on the possible data types, ranges of parameters, subclasses of functions which can be treated by the schema).

2. *Section conditions*, which are assertions about the program sections which must be substituted for free variables.

3. *Result assertions*, indicating what the schema can achieve. The result assertions can be classified as

   - *postassertions* — which define, in terms of the abstract entities and the input, some conditions that hold after execution of the schema.
   - *invariant-assertions* — claimed to be true throughout the execution of the schema.
   - *liveness claims* — in cases the schema ensures that some events will occur in any program derived from it.

The *presentation* of a schema includes the text of the schema, the abstract entities set, a statement in temporal logic of all aspects of the schema specification, and a proof of correctness of the result assertions of the schema, assuming both the applicability conditions and the section conditions.

A *problem statement* consists of *requirements* about the needed computation and *facts* about the input of the concrete task and about the requirements (mathematical properties, etc.). These may have the same forms allowed for schema specifications, but will not include free variables or undefined functions, as does the schema specification.

The *matching* of a problem statement to a schema and its specification involves: demonstrating a possible substitution of named entities from the problem statement for each non-program abstract entity in the schema and the specification, and showing that (a) the facts of the problem statement imply the schema conditions for that substitution, and (b) when the substitution is made, the result assertions of the schema's specification imply the requirements of the problem statement.

Once the matching has been demonstrated, the *instantiation* of the schema to a solution of a problem statement may occur. This involves first carrying out the above-mentioned substitution, and then supplying program parts which satisfy the appropriate section conditions after the substitution has been done. Supplying the sections of program can either involve a recursive application of the schema methodology, or when the specification is sufficiently straightforward, be done directly. The resulting instance of the schema is a program which is guaranteed to be correct with respect to the problem statement—provided the supplied program parts are correct with respect to the section conditions. In this way the generic proof of the schema can also be instantiated to provide a proof for a specific instance of the schema.

2.2 The Implementation Criteria

The schema library is a list[3] of schema entries. As implied by the above definitions, each schema entry has five components: ENTITY LIST, APPLICABILITY CONDITIONS, RESULT ASSERTIONS, SECTION CONDITIONS, and SCHEMA BODY. We assume that the system and the user agree upon the vocabulary and syntax of how a schema entry is defined. At the present time, we have not yet specified exactly which keywords are contained in the vocabulary and what is the definition of each keyword, but the keyword library is extendable and the keywords we have so far defined are sufficient for the examples in the schema library.

The ENTITY LIST includes all abstract entities used in a schema. The entities will be interpreted based on the problem statement. Restrictions on the concrete entities which may be substituted for non-program abstract entities are listed in the APPLICABILITY CONDITIONS. The result of executing the schema (provided that all applicability conditions are satisfied) will satisfy the temporal logic assertions in the RESULT ASSERTIONS. The SECTION CONDITIONS contains specifications for each required program section; the specifications will be presented to the user so he/she can supply the program sections accordingly.

The SCHEMA BODY is a list of strings and atoms: constant parts of the schema are represented as strings and abstract entities as atoms. Eventually, these atoms will be

---

[3]Familiarity with basic LISPlike notations is assumed.

interpreted, either by replacing all of them with concrete entities or leaving some of them unspecified, and then all elements of the list are concatenated together to form a long string, which is the resulting program.

The most difficult questions for partially interpreted schemas involve the abstract and concrete specifications, as part of the presentation of a schema and of a concrete problem statement. The representation of an abstract specification, the problem statement and the match between them are crucial to the usability of the system. The philosophy adopted here is to be semi-interactive. This means that the user is to be protected as much as we are able from the inner workings, representations, and decision procedures of the system. However, when the automatic tools are inadequate, the user is to be consulted in as clear a manner as possible.

In order to avoid over-consultation, we required that the system interact with a theorem prover. Thus, the PARIS System uses the Boyer-Moore Theorem Prover [3] as a subsystem. Potentially, PARIS should "protect" the user from the vagaries of the Theorem Prover, and much work can be done in this direction. In the theoretical description of partially interpreted schemas [1], any temporal logic assertion can be part of a specification, as well as any quantified predicate as a precondition, postcondition, or invariant. In order to achieve matching, we need to check whether one such assertion implies another. Clearly, the full implications of temporal formulae could not be treated. Even more significantly, quantification is explicitly excluded by the Boyer-Moore system.

As an attempted solution, we use a keyword approach. The hypothesis underlying the approach is that there is a reasonable number of English words which will appear uninterpreted as far as the system is concerned but will be used for matching. Thus no general definitional facility such as algebraic specification is used. So far, keywords from three categories have been identified: domains (or abstract data types), mathematical properties, and specification operators. In the first category are terms such as *domain, integer, real, function, set, programsection, numberofarguments, numberofprocesses, givenvalue*; in the second, terms such as *associative, commutative, nonnegative, nonempty*; while the specification related terms include *eventually, always, invariant, terminated, forall, forsome, precondition, postcondition* [4]. The way in which these terms can be presented to the Theorem Prover are explained in [3].

In the specifications we have considered, both the quantification and use of temporal operators is very limited, and thus amenable to partial treatment by the Theorem Prover. Nevertheless, the potential user of the system as presently implemented, must present his/her problem

---

[4]Some of these keywords are modified in PARIS' current version to avoid confusion with the built-in functions of Franz LISP.

statement in a form which is similar to the abstract specification of the appropriate schema, or rely on the linear shopping list presentation of each schema specification as explained below. In a full implementation, with a large schema library, it would be reasonable to select classes of relevant schemas by only one or two properties. Although the system has only been demonstrated for CSP [7] schemas, in fact any language or computational model could be used, and the schemas could be divided into categories such as sequential, functional, parallel shared memory, distributed message passing, CSP, Raddle[6], etc. Another natural category would be the type of specification (e.g., functional, invariant property, etc.). Use of descriptive names for the schemas (e.g., *scheduler, queue, mutual-exclusion*) should also help the user select likely candidates. Note that none of these aids in the preliminary matching should replace the eventual check for a true match, which is essential to prevent misunderstandings of the potential applicability of a schema.

An extension in which use of the Theorem Prover could be restricted, called "problem statement by interrogation," could be incorporated into later versions of PARIS. In that mode, once a potential schema has been selected by a few basic criteria, the system would interrogate the user in order to internally construct a problem statement similar in form to the schema specification.

2.3 From Abstract Specification to Concrete Program

In this section, we first describe a typical PARIS session of producing a program from a problem statement by interpreting the abstract entities, then we go over the details of its system organization to get an overview about how the functionalities are achieved. Here we assume that the schemas have been correctly presented to the schema library, i.e., that a generic proof has been (or could be) devised to show that if the abstract entities are correctly instantiated, and program sections provided satisfying the section conditions, the result is guaranteed to satisfy the instantiated result assertions. Heuristics for developing schemas from specific instances of sequential programs may be found in [5].

To start a PARIS session, the user has to input a problem statement. A problem statement consists of three components: an ENTITY LIST, APPLICABILITY CONDITIONS, and RESULT ASSERTIONS. These three components look similar to, and have the same syntax as, the first three components of a schema entry in the library, except that they contain no abstract entities.

After a problem statement has been correctly specified, PARIS searches the schema library to find a possible candidate. If a candidate is found, then the interpretation of abstract entities is initiated. The interpretation is done in two stages: the non-program abstract entities

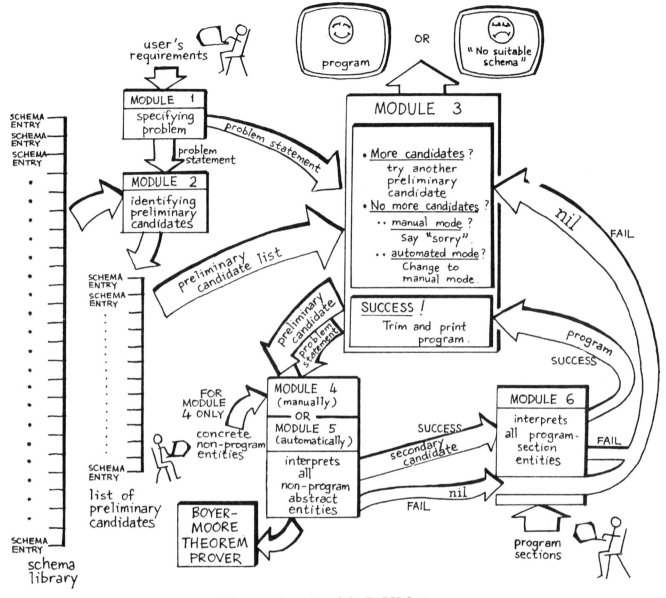

Figure 1: Overview of the PARIS System

are first interpreted and then the abstract program sections are interpreted. The replacement of **non-program** abstract entities can be done in two different manners: manual matching and automated matching, as discussed in the following two paragraphs.

If *manual* matching mode (also called *shopping list* mode) is selected to interpret the non-program abstract entities, then the system will present all possible candidates until the user chooses one or it fails to find another candidate. When a schema is presented, the user will decide whether to take it and supply all matching non-program entities, or to try another candidate. After

all non-program abstract entities have been replaced, and before the system prompts for entering program sections, the user has an option to ask the Theorem Prover to verify whether the choice and matchings satisfy the requirements of the problem statement.

If *automated* matching mode is selected, the system matches each non-program abstract entity in the schema with a concrete entity mentioned in the problem statement and invokes the Boyer-Moore Theorem Prover to carry out the verification. If the system finds a schema that satisfies the problem statement, then it will return a partially substituted schema (with all non-program abstract entities automatically replaced with concrete instances) and expect the user to fill in the program sections. On the other hand, if it fails to find one, the user will be informed about this situation.

In both matching modes, the preliminary matching (of non-program entities) is considered successful when the system displays section conditions and requires the user to input program sections. This insertion procedure is repeated until all abstract programs have been interpreted. In the current version, the replacement of **program section** abstract entities is done by the user manually supplying lines of code when the system displays conditions about a particular program section. At least theoretically by using the window manager, the user can suspend the activation, and recursively use the PARIS system to satisfy the section conditions from the schema library.

However, if the user fails to supply a program section, then PARIS will assume that the user can't correctly interpret the abstract program; hence, the schema will be incompletely interpreted and thus aborted; PARIS will then explore another possible candidate. The system displays the resulting program after all program section abstract entities have been correctly interpreted.

The approximately 70 LISP functions of the PARIS system can be grouped into six modules, whose interrelations are informally shown in Figure 1. The six modules can be summarized as follows:

Module 1. Specifying the problem: representing the user's requirements in a form understood by PARIS. The purpose of this module is to acquire a problem from the user and put it in an internal form understood by the other modules.

Module 2. Identifying the candidates: narrowing the choice by excluding irrelevant schemas. When the system encounters a problem statement, it builds a corresponding candidate list. Each schema entry (*preliminary candidate*) in the candidate list will be interpreted until either (i) a preliminary candidate is successfully constructed to be a program, or (ii) there are no more schema entries left in the candidate list. A schema entry in the library is included in this list iff the set of entities of the problem statement is a subset of the set of entities of the schema entry, considering the type declarations.

Module 3. Coordinating other modules: based on the requirements specified in the result of module 1, trying to build a program by interpreting candidates in the result of module 2. Interpretation of a candidate consists of two stages: matching of non-program abstract entities (either module 4 for manual mode or module 5 for automated mode) and insertion of program sections (module 6).

Module 4. Interpreting non-program entities— manual mode: interactive communication with the user to interpret non-program abstract entities.

After the manual matching is done, the user has the option of having the matchings checked by the Theorem Prover. However, if the Theorem Prover fails, the user can still override its result.

Module 5. Interpreting non-program entities— automated mode: permuting the abstract entity list to generate different matching instances of non-program entities, and invoking the Boyer-Moore Theorem Prover to verify every matching instance.

When an instance of the permutation is generated, the Theorem Prover is invoked to determine whether this matching of non-program entities will successfully build a *secondary candidate*. If it returns **true**, then the matching is used to substitute all non-program abstract entities, otherwise another instance of the permutation will be generated. The automated matching fails if none of the permutation instances causes the Theorem Prover to return **true**.

If all of the preliminary candidates fail to go through the automated matching, the user has an option to initiate a manual matching process.

Module 6. Inserting program sections: interactive communication with the user to interpret abstract program sections. This module interacts with the user to insert program sections into a secondary candidate (which was built from a preliminary candidate by having all of its non-program abstract entities interpreted).

If it detects that the user fails to supply a program section, the current candidate is aborted. When all program sections in a secondary candidate have been successfully interpreted, the result is the final program.

3 Examples of Schemas

3.1 A Schema for Linked List Insertion

The first example illustrates the specifications of a schema by means of a C program that inserts a new list node into a totally ordered linked list. A node in the list contains two fields: *next* and *data*. Next is the pointer to the next node and *data* is the value (which might be a complicated data structure) of the current node. The functions *leq*, *equal*, and f define a total ordering of the list nodes. The domain of function f is the set of possible data of list nodes and its range is the set of values for which the ordering of the predicate *leq* is defined. To maintain the ordering of the nodes in a list, both the applicability conditions and result assertions state that the list is ordered. The relation *equal* tests that two elements of $D1$ are identical.

The entity list contains all abstract entities, which will be replaced by concrete entities when the schema is interpreted. The applicability conditions impose some conditions on the functions and the requirement that the linked list should be ordered before an insertion is performed. The result assertions indicate that after the insertion is done, the list is ordered and the new node is inserted in the proper place.

The program section $S1$ assigns the value of inserted data to the allocated memory space. The assignment operation is abstracted because it may be in different forms based on the data structure of the data. The main program, which is another independent module, should satisfy the invariant that the list is ordered. It is left implicit that after an insertion is done, the list contains all the nodes it had before the insertion was done. The quantifications below relate to all nodes in the list.

The abstracted schema of the insertion module is shown below. Note that the user of such a schema need not understand the code of the schema body itself, as long as his/her instantiations of the abstract entities satisfy the specifications.

ENTITY LIST:
> function f
> function leq
> function $equal$
> domain $D1$, $D2$
> variable $data : D1$
> variable $newdata : D1$
> structure $node : D1 \times \textbf{pointer}(node)$
> programsec $S1$

APPLICABILITY CONDITIONS:
> $f : D1 \rightarrow D2$
> $leq : D2 \times D2 \rightarrow$ boolean
> $equal : D1 \times D1 \rightarrow$ boolean
> $\forall n : n \in node : n{-}{>}next \neq$ NULL $\Rightarrow$
> $\qquad leq(f(n{-}{>}data), f((n{-}{>}next){-}{>}data))$

RESULT ASSERTIONS:
> $[\ \exists n : n \in node : equal(n{-}{>}data, newdata)\ ] \wedge$
> $[\ \forall n : n \in node : n{-}{>}next \neq$ NULL $\Rightarrow$
> $\qquad leq(f(n{-}{>}data), f((n{-}{>}next){-}{>}data))\ ]$

SECTION CONDITIONS:
$S1$:   precondition: true
>   postcondition: $equal(new{-}{>}data, newdata)$

SCHEMA BODY:

```
struct node {struct node *next;
                 D1 data;}

insert(listhead, newdata)
struct node *listhead;
D1 newdata;
{
    struct    node *p, *q, *new;

    new = malloc (sizeof (struct node));

    /* assign newdata to new->data */
    S1
    if (listhead == NULL)
    {
        listhead = new;
        listhead->next = NULL;
    }
    else if ( leq(f(new),f(listhead)) )
    {
        new->next = listhead;
        listhead = new;
    }
    else
    {
        p = listhead;
        q = listhead->next;
        while ( !leq(f(new),f(q)) && q != NULL )
        {
            p = q;
            q = q->next;
        }
        p->next = new;
        new->next = q;
    }
}
```

This schema can be easily instantiated to handle different data types of the list nodes specified by $D1$. For example, if $D1$ is integer, then f will be the identity function and leq and $equal$ will be <= and ==, respectively; the assignment in $S1$ will be =. If $D1$ is character string (char* in C jargon), then the functions f, leq and $equal$ can be based on the C library string manipulation functions; and the assignment in $S1$ is simply the C library function strcpy. The three functions and the program section can also be "custom-made" to cope with more complicated data structures as the need arises.

3.2   A Distributed Snapshot Schema

We now look at a variant of a schema for the distributed snapshot algorithm of Chandy and Lamport [4]. In this algorithm, processes cooperate to detect global stable properties—that is, properties that, once they hold, continue to hold. A single communication skeleton will suffice to detect any kind of stable property. Therefore, we want a schema in which the basic communication skeleton is concrete, while the portion that detects the particular stable property is abstract.

We assume asynchronous message passing. To express the schema, we use a notation with nonblocking sends. A send is written "*send* (m, i)", meaning send message m to process i (along the appropriate outgoing channel). Receives are of the form "*receive* (m, i)", meaning receive message in m from a process, the identity of which is placed in variable i. We also use guarded commands, denoted by "*guard* $\rightarrow$ *action*". In each process i, "*channel_from* (j)" is true iff i has an incoming channel from process j, while "*channel_to* (j)" is true iff i has an outgoing channel to j. The number of incoming channels of the process is *innumber*. We assume there is at most one channel from any process i to another process j and that the channels are *fifo*.

To simplify this exposition, we assume the designation of an initiator—that is, when the schema is instantiated, one process is designated as the one which will initiate the detection algorithm. A more general (and complicated) schema would permit the dynamic selection of an initiator. We also restrict the algorithm to the detection of boolean conditions; the schema could be expanded to include an abstract domain for the stable property.

The schema given here will set local indicators to reflect a consistent global state. However, in order to actually determine the truth of the global predicate P, the values of the local indicators must be gathered together to a single process, using an additional schema. The global state satisfies $at(begin)$ when the schema is initiated, and $at(end)$ when $innumber = c$ for all the processes.

The entity list must include the abstract parts of the schema, namely:

- n is the the number of processes;
- 1 through n are processes;
- $S1$, $S2$, $S3$, $S4$, and $S5$ are program sections; and
- P and P_1 through P_n are predicates.
- p_1 through p_n are local variables (called *indicators*).

The applicability conditions are that:

- we have some global stable property, P;
- we have local properties P_1 through P_n;
- if the channels are empty and properties P_1 through P_n all hold in a global state, then P holds;
- communication is fair (i.e., that any message sent is eventually received).

The result assertions are that:

- if all local indicators p_1 through p_n hold at the end of the algorithm, then P also holds at that time,

- if P holds at the beginning of the algorithm, then the local indicators p_1 through p_n all hold at the end of the algorithm.

Our schema for the snapshot algorithm is:

ENTITY LIST:
   numproc n
   process $1 \cdots n$
   programsec $S1, S2, S3, S4, S5$
   predicate $P, P_1, \cdots, P_n$
   variable $p_1, \cdots, p_n$: local indicators

APPLICABILITY CONDITIONS:
   global P
   stable P
   local $P_1 \cdots P_n$
   (empty channels) $\wedge P_1 \wedge \cdots \wedge P_n \Rightarrow P$
   $\Box (\forall i, j (send_i(m, j) \Rightarrow \Diamond receive_j(m, i)))$

RESULT ASSERTIONS:
   $at(\text{end}) \wedge p_1 \wedge \cdots \wedge p_n \Rightarrow P$
   $at(begin) \wedge P \Rightarrow \Diamond at(end) \wedge p_1 \wedge \cdots \wedge p_n$

SECTION CONDITIONS:

$S1$ "boolean condition that, when it evaluates to true, causes the initiator to initiate the snapshot"

$S2$ "boolean expression within each process to detect the local property, P_i, in that process"

$S3$ "body of function that, given p, the current value of the local indicator for P_i, and m, a message that was received, determines the new value of local property P_i and assigns to *new_p*"

$S4$ "the desired action on the receipt of an incoming message (must NOT contain any receives)"

$S5$ "the non-receive code for the process, in the form of (*guard* $\rightarrow$ *action*)* (this code must NOT contain any receives)"

SCHEMA BODY:

```
process 1 ::   { the initiator }
   var p: boolean,
       c: integer,
       m: message,
       marker_recd: array [n] of boolean;
   const marker = "marker"; { the value of a marker }

   begin
      S1 -->
         p := S2; { detect whether local property Pi
                    holds }
         forall j (channel_from (j))
            marker_recd [j] := false;
         forall j (channel_to (j)) send (marker, j);
         c := 0; { count of markers received }
```

```
    receive (marker, j) -->
      { received marker from j }
      if not marker_recd [j] then
        marker_recd [j] := true;
        c := c + 1;
      fi;

    receive (m, j) ^ (m <> marker) -->
      if (c <> 0) ^ not marker_recd [j] then
        p := new_p (p, m);  { compute new value in
                              terms of old, message }
      fi;
      S4

    S5
  end;

process (i: 2 to n) ::   { the non-initiators }
  var p: boolean,
      c: integer := 0,
      m: message,
      marker_recd : array [n] of boolean;
  const marker = "marker";  { the value of a marker }

  begin
    receive (marker, j) ^ (c = 0) -->
      { received first marker }
      marker_recd [j] := true;
      p := S2;  { detect whether the local property
                  Pi holds }
      forall k (channel_to (k)) send (marker, k);
        { send a marker on all outgoing channels }
      forall k (channel_from (k) ^ (k <> j))
          marker_recd [k] := false;
      c := 1;

    receive (marker, j) ^ (c <> 0) -->
      if not marker_recd [j] then
        marker_recd [j] := true;
        c := c + 1;
      fi;

    receive (m, j) ^ (m <> marker) -->
      if (c <> 0) ^ not marker_recd [j] then
        p := new_p (p, m);  { compute new value in
                              terms of old, message }
      fi;
      S4

    S5
  end;

function new_p (p: boolean, m: message);
  begin
    S3
  end;

(1 || .. || n)
```

Note that, unlike those for the previous example, the section conditions for this particular schema are informal.

Let us consider instantiating the schema to determine whether all tokens in the system have disappeared. In other words, we want to detect the local condition, "there are no tokens in this process". Section condition $S1$ would be the condition that would cause the distinguished process to initiate the snapshot. $S2$ would be the code

in each process to determine whether any tokens resided in that process. $S3$ would be the body of a function to determine if an incoming message contained a token. $S4$ and $S5$ would be the regular code to handle receives and non-receives, respectively.

This example illustrates one of the problems with PARIS schemas: there is no easy way to deal with schemas when the schema code interleaves with the user-supplied code. In this example, for instance, we must prevent the user from adding his own receives, as we must intercept all receives along a channel after we take a local snapshot and before we receive a marker along that channel. One of the authors is currently investigating "superimposition", a means of interleaving code.

4 Concluding Remarks and Future Developments

Our experience in building the PARIS prototype indicates that transforming abstract logic expressions into precise implementational definitions is quite difficult. It is a non-trivial task to construct a system that is able to provide a friendly interface to the user and at the same time produce correct and efficient input to the theorem proving mechanism. Preparing a large schema is also a formidable challenge. As suggested in section 2.2, the practicality of use of a large-scale schema system depends upon the ability to quickly identify a subclass of schemas that might be relevant to a problem statement. Database techniques using keywords to identify the computational model, language, and intuitive role of the schema should be adequate for this task. A larger scale in itself therefore does not seem to pose a fundamental difficulty, but would require significant resources for its preparation.

In summary, to make this prototype really work to help software designers, it should be extended in the following directions:

- Adding more schemas into the library, for a variety of computational models.

- Classifying all schemas within the library to increase searching efficiency.

- Defining additional keywords in the system's vocabulary.

- Developing a user-friendly interface to add more convenience for the user to specify his/her problem statement and to provide more interactive communication during the process of matching and verification. In particular, when the Theorem Prover fails to prove one of the two implications needed for a successful matching, the user should not have to be an expert in automatic theorem proving in order to understand the reason for the failure.

- Augmenting the Theorem Prover with facts in the problem domain of the schemas, especially with facts about temporal logic assertions.

Despite the outlined problems and the remaining obstacles, using the system does provide (provably) correct programs, without burdening the average user with problems of proving the correctness of programs. It thus provides a first step towards automated reusability, short of program synthesis.

Acknowledgments. The authors would like to thank Les Belady, Ted Biggerstaff, Ira Forman, and Jim Peterson of the MCC Software Technology Program for their comments and suggestions; and also Chua-Huang Huang and Warren Hunt of the Dept. of Computer Sciences, The Univ. of Texas at Austin, for their efforts to get the authors acquainted with the Boyer-Moore Theorem Prover.

References

[1] O. BARUCH AND S. KATZ, "Partially interpreted schemas for CSP programming," Computer Science Dept., The Technion, Israel Inst. of Tech., Haifa, Israel, 1985.

[2] T. J. BIGGERSTAFF AND A. J. PERLIS, editors. Special issue on software reusability. *IEEE Trans. Software Eng.*, vol. SE-10, pp. 474–609, Sep. 1984.

[3] R. S. BOYER AND J S. MOORE, *A Computational Logic*. New York: Academic Press, 1979.

[4] K. M. CHANDY AND L. LAMPORT, "Distributed snapshots: determining global states of distributed systems," *ACM Trans. Comput. Syst.*, vol. 3, pp. 63–75, Feb. 1985.

[5] N. DERSHOWITZ, "Program abstraction and instantiation," *ACM TOPLAS*, vol. 7, pp. 446–477, July 1985.

[6] I. FORMAN, "On the design of large distributed systems," *Proc. International Conf. Comput. Lang.*, Miami Beach, FL, Oct. 1986.

[7] C. A. R. HOARE, "Communicating Sequential Processes," *Comm. ACM*, vol. 21, pp. 666–677, Aug. 1978.

[8] S. KATZ AND K. THE, "A preliminary report on the PARIS System: an implementation of software reusability concepts," MCC Technical Report *STP-114-85*, Oct. 1985.

[9] R. WILENSKY, *LISPcraft*. New York: W. W. Norton, 1984.

Domain-Specific Reuse:
An Object-Oriented and Knowledge-Based Approach

Neil Iscoe
University of Texas

Research Summary

Problem Statement

Although most would agree that a combination of programming knowledge and application knowledge is required to automate the construction of application programs, there is not yet agreement as to how to model an application domain. The problem is to create a model for domain knowledge that is general enough to be instantiated in several domains and expressive enough to specify and generate application programs. This model will then be used to build a meta-generation system that when instantiated for a particular domain can automate some of the aspects of application programming for that domain. Our research focuses on the aspects of the model related to program specification.

Expected Result

We are creating a system for gathering specifications and generating application programs within specific domains. The system will depend upon certain types of application domain knowledge. A model for representing this knowledge will be partially formalized, and portions of a methodology for gathering this information will be developed. The goal is to advance the basic groundwork for a meta-system—a program that after being instantiated with domain knowledge will allow persons who are neither computer programmers nor domain experts, but who are familiar with a domain, to declaratively specify, implement, and modify application programs within that domain. Characteristics and traits of domain knowledge that generalize across domains will be identified as will the algorithms and techniques that can be used to leverage this information across domains.

Conceptual Foundations

The research draws from several related areas. The model of application domain knowledge begins with an object-oriented view of the world. We assume that most of the critical domain knowledge within the target range of application domains can be represented by domain objects and the operations performed upon those objects. Scaling theory, a well defined mathematical system used for classification in other fields, forms the basis to characterize real world object attributes. Scales are the major mechanism used to retain the application knowledge usually lost in the mapping from user specification to hardware implementation. Transformation systems form the basis of the mapping from high-level user specifications to primitives that can be executed by a type-manager.

Research Approach

After completing the creation of the underlying model, a system will be implemented in enough detail to be instantiated in at least two domains. The implementation is intended to be sufficient to serve as a vehicle for successively refining the model as well as to provide a means for comparison of the similarities and differences between the knowledge required for the domain instantiations.

This article is a revised and updated description of current research. Portions of this paper appeared in "A Knowledge-Based and Object-Oriented Approach to Reusability Within Application Domains," Proceedings of the Workshop on Software Reuse, October 1987.
© Neil Iscoe, 1988. Reprinted with permission of author.
Electronic mail address: iscoe@cs.utexas.edu
US mail address: Department of Computer Sciences, University of Texas, Austin, TX 78712

Introduction

This paper describes our research into creating a model of application domain knowledge for the purpose of specifying and generating programs. We begin by describing three reasons why a model of domain knowledge is needed:

- The Mapping Process Is Hard To Control
- Requirements and Specifications are Difficult To Gather
- Requirements and Specifications Change

The paper then describes our research goals and the plan for achieving those goals. The model is outlined within the context of the plan, and certain salient aspects of the plan are explained. The paper concludes with a review of the related work in this area.

The Mapping Process Is Hard To Control

Creating an application program is a process that begins with a person's conception of an imagined program, and ends with a binary representation of information that can be executed by a machine. This mapping process can be viewed as beginning with a set of requirements and ending with a composition of primitive operations. Producing a successful mapping is a process that is intrinsically difficult, usually iterative, and often never terminates. Furthermore, the stages of the process tend to blur as decisions made in the various stages of implementation inevitably effect and change the original specifications [Swartout 82].

Requirements & Specification

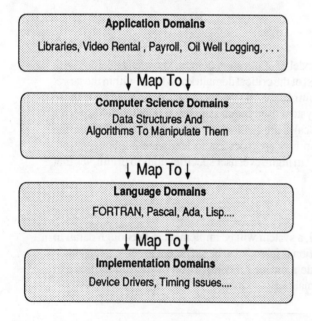

Implementation

Figure 1 - Mapping Requirements To Implementation

Figure 1 shows a view of the mapping process as it progresses from requirements and specifications expressed in terms of an application domain through computer science and programming language domains to a final level of implementation. While the figure is a rough abstraction, it provides an outline to which we will refer in future sections of this paper.

Application Programming

Creating application programs within well understood domains is a *programming in the small* process that can be accomplished by people who understand both programming and a specific application domain. Although, there is a general belief [Neighbors 84], [Barstow 84], [Adelson 85], [Prieto-Diaz 87], that knowledge of a domain is a prerequisite to being able to write good programs within that domain, the specificity of this knowledge means that it in addition to learning programming, programmers must often spend years learning the characteristics of a particular domain [Curtis 88]. This knowledge is used to build application programs, but is rarely codified in a way that allows it to be *well understood* enough to be reused by others.

Even when a domain is well understood, application programming is a difficult process that extends into the real world of human computer users. Most real world domains are neither well defined nor clearly bounded and consequently large amounts of effort are required to elicit and clarify the users image of an application program. While today's professional programmer is more likely than his or her predecessor to be able to construct and verify the correctness of a particular section of code, the gathering and refining of the specifications for that piece of code is still a black art—a skill that is not yet well enough understood to automate or even formalize.

Automating the Mapping

Information about each of the domain levels is normally lost between mappings because the information needs of each domain result in different representations. The lack of a formal model to represent information at the application domain level results in a severe information loss during the mapping process. Consequently, our focus is on modelling application domains which are shown at the top of figure 1.

Because one of our goals is to remove the application programmer from specific application programming tasks, this area of research is sometimes referred to as automatic programming, which [Barstow 84] explains as a, "*system [that] allows a computationally naive user to describe problems using the natural terms and concepts of a domain, with informality, and imprecision, and omission of the system details.*" Consequently, "... "*a primary goal of automatic programming research should be the development of a model of domain-specific programming and techniques for building domain-specific automatic programming systems.*"

It is interesting to look at the use of the term *automatic programming* as presented from a figure in the 1958 CACM. In Figure 2, FORTRAN is listed as the highest level automatic programming system then available.

Adapted from: *Communications of the ACM,*
Volume 1, #4, April 1958

Automatic Programming Systems		
Computer	In Library	Do not have
704	AFAC, CAGE FORTRAN, NYAP, PACT LA REG-SYMBOLIC SAP	ADES FORC KOMPILER 3

•
•
•

from Rich and Waters, *AI and Software Engineering,* 1986, p. xi.

Figure 2 - Automatic Programming 30 Years Ago

How has the view of automatic programming changed over the last 30 years? Through the development of programming languages, computer science has given programmers progressively better tools with which they can map their understanding of program specifications more directly to the computer by using high level constructs instead of machine specific operation codes.

The first step in automating programming was the development of assemblers that could assist in the task of composing these operation codes. Compilers immediately followed assemblers, and were viewed by many as an interesting, though originally inefficient, scheme for allowing programmers to work at a higher level of abstraction than is possible with assembly language. The construction of early compilers was ad hoc, but researchers have changed the construction process from a craft to a science, and have directed research towards specific subjects such as grammar types, parser construction, code optimization and so on. By separating the concerns of compiler construction from the issues of language design, the computer science community has been able to proceed with investigations into substantive language issues without usually having to carry the baggage of compiler or interpreter design. But even as languages reach to higher and higher levels, as [Smoliar 83] points out, "no matter how high the level, it's still programming."

Users Must Create Their Own Programs

Users must begin to directly create and maintain their own programs because it is unreasonable to expect that there will ever be enough professional programmers to meet the continually increasing demands for software. The problem is somewhat analogous to the difficulties that occurred with the proliferation of telephones during the early part of this century; it was predicted that if the telephone growth rate continued, eventually every man, woman, and child in the United States would have to become a telephone operator. And of course everyone eventually did. Networking technology eliminated the need for patch boards by solving the procedural

aspects of call routing, but placed the burden of declarative specification (i.e. specifying a phone number to be called) on the enduser. A similar solution to the problem of creating and maintaining complete programs within well understood application is both necessary and achievable.

Application Domain Knowledge

Software designers implicitly use and reuse application domain knowledge to prevent specification errors, and it is the absence of this knowledge that allows many types of errors to occur. But, what is application domain knowledge? How can it be represented? What kind of errors can it prevent? How can it help in the design and construction of application programs? This paper outlines an approach to answering portions of these questions.

Specifications Are Difficult To Gather

The failure to capture domain knowledge results in a variety of different problems in the creation of specifications. Examples of some of these problems are given in the remainder of this section, and are summarized as follows:

- An inadequate understanding of the mapping between specifications and code.
- The failure to recognize errors in specifications.
- Misunderstanding of terms that are operationally defined within a particular domain.
- The difficulty of communicating with the people who are going to be using the system.
- An insufficient understanding of the implementation level resource tradeoffs that are inherent in a specification.

Specification Errors Result From A Lack of Domain Knowledge

Problems result when a programmer neglects to acquire enough domain experience. One modern software engineering tale concerns the navigational system of the F-16 fighter plane. In this story, an F-16 flipped 180 degrees during a simulation of a routine flight from the Northern to the Southern Hemisphere. The behavior happened at the equator, where the plane's navigational gear observed that the previously decreasing latitudes were now increasing, and flipped the plane accordingly.

What is it about the specification that caused, or failed to prevent, this mistake? Assuming that if the plane hadn't crossed the equator that there wouldn't have been a problem, the error was caused by the failure of the programmer to recognize that there are no negative latitudes. This might have been caused by the programmer visualizing the world as mapped to a Cartesian Coordinate Plane where the y-axis was latitude, and a latitude of zero represented a position at the bottom of the map. Other interpretations are possible, but the consistent point is that errors can result when domain knowledge is lost in the mapping process.

Reasonable Constraints Are Often Wrong

The next example illustrates a subtle problem of the dangers of believing specifications as they are given without using a broader domain-knowledge view to interpret those specifications. The following two constraints are taken from the statement of the definition of a library system [Kemmerer 85]:

Constraint 1
All copies in the library must be available for checkout or be checked out.
Constraint 2
No copy of the book may be both available and checked out at the same time.

These constraints seem reasonable, and when axiomatized in a specification system such as Larch [Wing 87], allow theorems such as the following to be proved:

If a book is not checked out and is not available, then it is not a library book at all :
(~checkedOut(l,b) ∧ ~available(l,b)) —> b ∉ allBooks(l)

But books that have been lost, or stolen, or damaged, can violate constraint 1. In our view, the specification is wrong because it was based on a library model where critical knowledge about the domain was not captured. Consequently proofs based on this constraint, while correct within the bounds of the proof system, are results that would not be acceptable for librarians.

Our concern is with the levels of the application domain that map to the real world. We believe that a formal model of a library application domain would prevent errors such as these, and are concerned with creating a model of an application domain that will avoid, among other problems, specification errors of the type demonstrated above.

Terms Are Ambiguous Without A Domain Context

The following example of a specification problem concerns the ambiguity of simple terms without clarification by domain-specific use.

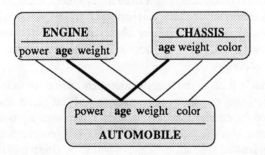

Figure 3 - Determining the Age of an Automobile

In figure 3, an engine has a power rating, an age, and a weight. A chassis also has an age and a weight, but does not have power and does have a color. Clearly, an automobile should have at least the properties *Power* (inherited from

Engine), and *Color* (inherited from Chassis). But what about *Weight* and *Age*? Assuming that the ages of *Engine*, *Body*, and *Automobile* are all measured in the same unit (say years), *automobile.age* could be calculated in at least the ways shown in figure 4.

Average_component_age
automobile.age := (engine.age + chassis.age)/2

Sum_of_component_ages
automobile.age := engine.age + chassis.age

Age_of_oldest_component
automobile.age := max(engine.age, chassis.age)

Ages_of_components
automobile.age :=set of {engine.age, chassis.age}

Age_since_manufacture
automobile.age := current_date - Automobile.create_date

Figure 4 - Some Interpretations of Age of a Car

Within the domain of car buyers, most people would say that automobile age would best be calculated by the *Age_since_manufacture* operation that uses the date that items are assembled to form the basis for the age. But what about other domains? For example, the following are all reasonable criteria for engine age in the domain of engine repair:

- Age of automobile engines is measured in miles .
- Age of automobile engines is measured in years.
- Age of boat and airplane engines is measured in hours.

Domain knowledge is used to answer this potentially ambiguous question about the age of an engine. This is one of the types of information, normally lost in the creation of an application program, that we will capture in our model.

Requirements and Specifications Change

Finally, requirements change. Even when requirements and specifications are correctly gathered, refined, and then transformed correctly into executable code, the nature of most real world applications is that requirements and specifications mutate throughout the existence of a program. These modifications are neither caused by the sometimes mercurial nature of endusers nor by sloppiness in the original design process, but are the result of natural occurrences such as workload modifications, environmental changes, new technologies, economic disturbances, legal mandates, and so on that remove old requirements and create new ones.

Automating the transformational mapping of specifications to code, and allowing the full program specification to be stored in terms of the domain will mean that users can change specifications and then regenerate their application program.

The Research

Figure 5 shows the research from the perspective of domain mappings. The box labeled current *research* represents the development of a model that will be instantiated in two domains. The ovals represent possible instantiations, and indicate that our results should generalize to more than just the instantiated domains. The *vertical integration* rectangle is part of the program generation paradigm, but is not the subject of this research. The remainder of this section details the research goals and the plan for achieving those goals.

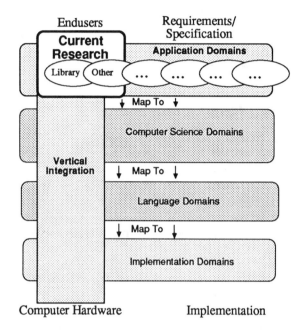

Figure 5 - Instantiations in Multiple Domains

Research Goals

The long-term research goal is to develop and partially formalize a development paradigm for application programming—an approach that will allow application designers who are neither computer programmers nor domain experts, to construct application programs by interactively and declaratively describing and refining the specifications for the program that they wish to construct. Application designers will vary in technical sophistication. We use the term to distinguish them from experts who are presumed to have an all encompassing view of the domain, and from endusers who are the class of users at the end of the development chain.

Specifically, the goals of the research are as follows:

• *The development and partial formalization of a paradigm for domain-specific application programming.*

    A System (Ozym[1]) that when instantiated with domain knowledge will allow application designers, who are neither computer programmers nor domain experts, to construct application programs by interactively describing and refining declarative specifications.

• *The creation of a model that is capable of capturing the*

relevant application domain knowledge necessary for the paradigm.

    General enough to be instantiated in several different domains.

    Expressive enough to be used and manipulated by application designers.

• *A detailed analysis and comparison of the instantiations of two different domains.*

    Identification of characteristics and traits that generalize across domains.

    Identification of algorithms and techniques that can be used across a class of domains.

The research is dedicated to finding a model powerful enough to capture those elements that constitute application programming domain knowledge, general enough that it could be instantiated in several different domains, and expressive enough to be used and manipulated by endusers. In the tradition of EMYCIN [van Melle 81], we plan to create and implement a model that can be instantiated in different domains by loading it with knowledge about those domains. Endusers will then be able to declaratively specify application programs in terms that both they and the machine will understand. Due to the system's knowledge about the application domain, it will be able to assist the enduser in constructive design of an application program and then convert that design into a composition of primitives that can be executed by a type manager.

After two different domain instantiations have been performed, we will analyze and compare the instantiations and attempt to generalize this information. Ideally, we will be able to begin to make the kind of high level characterizations about our model and domain-specific programming that researchers have been able to make about rule-based heuristic classification [Clancey 85]. Figure 6 shows a block diagram of the solution paradigm and Figure 7 refines this diagram to show individual components of the system.

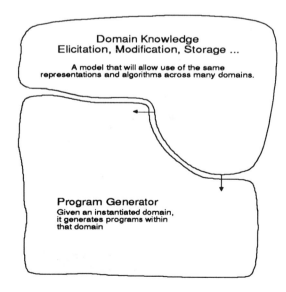

Figure 6 - The Solution Paradigm

Figure 7 can be viewed in several different ways. The darker blocks at the bottom (application specifications, transformation system, computer system) represent a program generation system. Given a set of application specifications, a transformation system can create a composition of primitive functions that can be executed by a type manager that operates within a computer system. This portion of the system completes the mapping from the application domain to the executable code.

Although we are interested in producing executable code, the research is not concerned with the mapping problem except insofar as to carry out the appropriate steps of the following research plan. Instead, the emphasis is on the top portion of figures 6 and 7. In particular, the major focus is on the model for representing domain knowledge. Domain instantiations are performed by a domain expert who loads a system with application domain knowledge. An application designer then uses a specialized version of the editor to produce program specifications that are then transformed into executable code.

Programming-in-the-large problems will not be considered. Programming-in-the-large problems are generally poorly defined, cover a number of domains, and have a host of other problems which exclude them from consideration. (see [Brooks 75], [Wegner 84], [Brooks 87], [Curtis 87] for views on the problems.) We explicitly mention this category only because we hope that portions of our methodology might eventually be able to be used for modelling and implementing solutions for particular portions of these type of problems. However, this research project is restricted only to programming-in-the-small problems.

The Research Plan

The research plan can be summarized as consisting of the following steps.

1. Create a model of domain knowledge 2. Implement the model. 3. Instantiate the system for the library domain 4. Specify and generate programs within the domain. 5. Instantiate the system for another related domain 6. Refine the Model. 7. Compare the instantiations. 8. Identification of characteristics and traits that generalize across domains. 9. Identification of algorithms and techniques that can be used across a class of domains.

The remainder of this paper will briefly discuss the current state of the research in terms of points 1, 2, 3, 5, and 8 of the plan. Further details about the research can be found in [Iscoe 88A].

Create a Model.

Two of the key questions in this research are: "*How can domain knowledge be structured for use by an automatic programming system?*" and "*How can the interaction between an automatic programming system and the user be modeled.*" [Barstow 84]. The model we are developing will serve as the vehicle for answering these questions. The model must allow for knowledge to be represented in a way that is understandable to the domain experts, the users, and to the computer. Informally, the model consists of objects and the operations performed upon those objects within a particular application domain. Objects are defined in terms of their measurable properties, are hierarchically organized, and rules exist for their composition, generalization, and specialization. The model also includes a methodology for domain analysis that helps the domain expert structure their domain knowledge in a way that helps realize the goal of a system that facilitates both end user comprehension and machine manipulation.

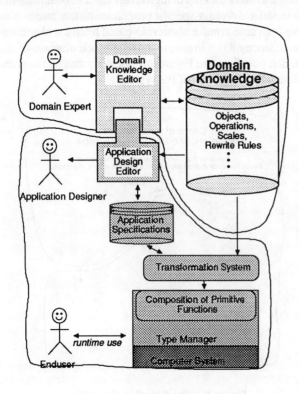

Figure 7 - System Overview

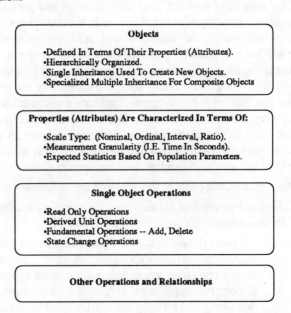

Figure 8 - Overview of the Model

Definitions of objects [Dahl 66];, [Goldberg 83];, [Jackson 83];, [Stefik 85];, [Cox 86], and [Wegner 88] differ in many areas, but most share at least the following definitional fragment: *An object, in an object-oriented model, is an abstraction of an entity that is characterized by its state and a set of operations that access or change that state. State is defined in terms of the properties or attributes of an object.*

Computer Scientists are accustomed to classifying state in terms of basic types like boolean, integer, real number, enumerated, and others that have been mapped up from computer architectures. These types are useful abstractions that provide more power and generality than simple bits. However, most of the formal discussion has been confined to the level of the types normally found in computer languages, and has not been particularly concerned with formalizing the process of mapping from the ambiguous but real world of requirements and specifications to an object-oriented model of the world.

Application domains contain entities that can be modeled in a variety of quantitative and qualitative ways. Each of these abstractions can represent only certain aspects of reality. Furthermore, implicit in any abstraction is a set of contexts for which the abstraction can be instantiated. Within the well-defined and bounded world of data structures, context can be made explicit and structures can be proved correct [Hoare 72]. However, mapping from a real world application domain into computer language data types often results in an information loss which cannot be corrected. This loss of information can create critical problems when high level specification changes can no longer be mapped into the code that implements those specifications.

Our Model

Our model adds domain knowledge to the standard object-oriented model by formalizing an application domain's natural scales and incorporating them into definitions of objects and operations. Starting with the definition of an object previously stated, the model is extended by adding: *An object, in an object-oriented model, is an abstraction of an entity that is characterized by its state and a set of operations that access or change that state. State is defined in terms of the properties or attributes of an object. Attributes and operations are defined in terms of their underlying scales, and when appropriate, units and granularity.* By quantifying attributes in terms of scales, we are able to capture, manipulate, and display domain knowledge in such a way as to be able to build a system that will accomplish our research goals.

Two theoretical aspects of our model differ significantly from most other object-oriented models. These areas are the scaling and units system used for the quantification of object attributes and operations, and a resultant new approach towards solving some of the problems of multiple inheritance.

In [Iscoe 88A], we give a more detailed explanation of objects within the model. We begin with a discussion of real world classification issues and their relation to specification, and then present a solution in terms of scaling theory and discuss its relation to attribute quantification. Scaling theory is a formal mathematical system used for classification in a variety of fields other than computer science. Seminal papers on scaling theory include [Stevens 46] and [Coombs 54].

After presenting a framework for quantifying the properties of objects, we introduce fundamental units, and fundamental operations that are found in many domains. Finally, we discuss how our representation of domain knowledge is sufficiently powerful to model tangible objects within different but related domains.

Implement the Model

Design work for this phase is currently in progress, and actual coding will begin in the Fall of 1988. It will be performed in enough detail to accomplish steps 7, 8, and 9. User interaction will be handled by a commercial front end. Prolog will be used as a back end. Our emphasis in this research is creating, analyzing, and generalizing a model of application domain knowledge. Consequently, issues of efficiency and user interaction while part of the overall paradigm, are not the subject of this research and are being implemented in only enough detail to allow analysis of the substantive research issues.

Instantiate the Library Domain

The library example is a classic software engineering problem that was introduced by Susan Gerhart and then published by [Kemmerer 85] who used it a sample problem to illustrate a specification language. It was used as a sample problem in the Fourth Annual Workshop on Specification and Design [IEEE 87]; which resulted in twelve separate papers each detailing their approach and solution. [Wing 88], an author of one of the twelve papers, gives a summary of the solutions presented at the conference. Another version of a library problem is found in [Jackson 83] and a summary of a reuse workshop in which this author participated can be found in [Neighbors 87]. The library domain will be the subject of a one day workshop on domain analysis which we have organized for the OOPSLA conference in September 1988.

Instantiate a Second Domain

Selecting a second domain is an important step that will have a direct effect on our ability to generalize results and to extend the model. Throughout this paper, the term *domain* means application domain—the sphere of knowledge that surrounds applications like accounts receivable systems, oil well logging systems, library checkout systems, and so on. Application domains are real world systems. Their structure defines the placement of boundaries on the knowledge represented within the system.

The domain must be capable of being so well understood by a domain expert he or she they would feel comfortable being able to specify and code *any* program within the domain that would normally be requested by an enduser. Since this is what we hope to achieve for our system, it is reasonable to restrict domain selection to domains which are well understood and routinely programmed by humans. This restriction excludes exploratory domains like the conference problem [Fickas 86], computer science research domains such as those requiring distributed or real-time solutions, and general purpose programs such as editors or spreadsheets that can be used in a variety of domains.

Identify Characteristics and Traits that Generalize Across Domains

The two instantiations will be compared for similarities and differences between the kind and content of information that was used for instantiation. Certain types of domain knowledge, while having different values within different domains, will generalize across domains. Scales are the primary means for achieving this generality. As the model is refined, we will specialize generalized scaling theory to more closely match the types of information found in application domains. In addition, the semantics of domain independent single and multiple object operations will generalize across multiple domains, and will be investigated further in this research.

Related Work

Space limitations prevent a complete discussion of all areas of related work. This section summarizes the related research on knowledge based systems and domain models. A further discussion of these and other related areas is contained in [Iscoe 88A].

Knowledge-Based Systems

We use the term knowledge-based to refer to systems that use a knowledge of a domain to facilitate the process of creating application programs. We have grouped this research into two categories: knowledge-based transformation systems and domain models. Transformation systems are a part of the solution paradigm, but are not a part of the current research. Domain models are directly related to the research, but generally have different goals then our particular project.

Knowledge-Based Transformation Systems use information about a domain to achieve good mappings when algorithmic methods are not yet well understood, don't exist, or are computationally intractable. Most existing knowledge-based transformation systems operate in, what we are calling *computer science and language domains* (the middle two boxes of Figure 1). This is a critical part of the overall solution paradigm, but is not part of this research.

The PSI project [Green 76], [Green 78], [Barstow 79A], [Barstow 79B], [Kant 81], [Kant 83] used a knowledge-based approach to synthesize programs within the domain of computer science. The PECOS component of PSI stored knowledge about the domain in terms of refinement rules. LIBRA helped create efficient programs by using its knowledge about costs of computation to limit the number of refinement rule expansions needed to create a program.

CHI [Green 82], [Westfold 84] was the successor to PSI, and used an internal representation of objects that served to structure the knowledge base. This structuring of knowledge helped organize the knowledge base. CHI also differed from

PSI in its approach to selection of transformations; it used user supplied information as opposed to the LIBRA style of cost calculation. CHI's successor is REFINE [Smith 85], a currently available commercial system.

GIST represents a fifteen year effort [Balzer 85] to produce a knowledge-based system for transforming program specifications to executable code. These specifications ranged from simple natural language type specifications [Balzer 78] to more formal specifications [Balzer 79]. Gist is further described in [Fickas 85], [Wile 83], and [Bruns 86A].

Draco [Neighbors 84] is another transformational system for programmers that maps through all four domains of Figure 1. It is further described in [Bruns 86B].

Domain Models

RML (Requirements Modelling Language) [Greenspan 82], [Greenspan 84], [Greenspan 86], and KATE [Fickas 86] are systems that model domain knowledge. However, these systems have slightly different goals from our own (and from each other). RML uses a frames, slots, and properties approach to develop domain models. It concentrates on the definition of concepts, data, user interaction, and transactions; it represents them in enough detail to have a system supply intuitions about requirements which have come from an SADT (Structured Analysis Design Technique) [Ross 77] analysis. However, RML does not provide an operational specification of an application program. It appears to be able to model certain domains, but it is not clear what level of effort is then required to be able to create its target in Taxis [Mylopoulous 84]

KATE [Fickas 86] is a project whose goal is to automate aspects of the software specification process. Working with the domain of conferencing, Fickas is building an interactive system that can help the user analyze their requirements and produce a reasonable specification. One way to view KATE is as an automated systems analyst.

Our goals are similar, but approach is substantively different, from that of the KATE project. We are attempting to generalize at an earlier stage than KATE, and are selecting domains that are better understood than conferencing to accomplish our goals. Furthermore, we do not plan to give policy advice of the type discussed in [Fickas 87].

Previous Work

For the purposes of this research, we assume that it is possible to produce a transformational system capable of completing the remaining mappings in a way that produces optimal executable output. Although this is not essential for research of this type, it has been a subject of some of our previous work. ACS [Iscoe 88B] is a transformational system operating in the domain of relational data base systems. Based on transformational rules developed by [Batory 87], the system also used LIBRA style cost estimation procedures to guide it to produce efficient possible implementations.

At the lowest level of the system, a type manager will implement the composition of primitive functions that are the actual application program. [Iscoe 86] describes CRTForm, a commercial system that produced type managers which implemented a set of primitive operations for forms on fields. Although that is not the emphasis of this research, it would be a critical part of large systems of this type. Other kernel implementations of what we would consider type managers are found in [Almes 83], [Pollack 81], and [Wulf 74].

Summary

Application domains are not currently represented in ways that are consistent or well enough understood for reuse to occur. Our research is dedicated to building a model of application domain knowledge that is general enough to be instantiated in different domains and expressive enough to allow programs to be specified and generated.

This paper has outlined the reasons why a model of domain knowledge is important, and our research plan for creating and evaluating a solution.

Acknowledgements

The current form of this paper would not have been possible without the assistance of John Werth and J.C. Browne. This research has been partially supported by DARPA Grant N00039-86-C-0167, Contract ONR N00014-86-K-0763, Dept of Energy Grant DE-FG05-85ER25010.

References

[Adelson 85] Adelson, B., Soloway, E., "The role of domain experience in software design, in *IEEE Transactions on Software Engineering*, Vol. 11, No. 11, Nov. 1985.

[Almes 83] Almes, Guy, Borning, Alan, and Messinger, Eli; "Implementing a Smalltalk-80 System on the Intel 432: A Feasibility Study; in *Smalltalk-80: Bits of History, Words of Advice*; Glen Krasner, Editor, Addison-Wesley, Mass.; 1983; pp. 299-322.

[Alws 85] Alws, K.H., Glasner-Schapeler, I.; "Experiences with Object-Oriented Programming"; *Proceedings of the International Joint Conference on Theory and Practice of Software Development* held in Berlin; Springer-Verlag;Mar 1985; pp. 435-452.

[Balzer 78] Balzer, R, Goldman, N, "Informality in Program Specifications", *IEEE Trans on SE*, Vol 4, No. 2, March 1978, pp. 94-102.

[Balzer 79] Balzer, R., Goldman, N., "Principles of Good Software Specification and Their Implications for Specification Languages," *Specification of Reliable Software Conference*, 1979, pp. 58-67.

[Balzer 85] Balzer, R., "A 15 year perspective on automatic programming, in *IEEE Transactions on Software Engineering*, Vol. 11, No. 11, Nov. 1985.

[Barstow 79a] Barstow, D., "The roles of knowledge and execution in program synthesis," in *Proceeding of the 6th International Joint Conference on Artifical Intelligence*, Tokyo, Japan, August 1979.

[Barstow 79b] Barstow, D., "An experiment in knowledge-based automatic programming", *Artificial Intelligence Journal*, (12) August 1979, pp. 73-119.

[Barstow 84] Barstow, D., "A perspective on automatic programming," AI Magazine, 5:1, pp. 5-27, Spring 1984.

[Barstow 85] Barstow, D, Shrobe, E., Sandewall, H. (eds.), *Interactive Programming Environments*, McGraw-Hill Book Co., 1984.

[Batory 87] Batory, Don, "A Mollecular Database Technology", University of Texas Technical Report, 1987.

[Brooks 75] Brooks, Frederick P. Jr., *The Mythical Man-Month: Essays on Software Engineering*, Addison-Wesley, 1975.

[Brooks 87] Brooks, F., "No silver bullet," *IEEE Computer*, 20(4), pp. 10-19.

[Bruns 86a] Bruns, Glenn, Bridgeland, David, Webster, Dallas, *Design Technology Assessment: Gist*. MCC Technical Report Number STP-369-86, Austin, TX, 1986.

[Bruns 86b] Design Technology Assessments: Affirm, CAEDE, Draco, PNUT, MCC Technical Report Number STP-197-87, Austin, TX, 1987.

[Clancey 85] Clancey, William, "Heuristic Classification", Artificial Intelligence, 27, 1985, pp. 289-350.

[Coombs 54] Coombs, C.H, H. Raiffa, and R.M. Thrall:"Some Views on Mathematical Models and Measurement Theory," *Psychological Review, Vol 61*, March 1954, pp.p. 132-144.

[Cox 86] Cox, Brad, *Object Oriented Programming*, Addison-Wesley, 1986.

[Curtis 87] Curtis, B., Krasner, H., Shen, V., Iscoe, N., "On building software process models under the lamppost," *Proceedings of the 9th International Conference on Software Engineering*, Washington, DC, *IEEE Computer Society*, pp. 96-103.

[Dahl 66] Dahl, O.J. and Nygaard, K.; "SIMULA—an Algol Based Simulation Language"; *Communications of the ACM* 9; 1966; pp. 671-678.

[Feather 82] Feather, M., "A System for Assisting Program Transformation," *ACM Transformations on Programming Languages and Systems*, V4#1, January 1982, pp. 1-20.

[Feather 86] Feather, M., "A Survey and Classifcation of Some Program Transformation Approaches and Techniques," *IFIP Working Conference on Program Specification and Transformation*, Bad Tolv Germany, April 1986.

[Fickas 85] S. Fickas. "Automating the transformational development of software", *IEEE Trans on Software Engineering*, November 1985.

[Fickas 86] Fickas, S., *A Knowledge-Based Approach to Specification Acquisition and Construction*, CIS-TR 85-13, Computer Science Department, University of Oregon, Eugene, Oregon.

[Fickas 87] Fickas, S., "Automating the Analysis Process: An Example," *Fourth International Workshop on Specification and Design*, April 1987, pp. 58-67.

[Goldberg 83] Goldberg, A., and Robson, D.; *Smalltalk-80: The Language and its Implementation"*; Addison Wesley, Reading, Massachusetts; 1983.

[Green 76] C. Green. The design of the PSI program synthesis system", *Second International Conference on Software Engineering*, 1976.

[Green 78] C. Green, D. Barstow. "On Program Synthesis Knowledge", *Artificial Intelligence Journal*, November 1978, pp. 241-279.

[Green 82] C. Green, "Knowledge-based programming self-applied", in J. Hayes, D.Miche, Y.-H Pao. *Machine Intelligence* 10, Wiley, 1982.

[Green 83] Green, C., Luckham, D., Balzer, R., Cheatham, T., Rich, C., "Report on a Knowledge-Based Software Assistant," RADC-TR-83-195, Rome Air Development Center, 1983.

[Greenspan 82] Greenspan, S., Borgida, A., Mylopoulos, J., "Capturing More World Knowledge in the Requirements Specification," *Proceedings of the 6th International Conference on Software Engineering*, Tokyo, Japan, 1982.

[Greenspan 84] Greenspan, S., "Requirements Modeling: A Knowledge Representation Approach to Software Requirements Definition, Ph.D. Thesis, Computer Science Department, Toronto, 1984.

[Greenspan 86] Greenspan, S., Borgida, A., Mylopoulos, J., "A Requirements Modeling Language and its Logic," *Information Systems*, V11#1, Pergammon Press, 1986, pp. 9-23.

[Hoare 72] Hoare, C.A.R.; "Proof of Correctness of Data Representations"; *Acta Informatica ,1* 1972, pp. 271-281.

[IEEE 87] Proceedings of the Fourth International Workshop on Software Specification and Design, California, April, 1987.

[Ingalls 78] Ingalls, D.H.; "The Smalltalk-76 Programming System: Design and Implementation"; *Conference Record of the Fifth Annual ACM Symposium on Principles of Programming Languages*, Tucson, AZ; Jan 1978; pp. 9-16.

[Ingalls 83] Ingalls, Daniel, "The Evolution of the Smalltalk Virtual Machine", in *Smalltalk-80, Bits of History, Words of Advice*, 1983.

[Iscoe 86] Iscoe, Neil, *CRTForm: An Object-Oriented Application Development System using Type and Type-Type Managers.* Masters Report, Dept of Computer Sciences, University of Texas, August 1986.

[Iscoe 88A] Iscoe, Neil "Domain-Specific Programming: An Object-Oriented and Knowledge-Based Approach to Specification and Generation"; Dissertation Proposal, Dept of Computer Sciences, University of Texas at Austin, June 1988.

[Iscoe 88B] Iscoe, Neil, "A Database Configuration System That Learns While It Optimizes," Proceedings of the Third Annual Rocky Mountain Conference On Artificial Intelligence, Denver, Colorado, June 1988.

[Jackson 83] Jackson, M., System Development, Prentice-Hall, 1983.

[Kant 81] Kant, E., Barstow, D., "Program Synthesis," in *IEEE Transactions on Software Engineering*, September, 1981, pp. 458-471.

[Kant 83] E. Kant. On the efficient synthesis of efficient programs," *Artificial Intelligence Journal*, 1983.

[Kemmerer 85] Kemmerer, R., "Testing Formal Specifications to Detect Design Errors, in *IEEE Transactions on Software Engineering*, Vol. SE-11(1):32-43, January, 1985.

[Mylopoulous 84] Mylopoulous, John, and Levesque, Hector, "An Overview of Knowledge Representation, in *On Conceptual Modelling*, (ed. Brodie & Mylopoulos), Springer Verlag, New York, 1984 pp. 3-17.

[Neighbors 84] Neighbors, J.M., "The Draco Approach to Constructing Software from Reusable Components," *IEEE Transactions on Software Engineering*, 10(5), September 1984, pp. 564-574.

[Neighbors 87] Neighbors, J.M., "Domain Analysis" in *Proceedings of the Workshop on Software Reuse*, October 1987, Boulder, Colorado.

[Pollack 81] Pollack, F.J., Kahn, K.C., Wilkinson, R.M.; "The iMAX-432 Object Filing System"; *Eighth Symposium on Operating Systems Principles*; 1981; pp. 137-147.

[Prieto-Diaz 87] Prieto-Diaz, Reuben, "Domain Analysis for Reusability," *Proceedings of COMPSAC 87*, October 1987.

[Ross 77] Ross, Douglass, Structured Analysis (SA): A Language for Communicating Ideas, IEEE Transactions on Software Engineering, Jan, 1977.

[Smith 85] Smith, D., Kotik, G., Westfold, S., "Research on Knowledge-Based Software Environments at Kestrel Institute," in *IEEE Transactions on Software Engineering*, Vol. SE-11, No. 11, November, 1985.

[Smoliar 83] Somliar, Stephen, Barstow, David, "Who needs Languages, and Why do They Need Them? or No Matter High The Level It's Still Programming," *SIGPLAN: Symposium on Programming Language Issues in Software Systems*, San Francisco, California, June 1983.

[Stefik 85] Stefik, & Bobrow, G. Object-Oriented Programming: Themes and Variations, *The AI Magazine*, Winter 1985, pp. 40-61.

[Stefik 86] Stefik, Mark J., Bobrow, Daniel, and Kahn, Kenneth, "Integrating Access-Oriented Programming into a Multiparadigm Environment," *IEEE Software*, January 1986, pp. 10-18.

[Stevens 46] Stevens, S.S. On the Theory of Scales of Measurement, *Science* 103: 1946, pp. 677-680.

[Swartout 82] Swartout, W. & Balzer, R. "An inevitable intertwining of specification and implementation, *"Comm of the ACM, 25:7*, July, 1982, pp. 438-446.

[van Melle 81] van Melle, W., Shortliffe, E., Buchanan, B., "EMYCIN: A domain-independent system that aids in constructing knowledge-based programs," Machine Intelligence, Infotech State of the Art Report " 9, no. 3, 1981.

[Waters 82] Waters, R., "The Prorgrammer's Apprentice: Knowledge Based Program Editing," in *IEEE Transactions on Software Engineering*, Vol. SE-8, no. 1, Jan. 1982, pp. 1-12.

[Wegner 84] Wegner, P., "Capital Intensive Software Technology — Part 2: Programming in the Large," in *IEEE Transactions on Software Engineering*, Vol. 1, No. 3, July 1984, pp. 24-32.

[Wegner 88] Wegner, P, "The Object-Oriented Classification Paradigm", *Research Directions in Object-Oriented Programming*, ed. Shriver & Wegner, MIT Press, 1988, pp. 479-560.

[Westfold 84] Westfold, S. "Very-high level programming of knowledge-based schemes," *Fourth National Conference of the American Association for Artificial Intelligence,* August 1984.

[Wile 83], Wile, David, "Program Developments: Formal Explanations of Implementations, *Communications of the ACM*, November, p. 191-200.

[Wing 87] Wing, J, "A Larch Specification of the Library Problem." In *Proceedings of the Fourth International Workshop on Software Specification and Design*, April 1987, pp. 34-41.

[Wing 88] Wing, J., "Study of Twelve Specifications of the Library Problem," Technical Report, Department of Computer Sciences, Carnegie Mellon University, 1988.

[Wulf 74] Wulf, W.A., et al; "Hydra: The Kernel of a Multiprocessor Operating System"; *Communications of the ACM*, Vol 17, No 6; Jun 1974; pp. 337-345.

Footnote

[1] The system name *Ozym* is a shortened form of *Ozymandias*.

*"My name is Ozymandias, king of kings:
Look on my works, ye Mighty, and despair!"
Nothing beside remains. Round the decay
Of that colossal wreck, boundless and bare,
The lone and level sands stretch far away.*
[Percy Shelly, 1817].

308

A KNOWLEDGE STRUCTURE FOR REUSING ABSTRACT DATA TYPES

David W. Embley
Scott N. Woodfield

Computer Science Department
Brigham Young University
Provo, Utah 84602

ABSTRACT

A knowledge structure for a software library consisting of abstract data types (ADTs) is defined. Both automatically-derived and explicitly-defined relationships are used to impose a knowledge structure on the ADTs. ADTs are defined by an ADT descriptor and one or more ADT implementations. Performance characteristics and default implementations are provided to assist users in choosing among alternatives. An explanation is given as to how the knowledge structure helps users find ADTs of interest, browse through similar ADTs to investigate alternatives, and build and customize executable software components from ADTs in the library.

Keywords: software reuse, reusability library, abstract data types, knowledge structure.

1. INTRODUCTION

In some software projects reuse of previously validated software components has increased programming productivity by 60 to 80 percent.[1] The potential impact of a 60 percent productivity increase is clear when we consider that the estimated $32 billion needed by the military in 1990 for software production could be cut to nearly $12 billion, a savings of almost 20 billion dollars!

Because the rewards of software reusability are likely to be great, there are several research groups investigating its possibilities and discovering ideas to help realize its potential. The September 1984 issue of *IEEE Transactions on Software Engineering,* for example, contains articles by Jones,[1] Horowitz and Munson,[2] and Standish,[3] which describe current efforts. Some of the topics presented are application-component libraries, organization and composition principles, language-based systems, application generators, and transformation systems.

While reusability issues can be diverse, for the purpose of this paper we restrict ourselves to software libraries and assume that the software components of the library are abstract data types (ADTs).[4] Horowitz and Munson[2] seem to imply that making software-component libraries the foundation for reusability is so fraught with problems that software libraries are not a suitable target of investigation. Although there are problems to be overcome, we believe that the problems are not insurmountable and that the potential rewards make the investigation worthwhile.

One of the reasons libraries consisting of general software components have been unsuccessful is that they have merely contained a large, mostly-unorganized set of functions and procedures. Often, the only means of finding a software component is by its function or procedure name. Finding a useful module under these circumstances is analogous to finding a book in a public library that has no card catalog but has all books arranged alphabetically -- without knowing the exact title, the search is almost certain to fail. Besides providing a card catalog to help patrons find books, a public library also facilitates patron browsing by arranging books according to subject matter. A public library also provides several facilities to help patrons in their quest for knowledge ranging from microfilm readers and copy machines to quiet reading rooms and simple checkout procedures. If a reusability library is to be successful, it must become more like a public library. In particular, it must be structured to help the user *find* modules of interest, *browse* through related modules to locate a module that best suits the current needs, and *build* a custom-tailored software component usable in the software system being developed.

In this paper we present a knowledge structure for a library of abstract data types that has facilities to help users succeed in these three basic tasks: finding, browsing, and building. Facilities for finding include search by name, search by keyword, and more sophisticated search features such as find a best match given a a description of an abstract data type in outline form. Facilities for browsing include the ability to follow aggregation, generalization, and classification links, to access ADTs used by and using some other ADT, and to view ADTs within a specified delta-distance. Facilities for building include automatic retrieval of all other required ADTs given that a particular ADT and implementation are selected for insertion into the software system under development, guidance for selection among various implementations of an ADT based on efficiency characteristics, and assistance in locating other modules that may need modification when an ADT is modified.

The basic organization of our library is a collection of ADTs contained within a knowledge structure supporting relationships among ADTs. In addition to containing data and operation definitions, the ADTs in the library include natural language descriptions and keywords to assist in finding and browsing activities and alternative implementations with efficiency definitions to assist in

Reviewed and recommended by:

Bertrand Meyer

building. ADTs are the only independent entities stored in the library. Algorithmic abstractions, implemented as procedures or functions, are not stored as independent entities, but are instead stored with the ADT to which they belong. Such an organization supports object-oriented design,[5,6,7] a design methodology which many claim is superior to function-oriented design.

Although the concepts explained in the paper are not language dependent, we choose Ada* as the implementation language. Ada packages are well suited for defining ADTs for inclusion in the library and nicely support the concepts of object-oriented design. Since not all constructs are applicable to all language environments, our examples are sometimes partial to Ada. Although not conceptually more difficult, additional overhead would be required to make the library applicable for multiple languages.

The remainder of this paper describes the organization of the library and its use to solve the find, browse, and build problems. In Section 2 we define an ADT as it appears in the library and the various explicit and implicit relationships that are supported. In Section 3 we explain how the library's knowledge structure can be used to facilitate software reusability and outline the features necessary to make the library convenient for users. We also briefly mention some tools that are useful for creating, maintaining, and updating the library. Finally, in the Section 4, we present our conclusions.

2. GENERAL LIBRARY ORGANIZATION

2.1. Objects

In our reusability library, an *abstract data type (ADT)* is a pair

(ADT-descriptor, ADT-implementation-set)

where an ADT-descriptor describes the ADT and an ADT-implementation-set is a set of one or more implementations for the ADT. Sample ADT descriptors are shown in Figures 1 and 2 and parts of corresponding ADT implementation sets are shown in Figures 3, 4, and 5. These ADTs will be used to exemplify ideas throughout the paper.

An *ADT-descriptor* consists of a name, zero or more instantiation parameters, a list of aliases, a natural language description, a list of keywords, a domain specification, and zero or more operation specifications. The ADT name ("bounded-queue" in Figure 1 and "person" in Figure 2) identifies an ADT for the system and user and thus must be unique within the reusability library.

Instantiation parameters allow an ADT to be generic. A generic instantiation parameter may be a generic type parameter (represented by the word "ADT"), a generic value (designated by an ADT name), or generic subprogram parameter (a full procedure or function specification).[8] In Figure 1 "item" is a generic type parameter and thus allows bounded queues of any type of defined item. The generic value parameter "size" is of type "positive_int", an ADT assumed to be defined elsewhere, and represents a value giving the upper bound on the size of the bounded queue.

Aliases are synonym names for the ADT name and are not necessarily unique within the reusability library (e.g., "bounded-list" and "list" in Figure 1). The natural

language description describes an ADT; it has no format or content constraints, but should be written to be as helpful as possible. The keyword list allows context words or phrases to be specified (e.g., "bounded", "first-in-first-out", and "FIFO" in Figure 1). Keywords are not considered to be aliases, but aliases are considered to be keywords, and thus the union of the set of alias names and the set of keywords constitutes the keywords for the ADT.

The domain specification is a regular expression whose atoms are ADTs in the library or ADT instantiation parameters of the ADT being defined. The domain specification thus defines a value set for an ADT. A particular value in the value set is obtained by selecting an ADT for each generic type parameter and a value for each generic value parameter, expanding the regular expression so that it contains only atoms, and replacing each atom with a value instance from its ADT.

To avoid ambiguity, we insist that an atom in a domain specification be mentioned at most once. An atom may be repeated in a sequence, as is "item" in Figure 1, which is repeated zero or more times up to "size" times, but the same atom cannot appear twice. For example, "birthdate" and "deathdate" in Figure 2 are both dates, but it would not be permissible to replace them both with "date". Normally, as is the case in Figure 2, multiple occurrences represent different roles which should be identified. This requires, of course, that "birthdate" and "deathdate" be separate ADTs in the library. Since they represent different concepts, we argue that they should be different even if they have the same syntactic specification.

Each operation is specified by giving its name, arguments, results, and exception conditions, if any. A list of aliases, which are also considered to be keywords for the operation, a natural language description of the operation, and a list of additional keywords accompanies each operation. Arguments and results must be names of ADTs in the library or ADT instantiation parameters in the ADT being defined, and every operation should include the name for the ADT being defined as an argument or result.

An *ADT-implementation-set* contains one or more implementations for an ADT. An implementation for an ADT is a pair:

(domain-implementation, operator-implementation-set) .

A *domain-implementation* is specified in terms of the implementation language (Ada for this paper) and is a mapping from the value set of an ADT to a set of representations defined in terms of previously-existing ADTs in the library, some of which may be given as ADT instantiation parameters. In Figure 3, the domain implementation for a bounded queue (Figure 1) is specified as an array of items, and in Figure 4, the domain implementation is specified as a circularly-linked list of items. In Figure 5, the domain implementation for a person (Figure 2) is a record and is a subset of the fields declared for a person (age can be computed and is thus not explicitly stored).

Given a domain implementation which references a set of ADTs A, an *operator-implementation-set* is a set of algorithms (one for each operator) that are written in the implementation language, invoke operators of elements of A, and make the same set of assumptions about the implementation behavior. In Figure 3 the set A consists

* Ada is a trademark of the Department of Defense.

```
ADT: bounded_queue(item: ADT; size: positive_int)

Aliases: bounded_list, bounded_line, queue, list, line.
Description: A bounded queue is a first-in-first-out list of at most
    "size" items. Items are appended to the back of the queue and removed
    from the front.
Keywords: bounded, first-in-first-out, FIFO.

Domain:

    item*size

Operations:

    create() → bounded_queue;
        Aliases: make, initialize, start-up.
        Description: Initializes the queue.

    remove(bounded_queue) → item, bounded_queue;
        Exception: queue_empty;
        Aliases: delete, service.
        Description: Removes the front item from the queue and returns it.
        Keywords: front.

    append(bounded_queue, item) → bounded_queue;
        Exception: queue_full;
        Aliases: add, insert.
        Description: Appends an item to the queue.

    empty(bounded_queue) → boolean;
        Description: Returns true if the queue is empty.
        Keywords: has nothing, contains none.
```

Figure 1. Sample ADT-Descriptor for a Bounded Queue.

of two existing ADTs: "bounded_list" which is an array and "integer". Both arrays and integers are built-in ADTs and have predefined sets of operations. In Figure 3, the bounded-queue operation "append" invokes the operators greater-than-or-equal, equal, plus, and array-reference, all of which are operators of elements of A. The operator implementation set in Figure 3 assumes that the bounded queue is stored in the array with "front" pointing at the first element and "back" pointing at the last element and retains the number of elements in the bounded queue in "count". The operator set in Figure 4 assumes that the bounded queue is a circularly-linked list with pointers pointing at successive elements (except the pointer in the last element which points at the first element) and with a pointer from the outside pointing at the last element. Since the two implementation sets make different assumptions, algorithms corresponding to the same operator are clearly not interchangeable. An example of interchangeable algorithms would be two sorting algorithms (e.g., one implementing quicksort and the other implementing heapsort).

Included within the code of an ADT-implementation-set are special comments. These special comments are notes to the library about an implementation. They are enclosed in opening and closing dollar-signs, "($ ... $)", and begin with a recognizable keyword, one of "Implementation", "Space", "Time", or "Default". In Figure 3, for example, the special comment "($Implementation #1 for bounded_queue$)" designates the implementation as implementation number one. Similarly, as is indicated in the special comment at the top of the Figure, Figure 4 is implementation number two.

To assist in selecting among the (possibly many) implementation choices, space efficiency characteristics are noted for each domain definition and time efficiency

and any additional space requirements are noted for each algorithm. In Figures 3 and 4 the space complexity of the domain implementations is "nm+c" and and "n(m+p)+c" respectively where the variables are explained within the special comments in the Figures. If there are few queue elements compared to the size of the bounded queue, then implementation #2 has better space characteristics, but if the number of queue elements is large compared to the size, then implementation #1 has better space characteristics. A programmer knowing the demands of the application being developed could make an intelligent choice between the two implementations.

One of the implementations is designated as the *default* implementation. This implementation is selected whenever a user does not specify which implementation is to be used. The special comment near the top of Figure 4 designates "Implementation #2" as the default implementation for the bounded queue. Similar default designations are also included in operation implementations if there is more than one implementation for an operator, given a particular domain implementation.

2.2. Relationships

Relationships in the ADT library are of two types: those implied by ADT information contained in the library and those not implied, which therefore must be explicitly provided. Relationships implied by ADT information are called *automatic* because they can be automatically derived given the ADTs. Relationships that must be explicitly provided are called *user-defined* because a user must explicitly assert these relationships. Although automatic relationships can be derived, they may, in some cases, be explicitly stored to increase operation efficiency. Notationally, automatic relationships have a prefix "a" and user-defined relationships have a

311

```
ADT: person

Aliases: human, individual.
Description: A person is a human being represented by attributes name, address,
      birth date, age, sex and death date.
Keywords: man, woman, adult, child.

Domain:

    name
    address
    birthdate
    age
    sex
    deathdate

Operations:

    make_person(name, address:=UNKNOWN, birthdate:=UNKNOWN, age:=UNKNOWN,
             sex:=UNKNOWN, deathdate:=UNKNOWN) → person;
       Exception: age_and_birthdate_inconsistent;
       Description: Initializes information about a person.  Parameters with
             default values are optional.  Birth date and age must be consistent.
       Keywords: make record, create, initialize.

    name_of(person) → name;
       Description: Returns a person's name.
       Keywords: name of person, person's name.

    address_of(person) → address;
       Description: Returns a person's address.
       Keywords: address of person, person's address.

    birthdate_of(person) → birthdate;
       Aliases: birthday, Bday.
       Description: Returns a person's birth date.
       Keywords: birthday of person, person's birthday.

    age_of(person) → age;
       Description: Returns a person's age.
       Keywords: how old, person's age, age of person.

    sex_of(person) → sex;
       Description: Returns a person's sex.
       Keywords: person's sex, sex of person.

    deathdate_of(person) → deathdate;
       Aliases: death day.
       Description: Returns a person's death date.
       Keywords: date of death, person's death date, death date of person.
```

Figure 2. Sample ADT-descriptor for a Person.

prefix "u". Library administrators have the responsibility to create and maintain user-defined relationships.

In presenting the following list of relationships, we observe that many others can be defined. Those listed appear to be most useful in assisting with the find, browse, and build activities for which the library is designed.

aDepends_on(*a*, *b*, *i*): ADT *a* (automatically) depends on ADT *b* in implementation *i* if and only if *i* is an implementation of *a* and *i* references *b*. An implementation *i* references an ADT *t* if an operation of *t* is invoked in one of the operation implementations of the operation implementation set of *i*, or if the domain implementation of *i* is defined in terms of the ADT *t*, or if at least one parameter, variable, type, or constant associated with any domain representation or operation implementation of *i* is defined in terms of the domain of *t*. For example, in Figure 5 the ADT "birthdate" is referenced in the ADT "person" and thus **"aDepends_on**(person, birthdate, #1)" holds. With the

aDepends_on relationship and the default implementation specifications, it is possible to recursively enumerate all ADTs needed for implementation of a particular ADT. It is thus possible to automatically build a complete, compilable software component for an ADT in the library.

uDepends_on(*a*, *b*, *i*, *r*): This relationship allows a library administrator to assert that ADT *a* depends on ADT *b* in implementation *i* because of reason *r*. If an implementation of an ADT for an expression-evaluation stack depends on a source-line ADT because it assumes that the bound on the (bounded) stack has a maximum that depends on the source-line length, then the library administrator might assert, for example, "**uDepends_on**(expression_evaluation_stack, source_line, #1, 'The maximum stack size is chosen to be two-thirds of the source-line length.')". We are assuming, of course, that source-line length is not exported and thus unavailable to be referenced by the ADT implementing the expression-evaluation stack. Since it cannot be refer-

```
                  -- ($Implementation #1 of bounded_queue$)
GENERIC
    TYPE item IS PRIVATE;
    size: IN positive;
PACKAGE bounded_queue_package IS
    TYPE bounded_queue IS PRIVATE;
    FUNCTION create RETURN bounded_queue;
    PROCEDURE remove(Q: IN OUT bounded_queue; removed_item: OUT item);
    PROCEDURE append(Q: IN OUT bounded_queue; new_item: IN item);
    FUNCTION empty(Q: IN bounded_queue) RETURN boolean;
    queue_empty: EXCEPTION;
    queue_full: EXCEPTION;
PRIVATE
    TYPE bounded_list IS ARRAY(1..size) OF item;
    -- Normally, bounded_list would be an imported ADT.
    TYPE bounded_queue IS RECORD
        list: bounded_list;
        front: integer RANGE 1..size;
        back: integer RANGE 1..size;
        count: integer RANGE 0..size;
    END RECORD;
    -- ($Space: nm+c where n (=size) is the size of the array, m is the
    --     size of an item, and c is the constant amount of space taken
    --     by the auxiliary variables.$)
END bounded_queue_package;

PACKAGE BODY bounded_queue_package IS
    FUNCTION create RETURN bounded_queue IS SEPARATE;
    PROCEDURE remove(Q: IN OUT bounded_queue; removed_item: OUT item) IS SEPARATE;
    PROCEDURE append(Q: IN OUT bounded_queue; new_item: IN item) IS SEPARATE;
    FUNCTION empty(Q: IN bounded_queue) RETURN boolean IS SEPARATE;
END bounded_queue_package;

-- ($Implementation #1 of append in bounded_queue_package, implementation #1.$)
SEPARATE(bounded_queue_package)
PROCEDURE append(Q: IN OUT bounded_queue; new_item: IN item) IS
-- ($Time: c where c is constant.$)
BEGIN
    IF Q.count >= size THEN
        RAISE queue_full;
    ELSE
        IF Q.back = size THEN
            Q.back := 1;
        ELSE
            Q.back := Q.back+1;
        END IF;
        Q.list(back) := new_item;
        Q.count := Q.count+1;
    END IF;
END append;
```

Figure 3. Implementation of a Bounded Queue Using an Array.

enced, there is a "hidden dependency" that cannot be recorded in the relationship **aDepends_on**. The **uDepends_on** relationship is provided to allow these hidden dependencies of importance to be recorded.

aClose(a, b, d): Let a-ADTs (b-ADTs) be the set of ADTs mentioned in the regular expression of the domain specification of ADT a (ADT b). Let a-ops (b-ops) be the set of operation names in ADT a (ADT b). Let a-set = a-ADTs $\cup$ a-ops and b-set = b-ADTs $\cup$ b-ops. Let x be either an ADT name or an operation name; the keyword set of x contains x and the ADT keywords (including aliases) if x is an ADT name or x and the keywords (including aliases) of operation x if x is an operation name. If y is an element of a-set and z is an element of b-set, we say $y \approx z$ if there exists a nonempty intersection of the keyword set of y and the keyword set of z, and we define a-set ~ b-set as the usual relative complement of b-set with respect to a-set based on the definition of $\approx$ for element equality. Now, ADT a is d-Close to ADT b if and only if $|a\text{-set} \sim b\text{-set}| + |b\text{-set} \sim a\text{-set}| \le d$. Intui-

tively, two ADTs are 1-close if they differ by at most 1 operation or domain ADT and n-close if they differ by at most n operations or domain ADTs. Observe that d-Close is reflexive and symmetric, but not transitive, and thus two d-Close ADTs can have different sets of d-Close ADTs. This makes it possible to move from ADT A to d-Close ADT B and then be able to move to yet another d-Close ADT C that is not in the d-Close set of ADTs of A. Other measures of closeness are also possible. For example, $(|a\text{-set} \sim b\text{-set}| + |b\text{-set} \sim a\text{-set}|)/(|a\text{-set}| + |b\text{-set}|)$ gives a measure of relative (rather than absolute) closeness.

uClose(a, b, r) This relationship allows a library administrator to assert that ADT a is close to ADT b because of reason r. For example, a hash-table ADT may be thought of as being close to a linear-list ADT (from the point of view of searching) and a linear-list ADT may be thought of as being close to a queue ADT (from the point of view of ordering and first and last element), but a hash-table ADT is not likely to be thought of as being

```
--  ($Implementation #2 of bounded_queue$)
--  ($Default implementation$)
GENERIC
    TYPE item IS PRIVATE;
    size: IN positive;
PACKAGE bounded_queue_package IS
    TYPE bounded_queue IS PRIVATE;
    FUNCTION create RETURN bounded_queue;
    PROCEDURE remove(Q: IN OUT bounded_queue; removed_item: OUT item);
    PROCEDURE append(Q: IN OUT bounded_queue; new_item: IN item);
    FUNCTION empty(Q: IN bounded_queue) RETURN boolean;
    queue_empty: EXCEPTION;
    queue_full: EXCEPTION;
PRIVATE
    TYPE circular_list_node;
    TYPE circular_list_node_pointer IS ACCESS circular_list_node;
    TYPE circular_list_node IS RECORD
        info: item;
        next: circular_list_node_pointer := NULL;
    END RECORD;
    TYPE bounded_queue IS RECORD
        back: circular_list_node_pointer;
        count: integer RANGE 0..size;
    END RECORD;
    -- ($Space: n(m+p)+c where n is the number of items in the queue,
    --    m is the size of an item, p is the size of a pointer, and
    --    c is the constant amount of space taken by the header node.$)
END bounded_queue_package;

PACKAGE BODY bounded_queue_package IS
    ...
    PROCEDURE append(Q: IN OUT bounded_queue; new_item: IN item) IS SEPARATE;
    ...
END bounded_queue_package;

-- ($Implementation #1 of append in bounded_queue_package, implementation #2.$)
SEPARATE(bounded_queue_package)
PROCEDURE append(Q: IN OUT bounded_queue; new_item: IN item) IS
-- ($Time: c where c is constant.$)
-- ($Space (additional): c where c is the space for pointer p.$)
    p: circular_list_node_pointer;
BEGIN
    IF count >= size THEN
        RAISE queue_full;
    ELSE
        IF Q.back = NULL THEN
            Q.back := NEW circular_list_node;
            Q.back.info := new_item;
            Q.back.next := Q.back;
        ELSE
            p := NEW circular_list_node;
            p.info := new_item;
            p.next := Q.back.next;
            Q.back.next := p;
            Q.back := p;
        END IF;
    END IF;
END append;
```

Figure 4. Implementation of a Bounded Queue Using Circular Linked Lists.

```
-- ($Implementation #1 of person$)
PACKAGE person_package IS
    TYPE person IS PRIVATE;
    FUNCTION make_person(new_name:   IN name;
                         addr:       IN address  := UNKNOWN;
                         b_date:     IN birthdate := UNKNOWN;
                         new_age:    IN age       := UNKNOWN;
                         new_sex:    IN sex       := UNKNOWN;
                         d_date:     IN deathdate := UNKNOWN) RETURN person;
    FUNCTION name_of(individual: IN person) RETURN name;
    FUNCTION address_of(individual: IN person) RETURN address;
    FUNCTION birthdate_of(individual: IN person) RETURN birthdate;
    FUNCTION age_of(individual: IN person) RETURN age;
    FUNCTION sex_of(individual: IN person) RETURN sex;
    FUNCTION deathdate_of(individual: IN person) RETURN deathdate;
PRIVATE
    TYPE person IS RECORD
        persons_name: name;
        addr:         address;
        b_date:       birthdate;
        persons_sex:  sex;
        d_date:       deathdate;
    END RECORD;
    -- ($Space: n where n is the sum of the sizes of the implementation of
    --     name, address, birthdate, sex, and deathdate.$)
END person_package;
```

Figure 5. Part of an Implementation for Person.

close to a queue ADT. The relationship **uClose** gives the library administrator the ability to establish relationships that are "conceptually close" even though the domain and operator specifications may be far apart.

aGeneralization(a, b)/**aSpecialization**(b, a): ADT a is an (automatic) generalization of ADT b if and only if the regular expression that specifies the domain for ADT a is a subexpression of a commuted regular expression that defines the domain for ADT b. For any regular expression, we allow concatenation (AND) and plus (OR) to be commutative and define a commuted regular expression of regular expression e to be any regular expression that can be derived from e by a sequence of zero or more commutative operations. If, for example, an ADT has a domain definition represented by the regular expression "(name sex birthdate)", then the ADT is a generalization of person because "(name sex birthdate)" is a subexpression of the expression "(name sex birthdate address age deathdate)" which is a commutated expression of the domain-defining regular expression for person. Observe that the generalization relationship is a partial ordering and thus imposes a generalization hierarchy on the ADTs in the library. ADT a is an (automatic) specialization of ADT b if and only if **aGeneralization**(b, a). Specialization is the converse of generalization and thus views the generalization hierarchy from the other direction.

uGeneralization(a, b, r)/**uSpecialization**(b, a, r): This relationship allows a library administrator to assert that ADT a is a generalization of ADT b because of reason r. Suppose, for example, that an ADT "working-person" has been declared with a domain definition whose regular expression is "(name address social-security-nr birthdate sex ethnic-origin handicap)". Although "working-person" is (conceptually) a specialization of person, according to the definition of **aSpecialization**, it is not an automatic specialization because it does not include age and deathdate. These types of conceptual generalizations and specializations can be recorded as user-defined generalizations and specializations. It would be best if the library could be established

such that automatic and conceptual generalizations/specializations are as much the same as possible.

aGeneric-of(a, b): ADT a is an (automatic) generic of ADT b if and only if b can be obtained from a by substituting one or more values for instantiation parameters of a. Observe that **Generic-of** is irreflexive, antisymmetric, and transitive and thus imposes a quasi ordering on the set of ADTs in the library. This quasi ordering induces a generic hierarchy on the ADTs in the library. There is no user-defined generic relationship. This is because the automatic generic relationship is itself user defined, but since the user must define the relationship in the syntax, it is always automatically detectable.

aAggregation(a, b): Here b is an ordered list of two or more ADTs. ADT a is an (automatic) aggregation of the list of ADTs b if and only if the regular expression that specifies the domain for ADT a is a commuted regular expression of the regular expression formed by concatenating the elements in the list of ADTs b. Like the generic relationship, aggregation does not have a user-defined counterpart because the user must define aggregation in the syntax.

uClassification(a, b, r): This relationship allows a library administrator to assert that ADT a is classified with ADT b because of reason r. For example, a classification may be constructed that includes all ADTs that have the operator "append", or a classification may be constructed that includes all ADTs that have been used in an accounting system. There is no automatic classification relationship because a classification cannot be established without a user-specified reason, which must be a predicate that classifies the ADTs. User-defined classification is general enough to permit almost any unforeseen relationships that may be deemed useful.

3. LIBRARY USE AND MANIPULATION

Based on the general library organization presented above, we have implemented an initial prototype for the library.[9] Although the prototype is only in its early stages of development, it already supports all of the ADT descriptor and implementation features and most of the relationships, both automatic and user-defined. Before beginning to experiment with actual users, however, additional features should be implemented including better user interfaces, more convenient tools to assist in inserting new ADTs and relationships into the library, and tools to automatically extract an ADT and its dependent ADTs to form compilable modules. These features are being developed and we now describe their main characteristics.

3.1. Find

The "find" operation is used to automatically find an ADT of interest, locate one that closely resembles a desired ADT, or indicate that a suitable ADT does not exist. To invoke the find operation, a user will fill out an ADT template whose form is similar to an ADT descriptor, containing fields for an ADT name, ADT parameters, general descriptions, keywords, and domain and operation definitions. All requested information need not be provided.

The collectible information allows several means by which an ADT can be located. One can search for an ADT by name, and although a library-administrator chosen name would not generally be widely known, automatic use of aliases makes the search more likely to succeed. General descriptions provided by a user can be compared with the natural-language descriptions associated with each ADT. This can be done much like a bibliographic search in which a function determines closeness by tallying the number and frequency of content words found in both the given and candidate descriptions. The time required to conduct a description search can be significantly reduced if a keyword search is used instead. A keyword search is similar to a general-description search except that the closeness function compares sets of keywords provided, with keywords (and aliases) associated with a candidate ADT. The user can also locate desired ADTs by providing partial domain definitions. The system would then search for any ADT with a domain definition containing some or all of the domain definition given. Since a user would rarely know exact attribute names, aliases are used. Operation definitions can also be used by providing whole or partial definitions for operations needed. The system then uses the operation names, parameter names, and type names or their aliases to search for fully or partially matching functions.

Based on an empirically-determined measure of closeness,[10] the system is to return the names of up to seven of the most similar ADTs that exceed a closeness threshold value. If none exceed the threshold value, the system so reports. If more than seven exceed the threshold value, the system reports how many exceed the value. Depending on the results, a user is to be able to edit the find template and again invoke the find command. Additional query-enhancement techniques including term truncation, term weighting, and broader or narrower terms can be borrowed from the research on automatic text-retrieval systems and incorporated into the library system.[11]

The success of the find operation will depend primarily on how well the automated search mechanisms can locate an ADT of interest. This can be measured using recall and precision ratios, metrics associated with bibliographic search.[12] The recall ratio is the number of ADTs of interest returned by the system compared to the number of ADTs of interest contained in the library. The precision ratio is the number of ADTs of interest returned by the system compared to the number of ADTs returned by the system. Together these two metrics determine if the search heuristics are returning what is needed and only what is needed. Since these metrics are subjective and difficult to measure in practice, they are best used to develop and fine-tune the search heuristics.

3.2. Browse

The "browse" operation allows a user to inspect a candidate ADT returned by a find (or browse) operation and follow relationship links to locate related ADTs. Two types of operations are provided: inspect and search, where the search is based on ADT relationships rather than on ADT descriptions.

A user will be able to inspect both an ADT-description and its corresponding ADT-implementation-set. To aid in inspection, multiple, scrollable windows are to be used to display different parts of ADT descriptor and implementation sets at the same time. Various subparts are to be suppressed so that they do not clutter the screen, and specific information, such as performance characteristics, are to be automatically found and displayed on request.

Using available relationships, a user will be able to search for related ADTs. Relationships are to be specified by pointing at relationship names listed on a screen and by providing necessary arguments as prompted. A list of active "reasons" for user-defined relationships is to be displayed on request. When a user specifies one or more relationships, the system displays a list of names of ADTs that satisfy all specified relationships. Since the search can continue from any one of the ADTs listed, a user can browse throughout the library following relationships.

3.3. Build

The "build" operation allows a user to extract ADTs from the library and integrate them into a software system. Before extracting and integrating an ADT into a software system, the user may customize the ADT to fit the needs of the application being developed.

The simplest type of extraction will not involve any customizing. A user who has found an "as-is-usable" ADT will be able to retrieve the ADTs default domain representation and operator implementation set. The system will also automatically retrieve the default implementation of all other ADTs necessary for implementation. Sometimes the user may not need all of the supporting ADTs because they may have already been retrieved to build a previously selected ADT. To prevent duplication, the system is to make a list of ADTs retrieved for a particular user and application and inform the user about duplicates so that the user can, if necessary, adjust the visibility of multiply-used ADTs.

It will be possible for the user to customize ADTs before retrieval. An ADT is customized by either selecting a non-default domain representation or operation implementation, or by deleting unwanted sub-domains or operations. When unwanted sub-domains are deleted, operations referencing unwanted sub-domains are to be automatically deleted. Deletion, of course, is localized to the customizing user so that the effects are not recorded in the library. Customizing by addition is also possible, but is beyond the scope of the library's responsibility.

3.4. Update

The library itself must be build, maintained, and updated. Capabilities to add new ADTs to the library, to modify existing ADTs, and perhaps to delete ADTs will be provided. The addition, modification, and deletion of relationships and types of relationships must also be possible.

Tools to assist library administrators perform these library updates will be provided. Some tools are a natural consequence of the library's organization. The automatic relationships, for example, can automatically be updated as changes are made. The find operation can be used to locate any existing ADTs that closely resemble a new ADT (two conceptually identical ADTs should not both reside in the library). Tools to assist library administrators recognize and establish useful user-defined relationships should also be provided. These tools could (perhaps) be based on statistics kept about the use of user-defined relationships (past usage is a reasonable guide to desired future usage).

4. CONCLUSIONS

Although much remains to be done, a significant step has been taken in defining and implementing a knowledge structure for an ADT software-reusability library. The objective of the knowledge structure is to help a user locate ADTs of interest and use them in a software system under development. ADTs are located with the "find" and "browse" capabilities of the library, and are extracted for use and customized with the "build" capability.

In creating the knowledge structure, we defined ADT-descriptors such that they would contain useful information for finding, browsing, and building. We also defined ADT-implementation-sets so that we could associate with each ADT one or more implementations. Since many implementations are possible, our definitions provide both for performance characteristics to assist users in choosing among alternatives and for default implementations to allow the system to automatically construct compilable software components when this is appropriate.

We also defined relationships among library ADTs to provide increased flexibility and power for finding, browsing, and building. Definitions for automatically determining closeness, generalizations, specializations, generics, and aggregations implicitly impose a useful structure on the library. In addition, library administrators may also define their own generalizations, specializations, and classifications to further aid the user.

References

1. T.C. Jones, "Reusability in programming: a survey of the state of the art," *IEEE Transactions on Software Engineering*, vol. SE-10, no. 5, pp. 488-493, September 1984.

2. E. Horowitz and J.B. Munson, "An expansive view of reusable software," *IEEE Transactions on Software Engineering*, vol. SE-10, no. 5, pp. 477-487, September 1984.

3. T.A. Standish, "An essay on software reuse," *IEEE Transactions on Software Engineering*, vol. SE-10, no. 5, pp. 494-497, September 1984.

4. S.N. Woodfield, D.W. Embley, G.L. Stokes, and K. Zhang, "Assumptions and issues of software reusability," *Proceedings Fifth Annual Phoenix Conference on Computers and Communications*, pp. 450-454, Phoenix, Arizona, March 1986.

5. G. Booch, "Object-oriented design," in *Tutorial on Software Design Techniques*, ed. A.I. Wasserman, IEEE Computer Society Press, Silver Springs, Maryland, 1984.

6. G. Booch, "Object-oriented development," *IEEE Transactions on Software Engieneering*, vol. SE-12, no. 2, pp. 211-221, February 1986.

7. V. Berzins, M. Gray, and D. Naumann, "Abstraction-based software development," *Communications of the ACM*, vol. 29, no. 5, pp. 402-415, May 1986.

8. G. Booch, *Software Engineering with Ada*, Benjamin/Cummings Publishing Company, Menlo Park, California, 1983.

9. K. Zhang, "A knowledge structure for object-oriented libraries," Master's Thesis, Brigham Young University, 1986.

10. Y.L. Kuo, "An empirical evaluation of closeness metrics for similar data abstractions," Master's Thesis, Brigham Young University, 1986. (in preparation)

11. G. Salton, "Another look at automatic text-retrieval systems," *Communications of the ACM*, vol. 29, no. 7, pp. 648-656, July 1986.

12. G. Salton, *Automatic Information Organization and Retrieval*, McGraw-Hill, New York, 1968.

SEE:
An Automated Tool to Facilitate Reuse in Ada(*) Project Development

Larry Latour
Asst. Prof. of Computer Science
University of Maine

Abstract

The definition of reusable software is a complex one. When a modular decomposition of a system is performed by an experienced program designer, it is done in such a way that the resulting modules are "implementable". The feel of the designer for what is implementable is drawn from experience with analogous systems and subsystems previously studied and/or implemented. These analogous systems are in this sense reusable.

The learning processes of a student and of a production programmer are similar in that they both consist of the construction of a personal set of analogies from which another system can then be constructed. Studying how programmers learn and how they construct these personal analogy knowledge bases will go far to help us define a **taxonomy for reusability** in a wide variety of application areas. Automated tools to capture these knowledge bases can be used both as aides to learning about system construction and as tools for organizing and presenting reusable (analogous) code. In this paper we describe one such tool: **SEE: A Student's Educational Environment**, specifically focusing upon **SeeGraph**, a network database with graphical interface language which we use to realize such knowledge bases described above.

(*) Ada is a registered trademark of the US Government AJPO

Introduction

SEE: A Student's Educational Environment is a set of environment tools that is equally useful in (1) helping novice programmers to learn how to reason about constructing systems and (2) helping production programmers to learn how to reason about constructing systems in unfamiliar application areas.

The primary tool of SEE and the focus of this paper is the **Analogy knowledge base**, a dynamically evolving predefined and user defined database of abstract program structures along with rules for their modification and usage. This knowledge base will serve a number of purposes. It will **facilitate project development** by providing a tool to organize and query knowledge about systems analogous to a particular target system. At the same time it will provide **a taxonomy for reusability** in a wide variety of application areas.

SEE was originally intended as a learning tool for students in a classroom setting, and was presented as such in [Latour 86]. However, gradually we became aware of it's value as an APSE tool in a production environment. The project is currently in the prototype development stage on a network consisting of a VAX/780 and Vaxstation II, Sun, and PC/AT workstations.

In addition to the Analogy knowledge base, other more standard APSE tools are supplied. These include a network of language subsets, on the style of the GNOME project at CMU, that must be assimilated in order to master the rich set of language facilities of Ada, and a structure oriented editor, combining elements of syntax direction and both incremental and batch syntax checking in a non-restrictive manner.

Knowledge Representation and The Analogy Knowledge Base

Typically software engineers tend to be guided to a problem solution by the constructs and limitations of their tools and techniques (requirements, specification, and design methodologies, programming languages and environments, etc) rather than by their "personal" knowledge base of analogous abstractions. This is very true of the novice but also is true of the experienced programmer who is working in an unfamiliar application area. In both cases the user's personal "analogy" knowledge base in the application area is limited in scope and/or form.

An important concept, and one that should be clear to anyone but the novice (our target), is that system development, at every step in the software life cycle, is carried out through analogy with past experience. A discussion of this idea is made by Scherlis and Scott in [Scherlis83]. The problem that arises when constructing an analogy knowledge base is twofold:

1) **What knowledge representation methodology or methodologies can be used to represent the analogies, and**
2) **What methods are provided for querying and modifying the knowledge base?**

Knowledge representation has been well studied and has become the central problem in the field of Artificial Intelligence (AI) [Bobrow and Collins75,Brachman85]]. Most efforts to represent knowledge result in the construction of **semantic networks**, collections of concepts connected in a network topology. We use a graphical methodology called **concept mapping** [Novak84] to realize semantic networks of abstract life cycle products analogous to the user's problem area. Concept mapping has been successfully applied to a number of learning situations and, although independent of the AI Knowledge Base domain of interest here, has roots in learning theory that suggest it's suitability for our project.

To realize our semantic networks, we have developed **SeeGraph** [Latour 87], a network database with a graphical query language allowing users to add and delete nodes and arcs in multiple windows. Nodes of SeeGraph networks represent life cycle products such as specifications or implementations of procedural or data abstractions, module interaction structures, etc. Arcs in turn represent similarities between the "analogous" products. To facilitate movement through the Seegraph network, operations for changing, magnifying, and reducing the user's current view are available. In addition, the user can create and manipulate text attributes of the nodes and arcs.

Information associated with SeeGraph nodes and arcs may be described in as formal or informal a manner as is desired. Informal descriptions of abstractions and their relationships might be used when initially extending the knowledge base as new domains are explored, while more formal abstraction descriptions might take the form of algebraic specifications, with their relationships taking the form of proofs relating these specifications. Existing interpretors may be used to construct logically correct specifications, and theorem provers may be used to develop theorems relating these specifications.

A parallel software engineering/learning project is underway by our group at UMaine to construct a Medical Technology System utilizing concept mapping techniques [Brody,Kopec,and Latour87]. The software engineering group assembled to construct SEE will also construct this system using SeeGraph along with other SEE subsystems.

Examples of Analogical Inference

As we previously stated, abstractions may be represented in a variety of ways in our knowledge base. We first consider how procedural abstractions are represented, and then see that the data abstraction representations are simply extensions of the former.

We think of procedural abstraction as defined by Wirth [Wirth71]. Subsets of our semantic network of analogies can be viewed as trees, where each node of the tree represents an abstract operation that is a more abstract, "generic" form of it's descendents, and where any two nodes in the tree are termed analogies. In Wirth's stepwise refinement methodology, a programmer makes some implementation commitment transforming an abstract operation into one that is less abstract, or less "generic".

Now, consider the abstract operation "Linearly search an array for the presence (or absence) of a key". If we analyze the commitments that were made to achieve this level of abstraction, we have the following tree:

```
                    Search a List until
                  a Condition becomes True
                /
          Condition =>
          List element
          equals key
              /
     Search a list for
     the Presence of a Key
        /              \
List => Array      List => Linked List
   ¦                   ¦
Search an Array    Search a Linked
for the Presence   List for the
of a Key           Presence of a Key
    /     \            /        \
Search =>  Search =>  Search =>  Search =>
 Linear     Binary     Linear     Binary
   ¦
Linearly Search
an Array for the
presence of a Key
```

In the analogy tree presented above, linearly searching an array for the presence of a key is **not** the same as, but **is** analogous to, searching a linked list for the presence of a key.

Abstract operations can be, and usually are, referred to by definitions (concepts) in the user's area of application. Consider for example the abstract operation "Test whether or not a number is prime". One of the many implementations of this abstraction (in Ada) is:

```
PRIME:= TRUE;
for I in 2..ARG-1 loop
   if {I divides equally into ARG} then
      PRIME:= FALSE;
      exit;
   end if;
end loop;
```

Using this implementation as a definition for prime numbers, we can add this abstraction and it's commitments to the previous tree, yielding:

```
                    Search a List until
                  a Condition becomes True
                /                      \
        Condition =>              Condition =>
        List element               List element divides
        equals key                 evenly into Arg(ument)
            /                           ¦
     Search a list for            Search a list for
     the Presence of a Key        the presence of a
            ¦                      List element that
            ¦                      divides evenly into Arg
            v                          /        \
```

```
                               /          \
              List => 2..Arg-1   List => 2..Arg/2 ...
                           !                 !
                      Search 1..Arg-1 for
                      the presence of an
                      integer that divides
                      evenly into Arg
                           !
                       Search => Linear
        !                    !
Linearly search         Linearly search 1..Arg-1
an Array for      <=>   for the the presence of
Presence of a Key       an integer that divides
                        evenly into Arg
```

The two abstract operations at the bottom of the tree are analogies (equated in the network by <=>), and experience with one leads to a fairly good understanding of the other.   In general, the "closer" analogies are to each other in the tree, the more understanding of one can be derived from understanding of the other.

We next consider data abstraction, the fundamental tool of object oriented design.   Suppose we have the following dictionary ADT:

```
    with WORDS; use WORDS;
    Package DICTIONARIES is
        type DICTIONARY is private;
        procedure CREATE(D: out DICTIONARY);
        procedure ADD(D: in out DICTIONARY;W: in WORD);
        function ALREADY_THERE(W: WORD;D: DICTIONARY) returns BOOLEAN;
        procedure ALPHABETIZE(D: in out DICTIONARY);
        procedure PRINT(D: DICTIONARY);
    private
        type DICTIONARY is {implementation dependent}
    end DICTIONARY;
```

Just as with procedural abstraction, we can represent a data abstraction as a node in an analogy tree, where the children of the node represent either other data abstraction nodes or procedural abstraction trees described previously.   In the case of the abstract data type DICTIONARY, commitment to a particular data structure for dictionary forces commitment to:

1) a search algorithm for ALREADY_THERE,
2) an insert algorithm for ADD,
3) the details of CREATE,
4) a subset of sort algorithms for ALPHABETIZE, and
5) the details of accessing words in PRINT.

Frequently a module designer has need for an abstract data type with functionality similar to (analogous to), but not quite the same as a well known ADT that has a number of available implementations.   Through our semantic network we can represent hierarchies of ADT specifications and implementations, i.e., those based on the sequence model - stacks, queues, deques, etc., along with the precise similarities and differences between

them. Allowing the designer to browse through this hierarchy of formally
specified ADTs will give him a better feel for expressing precisely the
functionality of his own ADT, as well as a better feel for the choices of
implementation available.

Module interconnection structures

A problem with a number of popular ADT library facilities is that they
provide a large number of ADTs out of context with respect to their
environment. We have begun looking at a number of interconnection
structures using a small class of popular ADTs in order to classify these
structures and store them as nodes in our knowledge base. One such
example is a cyclic command interpretor, a fairly simple module usually
found at the head of a "Uses" structure in most command driven applications.

Interconnection structures have similarities to other interconnection
structures, relationships to their component modules, and to some extent
influence the choice of module implementation.

Usage of the SeeGraph Analogy Knowledge Base

We envision SeeGraph and it's stored analogy knowledge base to be used
in a variety of ways:

1) Currently it is being used as a browser through a knowledge base of
predefined objects and relations. There are several conceptual advantages
to querying a network database in such a spatial fashion, browsing being
one. The relation of one node to another through a connecting arc in a
graph is unmistakable but limiting. This is the only relation it addresses.
SeeGraph gives the user a spatial dimension in which to give meaning to the
network at hand and show relation between it's many objects. Placement of
objects in groups to show a sharing of common characteristics, use of node
size to indicate hierarchy within groups, and thickening of arcs to show
path precedence are all spatial effects which allow the user to get a feel
for the logical representation of the network and how to best use it as an
interface to the underlying data objects.

Predefined procedure and data abstractions, those usually found
alphabetically listed in a program library, are being added by our students
as nodes in a semantic network containing subtrees as described earlier.

2) It can be constructed by a designer as he/she explores new application
areas. It can then be used by other designers to gain insight into the
semantic network constructed for these application areas. We are
considering testing the system in existing CAD/CAM software engineering
environments on campus to determine it's usefulness as an aid to such domain
analysis.

3) A number of designer defined networks can be merged and studied to
provide an integrated, permanent network for an application area.

4) As stated before, it can be used as a base for automated tools to
formally describe and automatically (semi-automatically) search for objects

having relevant characteristics.

Knowledge Base Construction

A team of both graduate and undergraduate students are participating in the implementation of this system as part of our software engineering, graphics, and AI curriculum programs.

We currently have a simple prototype of SeeGraph running on a Vaxstation II [Ferguson,Latour 86], written in Ada using the DEC/Ada compiler system. We are in the specification stage for additional facilities such as 1) a 3-D graphics interface, 2) multiple user/screen access to shared networks, 3) hierarchical graphs (ie., graphs whose nodes have graph attributes) with selective viewing, etc...

Bibliography

Bobrow,D.G. and Collins,A. (eds.),1975. Representation and Understanding. Academic Press, New York.

Brachman,R., Readings in Knowledge Representation. Kauffman, Menlo Park.

Brody,M.J.,Kopec,D.,Latour,L.,"Expert/Novice Learning Systems with Applications to Medical Technology", Grant Proposal in Process, 1987.

Ferguson,E. and Latour L.,"Explorations in Workstation Technology for Advanced Graphics and Automated Tools for APSEs", Digital Equipment Corporation Equipment Grant, 1986.

Latour,L.,"A Programming Environment for Learning - SEE: A Student's Educational Environment", IEEE Second Annual Conference on Ada Applications and Environments, Miami Beach, Fla, April, 1987.

Latour,L.,"SeeGraph: An APSE Tool For Organizing Reusable Abstractions - Software Description", University of Maine Computer Science Dept. Internal Report, July, 1987.

Minnow87,Proceedings: Tenth Minnowbrook Workshop on Software Reuse, July 28-31, Syracuse University Minnowbrook Conference Center.

Novak,J.D. and Gowin,D.B.,Learning How to Learn, Cambridge University Press, 1984

Sherlis,W.L. and Scott,D.S., "First Steps Towards Inferential Programming", Dept. of Computer Science, CMU, July 1983, CMU-CS-83-142.

Wirth,N., "Program Development by Stepwise Refinement", CACM, Vol. 14, April 1971, Pgs. 221-227.

MECHANISMS FOR EXTENDING THE APPLICABILITY OF REUSABLE COMPONENTS

Robert S. Arnold
Mark Blackburn
Terry Bollinger
John Gaffney

SPC–TN–87–013
VERSION 1.0

JULY 1987

This document may be distributed without restriction.

All complete or partial copies of this document must contain a copy of this page.

STATUS:	APPROVALS:		
Working Draft ☐	Author:	*Robert S. Arnold*	07/02/87
For Review ☐	V.P.:	*Bruce Barnes*	7/2/87
Final ☒	C.T.O.:	*William E. Riddle*	7/2/87

SOFTWARE PRODUCTIVITY CONSORTIUM
1880 CAMPUS COMMONS DRIVE, NORTH
RESTON, VIRGINIA 22091

Mechanisms for Extending the Applicability
of Reusable Components

Position Paper

Robert S. Arnold

Mark Blackburn

Terry Bollinger

John Gaffney

Software Productivity Consortium
1880 N. Campus Commons Drive
Reston, Virginia 22091

INTRODUCTION

The potential for reuse of components in new applications should be high to justify the initial costs of obtaining the components. By a "reusable component" we mean a software representation (e.g., specification, design, or source code) for which we have a specification, which is self–contained, and which is intended for integration into a variety of software systems. Our current work is on providing mechanisms to match problem descriptions with solutions incorporating reusable components. By letting the granularity of reuse be slight tailoring of reusable components, we hope to increase the applicability of the components.

NEED FOR EXTENDING THE APPLICABILITY OF REUSABLE COMPONENTS

The degree of reuse for a reusable component should be high for the creation of the component to be economically justified. We believe that a broad range of reusable components should be available for their use to be economical on a wide scale. Such a range of reusable components may be years away, because of the tremendous variety of applications and since many reusable components libraries are proprietary.

We feel that the applicability of reusable components can be significantly increased without expanding the size of the reusable components library. Below we indicate one way for doing this.

EXTENDING THE APPLICABILITY OF REUSABLE COMPONENTS

The process of finding, for a given application, candidate reusable components in a library involves matching information about the application domain with information about the reusable components. Once candidate reusable components are found, they must be integrated into the solution.

Our approach for performing this process is first to establish a knowledge base containing information about reusable components and about the application. Semantic descriptors are attached to each reusable component to characterize the contexts where it is most likely to apply. A semantic feature extraction program collects information from high-level, problem-oriented documents (e.g., text documentation, graphical designs, etc.) and puts this information into the knowledge base. Other information may be gained directly from the programmer. Problem-oriented information is then matched with reusable component information in the knowledge base.

When partial matches are found, tailoring mechanisms are invoked to create a new component which fully matches the problem-oriented information. The new component incorporates the partially matched reusable components. If high usage or high performance warrants, the new component may itself be made dynamically into a reusable component.

A major benefit of this approach is in handling modifications to software representations incorporating reusable components. Normally, if a piece of source code incorporating reusable components is arbitrarily modified, all the reusable components may have to be manually reexamined for applicability. However, if the system has a component-independent description of the properties the source code should possess, the system has some flexibility for automatically retailoring components to achieve the desired properties in a changed problem context. We feel that capturing programmers' software construction intentions gives component-independent information that is invaluable for aiding reuse in changed problem contexts.

SPECIFIC EXAMPLE

We are applying these ideas in a specific problem domain, optimization of Ada® source code. We first explain how we are approaching this problem, then why our approach is an instance of the reuse paradigm mentioned above.

In our optimization approach, we imagine a programmer sitting at a terminal, running the application program with test data, then using an execution profile tool (or program animation) to determine where the program is spending its time. Using our program optimization system, the programmer graphically indicates where he wants changes, then selects a "speedup" intention from a menu of change intentions. The system attempts to satisfy the speedup goal with its available optimization transformations. Once done, the system returns to the programmer for another round of optimization.

® Ada is a registered trademark of the Department of Defense (Ada Joint Program Office).

This continues until satisfactory performance is achieved, or the programmer gets tired. As a fallback, we plan to allow the programmer direct access to the optimized code version under controlled conditions.

We apply several constraints to the programmer. First, he is expected to view only a very easy-to-understand program version. Optimization never overtly changes this representation. The system keeps track of the optimized versions and conceals them from the programmer. The programmer is encouraged to think of his program through software performance metrics and program animation, not in terms of software efficiency constructs. Second, only functional changes, not speedup (or space) changes, generally can be made by the programmer directly on the easy-to-understand version. We rely on manual inspections to ensure that only functional changes are inserted and that understandability is preserved. Third, optimizations are performed by the system on behalf of the programmer. The optimizations are effected with optimization transformations. The system selects optimizations by using knowledge from the programmer's specified optimization intentions and the knowledge base of software and optimization information.

When the programmer functionally modifies the source code, the system will attempt to reapply the sequence of optimization intentions created when the code was first optimized. (Thus, optimization intentions become the most visible element of reuse and are tailored for changed problem contexts.) In this way, the need for the programmer to overtly reoptimize the entire program is reduced.

This optimization approach is an instance of the reuse paradigm mentioned earlier. The information in the knowledge base comes from the Ada source code, sequence of intentions specified by the programmer, values of software performance metrics, general and Ada-specific information about program optimization, and the optimization transformations themselves. The sequence of optimization intentions is the basis for finding partial matches with optimization transformations. Matches are made possible through the use of the semantic information in the knowledge base.

PERSPECTIVE

The ideas reported here represent ongoing research. We have no running tools yet. We are trying to anticipate problems with reusability and build tools to deal with those problems. We like knowledge bases for their flexibility in translating between different software representations, and for their ability to localize application-specific knowledge in a few parts of the system. We like transformations for their convenient encapsulation of procedural and non-procedural knowledge. We hope eventually to reload our system with knowledge from other domains (e.g., making Ada programs portable or conforming to Ada style guidelines). Eventually we hope to quantify the economic impact of providing some flexibility for reusable component libraries.

Reusing Design Histories
via Transformational Systems

Ira D. Baxter*

Advanced Software Engineering Project

Department of Information and Computer Science

University of California at Irvine

Irvine, California 92717

November 3, 1987

Abstract

Reuse is normally focused on reuse of code. We believe that reuse of other design artifacts is at least as important as the reuse of code. A *design history*, the sequence of decisions that determined an implementation, is a potentially reusable design artifact.

This paper outlines a method for reusing the transformational implementation of a specification, given a revised specification. While other methods actually *replay* a derivation history, this approach is unique in that it identifies only that part of the derivation history which needs to be changed, thus avoiding the replay effort. The few samples we have on transformational implementation suggest that even moderate size programs require tens of thousands of steps, and so avoidance is necessary for making maintenance on large transformationally-implemented systems practical. We argue that such an approach leads to a continuous design paradigm rather than the more conventional software lifecycle.

1   Introduction

This paper briefly outlines work on a method to minimize the designer interaction required and to speed the rate at which modifications can be made to software systems, if they have been implemented *transformationally*. The method may also lead to a practical instantiation of a *continuous design* software lifecycle rather than more traditional models.

The *transformational approach* to software implementation converts a *formal specification* to an implementation in a series of steps. Each step applies a *transform* (a re-writing rule) to the specification resulting from the previous step to generate a revised specification, usually with more implementation detail added [Balzer75]. The utility of the transformational

---

*This research was supported by the University of California and the National Science Foundation under contract DCR-85-21398

329

approach is that it provides an organizing principle to the generally nebulous process of software construction, and, with the aid of pre-constructed libraries of commonly used transformations, it promises potential productivity gains by reuse of hard-won implementation knowledge with the possibility of automated implementation. (Using a library of transforms is a significant form of re-use, but not the one we wish to emphasize here.) A very good overview of transformational systems can be found in [Partsch83] or [Agresti86]; a more recent index into the literature is [Feather86]. [1]

Because the branching factor in the design space is enormous ([Kant79], [Baxter86a]), and the number of transformations required to implement a specification is large [Boyle84b], [Baxter87a], finding a sequence of transformations that successfully converts the original specification to an implementation can be expensive. This is consistent with [Wile83]'s comment that the problem of *scale* is one of the most critical to handle.

Our expectation that software design is a hard problem makes the cost of initial implementation easier to accept. The notion that one should only modify specifications and re-implement a new program (transformationally) from the revised specifications rather than modify the originally implemented program is expounded in [Balzer82]. Paying a similar cost for a reimplementation from a slightly-changed specification is generally considered unacceptable. Because of the high cost of finding another sequence of transforms, [Feather83] suggests the importance of being able to reuse the transformational *development* on a modified specification.

We are interested in methods for accomplishing change in transformational implementations based on the specification of a change and reusing the derivation history of the previously implemented specification. We will sketch methods whose purpose is to achieve the small-change, small-reimplementation-effort property desired by practitioners[2], thereby enhancing the performance and therefore the utility of the transformational paradigm.

2 Replay of design histories

A naive method for re-using the original development is to capture the sequence of transformations which have been applied in the original implementation (called a *design history*), and to *replay* those transformations, in sequence, on the revised specification. Of course, we can only replay the derivation up to the point where a change is required; replaying from this point on is *blocked* because the original conditions no longer apply.

---

[1]Other interesting papers about the theory and practice of transformational systems include [Burstall77], [Green78], [Kibler78], [Feather82], [Boyle84a], [Neighbors84], [Smith86], and [Belkhouche86].

[2]We know this is not possible in general. We believe it to be a reasonable goal when the problem statement is made in terms of a domain whose implementation principles are well-understood.

A key insight is that the decisions, made beyond the point where a change is required in a design history, are not necessarily invalidated by the change.[3] We argue, in fact, that the very large scale of any transformational implementation ensures that many of the decisions beyond the change point are, in fact, applicable. Effective reuse of design histories requires reuse of decisions *beyond* the blocking point. Even those decisions which no longer apply directly may contain some useful information extractable by *analogy* [Carbonell85]. A consequence of these insights is that methods for replay hardly ever use the naive method outlined without some interesting variations.

Other researchers have investigated *replay* of a design history [Cheatham81], [Steinberg84], [Mostow87] or a *development* [Wile83].

[Partsch83] describes replay in Cheatham's system as repeated application of previously used refinement rules until none is applicable. The implication is that the transform sequence is also lost; this cannot be practical as many optimizing transformations in an implementation require other *conditioning* transformations be applied first [Fickas82], [Fickas85], so loss of sequencing must imply some lost of optimizations. Also, different early sequencing will lead to implementations radically different than the original, and this is surely not desired. We see that order is somehow important and must be preserved.

[Mostow87] constrains design histories to consist of recursive decompositions of a specification, so the history actually takes the form of a tree, with the root being the initial specification, and the set of branches emanating from a node specify the decomposition of that node into sub-nodes. Such tree-structured design histories can be replayed by replaying each branch until a blocking condition is reached along that branch.

The PADDLE ([Wile83]) system captures *program developments*, as a set of *goal structures* for implementation, in a language which shares some similarities to hierarchical planning systems like that of [Sacerdoti77]. Goals may be achieved by any of several subgoals, providing a method of handling decisions which no longer apply. Even so, PADDLE still blocks at the first decision it cannot handle, and it still replays each individual decision.

3 On Commutativity of Transformations

A practical system to reuse design decisions should reuse as many of the decisions from the design history as possible, and must also handle invalidated design decisions. Our work emphasizes the former. It is based on a simple formalization of a transformational implementation:

For any formal specification S, and implementation $I(S)$ which implements S, the transformation $S \rightarrow I(S)$ implements the specification. It is currently an article of faith that $I(S)$ can be composed of many smaller transformations t_i, such that

---

[3][Baxter86a] suggests that the actual historical order is not always relevant, and, in fact, hinders the ability to maximize the re-use of an established design.

$$I(S) = t_n(t_{n-1}(\ldots t_2(t_1(S))\ldots))$$

A major value of transformational systems is precisely this decomposability; we expect individual t_i to be reusable on other specifications. We believe that the t_i serve to capture implementation knowledge. The set of t_i are drawn, presumably, from a library of transformations (a set) T containing enough transformations to implement all the S_j of interest.

The transformations form a mathematical structure similar to an *algebra*; some of the transformations *commute*. Thus a particular design history can be commuted into many different orders without affecting the result. Given a revised specification, our approach is effectively to rewrite the design history of the previous implementation to "move" the affected transforms as far to the left (increasing n) as possible; if the lowest index of an affected transform is m, then transforms 1 to $m - 1$ are the set of reusable decisions. Transforms m through n must be handled by other methods, such as goal structures or analogies.

This viewpoint reduces the problem of identifying reusable transforms to that of discovering and recording commutativity between transforms.

4 Determining/Recording Commutativity

We use or are investigating several methods for determination of commutativity.

1. The transform composition operator directly forces many transforms to be commutative

2. Certain chains of transforms may not commute with one another, but may commute with other chains

3. *Bindings* of the transforms used may demonstrate commutativity of two transforms in the particular design history, even in the absence of condition 1)

[Baxter86b] gives a taxonomy of interactions between transforms which includes commutativity.

Given a specific, time-sequenced design history, the commutativity of the various transforms used in that history can be worked out using the above methods.

We follow the *dependency-directed backtracking* ([London78]) techniques used in *truth-maintenance systems* [Doyle78], [Martins86] and non-linear planners [Chapman85] to record the dependency (non-commutativity) of transforms on one another. Such a record is termed a *dependency network*. This captures the minimal (partial) ordering necessary.

The dependency network is rooted in the original specification and terminates in the implementation. A change to the original specification directly determines the set of transformations dependent on that part of the specification. Those parts of the specification must be re-implemented, generating a new implementation portion. Transformations (and the part of the implementation) not dependent on the changed part of the specification need NOT be inspected, leading to a fast identification of the part of the implementation needing change.

We assume the original transformation process was controlled by a high-level *performance* goal structure, which had detailed subgoal and plans instantiated during the construction process. The original implementation thus also depends on the instantiated goal/plan structure. Given a goal dependency network on this structure, high level performance goals that control how a portion of the implementation was created can be identified [Baxter87b].

Given both dependency networks and a specification change, the part of the implementation needing change can be identified and "undone"; performance goals the undone part of the original implementation can then be identified and reused to implement the change.

Work on a prototype system that implements these ideas has been started.

5   Conclusion

[Marks86] suggests the need for a software design environment in which design is a (nearly) continuous process over the lifespan of a software system. He proposes the separation between design and maintenance is imaginary; modifications to a system during the design phase are no different than modifications after release of the first implementation. [Baxter86c] suggests a basis for such an environment based on a transformational paradigm, using propagation of change ([Lehman84]) as the vehicle for managing design changes. This allows a system to start with an extremely vague specification which is refined over time by teams.

Reuse of design histories appears to be a promising method for implementing tools necessary for such a design environment.

These mechanisms, we believe, would significantly enhance the utility of transformational systems for software construction.

References

[Agresti86] "What are the New Paradigms?", William W. Agresti, in **New Paradigms for Software Development**, William W. Agresti, ed., IEEE, 1986, ISBN 0-8186-0707-6.

[Balzer75] "On the transformational approach to programming", R. Balzer, N. Goldman, and D. Wile, in **Proceedings of 2nd International Conference on Software Engineering**, 1976, pp. 337-343.

[Balzer82] "Operational Specification as the basis for rapid prototyping", R. Balzer, N. Goldman and D. Wile, ACM Sigsoft Software Engineering Notes, Vol. 7, No. 5, December 1982, pp. 3-16.

[Baxter86a] "TMM: Software Maintenance by Transformation", G. Arango, I. Baxter, P. Freeman, C. Pidgeon, IEEE Software, Vol. 3, Number 3, May 1986, page 27-39.

[Baxter86b] "Evolution Through Formal Transformations", G. Arango, I. Baxter, P. Freeman, C. Pidgeon, University of California at Irvine, Department of ICS, Advanced Software Engineering Project, September 1986.

[Baxter86c] "DOIT: A Domain-Oriented, Iterative Transformational architecture for LEONARDO", I. Baxter, M. Conner and J. Petersen, MCC Corporation proprietary document, October 1986.

[Baxter87a] "Propagation of Change in Transformational Systems", Ira D. Baxter, Advanced Software Engineering Project, Department of Computer Science, University of California at Irvine, January, 1987, Internal Research Memo.

[Baxter87b] "PCL: A Production Control Language", Ira D. Baxter, Technical Report, Microelectronics and Computer Technology Corporation, Software Technology Program, November, 1987.

[Belkhouche86] "Direct Implementation of Abstract Data Types from Abstract Specifications", Boumediene Belkhouche and Joseph E. Urban, IEEE Transactions on Software Engineering, Vol. SE-10, No. 5, May 1986, pp. 649-661.

[Boyle84a] "Reuseability through Program Transformation", J. M. Boyle and M. N. Muralidharan, IEEE Transactions on Software Engineering, Vol. SE-10(5), pp. 574-588.

[Boyle84b] "Lisp to FORTRAN – Program Transformation Applied", James. M. Boyle, in **Program Transformation and Programming Environments**, ed. Peter Pepper, Springer-Verlag, New York, 1984, pp. 291-298.

[Burstall77] "A Transformational System for Developing Recursive Programs", R. M. Burstall and John Darlington, Journal of ACM, Vol. 24, No. 1, January 1977, pp. 44-67.

[Carbonell85] "Derivational Analogy: A Theory of Reconstructive Problem Solving and Expertise Acquisition", J. Carbonell, Tech. Rep. CMU-CS-85-115, 1985.

[Chapman85] "Planning for Conjunctive Goals", David Chapman, MIT Technical Report 802, May, 1985.

[Cheatham81] "Program refinement by transformation", T. E. Cheatham Jr., G. H. Holloway, J. A. Townley, in **Proceedings of the Fifth International Conference on Software Engineering**, San Diego, California, pp. 430-437, March 1981, reprinted in **New Paradigms for**

Software Development, William W. Agresti, ed., IEEE, 1986, ISBN 0-8186-0707-6.

[Doyle78] "Truth Maintenance Systems for Problem Solving", Jon Doyle, TR-419, Massachusetts Institute of Technology, Artificial Intelligence Laboratory, January 1978.

[Feather82] "A system for assisting program transformation", Martin S. Feather, ACM Transactions on Programming Language and Systems, Vol. 4, Number 1, pp. 1-20.

[Feather83] "Reuse in the Context of a Transformation Based Methodology", Martin S. Feather, ITT Proceedings of the Workshop on Reusability in Programming, 1983, pp. 50-58, reprinted in **Tutorial: Software Reusability**, Peter Freeman, ed., IEEE Computer Society, 1987.

[Feather86] "A Survey and Classification of some Program Transformation Approaches and Techniques", Martin S. Feather, IFIP WG2.1 Working Conference on Program Specification and Transformation, Bad Toelz, Germany, April 1986, also available from USC/ Information Sciences Institute, Marina del Rey, CA.

[Fickas82] **Automating the transformational development of software**, Stephen Fickas, PhD Thesis, University of California at Irvine, 1982.

[Fickas85] "Automating the transformational development of software." IEEE Transactions on Software Engineering, 111(11):1268-1277, November, 1985

[Green78] "On Program Synthesis Knowledge", Cordell Green and David Barstow, Artificial Intelligence Vol. 10, 1978, pp. 241-279.

[Kant79] **Efficiency considerations in program synthesis: A knowledge-based approach**, Elaine Kant, PhD thesis, Computer Science Department, Stanford University, 1979.

[Kibler78] **Power, Efficiency, and Correctness of Transformation Systems**, Dennis F. Kibler, PhD Thesis, University of California at Irvine, Irvine California, 1978.

[Lehman84] "Another Look At Software Design Methodology", M. M. Lehman, V. Stenning, W. M. Turski, ACM Sigsoft Software Engineering Notes, Vol. 9, No. 2, April 1984, p. 38.

[London78] "A dependency-based modelling mechanism for problem solving", P. London, in **AFIPS Conference Proceedings, Vol 47**, pp. 263-274, 1978.

[Marks86] "What is Leonardo?", MCC Technical Report STP-141-86, Microelectronics and Computer Technology Corporation, May 1986.

[Martins86] "Theoretical Foundations for Belief Revision", Joao P. Martins and Stuart C. Shapiro, in **Proceedings of the 1986 Conference on Theoretical Aspects of Reasoning About Knowledge**, ed. Joseph Y. Halpern, Morgan-Kaufmann, 1986, ISBN 0-934613-04-4 pp. 383-398

[Mostow87] "Automated Reuse of Design Plans", Jack Mostow and Mike Barley, Rutgers AI/Design Project Working Paper Number 53, February, 1987, submitted to International Conference on Engineering Design, Boston, MA, August 1987.

[Neighbors84] "The Draco Approach to Constructing Software from Reusable Components", James Neighbors, IEEE Transactions on Software Engineering, Vol. SE-10, No. 5, September 1984.

[Partsch83] "Program Transformation Systems", H. Partsch and R. Steinbruggen, Computing Surveys, Vol. 15, No. 3, September 1983, pp. 199-236, reprinted in **New Paradigms for Software Development**, William W. Agresti, ed., IEEE, 1986, ISBN 0-8186-0707-6.

[Sacerdoti77] **A Structure for Plans and Behavior**, E. Sacerdoti, Elsevier North-Holland, New York, 1977, ISBN 0-444-00209-X.

[Smith86] "Research on Knowledge-Based Software Environments at Kestrel Institute", D. R. Smith, G. B. Kotik and S. J. Westfold, IEEE Transactions on Software Engineering, November 1985, Volume SE-11, Number 11, pp. 1278-1295.

[Steinberg84] "A Knowledge Based Approach to VLSI CAD: The Redesign System", Louis I. Steinberg and Tom M. Mitchell, 21st Design Automation Conference, IEEE 1984, pp. 412-418.

[Wile83] "Program Developments: Formal Explanations of Implementations", D. Wile, Comm. ACM, Vol. 26 No. 11, November 1983, pp. 902-911.

Parameterized Programming in OBJ2" by K. Futatsugi, J. Goguen, J. Meseguer, and K. Okada from *Proceedings of the Ninth International Conference on Software Engineering*, 1987, pages 51–60. Copyright 1987, Association for Computing Machinery, Inc., reprinted by permission.

Parameterized Programming
in
OBJ2

Kokichi Futatsugi, Joseph Goguen, José Meseguer,
and Koji Okada

Electrotechnical Laboratory
1-1-4 Umezono, Tsukuba Science City, Ibaraki 305, JAPAN
and
SRI International
333 Ravenswood Ave., Menlo Park, California 94025, U.S.A.

ABSTRACT

Parameterized programming [9] is a powerful technique for the construction, maintenance, and reuse of software. In this technique, modules may be parameterized over very general interfaces that describe what properties of an environment are required for the module to work correctly. Ease of construction, maintenance, and reuse of software are all enhanced by the flexibility of the parameterization mechanism provided.

OBJ2 [8] is designed to support parameterized programming, using algebraic specification techniques [2,16,17]; it provides facilities for user-definable abstract data types, parameterized abstract objects, and interactive programming. OBJ2 is a functional programming language based on equational logic, rather than on general first order logic; because equations can be interpreted directly as rewrite rules [18], it is easy to see their computational significance as well as their logical significance.

This paper describes parameterized programming in OBJ2 with some simple examples. These techniques would also be effective in constructing a library system [10] for a conventional procedural language such as Ada [5] or Modula-2 [21], as well as for adding a module system to so-called logic programming languages such as Prolog [3,11].

1 INTRODUCTION

The basic idea of parameterized programming [9] is to maximize program reuse by creating and storing programs in as general a form as possible. One can then construct new program modules from old ones just by instantiating parameters; moreover, debugging, maintenance, readability and portability are all enhanced. For this to work, we need a suitable notion of parameterized module, along with the capability for instantiating parameters, and the capability for encapsulating code within modules.

OBJ2 [8] is designed to support parameterized programming. OBJ2's modularization and parameterization mechanisms are based on algebraic specification techniques [2,16,17] and can provide powerful and clear techniques for hierarchically structuring software. For example, the interface declarations of OBJ2's parameterized modules are not purely syntactic, but may contain semantic requirements that actual modules must satisfy before they can be meaningfully substituted. This can prevent many subtle bugs. Views and theories support this semantic interface in OBJ2.

An unusual feature of OBJ2 is the commands that it provides for modifying and combining program modules. A key for this is the systematic use of module expressions for describing and creating complex combinations of modules. Module expressions are similar to the usual arithmetic expressions, except that parameterized modules act like operators such as "+" or "*", and fully instantiated modules act like constants such as "2" or "1.5". It often happens that there is a software part that we want to reuse, but it is not in exactly the right form. One

Reviewed and recommended by:
Pamela Zave

way to get it into the right form is to
apply some transformations. An important
aspect of the parameterized programming
paradigm is to permit parameterized
modules to be modified, either before or
after instantiation, so that they can fit
to a wider variety of applications. OBJ2
provides the following transformations:
(1) enrich a module, by adding to its
functionality; and (2) rename part of the
interface of a module.

This paper describes parameterized
programming in OBJ2 in a rather concrete
fashion, using simple but "real" OBJ2
programs. That is, all our examples have
been running on the OBJ2 system. Section
2 provides the basics of OBJ2 needed to
understand the examples. Section 3
explains parameterized programming in OBJ2
and its applications to formalizing and
automating the software construction
process. Section 4 gives some concluding
remarks.

2 BASICS OF OBJ2

An OBJ2 program is a sequence of
"objects," each of which may define one or
more new sorts of data, together with
associated operations that may create,
select, interrogate, store, or modify
data. Such an object may use existing
objects with their sorts of data and
operations. An object defines both
"types" (in the programming language sense
of a domain of values for variables
together with operations to construct and
access those values) and algorithms that
manipulate values.

2.1 OBJECTS

OBJ2's basic entity is the "object", which
is a (possibly parameterized) module
encapsulating executable code; objects
generally introduce new sorts of data and
new operations upon that data. An object
has three main parts: (1) a "header",
containing its name, parameters, interface
requirements, and imported module list;
(2) a "signature", declaring its new
sorts, subsort relationships, and
operations; and (3) a "body", containing
its code, consisting of equations.

For example, the following BITS object
introduces sorts Bit and Bits (for Bit
Sequence) with a length operation which
gives the length of sequences; these
sequences have syntax using dot and nil.

```
obj BITS is
   extending INT .
   sorts Bit Bits .
   ops 0 1 :     -> Bit .
   op nil :      -> Bits .
   op (_ . _) : Bit Bits -> Bits .
   op length_ : Bits -> Int .
      --- the sort Int stands for
      --- Integers and is imported from
      --- the INT object
      --- a comment starts with "---" and
      --- ends at <end-of-line> in OBJ2
   var B : Bit
   var S : Bits
   eq : length nil = 0 .
   eq : length (B . S) = 1 + length S .
endo
```

Each line in this example begins with an
OBJ2 keyword. The first line gives the
name BITS of the object. The second line
indicates that the built-in object INT
(for integers) is imported by BITS. The
keyword "extending" indicates that certain
static checks are to be performed. The
"ops" line declares the two Bit constants
0 and 1, the next line declares the empty
string nil, the next a "cons" operation
(which adds a Bit to some Bits) with "dot"
syntax, and the next a length operation
using the sort Int from INT. Then,
variables of sorts Bit and Bits are
declared and used in equations which give
semantics for the length function.

An OBJ2 user can define any desired
prefix, postfix, infix, or more generally,
mixfix syntax for an operation. The sorts
of the arguments and value of an operation
are defined at the same time as the form
for its syntax. We use a notation for
syntactic forms which is similar to that
used in algebra. For example, consider
the following declarations of operators
and expressions which are constructed
using them (enumerated with letter "a"):

```
    (1) op push : Int Stack -> Stack .
    (1a) push(3, S)
or  (2) op top_ : Stack -> Int .
    (2') op (top _) : Stack -> Int .
    (2a) top push(3, S)
or  (3) op {_} : Int -> Set .
    (3') op ({ _ }) : Int -> Set .
    (3a) { 4 }
or  (4) op _+_ : Int Int -> Int .
    (4') op (_ + _) : Int Int -> Int .
    (4a) 2 + 4
or  (5) op if_then_else_fi :
                Bool Int Int -> Int .
    (5') op (if _ then _ else _ fi) :
                Bool Int Int -> Int .
    (5a) if prime?(I) then 1 else 0 fi
```

The first example indicates the usual
parenthesized-prefix-with-commas notation,
as the expression "push(3, S)" of sort
Stack for 3 of sort Int and S of sort
Stack. Other syntactic forms make use of
place-holders, for which we use an
underbar "_", as in the prefix declaration
of the second example for top operation.
Similarly, the outfix form of the

singleton set operation is defined in the third example, and infix form for addition is defined in the fourth example. The fifth example defines mixfix declaration for a conditional expression.

Obviously, there are many opportunities for ambiguity in parsing such a syntax. The OBJ2 convention is that an expression is well-formed if and only if it has exactly one parse. For example, the expression "1" in the object BITS is not a well formed term because it can be parsed as an Integer and as a Bit at the same time. On the other hand, the expression "length 1 . 1 . nil" is well formed term in the BITS object.

Basic naming conventions for OBJ2 are as follows: each module must have a globally unique name; each sort name must be unique within its module, and may be qualified by the module name to provide a globally unique name; an operation name is taken to include its distribution of keywords (which is called its "pattern") and its "arity" (which is its list of argument sorts), and its "coarity" (which is its value sort), and must be unique within a module; an operation name may be qualified by the name of its module to produce a globally unique name. Note that, same pattern may have several arities, as in Section 2.2 below.

2.2 SUBSORTS

OBJ2 is strongly typed (or strongly "sorted" in OBJ2 jargon). As in many other languages, users can introduce their own sorts and operations, thus supporting user defined ADTs. However, OBJ2 also permits users to declare that some sorts contain (or are contained in) others. For example, we can define BITS in a different way as follows.

```
obj BITS' is
    extending INT .
    sorts Bit Bits
    subsorts Bit < Bits .
        --- Bit is subsort of Bits
    ops 0 1 : -> Bit .
    op (_ _) : Bit Bits -> Bits .
    op length_ : Bits -> Int .
    var B : Bit
    var S : Bits
    eq : length B = 1 .
    eq : length B S = 1 + length S .
endo
```

In this object sort Bit is declared to be a subsort of sort Bits and the Bit constants 0 and 1 can be "coerced" to Bits automatically. So an expression like "length 1 1 1 0" is a well formed term in this object.

There are many cases where one sort of data is contained in (or contains) another, e.g., the natural numbers are contained in the integers, which are contained in the rationals; then the sort Nat is a subsort of Int, and Int is a subsort of Rat (or Int is a supersort of Nat, etc.), written Nat < Int < Rat. Moreover, an operation may restrict to subsorts of its arity and coarity, and still be "the same" operation. For example, each addition operation _+_ : Rat Rat -> Rat, _+_ : Int Int -> Int, _+_ : Nat Nat -> Nat is a restriction of the preceding one.

2.3 OPERATIONAL AND MATHEMATICAL SEMANTICS

OBJ2 code is executed by interpreting equations as rewrite rules: the lefthand side is regarded as a pattern to be matched within an expression (variables can match any subexpression of appropriate sort); when a match occurs, the subexpression matching the lefthand side is rewritten to the corresponding substitution instance of the righthand side. This process continues until there are no more matches, and then the expression is said to be "reduced" or in "normal form". For example, writing

```
reduce in BITS as Int :
        (length 1 . 0 . 1 . nil) .
```

at OBJ2's top level causes calculation of the reduced form of the term "(length 1 . 0 . 1 . nil)" using equations in the object BITS as rewrite rules, and OBJ2 replies with

```
as Int.INT : 3
```

to show that the reduced form is 3 of sort Int in the object INT. Henceforth, we will write

```
reduce in BITS as Int :
        (length 1 . 0 . 1 . nil) .
==> as Int.INT : 3
```

to show reductions in objects.

OBJ2's mathematical semantics is so-called Initial Algebra Semantics (IAS) [16] which is implemented by an operational semantics based on rewrite rules [18]. IAS provides a standard interpretation characterized by the properties of (1) having "no junk", meaning that all data values are denoted by terms in the available operation symbols; and (2) having "no confusion", meaning that two terms denote the same data value if and only if they can be proved equal with standard equational reasoning from the available equations.

In fact, the initial algebra semantics underlying OBJ2 uses order-sorted algebra [12], which generalize many-sorted algebra by allowing subsorts and operator overloading; these features make OBJ2 much more expressive than standard algebraic notation. There is also a fully developed operational semantics for the order-sorted algebra based on rewrite rules [14]

The Church-Rosser and termination properties for rewrite rules [18] guarantee a unique reduced form is always produced. Experienced programmers usually write rules that satisfy these properties except for some special operations such as if_then_else_fi. Term rewriting may seem a specialized computational paradigm, but in fact it is completely general, because any computable function over any computable data types can be so realized [19].

2.4 HIERARCHY OF MODULES

OBJ2 modules can import other modules in three different ways by "using", "extending" and "protecting". These define three different restrictions on properties of the imported module that are preserved, and they define three corresponding partial orders among modules.

An importation may fail to preserve the "no confusion" property for the data elements of the imported module. For example, if we define the integers modulo 7 by importing the integers and adding the equation "7=0", then the integer data elements become confused. Similarly, the "no junk" property may be violated by operations that create new data elements of imported sorts. For example, a Bool-valued operation "prime?" can create "Boolean junk" like "prime?(14)" if a user gives incomplete equations for "prime?".

"Protecting" is the most restrictive relation, indicating that both the "no confusion" and "no junk" properties are preserved, and thus the imported module remains unchanged. "Extending" is a relation requiring that only the "no confusion" condition is preserved. "using" does not guarantee anything, it just copies the imported modules.

3 PARAMETERIZED PROGRAMMING IN OBJ2

The only top level OBJ2 entities are "modules" (which are either "objects" or "theories") and "views" (which relate theories to modules); objects contain executable code, while theories contain nonexecutable assertions. Thus, executable code and nonexecutable

assertions are both modularized, and are closely integrated with each other. Theories and views make it possible to construct a wide varieties of module expressions, and provide powerful tools for parameterized programming.

3.1 PARAMETERIZED MODULES AND THEORIES

Modules group together the data and operations used for particular problems such as sorting, matrix manipulation, or graphics. Parameterized modules maximize reusability by permitting "tuning" to fit a variety of applications. For example, we can define a parameterized sequence module SEQ in OBJ2 as follows:

```
th TRIV is sort Elt . endth

obj SEQ[X :: TRIV] is
   protecting BOOL .
   sort NeSeq . --- non-empty sequences
   sort Seq .
   subsorts NeSeq < Seq .
   op . : -> Seq . --- the empty sequence
   op (_ _) : Elt Seq -> NeSeq . --- cons
   op head_ : NeSeq -> Elt .
   op tail_ : NeSeq -> Seq .
   op _$_ : Seq Seq -> Seq .
      --- concatenation
   vars S S' : Seq .
   var E : Elt .
   eq : head E S  = E .
   eq : tail E S = S .
   eq : (. $ S) = S .
   eq : (E S) $ S' = E (S $ S') .
endo
```

The parameter of SEQ is characterized by the theory TRIV. TRIV is the requirement theory for an interface that only requires a designated sort corresponding to Elt from an actual object. Using this generic SEQ object we can define integer sequence SEQInt only by instantiating TRIV with INT with

```
obj SEQint is protecting SEQ[INT] . endo
```

In the object SEQint, the following reductions may occur:

```
reduce in SEQint as Int : (head 1 2 3 .)
==> as Int.INT : 1
reduce in SEQint as Seq :
  (1 2 . $ 3 4 .)
==> as Seq.SEQ_2_SEQint :
     (1 (2 (3 (4 .))))
        --- the reduced output term is
        --- fully parenthesized
        --- module names which contain
        --- "_" such as SEQ_2_SEQint are
        --- generated by the OBJ2 system
```

As a more interesting generic module, we write a parameterized sorting module

SORTING in OBJ2. The parameter of SORTING should range over ordered sets. As explained above, in OBJ2 the requirements for parameters are given as theories. The requirement theory for SORTING is given as a theory TOSET (Totally Ordered SET):

```
th TOSET is
  protecting BOOL .
  sort Elt .
  op _<_ : Elt Elt -> Bool .
  vars E E' E'' : Elt .
  eq Bool : E < E = false .
  eq Bool :
    (E < E') or (E' < E) or (E == E') =
      true .
  eq Bool :
    (E < E' and E' < E'')
      implies (E < E'') =
        true .
endth
```

In the second equation, "==" is a built-in equality such that for two terms t, t' of the same sort, t == t' is true if they have the same reduced form, and is false otherwise. == implements the decision procedure for equality that is automatically associated with every sort.

Using the theory TOSET, a generic sorting object is written as follows, using the binary sorting algorithm:

```
obj SORTING [ELT :: TOSET] is
  extending SEQ[ELT] .
  op sort_ : Seq -> Seq .
  sort Btree .
   --- binary tree for storing elements
   --- in order
  op makeBtree_ : Seq -> Btree .
  op flatten_ : Btree -> Seq .
  var L : Seq .
  eq : sort L = flatten makeBtree L .
  op nil : -> Btree .
  op _#_#_ : Btree Elt Btree -> Btree .
  op insert_to_ : Elt Btree -> Btree .
  vars E E' : Elt .
  eq : makeBtree(.) = nil .
  eq : makeBtree(E L) =
        insert E to (makeBtree L) .
  vars T T' : Btree .
  eq : insert E to nil = nil # E # nil .
  eq : insert E to (T # E' # T') =
    if E < E' or E == E'
    then (insert E to T) # E' # T'
    else T # E' # (insert E to T')
    fi .
  eq : flatten nil = (.) .
  eq : flatten(T # E # T') =
        (flatten T) $ (E flatten T') .

endo
```

Here, if_then_else_fi is a polymorphic conditional, provided for every sort by a built-in control structure object. As can be seen from these examples, an OBJ2 module interface is described by a

requirement theory, giving both syntax for the interface and axioms, so that an object is an admissible actual only if it satisfies the axioms.

By instantiating the parameter of the SORTING object with a built-in object INT, one can easily define a sorting program over sequences of integers (instantiation is explained in more detail in the next section):

```
obj INTsorting is
  protecting SORTING[INT] .
endo

reduce in INTsorting as Seq :
  (sort 1 4 2 3 .)
==> as Seq.SEQ_4_INTsorting :
    (1 (2 (3 (4 .))))
```

A parameterized object may have one or more requirement theories; these are given in square brackets after its name. Since more than one parameter may be subject to the same requirements, different instances of the same theory may be needed. For example, the following TABLE object has two TRIV requirement theories, INDEX and VAL, with Elt.INDEX and Elt.VAL their corresponding sorts; this illustrates OBJ2's qualified sort name convention. The supersort ErrVal of Elt.VAL accommodates error messages for lookups of an index where no value is stored.

```
obj TABLE [INDEX :: TRIV, VAL :: TRIV] is
  protecting BOOL .
  sorts Table ErrVal .
  subsorts Elt.VAL < ErrVal .
   --- error handling using the subsort
   --- mechanism; ErrVal contains error
   --- messages for undefined values and
   --- is a super sort of Elt.VAL
  op empty : -> Table .
  op put : Elt.VAL Elt.INDEX Table ->
          Table .
  op _[_] : Table Elt.INDEX -> ErrVal .
  op undef : Elt.INDEX -> ErrVal .
  vars I I' : Elt.INDEX
  var V : Elt.VAL
  var T : Table
  eq : put(V,I,T)[ I' ] =
        if I == I'
        then V else T [ I' ] fi .
  eq : empty [ I ] = undef(I) .
endo
```

Using the TABLE object, we can define the object TABLEidInt by

```
obj TABLEidInt is
  protecting TABLE[ID,INT] .
endo
```

and then the following reductions take place in it:

```
reduce in TABLEidInt as :
  --- the sort name can be omitted in a
  --- reduction command if no
  --- ambiguities occur
(put(1,a,put(2,b,put(3,c,empty)))) [ b ])
==> as Int.INT : 2

(put(1,a,put(2,b,put(3,c,empty)))) [ d ])
==> as ErrVal.TABLE_6_TABLEidInt : undef(d)
```

3.2 VIEWS AND MODULE EXPRESSIONS

Parameterized programming permits building
complex modules from simple ones by
applying parameterized objects, to actuals
that are themselves instantiations of
other parameterized objects and so on
recursively; a similar approach using
module construction operations occurs in
previous OBJ languages [13,15] and in
the HISP specification language [6,7].

Instantiating a parameterized object means
providing actual objects satisfying each
of its requirement theories. In OBJ2, the
actual objects are provided through views,
which bind required sorts and operations
to those actually provided in such a way
that all the axioms of the requirement
theory are satisfied. That is, views map
the sort and operation symbols in the
formal requirement theory to those in the
actual object. More generally, a view can
map an operation symbol in the formal to
an expression in the actual, as
illustrated in the following views from
TOSET to INT.

```
view INTdesc of INT as TOSET is
  sort Elt to Int .
    --- Elt should be mapped to Int
  vars X Y : Elt .
  op : X < Y to : Y < X .
  --- (X < Y) should be mapped to
  --- (Y < X)
endview
```

The view INTdesc views INT with descending
order as a TOSET; in "(op : X < Y to : Y <
X)" the first "<" is the one from TOSET
while the second "<" is from INT. Note
that, in general, there can be more than
one view from a theory to an actual.

Instantiating a parameterized object with
a view is indicated by replacing the
parameter part with the view name. Thus,
instantiating the generic sorting object
SORTING[X :: TOSET] for sorting integers
in descending order is indicated by
SORTING[INTdesc]. The following examples
shows how instantiations are written in
OBJ2, with a reductions on the
instantiated object.

```
obj SORTintDesc is
  protecting SORTING[INTdesc] .
endo
```

```
reduce in SORTintDesc as :
  (sort 2 1 4 3 .) .
==>
  as Seq.SORTING_4_SORTintDesc :
    (4 (3 (2 (1.))))
```

Sometimes a view can be inferred from a
partial description, using syntactic
similarities between the theory and the
object. We call such a view description
an "abbreviated view"; it is a "default
view" if abbreviated to nothing.(see [9]
for a precise description.) For example,
there is a default view of INT as TOSET
that maps Elt to Int and "op _<_ : Elt Elt
-> Bool ." to the usual ordering _<_ on
the integers. To instantiate a
parameterized object with a default view,
it suffices to place the actual in the
parameter part. Thus the object
SORTING[INT] sorts natural numbers in
ascending order and SORTING[ID] sorts
identifiers in the built-in lexicographic
ordering of OBJ2's built-in identifier
object ID. The INTsorting object in the
previous section was also defined using
this default view mechanism.

Using the default view mechanisms, the
module expression

```
SORTING[LEX[ID]] *
  (op (sort_) to (_lex-sort))
```

defines an object which lexicographically
sorts sequences of sentences (which are
sequences of identifiers). Here, LEX[X ::
TOSET] is a parameterized object which
provides lexicographic ordering for
sequences of elements from an ordered set
X. This module expression uses several
default conventions. In LEX[ID], a
default view maps the sort of LEX's
requirement theory to the sort Id and maps
its ordering to the built-in ordering for
identifiers. Another default view maps
the sort of the object SORTING's
requirement theory to the Seq sort of
LEX[ID], and maps its ordering to the
lexicographic ordering from LEX[ID]. "M *
(...)" is another module expression
construct which renames sorts and
operations of module M according to (...).
In this example, we rename the prefix
operation (sort_) of SORTING to postfix
(_lex-sort).

We now show this using real OBJ2 code.
First comes a definition of the
parameterized object LEX. LEX has a
parameter which is required to be a
totally ordered set, and it defines a
lexicographic ordering on sequences of it,
so it also yields a totally ordered set.

```
obj LEX[X :: TOSET] is
  protecting BOOL .
  extending SEQ[X] .
```

```
op _<_ : Seq Seq -> Bool .
var S S' : Seq .
var E E' : Elt .
eq : . < . = false .
eq : E S < . = false .
eq : . < E S = true .
eq : E S < E' S' =
        if E < E'
        then true
        else (if E == E'
                then S < S'
                else false fi) fi .
endo
```

Using this LEX object the object for
sorting sentences in lexicographic
ordering is defined by

```
obj SORTsentence is
  protecting
    SORTING[LEX[ID]] *
      (op (sort_) to (_lex-sort)) .
endo
```

The following reduction takes place in
SORTsentence.

```
red in SORTsentence as :
  (((Merry likes cherries .)
    (Tom peels bananas .)
    (Ken eats cherries .)
    (Ken loves apples .) .) lex-sort) .
==>
  as Seq.SEQ_14_SORTsentence :
  ((Ken (eats (cherries (.))))
  ((Ken (loves (apples (.))))
  ((Merry (likes (cherries (.))))
  ((Tom (peels (bananas (.))))
    (.)))))
```

As another typical example of module
expression, we show how to define
SYMBOLtable using OBJ2's module
expressions. First, a parameterized STACK
object is defined; then SYMBOLtable is
defined using ID, INT, TABLE, and STACK:

```
obj STACK[X :: TRIV] is
  protecting INT .
  sort NeStack Stack .
  subsorts NeStack < Stack
  op empty : -> Stack .
  op push_to_ : Elt Stack -> NeStack .
  op top_ : NeStack -> Elt .
  op pop_ : NeStack -> Stack .
  op length_ : Stack -> Int .
  var E : Elt
  var S : Stack
  eq : length empty = 0 .
  eq : length (push E to S) =
        1 + length S .
  eq : top push E to S = E .
  eq : pop push E to S = S .
endo

obj SYMBOLtable is
  protecting
    STACK[TABLE[ID,INT]]
```

```
    * (sort Table to Layer,
        op (empty) to (#),
        op (put) to (_at_ _))]
  * (sort Stack to Env,
      op (empty) to (#),
      op (push_to_) to (_$_)) .
endo
```

The following reductions show how
SYMBOLtable works:

```
reduce in SYMBOLtable as :
  (1 at a 2 at b 3 at c # [ c ])
  ==> as Int.INT : 3
  (1 at a 2 at b 3 at c # [ d ])
  ==> as ErrVal.TABLE_1_SYMBOLtable :
      undef(d)
  (top pop (1 at a 2 at b 3 at c # $
        4 at a 5 at b 6 at c # $ #)
  [ c ]) .
  ==> as Int.INT : 6
```

3.3 LIBRARY CARD SORTING EXAMPLE

Using module expressions, we can defined a
wide variety of objects of similar nature
very easily. To show this by a simple but
more realistic example, let us write a
library card sorting program in OBJ2.
First, let library cards be modeled by the
following:

```
obj LIBcard is
  extending
    LEX[ID] *
      (sort Seq to Text, op (.) to (,)) .
  extending INT .
--- sort LibCard together with four
--- operations on it can be obtained
--- by only renaming an OBJ2's
--- built-in object 4TUPLE, but we
--- write them down directly here
  sort LibCard .
  op (author = _ title = _
      publisher = _ year = _) :
        Text Text Text Int -> LibCard .
  op authorOf_ : LibCard -> Text .
  op titleOf_ : LibCard -> Text .
  op publisherOf_ : LibCard -> Text .
  op yearOf_ : LibCard -> Int .
  vars X Y Z : Text .
  var I : Int .
  eq : authorOf(author = X title = Y
              publisher = Z year = I)
      = X .
  eq : titleOf(author = X title = Y
              publisher = Z year = I)
      = Y .
  eq : publisherOf(author = X title = Y
              publisher = Z year = I)
      = Z .
  eq : yearOf(author = X title = Y
              publisher = Z year = I)
      = I .
--- some examples of LibCard
  ops lc1 lc2 lc3 lc4 : -> LibCard .
  eq : lc1 =
```

```
              (author = Boyer, R.
                   and Moore, J. S.,
          title = A Computational Logic,
          publisher = Academic Press,
          year = 1980) .
     eq : lc2 =
          (author = Arbib, M. A.
                   and Manes, E.,
          title = Arrows, Structures and
                   Functors,
          publisher = Academic Press,
          year = 1975) .
     eq : lc3 =
          (author = McCarthy, J.,
                   Levin, M.  et al.,
          title = LISP 1.5 Programmer's
                   Manual,
          publisher = MIT Press,
          year = 1966) .
     eq : lc4 =
          (author = Stoy, J.,
          title = Denotational Semantics
                   of Programming
                   Languages,
          publisher = MIT Press,
          year = 1977) .
   endo
```

Depending on which component you want to use for key to sort the cards, you can define four views of LibCard as TOSET corresponding to the four components of LibCard:

```
  view ByTitle of LIBcard as TOSET is
     sort Elt to LibCard .
     vars X Y : Elt .
     op : X < Y to :
          titleOf X < titleOf Y .
     --- we assume that there are no two
     --- library cards with same title
     --- the "<" operator in the right hand
     --- is the lexicographic ordering on
     --- the Text
  endview
```

```
  view ByAuthor of LIBcard as TOSET is
     sort Elt to LibCard .
     vars X Y : Elt .
     op : X < Y to :
          (authorOf X < authorOf Y) or
          ((authorOf X == authorOf Y)
            and (titleOf X < titleOf Y)) .
     --- the "<" operators in the right
     --- hand is the lexicographic ordering
     --- on the Text
  endview
```

The views ByPublisher and ByYear are defined in the same manner.

```
  view ByPublisher of LIBcard as TOSET is
     sort Elt to LibCard .
     vars X Y : Elt .
     op : X < Y to :
          (publisherOf X < publisherOf Y) or
          ((publisherOf X == publisherOf Y)
            and titleOf X < titleOf Y) .
```
```
     --- the "<" operators in the right
     --- hand is the lexicographic ordering
     --- on the Text
  endview
```

```
  view ByYear of LIBcard as TOSET is
     sort Elt to LibCard .
     vars X Y : Elt .
     op : X < Y to :
          (yearOf X < yearOf Y) or
          ((yearOf X == yearOf Y)
            and titleOf X < titleOf Y) .
     --- the first "<" operator in the right
     --- hand is the ordering on the Integers
     --- the second "<" operator in the right
     --- hand is the lexicographic ordering
     --- on the Text
  endview
```

Using the object LIBcard and the four view of it as totally order sets, the object LIBcardSorter is defined as follows. This object provides four sorting routines corresponding to the four views of LIBcard as TOSET, which are named sortByAuthor, sortByTitle, sortByPublisher, and sortByYear respectively.

```
  obj LIBcardSorter is
     protecting
       SORTING[ByAuthor] *
         (op (sort_) to (sortByAuthor_))
       + SORTING[ByTitle] *
         (op (sort_) to (sortByTitle_))
       + SORTING[ByPublisher] *
         (op (sort_) to
             (sortByPublisher_))
       + SORTING[ByYear] *
         (op (sort_) to (sortByYear_)) .
  endo
```

Here, the "+" is another module expression construct for creating a module which is defined as an "union" of two modules. The following examples of reductions show how the object LIBcardSorter works:

```
  reduce in LIBcardSorter as :
  (sortByAuthor lc1 lc2 lc3 lc4 .)
  ==>
  as Seq.SEQ_9_LIBcardSorter :
  ((author =
     (Arbib (, (M. (A.
     (and (Manes (, (E. (,)))))))))
   title =
     (Arrows (, (Structures
     (and (Functors (,))))))
   publisher =
     (Academic (Press (,)))
   year = 1975)
  ((author =
     (Boyer (, (R.
     (and (Moore (, (J. (S. (,)))))))))
   title =
     (A (Computational (Logic (,))))
   publisher = (Academic (Press (,)))
   year = 1980)
  ((author =
```

```
  (McCarthy (, (J. (, (Levin (, (M.
    (et (al. (,)))))))))))
  title =
  (LISP (1.5 (Programmer's
    (Manual (,)))))
  publisher = (MIT (Press (,)))
  year = 1966)
 ((author = (Stoy (, (J. (,))))
   title =
   (Denotational (Semantics (of
     (Programming (Languages (,))))))
   publisher = (MIT (Press (,)))
   year = 1977)
   (.)))))

(sortByTitle lc1 lc2 lc3 lc4 .)
==>
--- as expected

(sortByPublisher lc1 lc2 lc3 lc4 .)
==>
as Seq.SEQ_19_LIBcardSorter :
((author =
    (Boyer (, (R.
    (and (Moore (, (J. (S. (,)))))))))
  title =
    (A (Computational (Logic (,))))
  publisher = (Academic (Press (,)))
  year = 1980)
 ((author =
    (Arbib (, (M. (A.
    (and (Manes (, (E. (,)))))))))
  title =
  (Arrows (, (Structures
    (and (Functors (,))))))
  publisher =
  (Academic (Press (,)))
 year = 1975)
 ((author = (Stoy (, (J. (,))))
   title =
   (Denotational (Semantics (of
     (Programming (Languages (,))))))
   publisher = (MIT (Press (,)))
   year = 1977)
  ((author =
   (McCarthy (, (J. (, (Levin (, (M.
   (et (al. (,)))))))))))
   title =
   (LISP (1.5 (Programmer's
     (Manual (,)))))
   publisher = (MIT (Press (,)))
   year = 1966)
   (.)))))

(sortByYear lc1 lc2 lc3 lc4 .)
==>
--- as expected
```

4 CONCLUDING REMARKS

Whatever method may be used, it is not
easy to give software systems good
hierarchical structure. It might be said
that the most difficult part of the design
of software systems is the determination
of the structure of the system.
Parameterized programming provides a good

method for giving software systems good
hierarchical structure. If the system is
hierarchically well-structured and
parameterized, a large part of the
description could be later used for the
construction of the actual software
system. The combination of parameterized
programming with transformational
programming [1] would provide a good
framework for accumulating typical
software for general use.

Parameterized programming in OBJ2 seems to
provide a powerful apparatus for
formalizing and automating a large part of
software process. For example, we can use
OBJ2's parameterization mechanism to
formalize stepwise refinement [4,20] by
considering theories as prototypes and
instantiated actual objects as a refined
final program. For this analogy to work,
it might be better to make theories
executable. The present OBJ2 semantics
does not require that theories be
executable, but there is no problem for
the OBJ2 system to support executable
theories if users write executable
theories as prototypes. We have already
written some examples using this "stepwise
refinement mechanism" in OBJ2.

OBJ2 was first designed and implemented in
1984 by K. Futatsugi, J.Goguen,
J.-P.Jouannaud, and J.Meseguer [8] based
on the previous experience of OBJ and HISP
languages [6,7,13,15]. Since then some
improvements were incorporated into it and
all the examples in this paper are now
running on the present OBJ2 system. The
original system was written in Maclisp.
ZetaLisp and Common Lisp version are also
available now. This paper concentrates on
the methodological aspect of OBJ2, that
is, on parameterized programming with
abstract objects in OBJ2. For other
aspects of OBJ2, see [8].

REFERENCES

[1] Balzer,R., Goldman,N., and Wile,D., On
the transformational implementation
approach to programming, Proc. of 2nd
International Conf. on Software Eng.,
pp.337-344, 1976

[2] Burstall,R.M., and Goguen,J.A.,
Putting theories together to make
specifications, Proc. of 5th Int. Joint
Conf. on Artificial Intelligence, Jul.
pp.1045-1058, 1977

[3] Clockin,W.F. and Mellish,C.S.,
"Programming in Prolog", Springer-Verlag,
1981

[4] Dijkstra,E.W., Notes on structured
programming, in "Structured programming",
Academic Press, 1972

[5] United States Department of Defense, Reference Manual for the Ada programming language, ANSI/MIL-STD-1815 A, 1985

[6] Futatsugi,K. and Okada,K., Specification writing as construction of hierarchically structured clusters of operators, Proc. of IFIP Congress 80, Tokyo, Oct. pp.287-292, 1980

[7] Futatsugi,K. and Okada,K. A Hierarchical Structuring Method for Functional Software Systems, Proceedings, 6th International Conference on Software Engineering, pp.393-402, 1982

[8] Futatsugi,K., Goguen,J., Jouannaud,J.-P., and Meseguer,J., Principles of OBJ2, Proceedings, 1985 Symposium of Principles of Programming Languages, ACM, pp.52-66, 1985

[9] Goguen,J.A., Parameterized Programming, IEEE Trans. Software Engineering, Vol.SE-10, No.5, pp.528-543, Sept.1984

[10] Goguen,J.A., Reusing and interconnecting software components, IEEE Computer, Vol.19, No.2, pp.16-28, 1986

[11] Goguen,J. and Meseguer,J., Equality, Types, Modules and (Why Not?) Generics for Logic Programming. The Journal of Logic Programming, Vol.1, No.2, pp.179-210, 1985

[12] Goguen,J.A. and Meseguer,J., Order-sorted algebra I: partial and overloaded operators,errors and inheritance, Technical Report, SRI International, 1986

[13] Goguen,J.A. and Tardo,J., An introduction to OBJ: a language for writing and testing software specifications, in Specification of Reliable Software, IEEE Press, pp.170-189, 1979

[14] Goguen,J.A., Jouannaud,J.-P. and Meseguer,J., Operational semantics of order-sorted algebra. in Proc. ICALP'85, Springer LNCS 194, pp.221-231, 1985

[15] Goguen,J.A., Meseguer,J. and Plaisted,D., Programming with parameterized abstract objects in OBJ, in "Theory and Practice of Software Technology", ed. Ferrari,D., Bolognani,M. and Goguen,J., North-Holland, pp.163-193, 1983

[16] Goguen,J.A., Thatcher,J.W. and Wagner,E.G., An initial algebra approach to the specification, correctness, and implementation of abstract data types, in "Current trends in programming methodology, Vol.IV: Data Structuring", R.T.Yeh, Ed., Prentice-Hall, 1978

[17] Guttag,J.V., The specification and application to programming of abstract data types, CSRG-89, Univ. of Toronto, 1975

[18] Huet,G. and Oppen,D.C., Equations and rewrite rules: a survey, in "Formal Language Theory: Perspectives and Open Problems", R.Book.,Ed., Academic Press, 1980

[19] Meseguer,J. and Goguen,J.A., Initiality, induction and computability, in "Algebraic Methods in Semantics", Cambridge University Press, pp.459-540, 1984

[20] Wirth,N., Program development by stepwise refinement, Comm. ACM, Vol.14, No.4, pp.221-227, 1971

[21] Wirth,N., "Programming in Modula-2", Springer-Verlag,1985

DOMAIN ANALYSIS FOR REUSABILITY

Rubén Prieto-Díaz

GTE Laboratories Incorporated
40 Sylvan Road
Waltham, Massachusetts 02254
(617)466-2933

ABSTRACT

Domain analysis is a knowledge intensive activity for which no methodology or any kind of formalization is yet available. Domain analysis is conducted informally and all reported experiences concentrate on the outcome, not on the process. We propose a model domain analysis process derived from analyzing some domain analysis cases and two existing approaches. After decomposition of the activities analyzed, we were able to capture the domain analysis process in a set of data flow diagrams. The model identifies intermediate activities and workproducts for which support tools can be developed. A project is currently under way to verify our model.

1. INTRODUCTION

A major problem in reusability is the creation of components that can be reused in applications other than the application for which they were originally designed. In previous works [Prie85, Prie86] where we discussed the classification and retrieval problem in great detail, it was assumed that reusable components were readily available. A typical complaint is that, in spite of having software components available for reuse, programmers have preferred to create their own because available components are difficult to understand and adapt to new applications. In this paper we discuss domain analysis as a fundamental step in creating real reusable components. Organizations that have conducted domain analysis prior to creating reusable components have shown greater success in reusability [Lane79, Mats86]. Components that result from domain analysis are better suited for reusability because they capture the essential functionality required in that domain; thus, developers find them easier to include in new systems. We believe that domain analysis is a key factor in the success of reusability.

In this paper we explore current approaches, and propose the development and validation of a model domain analysis (DA) process. The paper starts with a brief explanation of our idea of domain analysis and illustrates how DA is related to the areas of knowledge acquisition, modeling, and object oriented programming. A simple example, drawn from library science, is presented to illustrate the DA process. Next, an analysis of some cases where DA was conducted for reusability purposes is presented followed by the analysis of two proposed approaches to DA. As a result of these analyses, a detailed DA process with identifiable intermediate activities and workproducts is presented. The paper concludes by presenting a current project undertaken to validate the approach.

2. WHAT IS DOMAIN ANALYSIS

Domain analysis can be conceived of as an activity occurring prior to systems analysis and whose output (i.e., a domain model) supports systems analysis in the same way that systems analysis output (i.e., requirements analysis and specifications document) supports the systems designer's tasks.

In the conventional waterfall model of software development, a systems designer's task is to produce a particular design from a set of requirements and specifications. A systems analyst's task, in the same model, is to create a model of an existing system and propose alternatives for automation or improvement. Both activities focus on a specific model for a particular system. In DA, in contrast, we try to generalize all systems in an application domain by means of a domain model that transcends specific applications. DA is thus at a higher level of abstraction than systems analysis. In domain analysis, common characteristics from similar systems are generalized, objects and operations common to all systems within the same domain are identified, and a model is defined to describe their relationships.

If we succeed in identifying the objects and operations in a domain, the next step is to define a domain specific language. This language becomes our domain model and is used to describe objects and operations common to that domain. If we consider for example the domain of airline reservation systems, typical objects are seats, flights, dates, airports, crews, etc. Operations or actions are schedule a flight, reserve a seat, assign crew to a flight, etc. A language with syntax and semantics designed to represent all valid actions and objects in a particular domain is called a domain specific language. With a domain specific language we can specify, talk about, and model systems within that domain.

If a domain language exists that can acceptably describe the objects and operations of a required system, then the systems analyst has a framework on which to hang the new specification. This is the *reuse of analysis of information,* and in our opinion it is the most powerful sort of reuse.

The crux of the problem, however, is how to analyze a domain and build a domain specific language. The typical and usually very involved approach consists of identifying an appropriate set of objects and operations by consulting an expert.

One of the basic problems in DA is defining a domain boundary; i.e., where one domain stops and another domain begins. If we look at the airline reservation system, there are several domains involved; e.g., the domain of database systems, scheduling, path optimization, etc. Where do we separate the action of reserving a seat in the airline reservation domain from the action of updating a file in the database domain? How do we interconnect domains so that modeling a system in one domain translates to objects and operations in another domain? All these are questions pertinent to DA.

3. RELATED AREAS

There is a strong relationship between DA and knowledge acquisition. Building a knowledge base and defining heuristics for an expert system are basically the same problems as DA [Hay83]. The final product of DA in knowledge acquisition is a knowledge base (either in the form of a semantic net or production rules) where objects and operations related to a particular domain are encapsulated and can be used to explain or to talk about events in that domain.

Domain knowledge acquisition is also a requirement for complete functional specifications. Borgida et al. [Borg85] indicate that "...while it may seem obvious that to describe a system's requirements, it is first necessary to understand the real world concepts involved, techniques for explicitly capturing this information have yet to be adopted in software engineering."

The need for DA is also evident when constructing frame-based knowledge bases. Fikes and Kehler [Fike85] indicate the necessity of "many different kinds of knowledge about a domain" in order to design a proper set of frames in a frame based knowledge system.

In modeling, DA is essential. Thompson and Clancey [Thom86], developed their 'Caster' expert system by reusing the MYCIN skeleton and found that the most crucial step in their experiment was DA. They had to encapsulate all available knowledge in the sandcasting domain into a qualitative model. Based on 15 major classes of sandcasting malfunctions that cause shrinkage cavities, they used manuals, textbooks, and expert consultation to identify the abnormal processes that could cause shrinkage and then organized them into a classification hierarchy. "Only after we really understood the causality behind shrinks could we put that knowledge in the language used by our system." This process took the longest time. They call this crucial step the "acquisition bottleneck."

Another example of modeling is in the area of robot vision. Parts-recognition systems are based on matching previously defined parts models with parts presented to them. The general problem of matching may be regarded as finding a set of features in the given image that approximates one model's features. Chin and Dyer [Chin86] observe that the problem of selecting the geometric features that are the components of the model is integrally related to the problem of model definition. In this case, DA consists of selecting the geometric properties that would make a model distinct from the models of other parts and at the same time capture the essential visual features that characterize the part.

In object oriented programming, identifying objects, operations, and their relationships in large systems is not a trivial task as it is usually assumed to be [Booc86]. We often have to deal with objects at different levels of abstraction, define abstraction boundaries, find complex relationships, and find all possible operations performed on a given object. We have moreover, to identify classes of objects and identify their common attributes. All these tasks are pertinent to DA.

4. DOMAIN ANALYSIS AND CLASSIFICATION

Classification is the act of grouping like things. Typically, classification starts by identifying characteristics common to more than one object in a given collection. Objects that share the same characteristics are grouped together and regrouping may occur several times until the organization of the collection satisfies the classifier. Identification of common characteristics depends on the intended use of the objects in the collection.

Classification is the product of integrating the knowledge inherent to the objects of the collection with the knowledge of the domain where the collection is going to be used. With classification we are identifying the objects and operations of a domain. We are also identifying the common characteristics of these objects and operations, which allows us to make generalizations about them.

The specialized faceted classification schemes of library science are based on a process similar to DA called *literary warrant.* Literary warrant consists in selecting a random sample of titles from the collection to be classified, listing individual terms from the titles, grouping related terms into common classes, and organizing the common classes into a classification scheme. This process implies knowledge of the domain and of the intended use of the collection. The selected terms and their relationships can be considered as a domain specific language used to express activities in the domain of the specialized library. Literary warrant, is one approach to DA.

Although literary warrant is a systematic approach for constructing faceted schemes, we can reuse some of it for domain analysis. The objective in literary warrant is to identify individual terms from an existing collection of titles and group them for classification. We consider this a simple minded approach where some knowledge about the domain is available by 'evidence' found in the collection. We briefly illustrate this process.

Assume we are asked to build a classification for a list of zoology related titles (i.e., books). The first step is to select a representative sample from the collection. Let us assume we select the following titles:

"Essays on the physiology of marine fauna"
"Animals of the mountains"
"Amphibious animals"
"Desert reptiles"

"Migratory birds"
"Salt water fish"
"Mammalian reproduction"
"Snakes of the Amazon river"
"Experimental reports on the respiration of vertebrates"
"Tropical leaf moths"

The next step is to group common terms together.

physiology, reproduction, respiration
tropical, desert, mountains, salt water
marine, amphibious
fauna, animals, vertebrates, reptiles, snakes, birds, fish, moths, mammals
essays, experimental reports

The groups are then identified and ordered by their relevance to the collection's users, and terms in each group are listed in a logical order. The result of this process, called a classification scheme, is shown below.

DOMAIN → animals/fauna

{by habitat}	{by element}	{by taxonomy}	{by process}	{by literary form}
land	marine	anaimals/fauna	physiology	essays
tropic	:	invertebrates	respiration	:
desert	:	insects	reproduction	:
moutain	amphibious	moths	:	reports
:	:	:	:	experimental
:	:	vertebrates	:	:
water		mammals		
sea		:		
river		birds		
Amazon		:		
:		reptiles		
:		snakes		
		:		
		fish		

Five groups or classes (facets in library science terminology) were identified: by processes, by habitat, by element, by taxonomy, and by literary form. These classes are ordered from left to right by relevance to the hypothetical user of the collection. We assumed in this example that the users are environmentalists; habitat becomes the most relevant. Terms within each class are arbitrarily ordered to show some logical relationship among them, like in taxonomy– from general to specific.

We can now systematically use this scheme to describe each title of the collection. To describe a title, we match by order of relevance each term in the title to the terms in the scheme. For example

Essays on the physiology of marine fauna -> marine/animals/physiology/essays

Animals of the mountains -> mountain/animals

Desert reptiles -> desert/reptiles

As new titles enter the collection, new facets may be defined and new terms added to the scheme. This is, briefly illustrated, the core of literary warrant. Resulting schemes are used for

classification. Buchanan [Buch79] and Vickery [Vick60] present detailed tutorials of this approach.

From the DA perspective, the collection's user now has a standard vocabulary and some elementary rules to describe titles in the collection. We have a primitive domain language to describe titles in the domain of animals/fauna for a specific audience.

5. DOMAIN ANALYSIS CASES

If we look closely at the process of literary warrant we identify the following activities:

● Selection of representative items from a collection of similar items
● Analysis of each item
● Decomposition
● Grouping
● Abstraction
● Arrangement
● Definition of rules of use

These activities, as we show below, are basically the same activities conducted in domain analysis for reusability. We present the analysis of two cases that have lead to a successful reuse of software.

The Raytheon Experience

Lanergan and Poynton [Lane79] developed a unique methodology to reuse code in business applications development within Raytheon. They analyzed several business applications and found out that most modules fall into only three major classes common to most business applications. They documented, cataloged, and classified each into a library and made the library available to the programmers. They also discovered that most programs fall in one of three 'logic structures' or a combination of them (they have defined 85 different logic structures combinations). They identified common functions in the domain and then abstracted these functions and their relationships to form the three logic structures.

We can trace their DA process through the following activities:

● Identify common functions across business applications
● Group them by classes
● Organize into a library
● Analyze business systems structures
● Identify common structures
● Abstract such structures
● Use structures and components to build new systems.

This is essentially a DA process where the library of functions are the objects and the logic structures are equivalent to the rules or glue to articulate such functions into a particular business system.

NEC of Japan has followed a very similar approach, albeit independent from Raytheon [Mats86]. Their DA process can also be traced through the same activities we listed for the Raytheon experience.

The CAMP Experience

The Common Ada Missile Packages (CAMP) Project [Camp84, McNic86] has as one of its objectives the identification of common missile functions and the design of reusable Ada parts. Their commonality analysis is basically an analysis of the missile systems domain. They analyzed eleven tactical missile systems, identified several components common to most of them, and grouped them by their functionality.

The approach to DA followed in this case can be characterized by the following activities:

• Identification of similar systems
• Functional decomposition
• Functional abstraction
• Interface definition
• Component encapsulation

Essentially, we have surveyed the DA process to search for common features. Our survey is rather small and we cannot claim to have done a thorough DA, but with these few cases we have identified some of the key steps in the DA process. Before we present our approach to DA, we introduce two proposed approaches to DA: McCain's [McCa85, McCa86] and Arango's [Aran86].

6. EXISTING PROPOSALS FOR DOMAIN ANALYSIS

McCain did an extensive study on reusability where he proposed a paradigm for developing reusable components. One of the key tasks in this paradigm is domain analysis. He divides the DA process into three activities:

• Define reusable entities which include reusable objects such as stacks and sets and reusable non-objects which are collections of related independent reusable operations such as mathematical subroutines.

• Define reusable abstractions; i.e., identify common operations on objects and object to object relationships. It is not clear how to do this nor what is the output.

• Perform classification of reusable abstractions, which results in a classification hierarchy that supposedly is used as a navigation aid in the selection of reusable components. It is not clear what are the nodes and what are the edges in this classification graph, nor how the relationships among objects are defined.

After completing DA, McCain proposes to do component DA which is basically a DA of each identified abstraction to define an abstract interface, essential constraints, limitations, and customization requirements. This process ensures proper encapsulation and is intended to guarantee reusability.

Arango proposes a more systematic approach to domain analysis. He indicates that to become practical domain analysis must be decomposed into a set of intermediate activities with well-defined workproducts to support a controlled transition from initial analysis to the actual encapsulation of reusable components.

The first step is bounding the domain; that is, defining the boundaries of the domain in order to limit the type and amount of information to be treated in the analysis. The next step is collecting standard examples of implementations in the domain and performing systems analysis of each. The domain analyst's next task is to identify potential abstractions and map them into formal representations using conceptual modeling languages. An extension of this task is to identify possible abstract implementations that can be carried out by refining domain specific abstractions into a sequence of subsidiary domains until an operational domain is reached. Arango's proposed next step is to collect these abstractions and define some guidelines for encapsulation into reusable components, similar to McCain's component DA.

Both approaches are in the proposal stage with no examples or test cases provided. In a DA of the DA process however, we integrated some of these ideas with the domain analysis activities identified in the previous case studies. As a result we propose a DA process aimed at the production of reusable components and where most intermediate activities and workproducts are identified. The breakdown of the DA process allows us to identify potential tools to assist the domain analyst.

7. A DOMAIN ANALYSIS PROCESS

In our approach we identify a set of activities prior to domain analysis, follow this by DA, and conclude with post-DA activities. Pre-DA activities include defining and scoping the domain, identifying sources of knowledge and information about the domain, and defining the approach to DA.

The two types of DA (evidential and synthetic) both have three basic activities: identification of objects and operations, abstraction, and classification.

The first step in DA activities is to find abstractions for groups or classes of groups. The attributes selected to characterize these abstractions should be relevant to the intended use of the expected components and also relevant to the expected audience using them. The output of this activity are frames that describe abstractions and that group specific instances of these abstractions. Frames seem to be a natural representation of domain objects and functions and provide the necessary mechanisms to express relationships.

Classification is the next step in DA. A classification structure can be derived for the complete domain or it can be broken into partial classifications. The relationships among frames used to define the classification can be found during this process. The output of this process is a taxonomy of the domain and a structure of relationships that can be used as a model to describe or talk about objects and operations in the domain. A desirable outcome of this activity would be a domain language. A domain language is a collection of rules that relate objects and functions and which can be made explicit and encapsulated in a formal language and further used as a specification language for the construction of systems in that domain.

Post-DA activities include encapsulation and producing reusability guidelines. Encapsulation is the identification and implementation of reusable components based on the domain structure or model. Each frame is a candidate for encapsulation. The approach is similar to that used in object-oriented programming or in McCain's object domain analysis; it includes definition of interface and constraints. Reusability guidelines consist basically of documentation for the reuser.

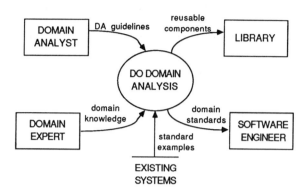

Figure 1- Context Diagram for DA

We capture the DA process in a set of DeMarco data flow diagrams (DFDs) shown in figures 1 through 5. The context DFD of the DA process is shown in figure 1. The domain analyst and the domain expert are the two actors responsible for DA. The domain analyst has the procedural know-how on DA. A set of guidelines are used to extract relevant knowledge from the domain expert and from existing systems. The product of DA is a collection of domain specific reusable components and domain standards used by software engineers for building new systems in that domain.

The three high level activities in DA are shown in figure 2– Do Domain Analysis. Key intermediate products are a DA requirements document customized for the particular domain, a domain taxonomy, and domain frames. A domain model and a domain language are optional products because not many domains can be modeled and because deriving a domain language is yet a difficult and uncertain activity. The DA requirements document (figure 3) is the product of applying

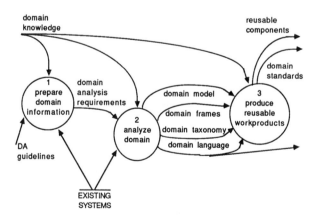

Figure 2- DFD Level 0: Do Domain Analysis

general DA guidelines to a well defined and bounded domain. This document should include a high level breakdown of activities in the domain, which part of the domain to analyze, potential areas to modularize, standard examples of available systems, and any issues relevant to that domain.

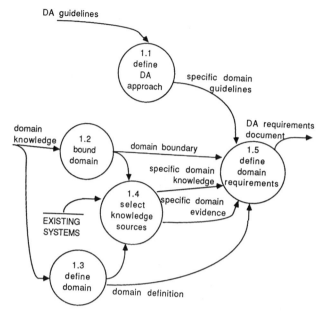

Figure 3- DFD Level 1: Prepare Domain Information

Figure 4– Analyze Domain is the central activity. We break it down into specific sub-activities with well defined intermediate outputs. The flow is logical; selection (2.1, 2.2), abstraction (2.3, 2.4, 2.5), and classification (2.6). The basic outputs are domain frames and taxonomy.

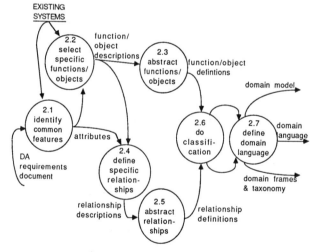

Figure 4- DFD Level 2: Analyze Domain

To illustrate these activities we can use the airline reservation example. In identifying common features (activity 2.1), the domain analyst selects activities common to the existing systems analyzed such as seat reservation, flight scheduling, ticket sale. Some of the systems may perform some activities not common to the rest such as crew assignment or scheduling of preventive repairs for the fleet. This identification process is coupled with the bounding and defining of the domain shown in DFD Level 1 (1.2 and 1.3 in figure 3). Some of the non-common activities may either be left out or included as part of the domain.

Some of the function/objects in this example (output of 2.2) may be assign/seat, schedule/flight, sell/ticket, write/ticket, etc. (more specific descriptions are passenger *assign-to* seat, ticket *sell-to* passenger and passenger *schedule-to* flight.) Abstract activities (2.3) such as flight reservation can be defined in terms of these more specific functions and objects. In fact, flight reservation may include all of the above.

Specific relationship descriptions (output of 2.4) could be flight descriptions as defined in the existing systems such as: Flight 42, BOS-LAX, C15. From these descriptions the analyst may abstract relationships like: flight *has* number, flight *has* departure, flight *has* destination, flight *has* seats, flight *is-a* feature, etc. These would be typical outputs of 2.5.

In classification we create a domain taxonomy from the common objects, functions and their relationships. Reserving a flight may be considered a primitive function in our airline reservations example domain and it may be generalized and used as a building block for new systems.

A domain taxonomy can have different levels of complexity and can be developed incrementally as domain knowledge is acquired. The most obvious and simple domain classes are used as a starting set for the taxonomy. The taxonomy structure we propose may be a single hierarchy, a collection of semantic nets, a faceted classification scheme, or a combination of all three.

A hierarchy has objects and/or functions at the nodes and different kinds of relationships at the edges. Simple domain taxonomies can be represented with a module interconnection language (MIL) or a more typical inverted tree structure of classes. Semantic nets are used to represent some complex taxonomies and frames are used to represent some nodes in the net. We illustrate a semantic net representation in Figure 5. To complement our airline reservation example we are including an example from the compilers domain which shows a partial generic model of parsers as components of a generic compiler in the form of a semantic net. This net could very well be presented as a frame which could itself be a node of yet a larger generic compiler net. The values in each box are instances of a particular parser and circles are attribute values. This example is a particular instantiation of the P-Parser but the structure remains the same if a different parser is instantiated.

Selection of a particular representation structure would depend on the kind of domain analyzed. Different forms could be used within the same domain depending on its size. A high level domain model could be in the form of a faceted scheme or a simple hierarchy with semantic nets and frames used for lower level domain elements.

With frames, a taxonomy, and a possible domain model in hand, production of reusable workproducts (figure 6) is straightforward. Elements that offer the most potential for reusability are selected first for encapsulation (3.1). Encapsu-

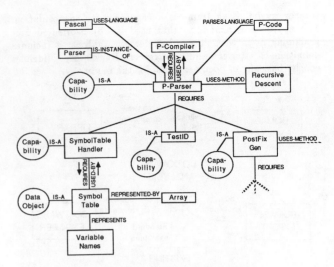

Figure 5- Partial Semantic Net for the P-Parser

lation consists of making specific components reusable by proper structuring, modularization, and standardization (3.2). Reuse guidelines (3.3) indicate how to reuse individual components, list performance considerations, limitations, and potential for reuse (e.g., where can they be reused). Domain standards (3.4) are refinements of the guidelines focusing on standards to build systems in the domain. Standards include the set of reusable components available, definitions of logic structures and guidelines to integrate reusable components into systems. Interface and interconnection problems are also part of the domain standards. If a domain language is available, sets of refinements can also be defined. In this context, refinements are transformations of domain language statements into intermediate domains and through an operational representation.

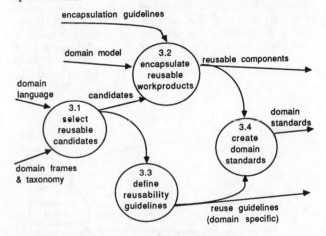

Figure 6- DFD Level 3: Produce Reusable Workproducts

Implicit in the DA process is a continuous iteration in the domain knowledge acquisition activity in particular and in each of the other activities through feedback from subsequent activities. The purpose of these DFDs is to show what is done in DA.

8. VALIDATION

In order to verify the proposed DA approach, it is necessary to try it. A project at GTE Laboratories is under way to test this DA process. A small, well understood application domain from the area of telecommunications is being considered. We are tuning the process as we conduct the experiment and will provide a domain analysis guidelines document as the end product.

We are taking advantage of an existing library system [Prie86] to monitor the reusability of the resulting components. This feedback will also be used to tune the products of the DA and the DA methodology. Each DA activity is being recorded and plans for DA support tools are being proposed. We are working to develop the methodology into a set of tools and procedures.

9. CONCLUSIONS

DA is a knowledge intensive activity for which no methodology or any kind of formalization is yet available. DA is conducted informally and all reported experiences concentrate on the outcome, not on the process.

In this report we have barely scratched the surface of the problem. We approached DA as an information system where certain activities are performed. We surveyed the field and applied DA techniques on DA to acquire knowledge. Decomposition techniques were then applied as is done in systems analysis to uncover DA internal activities and to define some of the intermediate products. The analysis resulted in a detailed set of activities and products that model the DA process.

An experiment is under way at GTE Laboratories to test this methodology and to build tools that support the intermediate stages of the DA process.

10. REFERENCES

[Aran86]   G. Arango, personal communication, Irvine CA, September 25, 1986.

[Booc86]   G. Booch, "Object-Oriented Development," *IEEE Transactions on Software Engineering*, **SE-12**(2)211-221, February, 1986.

[Borg85]   A. Borgida, S. Greenspan, and J. Myopoulos, "Knowledge Representation as the Basis for Requirements Specifications," *IEEE Computer*, **18**(4)82-91, April 1985.

[Buch79]   B. Buchanan, *Theory of Library Classification*. Clive Bingley, London, 1979.

[Camp84]   *Common Ada Missile Packages (CAMP)*, Technical Proposal, Vol. 1. Prepared by Raytheon Company, Missile Systems Division, Bedford, Mass. May 7, 1984.

[Chin86]   R.T. Chin and C.R. Dyer, "Model-Based Recognition in Robot Vision," *ACM Computing Surveys*, **18**(1)67-108, March 1986.

[Fike85]   R. Fikes and T. Kehler, "The Role of Frame-Based Representation in Reasoning," *Communications of the ACM,"* **28**(9)904-920, Sept. 1985.

[Haye83]   F. Hayes-Roth, D. Waterman, and D. Lenat, eds., *Building Expert Systems*, Addison-Wesley, New York, 1983.

[Lane79]   R.G. Lanergan and B.A. Poynton, "Reusable Code: The Application Development Technique for the Future." In *Proceedings of the IBM SHARE/GUIDE Software Symposium*, IBM, Monterey, CA, October, 1979.

[Mats86]   M. Matsumoto, "Reusable Software Parts Paradigm and Automatic Program Synthesis Using Them," talk presented at the National Conference on Software Reusability and Maintainability, Tysons Corner, VA, Sept. 10-11, 1986. Proceedings available from The National Institute for Software Quality and Productivity, Inc., Suite 320, 655 15th St.NW, Washington, D.C. 20005.

[McCa85]   R. McCain, "A Software Development Methodology for Reusable Components," Proc. of the 1985 Hawaii International Conference on Systems Science, January, 1985.

[McCa86]   R. McCain, "Reusable Software Component Construction: A Product-Oriented Paradigm," (unpublished) IBM Federal Systems Division, Houston TX, 1986.

[McNic86] D. McNichol, "CAMP: Common Ada Missile Packages," talk presented at the National Conference on Software Reusability and Maintainability, Tysons Corner, VA, Sept. 10-11, 1986. Proceedings available from The National Institute for Software Quality and Productivity, Inc., Suite 320, 655 15th St.NW, Washington, D.C. 20005.

[Neigh84] J. Neighbors, "The Draco Approach to Constructing Software from Reusable Components," *IEEE Transactions on Software Engineering*, SE-10(9)564-573, Sep. 1984.

[Prie85]   R. Prieto-Diaz, *A Software Classification Scheme*, Ph.D. Disertation, Department of Information and Computer Science, University of California, Irvine CA, 1985.

[Prie86]   R. Prieto-Diaz, "Classifying Software for Reusability," *IEEE Software*, 4(1):6-16, January, 1987.

[Thom86]   T.F. Thompson and W.J. Clancey, "A Qualitative Modeling Shell for Process Diagnosis," *IEEE Software*, **3**(2)6-15, March 1986.

[Vick60]   B.C. Vickery, *Faceted Classification: A Guide to Construction and Use of Special Schemes*. Aslib, 3 Belgrave Square, London, 1960.

The Domain-Oriented Software Life Cycle: Towards an Extended Process Model For Reusability

Mark A. Simos
Unisys Corporation--System Development Group
Paoli Research Center, Box 517, Paoli PA 19301
Submitted to: RMISE 1987 Workshop on Software Reuse

1. Introduction

Despite a growing interest in software reusability, spurred by the much-discussed software productivity crisis, software reuse on a large scale has proved an elusive goal. A number of different technical approaches to achieving increased levels of software reuse have been advocated, each likely to prove fruitful in at least some domains of application [HOROWITZ,IEEE,SIM1]. However, technical challenges to reusability are closely intertwined with management issues, organizational philosophy, contractual and economic considerations. Technical innovations will lead to significant increases in software productivity only if accompanied by shifts in the broader organizational and methodological framework within which large-scale software development takes place. In recognition of this close interdependence of technical and non-technical issues, this paper will first report on one specific technology developed within Unisys, an attribute grammar-based generative approach to reusability, then outline an extended view of the software life cycle that provides an integral role for this and a variety of other techniques supporting software reuse.

At Unisys, we have developed an approach to reusability, based on program generation techniques, that offers several advantages over the conventional notion of a library of reusable software components. In participation at previous industry workshops we have presented our experience with these techniques and urged that they be included, along with the "parts library" approach, in a general taxonomy and set of strategies for support of software reuse [SIM1]. The first portion of this paper will briefly summarize relevant aspects of our technical approach and the results we have achieved.

As this technology has matured, we are confronting more issues of methodology and technology transfer in widening its acceptance and use. We believe many of these issues relevant not only to our specific technical approach, but to reusability in general. One fundamental problem is the difficulty of integrating reusability into a conventional top-down "waterfall" life cycle model of software development. The main objective of this position paper will be to outline some general characteristics that we believe an extended life cycle model must have. These characteristics include the following:

- a perspective centered, not on the single project life cycle, but on the notion of what can loosely be termed "domains": "families" of related programs or systems

Reprinted with permission from *Proceedings of the Workshop on Software Reusability and Maintainability,* October 1987. Copyright ©1987 by The National Institute of Software Quality and Productivity. All rights reserved.   354 supporting particular application areas.

- concentration on application specificity, or "narrow-band" reuse within specific application domains, as the best means of achieving significant productivity increases in the near term for "reusability in the large".

- recognition that a spectrum of techniques for reusable software and other work products of software development activities are needed: ad hoc reuse (ranging from large-scale to small-scale reuse); libraries; code generation techniques; and even advanced approaches such as the use of knowledge-based techniques [BEACON,CHEATHAM,SIM1,RICH].

This perspective should provide a foundation for a general methodology to aid in the incremental development of reusable resources within given domains—aiding in identifying potential domains for reuse, and determining which technologies are appropriate based on characteristics of the application area.

2. Technical Approach: Application-Specific Languages

At Unisys, our technical approach to software reusability is founded on the use of *application-specific languages*, or ASLs— very high-level non-procedural specification languages that employ syntax and terminology suitable for a specific, narrow-band domain of application. We have produced a number of ASL processors for diverse domains such as computer system configuration and message format translation/validation [POLLACK1]. These processors translate specifications written in an ASL to efficient, maintainable high-level language code.

Generation of high-level code from ASL specifications has proved a better approach to software reuse than libraries of reusable components in these domains, due to many factors. Besides the productivity gain obtained from use of a concise, declarative description, ASLs permit the generated code to be driven by the specification in a far more complex way than is permitted by parameterization in a general-purpose programming language (even Ada*, with features such as default parameters designed to be particularly supportive of reuse). Semantic checks peculiar to the application domain can be incorporated into the structure of the ASL; moreover, by embedding domain-specific algorithms and expertise in the code generation component, generated high-level source code can be of comparable efficiency to a hand-written implementation [MFPL]. This makes ASLs potentially more viable in the near term than general-purpose "automatic programming" systems; such systems tend to employ highly formal, abstract syntax, and cannot draw as readily on efficient application-specific code generation techniques.

We believe that ASLs can be most effective when there is an automated mechanism for creating ASL translators. At Unisys, we have developed a proprietary

---

*Ada is a registered trademark of the Ada Joint Program Office.

attribute grammar-based generation system called SSAGS (Syntax and Semantics Analysis and Generation System [KNUTH, KELLER]). SSAGS is in fact a meta-generation system (i.e., a generator of generators in the sense of a compiler-compiler) that enables many portions of an ASL language processor to be generated from a formal specification of the ASL. SSAGS (which, like any respectable compiler, is written in its own specification language) is operational on Unisys mainframes as well as Sun workstations and VAX computers running under Berkeley UNIX*, and generates Ada source code. Through the use of SSAGS and the attribute grammar formalism [KASTENS], which provides a clean separation between the syntactic, semantic, and back-end portions of the translators, we have significantly reduced the effort required to develop, maintain, and retarget ASL translators. For example, SSAGS will generate an associated toolset (including a specification-oriented debugger and syntax-directed editor) specific to each ASL defined. In addition, syntactic variants of an ASL can be created which share the same semantic and back-end processing [POLLACK2, SOLDERITSCH]. Recent work has reduced the amount of hand-implementation required in the code generation portion of the SSAGS system, and has made it easier to retarget ASL translators to new output languages [BESL].

Technology Transfer Issues

As our ASL technology has matured, we are beginning to confront strategic issues of technology transfer, such as the problem of identifying candidate domains where the ASL approach can be cost-effective (and can be demonstrated to be so). Though there are numerous areas of potential application for ASLs, choice of an appropriate domain and the proper functional scoping of the ASL to be produced are vital to the success of the endeavor. Definition and implementation of an ASL involves a process of capturing domain-specific expertise somewhat akin to the knowledge engineering phase of expert systems development. Though the criteria of a good domain for an expert system and an ASL are not the same, both technologies depend heavily on a good choice of domain [CAMP].

The ASL or source code generation approach is certainly not new. Fourth-generation languages, or 4GLs, are an accepted way of doing business in transaction analysis-oriented EDP domains. They emerged in EDP domains which were comparatively stable and mature (e.g., the procedures for payroll processing), and where there was a high degree of commonality across applications. Gradually, applications in these domains were carved into well-defined sub-domains, such as report generation, screen management, database access, etc., each of which was supported by a different specialized language. Furthermore, there was enough flexibility in the performance/efficiency demands of these applications, relative to available processing power, that code generation techniques were able to be applied relatively early.

---

*UNIX is a registered trademark of AT&T Bell Laboratories.

We view 4GLs as particular instances of ASLs—or rather, integrated "clusters" of ASLs [SIM2], particularly tailored to certain database-intensive application areas for some of the historical reasons discussed above. Our research priorities support the goal of transferring this 4GL-like approach to non-data-processing domains [SIM2]. However, the differing requirements of real-time domains have necessitated advances in the technology of code generation before this technology transfer could be achieved. By concentrating on the refinements of program generation techniques summarized above, we have reduced the extra investment needed to create ASL processors. For example, the level of effort required to implement an ASL translator for the generation of message format and validation routines was roughly comparable to the effort required to implement one such program by hand [MFPL]. Thus, the assumption that investment in reusability can only be justified across multiple projects no longer holds in many domains of interest. A converging trend supporting this shift is the expanding size, complexity, and longevity of systems, effectively creating many applications within the scope of a single contract. (That is, if "domain" is taken to mean an anticipated family of related but separate applications, then such "domains" will be increasingly found within the scope of a single project.)

Though investment in ASL technology can be justified economically even within a single project's scope, a key problem faced in transferring ASLs into use on large projects is accommodating the notion of source code generation systems within the typical single-project life cycle model. Since this is the model driving most current large-scale development efforts (particularly in a government contracting environment), a realistic strategy for maximizing "reusability in the large" must begin with an extended life cycle model that provides an integral (not a token) role for reuse. The lack of an adequate process model for software development that incorporates reusability (in the dual sense of developing and making use of reusable resources) is a fundamental problem, not only for the transition of ASL technology, but software reuse in general. An extended view of the software development process is needed, one rich enough to account for differences between domains, to facilitate the identification of discrete sub-domains within larger application areas, and to suggest appropriate matches of domain criteria with technical approaches. The remainder of this paper will address these issues from the standpoint of software reusability in general.

3. A Proposed Extended Model for Reuse

Limitations of the Waterfall Model

There are three particular points of divergence that make it difficult to incorporate the notion of reusability into the typical top-down, single-project view of system development.

- Software reuse is not inherently "top-down";

- it involves a perspective that necessarily looks beyond the development of single projects or systems;
- it involves the exploitation of commonality at many levels of abstraction besides that easily captured in code.

Software reuse is not specifically addressed in the conventional top-down model, in which systems are designed via a process of modular decomposition. Hence, structured methodologies rarely include specific techniques for analyzing domains to extract maximally reusable components (though object-oriented design methods may rightly claim to improve this state of affairs to a great extent [MEYER]). Since most applications are in fact hybrids of reuse and new design, de facto reuse does occur; yet it is often confined to ad hoc, informal contexts that fall between the cracks of the "official" methodology being followed by the project, and is dependent on developers' intuitive grasp of common functionality within the semantics of the application.

What is needed is a process model that allows for iteration between the top-down, "problem-driven" approach and a bottom-up, "parts-driven" perspective (terms elucidated more fully in the draft STARS Reusability Guidebook [GUIDE]). Such a process model would correspond more closely to the real state of practice in software development than the current model, and would at least initially have a less prescriptive, more descriptive, flavor. Viewed in this iterative way, large-scale system design involves exceedingly complex features, including: inherent parallelism (project team interaction); non-monotonic reasoning (as system requirements change over time, design cul-de-sacs are discovered and accommodated); and both forward-chaining (or data-driven) and backward-chaining (or goal-driven) reasoning, respectively supporting part-exploitation and problem-decomposition design tasks. As these features are directly analogous to many design problems at the frontier of current AI research, we are clearly a long way from formalizing such a process model into a methodology.

Beyond a Project Orientation

To fully understand that aspect of system design that is driven by existing parts requires a perspective that looks beyond the single project life cycle. The software life-cycle model has already evolved considerably from a too-restrictive focus on the programming phase to an acknowledgement of the full software life cycle incorporating requirements, design, testing, and maintenance. In addition the predominating role of "maintenance" activities (including post-deployment debugging, enhancements, adaptation and evolution of older systems to meet new requirements) in over-all development efforts is receiving more acknowledgement, as a result of our experience with aging systems in the field and our desire to build longer-lived, more evolvable systems.

Yet even this longer-range perspective is still centered on the notion of maintaining and evolving a particular system. In the general case, the additional capital investment necessary to accumulate and use reusable resources must be amortized over a number of intended applications. We use the term "domain" to refer to a designated collection of existing applications (the population) and anticipated opportunities for future applications (the market) with common functionality in one or more areas. The quantity and form of reusable resources available to an individual project within a domain, and the new resources contributed as a by-product of project development, alters the individual project life cycle both quantitatively and qualitatively. We refer to this multi-project evolutionary pattern as the *domain-oriented software life cycle*; a domain life cycle model formalizes typical patterns in the development of related series of applications and the persistence of information from one application to the next. As noted earlier, reuse is justifiable on a per-project basis in an increasing number of domains due to advances in technology and expansion of system scope; nevertheless, this multi-project view is an essential foundation for a general model of reusability. To actually develop and refine this extended life cycle model, much basic research needs to be done, much of which should be in the form of extended case studies of particular domains.

Domain Traceability

The perspective of the full project life cycle reveals problems stemming from a breakdown of information traceability across individual project phases (e.g., requirements to design). In a similar way, viewing the development of a series of related applications within an enterprise as a larger evolutionary cycle reveals a different sort of flow of information, previously implicit in the state of practice. Information relevant to the domain life cycle persists to a large extent in the form of individual human expertise about the application area. Such expertise might take the form of specific routines, templates, algorithms, generic design schemata, or heuristics (such as typical loopholes or "gotchas" to check for in a requirements specification for particular types of applications). A purely top-down design methodology does not account for the role of this available repertoire in designing a new system. Because this information (or knowledge) is rarely captured in any explicit form, what could be an accumulating corpus of reusable components, methods, and domain expertise is often diluted by the organizational framework in which successive systems are built.

Methodology For Domain Analysis

Starting from a domain life cycle model as outlined above, the next step is to develop a methodology by which a software engineer, project manager, or strategic technical planner for an organization can identify coherent "domains" within current or proposed lines of business, determine which techniques or combination of techniques supporting reusability are appropriate for those domains, and take steps to put the necessary resources into place. We see needs for at least the following kinds of methodological support in this task:

(1) Taxonomic: classification schemes for characterizing different application domains. For example, application areas exhibiting "abundant redundant code", such as the message-processing domain, may be ideal for the application of an ASL approach. Conversely, some "horizontal" domains [CAMP] that cut across application areas, such as the area of statistical routines, may be best supported by a library approach, because usage will be sparsely distributed throughout typical applications.

(2) Analytic: techniques for decomposing large, variegated application areas into sub-domains of the right granularity to apply a particular technique for reuse [GUIDE,CAMP]. For example, our message-processing ASL [MFPL] was defined to support a narrow but labor-intensive niche within the larger domain of message-switching applications. Unisys has now initiated an internal research project to investigate alternative techniques for reusability for the message-switching domain as a whole, one of the company's long-established lines of business.

(3) Diachronic: distinguishing typical phases in the *maturation* of specific application areas. The process of system specification and implementation is not a constant, but is gradually transformed as enterprises gain experience with delivering certain types of systems. In addition, whereas the waterfall model is often presented as a uniform model for software project development, we should expect that application domains with different characteristics may follow different evolutionary patterns.

Methodological advances in each of these areas are essential to a rational strategy of reuse. At different stages in the maturation of application domains, different techniques of reuse will be most appropriate. For example, a library of discrete modules may be a natural precursor to a part generation system, which arises after interface standards have stabilized to the necessary extent. Attempting to introduce a technology such as an ASL or a software components library in support of a domain that has not yet stabilized in the necessary ways may be premature, hence less effective.

As a suggestion of what a typical diachronic pattern might look like, consider the common progression by which a system built initially on a one-time-only, single-contract basis, once complete, serves as a magnet for new contracts with similar requirements. After a certain number of ad hoc customizations for new users, the frustrated developers in the trenches may be allowed to re-engineer a tailorable or semi-generic system, which eventually may evolve into a standard product. An important by-product of this productization cycle is the emergence of a standard product specification by developers, characterizing and constraining the available "flavors" of the system. This marks an important threshold in the domain, as the developing organization now provides a structure into which *customers* must fit their requirements. Such specifications thus become reusable components (i.e., "reusable requirements") as important or more important than reusable software per se. As this scenario indicates, by viewing reusability in this wider context, it is easier to see concrete examples of how life cycle work products other than source code might be reused. Also, the domain life cycle perspective allows us to see instances of reuse in the current state of practice that were not previously recognized as such.

Implications For Environments

Just as the software project life cycle has had a significant impact on the notion of software engineering environments, the implications of the domain life cycle model for support environments are manifold. The domain life cycle model provides a necessary framework for automated support to capture and reuse domain-specific knowledge across applications, thereby accelerating and rendering manageable the informal process of reuse that currently occurs.

Though detailed discussion of this topic is beyond the scope of this paper, we will briefly sketch some characteristics of such automated support. A "domain-specific environment" would support reuse across a family or series of related applications (including variants and upgrades), facilitating the incremental incorporation of domain-specific knowledge into the environment framework itself with each successive system. Such an environment or support system would need to support the encapsulation of domain-specific knowledge in many forms, including libraries of static components, ASLs, and system architectures tailored to the specifics of the applications being developed (e.g., "generic" compiler architectures). Furthermore, the environment would need to support the integration and hybridization of these various forms of reusable resources, and the transformation of one form into another (for example, the specification of an ASL as an "envelope" to an over-populated library [SIM1]).

We believe that a critical factor to the successful application of any of these advanced reusability techniques is the maintenance of an explicit representation of domain knowledge as part of the environment framework. This explicit semantic model of the supported domain, along the lines of knowledge-based or expert systems, would serve as a structuring framework for the other components in the environment. It is somewhat of a paradox, yet seems appropriate as well, that large-scale increases in reusability could be accomplished by applying advanced knowledge-engineering techniques to the "experts" who implement conventional software systems. Whether domain-specific environments of this kind could be developed to support the work of the knowledge engineers themselves is a question for further down the road.

References

[BATZ]
J. C. Batz, P. M. Cohen, S. T. Redwine, J. R. Rice, "The Application-Specific Task Area", *IEEE Computer*, **16**:11, pp. 78-85, November 1983.

[BEACON]
Freeman, M., "Case Study of the BEACON Project", illustrated presentation script, IEEE Videoconference Seminar "Expert Systems and Prolog", The Learning Channel, December 1985.

[BESL]
Solderitsch, J., "Application-Specific Language System for Code Generation via Tree Traversal", Unisys Internal Report, December 1986.

[CAMP]
Anderson, C. M., McNicholl, D. G., "Contract FO 8635-84-C-0280, Common Ada Missile Packages (CAMP): Preliminary Technical Report, Vol. 1", in *STARS Workshop Proceedings*, April 1985.

[CHEATHAM]
Cheatham, T. E., "Reusability through Program Transformations", *IEEE Trans. on Software Engineering*, Special Issue on Software Reusability, **SE-10**:5, September 1984.

[GUIDE]
STARS Applications Task Area Reusability Guidebook Draft V4.0

[HOROWITZ]
Horowitz, E., Munson, J. B., "An Expansive View of Reusable Software", *IEEE Trans. on Software Engineering*, Special Issue on Software Reusability, **SE-10**:5, September 1984, pp. 477-487.

[IEEE]
IEEE Trans. on Software Engineering, Special Issue on Software Reusability, **SE-10**:5, September 1984.

[KASTENS]
Kastens, U., "Ordered Attribute Grammars", *Acta Informatica*, Volume 13, 1980, pp. 229-256.

[KELLER]
Keller, S.E., J. A. Perkins, T. F. Payton, S. P. Mardinly, "Tree Transformation Techniques and Experiences", *Proceedings of the SIGPLAN '84 Symposium on Compiler Construction*, June 1984, pp. 190-201.

[KNUTH]
Knuth, D., "Semantics of Context-Free Languages", *Math. Systems Theory*, **5**:1, 1971, pp. 127-145.

[MEYER]
Meyer, B., "Reusability: The Case for Object-Oriented Design", *IEEE Software* Volume 4.2, March 1987.

[MFPL]
Pollack, R. H., J. Solderitsch, W. P. Loftus, "MFPL: A Case Study in Software Generation from Specification", Unisys Internal Report, 1987.

[POLLACK1]
Pollack, R. H., *Message Format Specification Language Reference Manual*, Unisys Internal Report, 1986.

[POLLACK2]
Pollack, R. H., M. A. Simos, W. P. Loftus, "A Tree-Transformation Approach to Implementing Syntactic Dialects", Unisys Internal Report, January 1986.

[RICH]
Richter, C., "The Application of KL-ONE to Software Design Information: A Case Study", MCC Technical Report Number STP-440-86.

[SIM1]
Simos, M.A., "Alternative Technologies for Software Reusability", presented to 3rd STARS Workshop on Applications Systems and Reusability.

[SIM2]
Simos, M.A., R. H. Pollack, W. P. Loftus, "Integration of Fourth Generation Languages and Ada", Proceedings of the USAISEC Technology Strategies '87 Conference, Alexandria, Virginia, February 1987.

[SOLDERITSCH]
Solderitsch, J., *English-Language Dialect Message Format Specification Language Reference Manual*, Unisys Internal Report, 1986.

Part 5: Bibliography

The following list of articles and papers focus on software reuse and related technologies. In particular, the following auxiliary topics are addressed:

- software factories
- application generators
- object-oriented programming
- transformation systems

The bibliography has been broken down chronologically into four sections:

- pre-ITT workshop (up until 1983)
- ITT workshop and pre-STARS workshops (1983-1984)
- early STARS workshops and reuse conferences/sessions (1985-1986)
- recent activities (1987-)

Other bibliographies on software reuse may be found in Peter Freeman's *Tutorial: Software Reusability* (IEEE Computer Society Press), Grady Booch's *Software Components with Ada* (Benjamin/Cummings), Ted Biggerstaff and Alan Perlis' *Software Reusability* (Addison-Wesley), and Logicon's *Collection of Abstracts for Reusability and Very-High-Level Languages Technical Report*.

Software Reuse 1969-1982

The modern roots of software reuse can be traced back to Doug McIroy's 1969 visionary paper on software reuse, "Mass Produced Software Components." After the publication of some foundational work by Goodenough, Parnas, Kernighan, and later Cheatham, Balzer, and Waters, the social conscience of software reuse was raised by short contributions by Glass and Denning. The seminal work of Lanergan at Raytheon appeared at the end of the 1970s, demonstrating dramatic results. Peter Freeman and Jim Neighbors entered the software reuse arena at the beginning of the decade (when Jim wrote the first Ph.D. dissertation on reusable software) and have continued to be strong players throughout the 1980s. The impact of Ada also started raising new issues in the early 1980s, as reflected in the papers by Meyer, Abbott, and Bowles.

[1]   Abbott, R.J. Style Guide and Documentation Standard for the Programming Language Ada. In *Proceedings of the Software Engineering Standards Application Workshop*, pages 108-114. IEEE Computer Society Press, Washington, D.C., August 18-20, 1981.

[2]   Balzer, R.M, Goldman, and N.M, Wile, D. On the Transformational Implementation Approach to Programming. In *Proceedings of 2nd International Conference on Software Engineering*, pages 58-67. IEEE Computer Society Press, Washington, D.C., 1980.

[3]   Balzer, R.M. Transformational Implementation: An Example. *IEEE Transactions on Software Engineering* SE-7(1):3-14, January, 1981.

[4]   Bjorklund, H.A., and Averill, E. L. Reusable Software Engineering. In *Proceedings of the IEEE 1982 National Aerospace and Electronics Conference*, pages 1178-1184. May 18-20, 1982.

[5]   Bousley, R.F. Reusable Avionics Executive Software. In *Proceedings of the IEEE 1981 National Aerospace and Electronics Conference*, pages 31-36. IEEE, New York, May 19-21, 1981.

[6]   Bowles, K. Linked Ada Modules Shape Software System. *Electronic Design* (7), July, 22, 1982.

[7]   Bratman, H. and Court, T. The Software Factory. *IEEE Computer* 8(5):28-37, May, 1975.

[8]   Chandersekaran, C.S. Survey of Reusable Software. 1982.Unpublished IBM Technical Report.

[9]   Cheatham, T.E., Holloway, G.H, and Townley, J.A. Program Refinement by Transformation. In *Proceedings of 5th International Conference on Software Engineering*, pages 430-437. IEEE Computer Society Press, Washington, D.C., 1981.

[10]   Denning, P.J. Throwaway Programs. *Communications of the ACM* 24(2):259-260, February, 1981.

[11]   Engelland, J.D. et al. *Operational Software Concept (Phase One) Volume I - Introduction and Summary*. Technical Report AFAL-TR-74-168, Air Force Avionics Laboratory, Wright Patterson AFB, Dayton, Ohio, 1974.

[12]   Freeman, P. *Reusable Software Engineering: A Statement of Long-Range Research Objectives*. Technical Report 159, Department of Information and Computer Science, University of California, Irvine, Irvine, Calif., November, 10, 1980.

[13]   Glass, R.L. Software Parts Nostalgia. *Datamation* :245-247, November, 1981.

[14]   Goodenough, J.B. and Zara, R.V. *The Effect of Software Structure on Software Reliability, Modifiability, and Reusability: A Case Study and Analysis*. Technical Report DAAA 25-72C 0667, SofTech, Inc., Waltham, Mass., 1974.

[15] Gordon, R.D. The Modular Application Customizing System. *IBM Systems Journal* 19(4):521-541, 1980.

[16] Hammer, M.M., House, W.G., and Wladawsky, I. An Interactive Business Definition System. In *Proceedings of Symposium on Very High Level Languages*, pages 25-33. 1974.

[17] Kernighan, B. and Plauger, P. *The Elements of Style*. New York: McGraw-Hill, 1978.

[18] Lanergan, R. and Poynton, B. Software Engineering with Standard Assemblies. In *Proceedings of the ACM Annual Conference*, pages 507-514. Association for Computing Machinery, Inc., New York, December, 1978.

[19] Lanergan, R. and Poynton, B. Reusable Code - The Application Development Technique of the Future. In *Proceedings of IBM GUIDE/SHARE Application Symposium*, pages 127-136. SHARE, Inc., Chicago, Il., 1979.

[20] Matsubara, T., Sasaki, O., Nakajim, K., Takezawa, K., Yamamoto, S. and Tanaka, T. SWB System: A Software Factory. In *Software Engineering Environments*, pages 305-318. North-Holland Publishing Company, 1981.

[21] McIlroy, M. D. Mass Produced Software Components. In Naur, P., Randell, B. and Buxton, J.N. (editors), *Proceedings of NATO Conference on Software Engineering*, pages 88-98. Petrocelli/Charter, New York, 1969.

[22] Meyer, B. Principles of Package Design. *Communications of the ACM* 25(7):419-428, July, 1982.

[23] Neighbors, J.M. *Software Construction Using Components*. PhD thesis, University of California, Irvine, 1980.

[24] Neighbors, J.M. *Software Construction Using Components*. Technical Report 160, Department of Information and Computer Science, University of California, Irvine, Irvine, Calif., 1982.

[25] Parnas, D.L.. On the Design and Development of Program Families. *IEEE Transactions on Software Engineering* SE-2(1):1-9, March, 1976.

[26] Rauch-Hindin, W. Software Tools: New Ways to Chip Software into Shape. *Data Communications* 11:83-88, April, 1982.

[27] Schappelle, S.J. *Reusable Software Definitions*. Technical Report 82-550-006, IBM Technical Reports Center, Owego, N.Y., June 11, 1982.

[28] Schappelle, S.J. A Methodology for Reusable Software. 1982.Unpublished IBM Technical Report.

[29] Sizer, P.D. Software Engineering and Guide Lines for the Production of Reliable Software. *Macroni Review* 44(223):204-224, 1981.

[30] Tajima, D. and Matsubara, T. The Computer Software Industry in Japan. *IEEE Computer* :89-96, May, 1981.

[31] Waters, R.C. The Programmer's Apprentice: Knowledge Based Program Editing. *IEEE Transactions on Software Engineering* SE-8(1):1-12, January, 1982.

Software Reuse 1983-1984

Interest in reuse burst onto the software scene in 1983 with the landmark ITT Workshop on Reusability in Programming. Ted Biggerstaff and Alan Perlis succeeded in attracting a critical mass of leading researchers and industry representatives to this meeting. The best papers were then refined and subsequently published in a special issue of *IEEE Transactions on Software Engineering* the following year.

1983 also saw the Ada Program Libraries Workshop at the Naval Post Graduate School in Monterey, California chaired by Joseph Goguen and Karl Levitt of SRI International. Not surprising, the two master's thesis on reuse appeared the following year from the same location. COMPSAC 84 featured the first paper session on software reuse and Wegner's paper on "Capital-Intensive Software Technology" in *IEEE Software* shed new light on software reuse. Finally, much

of the work of Lanergan was being refined (and reused) by EDP programmers. Their successes appeared in a series of articles published by *Computerworld*.

[1] Anonymous. Reusable Code Writes Finis to Productivity Woes. *Computerworld* 17(37):65, September 12, 1983.

[2] Anonymous. CAP Accelerates COBOL Production. *Computer Data* 9(2):8, February, 1984.

[3] Archibald, J.L., Leavenworthe, B.M., and Power, L.R. Abstract Design and Program Translator: New Tools for Software Design. *IBM Systems Journal* 32(3):170-187, 1983.

[4] Balzer, R. Evolution as a New Basis for Reusability. In *Proceedings of ITT Workshop on Reusability in Programming*. ITT, Startford, Conn., September 7-9, 1983.

[5] Balzer, R.M., Cheatham, T.E., and Green, C. Software Technology in the 1990's: Using a New Paradigm. *IEEE Computer* :39-42, November, 1983.

[6] Barnes, J. Using Ada for Compilers and Operating Systems. *Data-Processing* 26(6):22-24,29, July/August, 1984.

[7] Bassett, P. and Glon, J. Computer Aided Programming. In *Proceedings of Softfair 83*, pages 9-20. IEEE Computer Society Press, Washington, D.C., July 25-28, 1983.

[8] Bassett, P. Design Principles for Software Manufacturing Tools. In *Proceedings of the ACM 84 Annual Conference*, pages 85-93. Association for Computing Machinery, Inc., New York, October, 1984.

[9] Batz, J. C., Cohen, P.M., Redwine, S.T., and Rice, J.R. Application-Specific Task Area. *Computer* 16(11):78-85, November, 1983.

[10] Biggerstaff, T.J. A Radical Hypothesis: Reusability Is the Essence of Design. In *Proceedings of COMPSAC 84*, pages 474-475. IEEE Computer Society Press, Washington, D.C., October, 1984.

[11] Biggerstaff, T.J. and Perlis, A.J. Forward: Special Issue on Software Reusability. *IEEE Transactions on Software Engineering* SE-10(5):474-476, September, 1984.

[12] Booth, T. L. Software Is the Limitation. *IEEE Spectrum* 21(1):36-37, January, 1984.

[13] Bowles, K. Reusability in Ada. In *Proceedings of ITT Workshop on Reusability in Programming*. September 7-9, 1983.

[14] Boyle, J.M. and Muralidharan, M.N. Program Reusability through Program Transformation. *IEEE Transactions on Software Engineering* SE-10(5):574-588, September, 1984.

[15] Cameron, R.D. and Ito, M.R. Grammar-Based Definition of Metaprogramming Systems. *ACM Transactions on Programming Languages and Systems* 6(1):20-54, January, 1984.

[16] Cavaliere, M.J. and Archambeault, P.J. Reusable Code at The Hartford Insurance Group. In *Proceedings of ITT Workshop on Reusability in Programming*. ITT, Startford, Conn., September 7-9, 1983.

[17] Chandersekaran, C.S. and Perriens, M.P. Towards an Assessment of Software Reusability. In *Proceedings of ITT Workshop on Reusability in Programming*. ITT, Startford, Conn., September 7-9, 1983.

[18] Cheatham, T.E. Jr. Reusability Through Program Transformations. *IEEE Transactions on Software Engineering* SE-10(5):589-594, September, 1984.

[19] Cheng, T.T., Lock, E.D., and Prywes, N.S. Use of Very High Level Languages and Program Generation by Management Professionals. *IEEE Transactions on Software Engineering* SE-10(5):552-563, September, 1984.

[20] Clapp, J. Software Reusability: A Management View. In *Proceedings of COMPSAC84 Conference*, pages 479. IEEE Computer Society Press, Washington, D.C., 1984.

[21] Cox, B.J. An Evolutionary Change in Programming Technology. *IEEE Software* 1(1):50-61, January, 1984.

[22] Curry, G.A. and Ayers, R.M. Experience with Traits in the Xerox Star Workstation. *IEEE Transactions on Software Engineering* SE-10(5):519-527, September, 1984.

[23]   Curtis, B. Cognitive Issues in Reusability. In *Proceedings of ITT Workshop on Reusability in Programming*. ITT, Startford, Conn., September 7-9, 1983.

[24]   Deutsch, L.P. Reusability in the Smalltalk-80 Programming System. In *Proceedings of ITT Workshop on Reusability in Programming*. ITT, Startford, Conn., September 7-9, 1983.

[25]   Doberkat, E. Dubinsky, E., and Schwartz, J.T. Reusability of Design for Complex Programs: An Experiment with the SETL Optimizer. In *Proceedings of ITT Workshop on Reusability in Programming*. ITT, Startford, Conn., September 7-9, 1983.

[26]   Druffel, L.E. Redwine, S.T., and Riddle, W.E. The STARS Program: Overview and Rationale. *Computer* 16(11):21-29, November, 1983.

[27]   Ellis, W. Programming Templates for Software Productivity and Quality. December, 1983.IBM-FSD Technical Report.

[28]   Evanczuk, S. New Tools Boost Software Productivity. *Electronics Week* 57(22):67-74, Sept. 10, 1984.

[29]   Feather, M.S. Reuse in the Context of a Transformation Based Methodology. In *Proceedings of ITT Workshop on Reusability in Programming*. ITT, Startford, Conn., September 7-9, 1983.

[30]   Freeman, P. Reusable Software Engineering: Concepts and Research Directions. In *Proceedings of ITT Workshop on Reusability in Programming*. ITT, Startford, Conn., September 7-9, 1983.

[31]   Fujibayasi, S. et al. Early Experiences Regarding SDMS Introduction into Software Production Sites. *NEC Research and Development* (68):51-60, January, 1983.

[32]   Gerhart, S.L. Reusability Lessons from Verification Technology. In *Proceedings of ITT Workshop on Reusability in Programming*. ITT, Startford, Conn., September 7-9, 1983.

[33]   Giddings, N. Reusable Components Based on Separating Knowledge and Control. December 11, 1984.Honeywell Technical Report.

[34]   Gillin, P. T. Capers Jones on Life Without Programmers. *Computerworld* 18(22):3,6, May 28, 1984.

[35]   Gladney, H.M. A CONCISE Experiment in Program Reusability. In *Proceedings of ITT Workshop on Reusability in Programming*. ITT, Startford, Conn., September 7-9, 1983.

[36]   Goguen, J.A. and Levitt, K.N. (editors). *Report On Program Libraries Workshop*. SRI International, Menlo Park, Calif., 1983.

[37]   Goguen, J.A. Parameterized Programming. *IEEE Transactions on Software Engineering* SE-10(5):528-543, September, 1984.

[38]   Goodell, M. Quantitative Study of Functional Commonality in a Sample of Commercial Business Applications. In *Proceedings of ITT Workshop on Reusability in Programming*. ITT, Startford, Conn., September 7-9, 1983.

[39]   Grabow, P.C., Noble, W.B., and Huang, C. *Reusable Software Implementation Technology Reviews*. Technical Report N660001-83-D-0095, NOSC and Hughes Aircraft Company, San Diego, Calif., December, 1984.

[40]   Horowitz, E. and Munson, J.B. An Expansive View of Reusable Software. *IEEE Transactions on Software Engineering* SE-10(5):477-487, September, 1984.

[41]   Horowitz, E., Kemper, A., and Narasimhan, B.. Application Generators: Ideas for Programming Language Extensions. In *Proceedings of the ACM'84 Annual Conference*, pages 94-101. October, 1984.

[42]   IBM. Reusable Software Implementation Program (RSIP) Software Development Methodology Reviews. 1984.Unpublished IBM Technical Report.

[43]   Biggerstaff, T.J. and Cheatham, T.E. Jr. (editors). *Workshop on Reusability in Programming*. ITT, Stratford, Conn., 1983.

[44]   Iwamoto, K., et al. Early Experiences Regarding SDMS Introduction into Software Production Sites. *NEC Research and Development* (68):51-60, January, 1983.

[45]   Johnson, W.C. Reusable Software. Master's thesis, Naval Postgraduate School, March, 1984.

[46]   Jones, G. Software Reusability: Approaches and Issues. In *Proceedings of COMPSAC84 Conference*, pages 476. IEEE Computer Society Press, Washington, D.C., 1984.

[47]   Jones, T.C. Reusability in Programming: A Survey of the State of the Art. *IEEE Transactions on Software Engineering* SE-10(5):488-493, September, 1984.

[48]   Jones, T.C. Laying the Groundwork with Reusable Code. *Computerworld* :12-16, June, 1984.

[49]   Kandt, K. Pegasus: A Tool for the Acquisition and Reuse of Software Designs. In *Proceedings of COMPSAC84 Conference*, pages 288. IEEE Computer Society Press, Washington, D.C., 1984.

[50]   Kernighan, B. W. The Unix System and Software Reusability. *IEEE Transactions on Software Engineering* SE-10(5):513-518, September, 1984.

[51]   Kim, K.H. A Look at Japan's Development of Software Engineering Technology. *IEEE Computer* :26-37, May, 1983.

[52]   Kok, J. and Symm, G.T. A Proposal for Standard Basic Functions in Ada. *Ada Letters* IV(3):44-52, November-December, 1984.

[53]   Kuo, H.C., Chow, A.L., and Kishimoto, Z. An Approach to Flexible Software System Design Using Generic Capabilities. In *Proceedings of COMPSAC84 Conference*, pages 294. IEEE Computer Society Press, Washington, D.C., 1984.

[54]   Lanergan, R.G. and Grasso, C.A. Software Engineering with Reusable Design and Code. *IEEE Transactions on Software Engineering* SE-10(5):498-501, September, 1984.

[55]   Ledbetter. Reusability of Domain Knowledge in the Automatic Programming System O. In *Proceedings of ITT Workshop on Reusability in Programming*. ITT, Startford, Conn., September 7-9, 1983.

[56]   Litvintchouk, S.D. and Matsumoto, A.S. Design of Ada Systems Yielding Reusable Components: An Approach Using Structured Algebraic Specification. *IEEE Transactions on Software Engineering* SE-10(5):544-551, September, 1984.

[57]   Maiden, G.S. Source Translation in a Multi-Language Compiling System. In *Proceedings of ITT Workshop on Reusability in Programming*. ITT, Startford, Conn., September 7-9, 1983.

[58]   Martin, R.D. Customized Automatic Test System Software Without Redesign. In *Proceedings of AUTOTESTCON '83*, pages 471-477. IEEE, New York, November 1-3, 1983.

[59]   Matsumoto, Y. Some Experience in Promoting Reusable Software: Presentation in Higher Abstract Levels. *IEEE Transactions on Software Engineering* SE-10(5):502-512, September, 1984.

[60]   Matsumoto, Y. Management of Industrial Software Production. *IEEE Computer* 17(2):59-70, February, 1984.

[61]   McDermott, D. NISP - A Portable LISP with Compile-Time Types. In *Proceedings of ITT Workshop on Reusability in Programming*. ITT, Startford, Conn., September 7-9, 1983.

[62]   McFarland, C. and Rawlings, T. DARTS: Software Manufacturing Technology. In *AIAA 21st Aerospace Sciences Meeting*, pages 6. January 10-13, 1983.

[63]   Metcalf, S.G. Software Library: A Reusable Software Issue. Master's thesis, Naval Postgraduate School, June, 1984.

[64]   Munson. Software Technology Lagging Behind Hardware. *Computerworld* 18(22):24,26, May 28, 1984.

[65]   Neighbors, J.M. The Draco Approach to Constructing Software from Reusable Components. *IEEE Transactions on Software Engineering* SE-10(5):564-573, September, 1984.

[66]   Oskarsson, O. Software Reusability in a System Based on Data and Device Abstractions - A Case Study. In *Proceedings of ITT Workshop on Reusability in Programming*. ITT, Startford, Conn., September 7-9, 1983.

[67]   Osterweil, L.J. Toolpack - An Experimental Software Development Environment Research Project. *IEEE Transactions on Software Engineering* SE-9(6):673-685, November, 1983.

[68]   Parish, S., and Rudmik, A. DCP (Distributed Software Engineering Control Process) - Experience in Bootstrapping an Ada Environment. In *Proceedings of the 2nd Annual Conference on Ada Technology*, pages 62-69. March, 1984.

[69]   Parnas, D.L., Clements, P.C., and Weiss, D.M. Enhancing Reusability with Information Hiding. In *Proceedings of ITT Workshop on Reusability in Programming*. ITT, Startford, Conn., September 7-9, 1983.

[70]   Partsch, H. and Steinbruggen, R. Program Transformation Systems. *ACM Computing Surveys* 15(3):199-236, March, 1983.

[71]   Paul, L. Factory Approach: New Way to Build Software. *Computerworld* 17(9):4, February 28, 1984.

[72]   Pedersen, J.T. Kongsberg Approach to Achieve Reusable Application Software. In *Proceedings of the 1st International Conference on Computers and Applications*, pages 787-794. IEEE Computer Society Press, Washington, D.C., June 20-22, 1984.

[73]   Platek, R. Use of Ada as an Implementation Language in Formally Specified Systems. In *Proceedings of the Symposium on Security and Privacy*, pages 107-110. IEEE Computer Society Press, Washington, D.C., April 29-May 2, 1984.

[74]   Presson, P.E., Tsai, J., Bowen, T.P., Post, J.V., and Schmidt, R. *Software Interoperability and Reusability*. Technical Report RADC-TR-83-174, Boeing Aerospace Company, Seattle, Wash., July, 1983. Two volumes.

[75]   Rauch-Hindin, W.B. Reusable Software. *Electronic Design* 31(3):176-193, February, 3, 1983.

[76]   Rice, J.R. and Schwetman, H.D. Interface Issues in a Software Parts Technology. In *Proceedings of ITT Workshop on Reusability in Programming*. ITT, Startford, Conn., September 7-9, 1983.

[77]   Rice, J.R. Remarks on Software Components and Packages in Ada. *SIGSOFT Software Engineering Notes* 8(2):9-10, March, 1983.

[78]   Rich, C. and Waters, R.C. Formalizing Reusable Software Components. In *Proceedings of ITT Workshop on Reusability in Programming*. ITT, Startford, Conn., September 7-9, 1983.

[79]   Romberg, F.A. and Thomas, A.B. Reusable Code, Reliable Software. *Computerworld* 18(13):17-26, March 26, 1984.

[80]   Saward, M.P. Programming Support: Tools of the Trade. *Electronic Communication* 57(4):289-294, 1983.

[81]   Soloway, E. and Ehrlich, K. What Do Programmers Reuse? Theory and Experiment. In *Proceedings of ITT Workshop on Reusability in Programming*. ITT, Startford, Conn., September 7-9, 1983.

[82]   Soloway, E. and Ehrlich, K. Empirical Studies of Programming Knowledge. *IEEE Transactions on Software Engineering* SE-10(5):595-609, September, 1984.

[83]   Standish, T.A. An Essay on Software Reuse. *IEEE Transactions on Software Engineering* SE-10(5):494-497, September, 1984.

[84]   Sterne, D.F. Applied Research in Ada. *John Hopkins APL Technical Dialogue* 5(3):266-269, July-September, 1984.

[85]   Sunfor, S. *Reusable Software Engineering: A Survey of Concepts and Approaches*. Technical Report RTP017, University of California, Irvine, Department of Information and Computer Science, Irvine, Calif., 1983.

[86]   Tajima, D. and Matsubara, T. Inside the Japanese Software Industry. *IEEE Computer* :34-43, March, 1984.

[87]   Tracz, W.J. Confessions of a Used Program Salesman. *Computer* 16(4):100, April, 1983.

[88]   Wegner, P. Varieties of Reusability. In *Proceedings of ITT Workshop on Reusability in Programming*. ITT, Startford, Conn., September 7-9, 1983.

[89]   Wegner, P. Capital-Intensive Software Technology. *IEEE Software* 1"(3):7-32, July, 1984.

[90]   Wenia, R.P. When to Use Used Software. *Computing Canada* 9(22), October 27, 1983.

[91]   Wile, D.S. Program Developments: Formal Explanations of Implementations. *Communications of the ACM* 26(11):902-911, November, 1983.

[92]   Yeh, R.T., Roussopoulos, N., and Chu, B. Management of Reusable Software. In *Proceedings of COMPCON 84 Fall: The Small Computer (R)Evolution*, pages 311-320. IEEE Computer Society Press, Washington, D.C., September 16-20, 1984.

[93]   Zelkowitz, M.V., Yeh, R.T., Hamlet, R.G., Gannon, J.D., and Basili, V.R. Software Engineering Practices in the US and Japan. *IEEE Computer* :57-66, June, 1984.

Software Reuse 1985-1986

Interest in software reuse continued to escalate, partially spurred by the high interest (and funding levels) of the U. S. Department of Defense and the recognition that the Japanese were achieving some remarkable success employing the software factory principles heralded by McIlroy almost two decades ago. The years of 1985 and 1986 witnessed no fewer than seven workshops on software reuse (four sponsored by STARS alone). Meanwhile, special sessions at conferences, such as COMPSAC and Ada Applications for NASA Space Station, continued to feature the work of researchers and industrial developers. At this point in time, the merits of object-oriented approaches to software development as well as libraries for reusable components started to draw attention of programmers.

[1]   Afsar, S.K. Software Reuse Via Source Transformations. In *Proceedings of COMPSAC 85*, pages 54-61. IEEE Computer Society Press, Washington, D.C., October 9-11, 1985.

[2]   Alexandridis, N.A. Adaptable Software and Hardware: Problems and Solutions. *Computer* 19(2):29-39, February, 1986.

[3]   Anderson, L.A. and Hudson, S.S. Project Requirements For Reusable Software. In *Proceedings of Software Technology for Adaptable Reliable Systems (STARS) Workshop*, pages 1-54. STARS Program Office, Washington, D.C., April 9-12, 1985.

[4]   Anderson, C.M. and Henne, M. Reusable Software - A Concept for Cost Reduction. In *Proceedings of Software Technology for Adaptable Reliable Systems (STARS) Workshop*, pages 243-270. STARS Program Office, Washington, D.C., April 9-12, 1985.

[5]   Anonymous. A Program Generator ARIES/I by Automatic Fabrication of Reusable Program Components. *Transactions on Information Processing (JAPAN)* 27(4):417-424, 1986.

[6]   Arkwright, T.D. Macro Issues in Reuse from a Real Project. In *Proceedings of Software Technology for Adaptable Reliable Systems (STARS) Workshop*, pages 55 74. STARS Program Office, Washington, D.C., April 9-12, 1985.

[7]   Baker, P.L. Ada Seen as Essential to Design. In *Proceedings of IEEE Computer Society Second International Conference on Ada Applications and Environments*. IEEE Computer Society Press, Washington, D.C., April, 1986.

[8]   Balzer, R.M, Goldman, N.M, Wile, D. On the Transformational Implementation Approach to Programming. In *Proceedings of 2nd International Conference on Software Engineering*, pages 58-67. IEEE Computer Society Press, Washington, D.C., 1986.

[9]   Barbacci, M.R., Habermann, A.H., and Shaw, M. The Software Engineering Institute: Bridging Practice and Potential. *IEEE Software* :4-21, November, 1985.

[10]   Barbacci, M. The Software Factory Project at the Software Engineering Institute. In *Proceedings of 1986 National Computer Conference*, pages 94-95. AFIPS Press, Reston, Va., 1986.

[11]   Barbuceanu, M. Knowledge Based Development of Evolutionary and Reusable Software. In *Proceedings of 6th International Workshop on Expert Systems and Their Applications* . 1986.

[12]   Barra, S., Ghisio, O., Gouthier, P., Truzzi, S. Assisted Reusability of CHILL Programs. *CSELT Technical Reports* XIV(2):111-115, April, 1986.

[13]   Barra, S., Ghisio, O., Gouthier, P., and Truzzi, S. An Environment Providing Assistance in Code Reusability. In *Proceedings of Sixth International*

Conference on Software Engineering for Telecommunication Switching Systems, pages 221-225. 1986.

[14]   Basili, V.R.,Bailey,J.,Joo,B.-G., and Rombach, H.D. Software Reuse: A 'Framework for Research. September, 1986.University of Maryland.

[15]   Bassett, P.G. SW Model Needs Rethinking. *Canadian Datasystems* 18(3):94, March, 1986.

[16]   Bassett, P. More on Reusability. *System Development* 5(11):5-6, January, 1986.

[17]   Berard, E.V. Creating Reusable Ada Software. In *Proceedings of National Conference on Software Reuseability and Maintainability*. National Institute of Software Quality and Productivity, Washington, D.C., September 10-11, 1986.

[18]   Bieniak, R.M., Griffin, L.M., and Tripp, L.R. Automated Parts Composition. In *Proceedings of Software Technology for Adaptable Reliable Systems (STARS) Workshop*, pages 107-128. STARS Program Office, Washington, D.C., April 9-12, 1985.

[19]   Bond, R.M. Reusable Component Definition (A Tutorial). In *Proceedings of Software Technology for Adaptable Reliable Systems (STARS) Workshop*, pages 99-106. STARS Program Office, Washington, D.C., April 9-12, 1985.

[20]   Bott, F. A Survey of Reuse and its Problems. Presentation at the Workshop on Software Reuse Held at Hereford, UK. May 1-2, 1986

[21]   Bowen, T.P. Design Considerations for Reusable Software. In *Proceedings of COMPSAC 85*, pages 203. IEEE Computer Society Press, Washington, D.C., October 9-11, 1985.

[22]   Bowen, T. Workshop on Reusable Components of Application Software. In *Proceedings of Software Technology for Adaptable Reliable Systems (STARS) Workshop*, pages 75-82. STARS Program Office, Washington, D.C., April 9-12, 1985.

[23]   Braun, C.L., Goodenough, J.B., and Eanes, R.S. *Ada Reusability Guidelines*. Technical Report 3285-2-208/2, SofTech, Inc., April, 1985.

[24]   Braun, U. *An Expert System for the Retrieval of Software Building Blocks*. Technical Report TR 05.373, IBM Laboratory, Boeblingen, West Germany, 1986. In German.

[25]   Burton, B.A. and Broido, M.D. A Phased Approach to Ada Package Reuse. In *Proceedings of Software Technology for Adaptable Reliable Systems (STARS) Workshop*, pages 83-98. STARS Program Office, Washington, D.C., April 9-12, 1985.

[26]   Burton, B.A. A Practical Approach to Ada Reusability. In *Proceedings of National Conference on Software Reuseability and Maintainability*. National Institute of Software Quality and Productivity, Washington, D.C., September 10-11, 1986.

[27]   Burton, B. and Broido, M. Development of an Ada Package Library. In *Proceedings of First International Conference on Ada Programming Language Applications for the NASA Space Station*, pages E.1.3.1-E.1.3.13. University of Houston at Clear Lake, Clear Lake, Tex., June 2-5, 1986.

[28]   Card, D. N., Church, V.E., and Agresti, W.W. Emperical Study of Software Design Practices. *IEEE Transactions on Software Engineering* SE-12(2):264-271, February, 1986.

[29]   Chao, A. A Modular Approach to Real-Time Software. *Computer Design* :85-88, October, 1, 1986.

[30]   Chen, Y.F. and Ramamoorthy, C.V. The C Information Abstractor. In *Proceedings of 10th Anniversary COMPSAC '86*, pages 291-298. IEEE Computer Society Press, Washington, D.C., 1986.

[31]   Cohen, P.F. The Transformation of Functional Decompositions to Object-Oriented Designs. Presentation Slides at Ada Expo '86. November 21, 1986

[32]   Cohen, S.G. Reusable Software Parts and the Semi-Abstract Data Type. In *Proceedings of First International Conference on Ada Programming Language Applications for the NASA Space Station*, pages G.3.2.1-G.3.2.2. University of Houston at Clear Lake, Clear Lake, Tex., June 2-5, 1986.

[33]   Conn, R. Overview of DoD Ada Software Repository. *Dr. Dobbs Journal* :60-61,86-91, February, 1986.

[34]   Conn, R. (editor). *Ada Software Repository Master Index*. Echelon, Inc., Los Altos, Calif., 1988.

[35]   COSMIC. *COSMIC: A Catalog of Selected Computer Programs*. National Aeronautics and Space Administration Technology Utilization Office, Washington, D.C., 1986.

[36]   Cox, B.J. Object-oriented Programming, Software-ICs and System Building. In *Proceedings of National Conference on Software Reuseability and Maintainability*. National Institute of Software Quality and Productivity, Washington, D.C., September 10-11, 1986.

[37]   Cox, B.J. *Object-oriented Programming*. Addison-Wesley Publishing Company, Reading, Mass., 1986.

[38]   DaGraca, J.J. A Discussion of Ada Experience at General Dynamics Data Systems Division. In *Proceedings of Software Technology for Adaptable Reliable Systems (STARS) Workshop*, pages 129-144. STARS Program Office, Washington, D.C., April 9-12, 1985.

[39]   Dierickx, W. and Philips, B. Rewriting Programs to Have a Base for New Software. *Microprocessing and Microprogramming* 16:211-214, 1985.

[40]   Dillehunt, D., Nise, N.S., and Giffin, C. Reusable Software Development. March, 1985.Rockwell International.

[41]   Doe, D.D. and Bersoff, E.H. The Software Productivity Consortium (SPC): An Industry Initiative to Improve the Productivity and Quality of Mission Critical Software. *Journal of Systems and Software* 6(4):367-378, November, 1986.

[42]   Anonymous. Guideline for Writing Reusable Ada. ECLIPSE Technical Report. 1986

[43]   Rliot, L. B., and Scacchi, W. Towards a Knowledge Based System Factory: Issues and Implementation. *IEEE Expert* 1(4):51-58, Winter, 1986.

[44]   Elston, J.R. The Boeing Automated Software Engineering (BASE) Environment. In *Proceedings of Software Factory Forum*. Software Engineering Institute, Pittsburgh, Pa., February 18-19, 1986.

[45]   EVB. GRACE Bounded Stack. Pamphlet. 1985

[46]   Fatasugi, K., Goguen, J.A., Jouannaud, J.P., and Meseguer, J. Principles of OBJ2. In *Proceedings of Symposium on Principles of Programming Languages*, pages 52-66. Association for Computing Machinery, Inc., New York, 1985.

[47]   Frbes, J.E. Architectural Design for Automation: Functions and Interfaces. *IBM Manufacturing Technology Digest* 4(1):66-74, 1986.

[48]   Frankowski, E. N., and Anderson, C. Design/Integration Panel Report. 1985.STARS Application Workshop.

[49]   Frankowski, E., Spinrad, M., and Stachour, P. Rapid Prototyping with Reusable Source Code. In *Proceedings of Software Technology for Adaptable Reliable Systems (STARS) Workshop*, pages 145-154. STARS Program Office, Washington, D.C., April 9-12, 1985.

[50]   Frankowski, E.N., Abraham, C.L., Onuegbe, E., Spinrad, M., St.Dennis, R., and Stachour, P. *RaPIER (Rapid Prototyping to Investigate End-user Requirements: A Report of 1985 Technical Activities*. Technical Report CSC-86-4:82313, Honeywell Computer Sciences Center, Golden Valley, Minn., March, 1986.

[51]   Frankowski, E. N. *Why Programs Built from Reusable Software Should be Single Paradigm*. Technical Report, Honeywell Computer Sciences Center, Golden Valley, Minn., March 6, 1986.

[52]   Gaube, W., Mayr, H.C., and Lockemann, P.C. Retrieval in a Module Library Using Formal Specifications: Preliminary Search Using Syntactic Properties. In *Proceedings of EUROCAL' 85. European Conference on Computer Algebra*, pages 181-196. 1985.

[53]   Gautier, B. A Component Description Language. Presentation at the Workshop on Software Reuse Held at Hereford, UK. May 1-2, 1986

[54]   Gautier, B. Guidelines for Writing Reusable Components in Ada. Presentation at the Workshop on Software Reuse Held at Hereford, UK. May 1-2, 1986

[55]   Gerhardt, M.S. Reuseable Components and Ada. Presentation Foils from SIGAda Tutorial, July 22, Pittsburgh, PA. 1986

[56]   Goguen, J.A. Reusing and Interconnecting Software Components. *Computer* 19(2):16-28, February, 1986.

[57]   Goldberg, R. Software Engineering: An Emerging Discipline. *IBM Systems Journal* 25(3/4):334-353, 1986.

[58]   Goltz, A. Safety Demands Formal Software Engineering. *Railway Gazette International* 142(7):495-497, July, 1986.

[59]   Grabow, P., and Noble, W. Reusable Software Concepts and Software Development Methodologies. In *Proceedings of the AIAA/ACM/NASA/IEEE Computers in Aerospace V Conference*, pages ??. October, 1985.

[60]   Grabow, P.C. Software Reuse: Where Are We Going? In *Proceedings of COMPSAC 85*, pages 202. IEEE Computer Society Press, Washington, D.C., October 9-11, 1985.

[61]   Grabow, P., Noble, W., Huang, C., and Winchester, J. Reusable Software Implementation Technology Reviews. In *Proceedings of Software Technology for Adaptable Reliable Systems (STARS) Workshop*, pages 823-854. STARS Program Office, Washington, D.C., April 9-12, 1985.

[62]   Grabow, P.C. and Nobles, W,B. Reusable Software Concepts and Software Development Methodologies. In *Proceedings of National Conference on Software Reuseability and Maintainability*. National Institute of Software Quality and Productivity, Washington, D.C., September 10-11, 1986.

[63]   Grau, J.K. Variations of a Reusable Software Component. In *Proceedings of Software Technology for Adaptable Reliable Systems (STARS) Workshop*, pages 195-208. STARS Program Office, Washington, D.C., April 9-12, 1985.

[64]   Hansen, G.A., Spaulding, S.D., and Edgar, G. Certification of Ada Parts for Reuse. In *Proceedings of First International Conference on Ada Programming Language Applications for the NASA Space Station*, pages E.1.2.1-E.1.2.6. University of Houston at Clear Lake, Clear Lake, Tex., June 2-5, 1986.

[65]   Harandi, M.T. and Young, F.H. Template Base Specification and Design. In *Proceedings of Third International Workshop on Software Specification and Design*, pages 84. IEEE Computer Society Press, Washington, D.C., 1985.

[66]   Harrison, W. *A Program Development Environment for Programming by Refinement and Reuse*. Technical Report RC 11253, IBM TJ Watson Research Center, Yorktown Heights, N.Y., September 3, 1985.

[67]   Heilbronner, F.D. Reusable Software in Simulation Applications. In *Proceedings of Software Technology for Adaptable Reliable Systems (STARS) Workshop*, pages 227-242. STARS Program Office, Washington, D.C., April 9-12, 1985.

[68]   Hobson, T. A Unified Systems Engineering Approach to Software Reusability. In *Proceedings of Software Technology for Adaptable Reliable Systems (STARS) Workshop*, pages 271-296. STARS Program Office, Washington, D.C., April 9-12, 1985.

[69]   Howey, R.A. and Meredith, L.M. Issues In Reusing Software. In *Proceedings of Software Technology for Adaptable Reliable Systems (STARS) Workshop*, pages 297-320. STARS Program Office, Washington, D.C., April 9-12, 1985.

[70]   Isoda, S. Quality Assurance and Software Reuse Activities with Multi-Firm Joint Teams. In *Proceedings of 10th Anniversary COMPSAC '86*, pages 179. IEEE Computer Society Press, Washington, D.C., 1986.

[71]   Jackson, M. Formal Notations for Representing Software Components - Some Problems. Presentation at the Workshop on Software Reuse Held at Hereford, UK. May 1-2, 1986

[72]   Johnson, R.E. and Kaplan, S.M. Towards Reusable Software Designs and Implementations. In *Proceedings of Workshop on Future Directions in Computer Architecture and Software*. ARO, Washington, D.C., May, 1986.

[73]   Johnson, C.S. Some Design Constraints Required for the Use of Generic Software in Embedded Systems. In *Proceedings of First International Conference on Ada Programming Language Applications for the NASA Space Station*, pages B.4.3.1 - B.4.3.10. University of Houston at Clear Lake, Clear Lake, Tex., June 2-5, 1986.

[74]   Johnson, C.S. Some Design Constraints Required for the Assembly of Software Components. In *Proceedings of First International Conference on Ada Programming Language Applications for the NASA Space Station*, pages E.1.1.1-E.1.1.12. University of Houston at Clear Lake, Clear Lake, Tex., June 2-5, 1986.

[75]   Jones, T.C. Reusable Code Paying Off in Variety of Applications. *Computerworld* 19(34):6-7, August 26, 1985.

[76]   Jones, T. C. *Programming Productivity*. McGraw-Hill Book Company, New York, 1986.

[77]   Jones, D. Ada Software Engineering Examples by Do-While Jones. *Journal of Pascal, Ada and Modula 2* 5(2):7-23, March-April, 1986.

[78]   Kaneko, S., et al. Technology for Development and Reuse of Software Parts. *Toshiba Review* 42(8):11-14, 1986. in Japanese.

[79]   Kaplan, J. Using Ada Design Language to Achieve Internal Reuse. Presentation Slides at Ada Expo '86. November 21, 1986

[80]   Katoh, H., Yoshida, H., and Sugimoto, M. Logic Based Retrieval and Reuse of Software Modules. In *Proceedings, Fifth Annual International Phoenix Conference on Computers and Communications*, pages 445-449. IEEE, New York, 1987.

[81]   Horowitz, E., Kemper, A., and Narasimhan, B. A Survey of Application Generators. *IEEE Software* 2(1):40-54, January, 1985.

[82]   Komatsuara, A. Human Factors Approach to Improve the Environment in Software Factory. In *Proceedings of COMPSAC 85*, pages 199. IEEE Computer Society Press, Washington, D.C., October 9-11, 1985.

[83]   Ledbetter, L., and Cox, B. Software ICs. *Byte* 10(6):307-316, June, 1985.

[84]   Levy, L.S. A Metaprogramming Method and Its Economic Justification. *IEEE Transactions on Software Engineering* SE-12(2):272-277, February, 1986.

[85]   Link, A., and Lanphar, R. The Hughes Software Development Environment. In *Proceedings of Software Factory Forum*. Software Engineering Institute, Pittsburgh, Pa., February 18-19, 1986.

[86]   Litke, J.D. Searching and Retrieval for Automated Parts Libraries. In *Proceedings of Software Technology for Adaptable Reliable Systems (STARS) Workshop*, pages 321-334. STARS Program Office, Washington, D.C., April 9-12, 1985.

[87]   Litke, J.D. A Design of Ada Reusable Packages. In *Proceedings of First International Conference on Ada Programming Language Applications for the NASA Space Station*, pages E.1.4.1-E.1.4.10. University of Houston at Clear Lake, Clear Lake, Tex., June 2-5, 1986.

[88]   Loesh, R.E. Improving Productivity Through Standard Design Templates. *Data Processing* 27(9):57-59, November, 1985.

[89]   Logicon. *Collection of Abstracts for Reusability and Very-High-Level Languages*. Technical Report, Logicon Inc., Arlington, VA., March, 1986.

[90]   Love, T. The Concepts of Object Oriented Programming. In *Proceedings of DSSD User's Conference - Feedback '86*, pages P3/1-13. 1986.

[91]   Lubars, M.D. Reusability in the Large versus Code Reusability in the Small. *ACM SIGSOFT Software Engineering Notices* 11(1):21-27, January, 1986.

[92]   Lubars, M.D. Affording Higher Reliability Through Software Reusability. *ACM SIGSOFT Software Engineering Notices* 11(5):39-42, October, 1986.

[93]   Machida, S. Approaches to Software Reusability in Telecommunications Software System. In *Proceedings of COMPSAC 85*, pages 206. IEEE Computer Society Press, Washington, D.C., October 9-11, 1985.

[94]   Maginnis, N.B. Specialist: Renewable Code Helps Increase Productivity. *Computerworld* 20(47):19-20, November 24, 1986.

[95]   Mair, P. The BSI Working Party on Reuse. Presentation at the Workshop on Software Reuse Held at Hereford, UK. May 1-2, 1986

[96]   Manley, J.H. Waves of the Future in Software Engineering. In *Proceedings of DSSD User's Conference - Feedback '86*, pages P1/1-9. 1986.

[97]   Mathis, R.F. Transportable Software Designs Using Expert System Technology. In *Proceedings of National Conference on Software Reuseability and Maintainability*. National Institute of Software Quality and Productivity, Washington, D.C., September 10-11, 1986.

[98]   Mathis, R.F. The Last 10 Percent. *IEEE Transactions on Software Engineering* SE-12"(6):705-712, June, 1986.

[99]   Matsumoto, M. Reusable Parts Paradigm and Automatic Program Synthesis Using Them. In *Proceedings of National Conference on Software Reuseability and Maintainability*. National Institute of Software Quality and Productivity, Washington, D.C., September 10-11, 1986.

[100]   Matsumoto, Y. Experiences in Software Manufacturing. In *Proceedings of 1986 National Computer Conference*, pages 93-94. AFIPS Press, Reston, Va., 1986.

[101]   Matsumoto, Y. and Yamamoto, S. Software Production Systems for Industrial Control Systems. *Toshiba Review* 41(8):697-700, 86.

[102]   Mayr, H.C., Lockemann, P.C., Beyer, M. Framework for Application Systems Engineering. *Information Systems* 10(1):97-111, 1985.

[103]   McBride, J.G. Reusable Software Implementation Program: Response to Request for Information. In *Proceedings of Software Technology for Adaptable Reliable Systems (STARS) Workshop*, pages 335-360. STARS Program Office, Washington, D.C., April 9-12, 1985.

[104]   McCain, R. Reusable Software Component Construction. Presentation Foils. 1985

[105]   McCain, R. Reusable Software Component Construction - A Product-Oriented Paradigm. In *Proceedings of the AIAA/ACM/NASA/IEEE Computers in Aerospace V Conference*. October, 1985.

[106]   McCain, R. A Software Development Methodology for Reusable Component. In *Proceedings of Software Technology for Adaptable Reliable Systems (STARS) Workshop*, pages 361-384. STARS Program Office, Washington, D.C., April 9-12, 1985.

[107]   McCain, R.C. Reusable Software Component Engineering. In *Proceedings of National Conference on Software Reuseability and Maintainability*. National Institute of Software Quality and Productivity, Washington, D.C., September 10-11, 1986.

[108]   McCain, R. Software Development Methodology for Reusable Components. In *Proceedings of the Eighteenth Hawaii International Conference on System Science*, pages 319-324. Western Periodicals, San Francisco, Calif., January 2-4, 1986.

[109]   McNamara, D.M. The Japanese Software Factories. In *Proceedings of Software Factory Forum*. Software Engineering Institute, Pittsburgh, Pa., February 18-19, 1986.

[110]   McNicholl, D.G., et al. *Common Ada Missile Packages*. Technical Report AFATL-TR-85-17, Eglin Air Force Base, FL, Elgin, Fla., June, 1985.

[111]   McNicholl, D.G. and Anderson, C.M. Preliminary Technical Report - Study Results. In *Proceedings of Software Technology for Adaptable Reliable Systems (STARS) Workshop*, pages 385-412. STARS Program Office, Washington, D.C., April 9-12, 1985.

[112]   McNicholl, D.G. CAMP: Common Ada Missile Packages. In *Proceedings of National Conference on Software Reuseability and Maintainability*. National Institute of Software Quality and Productivity, Washington, D.C., September 10-11, 1986.

[113]   Mebus, G.W. Encouragement of Software Reusability. In *Proceedings of Software Technology for Adaptable Reliable Systems (STARS) Workshop*, pages 413-428. STARS Program Office, Washington, D.C., April 9-12, 1985.

[114]   Mellby, J.R. Composition of Reusable Software. In *Proceedings of Software Technology for Adaptable Reliable Systems (STARS) Workshop*, pages 429-442. STARS Program Office, Washington, D.C., April 9-12, 1985.

[115]   Mendal, G.O. Micro Issues in Reuse from a Real Project. In *Proceedings of Software Technology for Adaptable Reliable Systems (STARS) Workshop*, pages 443-520. STARS Program Office, Washington, D.C., April 9-12, 1985.

[116]   Mendal, G.O. Designing For Ada Reuse: A Case Study. In *Proceedings of IEEE Computer Society Second International Conference on Ada Applications and Environments*. IEEE Computer Society Press, Washington, D.C., April, 1986.

[117]   Meng, B. Systems Architecture: Programming Gets Object Oriented. *Digital Design* 16(10):28-31, September, 1986.

[118]   Meyer, B. Genericity versus Inheritance. In *Proceedings of OOPDLS' 86*, pages 391-405. November, 1986. ACM SIGPLAN Notices, vol. 21, no. 11.

[119]   Mickel, S. Achieving Reusability of Ada Packages. In *Proceedings of Software Technology for Adaptable Reliable Systems (STARS) Workshop*, pages 521-536. STARS Program Office, Washington, D.C., April 9-12, 1985.

[120]   Miller, M.R., Habereder, H.L., and Keeler, L.O. Software Validation of Signal Processing Systems and Its Impact on Reusability. In *Proceedings of Software Technology for Adaptable Reliable Systems (STARS) Workshop*, pages 209-226. STARS Program Office, Washington, D.C., April 9-12, 1985.

[121]   Minkowitz, C. Reuse of Specification Components. Presentation at the Workshop on Software Reuse Held at Hereford, UK. May 1-2, 1986

[122]   Mortison, J.E. Software Reusability. In *Proceedings of Software Technology for Adaptable Reliable Systems (STARS) Workshop*, pages 537-598. STARS Program Office, Washington, D.C., April 9-12, 1985.

[123]   Munsil, W. The Language Translation Task: Toward Reusable Components. In *Proceedings of Fourth International Conference: Phoenix Conference on Computers and Communications*, pages 46-52. IEEE Computer Society Press, Washington, D.C., 1985.

[124]   Newport, J.P. A Growing Gap in Software. *Fortune* :132-142, April 28, 1986.

[125]   Nise, N., McKay, C., Dillehunt, D., Kim, N., and Giffin, C. A Reusable Software System. In *Proceedings of the AIAA/ACM/NASA/IEEE Computers in Aerospace V Conference*, pages ??. October, 1985.

[126]   Nise, N.S. Ada Technology Objectives and Plans (Atop). In *Proceedings of Software Technology for Adaptable Reliable Systems (STARS) Workshop*, pages 599-636. STARS Program Office, Washington, D.C., April 9-12, 1985.

[127]   Nise, N.S. and Giggin, C. Considerations for the Design of Ada Reusable Packages. In *Proceedings of First International Conference on Ada Programming Language Applications for the NASA Space Station*, pages E.1.6.1-E.1.6.10. University of Houston at Clear Lake, Clear Lake, Tex., June 2-5, 1986.

[128]   Nourani, C.F., and Jones, G.A. Software Reusability - A Perspective. In *Proceedings of the Eighteenth Hawaii International Conference on System Science*, pages 447. Western Periodicals, San Francisco, Calif., January 2-4, 1986.

[129]   Orme, T. How to Succeed with Ada. *Data Processing* 28(5):236-240, June, 1986.

[130]   Palmer, J.D. and Nguyen, T. A Systems Approach to Reusable Software Products. In *Proceedings of the 1986 IEEE Conference on Systems, Man, and Cybernetics*, pages 1410-1414, Vol. 2. IEEE, New York, 1986.

[131]   Penedo, M.H., and Wartik, S.P. Reusable Tools for Software Engineering Environments. In *Proceedings of the AIAA/ACM/NASA/IEEE Computers in Aerospace V Conference*. October, 1985.

[132]   Polak, W. Maintainability and Reusable Program Designs. In *Proceedings of National Conference on Software Reuseability and Maintainability*. National Institute of Software Quality and Productivity, Washington, D.C., September 10-11, 1986.

[133]   Polster, F.J. Reuse of Software Through Generation of Partial Systems. *IEEE Transactions on Software Engineering* 12(3):402-416, March, 1986.

[134]   Poston, R.M. Improving Software Quality and Productivity. *IEEE Software* 2(3):74-75, May, 1986.

[135]   Prieto-Diaz, R. *A Software Classification Scheme*. PhD thesis, University of California, Irvine, 1985.

[136]   Prieto-Diaz, R., and Neighbors, J.M. Module Interconnection Language. *Journal of Systems and Software* 6(4):307-344, November, 1986.

[137]   Przybylinski, S.M. Archetyping - A Knowledge-Based Reuse Paradigm. In *Proceedings of Workshop on Future Directions in Computer Architecture and Software*. ARO, Washington, D.C., May, 1986.

[138]   Ramamoorthy, C.V., Usuda, Y., Wei-Tek, T., and Prakash, A. GENESIS: An Integrated Environment for Supporting Development and Evaluation of Software. In *Proceedings of COMPSAC 85*, pages 472-479.

IEEE Computer Society Press, Washington, D.C., October 9-11, 1985.

[139] Ramamoorthy, C.V., Garg, V., and Prakash, A. Programming in the Large. *IEEE Transactions on Software Engineering* SE-12(7):769-783, July, 1986.

[140] Ramamoorthy, C.V., Garg, V., and Prakash, A. Support for Reusability in Genesis. In *Proceedings of 10th Anniversary COMPSAC '86*, pages 299-305. IEEE Computer Society Press, Washington, D.C., 1986.

[141] Rickert, N.W. Preconditions for Widespread Reuse of Code. *ACM Software Engineering Notes* 11(2):21, April, 1986.

[142] Rosene, A.F. Workshop on Reusable Components of Application Programs. In *Proceedings of Software Technology for Adaptable Reliable Systems (STARS) Workshop*, pages 637-662. STARS Program Office, Washington, D.C., April 9-12, 1985.

[143] Scherlis, W.L. Abstract Data Types, Specialization, and Program Reuse. In *Proceedings of International Workshop on Advanced Programming Environments*, pages 1-21. Springer-Verlag, April, 1986.

[144] Schwederski, T. and Siegel, H.J. Adaptable Software for Supercomputers. *IEEE Computer* 19(2):40-48, February, 1986.

[145] MAnley, J.H. (editors). *Software Factory Forum*. Software Engineering Institute, Pittsburgh, Pa., 1986.

[146] Seppanen, V. *Design and Implementation of Embedded Software in an Integrated Software Engineering Environment*. Technical Report, Technical Research Centre, Finland, June, 1986.

[147] Shaw, M. Beyond Programming-in-the-Large: The Next Challenges for Software Engineering. April, 1986.Software Engineering Institute.

[148] Shaw, M. Challenges and Directions for Software Engineering. In *Proceedings of Software Factory Forum*. Software Engineering Institute, Pittsburgh, Pa., February 18-19, 1986.

[149] Sievert, G.E. Specification - Based Software Engineering with Tagsotm. In *Proceedings of Software Technology for Adaptable Reliable Systems (STARS) Workshop*, pages 663-682. STARS Program Office, Washington, D.C., April 9-12, 1985.

[150] Silverman, B. Software Cost and Productivity Improvements: An Analogical View. *IEEE Computer* 18(5):86-96 , May, 1985.

[151] Simcox, L. N., and Ball, R. G. *Reusable Software*. Technical Report 3884, Royal Signals and Radar Establishment, Orpington, England, 1985.

[152] Smith, D.D. Designing Generics for Compatibility and Reusability. In *Proceedings of First International Conference on Ada Programming Language Applications for the NASA Space Station*, pages E.1.5.1-E.1.5.11. University of Houston at Clear Lake, Clear Lake, Tex., June 2-5, 1986.

[153] Snodgrass, J.G. Fundamental Technical Issues of Reusing Mission Critical Application Software. In *Proceedings of Software Technology for Adaptable Reliable Systems (STARS) Workshop*, pages 707-720. STARS Program Office, Washington, D.C., April 9-12, 1985.

[154] Squire, J.S. Response to the Tri-Service Working Group Workshop Reusable Components of Application Software. In *Proceedings of Software Technology for Adaptable Reliable Systems (STARS) Workshop*, pages 721-732. STARS Program Office, Washington, D.C., April 9-12, 1985.

[155] Stanley, M. Some Practical Aspects of Software Reuse. Presentation at the Workshop on Software Reuse Held at Hereford, UK. May 1-2, 1986

[156] STARS. STARS Reusability Guideline V4.0. 1986.

[157] Startzman, E.T. Ada Software Reuse Issues. In *Proceedings of Software Technology for Adaptable Reliable Systems (STARS) Workshop*, pages 733-756. STARS Program Office, Washington, D.C., April 9-12, 1985.

[158] St. Dennis, R. J., Stachour, P., Frankowski, E., Onuegbe, E. Measurable Characteristics of Reusable Ada Software. *Ada Letters* 5(2):41-49, March/April, 1986.

[159] St. Dennis, R. *A Guidebook for Writing Reusable Source Code in Ada*. Technical Report, Honeywell Inc., Golden Valley, Minn., March, 1986.

[160] Stix, G. Breaking out of the DP Mold. *Computer Decisions* 17(13):64-68, July 2, 1985.

[161] Thomson, M.K. A Discussion of Methodologies for the Development of Reusable Software. In *Proceedings of Software Technology for Adaptable Reliable Systems (STARS) Workshop*, pages 773-798. STARS Program Office, Washington, D.C., April 9-12, 1985.

[162] Thomson, M.K. A Discussion of Prototyping in the Software Development Cycle. In *Proceedings of Software Technology for Adaptable Reliable Systems (STARS) Workshop*, pages 757-772. STARS Program Office, Washington, D.C., April 9-12, 1985.

[163] Tracz, W.J. Confessions of a Used Program Salesman: An Update. *Computer* 19(5):91, June, 1986.

[164] Tracz, W.J. Confessions of a Used Program Salesman: The Loves in My Life. *ACM SIGPLAN Notices* 21(5):79-81, June, 1986.

[165] Tracz, W.J. Why Reusable Software Isn't. In *Proceedings of Workshop on Future Directions in Computer Architecture and Software*. ARO, Washington, D.C., May, 1986.

[166] Utter, D.F. Reusable Software Requirements Documents. In *Proceedings of COMPSAC 85*, pages 204. IEEE Computer Society Press, Washington, D.C., October 9-11, 1985.

[167] VanNeste, K.F. Ada Coding Standards. *ACM Ada Letters* VI(1):41-48, January/February, 1986.

[168] VanVolkenburgh, G. Information Package for Workshop on Reusable Components of Applications Software. In *Proceedings of Software Technology for Adaptable Reliable Systems (STARS) Workshop*, pages 799-822. STARS Program Office, Washington, D.C., April 9-12, 1985.

[169] Wald, E. A System Building Strategy with Reusable Software Components. In *Proceedings of National Conference on Software Reuseability and Maintainability*. National Institute of Software Quality and Productivity, Washington, D.C., September 10-11, 1986.

[170] Wald, E., et al. STARS Reusability Guidebook. September, 1986.Draft Version 4.0, Sept. 1986 Workshop Product.

[171] Wallis, Peter. Ada and Software Reuse. Presentation at the Workshop on Software Reuse Held at Hereford, UK. May 1-2, 1986

[172] Wartik, S.P., and Penedo, M.H. Fillin: A Reusable Tool for Form-Oriented Software. *IEEE Software* ():61-69, March, 1986.

[173] Welch, P. Building Systems out of Reusable Processes. Presentation at the Workshop on Software Reuse Held at Hereford, UK on. May 1-2, 1986

[174] Wichmann, B.A. and Meijerink, J.G. Converting to Ada Packages. In *Proceedings of the Third Joint Ada Europe and AdaTEC Conference*. 1985.

[175] Williams, D. L. A Mathematical Software Environment. *SIGNUM Newsletter* 21(3):2-12, July, 1986.

[176] Willman, H. Issues in Software Reusability - A Report of the Software Reusability Working Group. *SIGADA Notes* V(1), January, 1985.

[177] Wolfe, A. Software Productivity Moves Upstream. *Electronics* :80-86, July 10, 1986.

[178] Wong, W. *Management Overview of Software Reuse*. Technical Report PB87-109856/XAB, National Bureau of Standards, Gaithersburg, Md., 1986.

[179] Wood, M. Knowledge Based Techniques for Cataloging Components. Presentation at the Workshop on Software Reuse Held at Hereford, UK. May 1-2, 1986

[180] Yamamoto, S. and Isoda, S. SoftDA: A Reuse Oriented Design System. In *Proceedings of 10th Anniversary COMPSAC '86*, pages 284-290. IEEE Computer Society Press, Washington, D.C., 1986.

[181] Yourdon, E. Impact of the Computer Revolution: 1985-2001. In *Proceedings of the 1985 ACM Computer Science Conference*. Association for Computing Machinery, Inc., New York, March 12-14, 1985.

[182] Yudkin, H.L. Software Reuseability and Maintainability. In *Proceedings of National Conference on Software Reuseability and Maintainability*. National Institute of Software Quality and Productivity, Washington, D.C., September 10-11, 1986.

Software Reuse 1987-

Interest in software reuse showed no signs of slowing in 1987. At least seven workshops, institutes, seminars, or conferences, four tutorials, and six sessions at conferences were held, somewhat saturating the field but also serving to separate the technical from the non-technical issues and to force researchers to focus on the key characteristics that distinguished reusable software from regularly produced code and to look beyond code reuse to reusing designs, specifications, and other software artifacts (see the RMISE workshop summary in Part 1).

[1]   Ada Europe Reuse Working Group. Studies in Ada Reuse. A book for the Ada Companion Series. 1987

[2]   Agresti, B. and McGarry, F. Defining Leverage Points for Increasing Reuse. In *Proceedings, Tenth Minnowbrook Workshop: 1987 Focus: Software Reuse*. Syracuse University, Syracuse, N.Y., July 28-31, 1987.

[3]   Angier, R.A. Large-Scale Parts-Based Software Reuse in the Space Shuttle Program. In *Proceedings, National Conference on Software Reuseability*. National Institute of Software Quality and Productivity, Washington, D.C., April 13-14, 1988.

[4]   Antoy. S., Forcheri, P., Kowalchack, B., Molfino, M.T., Pearlman, S., and Zelkowitz, M. Executable Specifications as a Basis for Software Reuse. In *Proceedings, Tenth Minnowbrook Workshop: 1987 Focus: Software Reuse*. Syracuse University, Syracuse, N.Y., July 28-31, 1987.

[5]   Arkwright, T.D. Reuse as a Viable Business Proposition. Unpublished Technical Paper. 1987

[6]   Arnold, S.P. and Stepoway, S.L. The Reuse System: Cataloging and Retrieval of Reusable Software. In *Proceedings, COMPCON '87*, pages 376-379. IEEE Computer Society Press, Washington, D.C., February 23-27, 1987.

[7]   Arnold, R.S., Blackburn, M., Bollinger, T., and Gaffney, J. Mechanisms for Extending the Applicability of Reusable Components. In *Proceedings, RMISE Workshop on Software Reuse*. Rocky Mountain Institute of Software Engineering, Boulder, Colo., October 14-15, 1987. Also SPC-TN-87-013.

[8]   Bailey, S., Burton, B., and Mayer, L. A Design Tool to Support Reuse of Existing Software Components. In *Proceedings, National Conference on Software Reuseability*. National Institute of Software Quality and Productivity, Washington, D.C., April 13-14, 1988.

[9]   Bailin, S.C. Informal Rigor: A Practical Approach to Software Reuse. In *Proceedings, RMISE Workshop on Software Reuse*. Rocky Mountain Institute of Software Engineering, Boulder, Colo., October 14-15, 1987.

[10]   Bailin, S.C. An Environment for Reusing Software Life-Cycle Products. In *Proceedings, National Conference on Software Reuseability*. National Institute of Software Quality and Productivity, Washington, D.C., April 13-14, 1988.

[11]   Bailin, S.C., Moore, J.M. A Software Reuse Environment. In *Proceedings, Bass Harbor/Minnowbrook Workshop on Tools and Environments for Reuse*. University of Maine Department of Computer Science, Orono, Me., June 21-24, 1988.

[12]   Bardin, B. and Thompson, C. Composable Ada Software Components and the Re-Export Paradigm - Part 1. *ACM SIGAda Letters* VIII(1):58-79, January/February, 1988.

[13]   Bardin, B. and Thompson, C. Composable Ada Software Components and the Re-Export Paradigm - Part 2. *ACM SIGAda Letters* VIII(2):39-54, March/April, 1988.

[14]   Barnes, B., Durek, T., Gaffney, J., and Pyster, A. A Framework and Economic Foundation for Software Reuse. In *Proceedings, RMISE Workshop on Software Reuse*. Rocky Mountain Institute of Software Engineering, Boulder, Colo., October 14-15, 1987. Also SPC-TN-87-011.

[15]   Barnes, B., Durek, T., Gaffney, J., and Pyster, A. Cost Models for Software Reuse. In *Proceedings, Tenth Minnowbrook Workshop: 1987 Focus: Software Reuse*. Syracuse University, Syracuse, N.Y., July 28-31, 1987.

[16]   Barsotti, G., and Wilkinson, M. Reusability - Not An Isolated Goal. In *Proceedings, National Conference on Software Reusability and Maintainability*. National Institute of Software Quality and Productivity, Washington, D.C., March 4-5, 1987.

[17]   Basili, V.R., Bailey, J., Joo, B.G., and Rombach, H.D. Software Reuse: A Framework. In *Proceedings, Tenth Minnowbrook Workshop: 1987 Focus: Software Reuse*. Syracuse University, Syracuse, N.Y., July 28-31, 1987.

[18]   Bassett, P.G. Frame-Based Software Engineering. *IEEE Software* 4(4):9-16, July, 1987.

[19]   Baxter, I.D. Reusing Design Histories via Transformational Systems. In *Proceedings, RMISE Workshop on Software Reuse*. Rocky Mountain Institute of Software Engineering, Boulder, Colo., October 14-15, 1987.

[20]   Belanger, D.G., Dudgeon, C.R., and Vo, K. A Tool Based Approach to Building Application Software. Unpublished Technical Paper. 1987

[21]   Bennett. Building Software from Standard Components: Restructuring Software Development. In *Proceedings, National Conference on Software Reusability and Portability*. National Institute of Software Quality and Productivity, Washington, D.C., September 16-17, 1987.

[22]   Benson, E.D. Software Cost Reductions in Air Defense Projects through Software Reusability. In *Proceedings, National Conference on Software Reusability and Portability*. National Institute of Software Quality and Productivity, Washington, D.C., September 16-17, 1987.

[23]   Berard, E.V. DoD and Reusable Software - Part 2. Info-Ada@SIMTEL20 (arpanet) message. March 6, 1987

[24]   Berard, E.V. Does the DoD Really Want Reusable Software. Info-Ada@SIMTEL20 (arpanet) message. March 5, 1987

[25]   Berard, E.V. Software Reusability Cannot Be Considered in a Vacuum. In *Proceedings, COMPCON 87*, pages 390-393. IEEE Computer Society Press, Washington, D.C., February 23-27, 1987.

[26]   Berard, E.V. Reusable Ada Software: from Start to Finish. In *Proceedings, National Conference on Software Reusability and Portability*. National Institute of Software Quality and Productivity, Washington, D.C., September 16-17, 1987.

[27]   Biggerstaff, T. and Richter, C. Reusability Framework, Assessment and Directions. In *Proceedings, The Hawaii International Conference on System Sciences*, pages 502-512. Western Periodicals, San Francisco, Calif., January 7-10, 1987.

[28]   Biggerstaff, T. and Richter, C. Reusability Framework, Assessment and Directions. *IEEE Software* 4(2):41-49, March, 1987.

[29]   Blum, B.I. Experience with an Atypical Development Based Upon Reuse. In *Proceedings, Tenth Minnowbrook Workshop: 1987 Focus: Software Reuse*. Syracuse University, Syracuse, N.Y., July 28-31, 1987.

[30]   Bodine, J.E. Tools for Creating Object-Oriented Libraries. In *Proceedings, National Conference on Software Reuseability*. National Institute of Software Quality and Productivity, Washington, D.C., April 13-14, 1988.

[31]   Booch, G. *Software Components with Ada*. Benjamin/Cumming, Menlo Park, Calif., 1987.

[32]   Booch, G. The Design of Ada Systems for Reusable Components. In *Proceedings, COMPCON 87*, pages 352. IEEE Computer Society Press, Washington, D.C., February 23-27, 1987.

[33]   Bowen, T.P. E-3 Reusable Software Catalog. In *Proceedings, Tenth Minnowbrook Workshop: 1987 Focus: Software Reuse*. Syracuse University, Syracuse, N.Y., July 28-31, 1987.

[34]   Braun, C.L. and Ruegsegger, T.B. Software Reusability and Ada. Unpublished Technical Paper. 1987

[35]   Brown, G. and Quanrud, R. The Generic Architecture Approach to Reusable Software. In *Proceedings, Sixth National Conference on Ada Technology*. U.S. Army Communications-Electronics Command, Ft. Monmouth, N.J., March 14-17, 1988.

[36]   Burton, B.A., Aragon, R. W., Bailey, S.A., Koehler, K.D., and Mayes, L.A. The Reusable Software Library. *IEEE Software* 4(4):25-33, July, 1987.

[37]   Burton, B.A. Integrating Diverse Libraries of Reusable Software. In *Proceedings, National Conference on Software Reusability and Maintainability*. National Institute of Software Quality and Productivity, Washington, D.C., March 4-5, 1987.

[38]   Card, D.N., Clark, T.L., and Berg, R.A. Improving Software Quality and Productivity. In *Proceedings, Tenth Minnowbrook Workshop: 1987 Focus: Software Reuse*. Syracuse University, Syracuse, N.Y., July 28-31, 1987.

[39]   Carle, R., and Fischer, L.P. Missile Software Reusability. In *Proceedings, Tenth Minnowbrook Workshop: 1987 Focus: Software Reuse*. Syracuse University, Syracuse, N.Y., July 28-31, 1987.

[40]   Carrio, M. Capturing Reusable Program Elements. In *Proceedings, National Conference on Software Reusability and Maintainability*. National Institute of Software Quality and Productivity, Washington, D.C., March 4-5, 1987. Presentation only.

[41]   Carrio, M.A., Jr. Creating Reusable, Transportable Software Design Components. In *Proceedings, National Conference on Software Reusability and Portability*. National Institute of Software Quality and Productivity, Washington, D.C., September 16-17, 1987.

[42]   Cartensen, H.B., Jr. A Real Example of Reusing Ada Software. In *Proceedings, National Conference on Software Reusability and Maintainability*. National Institute of Software Quality and Productivity, Washington, D.C., March 4-5, 1987.

[43]   Carter, J.R. MMAIM: A Software Development Method for Ada. *ACM SIGAda Letters* VIII(3):107-114, May/June, 1988.

[44]   Chan, Y.K. Lessons in Software Reusability in Large Complex Systems. In *Proceedings, National Conference on Software Reusability and Portability*. National Institute of Software Quality and Productivity, Washington, D.C., September 16-17, 1987.

[45]   Chmura, A. Identifying Existing Software Components for Reuse. Unpublished Technical Paper. 1987

[46]   Christensen, D.G. The Search for Effective Design Units. In *Proceedings, National Conference on Software Reusability and Portability*. National Institute of Software Quality and Productivity, Washington, D.C., September 16-17, 1987.

[47]   Colbert, E. Defining Reusability in Measurable Terms. June, 1988 Presentation foils.

[48]   Conn, R. Ada Software Repository and Software Reusability. In *Proceedings, Fifth National Conference on Ada Technology and Fourth Washington Ada Symposium*. U.S. Army Communications-Electronics Command, Ft. Monmouth, N.J., March 17-19, 1987.

[49]   Conn, R. The Ada Software Repository. In *Proceedings, COMPCON 87*, pages 372-375. IEEE Computer Society Press, Washington, D.C., February 23-27, 1987.

[50]   Cook, R.P. Tools and Environments for Reuse. In *Proceedings, Bass Harbor/Minnowbrook Workshop on Tools and Environments for Reuse*. University of Maine Department of Computer Science, Orono, Me., June 21-24, 1988.

[51]   Cox, B. Building Malleable Systems from Software 'Chips'. *Computerworld* 21(13):59-62, 64-68, March 30, 1987.

[52]   Cox, B.J. The Objective-C Environment: Past, Present, and Future. In *Proceedings, COMPCON 88*, pages 166-170. IEEE Computer Society Press, Washington, D.C., February 29-March 4, 1988.

[53]   Dobbins, J. ASA: An Automated Tool for Evaluating Reusability at the Requirements Level. In *Proceedings, National Conference on Software Reusability and Portability*. National Institute of Software Quality and Productivity, Washington, D.C., September 16-17, 1987.

[54]   Dobbins, J. Logiscope: A Tool for Evaluating Candidate Components for Reusability. In *Proceedings, National Conference on Software Reusability and Portability*. National Institute of Software Quality and Productivity, Washington, D.C., September 16-17, 1987.

[55]   Dobbs, V. Reusable Ada Modules for Artificial Intelligence Applications. In *Proceedings, Sixth National Conference on Ada Technology*. U.S. Army Communications-Electronics Command, Ft. Monmouth, N.J., March 14-17, 1988.

[56]   Embley, D. W. and Woodfield, S.N. A Knowledge Structure for Reusing Abstract Data Types. In *Proceedings, 9th Annual International Conference on Software Engineering*, pages 360-368. IEEE Computer Society Press, Washington, D.C., March 30 - April 2, 1987.

[57]   Embley, D.W. and Woodfield, S.W. Conceptual Modeling in Software Reuse. In *Proceedings, Bass Harbor/Minnowbrook Workshop on Tools and Environments for Reuse*. University of Maine Department of Computer Science, Orono, Me., June 21-24, 1988.

[58]   Evans, M.W. Building Reusability into the Life-Cycle. In *Proceedings, National Conference on Software Reusability and Portability*. National Institute of Software Quality and Productivity, Washington, D.C., September 16-17, 1987.

[59]   Evans, M.W. and Callender, E.D. A Reusable Software Environment. In *Proceedings, Tenth Minnowbrook Workshop: 1987 Focus: Software Reuse*. Syracuse University, Syracuse, N.Y., July 28-31, 1987.

[60]   EVB Software Engineering, Inc. Generic Reusable Ada Components. In *Proceedings, National Conference on Software Reusability and Maintainability*. National Institute of Software Quality and Productivity, Washington, D.C., March 4-5, 1987.

[61]   Fischer, G. Cognitive View of Reuse and Redesign. *IEEE Software* 4(4):60-73, July, 1987.

[62]   Fischer, G., Lemke, A., and Rathke, C. From Design to Redesign. In *Proceedings, 9th Annual International Conference on Software Engineering*. IEEE Computer Society Press, Washington, D.C., March 30 - April 2, 1987.

[63]   Ford Aerospace Corporation. A Library Tool for Organizing and Identifying Reuseable Software Components. In *Proceedings, National Conference on Software Reusability and Maintainability*. National Institute of Software Quality and Productivity, Washington, D.C., March 4-5, 1987. Presentation only.

[64]   Frakes, W.B. and Nejmeh, B.A. Software Reuse Through Information Retrieval. In *Proceedings, COMPCON 87*, pages 380-384. IEEE Computer Society Press, Washington, D.C., February 23-27, 1987.

[65]   Frakes, W.B. and Nejmeh, B.A. Software Reuse Through Information Retrieval. In *Proceedings, The Hawaii International Conference on System Sciences*, pages 530-535. Western Periodicals, San Francisco, Calif., January 7-10, 1987.

[66]   Frakes, W.B. and Fox. C.J. An Approach to Integrating Expert System Components into Production Software. In *Proceedings, FJCC 87*, pages 50-56.

IEEE Computer Society Press, Washington, D.C., October, 1987.

[67]   Frakes, W.B., and Nejmeh, B.A. An Information System for Reuse. In *Proceedings, Tenth Minnowbrook Workshop: 1987 Focus: Software Reuse.* Syracuse University, Syracuse, N.Y., July 28-31, 1987.

[68]   Frakes, W.B. and Gandel, P.B. Classification, Storage and Retrieval of Reusable Components. In *Proceedings, Bass Harbor/Minnowbrook Workshop on Tools and Environments for Reuse.* University of Maine Department of Computer Science, Orono, Me., June 21-24, 1988.

[69]   Frankowski, E.N. Rapid Prototyping with Reusable Source Code. Unpublished Technical Paper. 1987

[70]   Freeman, P. Reusable Software Engineering. Handouts for Tutorial at COMPCON 87. February, 1987

[71]   Freeman, P. Advanced Software Engineering Project (Formerly the Reuse Project) Project Introduction and Research Technical Publications. University of California, Irvine. February 24, 1987

[72]   Peter Freeman (editor). *Tutorial: Software Reusability.* IEEE Computer Society Press, Washington, D.C., 1987.

[73]   Freeman, P. A Conceptual Analysis of the Draco Approach to Construction Software Systems. *IEEE Transactions on Software Engineering* SE-13(7):830-844, July, 1987.

[74]   Freeman, P. A Perspective on Reusability. In Peter Freeman (editor), *Tutorial: Software Reusability*, pages 2-8. IEEE Computer Society Press, Washington, D.C., 1987.

[75]   Fujino, K. Software Factory Engineering: Todays and Future. In *Proceedings, FJCC 87*, pages 262-270. IEEE Computer Society Press, Washington, D.C., October, 1987.

[76]   Gargaro, A., and Pappas, T.L. Reusability Issues in Ada Software. *IEEE Software* 4(4):43-51, July, 1987.

[77]   Gautier, R.J. A Language for Describing Ada Software Components. In *Proceedings, Ada-Europe Conference.* May 26-28, 1987.

[78]   Ghisio, O., Gouthier, P., and Truzzi, S. An Extended Approach to Reusability. Unpublished Technical Paper. 1987

[79]   Ghisio, O., Gouthier, P., and Truzzi, S. An Extended Approach to Reusability. In *Proceedings, COMPCON 87*, pages 385-389. IEEE Computer Society Press, Washington, D.C., February 23-27, 1987.

[80]   Ghisio, P., Gouthier, P., and Truzzi, S. New Approach to Software Reusability. *CSELT Technical Reports* 16(1):53-60, February, 1988.

[81]   Grabow, P.C., Huang, C., and Noble, W.B. Concepts of Software Reuse and A Software Methodology Review Framework. Unpublished Technical Paper. 1987

[82]   Grau, J.K. Impact of Types of Reusable Components on Automation. In *Proceedings, Bass Harbor/Minnowbrook Workshop on Tools and Environments for Reuse.* University of Maine Department of Computer Science, Orono, Me., June 21-24, 1988.

[83]   Guerrieri, E. Searching for Reusable Software Components with the Rapid Center Libary System. In *Proceedings, Sixth National Conference on Ada Technology.* U.S. Army Communications-Electronics Command, Ft. Monmouth, N.J., March 14-17, 1988.

[84]   Haberman, A.N. Programming Environments for Reusability. In *Proceedings, 21st Annual Hawaii International Conference on System Sciences - Software Track*, pages 1-10. IEEE Computer Society Press, Washington, D.C., January, 1988.

[85]   Harrison, G.C. An Automated Method of Referencing Ada Reusable Code Using LIL. In *Proceedings, Fifth National Conference on Ada Technology and Fourth Washington Ada Symposium.* U.S. Army Communications-Electronics Command, Ft. Monmouth, N.J., March 17-19, 1987.

[86]   Hess, G.K. Jr., Knowles, H.B. Jr., and Branyon, S.A. Kalman Filters in Generic Ada Packages. In *Proceedings, Sixth National Conference on Ada Technology.* U.S. Army Communications-Electronics Command, Ft. Monmouth, N.J., March 14-17, 1988.

[87]   Hocking, D.E. The Next Level of Reuse. In *Proceedings, Sixth National Conference on Ada Technology.* U.S. Army Communications-Electronics Command, Ft. Monmouth, N.J., March 14-17, 1988.

[88]   Hori, Y., Kimura, S., and Matsuura, H. Reusable Design Methodology for Switching Software. In *Proceedings, International Switching Symposium 1987*, pages 291-295. IEEE Computer Society Press, Washington, D.C., March 15-20, 1987.

[89]   Howey, R.A. Software Reuse and Ada. Unpublished Technical Paper. 1987

[90]   Howey, R.A. Reusing Code and Documentation in Real-Time Military (DoD 2169) Environments. In *Proceedings, National Conference on Software Reuseability.* National Institute of Software Quality and Productivity, Washington, D.C., April 13-14, 1988.

[91]   Hrycej, T. A Knowledge-Based Problem-Specific Program Generator. *ACM SIGPLAN Notices* 22(2):53-61, February, 1987.

[92]   Iscoe, N. A Knowledge Based and Object-Oriented Approach to Reusability Within Application Domains. In *Proceedings, RMISE Workshop on Software Reuse.* Rocky Mountain Institute of Software Engineering, Boulder, Colo., October 14-15, 1987.

[93]   Isoda, S. SoftDa - A Computer-Aided Software Engineering System. In *Proceedings, FJCC 87*, pages 147-151. IEEE Computer Society Press, Washington, D.C., October, 1987.

[94]   Johnson, B. A Retrieval System for Reuse. In *Proceedings, Bass Harbor/Minnowbrook Workshop on Tools and Environments for Reuse.* University of Maine Department of Computer Science, Orono, Me., June 21-24, 1988.

[95]   Jones, G. Methodology/Environment Support for Reusability. In *Proceedings, RMISE Workshop on Software Reuse.* Rocky Mountain Institute of Software Engineering, Boulder, Colo., October 14-15, 1987.

[96]   Jones, G., and Prieto-Diaz, R. Classification and Library Support for Reusability. In *Proceedings, Tenth Minnowbrook Workshop: 1987 Focus: Software Reuse.* Syracuse University, Syracuse, N.Y., July 28-31, 1987.

[97]   Jones, G.A. Building a Library System for Managing Life-Cycle Software Developmment Components. In *Proceedings, National Conference on Software Reuseability.* National Institute of Software Quality and Productivity, Washington, D.C., April 13-14, 1988.

[98]   Kaiser, G.E. and Garlan, D. Melding Software Systems from Reusable Building Blocks. *IEEE Software* 4(4):17-24, July, 1987.

[99]   Kaiser, G.E. and Garlan, D. Composing Software Systems from Reusable Building Blocks. In *Proceedings, The Hawaii International Conference on System Sciences*, pages 536-545. Western Periodicals, San Francisco, Calif., January 7-10, 1987.

[100]   Latour, L. SEE: An Automated Tool to Facilitate Reuse in Ada Project Development. In *Proceedings, RMISE Workshop on Software Reuse.* Rocky

Mountain Institute of Software Engineering, Boulder, Colo., October 14-15, 1987.

[101]   Latour, L. An Automated Tool to Facilitate Ada Project Development. In *Proceedings, Tenth Minnowbrook Workshop: 1987 Focus: Software Reuse.* Syracuse University, Syracuse, N.Y., July 28-31, 1987.

[102]   Latour88. But How Can I be Sure It's the Module for Me? In *Proceedings, Bass Harbor/Minnowbrook Workshop on Tools and Environments for Reuse.* University of Maine Department of Computer Science, Orono, Me., June 21-24, 1988.

[103]   Lenz, M., Schmid, H., and Wolf, P. Software Reuse Through Building Blocks: Concepts and Experience. *IEEE Software* 4(4):34-42, July, 1987.

[104]   Lenz, M. Endres, A., and Prescher, P. Software Reuse through Building Blocks. In *Proceedings, National Conference on Software Reuseability.* National Institute of Software Quality and Productivity, Washington, D.C., April 13-14, 1988.

[105]   Levy, P. and Ripken, K. Experience in Constructing Ada Programs from Nontrivial Reusable Modules. In *Proceedings, Ada-Europe Conference.* May 26-28, 1987.

[106]   Lieberherr, K.J. and Riel, A.J. Demeter: A Case Study of Software Growth through Parameterized Classes. In *Proceedings, 10th Annual International Conference on Software Engineering*, pages 254-264. IEEE Computer Society Press, Washington, D.C., April 11-15, 1988.

[107]   Litke, J.D. and Benedict, P.A. A Design for a Reusable Ada Library. Unpublished Technical Paper. 1987

[108]   Liu, D.B. A Knowledge Structure of a Reusable Software Component in LIL. In *Proceedings, Sixth National Conference on Ada Technology.* U.S. Army Communications-Electronics Command, Ft. Monmouth, N.J., March 14-17, 1988.

[109]   Love, T. The Economics of Reuse. In *Proceedings, COMPCON 88*, pages 238-241. IEEE Computer Society Press, Washington, D.C., February 29-March 4, 1988.

[110]   Lubars, M.D. Wide-Spectrum Support for Software Reusability. In *Proceedings, RMISE Workshop on Software Reuse.* Rocky Mountain Institute of Software Engineering, Boulder, Colo., October 14-15, 1987.

[111]   Luqi. Normalized Specifications for Identifying Reusable Software. In *Proceedings, FJCC 87*, pages 46-48. IEEE Computer Society Press, Washington, D.C., October, 1987.

[112]   Mac an Airchinnigh, M. Reusable Generic Units of Degree 2 An Effective Construction Method. In *Proceedings, Ada-Europe Conference.* May 26-28, 1987.

[113]   Maley, B. Software Reuse at Eastman Kodak. In *Proceedings, Bass Harbor/Minnowbrook Workshop on Tools and Environments for Reuse.* University of Maine Department of Computer Science, Orono, Me., June 21-24, 1988.

[114]   Mano, N. Modeling of Data-Processing Software for Generating and Reuseing Their Programs. In *Proceedings, 10th Annual International Conference on Software Engineering*, pages 231-240. IEEE Computer Society Press, Washington, D.C., April 11-15, 1988.

[115]   Margono, J. and Berard, E.V. A Modified Booch's Taxonomy for Ada Generic Data Structure Components and Their Implementation. In *Proceedings, Ada-Europe Conference.* May 26-28, 1987.

[116]   Mathis, R.F. Reusability, Prototyping and Program Evaluation. In *Proceedings, National Conference on Software Reusability and Portability.* National Institute of Software Quality and Productivity, Washington, D.C., September 16-17, 1987.

[117]   Matsumoto, Y. A Software Factory: An Overall Approach to Software Production. In Peter Freeman (editor), *Tutorial: Software Reusability*, pages 155-178. IEEE Computer Society Press, Washington, D.C., 1987.

[118]   Matsumoto, Y. and Ohfude, Y. Software Reuse Based on a Process Programming System. In *Proceedings, FJCC 87*, pages 254-261. IEEE Computer Society Press, Washington, D.C., October, 1987.

[119]   Matsumura, K., Furuya, K., Yamashiro, A., and Obi, T. Trend Toward Reusable Module Component: Design and Coding Technique 50 SM. In *Proceedings, COMPSAC 87*, pages 45-52. IEEE Computer Society Press, Washington, D.C., October, 1987.

[120]   McBride, J.G. The Graph Analysis and Design Technique. Unpublished Technical Paper. 1987

[121]   McGarry, F. and Agresti, B. A Users Perspective of Software Reuse. In *Proceedings, Tenth Minnowbrook Workshop: 1987 Focus: Software Reuse.* Syracuse University, Syracuse, N.Y., July 28-31, 1987.

[122]   Meyer, B. EIFFEL: Programming for Reusability and Extendability. *ACM SIGPLAN Notices* 22(2):85-94, February, 1987.

[123]   Meyer, B. Software Reusability: The Case for Object-Oriented Design. *IEEE Software* 4(2):50-64, March, 1987.

[124]   Meyer, B. Constructing Reliable, Reusable Software Components Using the EIFFEL Language and Environment. In *Proceedings, National Conference on Software Reusability and Portability.* National Institute of Software Quality and Productivity, Washington, D.C., September 16-17, 1987.

[125]   Mittermeir, R.T. and Rossak, W. Software Bases and Software Archives: Alternatives to Support Software Reuse. In *Proceedings, FJCC 87*, pages 21-28. IEEE Computer Society Press, Washington, D.C., October, 1987.

[126]   Miyamoto, I. A Prototyping Tool for Graphical Software Engineering Tools. In *Proceedings, Tenth Minnowbrook Workshop: 1987 Focus: Software Reuse.* Syracuse University, Syracuse, N.Y., July 28-31, 1987.

[127]   Murine, G.E. Recent Japanese Advances in Software Reusability and Maintainability. In *Proceedings, National Conference on Software Reusability and Maintainability.* National Institute of Software Quality and Productivity, Washington, D.C., March 4-5, 1987.

[128]   Musser, D.R. and Stepanow, A.A. Generic Algorithms + Generic Data Structures = Reusable Software. In *Proceedings, Tenth Minnowbrook Workshop: 1987 Focus: Software Reuse.* Syracuse University, Syracuse, N.Y., July 28-31, 1987.

[129]   Musser, D.R. and Stepanow, A.A. Using Generic Algorithms to Build Reusable Software Components. In *Proceedings, Tenth Minnowbrook Workshop: 1987 Focus: Software Reuse.* Syracuse University, Syracuse, N.Y., July 28-31, 1987.

[130]   Nise, N.S. and Giffin, C. Reusable Software Vs. Software: The Difference. Unpublished Technical Paper. 1987

[131]   Notkin, D., and Griswold, W.G. Extension and Software Development. In *Proceedings, 10th Annual International Conference on Software Engineering*, pages 274-285. IEEE Computer Society Press, Washington, D.C., April 11-15, 1988.

[132]   Odaka, T, and Uchiyama, A. A Programming Language Support for Reuse of Software. *Trans. Inst. Electron. Inf. Commun. Eng. (Japan)* J70D(8):1693-1696, August, 1987. in Japanese.

[133]   Onuegbe, E.O. Software Classification as an Aid to Reuse: Initial Use as Part of a Rapid Prototyping System. In *Proceedings, The Hawaii International Conference on System Sciences*, pages 521-529. Western Periodicals, San Francisco, Calif., January 7-10, 1987.

[134] Ower, G.S., Gagliano, R., and Honkanen, P. Functional Specifications of Reusable MIS Software in Ada. In *Proceedings, Fifth National Conference on Ada Technology and Fourth Washington Ada Symposium*. U.S. Army Communications-Electronics Command, Ft. Monmouth, N.J., March 17-19, 1987.

[135] Perry, J.M., Roder, J., and Rosene, F. Reusability Benefits of a Structure which Supports a Development Methodology and Environment. In *Proceedings, RMISE Workshop on Software Reuse*. Rocky Mountain Institute of Software Engineering, Boulder, Colo., October 14-15, 1987.

[136] Pope, S.T., Goldberg, A., and Deutsch, L.P. Object-Oriented Approaches to the Software Lifecycle Using the Smalltalk-80 as a CASE Toolkit. In *Proceedings, FJCC 87*, pages 13-20. IEEE Computer Society Press, Washington, D.C., October, 1987.

[137] Prieto-Diaz, R. and Freeman, P. Classifying Software for Reusability. *IEEE Software* 4(1):6-16, January, 1987.

[138] Prieto-Diaz, R. Domain Analysis for Reusability. In *Proceedings, COMPSAC 87*. IEEE Computer Society Press, Washington, D.C., October, 1987.

[139] Prieto-Diaz, R. Deriving Classification Schemes: A Proposal for a Tool. In *Proceedings, Bass Harbor/Minnowbrook Workshop on Tools and Environments for Reuse*. University of Maine Department of Computer Science, Orono, Me., June 21-24, 1988.

[140] Pyster, A., and Barnes, B. The Software Productivity Consortium Reuse Program. In *Proceedings, COMPCON 88*, pages 242-248. IEEE Computer Society Press, Washington, D.C., February 29-March 4, 1988.

[141] Ratcliffe, M. Report on a Workshop on Software Reuse Held at Hereford, UK on 1,2 May 1986. *SIGSOFT Software Engineering Notes* 12(1):42-47, January, 1987.

[142] Reilly, A. Roots of Reuse. *IEEE Software* 4(1):4, January, 1987.

[143] Richter, C., Katz, S., and The, K. PARIS: A System for Reusing Partially Interpreted Schemas. In *Proceedings, 9th Annual International Conference on Software Engineering*. IEEE Computer Society Press, Washington, D.C., March 30 - April 2, 1987.

[144] Richter, C. Solving the Representation Problem. In *Proceedings, RMISE Workshop on Software Reuse*. Rocky Mountain Institute of Software Engineering, Boulder, Colo., October 14-15, 1987.

[145] Rogers, G. Software Reuse at NASA/Ames Research Center. In *Proceedings, Tenth Minnowbrook Workshop: 1987 Focus: Software Reuse*. Syracuse University, Syracuse, N.Y., July 28-31, 1987.

[146] Rogers, G. Software Reuse at NASA/Ames Research Center. In *Proceedings, Bass Harbor/Minnowbrook Workshop on Tools and Environments for Reuse*. University of Maine Department of Computer Science, Orono, Me., June 21-24, 1988.

[147] Rogerson, A.M. and Balin, S.C. Software Reusability Environment Prototype: Experimental Approach. In *Proceedings, Tenth Minnowbrook Workshop: 1987 Focus: Software Reuse*. Syracuse University, Syracuse, N.Y., July 28-31, 1987.

[148] Rombach, H. D. A Controlled Experiment on the Impact of Software Structure on Maintainability. *IEEE Transactions on Software Engineering* SE-13(3):344-354, March, 1987.

[149] Ruesegger, T.D. A Center of Excellence for Software Reuse: Organizational Issues. In *Proceedings, National Conference on Software Reuseability*. National Institute of Software Quality and Productivity, Washington, D.C., April 13-14, 1988.

[150] Russell, G. Experiences Implementing a Reusable Data Structure Component Taxonomy. In *Proceedings, Fifth National Conference on Ada Technology and Fourth Washington Ada Symposium*. U.S. Army Communications-Electronics Command, Ft. Monmouth, N.J., March 17-19, 1987.

[151] Rzepka, W. Opportunities for Reuse in the Requirements Engineering Process. In *Proceedings, Tenth Minnowbrook Workshop: 1987 Focus: Software Reuse*. Syracuse University, Syracuse, N.Y., July 28-31, 1987.

[152] Scheff, B.H. Reusable Software Development Templates for DoD Data Items. In *Proceedings, National Conference on Software Reuseability*. National Institute of Software Quality and Productivity, Washington, D.C., April 13-14, 1988.

[153] Selby, R.W. Analysing Software Reuse at the Project and Module Design Levels. In *Proceedings, ESEC 87*, pages 227-236. September, 1987.

[154] Seppanen, V. Reusability in Software Engineering. In Peter Freeman (editor), *Tutorial: Software Reusability*, pages 286-297. IEEE Computer Society Press, Washington, D.C., 1987.

[155] Shaw, M. Purposes and Varieties of Software Reuse. In *Proceedings, Tenth Minnowbrook Workshop: 1987 Focus: Software Reuse*. Syracuse University, Syracuse, N.Y., July 28-31, 1987.

[156] Shriver, B.D. Reuse Revisited. *IEEE Software* 4(1):5, January, 1987.

[157] Simos, M.A. The Domain-Oriented Software Life Cycle: Towards an Extended Process Model for Reusability. In *Proceedings, Tenth Minnowbrook Workshop: 1987 Focus: Software Reuse*. Syracuse University, Syracuse, N.Y., July 28-31, 1987.

[158] Simos, M.A. A Hybrid Knowledge-Based Technology and Methodology for Software Reuse. In *Proceedings, National Conference on Software Reuseability*. National Institute of Software Quality and Productivity, Washington, D.C., April 13-14, 1988.

[159] Simos, M.A. Workshop on Reuse Tools and Environments: Approaches and Goals. In *Proceedings, Bass Harbor/Minnowbrook Workshop on Tools and Environments for Reuse*. University of Maine Department of Computer Science, Orono, Me., June 21-24, 1988.

[160] Simos, M.A. STARS Databases/Reusability Foundations Area. In *Proceedings, Bass Harbor/Minnowbrook Workshop on Tools and Environments for Reuse*. University of Maine Department of Computer Science, Orono, Me., June 21-24, 1988.

[161] Snodgrass, J.G. and Yun, D.Y.Y. Reuse: Engineers' Natural Approach to Software Development. Unpublished Technical Paper. 1987

[162] Sobrinho, F.J. and Ferraretto, M.D. Software Plant: The Brazilian Software Consortium. In *Proceedings, FJCC 87*, pages 235-243. IEEE Computer Society Press, Washington, D.C., October, 1987.

[163] St. Dennis, R.J. Reusable Ada (R) Software Guidelines. In *Proceedings, The Hawaii International Conference on System Sciences*, pages 513-520. Western Periodicals, San Francisco, Calif., January 7-10, 1987.

[164] Stotts, P.D. Achieving Software Reusability with Formal Semantic Model of Real-Time, Concurrent Computation. In *Proceedings, Tenth Minnowbrook Workshop: 1987 Focus: Software Reuse*. Syracuse University, Syracuse, N.Y., July 28-31, 1987.

[165] Sugimoto, A. Object-Oriented Approach and Environment for Software Reusability. *System Control (Japanese)* 31(9):674-681, September, 1987. in Japanese.

[166] Swanson, M. and Curry, S. Results of an Asset Engineering Program: Predicting the Impact of Software Reuse. In *Proceedings, National Conference on Software Reusability and Portability*. National Institute of Software Quality and Productivity, Washington, D.C., September 16-17, 1987.

[167] Tarumi, H., Agusa, K., and Ohno, Y. A Programming Environment Supporting Reuse of Object-Oriented Software. In *Proceedings, 10th Annual International Conference on Software Engineering*, pages 265-273. IEEE Computer Society Press, Washington, D.C., April 11-15, 1988.

[168] Topping, P., McInroy, J., Lively, W., and Sheppard, S. Express - Rapid Prototyping and Product Development via Integrated Knowledge-Based Executable Specifications. In *Proceedings, FJCC 87*, pages 3-9. IEEE Computer Society Press, Washington, D.C., October, 1987.

[169] Tracz, W. Software Reuse: The State of the Practice. Handouts for Tutorial at COMPCON 87. February, 1987

[170] Tracz, W. Ada Reusability Efforts - A Survey of the State of the Practice. In *Proceedings, Fifth National Conference on Ada Technology and Fourth Washington Ada Symposium*. U.S. Army Communications-Electronics Command, Ft. Monmouth, N.J., March 17-19, 1987.

[171] Tracz, W.J. Software Reuse: Motivators and Inhibitors. In *Proceedings, COMPCON 87*. IEEE Computer Society Press, Washington, D.C., February, 1987.

[172] Tracz, W. RECIPE: A Reusable Software Paradigm. In *Proceedings, The Hawaii International Conference on System Sciences*, pages 546-555. Western Periodicals, San Francisco, Calif., January 7-10, 1987.

[173] Tracz, W. Software Reuse Myths. In *Proceedings, RMISE Workshop on Software Reuse*. Rocky Mountain Institute of Software Engineering, Boulder, Colo., October 14-15, 1987.

[174] Tracz, W. Confessions of a Used-Program Salesman: Fringe Benefits. *IEEE Computer* 20(5):109, May, 1987.

[175] Tracz, W. Confessions of a Used-Program Salesman: Excuses. *IEEE Computer* 20(4):104, April, 1987.

[176] Tracz, W. Confessions of a Used-Program Salesman: The RISC versus CISC Debate. *IEEE Computer* 20(11):90, November, 1987.

[177] Tracz, W. Reusability Comes of Age. *IEEE Software* 4(4):6-8, July, 1987.

[178] Tracz, W. Confessions of a Used-Program Salesman: Programming-in-the-New. *IEEE Computer* 21(5):74, May, 1988.

[179] Van Katwijk, J. and Dusink, E.M. Reflections on Reusable Software and Software Components. In *Proceedings, Ada-Europe Conference*. May 26-28, 1987.

[180] Vesper, N. Software Reusability and the Strategic Defense Initiative. In *Proceedings, National Conference on Software Reusability and Portability*. National Institute of Software Quality and Productivity, Washington, D.C., September 16-17, 1987.

[181] Vo, K. Rapid Prototyping via the Interpretive Frame System and Reusable Design Components. In *Proceedings, National Conference on Software Reuseability*. National Institute of Software Quality and Productivity, Washington, D.C., April 13-14, 1988.

[182] Wald, E.E. Software Engineering with Reusable Parts. In *Proceedings, COMPCON 87*, pages 353-356. IEEE Computer Society Press, Washington, D.C., February 23-27, 1987.

[183] Wald, E. STARS Program: New Thrusts in Reusing Ada Components. In *Proceedings, National Conference on Software Reusability and Portability*. National Institute of Software Quality and Productivity, Washington, D.C., September 16-17, 1987.

[184] Wartik, S. Reuse and Object-Oriented Development. In *Proceedings, Bass Harbor/Minnowbrook Workshop on Tools and Environments for Reuse*. University of Maine Department of Computer Science, Orono, Me., June 21-24, 1988.

[185] Weiner, J. Making Engineering Easy. *Computerworld* 21(13):63, March 30, 1987.

[186] Welch, P.H. Parallel Processes as Reusable Components. In *Proceedings, Ada-Europe Conference*. May 26-28, 1987.

[187] Williams, L.G. Software Reuse. In *Proceedings, 10th Annual International Conference on Software Engineering*, pages 320. IEEE Computer Society Press, Washington, D.C., April 11-15, 1988.

[188] Woodfield, S.N. and Embley, D.W. A Knowledge Structure for Reusing Abstract Data Types in Ada Software Production. In *Proceedings, Fifth National Conference on Ada Technology and Fourth Washington Ada Symposium*. U.S. Army Communications-Electronics Command, Ft. Monmouth, N.J., March 17-19, 1987.

[189] Woodfield, S.N., Embley, D.W. and, Scott, D.T. Can Programmers Reuse Software? *IEEE Software* 4(4):52-59, July, 1987.

[190] Woodfield, S.N. and Embley, D.W. Reusability for ADT-Based Software Systems. In *Proceedings, RMISE Workshop on Software Reuse*. Rocky Mountain Institute of Software Engineering, Boulder, Colo., October 14-15, 1987.

[191] Woodfield, S.N. and Embley, D.W. A Software Developer's Assistant. In *Proceedings, Bass Harbor/Minnowbrook Workshop on Tools and Environments for Reuse*. University of Maine Department of Computer Science, Orono, Me., June 21-24, 1988.

[192] Yeh, R.T. and Welch, T.A. Software Evolution: Forging a Pardigm. In *Proceedings, FJCC 87*, pages 10-12. IEEE Computer Society Press, Washington, D.C., October, 1987.

[193] Yin, W., Tanik, M.M., Yun, D.Y.Y., Lee, T.J., and Dale, A.G. Software Reusability: A Survey and a Reusability Experiment. In *Proceedings, FJCC 87*, pages 65-72. IEEE Computer Society Press, Washington, D.C., October, 1987.

THE COMPUTER SOCIETY
A member society of the Institute of Electrical and Electronics Engineers, Inc.

Purpose

The Computer Society strives to advance the theory and practice of computer science and engineering. It promotes the exchange of technical information among its 90,000 members around the world, and provides a wide range of services which are available to both members and nonmembers.

Membership

Members receive the highly acclaimed monthly magazine *Computer*, discounts on all society publications, discounts to attend conferences, and opportunities to serve in various capacities. Membership is open to members, associate members, and student members of the IEEE, and to non-IEEE members who qualify as affiliate members of the Computer Society.

Publications

Periodicals. The society publishes six magazines (*Computer, IEEE Computer Graphics and Applications, IEEE Design & Test of Computers, IEEE Expert, IEEE Micro, IEEE Software*) and three research publications (*IEEE Transactions on Computers, IEEE Transactions on Pattern Analysis and Machine Intelligence, IEEE Transactions on Software Engineering*).

Conference Proceedings, Tutorial Texts, Standards Documents. The society publishes more than 100 new titles every year.

Computer. Received by all society members, *Computer* is an authoritative, easy-to-read monthly magazine containing tutorial, survey, and in-depth technical articles across the breadth of the computer field. Departments contain general and Computer Society news, conference coverage and calendar, interviews, new product and book reviews, etc.

All publications are available to members, nonmembers, libraries, and organizations.

Activities

Chapters. Over 100 regular and over 100 student chapters around the world provide the opportunity to interact with local colleagues, hear experts discuss technical issues, and serve the local professional community.

Technical Committees. Over 30 TCs provide the opportunity to interact with peers in technical specialty areas, receive newsletters, conduct conferences, tutorials, etc.

Standards Working Groups. Draft standards are written by over 60 SWGs in all areas of computer technology; after approval via vote, they become IEEE standards used throughout the industrial world.

Conferences/Educational Activities. The society holds about 100 conferences each year around the world and sponsors many educational activities, including computing sciences accreditation.

European Office

This office processes Computer Society membership applications and handles publication orders. Payments are accepted by cheques in Belgian francs, British pounds sterling, German marks, Swiss francs, or US dollars, or by American Express, Eurocard, MasterCard, or Visa credit cards.

Ombudsman

Members experiencing problems — late magazines, membership status problems, no answer to complaints — may write to the ombudsman at the Publications Office.